CHAMBERS

DICTIONARY OF
Idioms

Compiled by
Penny Hands

GW00646707

CHAMBERS
English

CHAMBERS
An imprint of Chambers Harrap Publishers Ltd
7 Hopetoun Crescent, Edinburgh EH7 4AY

Copyright © Chambers Harrap Publishers Ltd 1996

Reprinted 1998, 1999

A CIP catalogue record for this book is available from the British Library.

ISBN 0 550 10730 4

We have made every effort to mark as such all words which we believe to be
trademarks. We should also like to make it clear that the presence of a word in
the dictionary, whether marked or unmarked, in no way affects its legal status
as a trademark.

The British National Corpus® is a collaborative initiative carried out by Oxford
University Press, Longman, Chambers Harrap, Oxford University Computing
Services, Lancaster University's Unit for Computer Research in the English
Language, and the British Library. The project received funding from the
UK Department of Trade and Industry and the Science and Engineering
Research Council, and was supported by additional research grants from
the British Academy and the British Library.

Typeset in Great Britain at Hewer Text Composition Services, Edinburgh
Printed in Singapore by SNP Printing Pte Ltd

CONTENTS

Contributors   *iv*

Introduction

    What is an idiom? The scope of this dictionary   *v*

    Labelling   *v*

    How to find an idiom   *v*

    The subject index   *vi*

    The corpus – what is it?   *vii*

    How is the corpus used in this dictionary?   *vii*

    The corpus and examples   *viii*

Organization of entries   *ix*

The dictionary   **1**

Subject index   **389**

CONTRIBUTORS

Publishing Director
Robert Allen

Managing Editor
Elaine Higgleton

Senior Editor
Anne Seaton

Compilers
Penny Hands
Imogen Preston

Computer Officer
Ilona Morison

INTRODUCTION

What is an idiom? - the scope of the dictionary

The term 'idiom' is not an easily defined one - it can refer to many kinds of words and phrases. The traditional definition of an idiom is 'a group of words which has a different meaning from the sum of its parts'. This means that knowing the meanings of all the words in a phrase will not necessarily help you to understand the meaning of the whole phrase. In some cases it is possible to make a good guess at the meaning of an idiom, because the image created is an obvious one, eg, *look like thunder* [= look angry], but in others it is virtually impossible to do so.

In this dictionary, we have covered 5 main kinds of idiom. These are:

- metaphorical expressions, for example, **make someone's blood boil** or **knock it off!**
- sayings, for example, **that's the way the cookie crumbles**.
- some phrasal verbs which have a fixed element, for example, **live it up**.
- proverbs and variations on proverbs, for example **a bird in the hand...**
- some foreign or Latin phrases which are commonly used in English, for example, **fait accompli** and **ad infinitum**.

What is not included in this dictionary?

Some less 'colourful' phrases, such as *if only* and *up till now* have not been included. These and many more are fully dealt with in the *Chambers Essential English Dictionary* (*CEED*). Phrasal verbs, similarly, are dealt with elsewhere, both in *CEED*, and in greater detail in the *Chambers Dictionary of Phrasal Verbs*.

Labelling

The principle behind the dictionary throughout has been that it should be easy for the learner to use. This is why we have avoided the use of complicated coding and terminology. The only labelling we have kept is that which describes the register of language to which an idiom belongs, for example, *formal, informal, disrespectful, vulgar,* or *offensive*.

How to find an idiom

In order to make the dictionary as simple as possible to use, we have devised a rigorous ordering system. Under this system, any idiom that you are looking for which contains a noun will be found under the ***first noun*** that occurs within it. So, **up in arms** will be found under **arms**, and **go to the devil** will be found under **devil**. If there is no noun in the idiom, look for the ***first verb***. An example of this kind of idiom would be **snuff it** [= die], where **snuff** is the first (and only) verb. So this idiom will be found under **snuff**. If there is no noun or verb in the idiom you are looking for, it will be found under the ***first adjective***. So **above and beyond** will be found under **above**. If there is no noun, verb, or adjective, look for the ***first adverb***. An example of this kind of idiom would be **slowly but surely**, which will be found under **slowly**.

Remember:

- first noun
- first verb
- first adjective
- first adverb

⎫
⎬ ordering system
⎭

There is one notable exception to this rule. This is that idioms of the type **white as a sheet** or **bald as a coot**, although they contain a noun, will always be found under the ***first adjective***. This is because there are often several possible nouns which can go with the adjective, and so it is more useful to see them grouped together.

Finally, note that an idiom will always be found under its headword in the form in which it occurs within the idiom. This means that **caught short** will be found under **caught**, not **catch**, and **up in arms** will be found under **arms**, not **arm**. If the verb or noun is variable within the idiom, it will be found under the base form; for example, if you want to know the meaning of *fluff it* in *I fluffed it*, you will find the idiom under **fluff**.

Ordering within an entry

Within entries, idioms are ordered alphabetically. The only words that are ignored under the system are *a*, *an*, and *the*. A typical example of ordering would be the following:

death
at death's door
catch your death
the death of someone
dice with death, etc...

The subject index - expanding your knowledge of idioms in English

The main part of this dictionary has been designed so that you can look for the meanings of idioms that you have heard or read. However, many students, rather than always waiting for idioms to come along, will wish to expand their knowledge of idioms on their own initiative. The subject index allows you to do just this. Containing over 100 categories, it lists those subject areas where the idioms in this dictionary most commonly occur. Let's say you want to express how angry you feel about something. Turn to the back of the book, and under **anger** you will find a section called **things people say when they are angry or annoyed**. Here you will find plenty of expressions that you can use to express your anger. Once you have found the idioms that interest you, check their entries in the main part of the dictionary. Here you will find information regarding the register or level of language to which the idioms belong, as well as their definitions, any notes on usage or history, and any synonyms or near-synonyms.

The corpus - what is it?

The British National Corpus is a large collection or 'database' of English language, both spoken and written. It has been recorded and gathered from books, magazines, newspapers, radio and TV, formal meetings, and ordinary people's everyday conversations. It contains 100 million words.

How is the corpus used in this dictionary?

Access to such a language corpus has revolutionized dictionary-making, helping us to learn a lot of new things about the English language. Learners, of course, can benefit directly from this new-found knowledge. It helps our task in the following ways:

- **new meanings**
  The corpus frequently shows us new meanings of words or idioms.
- **frequency**
  It shows us how frequently a word or idiom occurs, for example, once or twice within 100 million words, or thousands of times.
- **collocation**
  It shows us which words are normally used with a particular idiom, for example, a search on the term *scot-free* shows us that people *go, get off,* or *escape, scot-free.*
- **context**
  It shows us in what sort of situations certain idioms are used, for example, on television, at a business meeting, or in a conversation between friends.
- **spoken versus written language**
  It enables us to see if an idiom occurs more frequently in spoken or written language.
- **gender, age, status**
  It enables us to see what kinds of people use certain idioms.

The corpus and examples

In addition, the corpus has been used extensively in this dictionary to provide material for examples. These examples serve to support the definition (that is, help to show meaning), to show collocation, to show context, and to illustrate level of language. Where possible, material is authentic in that it is transferred directly from the corpus. However, in order to keep the examples clear and useful, the language has sometimes been modified or graded.

We hope that you will enjoy using this dictionary both as a reference book, and as a helpful and productive learning tool. Similarly, it is hoped that teachers will find it useful as an aid to devising classroom activities.

Penny Hands 1996

ORGANIZATION OF ENTRIES

Definitions are written as whole sentences, showing the idiom being used in a natural and grammatically correct way.

eagle
the eagle eye of 'so-and-so

You are under **the eagle eye** of a certain person if they are watching you very carefully to make sure that you do not do anything wrong: *Nothing ever escaped the eagle eye of our 'maths teacher.*

The mark ' shows where the main stress occurs in the idiom. If the main stress shifts to another part of the sentence in speech, this is shown in the example.

legal 'eagle

If you describe a lawyer as a **legal eagle**, you mean that they are well-known for being exceptionally good at, and enthusiastic about, their job: *Leigh Lawson, alias TV legal eagle Kinsey.*

Cross-references to other headwords help you to find the idiom you are looking for.

ear (*see also* ear)
bend someone's 'ear (*informal*)

You **bend someone's ear** when you force them to listen while you talk to them for a long time about something: *Whenever I meet her, she bends my ear about how things have changed since the good old days.*

catch someone's 'ear

When a sound **catches your ear**, you suddenly notice it for some reason: *A noise on the pavement behind me caught my ear and I turned round.*

◇ SEE ALSO **catch someone's eye** ▷ EYE

Cross-references to other idioms are marked with a diamond and introduced with the words SEE ALSO. They draw your attention to variations and other idioms with similar meanings, to help you to expand your knowledge in particular subject areas. The arrow ▷ tells you where to find the idiom.

Register labels show if an idiom is formal, informal, disrespectful or vulgar. They will also tell you if the idiom is used humorously, or if it was more commonly used in the past.

'ear-bashing (*informal*)

Someone gives you an **ear-bashing** if they tell you, forcefully and without listening to your comments, how much they disapprove of something: *I picked up the phone and gave him an ear-bashing.* □ *Evelyn was inclined to appease Samuel rather than endure his ear-bashing tantrums.*

Examples supported by the British National Corpus show the range of ways in which the idiom can be used.

have your 'ear to the ground or keep your 'ear to the ground

You **have**, or **are keeping, your ear to the ground** if you are taking care to be well-informed about what is happening around you: *You must keep your ear to the ground and contact me if you discover anything suspicious.*

Variants are always given in full.

> Red Indians used the method of listening with an ear next to the ground to help them discover the position of other people or animals.

Notes of interest (i) explain the history of certain idioms, (ii) define words within idioms and (iii) give variants and information on usage.

A

go from A to 'B or **get from A to 'B**
You **go** or **get from A to B** when you go
from one place to another: *How long does it
take to get from A to B?*

A to 'Z
From **A to Z** means from the beginning to
the end or, of a subject, covered thoroughly: *She went through the whole explanation again from A to Z.* □ *An Illustrated A
to Z of Garden Plants.* □ *an A to Z of
London.* [=book of maps showing all the
roads in London]

the AB'C
The ABC of a subject is the basic facts or
principles of it; **the ABC** is also the alphabet
and the first lessons in reading taken at
primary school: *The ABC of Practical Wood-
working.* □ *The first schools just taught the
ABC and counting.*

ability

to the best of your a'bilities or **to the best of
your a'bility**
You do something **to the best of your
abilities** or **ability** when you do it as well
as you can: *I know you haven't had much
practice yet, but just do it to the best of your
ability; don't worry if you make mistakes.*

abode

no fixed a'bode
Someone is of **no fixed abode** when they do
not have a regular place to live: *It's hard to
get a job when you have no fixed abode.*

about

how a'bout or **what a'bout**
1 You say to someone **'how about'** or **'what
about'** something when you are suggesting
doing it or having it: *How about going for a
walk?* □ *How about a drink?* □ *What about
the restaurant round the corner? They do
good pizzas.* **2** You say to someone **'how
about'** or **'what about'** something when you
are reminding them of it or asking them to
consider it: *We've got enough food for
today, but what about tomorrow?*

not about to
You say you are **not about to** do something
when you are determined not to do it, or
when it is not your intention to do it: *'I'm
not about to become one of those husbands
who shops with his wife on Saturday mornings and cuts the grass on Sunday
after'noons.'* □ *I'm not about to dismiss
their arguments com'pletely, but I do see
some problems in what they suggest.*

that's about 'it
You say **'that's about it'** when you have
finished doing something, for example,
telling someone something: *Well, that's
about it; does anybody have any questions?*

above

above and be'yond
Something which is done or required **above
and beyond** the normal level is done or
required in addition to the normal level:
*They often needed money above and beyond
their budget.*

◇ SEE ALSO **over and above** ▷ OVER

a'bove yourself
People say you are **above yourself** or that
you are getting **above yourself** if they think
you are too pleased with yourself, or rather
conceited: *These small-time villains have a
habit of getting above themselves, laying
themselves open to easy detection.*

accident

an accident waiting to 'happen
You can say that someone or something is
an accident waiting to happen if you feel sure
that they are going to be involved in some
kind of disaster at some time: *That son of
theirs is an accident waiting to happen.*

by 'accident
Something, whether good or bad, happens
by accident if it happens unexpectedly,
without planning: *In 1928, Alexander Flem-
ing discovered penicillin, purely by accident.*
□ *Occasionally we would meet by accident in
a corridor or out in the street.*

more by accident than de'sign
Something desirable that happens **more by
accident than design**, happens more

through chance than because of any skill or judgement used by anyone: *He got the job more by accident than design, since it was he who had to take over when his boss first went off sick.*

◇ SEE ALSO **more by luck than judgement** ▷ LUCK

accidents

accidents will 'happen

If you say that **accidents will happen**, you mean that things can always go unexpectedly wrong, even when people have taken the strictest precautions: *The system is tested to the highest possible levels, but accidents will happen, so we recommend that you still take out some sort of insurance.*

accord

of your own ac'cord

You do something **of your own accord** if you do it without anyone asking you to: *He'll soon get tired of screaming and stop of his own accord.*

account

bring someone to ac'count or call someone to ac'count

You **bring**, or **call**, **someone to account** when you make them explain their actions and perhaps punish them: *The police have assured us that they will do all they can to see that those responsible are brought to account.*

of no ac'count

You say something is **of no account** if it is not important, or does not matter: *Whether or not you see him again is of no account to me.*

on someone's ac'count or on something's ac'count or on account of 'someone or 'something

Someone does something **on someone's** or **something's account** or **on account of someone** or **something** when they do it because of them, or for them only: *Please, don't make anything on my account; I'll only eat if everyone's having something.* □ *He walked slowly on account of his heart.*

on no ac'count

1 You say that **on no account** will you do something, or will something happen, when you will not do it or it will not happen under any circumstances: *On no account will I ask them for money.* **2** You say that something should **on no account**, or **not on any account**, be done, if it must never be done: *Don't on any account switch off the computer.*

settle an ac'count

You **settle an account** with someone when you do something to harm them in return for something unpleasant that they have done to you in the past: *It has been suggested that the murder was committed as a way of settling an account between the two gangs.*

take account of 'such-and-such or take such-and-such into ac'count

You **take account of** a certain thing, or **take** a certain thing **into account** if it is one of the things you consider when making a decision, judgement or statement: *Have you taken account of staff holidays in the schedule?* □ *Remember to take your travelling expenses into account when you submit your bill.*

turn something to good ac'count or put something to good ac'count

You **turn**, or **put**, **something to good account** when you use a situation or opportunity to your advantage: *But couldn't all this be turned to good account? Let's think about it in a positive way.*

accounts

by all ac'counts

You say that something is true **by all accounts** if it is the general opinion of the people you are inclined to believe: *By all accounts it's an excellent reference book for teachers and language learners alike.*

ace

have an ace up your 'sleeve

You **have an ace up your sleeve** when you have a secret or hidden advantage that you can use against an opponent: *I bet he's got an ace up his sleeve; he wouldn't let anybody beat him that easily.*

aces

have all the 'aces or hold all the 'aces

You **have**, or **hold**, **all the aces** when you are in a dominant position because you have certain advantages over someone else: *It's a difficult situation: he's a lot brighter than his teacher, but the teacher's the one who holds all the aces.*

acquaintance

make the ac'quaintance of someone

You **make the acquaintance of someone** when you meet them and get to know them: *I made his acquaintance at University.*

a passing ac'quaintance

You have **a passing acquaintance** with someone if you know them slightly: *He never found work, made no male friends* *and had only a passing acquaintance with people in a local pub.*

act

act of 'God
An **act of God** is a totally unexpected natural event, such as an earthquake, which you could not have predicted or prevented: *Famine caused by drought is not an unstoppable act of God. It is simply the most dramatic manifestation of soil degradation, caused by poor agricultural techniques.*

'**Act of God**' is a legal term referring to events for which you cannot expect compensation from insurance.

catch someone in the 'act
You **catch someone in the act** when you discover them while they are doing something wrong:
◇ SEE ALSO   **catch someone red-handed**
▷ CATCH

clean up your 'act
Someone **cleans up their act** when they start complying with general standards of behaviour: *I think it's about time I cleaned up my act and started taking my responsibilities a bit more seriously.*

get in on the 'act
You **get in on the act** when you get yourself involved in some profitable deal or activity in order to share the benefits: *Everybody's getting in on the act now; the market's totally flooded with computer games of this type.*

get your 'act together
You **get your act together** when you organize yourself, your time and your work efficiently: *We're going to have to get our act together if we want to finish this job by the end of the month.*

a hard act to 'follow
You say that someone or something is **a hard act to follow** when they set such a high standard that others will find it difficult or impossible to match them: *It won't be easy taking over from the old managing director; he's quite a hard act to follow.*

'**Act**', here, refers to a performance in the theatre or a cabaret, for example.

put on an 'act
Someone **puts on an act** when they behave in an elaborately false or artificial way: *The most uncomfortable part now is the interviews, because I can't put on an act, particularly on TV. I get really embarrassed.*

This expression often occurs in the negative, and is used to talk about not being able to, or not wanting to, change one's natural behaviour.

action

in 'action
Someone or something is **in action** when they are working or carrying out a particular activity.

out of 'action
A machine or vehicle is **out of action** if you cannot use it because it is broken or not working: *I'm afraid I can't give you a lift; my car's out of action at the moment.*

actions

actions speak louder than 'words
If you say '**actions speak louder than words**', you mean that what people do is more important and effective than what they say: *Okay, well, since actions speak louder than words, I think we should consider a one-day strike.*

actress

as the actress said to the 'bishop
If you say '**as the actress said to the bishop**', you are indicating a sexual double meaning in a seemingly ordinary remark: *'Admiring my equipment, I see.' 'As the actress said to the bishop.'*

Adam

not know someone from 'Adam
If you say that you do **not know someone from Adam**, you mean that you do not have any idea who they are: *You can't be suggesting I was with him last night; I don't know him from Adam.*

According to the Bible, Adam was the first man on earth, and therefore someone you could not possibly know.

add

add 'up
Facts, or aspects of a situation, **add up** when you realize that they make sense: *Suddenly it all added up; they were planning to take the money and leave the country.* □ *It just doesn't add up – why would he give up everything he's always worked for?*

ado

without more a'do or without further a'do
(*formal*)
You announce that you are about to do something, especially perform some official ceremony, **without more ado**, or **without further ado**, when you intend to do it immediately, without any more delay:

You must all be getting impatient to know the results, so without further ado I shall ask Mrs Rennie to read out the names of the winners.

advantage

take ad'vantage of

1 You **take advantage of** an opportunity or situation when you make the best use of it: *Why don't you take advantage of his offer while it lasts?* **2** You **take advantage of** a person when you treat them unfairly or make selfish use of their kindness or good nature: *I get the feeling he's taking advantage of you; are you sure he really cares for you?*

to best ad'vantage

Something is seen or used **to best advantage** when it is likely to impress you because its best qualities are particularly evident: *It is designed to display both dancer and dance to best advantage from the audience's point of view.*

◇ SEE ALSO **to best effect** ▷ EFFECT; **in a good light** ▷ LIGHT

to your ad'vantage

Something is **to your advantage** if it would be useful or beneficial to you: *It would be to your advantage to get experience in English-teaching abroad.*

afar

from a'far

From afar means from a long distance away; you admire someone **from afar** when you find them interesting or attractive, but you do not have the opportunity to develop your relationship with them: *He had admired her from afar but never dared speak to her.*

after

after 'all

1 You use '**after all**' with the meaning 'in spite of what was expected' when stating something surprising: *She didn't get the job after all.* **2 After all** also means 'because it must be remembered that': *You can't expect to master English in a few days – after all, it's not easy to learn a language.*

after 'you

You say '**after you**' politely to someone to ask them to go in front of you, for example, through a door.

be 'after someone

1 You **are after someone**, or **go after someone** if you are looking for them or chasing them, especially in order to catch or punish them: *The police are after two boys who stole a car and drove it straight into the*

owner's garden wall. **2** You are also **after someone** if you are attracted to them and want to start a relationship with them: *I can tell he's after you by the way he looks at you when you're talking to other men.*

be 'after something

Someone who **is after something** is looking for, or hoping to be given something: *Hello, I'm after something for removing wine stains.*

again

again and a'gain

Something happens **again and again** if it happens often or repeatedly: *I've told her again and again to switch off the computer at night.*

◇ SEE ALSO **time and time again** or **time and again** or **time after time** ▷ TIME; **over and over** or **over and over again** ▷ OVER

then a'gain or there a'gain

You use '**then again**' or '**there again**' when making a comment that conflicts with something that has just been said: *I know the children shouldn't eat so many chips; there again, there isn't much else they actually like.* □ *He says he'll come, but then again he may not manage to.*

against

as a'gainst

You use **as against** when making comparisons: *Our sales total this year was $5 000 000, as against last year's $4 000 000.*

have something a'gainst

You **have something against** someone or something if you have a reason for disliking or disapproving of them: *Greg was once more conscious of the man's eye on him – watchful, anxious, distrustful. 'What's he afraid of?' he wondered. 'What's he got against me?'*

◇ SEE ALSO **not have a good word to say about** ▷ WORD

age

act your 'age

If you tell someone to **act their age** you are telling them to stop being childish or silly: *Why don't you just act your age for once?*

age of con'sent

The **age of consent** is the age at which a person may legally agree to have sexual relations: *They have pledged to create a common age of consent, regardless of gender or sexual orientation.*

come of 'age

1 You **come of age** when you become legally old enough to have an adult's rights and duties: *I came of age in the '60s, when there*

were chances, when it was all there waiting. Now they come out of school to nothing. **2** Someone or something **comes of age** when they reach a level at which they are recognized as being fully mature, developed, or independent: *I regard it as the moment in my career when I truly came of age as a butler.* □ *The English-language feature film came of age in the 1930s, because of its singularity as a piece of entertainment.*

feel your 'age or look your 'age

You **feel**, or **look, your age** if you feel or look as old as you are; you also **feel your age** if you feel tired or unhealthy: *Some days, you feel your age. Other times you don't feel your age at all. If it's a good day, I feel on top of the world. I do all I can on my good days.*

a ripe old 'age or a grand old 'age or the grand old age of 'such-and-such or the ripe old age of 'such-and-such

Someone who has lived to **a ripe**, or **grand, old age**, or to **the ripe**, or **grand, old age of** a certain number of years, has lived to a very old age: *She lived to the grand old age of 91.* □ *We have all heard of cases where someone has smoked 60 cigarettes a day and still lived to a ripe old age – but is it really worth taking the chance?*

under 'age

Someone who does something when they are **under age** is too young to be legally allowed to do it: *the problem of under-age drinking.*

agree

agree to 'differ

Two people **agree to differ** when they decide to stop arguing with each other because neither of them is prepared to change their opinion: *I think we're just going to have to agree to differ, don't you?*

agreed

be a'greed

People **are agreed** when they have made a decision and all know what they have decided: *Are we all agreed on the plan for the day?*

agreement

in a'greement

You are **in agreement** with someone if you have the same opinion as they do: *Oh dear, I thought we were all in agreement; what's the problem?*

aid

aid and a'bet *(formal)*

You **aid and abet** someone when you help them to do something which is wrong or against the law: *He was convicted of murder and his wife was given ten years' imprisonment for aiding and abetting.*

in aid of

1 An event is held **in aid of** something such as a charity if the money made by the event is to be given to it: *a ball held in aid of Amnesty Inter'national.* **2** You ask what something is **in aid of** when you want to know the reason for it: *What's all this 'noise in aid of?*

to the aid of someone or to someone's 'aid

You go **to the aid of someone,** or **to someone's aid,** when you go and help them: *We ran to the aid of the people on the 'boat.* □ *Thanks for coming to my aid.*

with the aid of

You do something **with the aid of** a person or thing when they help you to do it or support you: *He walks with the aid of a 'stick.*

aim

take 'aim

You **take aim** when you point a weapon or missile at someone or something, so as to hit them when you throw or shoot.

air

clear the 'air

Something such as a quarrel or argument **clears the air** if it gives people the opportunity to express their opinions frankly, and so reduces tension: *A good argument often clears the air.*

◇ SEE ALSO **get something off your chest** ▷ CHEST

go up in the 'air

You **go up in the air** if you are extremely angry about something: *I daren't tell my Mum; she'll go up in the air.*

hot 'air

Hot air is a derogatory term referring to claims and promises made by someone who does not intend to keep them: *It was an impressive speech, but how much of it was just hot air?*

in the 'air

1 A possibility is **in the air** if you hear people discussing it a lot: *Talk of an election was in the air.* **2** A project is still a bit in **the air** if its future is doubtful or undecided: *It's all a bit in the air still, but we'll have to make some definite decisions pretty soon.* **3** Something is **in the air** when people can feel that it is present, but they do not mention it directly: *There is a spirit of unrest in the air, violence, lawlessness and corruption.*

into thin 'air

Someone or something disappears **into thin air** if they disappear suddenly and completely: *My keys seem to have disappeared into thin air.*

on the 'air
Someone is **on the air** when they are being broadcast on radio or television.

out of thin 'air
Someone or something appears **out of thin air** if they appear suddenly and unexpectedly: *Then suddenly, out of thin air, she appeared in the room.*

walk on 'air
You **are walking on air** when you are extremely happy: *He's been walking on air ever since he met Julia.*
◇ SEE ALSO **thrilled to bits** ▷ BITS; **on cloud nine** ▷ CLOUD; **in seventh heaven** ▷ HEAVEN; **over the moon** ▷ MOON; **on top of the world** ▷ TOP

airs

put on airs and 'graces
Somebody puts on **airs and graces** when they behave in a way that suggests that they want people to think that they are more important or sophisticated than they really are: *Bella never put on airs and graces, remaining a real Blackpool girl. The stars must have enjoyed her infectious laughter.*

aitches

drop your 'aitches
Someone who **drops their aitches** does not pronounce the letter 'h', especially at the beginning of words: *Don't drop your aitches, and remember to say please and thank you.*

Dropping your aitches is considered a typical feature of uneducated speech.

alarm

alarm bells start to 'ring or **warning bells start to 'ring**
You say that **alarm bells**, or **warning bells**, **start to ring** when you begin to sense that something is going wrong: *The warning bells started to ring for me when I noticed she seemed to have a lot more money than usual.*

false a'larm
A **false alarm** is a situation where you think something bad or dangerous is going to happen, or has happened, but you then discover that nothing is wrong after all: *'Did the police find your car?' 'Oh, actually it was a false alarm; I'd just forgotten where I'd parked it.'*

raise the a'larm or **sound the a'larm**
You **raise**, or **sound**, **the alarm** when you warn people of trouble or danger, or report an alarming circumstance, for example, to

the police: *It was seven-year-old Jenny Curtis who raised the alarm when she called the police from a phone box on the way home from school.*

aleck

smart 'aleck or **smart 'alec**
A **smart aleck** or **alec** is a person who has a very high opinion of themselves, and who thinks they know everything: *a right little smart aleck.*
◇ SEE ALSO **clever clogs** ▷ CLOGS; **clever dick** ▷ DICK; **know-all** or **know-it-all** ▷ KNOW

alert

on the a'lert
You are **on the alert** when you are watching for trouble or danger, or for developments of other kinds: *Teachers have to be constantly on the alert for signs of confusion and misunderstanding in their pupils.*

alive

alive and 'kicking
Someone is **alive and kicking** when they are still alive and in a strong and healthy condition: *No, he's not dead, he's alive and kicking, and living in North London with his family.*

all

all a'long
Something has been the case **all along** if it has been so since the beginning without people realizing it: *The truth was staring us in the face all along and we couldn't see it.* □ *To think I was right all along.*

all and 'sundry
All and sundry refers to everybody indiscriminately: *Rodney had found a much larger place than usual and invited all and sundry to join them.*

all but
You **all but** do something when you almost do it: *We all but suc'ceeded.* □ *The news all but 'killed her.*

all for
You are **all for** something if you are enthusiastically in favour of it: *I'm all for bringing boys and girls up in the same 'way.*

all 'in
1 Someone is **all in** when they are exhausted: *You look all in.* **2** Something such as a holiday costs a certain amount **all in** if all the major expenses are included in the price: *an all-in price.*
◇ SEE ALSO **done in** ▷ DONE

all in 'all
You use **'all in all'** to sum up what you think, or give your conclusion: *All in all, we did pretty well.*

all of 'such-and-such

1 Someone or something is **all of something**, for example, a size, weight, distance, etc, when it is not less than that size, weight, distance, etc, and is often used to express surprise at how large, heavy, tall, etc, they are: *It must be all of two hours' drive from here to Aberdeen.* □ *He must be all of six foot tall!* **2 'All of'** is often used in an ironic sense, when the quantity referred to is surprisingly small: *Ooh look, I've got all of 50p left in my purse to buy food for this evening!*

all 'out

You go **all out** to achieve something when you try as hard as you can to do so: *We went all out to get the best position in the market this year.*
all-out: *make an all-out effort.*

all 'over

1 An event is **all over** when it is finished: *We'll discuss it again when the excitement is all over.* **2** You say that something is someone **all over** if you think it is typical of them: *That kind of generosity is her all over.*

all 'over someone

You are **all over someone** if you treat them with great or excessive friendliness or affection: *It's a bit embarrassing being with them; they're constantly all over each other.*

all 'there

Someone is **all there** if they are intelligent and alert; if you say someone is not **all there**, you mean they are not completely sane.

allowances

make al'lowances for

You **make allowances for** something or someone when you take someone's special circumstances into consideration before making a judgement: *I'm tired of making allowances for her lack of experience.*

along

along with

1 You do something **along with** others if you are one of a number doing it: *Along with hundreds of 'others he had invested money in the venture.* **2** You deal with something **along with** something else when you deal with the two things together, or at the same time: *I returned his book along with his file of 'notes.*

also

an 'also-ran

Someone or something that is described as **an also-ran** is unsuccessful and unimpor-

tant: *Both projects aim to make Microsoft an also-ran in tomorrow's markets.*

amends

make a'mends

You **make amends** for harm you have done by doing something to help or please the person you have hurt or upset: *My colleagues sensed my unhappiness and tried to make amends for their own earlier contribution to this state of affairs.*

amiss

take a'miss *(formal)*

You **take** something such as a remark **amiss** if you are offended or upset by it: *Please do not take it amiss if I describe you as veterans; I do so with the utmost respect.* □ *I trust you will not take amiss my recommendation of a good hairdresser.*

would not come a'miss or would not go a'miss

You say that something **would not come**, or **go**, **amiss** when you want it or would welcome it: *A little patience wouldn't come amiss.* □ *Even a bit of flattery doesn't go amiss.*

analysis

in the final a'nalysis

You say that something is so **in the final analysis** when you are stating what you believe to be the key fact in a situation: *The time has come for the party to choose and, in the final analysis, it has two coherent policies to choose from.*

answers

know all the 'answers

You say that someone **knows all the answers** if they are in complete command of a situation, especially if they seem to be too proud of this ability: *She was the sort of person who knew all the answers, insisting I should get on with my life and forget all about him.*

ants

'ants in your pants

You say that someone has got **ants in their pants** when they cannot stop moving around or when they are very restless in general: *It rained all day, and by the end of the afternoon we all had ants in our pants.* □ *If you've got ants in your pants, why don't you take some time off and go and do some travelling?*

any

'any old how

Something that is done **any old how** is done in a careless or unmethodical way: *You can't just write a business letter any old how; there are rules to follow and set expressions to use.*

anyone

anyone who's 'anyone

You say **anyone who's anyone** to refer to the most influential or well-known people: *It's going to be a very special event; anyone who's anyone is going to be there.*

anything

anything 'but

You describe something as **anything but** something to indicate that the opposite would be truer: *This is anything but easy.* □ *'Was the weather nice?' 'Anything but.'*

like 'anything or like 'mad

Someone or something carries out an activity **like anything**, or **like mad**, if they do it a lot, very much, or very hard: *They wept like anything.* □ *All these people are watching us and clapping like mad because they're so happy and proud of us.*

not anything 'like

You say that someone or something is **not anything like** someone or something else if they are a long way from it in relationship: *She's not anything like as pretty as she looks in photos.*

◇ SEE ALSO **not anywhere near** ▷ ANYWHERE; **nothing like** ▷ NOTHING

anywhere

not anywhere 'near

You say that someone or something is **not anywhere near** someone or something else if they are a long way from it in relationship: *That's not anywhere near the right colour to go in the kitchen.*

◇ SEE ALSO **not anything like** ▷ ANYTHING; **nothing like** ▷ NOTHING

appearance

put in an ap'pearance

You **put in an appearance** at an event such as a meeting or party when you attend it briefly: *He didn't put in an appearance at the parents' meeting. I would like to see him.*

appearances

keep up ap'pearances

You **keep up appearances** when you pretend to be cheerful, or in good health, or financially well off, while suffering private misfortunes and worries: *Her deep sense of*

duty and obligation impelled her to keep up appearances for the sake of the public.*

to all ap'pearances or by all ap'pearances

You say that something is so **to**, or **by, all appearances** if you believe it is so from what you have observed: *It was an expensive wedding by all appearances.*

apple

the apple of someone's 'eye

If someone is **the apple of your eye**, you love them more than others and you are very proud of them: *Of course he loves all his daughters, but Katy is definitely the apple of his eye.*

◇ SEE ALSO **blue-eyed boy** ▷ BOY **pride and joy** ▷ PRIDE

> **'Apple'**, here, originally referred to the pupil of the eye [= the round, black part]. The person in question was therefore as important to you as your own eyes.

upset the 'applecart

Someone **upsets the applecart** when they spoil someone's plans: *Mr Lamont is anxious not to upset the applecart by cutting the present 7% lending rate too quickly.*

April

April 'fool

An **April fool** is a trick traditionally played on someone on April Fools' Day (1st April) or the person who is tricked: *Commiserations to all readers who were taken in by our April fool. But you were not alone!*

apron

tied to someone's 'apron strings

Someone who is **tied to someone's apron strings** is under the control of, or dependent on, a woman, especially their mother: *We have all met adults who are tied to mother's apron strings, often in many subtle, insidious little ways.*

> An **apron** is a piece of clothing that covers the front of you, which you tie round your waist over your clothes to stop them getting dirty when you are cooking.

appointment

by ap'pointment

You see someone, or do something, **by appointment** when you arrange in advance when to do it: *Visits to the cathedral library are by appointment only.*

area

'grey area

A **grey area** is a situation which is not clear or where people are not sure of the rules: *The issue of where to use '-ize' and where to use '-ise' is something of a grey area in English spelling.*

no 'go area

A **no go area** is a place where you are not supposed or allowed to go: *Bus services are operating normally during the daytime, but at night the estate becomes a no go area.*

ark

like something out of the 'ark

You say that a thing is **like something out of the ark** when it is extremely old-fashioned: *Mum was still using that old iron. It's like something out of the ark.*

> The **ark**, here, refers to Noah's ark in the Bible, in which two of every sort of animal went, to shelter from floods. Something out of the ark, therefore, is very old.

arm

an arm and a 'leg

Something costs you **an arm and a leg** when it is very expensive: *I can't believe these shoes have broken already; they cost me an arm and a leg.*

◇ SEE ALSO **a pretty penny** ▷ PENNY

arm in 'arm

You walk **arm in arm** with someone when you walk with one arm linked through one of theirs: *They both left the shop, laughing, arm in arm.*

at arm's 'length

1 You hold something that you are reading or looking at **at arm's length** when you hold it away from your body: *Hold the firework at arm's length as you light it, then quickly move back.* **2** You keep someone **at arm's length** when you behave in a cool or unfriendly manner towards them, to avoid becoming involved: *I'd keep him at arm's length if I were you; he hasn't got a very good reputation.*

◇ SEE ALSO **give a wide berth to** ▷ BERTH; **steer** or **stay clear of** ▷ CLEAR; **keep your distance** ▷ DISTANCE

chance your 'arm

You **chance your arm** when you take a risk: *You'll never get anything done in this life if you don't chance your arm occasionally.*

give your right 'arm

You say that you would **give your right arm** for something, or to do something if you would like it very much: *I would have given my right arm to be there with a camera.*

◇ SEE ALSO **give your ears** ▷ EARS; **give your eyeteeth** ▷ EYETEETH; **give your right hand** ▷ HAND; **give the world** ▷ WORLD

twist someone's 'arm

You **twist someone's arm** when you try hard to persuade them to do something; people often say, humorously, that someone has twisted their arm if they accept an offer readily: *'Have another drink.' 'Oh go on then, you've twisted my arm.'*

with open 'arms

You welcome someone or something **with open arms** if you show that you are delighted or relieved at their arrival: *Would you welcome them with open arms? Or would you tell them in no uncertain terms to leave immediately?*

arms

fold your 'arms

You **fold your arms** when you cross them over your chest and tuck your hands, one into, and the other under, your elbows: *He folded his arms, leaned back in his chair, and sighed.*

throw up your 'arms

You say that someone **throws up their arms** when they express a strong emotion such as anger or despair: *She threw up her arms in despair when I told her I'd crashed the car again.*

◇ SEE ALSO **throw up your hands** ▷ HANDS

up in 'arms

People are **up in arms** when they are very angry, and are protesting about something: *My lads are really up in arms. Nobody believes this story about the sacking incident.*

around

have been a'round

Someone who **has been around** has had a lot of experience of life: *I had an interesting conversation with Tom this morning; he's really been around, hasn't he?*

arrears

in ar'rears *(formal)*

1 You are **in arrears** with a regular payment, or it is **in arrears**, if you failed to pay an instalment of it when it became due for payment and you still owe it: *The rent is already three months in arrears.* **2** To pay an employee **in arrears** is to pay them at the end of the period for which they have earned their wages.

arrest

under ar'rest

Someone who is **under arrest** has been caught by the police and is being kept in a secure place.

arse

get your 'arse in gear (*very informal*)
If you tell someone to **get their arse in gear**, you mean that they should make an effort and try harder, or work harder: *It's taken that long for him to get his arse in gear and he's so slow.*
◇ SEE ALSO **pull your socks up** ▷ SOCKS

art

get something down to a fine 'art
You say you **have got something down to a fine art** if after a lot of practice you have discovered the best way of doing it: *Over the years I've got it down to a fine art. I make lists.*

as

as it 'were
You use '**as it were**' to mean 'in a sense', or to indicate that you are speaking metaphorically: *She was releasing me from the nest, as it were.*

ask

'ask after someone
You **ask after someone** when you ask how they are: *By the way, my Mum was asking after you this morning; I told her you're much better now.*

if you ask 'me
You use '**if you ask me**' when offering your own opinion: *She was just pretending, if you ask me.*
◇ SEE ALSO **for my money** ▷ MONEY

asking

'asking for it or **'asking for trouble**
You say that someone is **asking for it** or **asking for trouble** when the way they are behaving is bound to get them into trouble or difficulties: *Going out and leaving the back door unlocked is, frankly, asking for it.* □ *He'd never started a fight in his life. It was asking for trouble especially if you wore glasses like him.*

someone's for the 'asking
Something that is **yours for the asking** is there for you if you want it: *That job is yours for the asking; all you have to do is send in a letter of application.*

aspersions

cast as'persions (*formal*)
You **cast aspersions** on something when you make critical or derogatory remarks about it: *Under the censorship rules in force throughout the 1930s, they would not have been able to cast aspersions on a foreign power.*

atmosphere

you could have cut the atmosphere with a 'knife
You say that **you could have cut the atmosphere with a knife** when you are describing a situation in which you felt that there were very unpleasant or unfriendly feelings between people there: *I think they must have been having a row just before I arrived – you could have cut the atmosphere with a knife in there.*

attack

on the at'tack
You are **on the attack** when you are making an attack: *The away team were on the attack throughout the second half.*

attendance

dance at'tendance on
One person **dances attendance on** another when they follow them about and attend to all their needs and wishes: *The waiter went out of his way to dance attendance on them.* □ *'I'm not prepared to waste my youth dancing attendance on a woman!' he cried.*

in at'tendance (*formal*)
One person is **in attendance** on another if they are looking after them: *Four bridesmaids were in attendance.*

attention

bring something to someone's at'tention
or **draw someone's at'tention to something**
You **draw someone's attention to something**, or **bring something to someone's attention**, when you mention it to them or point it out: *Thank you for bringing the error to our attention.*

stand to at'tention
Soldiers are told to **stand to attention**, or given the command '**Attention!**', when they are required to stand up straight with their arms at their sides: *When the Inspector came along, all the men stood to attention, and the sergeant said, 'All correct, sir.'*

aunt

Aunt 'Sally
An **Aunt Sally** is a person or thing that people laugh at, express their anger at, or use as an excuse to show their frustration: *I'm pleased that we've finally managed to get rid of the Aunt Sally label the media have been giving us.*

An **Aunt Sally** was originally a model of a woman's head on a stick which people threw things at in order to win a prize at a fair, for example.

auspices

under the 'auspices of (*formal*)

Something is done **under the auspices of** an organization if it has been arranged by them, or is done with their official support, encouragement and approval: *The recommendations will be put to the 19 ministers gathered under the auspices of the European Conference of Ministers of Transport.*

avail

to no a'vail

You do something **to no avail** when you do not get the desired result: *I have scoured magazines for any information on this subject, but so far, to no avail.*

average

on 'average

On average means as the average of a range of numbers or quantities: *On average, women can expect to live five years longer than men.*

awake

wide a'wake

You are **wide awake** when you are fully awake: *I was still wide awake an hour later so took a gulp of wine to help me sleep.*

awakening

a rude a'wakening

You experience **a rude awakening** when you have an unpleasant surprise: *Jones is an idealist, and will probably face a rude awakening when confronted with the realities of the economy and bureaucracy.*

away

have it a'way with someone

Someone who **has it away with someone** else has sex with them: *We know as well as you do that Parkin was having it away with Nicola Sharpe. The question is – did he murder her or was it the husband?*

◇ SEE ALSO **get** or **have your end away** ▷ END; **get laid** ▷ LAID **have it off with someone** ▷ OFF

axe

have an 'axe to grind

You **have an axe to grind** when you have a strong belief or desire that something should happen, and you keep telling people about it, and trying to persuade them to see its importance; you **have no axe to grind** if you are not very concerned about a particular matter, or if you do not disapprove of it: *We all have an axe to grind now that our working conditions have become so unbearable.* □ *Mr Doe insists that he is no opponent of privatization as such and has no political axe to grind.*

awe

be in 'awe of or **stand in 'awe of**

You **are in awe of** someone or something, or **stand in awe of** them, if you feel deep respect for them, to the point of being rather afraid of them: *She still felt a little in awe of Mrs Miller who had an air of remoteness, her tone of voice always brisk and businesslike.*

b

baby

someone's 'baby

A project is a certain person's **baby** if they are responsible for it, and have put a lot of work into it: *He said I mustn't forget this product was his baby and that he wouldn't be happy until he saw it in the shops.*

'baby boom

A **baby boom** is a large increase in the number of babies born over a particular period, for example after a war: *the post-war baby boom.*

'baby-boomer

A **baby-boomer** is someone who was born during a baby boom: *baby-boomers of the post-war period.*

'cry-baby (*informal*)

If you call someone, usually a child, a **cry-baby**, you are saying that you think they are silly because they cry a lot for no good reason: *Don't be such a cry-baby; now eat your vegetables.*

leave someone holding the 'baby

You **leave someone holding the baby** when you stop working on a problem or project, and leave someone else to deal with it on their own; you are **left holding the baby** when you are the person who has to deal with a problem or organize something because everyone else has left you to do it on your own: *I've been left holding the baby; jobless, practically penniless, worrying about how I'm going to pay the rent.*

◇ SEE ALSO **leave someone in the lurch** ▷ LURCH

sleep like a 'baby

You **sleep like a baby** when you have a long, deep, and uninterrupted sleep: *At the end of every day his back was tired and his legs hurt, but he slept like a baby.*

◇ SEE ALSO **sleep like a log** ▷ LOG; **sleep like a top** ▷ TOP

throw the baby out with the 'bathwater

You **throw the baby out with the bathwater** when you are so enthusiastic about change and getting rid of old ideas that you destroy or dispose of things that remain essential: *The more ambitious supporters of the new method threw the baby out with the bathwater.*

back

back and 'forth

Back and forth means 'backwards and forwards', and is often used to talk about a trip that is made several times in a particular period: *I spent years going back and forth between the two flats, until we finally decided to move in together.* □ *Inspector Frank Gregson paced slowly back and forth from one side of his office to the other.*

◇ SEE ALSO **backwards and forwards** ▷ BACK-WARDS **to and fro** ▷ TO

the back of be'yond (*informal*)

A place that is in, or at, **the back of beyond** is a long way from any public facilities or houses: *You feel as if you're in the back of beyond, yet it's only forty-five minutes from London.*

◇ SEE ALSO **in the middle of nowhere** ▷ MIDDLE **out in the sticks** ▷ STICKS; **off the beaten track** ▷ TRACK; **out of the way** ▷ WAY

> This idiom is often used to speak about a place in a critical way.

back to 'front

You have clothing on **back to front** if you are wearing it the wrong way round, with the back on the front of your body: *You've got your pullover on back to front.*

behind someone's 'back

Someone does something **behind your back** when they do it secretively, without telling you, or without asking your permission: *I was obsessed with the fact that she might be up to something behind my back.* □ *I should have realized that he'd go behind my back, try to handle the whole thing by himself.*

break your 'back

You **break your back** doing something when you put a great deal of effort into getting it done: *No-one these days would break their back over such meticulous household chores.*

◇ SEE ALSO **sweat blood** ▷ BLOOD; **bust a gut** ▷ GUT; **work your guts out** ▷ GUTS

break the 'back of something

You say you **have broken the back of something**, such as a task, when you have completed most of it, or the most difficult part of it: *They are confident that they have finally broken the back of the technical problem they were experiencing.*

get off someone's 'back (*informal*)
If you tell someone to **get off your back** you mean that you want them to stop criticizing and pressurizing you: *If I can just pay this last instalment, the bank manager might get off my back for a while.*

have your back to the 'wall
You have your back to the wall when you are forced into a difficult situation which you feel you cannot escape from: *Of course, if your back is to the wall and you have to fight, then that is also classed as self-defence. □ They insisted that fascism was simply capitalism with its back to the wall.*

> This idiom comes from sword fighting, when the person who is losing has walked backwards as far as they can go, and must continue to defend themselves from a fixed position.

in the back of your 'mind or at the back of your 'mind
Something is **in**, or **at, the back of your mind** when you are aware of it, but are not thinking about it actively: *She had a little nagging worry at the back of her mind, but she pushed it away impatiently. □ As he left, he felt, in the back of his mind, that he would never come back.*

know something like the back of your 'hand
You **know** a place, for example, **like the back of your hand** if you know it very well and in great detail: *I know this city like the back of my hand, and I love every bit of it.*

put your 'back into something (*informal*)
You **put your back into something** when you try hard to do it well: *If he really made an effort and put his back into it, he'd be finished within three years.*

put someone's 'back up (*informal*)
You **put someone's back up** if you annoy them: *I think I put her back up a bit when I remarked on her being late.*

> When a cat is angry, it raises its back into the shape of an arch.

see the 'back of (*informal*)
You are glad to **see the back of** someone or something unpleasant and annoying if you are relieved to have finished with them: *I bet you'll be glad to see the back of that place when you graduate, won't you?*

> When someone walks away from you, you see their back.

short back and 'sides
A **short back and sides** is a traditional short haircut: *Oh, nothing fancy. Just a short back and sides, please.*

stab someone in the 'back
Someone **stabs you in the back** if they appear to be friendly when they are with you, but then say unpleasant or harmful things about you when you are not there: *She trusted Robert; he was so unlike Graham, who was probably stabbing her in the back at that very moment.*
'back-stabber: *I don't mind a person who gossips, but if there's one thing I hate it's a back-stabber.*
'back-stabbing: *I couldn't stand all the back-stabbing that went on in that place; that's why I left.*
◇ SEE ALSO **backbiting** ▷ BACKBITING

turn your 'back on
You **turn your back on** someone or something when you abandon them, leave them or refuse to help them in return: *No-one would have predicted that success would lead him to turn his back on his own people like this.*

you scratch my back and I'll scratch 'yours
If you say to someone, '**you scratch my back and I'll scratch yours**' you mean that if they do favours for you, you will do favours for them: *After all, you scratch my back and I'll scratch yours; that's what business is about, they tell me.*
'backscratching: *In the world of finance, backscratching plays a role in many transactions.*

backbiting
'backbiting
Backbiting is the activity of saying unpleasant or harmful things about someone when they are absent.
◇ SEE ALSO **backstabbing** ▷ BACK

backroom
The 'backroom boys
The backroom boys are the people, usually scientists or technicians, in an organization, who do the kind of work which is important but does not bring them into contact with people outside that organization: *There were also Oscars for the backroom boys behind 'The Commitments' and 'Dances With Wolves'.*

backside
get off your 'backside
If you tell someone to **get off their backside**, you mean that they should stop being lazy and be more active: *Instead of complaining,*

why don't you just get off your backside and do something about it?

Your **backside** is your bottom, or buttocks.

backward

backward in coming 'forwards or **backward at coming 'forwards**
Someone who is not **backward in**, or **at**, **coming forwards** is a bit too confident in expressing their own opinion or taking charge of a situation: *She wasn't exactly backward in coming forwards, was she?*

This idiom usually occurs in the negative.

backwards

backwards and 'forwards
To move **backwards and forwards** is to move first in one direction and then in the opposite direction: *I've been going backwards and forwards between my house and the office all day.* □ *He sat swinging his legs backwards and forwards.*
◇ SEE ALSO **back and forth** ▷ BACK; **to and fro** ▷ TO

bacon

bring home the 'bacon
You **bring home the bacon** when you succeed in doing something, such as earning money or winning a match: *The local team fulfilled their promise to bring home the bacon for retiring coach, Jim Rowark.* □ *They searched the globe for a market that would bring home the bacon.*

save someone's 'bacon (*informal*)
You can say you **have saved someone's bacon** if you have helped them to avoid getting into trouble or if you have helped them out of a dangerous situation: *There is also an 'undelete' command which will save your bacon if you have accidentally deleted a file from your disk.* □ *She didn't see how she could refuse his offer after he had saved her bacon.*

bad

go from bad to 'worse
A situation **goes from bad to worse** when it gets even worse than it was before: *Frankly, in the last few months, your work has gone from bad to worse.*

have got it 'bad (*informal*)
You say that someone **has got it bad** if they are so much in love that they act in a way that is not typical of their normal behaviour: *Oh dear, he's got it bad; he's taken to writing poetry now.*

not 'bad or **not too 'bad** (*informal*)
You describe something as **not bad**, or **not too bad**, if you think it is fairly good, or if you think it is okay: *That's not a bad drawing.* □ *'How's your sore throat?' 'Not too bad.'*

'Not bad' can, in fact, mean anything from 'quite good' to 'not very good at all', depending on the speaker's intonation.

take the bad with the 'good
If you say that you have to **take the bad with the good** you mean that you must accept the less pleasant things in life as well as the pleasant things: *Success as an actor means a lot of hard work, but you have to take the bad with the good; and most of the time it's a lot of fun.*
◇ SEE ALSO **take the rough with the smooth** ▷ ROUGH

too 'bad (*informal*)
You say **'too bad' 1** to comment rather rudely that nothing can be done to change a situation: *'I don't want to go to the concert tonight.' 'Well too bad, I've already bought the tickets.'* **2** to express sympathy: *That's too bad you can't come to the party tonight.*

badly

badly off for 'such-and-such
You are **badly off for something**, especially for money, if you need it and do not have much of it: *I know they're badly off for money at the moment, but they won't accept anything from me.*

bag

'bag lady (*informal*)
A **bag lady** is a woman who has no home, and who carries all her belongings around with her in plastic bags: *I feel like an old bag lady with all these things to carry!*

bag of 'bones
Someone who is described as a **bag of bones** is very thin: *Look at you. You're a bag of bones. What've they been feeding you on at that place?*
◇ SEE ALSO **skin and bone** ▷ SKIN

bag of 'tricks (*informal*)
Your **bag of tricks** is the set of things you need for a particular task: *This is my bag of tricks for making me look young and beautiful when I'm feeling old and tired.* □ *Creating the puzzle of how a seemingly impossible murder could have been committed is perhaps the most intriguing thing in the crime novelist's bag of tricks.*

in the 'bag (*informal*)
You say that something is **in the bag** if it is certain to be achieved or obtained: *All they*

have to do is tell the people what they want to hear; and their re-election's in the bag.

A phrase from hunting, where you put what you have shot in your bag.

mixed 'bag
A **mixed bag** is a group of people or things that vary a lot in type or quality: *We have a mixed bag of destinations and holiday choices for you.*

old 'bag (*very offensive*)
Old bag is a term for a woman whom you do not like or who has done something that you are not pleased about: *'What's your neighbour like?' 'She's a real old bag; never stops complaining and always shouting at the kids downstairs.'*

pull something out of the 'bag (*informal*)
You **pull something out of the bag** when you unexpectedly achieve something under difficult circumstances: *They always manage to pull something out of the bag when you think they can't possibly win.*

bags

'bags of something (*informal*)
You have **bags of something** if you have a lot of it: *We needn't hurry; there's bags of time yet. □ There are bags of odd jobs to do still. □ She should do well – she's got bags of personality.*

bait

rise to the 'bait or **take the 'bait**
You **rise to the bait**, or **take the bait**, if you let yourself get annoyed when someone is teasing you and trying to upset you: *Don't rise to the bait; they'll tease you even more.*

A phrase from fishing, where you put bait on to your hook to attract the fish.

balance

hold the balance of 'power
A group or person that **holds the balance of power** is in a position to make one or the other of two parties more powerful by giving it their support: *An 18% share of the votes would give the Greens a chance of holding the balance of power.*

in the 'balance
Something is **in the balance** if it is uncertain or in doubt: *The future of the school hangs in the balance till the governors reach a decision.*

A **balance** is an old-fashioned piece of equipment for weighing things, with two dishes which are level when the objects in them are of equal weights.

off 'balance
1 You are knocked, or thrown, for example, **off balance** when you are in an unsteady position and about to fall: *The wind blew me off balance.* 2 An unexpected remark or action throws, or catches, you **off balance** if it confuses you, or makes you feel uncomfortable: *'What about happiness?' 'Happiness?' Wilcox looked startled, caught off balance for the first time. □ He was suddenly thrown off balance by the hurried departure of one of his Ministers.*

on 'balance (*formal*)
You use **'on balance'** when stating a conclusion after considering all the evidence and possibilities: *On balance, it's probably not advisable to change the company's name.*

redress the 'balance
Something **redresses the balance** if it makes an unfair situation more equal: *Setting more adequate levels of child support goes some way to redressing the balance of the current situation, where the costs fall almost entirely on the mother.*

See note at **in the balance.**

strike a 'balance
You **strike a balance** when you find or create a situation which is not too extreme one way or another, and so satisfies all tastes: *We've had to strike a balance between offering people what they liked in the first movie, but coming up with something fresh.*

tip the 'balance
Something that **tips the balance** is enough to cause one thing from a range of possibilities to happen: *It was the price which finally tipped the balance for me.*

See note at **in the balance.**

bald

bald as a 'coot (*humorous*)
A person, especially a man, who is as **bald as a coot**, is completely bald: *Why would he need to go to the hairdresser's? He's bald as a coot.*

A **coot** is a bird with a spot of white feathers on its head.

ball (*see also* **balls**)

the ball is in 'so-and-so's court
You say that **the ball is in** a certain person's **court** when they are responsible for the next move in a situation: *I told them we were interested in buying, but at a lower price; so the ball's in their court now.*

In tennis, when the ball is in your court, it is on your side of the net and you must hit it back to the other player.

have a 'ball (*informal*)

You **are having a ball** if you are having an enjoyable time, usually socially: *Sounds like she's having a ball at that university of hers; I hope she's finding time to get some work done as well.*

◊ SEE ALSO **live it up** ▷ LIVE; **rave it up** ▷ RAVE; **have the time of your life** ▷ TIME

on the 'ball (*informal*)

You are **on the ball 1** if you have all the most recent information about something: *They're very much on the ball in this department where research is concerned.* **2** if you are paying attention to what you are doing: *He wasn't quite on the ball at the meeting this morning.*

play 'ball (*informal*)

You agree to **play ball**, or to **play ball with someone**, if you are willing to co-operate: *As long as you play ball you'll get what you want.*

set the 'ball rolling or **get the 'ball rolling** or **start the 'ball rolling**

You **set**, **get**, or **start**, **the ball rolling** when you cause some activity to begin; you **keep the ball rolling** when you make sure an activity continues: *To get the ball rolling, here are a few questions I've prepared.*

a whole new 'ball game or **a completely different 'ball game** or **a different ball game alto'gether** (*informal*)

A situation or activity which is **a whole new ball game, a completely different ball game**, or **a different ball game altogether**, is one which you are not used to: *Life's a completely different ball game once you've left home and have to look after yourself.*

◊ SEE ALSO **kettle of fish** ▷ KETTLE

This idiom refers to the fact that every game has its own separate set of rules.

balloon

go down like a lead ba'lloon (*humorous*)

Something such as a suggestion or a performance **goes down like a lead balloon** when it is not well received: *His sexist jokes went down like a lead balloon.*

◊ SEE ALSO **fall flat** ▷ FALL

ballpark

in the right 'ballpark, in the wrong 'ballpark (*informal*)

Something such as an estimate is **in the right ballpark** if it is likely to be more or less correct; an estimate is **in the wrong ballpark** if it is far from being correct: *We exclude*

those observations where the estimates were clearly in the wrong ballpark.

'ballpark figure: *The price they gave was only a ballpark figure* [= an estimate].

In baseball, the term **in the ballpark** means 'within the limits of the playing area'.

balls

'balls-up (*vulgar*)

A **balls-up** is a very bad mistake or misunderstanding; you make a **balls-up** of something when you do it very badly: *You've made a real balls-up and I want my money back.*

◊ SEE ALSO **cock-up** ▷ COCK

Balls is an informal name for testicles.

freeze the balls off a brass 'monkey or **freeze your 'balls off** (*humorous; may be considered vulgar*)

If the weather is cold enough to **freeze the balls off a brass monkey**, it is extremely cold; if you **are freezing your balls off**, you are very cold: *'God, it's cold enough to freeze the balls off a brass monkey!' he said, rubbing his hands together.*

brass-'monkey weather: *'Get yourself in, Pat, I've got the kettle on.' 'Oh, Sal, it's brass-monkey weather out there tonight!'*

Brass monkeys used to be found on ships, and were used for storing cannon balls. In very cold weather, the balls would contract and fall out.

bananas

be ba'nanas (*informal*)

If you say that someone **is bananas** you mean they are mad or stupid; people **go bananas** when they go mad or get wild with anger: *You paid £6000 for that? You must be bananas.* □ *His mum would go bananas if she saw him smoking.*

◊ SEE ALSO **off your trolley** ▷ TROLLEY; **off your chump** ▷ CHUMP; **off your rocker** ▷ ROCKER

bandwagon

jump on the 'bandwagon or **climb on the 'bandwagon**

People **jump**, or **climb**, **on the bandwagon** when they join in, or show interest in, a popular activity only because it is fashionable, and they hope to gain some advantage or public praise for doing so: *Channel 4's Saturday-night series showing favourite TV shows from the past has been so successful that the BBC have jumped on the bandwagon.*

A **bandwagon** was a large and beautiful vehicle for circus musicians, pulled by a horse in a circus procession.

bane

the bane of your 'life

Something that is **the bane of your life** causes you constant trouble and problems: *This weight problem has always been the bane of my life.*

bang

bang goes 'such-and-such (*informal*)

You say **bang goes** acertain thing when the probability of it happening or succeeding suddenly disappears: *Bang go my chances of promotion.*

bang 'on

Something is **bang on** when it is exactly right or precise; you are **bang on** something if you are in exactly the right place or situation at the right time: *That's right. You're bang on; how did you know that?* □ *The train left bang on 'time for once; just the day that I happened to be late.* □ *England's 34-32 half-time lead left them bang on 'target for the four-point margin required to win the cup.*

◇ SEE ALSO **spot on** ▷ SPOT

go with a 'bang (*informal*)

Something that **goes with a bang** is a great success: *In the end the evening went with a bang and everyone enjoyed themselves.*

bank

break the 'bank

Something that will not **break the bank** does not cost a lot of money: *We can get a sandwich for lunch if you like; that won't break the bank.*

This idiom usually occurs in the negative.

I wouldn't 'bank on it (*informal*)

You say '**I wouldn't bank on it**' if you think that the person you are speaking to is depending on something which may in fact not happen: *'It's okay, Henry will give me a lift to the airport.' 'I wouldn't bank on it, it's his afternoon off.'*

◇ SEE ALSO **don't bet on it** ▷ BET; **don't count your chickens before they are hatched** ▷ CHICKENS; **don't count on it** ▷ COUNT

bargain

drive a hard 'bargain

Someone who **drives a hard bargain** negotiates hard to get an agreement that will be of most benefit to themselves: *The new managers were warned that the union chiefs were likely to drive a hard bargain.*

into the 'bargain (*informal*)

You use '**into the bargain**' when you want to emphasize some additional and rather surprising element in a situation: *They are expected to be exemplary girlfriends, brilliant cooks, and to have a super job into the bargain.*

bargepole

not touch something with a 'bargepole (*informal*)

If you say that you **wouldn't touch something with a bargepole**, you mean that you refuse to have anything to do with it, for example, because it is not safe or reliable: *I warned against it at the time, telling investors not to touch it with a bargepole.*

A **bargepole** is a long pole used for moving a barge on a canal.

bark

someone's bark is worse than their 'bite (*informal*)

You say that **someone's bark is worse than their bite** if there is no need to be afraid of them because they are not as unkind or unpleasant as they seem: *Despite appearances, his bark is definitely worse than his bite.*

barrel

have someone over a 'barrel

Someone **has got you over a barrel** if they are in a position to get whatever they want from you: *If I don't pay now, they'll just keep putting the price up; basically they've got me over a barrel.*

scrape the 'barrel

You say you **are scraping the barrel** when you have to use, or take, poor-quality things or people because the best have already been used or taken, or because you can't get anything better: *You're scraping the barrel a bit with those old jokes, aren't you?*

If a barrel is almost empty you may have to scrape inside it to get the last of the contents out.

bars

behind 'bars

Someone who is **behind bars** is in prison: *The three men are now safely behind bars in a high-security prison.* □ *They were behind bars for fourteen years before their appeal was finally accepted.*

base

make first 'base or **get to first 'base** (*informal*)

You **make,** or **get to, first base** when you complete the first stage of a process: *They didn't even get to first base, since they hadn't prepared a clear proposal which the judges could approve of.*

In baseball, you **make,** or **get to, first base** when you complete the first of the four sections of a run.

bash

have a 'bash (*informal*)

You **have a bash,** or **have a bash at something,** when you try to do it: *I've never sung a solo in public before but I don't mind having a bash.*

◇ SEE ALSO **give something a go** or **have a go** ▷ GO; **have a crack** ▷ CRACK

basket

'basket case (*informal*)

1 If you call someone a **basket case** you mean that they are completely mad: *'That woman is a bit strange.' 'Not just strange; she's a basket case.'* **2** If you call a country or a company a **basket case,** you mean that it has serious financial problems: *The company now looks as if it is right down there in the corporate basket case category.*

◇ SEE ALSO **nut-case** ▷ NUT **head case** ▷ HEAD

basics

back to 'basics

You go **back to basics** when you concentrate again on the simple, bare, principles that underlie something, usually after being too concerned with the less important and more superficial matters: *It's time to get back to basics; children need more discipline at school and a good grounding in spelling and grammar.*

basis

on a certain 'basis

You do something **on a certain basis** if that is the system, arrangement or limit you are applying: *Other staff were hired on a seasonal basis. □ The kit had been issued to some army units on a trial basis. □ three- and four-year-olds who receive education on a part-time basis. □ The treatment would continue on a daily basis. □ the interpretation of archaeology on a world-wide basis.*

on the basis of 'such-and-such

You make a decision or form an opinion **on the basis of** a certain thing if that thing is the reason for your decision or opinion: *Students are able, on the basis of experience,* to choose which subjects to specialize in. □ It is on this basis alone that they support the change.

bat (*see also* **bats**)

like a bat out of 'hell

You go somewhere **like a bat out of hell** when you move at a great speed: *When I saw the headteacher coming I was out of there like a bat out of hell.*

off your own 'bat

You do something **off your own bat** when you do it without being told to, or without help: *I didn't ask her to prepare a forward plan; she did it off her own bat.*

bathroom

go to the 'bathroom

In American English, you say that you want to **go to the bathroom** when you want to go to the toilet: *I just need to go to the bathroom, and then I'll be ready.*

◇ SEE ALSO **powder your nose** ▷ NOSE; **spend a penny** ▷ PENNY

bats

have bats in the 'belfry or **be 'bats** (*humorous*)

Someone who **has bats in the belfry,** or who **is bats,** is slightly mad or eccentric.

batteries

recharge your 'batteries

You **recharge your batteries** when you have a rest, for example when you take a holiday, in order to regain your energy and enthusiasm for work: *Don't try to do too much when you're on holiday; this is a good chance for you to recharge your batteries.*

battle

battle of 'wills

Two people have a **battle of wills** when each one is determined not to do what the other one wants: *The debate was more a battle of wills than a discussion. □ I refuse to be drawn into a battle of wills with you over this; just do as I ask, please.*

◇ SEE ALSO **battle of wits** ▷ BATTLE

battle of 'wits

When two or more people have a **battle of wits** they use their intelligence to think quickly and try to defeat their opponents: *The detective story invites the reader to a battle of wits in arriving at the solution before the author makes it known. □ In the annual battle of wits between these two grand masters of chess, nothing is left to chance.*

◇ SEE ALSO **battle of wills** ▷ BATTLE

fight a losing 'battle

You **are fighting a losing battle** if you are trying to do something which is certain to fail: *I'm fighting a losing battle, trying to get Joanne to stay on at school.*

'half the battle

If you say that something is **half the battle**, you mean that it is an important step towards success: *'They've invited me in for an interview.' 'Oh well, that's half the battle, isn't it?'* □ *Actually admitting that you have an addiction is half the battle.*

bay

hold at 'bay or keep at 'bay (*formal*)

You **keep**, or **hold**, something or someone unwanted or threatening **at bay** when you keep them at a distance so that they do not harm or affect you: *Concentrating on her guests would keep her worries at bay for a little while.* □ *The best medicine for keeping colds at bay is a daily dose of your favourite tipple.* □ *In the last hour of play, however, he played with great accuracy to keep the Dutch grandmaster at bay.*

> This idiom comes from the French hunting term 'aux abois', describing the stage of the hunt when the animal can neither escape nor attack because it is just about to be caught.

be (*see also* **being**)

the be-all and 'end-all

The **be-all and end-all** of something is the final aim, or the most important part of that thing: *Don't worry about it; it's not the be-all and end-all.*

> This idiom comes from Shakespeare's *Macbeth.*

bean

not cost a 'bean (*informal*)

Something which **does not cost a bean** costs nothing: *My new flat is great and it doesn't cost me a bean. I'm looking after it for a friend of my mother's.*

◇ SEE ALSO **not cost a penny** ▷ PENNY

not worth a 'bean (*informal*)

Someone or something that is **not worth a bean** is of little or no value, and is not worth bothering with: *I wouldn't worry if I were you; his comments aren't worth a bean.*

beans

full of 'beans (*informal*)

You are **full of beans** if you are lively and cheerful: *'You're full of beans this morning.' 'I know; I think it must be the sun.'*

◇ SEE ALSO **bright-eyed and bushy-tailed** ▷ BRIGHT

spill the 'beans (*informal*)

You **spill the beans** about something when you tell people a secret, or when you finally tell them something that you have been keeping to yourself: *'Come on, Rosie, spill the beans. What's this all about?' 'It's something Mum said.'*

◇ SEE ALSO **let the cat out of the bag** ▷ BAG **blow the gaff** ▷ GAFF **give the game away** ▷ GAME

bear

like a bear with a sore 'head

You describe someone as being **like a bear with a sore head** if they are in a bad mood: *'You're looking thinner.' 'Must be a bug; Luke's got it, too, not to mention behaving like a bear with a sore head when I told him I wanted to take an early lunch.'*

bearing

have a bearing on 'such-and-such

One thing **has a bearing on** another when it has an effect on it or a connection with it: *Your decision will have a bearing on the rest of your life.*

bearings

find your 'bearings or get your 'bearings

You **find**, or **get**, **your bearings** when you discover where you are and what you need to do, or which direction you need to follow, next: *It always takes a few days to find your bearings when you start a new job.*

> This idiom refers to the use of a compass and a map to discover exactly where you are.

lose your 'bearings

You **lose your bearings** when you get lost or do not know what to do next: *They lost their bearings in the fog.*

> See note at **find your bearings** or **get your bearings**.

beat

beat someone 'hollow

You **beat someone hollow** when you defeat them easily: *I'd been beaten hollow all year on the squash court, and I was determined to get a bit fitter.*

◇ SEE ALSO **beat someone hands down** ▷ HANDS

'beat it (*informal*)

People **beat it** when they rush away, usually to avoid trouble; if you tell someone to **'beat it!'**, you mean, rather rudely, that you want them to go away: *Let's beat it, quick.* □ *Now beat it, before I call the police.*

□ *Beat it, you two, I've just about had enough of your silly behaviour.*
◇ SEE ALSO **hop it** ▷ HOP

beat someone 'to it
Someone **beats you to it** when they get to where you want to go, or do the thing you want to do, before you do: *At the office door I found that I was second in the queue, not first. Somehow Alec Davidson had beaten me to it.*

if you can't beat 'em, 'join 'em (*informal*)
If someone says '**if you can't beat 'em, join 'em**' they mean that if you can't persuade people to change their opinions, then the most sensible thing to do is to change your own opinion: *Melanie Simmonite says she started racing 20 years ago – her husband did it so it was a case of if you can't beat 'em join 'em.*

'Em, here, is the short, informal form of the word 'them'.

on the 'beat
A police officer is **on the beat** when he or she is on duty and is walking round, or patrolling, the area he or she is responsible for: *PC Tomlinson was on the beat when the burglary took place.*

beating

take a lot of 'beating or **take some 'beating** (*informal*)
You say that something such as an achievement or a performance will **take a lot of**, or **some**, **beating** if it is so good that it is difficult to find anything better: *What a brilliant performance. That'll take some beating.*

beats

it beats 'me (*informal*)
If you say '**it beats me**', you mean that you cannot understand or find a good explanation for the thing you are talking about: *What beats me is how he got into the hospital without anyone stopping him.*

beauty

beauty is in the eye of the be'holder
If you say that **beauty is in the eye of the beholder** you mean that things or people that are considered to be beautiful by one person are not necessarily considered beautiful by other people: *In the final analysis, beauty is in the eye of the beholder, and essentially a personal matter. What pleases me may not please you, and my recommendation may disappoint you.*

This idiom is often adapted to suit the needs of the speaker. You may therefore find expressions like 'perfection is in the eye of the beholder', or 'cleanliness is in the eye of the beholder' [= what is considered perfect, or clean, by one person is not necessarily considered to be so by another].

beauty is only skin 'deep
If you say that someone or something's **beauty is only skin deep** you mean that being physically attractive is not necessarily a good guide to a person's character: *Sometimes when you meet a beautiful woman, you know their beauty is more than skin deep, and so it was with Rachel.*

This idiom is often adapted to the speaker's needs; therefore you may find 'more than skin deep', 'little more than skin deep', or 'that skin-deep quality', for example.

the 'beauty of something
The **beauty of something** is the benefit or advantage it has: *The beauty of the plan is that it's so simple.*

'beauty sleep (*humorous*)
Your **beauty sleep** is the sleep that you need in order to feel well and to look good: *I have to get my beauty sleep or I'll be a wreck in the morning.*

beaver

beaver a'way
You **are beavering away** at something when you are working very hard at it: *There, beavering away in their individual boxes, were other Eurocrats surrounded by shelves full of files.*

Beavers are animals which are known for working very hard all the time.

eager 'beaver (*humorous*)
You call someone an **eager beaver** if they are enthusiastic about something, or very hard-working, in rather a childlike way: *We collected our boots and skis and went over to join the other eager beavers in our group.* □ *The company takes on a new set of young, ambitious eager beavers in September every year.*

See note at **beaver away**.

beck

at someone's beck and 'call
You are **at someone's beck and call** if you are always ready to carry out their orders or wishes: *I had to be at his beck and call, night and day. He often got me out of bed, late on an evening, to run an errand.*

become

what has become of

You wonder **what has become of** someone or something if you haven't heard of them for a long time, and wonder what has happened to them: *By the way, what became of that 'book you were planning to write?* □ *I haven't a clue what became of him after he went off to Aus'tralia.*

bed

get out of bed on the wrong 'side

You say that you **have got out of bed on the wrong side** when little things keep going wrong for you; you can also say that someone **got out of bed on the wrong side** when they seem to be in a bad mood: *I must've got out of bed on the wrong side today – that's the second cup of coffee I've spilt.* □ *What's the matter with Alan today? Did he get out of bed on the wrong side?*

◇ SEE ALSO **not be someone's day** ▷ DAY; **one of those days** ▷ DAYS; **get up on the wrong side of the bed** ▷ SIDE

go to 'bed with someone (*informal*)

To **go to bed with someone** means 'to have sex with someone': *He loves Esther and however many women he may go to bed with, he'll never love anybody else.*

in 'bed with (*informal*)

You say that two or more public figures or groups are **in bed with** each other if they have the same opinions or are helping each other without openly admitting it: *It's supposed to be a self-governing body, but everyone knows they're in bed with the Government.*

make the 'bed

You **make the bed** when you arrange the sheets and covers of a bed tidily after someone has slept in it: *After I've made the beds and done the hoovering, I go out to the shops.*

no bed of 'roses or **not a bed of 'roses**

1 If you tell someone that life is **no bed of roses**, or **not a bed of roses**, you mean that things in life are not always pleasant, and that we have to accept the unpleasant moments too. **2** If you say that a certain activity is **no**, or **not a, bed of roses**, you mean that it is unpleasant or difficult: *It's no bed of roses teaching in a secondary school.*

you've made your bed, now you'll have to 'lie in it

If you say to someone '**you've made your bed, now you'll have to lie in it**', you mean that they will have to suffer the unpleasant side of a situation which they have created themselves: *I'm sorry to sound unsympa-*

thetic, but you've made your bed, now you'll have to lie in it.

wet the 'bed

A person **wets the bed** when they accidentally urinate in bed while they are sleeping: *Our daughter is nearly three and she's been dry at night for over a year, but recently she's started to wet the bed at night. Is there anything we can do to stop her doing this?* **'bed-wetting:** *Bed-wetting, although essentially a childhood phenomenon, can occasionally be a problem for adults.*

bedpost

between you, me and the 'bedpost

You say '**between you, me and the bedpost**' when you are telling someone something that you don't want them to tell anyone else: *Between you, me and the bedpost, I think she's having an affair.*

◇ SEE ALSO **between you, me and the gatepost** ▷ GATEPOST

bee

a 'bee in your bonnet

You have **a bee in your bonnet** when you have an idea or belief that has become an obsession: *'Is she still worrying about my diet?' 'You know her – once she gets a bee in her bonnet she won't let the matter rest.'*

busy 'bee

A **busy bee** is someone who is cheerful, lively and hardworking: *'I've been organizing the tickets for our holiday, and I've got all this information from the library.' 'You have been a busy bee,' he said, irritatingly.*

think you are the bee's 'knees

If you say that someone **thinks they are the bee's knees**, you think they have too high an opinion of themselves: *And he thought he was the bee's knees, you see; he thought he knew everything.*

◇ SEE ALSO **think you are the cat's whiskers** ▷ CAT

beef

beef something 'up

You **beef something up** when you strengthen it or add to its size: *This soup needs something to beef it up a bit; more pepper I think.*

beeline

make a 'beeline for

You **make a beeline for** a particular place or person when you go towards them quickly and directly: *Victoria made a beeline for the orange juice and sandwiches.*

Bees fly in a straight line when they are returning to their hive.

beetle

beetle 'off or **beetle a'way** (*humorous*)
You **beetle off**, or **away**, when you go away
in a hurry: *'Where's Jean?' 'Oh, I just saw
her beetling off in that direction; I don't
suppose you'll catch her now.'*

Beetles run quite fast and always seem to
be in a hurry.

beetroot

go 'beetroot or **turn 'beetroot**
You **go**, or **turn, beetroot** when your face
gets extremely red because you are embarrassed or hot: *To Isobel's surprise he went
beetroot, flushing from the collar of his shirt
to the roots of his now receding hair.*
□ *Drinking wine always makes me go beetroot.*

beg

beg, borrow or 'steal something or **beg,
steal and 'borrow something**
You say that you will **beg, borrow or steal**,
or **beg, steal and borrow**, something if you
intend to obtain it by any means possible: *I
shall have to beg, borrow or steal the money
to get me through my last year of studies.*
□ *We have had to beg, steal and borrow
substantial funds to keep the football club
in existence.*

beg to 'differ (*formal*)
You say that you **beg to differ** with someone on a certain point, when you disagree
in a very formal way: *I'm afraid I must beg
to differ on this point.*
◇ SEE ALSO **with respect** or **with all due
respect** ▷ RESPECT

beggars

beggars can't be 'choosers
If you say that **beggars can't be choosers**,
you mean that people who have a great
need for something have to accept whatever is offered: *I didn't really want to take a
job like this again, but I suppose now that
I'm unemployed – beggars can't be choosers.*

begging

going 'begging (*informal*)
Something is **going begging** when it does
not belong to anyone and is therefore being
offered to any person who wants it: *There
are a few sandwiches going begging here; has
anybody still not had one?*

begin

not be'gin to
Something that you **do not**, or **cannot, begin
to** do is something that you do not, or

cannot do at all: *for reasons I can't begin
to understand.* □ *You don't even begin to see
the point, do you?*

beginner

beginner's 'luck
You have **beginner's luck** when you are
unexpectedly successful at an early stage
of learning something: *Congratulations to
our new Assistant Editor Richard Bath, who
(thanks to a large slice of beginner's luck!)
made accurate predictions for all of last
week's World Cup matches.*

beginning

beginning of the 'end
The **beginning of the end** is the point where
things start to go wrong, leading towards a
disaster which cannot be avoided: *The day I
found out that he had started drinking again
was the beginning of the end for me.*

behalf

on be'half of someone or **on someone's
be'half** (*formal*)
You do something **on behalf of someone**, or **on
someone's behalf**, when you do it for them, as
their representative: *I'm going to speak on
behalf of the 'company.* □ *On my husband's
be'half, I'd like to thank you for this award.*
□ *The winner can't be here tonight so his wife is
going to accept the prize on his be'half.*

behaviour

on your best be'haviour
You are **on your best behaviour** when you
make an effort to be particularly polite and
friendly with people: *Do you change a
situation when you know that you're doing
an evaluation? Do people make sure they're
on their best behaviour?*

behind

right be'hind someone
You are **right behind someone** when you
fully support them: *Don't listen to them –
we're right behind you on this.*

being

come into 'being
Something **comes into being** when it begins
to exist: *The company came into being in
1897.*

belief

beyond be'lief
Something which is **beyond belief** is incred-
ible: *His rudeness is beyond belief.*
◇ SEE ALSO **have to be seen to be believed**
▷ SEEN

to the best of your be'lief

You say that something is true **to the best of your belief** if you are almost but not completely sure that it is true: *To the best of my belief the body was placed in the water shortly after death.*

◇ SEE ALSO **to the best of your knowledge** ▷ KNOWLEDGE

believe

believe it or 'not

You say **'believe it or not'** when you are telling someone something you think will surprise them: *Believe it or not, he never even picked up a violin before the age of sixteen.*

believe 'me

You use **'believe me'** to emphasize what you are saying: *You expect it to get easier, but believe me, it doesn't.*

believe something when you 'see it

If you say about something that you will **believe it when you see it,** you mean that you are doubtful about the truth of it: *He said he's going to study harder this year, but I'll believe it when I see it.*

if you believe that, you'll believe 'anything

People say **'if you believe that, you'll believe anything'** when they think you would be foolish to believe what has just been said: *He said he would be sure to arrive on time, but then if you believe that, you'll believe anything.*

would you be'lieve

People sometimes use **'would you believe'** when telling you something surprising: *He's 92, would you believe, and just as bright as ever.*

bell

give someone a 'bell (*informal*)

You say that you will **give someone a bell** if you intend to phone them: *I'll give you a bell to let you know what time we're arriving.*

ring a 'bell (*informal*)

You say that something such as a name **rings a bell** if it is familiar or reminds you of something: *His name rings a bell.*

saved by the 'bell

People sometimes exclaim **'saved by the bell!'** when someone is rescued from an unpleasant or difficult situation by something which brings the situation suddenly to an end.

In boxing, a bell indicates the end of a round and the fight stops.

bells

with 'bells on

If someone, especially a child, says **'same to you with bells on'**, they are returning an insult or criticism.

◇ SEE ALSO **with brass knobs on** ▷ KNOBS

belle

the belle of the 'ball

The belle of the ball is the most attractive or best-dressed woman at a social event: *'Now you look pretty,' he said approvingly, 'We can have supper, now, and you'll be the belle of the ball.'*

Belle means 'beautiful' or 'beautiful woman' in French.

belt

below the 'belt

A remark or comment that is **below the belt** is unkind and unfair, or unacceptable: *'Perhaps, Mr Prentice, as you're obviously out of work, it would be better if you took a course in housekeeping.' That was below the belt, but she went on.*

In boxing, it is against the rules to hit your opponent below the level of the belt.

tighten your 'belt

You **tighten your belt** when you have to get used to having less money to spend than usual: *We have to do our best to pull ourselves out of this recession and tighten our belts.*

under your 'belt

You have something **under your belt** when you have done or achieved it, and will be able to use it to your advantage in the future: *If you have followed our training schedules thoroughly you will not just turn up on the day, unprepared and with no training under your belt.*

bend

bend over 'backwards

You **bend over backwards** to help someone when you do everything you can to help them: *They bent over backwards to make sure we were comfortable.*

◇ SEE ALSO **lean over backwards** ▷ LEAN

drive someone round the 'bend (*informal*)

You say that someone or something is **driving you round the bend** if they are annoying you intensely: *That noise outside is driving me round the bend.*

◇ SEE ALSO **get someone's goat** ▷ GOAT; **make someone's hackles rise** or **raise someone's hackles** ▷ HACKLES; **get on someone's nerves**

▷ NERVES; **get up someone's nose** ▷ NOSE; **rub someone up the wrong way** ▷ WAY; **get on someone's wick** ▷ WICK

round the 'bend (*informal*)

You say that someone is **round the bend** if you think they are mad.

◇ SEE ALSO **round the twist** ▷ TWIST

benefit

for the benefit of 'so-and-so

You do something **for the benefit of someone** when you do it specially for them: *She repeated her words of welcome for the benefit of those who had arrived late.*

give someone the benefit of the 'doubt

You **give someone the benefit of the doubt** when you accept that what they say is true, even though there is no evidence to support it: *I'll give you the benefit of the doubt this time, but you must bring your identification with you next time you come.*

berth

give a wide 'berth

You **give** someone or something **a wide berth** when you keep away from them, usually because they are unpleasant or dangerous: *Outside a mad woman was talking to herself. Passers-by gave her a wide berth.*

◇ SEE ALSO **at arm's length** ▷ ARM; **steer** or **stay clear of** ▷ CLEAR; **keep your distance** ▷ DISTANCE

> In shipping, a **berth** is the amount of space which a sailing ship needs to move and turn safely.

beside

be'side yourself with something

You are **beside yourself with** an emotion like worry or anger if that emotion is so strong that you cannot think and behave as you normally do: *He was beside himself with anxiety.*

best

all the 'best (*informal*)

People say '**all the best**' to express good wishes to someone, for example at the end of a letter.

as best you 'can

You do something **as best you can** when you try to do it even though the circumstances make it difficult: *crowds of refugees surviving as best they can on the bare hillside.*

at 'best

You describe something unsatisfactory as a certain thing **at best** if that is the most

optimistic or favourable way you can regard it: *It would be a setback at best if we were denied use of their software.*

at your 'best

Someone or something is **at their best** when they are performing at, or achieving, the highest standard they are capable of: *Shakespeare on the subject of jealousy is Shakespeare at his best.* □ *I'm not at my best late at night.*

do your level 'best

You **do your level best** when you try your hardest to do something: *I did my level best to persuade him, but he just refused to come.*

for the 'best or all for the 'best

If you say that something is **for the best**, or **all for the best**, you mean that although it may seem unsatisfactory, in fact it is to someone's advantage: *I think their separation was probably for the best.*

make the 'best of something

People **make the best of** difficult or unpleasant circumstances when they try to accept them as cheerfully as possible: *We were allowed one blanket apiece and had to make the best of it.*

bet

best 'bet

Someone's **best bet** is the action that you would recommend they take: *I'd say your best bet is to wait here until they arrive; if you go looking for them, you'll probably miss them.*

do you wanna 'bet? or wanna 'bet? (*informal*)

People say '**do you wanna bet?**' to someone to indicate to them that what they have assumed to be the case may not be so: *'Even you aren't cruel enough to push me off backwards.' 'Wanna bet?'*

> '**Wanna**' here, is the contracted form of 'want to'.

don't 'bet on it (*informal*)

You say '**don't bet on it**' to someone when they expect something to happen which you are doubtful about: *'They'll probably be here soon.' 'Don't bet on it; I don't think they've ever been on time in the ten years I've known them.'*

◇ SEE ALSO **I wouldn't bank on it** ▷ BANK; **don't count on it** ▷ COUNT **don't count your chickens before they are hatched** ▷ CHICKENS

I 'bet or I'll 'bet (*informal*)

I bet, or **I'll bet**, means 'I'm sure': *I bet she'll be late.*

you 'bet (*informal*)

You bet means 'yes, of course': *'Do you want to come too?' 'You bet.'*

bête

bête 'noire

Your **bête noire** is the thing which you fear or hate more than anything else: *As an example he cites Europe; his political passion – just as it would appear to be Mrs Thatcher's bête noire.*

Bête noire means 'black animal' or 'black beast' in French.

bets

hedge your 'bets

You **hedge your bets** when you do something to protect yourself from losing something, being criticized, etc: *I suggest you hedge your bets by applying for a university flat, whether you think you want one or not.*

In gambling, you **hedge your bets** when you make bets on both sides, to make sure that you do not lose any money whatever happens.

better

all the 'better or so much the 'better

You say it will be **all the better**, or **so much the better**, if a certain thing happens when that thing is not essential but you hope it will happen: *I'm sure we'll manage without you, but if you can come then so much the better.*

the better for 'such-and-such

You are **the better for** an experience if it has benefited you: *I was feeling somewhat the better for a proper night's rest.*

better late than 'never

You say '**better late than never**' 1 to someone to show that you are not very pleased that they are late. 2 if you think that it is preferable that something should happen late than not at all: *You will have to accept that some permanent damage may already have occurred. Better late than never, though.*

better 'off

You are **better off** 1 if you have more money: *a situation where those who do not work are better off than those who do.* 2 if you are in more satisfactory circumstances: *There are disturbed people in prison who'd be better off in hospital.*

better safe than 'sorry

You say '**better safe than sorry**' when you want to remind someone that it's worth taking precautions, or to tell them not to be afraid of raising the alarm if they see something suspicious: *You might as well take out holiday insurance; better safe than sorry.* □ *If you see someone acting suspi-ciously near vehicles ring the police immediately. Don't worry if it turns out to be a false alarm – it's always better to be safe than sorry.*

for the 'better

Things change **for the better** when they improve: *On the whole the alterations are a change for the better.*

for better or 'worse

Something that is the case **for better or worse** is the case whatever you may think of it: *For better or worse, the computer has taken control of our lives.*

get the 'better of someone

Someone **gets the better of you** when they defeat you, often because they are able to think faster than you; an emotion **gets the better of you** when you fail to control it: *Curiosity eventually got the better of him, and he approached to see what was happening.*

go one 'better

You **go one better** when you do the same thing as before, or as someone else, only better: *Bernard Tapie will be hoping to go one better than two years ago when they lost to Red Star Belgrade on penalties.*

◇ SEE ALSO **keep up with the Joneses** ▷ JONESES

had 'better

If you say you **had better** do something you mean you will have to do it: *We'd better hurry.* □ *We'd better not disturb her yet.* □ *You'd better assume that I won't arrive before nine.* □ *I'd better warn you; she's in a poor state.* □ *She'd better turn up soon or it'll be too late.*

beyond

be'yond you

Something is **beyond you** if it is too difficult for you to understand: *I can't help him with his homework any more; all that modern stuff is beyond me.* □ *It's beyond me how he can expect people to tolerate such nonsense.*

◇ SEE ALSO **over your head** ▷ HEAD

big

make it 'big

Someone who **has made it big** has become very successful, famous or rich: *I knew from a young age that I wanted to make it big in showbusiness.*

◇ SEE ALSO **make it** ▷ MAKE; **make a name for yourself** or **make your name** ▷ NAME

bigger

the 'bigger the 'better

The bigger the better means that the more you have of something, the happier you will be: *Tell them to bring their friends to the party – the bigger the better, and we can really have some fun.*

bike

on yer 'bike (*slang*)

People sometimes say '**on yer bike**' as a way of telling someone to go away: *'I'll give you £50 for it.' 'Oh, on yer bike.'*

> '**Yer**' here, means 'your'.

bill

bill and 'coo

Lovers **bill and coo** when they kiss and whisper loving words to each other: *One month they're billing and cooing about each other to the press, and the next thing we know they're announcing their divorce.*

> Some birds touch beaks [= bills], and make noises to each other [= coo].

fit the 'bill (*informal*)

Something **fits the bill** if it is suitable or what is required: *We need someone with some experience and an ability to mix well with all sorts of people; I think the first candidate fits the bill exactly.*

head the 'bill or top the 'bill

Someone who **heads**, or **tops, the bill**, is the person who is the most important performer in a show: *Who's topping the bill in this year's Christmas pantomime?*

> This idiom comes from the wording of theatrical notices, with the star performer's name at the top.

bird

'bird brain (*offensive*)

Bird brain is an offensive term for someone who does not think very clearly, or who is not very intelligent: *'What's she like?' 'Well, she seems like a bit of a bird brain, to tell you the truth.'*

bird's eye 'view

You have a **bird's eye view** of something when you are at a point above it from which you can see it very clearly: *I had a bird's eye view of the procession from the top of the lamp post.* 2 You get a **bird's eye view** of a subject when you get a general, but clear outline of it: *A good selective bibliography gives a bird's eye view of the subject literature.*

the bird has 'flown

If you say that **the bird has flown**, you mean that the person you are talking about has run away or escaped: *When the men went to call on Zukovsky, they found that the bird had flown.*

a bird in the 'hand is worth two in the 'bush

People say '**a bird in the hand is worth two in the bush**', or just '**a bird in the hand**', when they think that it is not worth giving up something you already have for only the possibility of getting something better.

early 'bird

An **early bird** is a person who gains some advantage by being early: *If you're an early bird you'll be able to see the sunrise from the top of the mountain.*

> This idiom is the shortened form of the saying 'the early bird catches the worm', meaning that people who get up for work early will be successful.

a little 'bird told me

People sometimes say '**a little bird told me**' when they don't want to tell you who really told them a piece of information: *'I hear you're getting promotion.' 'How did you know that?' 'Oh, a little bird told me.'* □ *A reliable little bird tells this column that Frank may not be staying around much longer either.*

birds

the birds and the 'bees

You tell a child about **the birds and the bees** when you explain the basic facts about sex to them: *Do you remember how old you were when your parents told you about the birds and the bees?* □ *Have you ever wondered where computer programmers come from? No, I don't want a lecture on the birds and the bees – I was just wondering where software companies find them.*
◊ SEE ALSO **the facts of life** ▷ FACTS

> The second example above is a joke based on the question often asked by children: 'Mummy, Daddy, where do babies come from?'

birds of a 'feather

You say '**birds of a feather**' to mean that people who have the same interests, personalities or backgrounds will often be friendly with each other: *'It's funny how people travel to the other side of the world, and then make friends with people of their own nationality, isn't it?' 'Yes, well, birds of a feather...'*

> This idiom is the shortened form of the proverb: 'Birds of a feather flock together'.

kill two birds with one 'stone (*informal*)

You **kill two birds with one stone** when you manage to achieve two things with a single action: *There are advantages to an appren-*

ticeship. You might as well kill two birds with one stone by doing and learning in parallel.

birth

give 'birth
A woman **gives birth** when she bears a baby: *She gave birth to her son in the back of a taxi.*

strangled at 'birth
If someone says that someone or something should have been **strangled at birth**, they mean that they think it is so bad, or that it has caused so many problems, that it would be better if it had never existed at all: *Many Liberals said that they thought the SDP should have been strangled at birth.*

birthday

in your 'birthday suit
You are **in your birthday suit** if you are naked: *He walked into the bathroom and found me standing there in my birthday suit.*

This idiom refers to the nakedness of a new-born baby.

biscuit

take the 'biscuit
You say that something **takes the biscuit** if it is the best, worst, strangest, etc, of its type that you have experienced: *I've heard some unusual excuses for lateness in my time, but this one takes the biscuit.*

This is a British variant of the US form 'take the cake', which probably comes from the giving of cakes as prizes in rural competitions.

bit *(see also* **bits***)*

bit by 'bit
Something that happens **bit by bit** happens gradually, or in stages: *She tidied the garden up bit by bit. □ Bit by bit the truth emerged.*

a bit 'much *(informal)*
Something that is a **bit much** is unacceptable, unreasonable, or unfair: *It's a bit much, her expecting me to wait for her and give her a lift home.*

a bit of a 'lad *(informal)*
People refer to a man as **a bit of a lad** if he acts in a noisy, arrogant way: *He's a nice guy, but he's a bit of a lad – not my type.*

a bit of all 'right *(informal)*
People humorously say that someone is a **bit of all right** if they find them physically attractive: *Who's that guy at the bar? He's a bit of all right, isn't he?*

a bit 'off *(informal)*
Something, such as a remark, is a **bit off** when it is rather rude: *'He said he'd give me a lift to the airport, but now at the last minute he says he's meeting a friend.' 'Oh, that's a bit off, isn't it?'*

bit on the 'side *(humorous or vulgar)*
Someone's **bit on the side** is a person with whom they are having extra-marital sexual relations: *You know I sometimes wonder if he's got a bit on the side.*

champ at the 'bit
You **champ at the bit** when you are extremely eager to start doing something: *Within three months Eva was champing at the bit. The doctor had said she could go back to work.*

This idiom refers to the way that horses 'chew the bit [= a metal bar which fits across a horse's mouth]' with impatience.

do your 'bit *(informal)*
You **do your bit** when you do your fair share of work: *You've certainly done your bit for the company.*

not a 'bit of it
If you say '**not a bit of it**' in reference to something you expected to be so, you mean that it is not so at all: *I expected her to be apologetic, but not a bit of it.*

take a bit of 'doing *(informal)*
Something that **takes a bit of doing** requires a lot of effort, work or care: *Keeping to the schedule will take a bit of doing.*

bite

a bite at the 'cherry or a bite of the 'cherry
You get **a bite at**, or **of, the cherry** when you get a chance to do something: *That could well have been their last bite at the cherry. □ These people would believe that we get just one bite at the cherry of human life. □ We had been quite successful on our first visit; now we were returning to have another bite at the cherry.*

Notice that this idiom is always preceded by a word like 'first', 'second', 'last', etc.

bite off more than you can 'chew
You **have bitten off more than you can chew** if you find that a project or piece of work you have decided to take on is too difficult for you to manage: *I'm going to have to travel up to London every day of the week. I'm beginning to wonder if I've bitten off more than I can chew.*

have a bite to 'eat *(informal)*
You **have a bite to eat** when you have a snack: *We'll have a bite to eat after the concert.*

bits

bits and 'bobs or **bits and 'pieces** (*informal*)
Bits and bobs, or **bits and pieces**, are small things of various kinds: *There are a few bits and bobs of yours still here; would you like me to send them to you?* □ *She showed me a few interesting bits and pieces she'd brought back from Africa.*

pull to 'bits
You **pull something to bits** when you criticize it strongly: *I've lost all confidence in my work since he pulled my last essay to bits.*
◇ SEE ALSO **pick holes in** ▷ HOLES; **pull** or **tear to pieces** ▷ PIECES; **tear** or **rip to shreds** ▷ SHREDS

thrilled to 'bits (*informal*)
You are **thrilled to bits** if you are surprised and very happy about something: *She looked at the happy faces of her companions, and knew they wanted to be alone. 'What marvellous news. I'm thrilled to bits.'*
◇ SEE ALSO **walk on air** ▷ AIR; **on cloud nine** ▷ CLOUD; **in seventh heaven** ▷ HEAVEN; **over the moon** ▷ MOON; **on top of the world** ▷ TOP

to 'bits
Something falls or comes **to bits** when it breaks, or separates, into several pieces: *The car's falling to bits.* □ *He took the keyboard to bits in order to clean it.*
◇ SEE ALSO **to pieces** ▷ PIECES

bitten

once bitten, twice 'shy
Someone who is **once bitten, twice shy** is afraid to attempt something again because of a previous bad experience: *He hasn't had a girlfriend now for two years; I think it's a case of once bitten, twice shy.*

black

black and 'blue
You are **black and blue** when you are covered with bruises: *Neil's mother, Sherie, 28, said, 'I couldn't believe it when I saw him. He was black and blue all over; he looked awful.'*

black and 'white
1 Something which is in **black and white** is written on paper, and therefore definite and cannot be legally stopped: *It sounds like an interesting proposal, but I'd like to see it in black and white before we go any further.* **2** People see something, such as an issue, in **black and white**, when they only look at the two main opposing views, without considering the points in between: *It's a very difficult moral question, and it does no good to talk as if it was a simple black and white issue.*

in the 'black
You are **in the black** if you do not owe anyone any money: *Business is starting to improve; this is the first time we've been in the black for two years.*
◇ SEE ALSO **in the red** ▷ RED

> It is customary to use black ink to write entries on the credit side of a ledger.

blame

to 'blame
You are **to blame** for something bad or wrong if you are the cause of it: *Critics argued that the Government itself had been largely to blame for the country's economic problems.*

blank

draw a 'blank
You **draw a blank** if you get no results, especially if you cannot find the person or thing you are looking for: *The police, who have been trying to track down the missing painting, have drawn a blank.*

> This idiom refers to picking a losing ticket in a lottery.

go a complete 'blank
Your mind **goes a complete blank** if you suddenly cannot think of anything appropriate to say or do: *He asked me who my favourite artists were, and my mind just went a complete blank.*

blanket

a wet 'blanket (*informal*)
A **wet blanket** is someone who does not want to have fun, and spoils other people's enjoyment by being dreary and pessimistic: *'I still think you're absolutely mad to embark on something so ambitious.' 'Oh Jenny, don't be such a wet blanket.'*

blast

blast from the 'past (*informal*)
A **blast from the past** is a person or thing from your past that you remember, but had almost forgotten about: *Oh yeah, Alvin Stardust, there's a blast from the past.*

full 'blast or at full 'blast
A machine is on **full blast**, or **at full blast**, when it is producing as much power, heat or sound as it can: *We had the heater on full blast but we were still cold.*

blazes

like 'blazes (*informal*)
You do something **like blazes** when you do it quickly or with great energy: *She worked*

like blazes to finish painting the walls by the evening. □ *You chuck in the rock salt when the kiln is very very hot, and then run like blazes, because it sends up hydrochloric acid.*
◇ SEE ALSO **like the clappers** ▷ CLAPPERS

bleed

bleed someone 'dry

Someone **bleeds you dry** when they use all your money: *Well, if they hadn't bled me dry we could afford a better place.*

bless

'bless you!

You say '**bless you!**' to a person who has just sneezed.

blessing

a blessing in dis'guise

If you describe something as **a blessing in disguise**, you mean that it proved to be the best thing that could have happened, despite having seemed like a disaster at first: *'The accident was probably a blessing in disguise,' admits Barbara. 'I had ideas, but no experience. I've had plenty of time to prepare.'*

a mixed 'blessing

A situation is **a mixed blessing** if it has both advantages and disadvantages: *Living here is a mixed blessing. Mixed because you can find real solitude in the mountains, but lack of people often means a lack of facilities.*

blessings

count your 'blessings

You **count your blessings** when you remember what is good in your life instead of complaining: *Count your blessings – you could have ended up in hospital.*
◇ SEE ALSO **half a loaf is better than no bread** ▷ LOAF; **thankful for small mercies** ▷ MERCIES; **look on the bright side** ▷ SIDE

blind

blind as a 'bat (*informal, humorous*)

Someone who is as **blind as a bat** does not have very good eyesight, or cannot see anything at all: *I am blind as a bat without glasses, and contact lenses are too expensive.*

the blind leading the 'blind

A situation may be described as a case of **the blind leading the blind** if the person who is supposed to be teaching or helping others knows little more than, or as little as, those being helped or taught: *'You gave me a lot of help at the beginning, explaining the theory.' 'That was the blind leading the blind. I don't know how I got through the exam myself.'*

blink

in the blink of an 'eye

Something happens **in the blink of an eye** when it happens very quickly: *He's good at spending a long time doing nothing, then becoming highly active in the blink of an eye.*
◇ SEE ALSO **in the twinkling of an eye** ▷ TWINKLING; **in the wink of an eye** ▷ WINK

on the 'blink (*informal*)

A machine is **on the blink** if it is not working properly: *Oh dear; the telly's on the blink again.*

> This idiom comes from the characteristic flickering of a faulty screen.

blood

bad 'blood

You say that there is **bad blood** between two or more people if there are bad feelings between them: *The court heard that there was a background of bad blood between the two families.* □ *Bad blood between these two politicians is a major barrier to progress.*

blood is thicker than 'water

When people say that **blood is thicker than water**, they mean that people are generally more loyal to members of their own family than to other people: *'We had a difference of opinion and she left home,' said Mr Harrison. 'But blood is thicker than water and I have been at the hospital waiting to hear how she is.'*

blood, sweat and 'tears

Blood, sweat and tears is the maximum amount of effort that you can put into an activity: *It all looks so easy, but it isn't easy and it isn't wonderful. It takes blood, sweat and tears to do it.*

fresh 'blood or new 'blood

The most recently joined, sometimes younger, members of a group, who bring original ideas and liveliness are sometimes called **fresh**, or **new, blood**: *She's rather young for such a responsible position, but then we could benefit from some new blood in the marketing department.*

in cold 'blood

Something is done **in cold blood** when it is done in a deliberately cruel or uncaring way: *At dawn they were shot down in cold blood by a firing squad in the woods behind the camp.*

> This idiom comes from the medieval belief that emotion raised the temperature of the blood.

like getting blood out of a 'stone or like trying to get blood out of a 'stone (*informal*)

You say that obtaining something is **like**

getting, or **trying to get, blood out of a stone**
if it is almost impossible to obtain: *Persuading them to give away any information is like trying to get blood out of a stone.*

make someone's 'blood boil (*informal*)
Someone or something **makes your blood boil** if they make you very angry: *It makes my blood boil to see how people are ruining the countryside.*

◇ SEE ALSO **drive someone mad** or **crazy** or **insane** ▷ DRIVE

make someone's blood run 'cold
Something **makes your blood run cold** if it makes you feel very frightened: *Her blood ran cold when she picked up the phone to hear that voice again.*

out for someone's 'blood or **after someone's 'blood** (*informal*)
You are **out for,** or **after, someone's blood** if you are very angry with them and want to fight them or argue with them: *He's out of prison – says there are people out for his blood.*

sweat 'blood (*informal*)
You **sweat blood** if you work very hard: *I've sweated blood to get him to agree to see me at all.*

◇ SEE ALSO **break your back** ▷ BACK; **bust a gut** ▷ GUT; **work your guts out** ▷ GUTS

blot

a blot on the 'landscape
Something such as a building can be described as **a blot on the landscape** if it is very ugly and spoils the view: *Yesterday's blot on the landscape is today's tourist curiosity, as lovers of modern architecture will tell you.*

blow (*see also* **blows**)

at one 'blow or **in a single 'blow**
Several people or things that are destroyed **at one blow,** or **in a single blow,** are destroyed in a single action: *These smaller losses may seem unimportant, but together they may add up to a total picture of her life which she feels has been shattered overnight by a single blow.*

blow someone a'way (*informal*)
Someone or something **blows you away** if it causes you to feel extremely strong emotions: *'She just blew me away,' he says. 'I was so impressed I asked her if she wanted to do some work immediately.'*

blow-by-'blow
A **blow-by-blow** account or description of something is a detailed and graphic one: *I didn't feel like hearing a blow-by-blow account of his courtship of Yvonne.*

blow hot and 'cold on
You **blow hot and cold on** someone or something when you keep changing your attitude towards them: *'You don't know where you are with him, do you?' said Dorothy. 'From one week to the next. Blowing hot and cold like that.'*

'blow it (*informal*)
You **blow it** when you lose your chance of success through your own fault: *'How did your interview go?' 'I blew it.'*

◇ SEE ALSO **fluff it** ▷ FLUFF

blow 'over
Bad feelings between people **blow over** when they pass and become forgotten: *I wouldn't worry too much if I were you – it'll all have blown over by Monday.*

blow something sky-'high
Someone **blows something sky-high** when they completely destroy it in an explosion: *The terrorist bomb blew the car sky-high.*

soften the 'blow or **cushion the 'blow**
A circumstance that **softens,** or **cushions, the blow** makes something bad that happens to you feel slightly less bad: *To cushion the blow, wages and pensions were increased.*

blowed

be 'blowed (*informal, old*)
1 People sometimes say 'Well, **I'll be blowed**', or 'Well, **I'm blowed**', to express astonishment. 2 If you say you **are blowed** if you're going to do something, you mean you are determined not to do it: *I'm blowed if I'm going to let her have her own way all the time.*

blower

on the 'blower (*slang*)
You are **on the blower** if you are on the telephone: *You'd better get on the blower to him now and tell him what's happened.*

blows

come to 'blows
People **come to blows** when they start fighting or arguing: *The geologists often came to blows with the Indians over the possession of the richest sites.*

◇ SEE ALSO **have a run-in with someone** ▷ RUN

blue

out of the 'blue
Something happens **out of the blue** when it happens without warning: *She appeared again out of the blue after fifteen years' absence.*

This idiom refers to lightning which strikes out of a clear sky.

blues

got the 'blues (*informal*)
You say that you've **got the blues** if you are feeling sad or depressed: *Whenever I get the blues I take a long walk in the hills or go for a bike ride.*

bluff

call someone's 'bluff
You **call someone's bluff** when you are not deceived by another person's attempts to trick you into doing something: *One day, some man is going to call her bluff and she's going to get hurt.*

> In poker, to **bluff** is to pretend to have cards of a greater value than you really have; to call someone's bluff is to force them to show their cards.

blushes

spare someone's 'blushes
You **spare someone's blushes** when you avoid saying something in public which might embarrass them: *We will omit the names in order to spare the blushes of those who made the biggest mistakes.*

board

above 'board
Something such as a deal is **above board** if it is legal, honest, and is known about by everyone whom it concerns or affects: *His name was linked to allegations that certain transactions were not totally above board.*

> This idiom comes from card games, where anything that takes place under the table is likely to be against the rules.

across the 'board
An arrangement that applies **across the board** applies to everyone: *Eventually no-one should wait longer than a year for treatment. We will first look at reducing waiting times to 18 months across the board.* **across-the-'board**: *There were to be across-the-board salary increases.*

go back to the 'drawing board
You **go back to the drawing board** when you have to abandon something you are working on, and start again at the planning stage: *Really radical change can be achieved only by going back to the drawing board, throwing away the previous design and starting again.*

go by the 'board (*informal*)
An arrangement **goes by the board** if it is ignored or abandoned: *The Government's 'spend less, earn more' policy meant that*

health, education, transport and other welfare spending went by the board.

> This was originally a nautical term, meaning 'to disappear over the side of the ship'.

sweep the 'board
You **sweep the board** in a series of competitions when you win all the prizes: *Suppose the Social Democratic Party moved in and swept the board, what would we do then?* □ *He swept the board with six wins, winning overall by 26 points.*

> This idiom refers to the board used in many games, where one player wins all the pieces or bets.

take something on 'board
1 You **take something on board** when you make yourself responsible for it: *Try not to take too much on board this year.* **2** You **take** an idea **on board** when you take it into consideration or accept it: *Thank you for your suggestions; we'll definitely take them on board when we start our next project.*

boards

tread the 'boards
Someone who **treads the boards** acts in plays: *I was 22 or 23 before I decided to tread the boards, and it was not until I was in my 40s that I first appeared at a West End theatre.*

boat

in the same 'boat (*informal*)
Two or more people who are **in the same boat** are having similar experiences or problems: *By meeting others who are in the same boat, they begin to feel less alone and different.*

miss the 'boat (*informal*)
You **miss the boat** when you do not get a chance to do or have something because you are too late in arriving or asking for it: *Even if we had celebrated in a small way we would have attracted tourists from all over the world. The council has really missed the boat.*

push the 'boat out
If you say that someone has decided to **push the boat out**, you mean that they are going to spend as much money as is necessary, and work as hard as they can to make a particular occasion successful: *When Andy Saville broke his arm after signing two weeks ago, a lot of people thought we would give up, but we pushed the boat out and bought John Thomas.*

◇ SEE ALSO **go to great lengths** ▷ LENGTHS; **go to town on something** ▷ TOWN; **go to a lot of**

trouble ▷ TROUBLE; **go out of your way**
▷ WAY

rock the 'boat (*informal*)

Someone **rocks the boat** when they disturb the balance or calmness of a situation, or cause trouble: *I don't want to rock the boat, but don't you think someone should bring this to the attention of the authorities?*

◇ SEE ALSO **make waves** ▷ WAVES

boats

burn your 'boats

You **burn your boats** when you destroy your chances of being accepted back into a situation: *The attraction of the concept was that it allowed him to advance the prospects of a political settlement without burning his boats in the eyes of the army.*

◇ SEE ALSO **blow your chance** ▷ CHANCE; **sign your own death warrant** ▷ DEATH

Bob

and Bob's your 'uncle (*informal*)

People say **'and Bob's your uncle'** to stress how easy something is: *Pour it in a glass and look at it, hold your breath, put it in your mouth, and Bob's your uncle! It's gone down!*

bode

bode 'ill or **not bode 'well**

Something that **bodes ill**, or **does not bode well**, is a bad sign for the future: *If they're arguing about such trivial things now, it bodes ill for their future together.*

bode 'well

Something **bodes well** if it is a good sign for the future: *Their success in the British Championships bodes well for next year's Olympic Games.*

body

keep body and 'soul together

You **keep body and soul together** when you are able to pay for food, housing, clothes, etc: *You are an actress, aren't you? And you were working there in order to keep body and soul together?*

over my dead 'body (*informal*)

You respond to some suggested future event with the words **'over my dead body'** to indicate that you are completely opposed to it and will try every means of preventing it: *'Looks like the takeover will be going ahead.' 'Over my dead body.'*

bogged

bogged 'down (*informal*)

You are **bogged down** if you have too much work to do, or if you are unable to make progress because you are paying too much

attention to detail: *I'm not getting anywhere with this essay; I think I'm getting too bogged down in the theoretical side of things.*

> This idiom refers to the way in which movement is slowed down by thick mud.

boil

go off the 'boil

1 A liquid **goes off the boil** when it stops boiling: *Don't let the water go off the boil.* **2** Someone **goes off the boil** if they go past the period of greatest activity or excitement: *For the past decade it has been the great talking point of French politics. Now it appears to have gone off the boil.*

it all boils down to 'such-and-such

You say that **it all boils down to** a certain thing when you state the basic reason for, or meaning of, something else: *It probably all boils down to the way you were treated as a child. Did your parents use to praise you, or criticize you?*

bold

be so bold as to (*very formal*)

People sometimes ask if they may **be so bold as to** do or suggest something as an extremely formal and polite way of asking permission: *Might I be so bold, Madam, as to suggest a little snakeskin 'handbag to match the shoes?*

bolt

a bolt from the 'blue

A bolt from the blue is a sudden, unexpected event: *Now, was this forty thousand pounds a bolt from the blue or did you know it was coming to you?*

◇ SEE ALSO **come as a shock** ▷ SHOCK

make a 'bolt for it (*informal*)

You **make a bolt for it** when you run away suddenly: *I thought he'd made a bolt for it. He looked bloody scared.*

bomb

cost a 'bomb

Something which **costs a bomb** is very expensive: *It costs a bomb to travel by train these days. I'd take a bus if I were you.*

◇ SEE ALSO **cost the earth** ▷ EARTH; **cost a packet** ▷ PACKET

go like a 'bomb (*informal*)

Someone or something **goes like a bomb** when it goes very well, very fast, or if it is very successful: *They used to work together as a team, and they went like a bomb.*

make a 'bomb (*informal*)

You **make a bomb** when you make or earn a lot of money: *I hear Keith's making a bomb* *in that new job of his.* □ *You could make a bomb if you sold that car now.*

◇ SEE ALSO **make a bundle** ▷ BUNDLE; **coin it** or **coin it in** ▷ COIN; **make a fortune** ▷ FORTUNE; **make a killing** ▷ KILLING; **make your pile** ▷ PILE

bone

as dry as a 'bone or bone 'dry

Something is **as dry as a bone**, or **bone dry**, if it is completely dry: *I've been out in the rain all day in these boots and my feet are still as dry as a bone.*

bone of con'tention

There is a **bone of contention** between two people when they disagree on something, which causes them to have regular disagreements: *The missile plant became a bone of contention between Margaret Thatcher and John Major in 1988.*

This idiom refers to the way that two dogs will fight over a bone.

chilled to the 'bone

You are **chilled to the bone** if you are extremely cold: *We stood on the summit, already close to exhaustion and chilled to the bone.*

◇ SEE ALSO **cold as ice** ▷ COLD; **chilled to the marrow** ▷ MARROW

close to the 'bone (*informal*)

A remark which is **close to the bone** is one which makes you feel uncomfortable, perhaps because it contains some truth that you would prefer people did not mention: *'Would I be right in saying that we haven't provided you with what you were looking for when you came here?' He was getting a little too close to the bone for my liking.*

have a 'bone to pick with someone (*informal*)

You say that you **have a bone to pick with someone** if you want to confront them about something they have done which has annoyed you: *By the way, I've got a bone to pick with you. Why did you go off and leave me on my own?*

◇ SEE ALSO **have it out with someone** ▷ HAVE

bones

bare 'bones

The **bare bones** of something are the basic or essential parts of it: *The company has worked out the bare bones of the agreement and needs to work on the details now.*

feel it in your 'bones (*informal*)

You say that you **feel something in your bones** if you are certain about it even though you have no definite proof: *It's*

all going to be perfect! I just know it! I can feel it in my bones.

make no 'bones about something

You **make no bones about something** if you are willing to say it or do it openly: *She made no bones about telling me to take my business elsewhere.*

book

bring someone to 'book

You **bring someone to book** for something when you make them explain their actions, or when you punish them: *The police assured the victims that they would do everything to ensure that the culprits were brought to book for this terrible crime.*

This idiom probably refers to an imaginary book in which crimes are listed.

by the 'book

You do something **by the book** when you do it exactly according to the rules, or in the way you are supposed to do it: *They make us do everything by the book, which doesn't give us much space for creativity.*

in 'my book (*informal*)

In my book means 'in my opinion': *In my book, what he said to you merits an apology.*

◇ SEE ALSO **in my view** ▷ VIEW

open 'book

You call someone an **open book** if it is very easy to see what they are feeling: *Helen had always been an open book. There were no secrets she could keep, no feelings she could not help but show.*

throw the 'book at someone

You **throw the book at someone** when you reprimand or punish them severely, especially for breaking the rules: *We can't do that; they'll just throw the book at us.*

This idiom refers to the idea of charging someone with all the crimes in 'the book'.

books

be in someone's 'bad books (*informal*)

You **are in someone's bad books** if they are annoyed with you: *I'd better be careful about what I say; I'm in everyone's bad books at the moment.*

be in someone's 'good books (*informal*)

You **are in someone's good books** if they are pleased with you: *I'm in his good books at the moment, so I'll ask him if you want.*

cook the 'books (*informal*)

Someone **cooks the books** when they change the numbers in their, or their company's, accounts in order to gain money for themselves or the company: *They are now saying that everyone is* *cooking the books. If it's true, it's a very serious allegation.*

◇ SEE ALSO **have your fingers in the till** ▷ FINGERS

boot

the boot is on the other 'foot (*informal*)
If you say **'the boot is on the other foot'**, you mean that the situation has changed dramatically, and probably that someone or something that was weak has gained power: *In the past, probably because she was four years older, Laura had always seemed the more dominant figure. But now the boot was on the other foot.*

◇ SEE ALSO **turn the tables** ▷ TABLES

give someone the 'boot (*informal*)
You are **given**, or **get, the boot**, when you are dismissed from your job: *'I thought you worked at the insurance company down the road?' 'Well I did, but I got the boot.'*

◇ SEE ALSO **give someone the elbow** ▷ ELBOW; **give someone the heave-ho** ▷ HEAVE **give someone the push** ▷ PUSH; **give someone the sack** ▷ SACK

put the 'boot in (*informal*)
Someone **puts the boot in 1** when they repeatedly kick a person who is already lying on the ground: *It seems that those thugs really put the boot in; he's had to be taken to hospital.* **2** when they say cruel or hurtful things to a person who is already feeling sad and upset: *You didn't need to go and put the boot in like that; you could see that she was in a bad way already.*

to 'boot
To boot means 'as well' or 'in addition': *She was a woman of uninspiring appearance and a dreadful bore to boot.*

boots

'bossy boots (*informal*)
You can call someone a **bossy boots** if they like telling other people what to do and organizing them: *It would be good to have a little wife, he thought. Mind you, she was a bossy boots. But he didn't mind.*

lick someone's 'boots (*informal*)
A person **licks someone's boots** when they flatter them and do everything they want: *I've had enough of licking their boots every time I need something; it's demoralizing and humiliating.*

tough as old 'boots (*informal*)
1 Someone who is as **tough as old boots** is very strong and not easily hurt, either physically or mentally: *Beneath her frail exterior, she's as tough as old boots.*

2 Food that is **tough as old boots** is difficult to eat because you have to chew it for a long time before you can swallow it: *I'm not going back to that restaurant; the steak they serve is tough as old boots.*

bored

bored 'stiff or **bored to 'death** or **bored to 'tears** (*informal*)
You are **bored stiff**, or **bored to death**, or **bored to tears**, if you are extremely bored: *We were bored stiff by the end of the lecture.* □ *Algebra used to bore me to death when I was a kid.*

born

born and 'bred
You are **born and bred** in a particular place if that is where you lived for at least the period of your childhood: *He's a Londoner, born and bred.* □ *She was born and bred on a remote island off the west coast of Scotland.*

not born 'yesterday (*informal*)
You say that you were **not born yesterday** if you do not believe what someone has told you, and you think that it is naïve of them to expect you to believe them: *Empty your pockets. Come on. I wasn't born yesterday, you know.*

bosom

in the 'bosom of
You are **in the bosom of** a group of people when you are surrounded and protected by them: *He was looking forward to spending the Christmas holidays back in the bosom of his family.*

Your most secret thoughts are supposed to be kept in your **bosom** [= your breast]; a bosom friend, or bosom buddy, is someone with whom you can talk about these things.

bother

no 'bother
You say **'no bother'** when you want the person to whom you are speaking to know that what you are doing for them is not a problem for you: *'Thanks ever so much for the lift.' 'No bother!'*

◇ SEE ALSO **no hassle** ▷ HASSLE **no problem** ▷ PROBLEM **no probs** ▷ PROBS

bothered

can't be 'bothered (*informal*)
You say that you **can't be bothered** to do something, or **can't be bothered** with it, if you intend not to do it, or concern yourself

with it, because it takes too much effort, or because it is unnecessary: *She couldn't be bothered with the niceties of drawing-room conversation.* □ *I can hardly be bothered to move.*

bottle

'bottle-feed
You **bottle-feed** someone when you help them to do everything, without leaving them to use their own common sense: *He's got no training and no experience, so you might need to bottle-feed him for the first few weeks.*

This idiom refers to the way in which we feed milk to babies.

bottle 'out or lose your 'bottle (*informal*)
You **bottle out** of something, or you **lose your bottle**, when you decide not to do it because you are afraid: *I was going to do this parachute jump, but I went and bottled out at the last minute.*

hit the 'bottle (*informal*)
Someone **hits the bottle** when they start to drink too much alcohol, usually because of problems that they are experiencing in their life: *All the pressures she was facing caused her to hit the bottle again.*
◇ SEE ALSO **drown your sorrows** ▷ SORROWS

bottom

at the 'bottom of
A person or thing that is **at the bottom of** something is the cause of it, or explanation for it: *'What's at the bottom of all this extra security?' she wondered.*

from the bottom of your 'heart
You feel something **from the bottom of your heart** if you feel it very deeply and sincerely: *I thank you from the bottom of my heart.*

get to the 'bottom of
You **get to the bottom of** a mystery, for example, when you find out its cause: *I'll talk to the member of staff concerned and get to the bottom of this.*

bottoms

bottoms 'up! (*informal*)
People sometimes say '**bottoms up!**' when they raise their glasses to drink together: *Bottoms up, and all the best for the coming year!*

'**Bottom**' here refers to the bottom of the glass.

bounce

bounce 'back
You **bounce back** after an unpleasant experience when you recover from it very quickly: *'It was the lowest point of my life. I'd sold everything to do this trip.' But Mark bounced back and in 1983 he went on an expedition to Indonesia.* □ *After the disappointment of the Arsenal defeat, we've bounced back with two very creditable performances.*

bounds

know no 'bounds
Something which **knows no bounds** seems to be limitless: *His generosity knows no bounds.* [= He is very generous.]

out of 'bounds
A place is **out of bounds** when people are not allowed to go there: *The playing fields are out of bounds to pupils during the lunch break.*

within 'bounds
You keep something **within bounds** when you keep it to acceptable limits: *The doctor said that drinking wine is fine, as long as it's kept within bounds.*

bow

bow and 'scrape
Someone **bows and scrapes** when they act in an excessively polite and submissive way towards someone in authority: *There'll be no need for anything like that. The only bowing and scraping you'll be doing in future will be for the customers.*

This idiom refers to the way in which someone might bend their head [= bow], and drag their foot across the floor [= scrape] as a sign of great respect.

bowled

be bowled 'over
You **are bowled over** if you are overcome by emotion, especially gratitude or admiration: *I was quite bowled over by all their kindness.*
◇ SEE ALSO **be taken with** ▷ TAKEN; **have a thing about** ▷ THING

boy

blue-eyed 'boy
Someone's **blue-eyed boy** is a man or boy that they like more than others, often to the point of not seeing their faults, and treating them in a special way: *They loved to spoil my new baby brother. I was no longer the blue-eyed boy of the family.*

◇ SEE ALSO **the apple of someone's eye**
▷ APPLE **pride and joy** ▷ PRIDE

boy next 'door or **girl next 'door**
You refer to someone as the **boy**, or **girl, next door** if they are very ordinary: *Jeans are a staple part of everyone's wardrobe – from the boy next door to the rich and famous.* ▢ *To some extent, our presenters are role models for young viewers, and we like them to have a girl- or boy-next-door image.*

boys

boys in 'blue (*old, informal*)
People sometimes affectionately refer to the police as the **boys in blue**: *The boys in blue had made a full-scale search of the area, but had come up with nothing. It seemed that the car had simply ceased to exist.*

boys will be 'boys
People say '**boys will be 'boys**' as a way of excusing boys' and men's noisy, rough behaviour, suggesting that this is the normal way for them to behave: *Many deviant and indeed criminal male roles either receive public approval ('boys will be boys') – or are at least positively portrayed.*

brain

the 'brain drain
The **brain drain** refers to the loss of experts to another country, usually because they can expect better salaries and conditions than they get in their own country: *Senior expatriate scientists representing Britain's 'brain drain' warned of severe economic and social consequences unless scientific research was given a higher priority.*

on the 'brain (*informal*)
You have something **on the brain** if you cannot stop thinking about it: *She'd got religion on the brain. In one way, it had its funny side, but there was too much of it, it went on all the time.*

brains

blow your 'brains out (*informal*)
Someone **blows their brains out** when they commit suicide by shooting themselves in the head: *It's a good film, but don't take your kids to see it; this guy blows his brains out in the very first scene.*
◇ SEE ALSO **end it all** ▷ END

pick someone's 'brains (*informal*)
You **pick someone's brains** when you ask them for information about a subject that they have a lot of knowledge and experience of: *I was deeply grateful for our con-*

versation yesterday morning and being able to pick your brains on the subject was an immense help.*

rack your 'brains (*informal*)
You **rack your brains** when you think very hard in order to remember something, or to find a solution to something: *A blonde girl waved at me from across the room. I waved back, racking my brains to remember who she was.*

> This idiom refers to the old instrument of torture, the rack, which stretched the body.

brainchild

so-and-so's 'brainchild
A great idea is a certain person's **brainchild** if it is they who thought of it: *The idea of the campaign was the brainchild of a schools' liaison officer. It's message is to think before getting into a car.*

brainstorm

have a 'brainstorm
Someone **has a brainstorm** when they experience a sudden mental disturbance: *'I can't understand why she's suddenly begun to behave like this. She must have had some kind of brainstorm.' 'Not a brainstorm,' Jessamy said drily. 'It's called love.'*

brainwave

have a 'brainwave
You **have a brainwave** when you suddenly have a good idea: *He had a brainwave one day when sitting at home watching his wife knitting stockings by hand. He invented a machine which made the job quicker and easier.*

brake

put a 'brake on or **put the 'brakes on**
You **put a brake**, or **the brakes**, **on** an activity when you stop it or slow it down: *This year, the company has had to put a brake on spending, especially with regard to training.*

brass

bold as 'brass (*informal*)
Someone who is **bold as brass** is very confident and not afraid to ask for things, often to the point of being disrespectful: *She came up to me, bold as brass, and asked me for the car keys.*

brave

brave it 'out or put on a brave 'face
You **brave something out**, or **put on a brave face**, when you do not show any fear about something: *I had to put on a brave face and try not to appear worried, but when I saw him I was shocked at how much he had changed.*

breach

in breach of 'such-and-such
You are **in breach of something**, for example a law, if you do not follow it or do not do what it says you must do: *I'm afraid you are in breach of the market traders' law by not holding a licence for this stall.*

bread

your bread and 'butter
Your **bread and butter** is the way you earn your living: *Most of them earn their bread and butter from market research.*

breadline

on the 'breadline
Someone is **on the breadline** if they are very poor: *People who had once been poor, often virtually on the breadline, were now much more elegantly dressed and had achieved a far higher standard of living.*

This idiom comes from the US. Breadlines were originally queues of very poor people, waiting for free food provided by the government.

break

break 'even
A business **breaks even** when it makes as much money as it spends, but does not make a profit: *Although we had broken even, we were unable to go on paying wages.*

break 'free or break 'loose
Someone or something **breaks free**, or **breaks loose**, when they escape from control: *He broke free from his guards and escaped into the crowd.* □ *Several sailing ships had broken loose from their moorings in the storm.*

◇ SEE ALSO **make a break** ▷ BREAK; **cut and run** ▷ CUT; **give someone the slip** ▷ SLIP

give me a 'break (*very informal, rather offensive*)
You say to someone '**Give me a break!**' if you want them to stop annoying you: *'Come on! Haven't you finished yet?' 'Oh, just give me a break, will you? I'll do it in my own time.'*

◇ SEE ALSO **knock it off** ▷ KNOCK; **give it a rest** ▷ REST

make a 'break or make a clean 'break
You **make a break**, or **make a clean break**, when you escape from a place or situation, or separate yourself completely from it: *I'll make a clean break from athletics in two years' time and I won't be competing any more.*

◇ SEE ALSO **break free** or **break loose** ▷ BREAK; **cut and run** ▷ CUT; **give someone the slip** ▷ SLIP

breakfast

have someone for 'breakfast or eat someone for 'breakfast (*informal*)
You say that someone will **have**, or **eat**, **someone for breakfast**, if they are likely to beat them easily in a contest, or if they easily gain control over people: *Have you seen the size of him? He'll have our Charlie for breakfast.* □ *I don't know if it's wise to ask for a rise today; he'll probably eat me for breakfast.*

breast

make a clean 'breast of it
You **make a clean breast of it** if you tell the truth about something wrong that you have done, thought or felt: *It's as well she made a clean breast of it when she did, especially since the tape recording confirms her guilt.*

◇ SEE ALSO **come clean** ▷ CLEAN

breath

a breath of 'air
You get **a breath of air** when you go outside for a short time: *I left the party for a breath of air, and it was then that I noticed something strange going on at the end of the garden.*

a breath of fresh 'air
You describe someone or something as **a breath of fresh air** if you feel that they have a fresh and positive influence on you and people in general: *They remember him as a 'breath of fresh air', as a manager who rejuvenated the team with his ability to motivate players.*

catch your 'breath
You **catch your breath** when you stop breathing for a moment, because of fear, amazement or pain, for example: *A sudden noise made her catch her breath; but it was only the wind in the eaves.*

don't hold your 'breath (*very informal*)
You say to someone '**Don't hold your breath**' if they are expecting something which you think is unlikely to happen:

'I'm sure she'll change her mind when she's thought about it.' 'Don't hold your breath; she's not known for her flexibility.'

get your 'breath back

You **get your breath back** when you begin to start breathing normally again, for example, after exercise: *I stopped to get my breath back and surveyed the valley below.*

hold your 'breath

You **hold your breath** when you stop breathing for a short period of time, for example, because you are worried, or to avoid being heard: *I held my breath; would she tell him the truth?*

in the same 'breath or **in the next 'breath**

You say something, especially something contradictory, **in the same**, or **next**, **breath** when you say it immediately after the first statement: *First you say that you want to be free from responsibility, and in the next breath you say that you want to be rich and successful.*

out of 'breath or **short of 'breath**

You are **out of breath**, or **short of breath**, if you are breathing quickly or with difficulty, especially because of exercise: *She was out of breath when she arrived; she had obviously been running.* □ *He tends to be a bit short of breath these days, but for a man of 85 he's extremely healthy.*

save your 'breath

You **save your breath** when you decide not to bother telling someone something, probably because you know they won't pay attention: *You might as well save your breath; whatever you say, they'll do exactly as they please.*

take someone's 'breath away

Something **takes your breath away** if you find it very beautiful, pleasing, surprising, shocking or exciting: *The scenery in the Alps will take your breath away.*

under your 'breath

You say something **under your breath** when you say it quietly or in a whisper: *'Leave this to me,' she said under her breath, and winked.*

waste your 'breath (*informal*)

You say that someone **is wasting their breath** if no-one is listening to, or taking any notice of, what they are saying: *You're wasting your time, wasting your breath. They'll just go their own way.*

with bated 'breath

You wait for something **with bated breath** when you wait in great anticipation: *She waited for a reply to her offer with bated breath.*

breathe

'breathe again or **breathe 'easily** or **breathe 'freely**

You **breathe again**, or **breathe easily**, or **breathe freely**, if you feel safe or relaxed after a period of worry or fear: *She felt she could breathe freely now the exams were over.*

breathe your 'last

Someone **breathes their last** when they die: *It was as she had wanted; at home, surrounded by friends and relatives, she breathed her last.*

◇ SEE ALSO **kick the bucket** ▷ BUCKET; **cash in your chips** ▷ CHIPS; **pop your clogs** ▷ CLOGS; **shuffle off this mortal coil** ▷ COIL; **bite the dust** ▷ DUST; **give up the ghost** ▷ GHOST; **depart this life** ▷ LIFE; **snuff it** ▷ SNUFF; **go the way of all flesh** ▷ WAY

breather

have a 'breather or **take a 'breather**

You **have**, or **take**, **a breather** when you stop doing something, especially something which is physically demanding, and have a rest: *We stopped to take a breather, and surveyed the magnificent mountain scene around us.*

breeze

shoot the 'breeze (*informal*)

You **shoot the breeze** when you spend time with people talking about unimportant things: *The two shop assistants stood shooting the breeze while the queue slowly grew in front of them.*

◇ SEE ALSO **chew the fat** ▷ FAT

brick

drop a 'brick (*informal*)

You **drop a brick** when you accidentally do or say something embarrassing in public: *I dropped a brick there when I asked her why we hadn't seen her husband recently.*

◇ SEE ALSO **drop a clanger** ▷ CLANGER; **put your foot in it** or **in your mouth** ▷ FOOT

bricks

shit 'bricks (*vulgar*)

You **are shitting bricks** if you are very frightened: *I was shitting bricks all alone at night in that spooky old house.*

bridge

cross that bridge when you 'come to it

If you say that you will **cross that bridge when you come to it**, you mean that you are going to deal with a problem when it arises and not before: *She lit another cigarette. What would she do when the secret was out? She would cross that bridge when she came to it.*

bright

bright and 'early

You do something **bright and early** when you do it very early in the morning: *We'll have to be up bright and early to avoid the rush-hour traffic.*

bright as a 'button or bright as a new 'penny

Someone is as **bright as a button**, or as **bright as a new penny**, if they are clever and quick or if they are fresh and wide awake: *Henry loved that boy of his – red-haired, bright as a new penny, full of life.* □ *Three hours later he was still as bright as a button, while Fouchard was dozing quietly in the corner, pretending to read a file.*

bright-eyed and bushy-'tailed (*informal*)

You are **bright-eyed and bushy-tailed** if you are feeling fresh, well-rested and eager to do something: *How can you be so bright-eyed and bushy-tailed on only three hours' sleep?*

◇ SEE ALSO **full of beans** ▷ BEANS

bring

bring someone 'round

You **bring someone round** when you 1 bring them back from unconsciousness: *They brought him round, slapping him on the face and feeding him small sips of whisky.* 2 persuade them to do something, or convince them of something: *I think I'm slowly bringing her round to the idea, but it's going to take her a while.*

brink

on the brink of 'such-and-such

You are **on the brink of something** frightening, terrible or exciting when you are just about to do it or experience it: *two countries on the brink of war.* □ *scientists on the brink of new discoveries.*

◇ SEE ALSO **teeter on the edge** ▷ EDGE

broad

it's as broad as it's 'long (*informal*)

If you say '**it's as broad as it's long**', you mean that there is no real difference between two things: *It's as broad as it's long – just do whatever you want.*

broke

go 'broke (*informal*)

A person or company **goes broke** when they lose all their money and cannot continue to work or trade properly.

◇ SEE ALSO **go bust** ▷ BUST

go for 'broke (*informal*)

You **go for broke** when you risk everything you have for a chance of being extremely successful: *After winning the gold in the under 16s' National Championships, he decided to go for broke and turn professional.*

◇ SEE ALSO **stick your neck out** ▷ NECK

stone 'broke or stony 'broke or flat 'broke (*informal*)

You are **stone broke**, or **stony broke**, or **flat broke**, if you have little or no money left: *Can I pay you next week? I'm afraid I'm stone broke now 'til the end of the month.*

brother

Big 'Brother

You refer to a person or a system as **Big Brother** if you have the impression that they are constantly watching and controlling people's actions: *He used to stand behind us, breathing down our necks like Big Brother, waiting to criticize us for the smallest error.*

This idiom refers to the ever-present dictator in George Orwell's book *1984*.

browned

browned 'off (*old, informal*)

You are **browned off** if you are either bored or annoyed: *I have to say I was a bit browned off when she didn't notice the difference; after all that work.*

brownie

'brownie points (*humorous*)

You score **brownie points** when you do something that pleases someone in authority, or someone who is not always easily pleased: *If he could encourage a less uniform snacks policy in pubs, he would doubtless win brownie points from some voters.*

This idiom refers to the organization for young girls; 'the Brownies', where the girls are expected to perform helpful tasks every day.

brows

knit your 'brows

You **knit your brows** when you bring your eyebrows together in a frown, because you

are thinking, or concentrating very hard:
*He knitted his brows as he tried to remember
what she had said.*

brunt

bear the 'brunt of something
You **bear the brunt of something**, such as a
blow or attack, when you receive the main
force or shock of it: *In previous downturns,
manufacturing workers bore the brunt of job
losses.* □ *In the last ten years of her life, her
two teenage sons bore the brunt of her bitter
and depressed spirit, while their father
turned to the bottle.*

brush

give someone the 'brush-off (*informal*)
Someone **gives you the brush-off** when they
do not act in a friendly and open way
towards you: *He's been giving her the
brush-off while she's trying to get back to
the way it used to be.*
◊ SEE ALSO **give someone the cold shoulder**
▷ SHOULDER

tarred with the same 'brush (*informal*)
Two or more people are **tarred with the
same brush** if they have the same faults: *You
never told me that! Not that I'm surprised;
they're all tarred with the same brush, that
family.*
◊ SEE ALSO **a chip off the old block** ▷ CHIP;
cut from the same cloth ▷ CLOTH; **have
something in common** ▷ COMMON; **cast in
the same mould as someone** ▷ MOULD

bubble

prick the 'bubble (*informal*)
Something **pricks the bubble** when it spoils
a good situation: *For many people living
through that time, 1968 was the pin that
pricked the bubble.*

buck

make a fast 'buck or make a quick 'buck
(*informal*)
Someone **makes a fast buck**, or **makes a
quick buck**, when they make money quickly
and easily, and often dishonestly: *The
streets were lined with small illegal traders, all trying to make a fast buck as the
wall came down.*

pass the 'buck (*informal*)
You **pass the buck** when you refuse to
accept responsibility for something,
especially when you refuse to deal with
a problem: *The industrialized nations
are manifestly the real environmental
villains. Shouldn't we now be acknowl-
edging blame rather than passing the
buck?*

This idiom comes from the card game,
poker, where the **buck** is an object passed
to the person who wins, in order to
remind them that they must start off
the new jackpot.

bucket

kick the 'bucket (*humorous*)
Someone **kicks the bucket** when they die:
*Honestly, I was so ill, I thought I was going
to kick the bucket.*
◊ SEE ALSO **breathe your last** ▷ LAST; **cash in
your chips** ▷ CHIPS; **pop your clogs** ▷ CLOGS;
shuffle off this mortal coil ▷ COIL; **bite the
dust** ▷ DUST; **give up the ghost** ▷ GHOST;
depart this life ▷ LIFE; **snuff it** ▷ SNUFF; **go the
way of all flesh** ▷ WAY

buckets

rain 'buckets
It **rains buckets** when it rains very hard: *Do
you remember that holiday we spent on the
west coast? It rained buckets.*
◊ SEE ALSO **bucket with rain** or **bucket rain** ▷
RAIN **rain cats and dogs** ▷ CATS **chuck it
down** ▷ CHUCK; **tip it down** ▷ TIP

weep 'buckets
You **weep buckets** when you cry a lot:
*'When they told us, I thought that was the
end. I wept buckets, night after night.'*
◊ SEE ALSO **cry your eyes out** ▷ EYES; **cry or
sob your heart out** ▷ HEART

bud

nip something in the 'bud (*informal*)
You **nip something in the bud** when you
make it stop at a very early stage: *Healing
massage may be instrumental in nipping the
disease process in the bud.* □ *Her dream of
Hollywood stardom was nipped in the bud
last night when critics in America savagely
criticized her first big movie.*

bug

get the 'bug (*informal*)
You **get the bug** when you start to have a lot
of enthusiasm for something: *At the age of
16 he travelled through the Far East and
went to Australia to work on a sheep station.
The travel bug had truly taken a firm hold.*
□ *At the end of last season I had decided to
finish my career playing rugby. But I got
myself extremely fit during the summer and
got the bug again.*

bugger

bugger 'all (*informal, vulgar*)
Bugger all means 'nothing at all': *'What do
you know about her, John?' 'Bugger all, at
the moment. I've just got a photograph.'*

'Then you know quite a lot, if it's a good one.'
◇ SEE ALSO **sod all** ▷ SOD

bugger 'off (*offensive*)
'Bugger off' is a rude way of telling someone to go away: *I wouldn't be as polite as you are. Just tell him to bugger off!*
◇ SEE ALSO **get lost** ▷ LOST; **sod off** ▷ SOD

buggers

play 'silly buggers (*very informal, rather offensive*)
Someone who **is playing silly buggers** is acting in a foolish way: *Hello? Who's there? Are you sleepwalking again? Come on, stop playing silly buggers.*

bulk

in 'bulk
You buy or sell something **in bulk** when you buy or sell very large quantities of it: *He bought in bulk from the manufacturers and sold to shops and stallholders in the markets.*

bull

hit the 'bull's-eye or score a 'bull's-eye
You **hit the bull's-eye**, or **score a bull's eye** when you make a remark or do something which is very appropriate to the situation: *Are you aware that you have just scored a marvellous bull's eye? Does your argument not prove that the Government are spending more on these services than before?*

The **bull's-eye** is the exact centre of a dartboard in the game of darts.

like a bull in a 'china shop
You describe someone as being **like a bull in a china shop 1** if they are very clumsy: *Anthony was always rushing about like a bull in a china shop, knocking things over, and generally causing havoc wherever he went.* **2** if they do not make any effort to be polite and tactful in social situations: *Politically, he often behaved like a bull in a china shop. Privately, he could be a man of great sensitivity.*

take the bull by the 'horns (*informal*)
You **take the bull by the horns** when you make a determined decision to do something: *Being the determined woman she was, she decided to take the bull by the horns and organize things for herself.*
◇ SEE ALSO **rise to the challenge** ▷ CHALLENGE; **grasp the nettle** ▷ NETTLE; **rise to the occasion** ▷ OCCASION; **pull out all the stops** ▷ STOPS

bullet

bite the 'bullet (*informal*)
You **bite the bullet** when you **1** decide to tolerate a situation rather than complain about it, since there is nothing you can do about it: *We have to bite the bullet a little now, but once the ground has been finished, we should start making profits again.* **2** decide that you must do something, even though it will be unpleasant: *Only so much can be done by discussion. Decisions have to be taken, and as director you have got to bite the bullet.*

This idiom refers to the practice used by army doctors of giving patients a bullet to put between their teeth while performing painful operations.

bun

'bun in the oven (*old or humorous*)
A woman who has got a **bun in the oven** is expecting a baby: *Looks like young Susie's got a bun in the oven.*
◇ SEE ALSO **up the duff** ▷ DUFF **up the spout** ▷ SPOUT **in the pudding club** ▷ PUDDING **in the club** ▷ CLUB

bunch

the best of a bad 'bunch
Someone or something that is **the best of a bad bunch** is the one you think is not as bad as the others in a group of people or things, none of which you like very much: *If none of the candidates is suitable, think twice before appointing the best of a bad bunch. You may be better advised to start again.*

give someone a bunch of 'fives (*old, humorous*)
A person **gives someone a bunch of fives** when they punch them: *Watch it you; or I'll give you a bunch of fives.*
◇ SEE ALSO **thick ear** ▷ EAR; **give someone a knuckle sandwich** ▷ KNUCKLE

bundle

bundle of 'nerves
You are a **bundle of nerves** if you are very anxious: *She was a bundle of nerves. She tried to calm herself. 'Now, madam, on the second of December, I understand that your husband was home with you all evening?'*

make a 'bundle (*informal*)
You **make a bundle** when you make a lot of money: *We made a bundle on that stall at the carnival last year.*
◇ SEE ALSO **make a bomb** ▷ BOMB; **coin it** or **coin it in** ▷ COIN; **make a fortune** ▷ FORTUNE; **make a killing** ▷ KILLING; **make your pile** ▷ PILE

Bundle here refers to banknotes.

not a bundle of 'laughs or a bundle of 'laughs (informal)

1 Someone or something that is **not a bundle of laughs**, is not very enjoyable or much fun: *Most of his films aren't exactly a bundle of laughs; but then they're not supposed to be.* 2 When people say that something is, or will be, **a bundle of laughs**, they usually mean, ironically, that it will not be very enjoyable at all: *If we go on treating the environment as we have been over the last years, life in the third millenium should be just a bundle of laughs.*

not go a 'bundle on something (informal)

You **don't go a bundle on something** when you are not keen on doing it: *They don't go a bundle on employing married women in this company.* □ *I don't go a bundle on discos, but I'll come with you if you want.*

◇ SEE ALSO **not your cup of tea** ▷ CUP

This idiom refers to the money that you would not like to bet on something.

bunk

do a 'bunk (informal)

Someone **does a bunk** when they run away from a place: *Several of the pupils did a bunk during the morning break.*

◇ SEE ALSO **do a moonlight flit** ▷ MOON-LIGHT

burner

put something on the back 'burner (informal)

You **put something on the back burner** when you delay doing it until later: *The company's activities have been put on the back burner until production can be resumed abroad with lower costs.*

This idiom is an old cooking term.

burst

fit to 'burst (informal)

1 You are **fit to burst** if you are very full from eating: *By the end of the meal we were all fit to burst.* 2 You are **fit to burst** with a particular emotion, when you are feeling it intensely: *I was fit to burst with joy.* □ *With a heart fit to burst through tension, at last, I heard a noise.*

bursting

bursting to 'do something (informal)

1 You are **bursting to do something** if you are extremely impatient to do it: *She met me at the door; opened it, and held it ready*

for me to come in; there was something she was bursting to tell me. 2 **'I'm 'bursting'** (informal) usually means 'I badly need to go to the toilet.'

bush

beat about the 'bush

You tell someone not to **beat about the bush** when you want them to speak openly and directly without hiding anything: *Come on, don't beat about the bush. What are you trying to say?* □ *I had the impression he was beating about the bush and there was something he wanted to tell me.*

'Beating the bush' is an activity carried out while hunting birds.

bush 'telegraph

The **bush telegraph** is the way in which news spreads fast from person to person: *How come everyone knows I'm getting married? The bush telegraph works fast round here.*

This was originally an Australian phrase.

business

back in 'business

Someone or something is **back in business** if they are working again after a period of inactivity: *When we get the electricity reconnected we'll be back in business.*

business as 'usual

It is **business as usual** in a place if people continue in the normal way despite disturbances: *It's business as usual in the local school, despite the storm which destroyed half the town in the night.*

'funny business

Funny business is tricks or dishonest behaviour: *They warned us not to try any funny business as we would be caught immediately.* □ *I think there's some funny business going on where these accounts are concerned; something isn't quite right.*

◇ SEE ALSO **monkey business** ▷ MONKEY; **foul play** ▷ PLAY; **sharp practice** ▷ PRACTICE

get down to 'business

People **get down to business** when they start dealing with, or discussing, something in a serious and practical way: *Right, let's get down to business. I think the first item on the agenda is this year's pay review.*

go about your 'business

People **go about their business** when they attend to their normal everyday tasks and duties: *We watched the small boats going about their business in the harbour.*

have no 'business

If you say that someone **has no business** doing something, you mean that they have no right to do it, or that they ought not to do it: *He had absolutely no business using the tapes without my permission.*

like 'nobody's business (*informal*)

You do something, or something happens, **like nobody's business** when you do it very well or fast, or if it happens a lot: *The phone's been ringing like nobody's business since we put that advert in the newspaper.* □ *She's working away like nobody's business to get that project finished on time.*

make it your 'business

You **make it your business** to do something when you deliberately try to do it: *She did not know the answer, but was going to make it her business to find out.* □ *We make it our business to learn all we can about our client's product.*

mean 'business (*informal*)

People **mean business** when they are seriously determined to do what they suggest or propose: *This time they were not just threatening; they clearly meant business.*

mind your own 'business (*informal, offensive*)

1 You say to someone '**Mind your own business!**', if you think they are being too curious and inquisitive about your private affairs: *'How did you vote in the last election?' 'Mind your own business.'* **2** You **are minding your own business** when you are concentrating on matters which concern you, and not paying attention to, or interfering in, other people's affairs: *I was so busy minding my own business that I didn't notice there was anything wrong.*

none of someone's 'business or **no business of 'someone's** (*informal*)

A matter is **none of someone's business**, or **no business of theirs**, if you think that they are being too curious about a private matter which does not concern them: *It's no business of mine how she gets the money for her foreign trips.* □ *I don't see that this is any business of yours.* □ *I know it's none of my business, but I don't want you to get hurt again.*

out of 'business

A company goes **out of business** when it stops trading, usually because it is losing money, or failing to make a profit: *Smaller firms are being forced out of business.*

busman

busman's 'holiday (*informal*)

You say that you are on a **busman's holiday** when you are doing something in your spare time which is too closely related to your work to be considered as leisure: *A fire crew's Christmas outing turned into a busman's holiday when their coach caught fire yesterday.*

bust

go 'bust (*informal*)

A company **goes bust** when it loses all its money and has to close down.

◇ SEE ALSO **go broke** ▷ BROKE

busy

busy as a 'bee

You are as **busy as a bee** when you are very busy.

buts

no buts a'bout it or **no 'buts**

You say that there are **no buts about it** if you will not accept any objections: *'But I live here,' said Charlie. 'No buts,' said the man and gave Charlie a shove in the chest which propelled him back into the street.*

butter

butter wouldn't melt in so-and-so's 'mouth

You say that **butter wouldn't melt in** a certain person's **mouth** when you want to comment that the person looks, or acts, as if they would never do anything wrong, often despite the facts to the contrary: *The boy was first arrested at the age of 10 for giving £1,000 to a drug dealer for heroin. The detective added: 'To look at him you'd think butter wouldn't melt in his mouth.'*

butterfingers

'butterfingers (*informal*)

You might call someone '**butterfingers**' when they have dropped something, or if they often drop things.

butterflies

have 'butterflies or **have 'butterflies in your stomach**

You **have butterflies**, or **have butterflies in your stomach**, if you have a nervous feeling in your stomach: *She's got butterflies about the exam.*

button

'button it! (*very informal, rather offensive*)
People sometimes say '**Button it!**' when they want someone to be quiet.

◇ SEE ALSO **put a sock in it** ▷ SOCK

right on the 'button (*informal*)
You are **right on the button** when you are exactly right about something: *Her description of him was right on the button; I recognized him immediately.*

buzz

give someone a 'buzz (*informal*)
You **give someone a buzz** when you call them on the telephone: *I'll give you a buzz as soon as I know what I'm doing.*

bygones

let bygones be 'bygones
You say '**let bygones be bygones**' to someone when you agree that you should both forget quarrels or problems from the past: *I expect auntie has told you everything, but please come now. We will let bygones be bygones. Daddy would have wanted it.*

◇ SEE ALSO **forgive and forget** ▷ FORGIVE

c

caboodle

the whole ca'boodle (informal)
The **whole caboodle** is a lot of different things which go together, including all the equipment you will need for a certain activity: *The whole caboodle, heavy and cumbersome, looked as though it might be more at home in a grand hotel than a north London flat.* □ *Of course it's yours truly that's got to clean the whole kit and caboodle.*

cackle

cut the 'cackle (informal)
If you tell a group of people to **cut the cackle**, you are telling them to be quiet and start working: *Okay now class, will you cut the cackle so we can get started.*

cage

rattle someone's 'cage (informal)
If someone seems unusually cross or unfriendly for no obvious reason, people sometimes ask what has **rattled their cage**: *What rattled his cage this morning? I said he looked well and he told me to mind my own business.*
◇ SEE ALSO **ruffle someone's feathers** ▷ FEATHERS

> Rattling the cage which an animal or a bird is living in will probably make it upset or angry.

cahoots

in ca'hoots
If two or more people are **in cahoots,** or **in cahoots with each other**, they are secretly working together to do something bad: *It all makes sense. He was in cahoots with the baker, and they used the bakery as a base.*

Cain

raise 'Cain
You **raise Cain** when you make a strong complaint about something, with the aim of punishing someone or getting what you want: *He guessed that his employer was used to having his own way, and would raise Cain if he didn't get it.*
◇ SEE ALSO **raise hell** ▷ HELL **kick up a stink** ▷ STINK

cake (see also **cakes**)

have your cake and 'eat it
If someone wants to **have their cake and eat it**, they want to do or have two things which are not usually possible together, instead of making a choice and being happy with just one of those things: *You can't have both. You can't have your cake and eat it.*
◇ SEE ALSO **the grass is always greener on the other side of the fence** ▷ GRASS **the best of both worlds** ▷ WORLDS

cakes

sell like hot 'cakes or go like hot 'cakes
A new product or item which **is selling**, or **going, like hot cakes** is so popular that a lot of people are buying it: *Cards depicting Santa are selling like hot cakes.*

call

the call of 'nature (humorous)
The **call of nature** is the need to go to the toilet; you answer **the call of nature** when you go to the toilet: *The driver moves the bus to reveal squatting passengers answering the call of nature.*

close 'call
You have a **close call** when a bad event almost happens, but you manage to avoid it just in time: *Bernadette Devlin had a close call, but she survived the assassination attempt against her.*
◇ SEE ALSO **narrow escape** ▷ ESCAPE; **close shave** ▷ SHAVE; **narrow squeak** ▷ SQUEAK; **close** or **near thing** ▷ THING

cold 'call
A **cold call** is a telephone call or visit made by a salesperson, to someone who is not expecting the call or visit: *They had heard of Oyston, who had originally been contacted as a cold call.* □ *Only certain types of investment may be the subject of a cold call.*

don't call us, we'll call 'you or **don't call 'us ...** (*humorous*)

The phrase **'don't call us, we'll call you'**, or **'don't call us ...'**, expresses a lack of interest on the part of the speaker in the person they are referring to, and a particular lack of enthusiasm for whatever that person has to offer: *Imagine your employer does not give you any work to do, perhaps sending you home and saying for some reason, 'Don't call us ...'*

This phrase was originally used by US film producers to discourage people who were taking part in an audition from contacting them. Today, you would never say it directly to the person you were talking about because it has become so insulting.

no 'call for something

If there is **no call for something** there is no need for it: *'Well there was no call to do that,' said his Mum.* □ *There was no call for him to bribe me.*

un'called for: *That remark was totally uncalled for.*

on 'call

A person such as a doctor is **on call** during the period when they can be contacted and have agreed to be available if anyone needs their services: *He had been on call for two days, and was feeling totally exhausted.* □ *In an emergency you can reach a doctor or nurse through our 24-hour on-call facility.*

pay someone a 'call

You **pay someone a call** if you visit them for a short time, probably at their home: *I thought I'd pay you a call as I was passing by. But you weren't in.*

calm

the calm before the 'storm

The **calm before the storm** is a time of quiet waiting that comes before a period of great activity or before some unpleasant event occurs: *Those who argue that Scotland is now experiencing the calm before the political storm could well be proved right.*

For a short time before a storm starts, the weather often becomes still.

camp

camp it 'up

A man who **is camping it up** is trying to imitate a woman in an artificial and amusing way, with movements of his body and hands, and with his voice: *His hands-on-hip simpering is beloved of pseudo comedians who, when in doubt, camp it up.*

can

can of 'worms

A situation which is a **can of worms** is full of hidden problems which have been left to get worse, because nobody noticed them or dealt with them while they were developing: *The prosecution could open a can of worms.* □ *They avoided any public probing into this can of worms.*

◇ SEE ALSO **Pandora's box** ▷ PANDORA; **poisoned chalice** ▷ CHALICE

A worm is a long, thin, cylindrical animal, with no backbone or legs, especially one that lives in the soil.

carry the 'can

You **carry the can** if you take the blame for something: *We were both equally at fault, but I had to carry the can.*

in the 'can (*informal*)

If something is **in the can**, it is already done or achieved: *By lunchtime we already had two complete runs of the play in the can.* □ *The boy already had one success in the can.*

candle

burn the candle at both 'ends

You **are burning the candle at both ends** if you are making yourself tired, probably by going to bed late at night and getting up early in the morning: *This month you are determined to live it up and have a good time, but you must watch your health and try not to burn the candle at both ends.*

hold a 'candle for someone

If you **hold a candle for someone**, you like them and hope that one day they may show interest in you, perhaps romantically: *Portillo still holds a candle for Margaret Thatcher in the cabinet.*

◇ SEE ALSO **have a crush on someone** ▷ CRUSH; **have a soft spot for someone** ▷ SPOT

not fit to hold a 'candle to

You can say that a person or thing is **not fit to hold a candle to** someone or something else if they are so much worse than them that the comparison is ridiculous: *As a Shakespearean actor he is very good, but he's not even fit to hold a candle to Jacobi.*

◇ SEE ALSO **in a class of your own** ▷ CLASS a **cut above** or a **cut above the rest** ▷ CUT **in a different league** ▷ LEAGUE

The literal meaning of this phrase is 'not even good enough to hold a light so that someone else can see to do a job'.

cannon

'cannon fodder

Cannon fodder is a name used to refer to people or workers whose lives are considered to be of such little value that they are being allowed to suffer or die: *The pressure to succeed will increase as schools compete on the exam league tables. Children will be cannon fodder to boost a school's image.* □ *Reports criticize the terrorists for using civilians as cannon fodder, to try to win sympathy for their cause abroad.*

canoe

paddle your own ca'noe

You **are paddling your own canoe** if, refusing help or control from anyone else, you do something your own way with great determination: *She had to paddle her own canoe, as she'd always done. 'It's not what happens to you, but how you cope with it that's important,' she told herself.*

cap

cap in 'hand

You go **cap in hand** to ask for something if you ask for it in a very humble way: *Shouldn't the elderly automatically receive a heating allowance every winter, instead of having to go cap in hand to the government?*
◇ SEE ALSO **on bended knee** ▷ KNEE

if the cap fits, 'wear it

If the cap fits, wear it, means 'If you recognize yourself in my description, then let that be the case': *'Are you calling me a traitor?' 'No, but if the cap fits, wear it.'* □ *'What do you mean, lowest of the low?' 'The cap fits, does it? They don't come much lower than you, Cullam.'*

put on your 'thinking cap

When you need to think hard about how to deal with a particular problem, you say that you will have to **put on your thinking cap**: *You will have to put on your own thinking cap and go through a whole array of techniques before you hit on the right one to catch this fish.*

set your 'cap at someone

You **set your cap at someone** who you are interested in romantically, when you decide to put a lot of effort into winning their affection: *It's obvious that he's set his cap at Julie. He's just not interested in any other women, is he?*

to cap it 'all

You introduce one last misfortune with the expression '**to cap it all**', if you have already mentioned a list of bad things that have happened: *Gray failed to realize how poor the team was, and then, to cap it all, he*

proceeded to spend £1,000,000 on rather an ordinary centre forward.
◇ SEE ALSO **to crown it all** ▷ CROWN **to make matters worse** ▷ MATTERS; **to top it all** ▷ TOP **what is more** ▷ WHAT

capacity

to ca'pacity

Something which is filled **to capacity** is full, with no room for any more: *The audience packed this room to capacity.*

capital

make 'capital of something or make 'capital out of something

Someone **makes capital of**, or **out of**, a situation or event if they use it for their own advantage: *She must not make capital out of her distress.* □ *He takes a rather gloating pleasure in turning over his secrets, deciding how to make capital of them.*

card

have a 'card up your sleeve or keep a 'card up your sleeve

You **have**, or **are keeping**, **a card up your sleeve** if other people think that you are in a difficult situation, but you have a secret solution which you plan to surprise them with: *Don't cry. Just wait and see. Your old grandad has still got plenty of cards up his sleeve.*

> When people cheat at cards they sometimes hide an extra card up their sleeve.

'wild card

A **wild card** is an action or thing whose chances of success are unknown; **wild card** is also a method of searching for information by computer, using a symbol [= the **wild card**] which represents a variable element in the search: *Paddy Agnew follows the success of the new wild card in Italy's World Cup team.* □ *We use an asterisk instead of the word ending for wild card searches.*

cards

the cards are stacked a'gainst someone

If **the cards are stacked against you**, you are in a situation which gives you very little hope of success: *He's giving his best effort to the election campaign, but the cards are stacked against him.*
◇ SEE ALSO **up against it** ▷ UP

have all the 'cards or hold all the 'cards

If you **have**, or **hold**, **all the cards** you have an advantage which puts you in control of a situation: *They know I hold all the cards, so I'll just wait and see what they do next.*

lay your 'cards on the table or **put your 'cards on the table**

You **lay**, or **put**, **your cards on the table** when you make your intentions known, rather than trying to keep them secret: *I'd be glad if you put your cards on the table.* ◇ SEE ALSO **lay it on the line** ▷ LINE

on the 'cards

If something is **on the cards** then all the signs make you believe that it is likely to happen: *His supporters believed that a decisive victory was on the cards.*

It is widely believed that it is possible to read the future with Tarot cards.

play your cards close to your 'chest or **keep your cards close to your 'chest**

You **are playing**, or **keeping**, **your cards close to your chest** when you do not give much information to other people about what you are doing: *The League's commercial director is playing his cards close to his chest.*

play your 'cards right (*informal*)

You **play your cards right** when you act in a way which will enable you to get what you want: *Tell Daniel that if he plays his cards right I'll bring him a drum back.*

care

in 'care

Someone who is **in care** is being looked after in an institution which is run by the state, rather than by their own family: *The children have been in care since Wednesday evening.*

take 'care

1 When you **take care**, you are being careful in a difficult or dangerous situation: *Take great care when you are driving abroad.* **2** '**Take care**' is also an informal way of saying goodbye to a friend: *'See you around.' 'Yeah, take care.'*

take 'care of

1 You **are taking care of** someone or something if you are looking after them: *I'm giving you my grandmother's ring because I know you'll take good care of it.* **2** To **take care of** something also means to deal with it or organize it: *Why don't you go out and enjoy yourself? I'll take care of the washing-up.* **3** Someone **takes care of** another person when they prevent them from causing any trouble, maybe by killing them: *I've taken care of him. I can guarantee he won't bother you again.*

take 'care to

You **take care to** do something if you make sure that you do it: *Always take care to lock the door when you go out.*

carpet

roll out the red 'carpet for someone or **give someone the red-'carpet treatment**

You **roll out the red carpet for someone** who is visiting you, or **give them the red-carpet treatment**, when you make a great effort to welcome them and treat them well: *What, a cream sponge for dessert? You're giving Gran the red-carpet treatment, aren't you?*

When an important person visits another country, a red carpet is sometimes put on the ground for them to walk on, as a sign of respect.

sweep something under the 'carpet or **brush something under the 'carpet**

You **sweep**, or **brush**, **something**, such as a problem, **under the carpet** when you ignore it or try to hide it from other people because you do not want to deal with it: *The secretary has said that his club will not allow the matter to be swept under the carpet.* □ *The row continued last week, despite deliberate efforts in Bonn to brush the affair under the carpet.*

carried

get carried a'way

You **get carried away** when you become so excited that you do things you would not normally do: *I got carried away today and spent £100 on clothes.*

carrot

a 'carrot

You promise something as **a carrot** for someone if it will be their reward for doing what you want, especially for working harder: *I'll tell her that she's due for a pay-rise. That'll be a bit of a carrot for her, I expect.*

A carrot is the traditional reward for a donkey that has done its work well.

carrot and 'stick

Carrot and stick describes a method of persuasion which involves both rewards and punishments: *There's nothing wrong with using a bit of the old carrot and stick on difficult children.*

See note at **carrot**.

carry (*see also* **carried**)

carry it 'off

You say that you **carried it off** if you know you did something badly, but you think that nobody else noticed your mistakes or weaknesses: *My speech wasn't very well prepared, but I think I carried it off.*

cart

put the cart before the 'horse

You **are putting the cart before the horse** if you try to do, plan, or say something before you have made the necessary preparations: *At times you appear to be over-optimistic and inclined to put the cart before the horse.*

carte

carte 'blanche

When someone gives you **carte blanche**, they are giving you the freedom to do something in whichever way you choose: *The landlord gave me carte blanche to redecorate his flat however I wanted.*

> In French, **carte blanche** means 'blank card' or 'white card'.

case

as the case may 'be or whichever the case may 'be (*formal*)

You use **'as the case may be'** or **'whichever the case may be'** to make it clear that what you are saying refers to both the possibilities which you have mentioned: *If the victim is in shock, it is not advisable to give him (or her, as the case may be) any alcohol.*

case in 'point (*formal*)

A particular example is a **case in point** if it proves or supports what you have said: *The EC fisheries policy is a mess, and the current dispute over who can fish where is a case in point.*

I rest my 'case (*formal*)

I rest my case means 'now you have proof, so there is no need for me to say anything else': *'He's a mean so-and-so.' 'He gave me a pair of socks for my birthday.' 'I rest my case!'*

> In a court of law, lawyers say 'I rest my case' when they have finished giving their statement.

in 'any case

1 You use **'in any case'** to make it clear that whatever has happened or may happen, what you say is true: *It's just a pity it was raining all day. In any case, I'm sure he enjoyed himself, and that's what counts.* **2** You also use **'in any case'** to limit the statement you are making to a narrower statement which you are sure is true: *Sea fishing, or in any case, fishing on the high seas, is a dangerous and lonely job.* **3** In any case is also used to introduce something which supports what you have just said: *He's got really fat, don't you think? In any case, he's put on a couple of stone.*

◇ SEE ALSO **in any event** ▷ EVENT **at all events** ▷ EVENTS **at any rate** ▷ RATE

in 'case

You do something **in case**, or **in case of something**, or **in case something happens**, if you do it to protect yourself from a possible problem in the future: *I'll put on the answer machine just in case she calls.*

in 'that case

You use **'in that case'** to show that you are acting as the result of some situation which you have just been informed of: *Did you say you could collect the kids from school? In that case, I don't have to miss my yoga class.*

◇ SEE ALSO **in which case** ▷ CASE

in which case

You use **in which case** to show that you are acting as the result of a possible situation which may happen: *He might arrive tomorrow, in which case I shall take the afternoon off' work.*

◇ SEE ALSO **in that case** ▷ CASE

open-and-shut 'case

An **open-and-shut case** is a problem which has a very obvious solution: *Oh, come on! Reduce motor traffic and air quality improves. It's an open-and-shut case.*

> In law, an **open-and-shut case** is one which is so easily dealt with that the trial is just a formality.

worst case sce'nario

The **worst case scenario** is the worst possible combination of events which could happen: *In the worst case scenario, the economic crisis may continue well into the next decade.*

◇ SEE ALSO **if the worst comes to the worst** ▷ WORST

cash

cash in 'hand

When you are paid **cash in hand** for work, you are paid in notes and coins instead of having money put into your bank account or getting a cheque: *The pay is usually appalling for those who don't speak any other language and want cash in hand.*

hard 'cash

Hard cash is money in notes and coins; **hard cash** is also money in a disposable form, rather than being tied up in equipment or property: *And I want the lot in hard cash. Fives and tens, okay?* □ *Part of the point of selling state business is to raise hard cash.*

castles

build castles in the 'air

You **are building castles in the air** when you make plans based on hopes and wishes which will probably never come true: *Unless she knows that she's got the job, all her plans are just castles in the air.*

◇ SEE ALSO **chase rainbows** ▷ RAINBOWS

cat (*see also* **cats**)

a cat may look at a 'king
A cat may look at a king means 'I shall look at you if I want to', and may be used as a rude reply, if someone asks you why you are looking at them.

the cat's 'mother (*informal*)
People say 'Who's "she"'? The cat's mother?', when they are commenting on the fact that someone has rudely used 'she', rather than the person's name, to refer to them: *'Mummy, she just hit me!'* *'Who's "she"? The cat's mother?'*

'copy cat (*insulting*)
Copy cat is a name, used by children, for someone who is trying to be the same, or to do the same things, as someone else: *'I've got a new pair of shoes.' 'They're the same as mine, you copy cat.'*

fat 'cat (*disrespectful*)
A fat cat is a person who is rich and important and has a high opinion of themselves: *Rather than fat cat developers benefiting from the countryside, small businesses and local people should have the main part to play in sensitive development.*
◇ SEE ALSO **big cheese** ▷ CHEESE; **big fish** ▷ FISH; **big noise** ▷ NOISE

fight like cat and 'dog
Two people fight like cat and dog when they argue fiercely whenever they are together: *My sister and I get on much better now, but when we were little we used to fight like cat and dog.*
◇ SEE ALSO **at each other's throats** ▷ THROATS

has the cat got your 'tongue? (*informal*)
If someone, probably a child, is refusing to speak or to answer a question, you can ask them if the cat has got their tongue: *She called after me, 'Cat got your tongue?'*

let the 'cat out of the bag
You let the cat out of the bag if you accidentally give away information which is supposed to remain a secret: *Mum and Dad found out about the party; someone let the cat out of the bag.*
◇ SEE ALSO **spill the beans** ▷ BEANS; **blow the gaff** ▷ GAFF; **give the game away** ▷ GAME

like a cat on hot 'bricks or **like a cat on a hot tin 'roof**
If you are so excited or anxious that you cannot sit still or concentrate properly, you are like a cat on hot bricks or a cat on a hot tin roof: *Fortescue is hopping like a cat on hot bricks, demanding that something should be done.*

like the cat that got the 'cream
Someone who looks like the cat that got the cream is looking very pleased with themselves: *He was smiling, Mr Barnes, smiling like the cat that got the cream.*

like something the 'cat brought in
A person who looks like something the cat brought in is looking very untidy: *You can't go out like that. You look like something the cat brought in.*

look what the 'cat's dragged in
If someone says 'look what the cat's dragged in' when another person enters a room, they mean that they are not at all pleased to see that person: *'Well, look what the cat's dragged in,' Moira said, gesturing to the bottom of the stairs. Maggie recognized a group of lads from the local boys' school.*

not have a cat in 'hell's chance or **not stand a cat in 'hell's chance** (*informal*)
You do not have, or stand, a cat in hell's chance if you are extremely unlikely to succeed: *We'd be stupid to climb in this weather. We wouldn't have a cat in hell's chance of reaching the top.*
◇ SEE ALSO **not have a hope in hell** ▷ HOPE; **not a snowball's chance in hell** ▷ SNOWBALL

play cat-and-'mouse with someone
If someone plays cat-and-mouse with a person less powerful than themselves, they tease them by repeatedly making them afraid and then letting them relax: *The Government is playing cat-and-mouse with political prisoners, releasing and re-imprisoning them.*

A cat which has caught a mouse often releases it several times to watch it run, before finally killing it.

set the cat among the 'pigeons or **put the cat among the 'pigeons**
If someone has set, or put, the cat among the pigeons, they have made a difficult situation even worse: *He said what? That's really set the cat among the pigeons now, hasn't it?*

swing a 'cat (*informal*)
If you say that you cannot swing a cat in a certain place, you mean that there is not much space there: *There's not even room to swing a cat in the kitchen.*

think you are the cat's 'whiskers or **the cat's py'jamas** (*informal, disrespectful*)
If you say that someone thinks they are the cat's whiskers, or the cat's pyjamas, you think they have too high an opinion of themselves: *She thinks she's the cat's whiskers, but she's no better than anyone else.*
◇ SEE ALSO **think you are the bee's knees** ▷ BEE

when the cat's away, the 'mice will play
If someone says 'when the cat's away, the mice will play', they mean that when the person who is normally in authority is absent, people will take advantage of the situation: *The boss is off sick, so we're all*

going to the pub for the afternoon. When the cat's away ...

catch (*see also* **caught**)

catch someone 'at it or catch someone red-'handed (*informal*)

You **catch someone at it**, or **catch someone red-handed**, when you find them in the act of doing something forbidden: *If I catch you boys at it again, I'm going to call the police, do you hear?* □ *Night patrols were started in some rural areas, and they sometimes caught burglars or cattle thieves red-handed.*

◇ SEE ALSO **catch someone with their trousers down** ▷ TROUSERS; **catch someone with their pants down** ▷ PANTS

'catch it (*old*)

'So-and-so will **catch it**', is an old-fashioned way of saying that someone will be punished: *'You'll catch it,' said Philip, then put his finger to his lips. But it was too late. His stepdad came into the shed.*

catch someone 'napping

You **catch someone napping** when you find them relaxing or distracted instead of working hard and paying attention; you **are caught napping** when another team, army, side, etc, launches a surprise attack that you are not prepared for: *The Oldham defence was caught napping when Paul Rideout's cross was flicked into the goal by John Ebbrell.*

◇ SEE ALSO **catch someone off guard** ▷ GUARD

Catch twenty-'two or Catch-twenty-'two situation

You are in a **Catch 22** or a **Catch-22 situation** if you have a problem that cannot be solved because the only possible solution is already part of that problem: *It's a Catch 22 if you are a single mum. You can't go to work unless you get a childminder, and you can't afford a childminder because you're not working.*

◇ SEE ALSO **vicious circle** ▷ CIRCLE **no-win situation** ▷ SITUATION

Catch 22 (1961) is a novel by J Heller.

what's the 'catch?

People ask '**what's the catch?**' if they think there must be a problem with something that seems good, and easy to obtain: *'I'll give it to you free of charge.' 'Really? So what's the catch?'* □ *Negotiations were long and painful. He was always looking for the catch.*

you won't catch 'so-and-so or you won't catch so-and-so 'dead (*informal*)

You say that **you won't catch so-and-so**, or **you won't catch so-and-so dead**, doing a certain activity, if you are sure that that person would never do, or even consider doing, it: *You won't catch my husband dancing. He says it's naff.* □ *You went to the Club Amoro? You wouldn't catch me dead in there. It's awful.*

cats

rain cats and 'dogs (*informal*)

It **is raining cats and dogs** if it is raining very hard: *It's been raining cats and dogs all morning!*

◇ SEE ALSO **rain buckets** ▷ BUCKETS **chuck it down** ▷ CHUCK **bucket with rain** or **bucket rain** ▷ RAIN; **tip it down** ▷ TIP

cause

a lost 'cause

A certain activity is **a lost cause** if it has no chance of succeeding: *We gave up the search as a lost cause after many fruitless hours.*

caution

throw caution to the 'wind

When you **throw caution to the wind**, you decide to take a risk, and not to worry about the possible bad result of your actions: *You cannot be tentative or apprehensive in your movements – you have to throw caution to the wind and 'attack' with your objective clearly in mind.*

cent

not have a red 'cent

If you do **not have a red cent**, you have no money at all: *I haven't a red cent till I get paid at the end of the month.*

◇ SEE ALSO **not have two ha'pennies to rub together** ▷ HA'PENNIES **not have two pennies to rub together** ▷ PENNIES **not have a penny to your name** ▷ PENNY

ceremony

stand on 'ceremony

If you agree not to **stand on ceremony**, you decide with someone that you will ignore certain formalities: *Well bring him in. We don't stand on ceremony in this house.*

certain

for 'certain (*informal*)

If you are sure about something, you can say it is **for certain**: *One thing's for certain. I never intend to live anywhere other than Scotland.*

◇ SEE ALSO **beyond all doubt** ▷ DOUBT; **without a doubt** ▷ DOUBT; **without question** ▷ QUESTION; **beyond any shadow of doubt** or **without any shadow of doubt** ▷ SHADOW; **sure as eggs is eggs** ▷ SURE

chalice

make 'certain

1 You **make certain**, or **make certain of something**, when you check that it is the case: *I just wanted to make absolutely certain that you will be coming.* **2** You **make certain** that something happens when you act so that there is no risk of it not happening: *I take the children to school and I collect them, to make certain that they get there and back safely.*

chalice

poisoned 'chalice

A **poisoned chalice** is something which seemed good at first but which turns out to be full of problems: *He took over as chairman of British Rail, a job described as a poisoned chalice, since there is so much trouble on the railways.*

◇ SEE ALSO **can of worms** ▷ CAN; **Pandora's box** ▷ PANDORA

chalk

like chalk and 'cheese

Two things or people that are **like chalk and cheese** are completely different.

chalk and 'talk

Chalk and talk is a traditional style of teaching, with the teacher giving a lot of written and spoken information, and the students listening: *Complete the following text pages in a chalk and talk way, stressing the 'golden rules'.*

not by a 'long chalk

If something is not the case **by a long chalk**, then it is not at all the case: *I'm afraid this essay doesn't deserve a pass mark. Not by a long chalk.*

challenge (see also **challenged**)

rise to the 'challenge

You **rise to the challenge** when pressure improves your performance, helping you to do something difficult better than everyone expected: *She didn't have much confidence at first, but she has risen to the challenge and is doing very well.*

◇ SEE ALSO **take the bull by the horns** ▷ HORNS; **grasp the nettle** ▷ NETTLE; **rise to the occasion** ▷ OCCASION; **pull out all the stops** ▷ STOPS

challenged

physically 'challenged

If you describe someone as **physically challenged** you mean that they have a physical problem or disability: *The organization as a whole became sensitized to the many debates which faced women artists who were physically challenged.*

This expression is one of a number of phrases describing problems, for example, 'lexically challenged' [= not good at reading] and 'visually challenged' [= blind, or partially blind] which used to be considered politically correct. Now a lot of people make jokes with this structure, using 'intellectually challenged' to mean 'stupid', and inventing expressions like 'follically challenged' [= bald] and 'rhinologically challenged' [= having a short nose].

chance (see also **chances**)

blow your 'chance (informal)

If someone **has blown their chance**, they have lost an opportunity by making a mistake or by doing the wrong thing: *She'd blown her chance to get close to Guy.*

◇ SEE ALSO **burn your boats** ▷ BOATS; **sign your own death warrant** ▷ DEATH

chance of a 'lifetime

If you have the **chance of a lifetime**, you have the kind of opportunity which is unlikely to come to you again: *You've been offered a teaching job with VSO? You've got to accept; it's the chance of a lifetime.*

chance would be a 'fine thing! (informal)

If someone wishes that the thing which has just been mentioned were true, and thinks that it is unlikely that they will be able to do it, they might say '**chance would be a fine thing!**': *How I would have liked to play that, I thought, but chance would be a fine thing.*

'fat chance (informal)

You say there is a **fat chance** or a **fat chance of something** if you are sure that that thing will not happen: *'Please stop loving me,' demands Smith at the album's climax. Fat chance. They'll love him even more.*

a fighting 'chance

You have **a fighting chance** if you have a small, but real, possibility of success: *If she can get through the first 24 hours, she's got a fighting chance of surviving.*

given the chance

If you say that someone would do something **given the chance**, you mean that they would do it if they had the opportunity: *Given the chance, I think he would prove himself to be an excellent worker.*

given half a 'chance

If you say that a person would do something, especially something considered to be unacceptable, **given half a chance**, you mean that they would do it happily at the slightest opportunity: *That Tom is such a womanizer. He'd be in bed with his own brother's wife, given half a chance.*

in with a 'chance

You are **in with a chance** if there is a good possibility that you will succeed or win: *This horse has got to be in with a chance. He has been racing well this season and the going is good.*

'jump at the chance

If someone says they would **jump at the chance** to do something, they mean they would certainly do it if they could: *I don't understand why you turned down that job. I'd jump at the chance to work abroad.*

not stand a 'chance

You **do not stand a chance** if you have no hope of succeeding or winning: *I've decided not to enter the competition. I don't stand a chance against the other contestants.*

on the 'off-chance

You do something **on the off-chance** when you hope it will be useful or successful but do not expect it to be: *Hi! I'm just calling you on the off-chance that you may be free this afternoon.*

a sporting 'chance

You have **a sporting chance** if you have at least as much chance of success as you do of failure: *Fox-hunting is so cruel. The fox doesn't even have a sporting chance against a pack of hounds.* □ *It's a theory which seems to me to have at least a sporting chance of being right.*

chances

chances 'are (*informal*)

You can say '**chances are**' or '**the chances are**' that something will happen if you think it is probable: *I don't know why I'm going. Chances are I'll have a horrible time.*

fancy your 'chances (*informal*)

You **fancy your chances** if you think you have a good chance of success: *If you fancy your chances, contact the public affairs officer, who will send you the necessary application forms.*

change

the change of 'life (*old*)

The change of life is an old-fashioned name for the menopause: *Many women dread the change of life simply because they are misinformed.*

for a 'change

If you do something which you do not usually do **for a change**, you are doing it because you want to try something different: *I usually drink red wine, but I'll try some white for a change.*

have a change of 'heart

When you **have a change of heart**, you decide not to do something which you had intended to do, or you change your opinion about something: *The British Government decided that Britain would remain independent, unless there was a genuine change of heart in Washington.*

◇ SEE ALSO **do a U-turn** ▷ U

make a 'change

1 Something **makes a change** when it is pleasantly different from what usually happens: *It makes a pleasant change to see her smiling.* **2** People say '**that makes a change**' if someone surprises them by doing something kind which they do not usually do: *Oh, you're offering to do the washing-up, are you? That makes a change.*

changes

ring the 'changes

You **ring the changes**, or **ring the changes on something**, when you change something or do something new for variety: *Why not ring the changes and freshen up your image with some of this season's fantasy jewellery?*

chapter

chapter and 'verse

You tell someone something **chapter and verse** if you know it so well that you can repeat it perfectly and say exactly where it comes from: *I can't give you chapter and verse, but I know the new law disallows unofficial gatherings like raves.*

a chapter of 'accidents

A chapter of accidents is a series of unfortunate incidents which happen to one person over a short period: *The whole affair has been a chapter of accidents from start to finish. We must accept some share of the blame ourselves, of course.*

character

in 'character

A certain action is **in character** for someone if it is what you would expect them to do: *Tony always gets aggressive when he's drunk. I'm afraid he was acting very much in character.*

out of 'character

A certain action is **out of character** for someone if it is the opposite of what you would expect them to do: *It's very out of character for him to be so quiet. He's usually such a mischievous little boy.*

charge

in 'charge

You are **in charge**, or **in charge of something**, if you have all the responsibility for it: *I have to go out for half an hour, Kay, and I'm leaving you in charge. All right?*

charity

in someone's 'charge (*formal*)
You are **in someone's charge** if they have all the responsibility for you: *I have to go now, but I am leaving you in Mr Smith's charge.*
◇ SEE ALSO **in the hands of such-and-such** or **in someone's hands** ▷ HANDS

charity

charity begins at 'home
If someone says '**charity begins at home**', they mean that you should concentrate on helping the people who are close to you instead of making an effort to help people you do not know: *Many believe that charity begins at home and prefer to donate to British, rather than overseas, relief.*

Charley

look a 'Charley or **feel like a 'Charley** (*old, informal*)
You **look**, or **feel like**, a **Charley** if an embarrassing event or situation makes you appear or feel foolish in public: *I felt a proper Charley when I got to the church and realized I had left the wedding rings at home.*

charm

work like a 'charm
Something that **works like a charm** works effectively and fast: *This new stain remover works like a charm.*

cheap

go 'cheap (*informal*)
Something which **is going cheap** is being sold at a reduced price: *Old models are going cheap, according to Rolls Royce dealer Reg Vardy, who has sold 18 second-hand ones this year against six new models.*

on the 'cheap (*informal*)
You do something **on the cheap** if you do it as cheaply as possible: *Holidaying on the cheap in such places as St Moritz, Zermatt or Gstaad is virtually impossible, whatever the tourist office there might say.*

cheek

cheek by 'jowl
When two very different things or people are **cheek by jowl**, they are beside each other or sharing the same space: *In Montmartre, you will find painters cheek by jowl with African traders and flower sellers.*

A dog's **jowls** are the hanging folds of loose skin which it has instead of cheeks.

turn the other 'cheek
You **turn the other cheek** when you accept the bad actions or words which someone directs at you without complaining or feeling angry with them: *The British have a reputation for not complaining. Turning the other cheek is the national pastime.*

In the Bible, Jesus instructs his followers to offer the other cheek if someone hits them on one of their cheeks.

cheese

big 'cheese (*disrespectful*)
A **big cheese** is a person who has a lot of influence, usually in a company or other kind of business organization: *Every year, the big cheeses from this London law firm meet for an expenses-paid dinner.*
◇ SEE ALSO **fat cat** ▷ CAT; **big fish** ▷ FISH; **big noise** ▷ NOISE

hard 'cheese (*informal*)
If someone says '**hard cheese**' about another person's misfortune, it is a rude way of saying that that person will just have to accept the situation: *'I don't want to come to the shops with you.' 'Hard cheese, you're coming.'*
◇ SEE ALSO **tough** or **hard** or **bad luck** ▷ LUCK; **tough** ▷ TOUGH

say 'cheese!
People tell you to '**say cheese!**' just before they take a photograph, to encourage you to smile:

When you say the 'ee' sound in cheese, you make a smiling shape with your mouth.

Cheshire

grin like a Cheshire 'cat
A person who **is grinning like a Cheshire cat** is smiling widely, in a rather foolish-looking way: *'It's over,' I said out loud. I turned to face Kathleen. She was smiling like a Cheshire cat. 'It's going to be all right now,' I told her.*
◇ SEE ALSO **grin from ear to ear** ▷ EAR

The Cheshire Cat is a character in Lewis Carroll's *Alice in Wonderland* (1865).

chest

get something off your 'chest
When you **get something off your chest**, you say something that you have been wanting to say for a long time: *Is something troubling you? Tell me about it, get it off your chest. It will make you feel better.*
◇ SEE ALSO **clear the air** ▷ AIR

chestnut

an old 'chestnut

An old chestnut is 1 an old joke which is no longer funny: *Nigel bent and kissed her hand, murmuring something about pretty, older sisters. Juliet cringed. Not that old chestnut!* 2 a subject that has been debated so much that people have become bored with it: *The subject under discussion is that old chestnut, public or private financing of the arts.*

chicken

the chicken and the 'egg

People call two things **the chicken and the egg** if they are closely linked, but it is difficult to tell which one causes the other: *Which came first, the chicken or the egg? The existence of a stable political culture in Britain may be due to the effectiveness of government. But what has enabled government to be effective?*
chicken-and-egg: *It's a chicken-and-egg situation. You can't get a job without having childcare. You can't pay for childcare without having a decent job.*

'chickenfeed

If something is **chickenfeed** to someone, it seems like a very small amount to them: *I know he spent £10,000 on their wedding, but that's chickenfeed to him.*

play 'chicken

When people **play chicken**, they play dangerous games to see who gets frightened first and takes action to avoid being injured or killed: *You can play chicken by driving two cars very fast towards each other to see who swerves first.*

chickens

count your chickens before they are 'hatched

If someone tells you not to **count your chickens before they** are hatched, they mean that you should not be sure that something good is going to happen until it has actually happened: *I wouldn't count your chickens, Mr Vass. I've agreed to sign the contract, but that's all I've agreed to.*
◇ SEE ALSO **I wouldn't bank on it** ▷ BANK
don't bet on it ▷ BET **don't count on it**
▷ COUNT

child

'child's play

Something that is described as **child's play** is so easy that you never worry about it: *It's child's play giving lectures. But I still get nervous when I have to give an after-dinner speech.*

◇ SEE ALSO **easy as ABC** or **anything** or

falling off a log or pie or winking ▷ EASY
kids' stuff ▷ KIDS **a piece of cake** or **a piece of piss** ▷ PIECE; **nothing to it**
▷ NOTHING

with 'child (*old*)

With child is an old-fashioned way of saying 'pregnant': *When I saw the young woman was with child, I took pity on her and bade her stay the night.*

childhood

second 'childhood

If an adult is in their **second childhood**, they are behaving like a child, probably because they are getting old and confused: *Senile dementia may result in a kind of second childhood.*

chill

a chill runs down your 'spine

Something which makes **a chill run down your spine** fills you with a strong feeling of fear or disgust: *The little girl's words made a chill run down his spine.*

chin

keep your 'chin up

If you tell someone to **keep their chin up**, you mean that they should try not to be unhappy or afraid: *Come on, keep your chin up. It can't be that bad.*
◇ SEE ALSO **keep your pecker up** ▷ PECKER

take it on the 'chin

If someone accepts something upsetting or discouraging, without complaining, you can say they **are taking it on the chin**: *See if he ever answers back, or, indeed, reacts in any other way other than to quietly stand and take it on the chin.*

chink

a chink in someone's 'armour

If you discover an aspect in an unfriendly or fiercely independent person which makes them seem weaker or more human, you have found **a chink in their armour**: *That would amount to an admission that he was right about her behaviour. It would widen the chink in her armour – and she didn't want it widened.*

chip

a chip off the old 'block

You say that someone, especially a man or boy, is **a chip off the old block** if, in behaviour or personality, he reminds you of his father: *From the doorstep she smiled at Jimmy, a chip off the old block with his grey eyes and a bit of his dad's twinkle.*

◇ SEE ALSO **tarred with the same brush**
▷ BRUSH; **cut from the same cloth**
▷ CLOTH; **have something in common** ▷ COM-
MON; **cast in the same mould as someone**
▷ MOULD

have a 'chip on your shoulder

Someone who **has a chip on their shoulder**,
or **a chip on their shoulder about something**,
privately resents something, and gets easily
upset or angry when they are reminded of
it: *He had a bit of a chip on his shoulder
because he felt that other people who were
not so good but who had the right background and connections had got ahead of
him.*

chips

cash in your 'chips (*informal*)

To **cash in your chips** is to die: *The old man
cashed in his chips last week. Funeral's on
Friday.*

◇ SEE ALSO **breathe your last** ▷ LAST; **kick the
bucket** ▷ BUCKET; **pop your clogs** ▷ CLOGS;
shuffle off this mortal coil ▷ COIL; **bite the
dust** ▷ DUST; **give up the ghost** ▷ GHOST;
depart this life ▷ LIFE; **snuff it** ▷ SNUFF; **go the
way of all flesh** ▷ WAY

> Gamblers usually **cash in their chips** [=
> exchange them for money], just before
> they leave the casino.

chips with 'everything (*humorous*)

1 Chips with everything is an expression
which makes fun of the eating habits,
and by extension the unexciting character, of a certain type of British person:
*Why bother going abroad if it'll just be
two weeks of nightclubbing and chips with
everything?* **2 Chips with everything** also
describes the meals which you are likely
to get in a rather bad canteen, for example
in a school: *It doesn't always have to be
chips with everything and meat with every
meal.*

have had your 'chips (*old*)

You say someone **has had their chips** if they
have had their chance of success and there
is no longer any hope for them: *Is this
subject not wholly appropriate for the Minister, because his Government have had their
chips?*

◇ SEE ALSO **curtains for** ▷ CURTAINS

when the chips are 'down (*informal*)

A period of time **when the chips are down** is
one when you have a particular need,
giving value to the people or things around
you: *It's when the chips are down that you
will find out what he's really capable of.*

◇ SEE ALSO **come to the crunch** ▷ CRUNCH;
when push comes to shove ▷ PUSH

In gambling, when the chips are down
[= on the table], you cannot change
your bet.

choice

by 'choice or out of 'choice

You do something **by**, or **out of**, **choice**, if
you do it freely, without being forced or
persuaded: *If I won a holiday in Turkey I'd
take it, but I wouldn't go there out of choice.
I can't stand the heat.* □ *I found myself
running, not by choice, but because I was
being chased by the mob behind.*

a such-and-such of your 'choice

If you are offered **a certain thing of your
choice**, you can choose any one item in a
particular group of things: *Season to taste
and serve with the salad of your choice.*

choose

nothing to choose between or little to choose between

When there is **nothing**, or **little**, **to choose
between** two or more things, there is no, or
very little, reason to prefer any one of those
things to the others: *There is nothing much
to choose between these two fishing rods in
terms of 'quality.* □ *There really wasn't much
to choose between them.* □ *But there is little
to choose between the two in terms of overall
per'formance.*

chop

chop and 'change

If someone is always **chopping and changing**, they never seem happy with their
decisions, and are continually changing
them: *Once you've made the choice
though, stick to it, don't chop and change
from one style to another.*

chop-'chop! (*informal*)

You say **'chop-chop!'** to someone, especially
a child, if you want them to hurry: *Chop-
chop, or we'll miss the train.*

for the 'chop (*informal*)

1 Something that is **for the chop** is going to
stop existing as the result of official action:
*I'm afraid housing benefit is probably next
for the chop.* **2** Someone who is **for the chop**
is going to lose their job: *We're going to a
company meeting today to find out who's for
the chop.*

get the 'chop (*informal*)

1 If something **gets the chop**, it suddenly
stops existing as the result of official action:
*How will the tourist industry survive if the
ferry service gets the chop?* **2** If someone
gets the chop, they lose their job suddenly:
*If Bill gets the chop I'm going to hand in my
notice too.*

chord

strike a 'chord

When something **strikes a chord**, or **strikes a chord with someone**, they have an understanding of it, or view it with sympathy, because it relates to something in their own experience: *Our appeal for rights to paternity leave struck a chord with many young fathers on the committee.*

touch a 'chord

When something **touches a chord**, or **touches a chord in someone**, it creates an emotional reaction in them: *The strange music touched a chord in him and brought tears to his eyes.*

Christ

Christ Al'mighty! (*informal, may be considered taboo*)

'**Christ Almighty!**' is an exclamation of great surprise, anger or annoyance: *Christ Almighty, Joe! Can't you keep your mouth shut for five minutes?*

◇ SEE ALSO **God Almighty!** ▷ GOD

Christ 'knows or **Christ a'lone knows** (*informal, may be considered taboo*)

1 People sometimes say '**Christ knows**' or '**Christ alone knows**' if they have no idea about something: *He disappeared last Wednesday, so Christ knows where he is now.* **2** You also use '**Christ knows**' to emphasize something you are about to say: *I don't know why she's asking for more money; Christ knows I give her enough as it is.*

◇ SEE ALSO **God knows** or **God alone knows** ▷ GOD **goodness knows** or **goodness only knows** ▷ GOODNESS **heaven knows** or **heaven alone knows** ▷ HEAVEN; **Lord knows** ▷ LORD

for Christ's 'sake (*informal, may be considered taboo*)

For Christ's sake is an exclamation that expresses great surprise, anger or annoyance, or that emphasizes what the speaker is saying: *For Christ's sake, get out of my way! This is an emergency!*

◇ SEE ALSO **for God's sake** ▷ GOD **for goodness sake** ▷ GOODNESS **for heaven's sake** ▷ HEAVEN **for Pete's sake** ▷ PETE **for pity's sake** ▷ PITY

Christmas

white 'Christmas

If there is snow on the ground or snow falling on Christmas day, it is a **white Christmas**: *While many children were hoping for a white Christmas, more than 500,000 families were packing their suitcases and heading for the sun.*

chuck

'chuck it down (*informal*)

It **chucks it down** when it rains very hard: *Look, it's chucking it down out there and I didn't bring my brolly!*

◇ SEE ALSO **rain buckets** ▷ BUCKETS **rain cats and dogs** ▷ CATS; **bucket with rain** or **bucket rain** ▷ RAIN; **tip it down** ▷ TIP

chump

off your 'chump (*informal*)

If someone does something which you consider to be foolish or extremely strange, you can say they are **off their chump**: *He paid £100 for that old thing? He must be off his chump!*

◇ SEE ALSO **be bananas** ▷ BANANAS **off your trolley** ▷ TROLLEY; **off your rocker** ▷ ROCKER

cinder

burnt to a 'cinder

When something has been burnt, especially by accident, until very little of it remains, it is **burnt to a cinder**; if food has been cooked for such a long time that it has become hard and black, you can say that it is **burnt to a cinder**: *Your dinner's in the oven, but it's probably burnt to a cinder by now.*

◇ SEE ALSO **burnt to a frazzle** ▷ FRAZZLE

circle (*see also* **circles**)

come full 'circle or turn full 'circle

If things **come**, or **turn**, **full circle**, a situation which existed in the past changes and develops, but then returns, probably in a slightly different form, in the present: *Sadly, events have come full circle and those who defended the university then must do so again.*

vicious 'circle

A **vicious circle** is an unpleasant situation from which you cannot escape, because the harder you try to improve things, the worse they get: *It's a vicious circle, really. The faster I work, the more work they send me.*

◇ SEE ALSO **Catch twenty-two** or **Catch-twenty-two situation** ▷ CATCH **no-win situation** ▷ SITUATION

circles

go round in 'circles or run round in 'circles

If someone is **going**, or **running, round in circles**, they are active or busy, but are not managing to get anything done: *You're in such a state that you're going round in circles. Sit down and have a cup of tea.*

circumstances

given the 'circumstances or in the 'circumstances or under the 'circumstances (*formal*)

You use '**given**, or **in**, or **under**, **the circumstances**' to show that you are considering the problems involved in a situation: *He was very ill at the time, and under the circumstances, I think we should award him a pass mark.*

under no 'circumstances (*formal*)

If you say that **under no circumstances** is something to happen, you are emphasizing that it must not happen, whatever the reason or situation: *Under no circumstances are you to answer the door, okay?*

city

city 'slicker (*disrespectful*)

A **city slicker** is someone who thinks they are better than people from the country because they live in, and understand, the life of the city, and dress in a fashionable way: *Once you get accustomed to life on the farm, it's hard to go back to being a city slicker.*

the Eternal 'City

Rome is sometimes called **the Eternal City**: *She saw herself in Rome; the Eternal City.*

claim

claim to 'fame

A **claim to fame** is something, usually a past event or achievement, which makes a person or thing special: *My only claim to fame is that my picture was in the local paper when I was six.*

This expression is usually used in a humorous way to talk about something which is not very special at all.

have a 'claim on

Someone or something **has a claim on** a particular thing when that thing belongs to them if they need it: *I'm afraid work matters have a big claim on my time at the moment, but we'll try to meet for lunch.*

lay 'claim to something

When someone **lays claim to something**, they insist that it is theirs: *What will happen when other individuals lay claim to the girl's affection and loyalty is another question.*

stake a 'claim or stake your 'claim

When someone **stakes a claim**, or **stakes their claim**, they make sure that nobody else is going to take something which they consider to be theirs: *Guy Sterne is one of the nicest men I know. If you want him, stake your claim. That's my advice.*

clam

shut up like a 'clam or clam 'up

If you **shut up like a clam**, or **clam up**, you refuse to speak about something: *I tried to find out if she knew anything, but she shut up like a clam.*

A **clam** is a type of shellfish whose shell is made of two halves which it closes together tightly when it senses danger.

clanger

drop a 'clanger

Someone **has dropped a clanger** if they have accidentally said or done something embarrassing in public: *I think I dropped a clanger when I told her she had lost weight. Was it the wrong thing to say?*

◇ SEE ALSO **drop a brick** ▷ BRICK **put your foot in it** or **in your mouth** ▷ FOOT

clap

a clap on the 'back

A **clap on the back** is an action or sign which shows someone your approval for something good they have done: *Well done, Jimmy. You deserve a clap on the back for all the work you've done.*

◇ SEE ALSO **a pat on the back** ▷ PAT; **a slap on the back** ▷ SLAP

clappers

go like the 'clappers (*old, informal*)

Something or someone which **is going like the clappers** is travelling very fast: *He saw a bicycle, quickly mounted it, and rode like the clappers.*

◇ SEE ALSO **like blazes** ▷ BLAZES

clappy

clappy 'happy (*humorous, insulting*)

Clappy happy is used for describing certain sections of the Christian church which are characterized by lively church worship and emphasis on bringing non-Christians to God: *'What did you think of Joe?' 'Oh, he's nice, but a bit clappy happy if you know what I mean.'*

class

in a class of your 'own

If you consider that someone or something is **in a class of their own**, you think that they are much better than any other in their area of activity: *Nureyev was in a class of his own. We shall never see a dancer like him again.*

◇ SEE ALSO **not fit to hold a candle to** ▷ CANDLE **a cut above** or **a cut above the rest** ▷ CUT **in a different league** ▷ LEAGUE

classes

the 'chattering classes (*disrespectful*)

The chattering classes are a certain social group of well-educated, middle class people who enjoy informal discussions on a variety of subjects and seem to have an opinion on everything: *The chattering classes are split between those in favour of, and those against, national identity cards.*

clean

clean as a 'whistle

Something that is as **clean as a whistle** is very clean.

come 'clean

When you **come clean**, you admit that you have done something wrong after telling lies about it for some time: *The Government has failed to add any convincing arguments to its feeble justifications for the changes, and dares not come clean about the real reasons.*

◇ SEE ALSO **make a clean breast of it** ▷ BREAST

cleaners

take someone to the 'cleaners (*informal*)

If someone **takes you to the cleaners**, their actions result in your losing or spending all or a lot of your money, or in your complete defeat: *His ex-wife really took him to the cleaners in the divorce settlement.* □ *His team were taken to the cleaners by a bunch of Australian students and farmers.*

cleanliness

cleanliness is next to 'godliness (*old, humorous*)

If someone says that **cleanliness is next to godliness**, they mean that they think it is important for people to keep themselves clean by washing: *'Cleanliness is next to godliness' is a message this generation has taken to heart. Enormous sums of money are now spent every year on washing powders and bleaches.*

clear

all-'clear

The **all-clear** is a signal, in the form of a statement or a sound, indicating that it is safe or possible to do something: □ *Councillor David Clark said, 'I am fairly confident that the new school will get the all-clear.'* □ *When the all-clear sounded, they came out of their buildings and stood on the street.*

◇ SEE ALSO **the coast is clear** ▷ COAST **go-ahead** ▷ GO

clear as a 'bell

A sound is as **clear as a bell** if you can hear

it very easily: *'Can you hear me?' 'Yes, you're as clear as a bell.'*

clear as 'mud (*informal*)

You say that something such as an explanation is as **clear as mud** if it is not very clear at all: *You discover which bits are clear as daylight and which are clear as mud.*

clear-'cut

Something such as a statement which is **clear-cut** is precise and easy to understand: *The shadow Chancellor is either unwilling or unable to give us a clear-cut answer on this question.*

in the 'clear

1 You are **in the clear** if you are no longer believed to have committed a crime: *Though it was finally agreed that I was in the clear, I never got a formal apology from the police.* **2** You are also **in the clear** if you no longer have a debt to pay: *If I watch what I spend for the next fortnight, I should be in the clear next month.*

steer 'clear of or stay 'clear of

You **steer**, or **stay, clear of** someone or something when you try to avoid them: *It was prudent to steer clear of political debate.*

◇ SEE ALSO **at arm's length** ▷ ARM; **give a wide berth to** ▷ BERTH; **keep your distance** ▷ DISTANCE

clever

'clever-clever (*disrespectful*)

If you call someone or something **clever-clever**, you mean that they are trying too hard to appear intelligent or interesting by the way they express themselves: *The film was a bit clever-clever for my taste.* □ *Don't give me any of your clever-clever answers, boy.*

too clever by 'half (*disrespectful*)

If you say that someone is **too clever by half**, you mean that their confident behaviour and high opinion of their own abilities annoys you: *He stood up, waved at Monica, winked at Paula and was gone. 'That man is too clever by half,' Paula commented.*

cloak

cloak-and-'dagger

Cloak-and-dagger actions or methods involve dishonesty and clever tricks: *A very cloak-and-dagger episode followed when I had to meet a colleague on shore after landing on a remote beach by a motor boat.*

In theatre, **cloak-and-dagger** is the name of a type of 17th century Spanish comedy, referring to the costume which was always worn by a particular character.

clock

against the 'clock
When you do something **against the clock**, you are doing it as fast as you can and recording how long it takes you: *It involves an arduous ten kilometre run preceded by a long assault course, against the clock.*

put the 'clock back
Something which **puts the clock back** brings back the conditions of an earlier time in history: *It would be putting the clock back 30 years to reintroduce the old eleven-plus exam in schools.*

round the 'clock
An activity which continues **round the clock** is one which continues all day and all night without stopping: *Twenty-four hours of aerobics, round the clock? I wouldn't do that, even for charity.* □ *Our round-the-clock information service gives timetables and fares for all destinations in the UK.*

turn the 'clock back
1 People say they wish they could **turn the clock back**, or imagine how things would be if they could **turn the clock back**, when they are imagining how things would be if they had behaved differently in the past: *If you could turn the clock back, would you change anything about your past?* □ *I wish I could turn the clock back; I've made such a terrible mistake.* **2** You **turn the clock back** if, instead of making progress, you make changes which involve returning to a past situation: *They would turn the clock back to policies that impoverished and divided our country.*

watch the 'clock
Someone who **is watching the clock** is not concentrating on their work, but spending their time counting the minutes until they can stop: *I was so excited that I couldn't stop watching the clock all morning.*
'clockwatcher: *You have to be willing to work long hours. There's no room in this company for clockwatchers.*
'clockwatching: *Advertising is not a nine-to-five job. Clockwatching has no place and everyone is expected to work as long as is necessary to do the job.*

clockwork

like 'clockwork
When something goes **like clockwork**, it happens exactly as planned with no problems: *The ceremony went like clockwork.*
◇ SEE ALSO **regular as clockwork** ▷ REGULAR

clogs

'clever clogs (*informal*)
If you call someone a **clever clogs**, you mean that they are annoying because they always seem to have an answer or an explanation for everything: *Okay then, clever clogs. Tell me what this means.*
◇ SEE ALSO **smart aleck or alec** ▷ ALECK; **clever dick** ▷ DICK; **know-all** or **know-it-all** ▷ KNOW

pop your 'clogs (*informal, humorous*)
To **pop your clogs** is to die: *I've started thinking about making my will, though I don't intend to pop my clogs for a few years yet.*
◇ SEE ALSO **breathe your last** ▷ LAST; **kick the bucket** ▷ BUCKET; **cash in your chips** ▷ CHIPS; **shuffle off this mortal coil** ▷ COIL; **bite the dust** ▷ DUST; **give up the ghost** ▷ GHOST; **depart this life** ▷ LIFE; **snuff it** ▷ SNUFF; **go the way of all flesh** ▷ WAY

close

come to a 'close or draw to a 'close
When something **comes to a close**, it finishes; if something **is drawing to a close**, it is about to finish: *The happy day had come to a close, and everyone went to bed.* □ *A millennium is drawing to a close, and we take this opportunity to look back on the past thousand years.*
◇ SEE ALSO **come**, or **draw**, **to an end** ▷ END

closet

come out of the 'closet
A homosexual person **comes out of the closet** when they tell everyone the truth about their sexuality: *When he finally came out of the closet, it came as a surprise to no-one.*
◇ SEE ALSO **come out** ▷ COME

cloth

'cloth-ears (*humorous, informal, old*)
If you call a person **cloth-ears**, you are saying that you think they did not hear what you just said: *Oy, cloth-ears, are you listening?*

cut from the same 'cloth
You say that two people are **cut from the same cloth** if the basic elements of their characters are similar: *Don't assume all women are cut from the same cloth.*
◇ SEE ALSO **tarred with the same brush** ▷ BRUSH; **a chip off the old block** ▷ CHIP; **have something in common** ▷ COMMON; **cast in the same mould as someone** ▷ MOULD

cloud

cast a 'cloud over something

If a particular event **casts a cloud over something**, it reduces the pleasure which that thing brings: *The recent death of her father cast a cloud over the wedding festivities.*

cloud 'cuckoo land (*informal*)

If you say that someone is in **cloud cuckoo land**, you mean that they are mad or that their idea of reality is not accurate: *It's always going to be like that here, and anyone who thinks differently is living in cloud cuckoo land.*

◇ SEE ALSO **never-never land** ▷ LAND

every cloud has a silver 'lining

If you say that **every cloud has a silver lining**, you mean that there is always a positive side to everything, however bad it may seem: *Now you've lost your job, at least you'll have more time for the kids. Every cloud has a silver lining.* □ *Reformed shopaholics almost always speak of a silver lining to the cloud which hung over their lives (and bank accounts).* □ *Then something happened – a silver lining on the cloud of doom.*

> Notice how this idiom can be adapted to suit the speaker's needs. People also sometimes just say '**Every cloud . . .**'.

on cloud 'nine

If you are **on cloud nine**, you are extremely happy: *When I was chosen to fight my first election in Birmingham, I was on cloud nine.*

◇ SEE ALSO **walk on air** ▷ AIR; **thrilled to bits** ▷ BITS; **in seventh heaven** ▷ HEAVEN; **over the moon** ▷ MOON; **on top of the world** ▷ TOP

under a 'cloud

If you are **under a cloud**, you are in trouble for something which you have done previously and which has caused strong disapproval: *I don't know the exact circumstances of her resignation, but she left under a bit of a cloud.*

clover

in 'clover (*informal*)

Someone who is **in clover** is living happily and in great comfort: *If Marcos was cynical, he was no more so than American foreign policy which kept him in power and in clover for 20 years.*

◇ SEE ALSO **in the money** ▷ MONEY; **quids in** ▷ QUIDS; **easy street** ▷ STREET

club

in the 'club (*informal, humorous, disrespectful*)

People sometimes use the expression '**in the club**' to mean pregnant: *Looks like Lucy Jones is in the club.*

◇ SEE ALSO **bun in the oven** ▷ BUN **up the duff** ▷ DUFF **in the family way** ▷ FAMILY **in the**

pudding club ▷ PUDDING **up the spout** ▷ SPOUT

join the 'club (*informal*)

You can say '**join the club**' if someone has just complained about something and you want to agree with them or to say that you are affected in the same way: *'I hate this new pedestrian crossing.' 'Join the club. It doesn't give you enough time to get over.'*

clue

not have a 'clue (*informal*)

1 You say you **do not have a clue** when you do not know something, or when you are ignorant about a certain subject: *Sorry, I haven't a clue about cars.* **2** Someone who **does not have a clue** in general is unable to do anything properly: *My God! Have you seen what he's wearing? He just doesn't have a clue, does he?*

◇ SEE ALSO **not have an earthly** ▷ EARTHLY **not have the foggiest** ▷ FOGGIEST; **not have the faintest** ▷ FAINTEST

clued

clued 'up (*informal*)

When you are **clued up**, you have a lot of knowledge about a particular thing: *Choosing the right sparkling wine can be a minefield if you are not clued up on the different brands available.*

coach

drive a coach and 'horses through something

If someone **drives a coach and horses through something** such as an argument or an official set of rules, they show or use its weak points in order to reduce its authority: *We drove a coach and horses through their new proposals, and they know it!*

> This expression uses the image of holes in an argument which are so large that a coach and horses can be driven through them.

coals

carry coals to 'Newcastle or take coals to 'Newcastle

If you **are carrying**, or **taking**, **coals to Newcastle**, you are taking something to a place where there is plenty of that thing already: *It was left to Western businessmen to manufacture the T-shirts which ended up on the Soviet black market, an acute case of carrying coals to Newcastle.* □ *Given his military background, such a task should have been in the nature of coals to Newcastle.*

Notice that simply saying **'coals to New-castle'** is often enough.

haul someone over the 'coals

You **haul someone over the coals** when you tell them severely that you disapprove of something they have done, in order to embarrass them: *I should have hauled him over the coals for not surrendering all of his files to me.*

◇ SEE ALSO **give someone a rap over the knuckles** ▷ RAP; **give someone a rough time** ▷ TIME

coast

the coast is 'clear

You say that **the coast is clear** when you consider that it is safe to do something because a certain person is absent or is not watching: *Once you're there, stay absolutely quiet – take slow, calm, soft breaths and don't move until you are sure that the coast is clear.*

coat

cut your coat according to your 'cloth

You **are cutting your coat according to your cloth** if you are being realistic about what you can do with the resources you have: *I'd like to redecorate the house completely, but we'll have to cut our coat according to our cloth.*

hang on someone's 'coat-tails

Someone who **hangs on another person's coat-tails** has achieved their position as a direct result of their friendship with that person, and not because they have deserved it independently.

cobwebs

blow the 'cobwebs away

When people say that going outside will **blow the cobwebs away**, they mean that it will make you feel better and more lively: *Why don't you go for a quick walk? That'll soon blow the cobwebs away.*

A **cobweb** is a network of threads made by a spider. Cobwebs gather in places that do not get used, or cleaned, very often.

cock

cock-and-'bull story

If you refer to someone's excuse or explanation as a **cock-and-bull story**, you mean that you don't believe it: *Last night, she had returned at some unearthly hour with some cock-and-bull story about having to work late.*

'cock-teaser (*vulgar*)

Cock-teaser is a vulgar and insulting name for a woman who enjoys the sexual interest of men but who has no intention of actually having sex with them: *Bit of a cock-teaser, your friend.*

Cock is vulgar slang for penis.

'cock-up (*vulgar*)

A **cock-up** is a very bad mistake or mis-understanding; you make a **cock-up** of something when you do it very badly: *Well, I'm only young. If I do make a cock-up of it, I can always do something else.*

◇ SEE ALSO **balls-up** ▷ BALLS

go off at half-'cock

Something which **goes off at half-cock** is unsuccessful because of lack of preparation: *My brother tends to rush into things, so his projects often go off at half-cock.*

On old guns, if the firing mechanism was **at half-cock** when the gun fired, the shot would be wasted.

cockles

warm the cockles of someone's 'heart (*old or humorous*)

You say that something **warms the cockles of your heart** if it makes you feel happy and sure that the world is full of good things: *If this was not a Government-inspired and briefed story, it must have warmed the cockles of the Ministry's heart.* □ *Talk of means-testing pensions hardly warms the cockles.*

Notice that just saying **'such-and-such warms the cockles'** is often enough.

cogs

cogs in a ma'chine or cogs in a 'wheel

If people are considered to be **cogs in a machine** or **wheel**, they are not regarded as individuals but as anonymous members of a very big group of workers: *The men were destined to remain cogs in a remorseless, unfeeling machine.* □ *People see themselves as not being simply cogs in a wheel.*

someone's mental 'cogs

If **someone's mental cogs** are turning, they are thinking hard and trying to understand something: *I think that the visit will be quick, but you may see something that will set your mental cogs turning again, and enable you to do a bit of detective work.*

coil

shuffle off this mortal 'coil or shuffle off the mortal 'coil (*humorous*)

To **shuffle off this**, or **the, mortal coil** is to die: *It was generally assumed that she would* *act as housekeeper to her brother Fred when Mrs Pendlebury finally shuffled off the mortal coil.*

◊ SEE ALSO **breathe your last** ▷ LAST; **kick the bucket** ▷ BUCKET; **cash in your chips** ▷ CHIPS; **pop your clogs** ▷ CLOGS; **bite the dust** ▷ DUST; **give up the ghost** ▷ GHOST; **depart this life** ▷ LIFE; **snuff it** ▷ SNUFF; **go the way of all flesh** ▷ WAY

From Shakespeare's *Hamlet.*

coin

'coin it or **'coin it in** (*informal*)
Someone who **is coining it** or **coining it in** is earning a lot of money: *He figured he could make a lot of money out of this room – he could charge £10 an hour and really coin it in.*

◊ SEE ALSO **make a bomb** ▷ BOMB; **make a bundle** ▷ BUNDLE; **make a fortune** ▷ FORTUNE; **make a killing** ▷ KILLING; **make your pile** ▷ PILE

pay someone back in their own 'coin
You **pay someone back in their own coin** when you punish them by giving them the same bad treatment that they have given you: *Paying Deana Davenport back in her own coin always seemed to backfire.*

◊ SEE ALSO **pay someone back with interest** ▷ INTEREST; **give someone a taste of their own medicine** ▷ TASTE

cold

cold as 'charity
You can say someone or something is as **cold as charity** if they are very unfriendly and unwelcoming: *Ewan Dean's as cold as charity, and that marriage has looked distinctly dodgy for a long time.*

cold as 'ice
1 Something that is as **cold as ice** is very cold: *The lemonade, cold as ice, in a deep earthenware jug with slices of lemon floating on top, was delicious.* **2** Someone who is as **cold as ice** is very unfriendly: *From then on his manner towards me was as cold as ice. I began to understand that this man could kill me, without feeling any guilt at all.* □ *'What I want to know,' she said in a voice as cold as ice, 'is when do I cease to be your mistress and become your wife?'*

◊ SEE ALSO **chilled to the bone** ▷ BONE; **chilled to the marrow** ▷ MARROW

come in from the 'cold
When someone **comes in from the cold**, they re-enter a group or rejoin an activity after a period of time when they were not permitted to do so: *Allegations of misconduct were dropped and the two MPs finally came back in from the cold.*

leave someone 'cold
If something **leaves you cold**, it has no effect on your emotions: *I'm afraid the film left me cold. I couldn't sympathize with either of the main characters.*

out 'cold
Someone who is **out cold** is unconscious: *I saw him fall, but when I got to him he was out cold.*

out in the 'cold
If people leave someone **out in the cold**, they ignore, or are unkind to, a person who wants to join their activities: *If he keeps behaving like this, he'll find himself out in the cold.*

collar

hot under the 'collar
If you are **hot under the collar**, you feel annoyed and become rather agitated: *There's no need to get so hot under the collar. I'm just slower than you, that's all. Now explain again, and explain slowly.*

colour

add 'colour to something
Something that **adds colour to something** else brings some energy, interest or variety to that thing: *His enthusiastic lecturing style adds colour to a subject that many people regard as dull.*

bring some 'colour to your cheeks
If something **brings some colour to your cheeks**, it makes you feel or look a lot better or more healthy: *Drink this nice bowl of soup, now. That'll soon bring some colour to your cheeks.*

◊ SEE ALSO **do you a world of good** ▷ WORLD

change 'colour
You **change colour** if your face becomes pale or red because of an emotion such as fear or anger: *She changed colour visibly at the mention of his name.*

lend 'colour to something
Something that **lends colour to** a story or argument, for example, makes it appear more likely, believable or reasonable: *It is essential that nothing is done that might lend colour to the suggestion that they are favouring any one section of the community.*

local 'colour
The **local colour** of a place is made up of all the traditions and typical activities which give the place its character and make it unique: *The traditional dances and customs of a particular country can give local colour and atmosphere to a plot or theme.*

off-'colour
If you are **off-colour**, you are not feeling very well, but you are not really ill either:

I've been feeling a bit off-colour ever since I came back from holiday.

◇ SEE ALSO **look like death warmed up**
▷ DEATH; **pale** or **green about the gills**
▷ GILLS

see the colour of someone's 'money (*informal*)

If you say that you want to **see the colour of someone's money**, you mean that you want them to prove that they can be believed or trusted by supporting what they say with money: *He says he'll buy it, but I'll wait to see the colour of his money before I take the advert down.*

colours

nail your colours to the 'mast

You **nail your colours to the mast** when you decide on an opinion or course of action in a way that makes it impossible to change your mind: *With this latest expression of support for Labour, the Lib Dems have nailed their colours to the mast.*

In battles at sea, a ship brings down its colours [= its flag] as an admission of defeat. If the colours are nailed to the mast, then they are fixed in that position and cannot be brought down.

someone's true 'colours

If someone shows **their true colours**, or if **their true colours** are showing, they have stopped pretending to be nicer than they really are, and are starting to show the unpleasant side of their character: *Careful, Luke, your true colours are beginning to show.* □ *Anyway, she's seen him in his true colours now, and she's lost interest.*

with flying 'colours

When you do something **with flying colours**, you do it easily and with great success: *She passed her exams with flying colours.*

come (*see also* comes *and* coming)

come 'such-and-such

You say '**come** a certain time' if you are looking ahead to something which will happen or be the case then: *Come the spring, we should have enough money to buy a car.* □ *Come this time next week, I'll know if I have passed my exams.*

come a'gain? (*informal*)

You say '**come again?**' when you want someone to repeat something they have just said, either because you did not hear it, or because you could not believe it: *'Meet me at five.' 'Come again?' 'At five o'clock. Okay?'* □ *'Len's got a girlfriend.' 'Come again?' 'I know. I didn't believe it at first, either.'*

come 'come or **'come now** (*old*)

If someone says '**come come**', or '**come now**', they mean that the person they are talking to should change their opinion or act in a more sensible way: *Come now, it can't be as bad as all that, can it?*

come 'off it! (*informal*)

If someone says '**come off it!**', they mean, rudely, that they do not believe, or agree with, what someone has just said: *'You saved all that money in two months?' 'Come off it Cullam, I couldn't save it in six.'*

◇ SEE ALSO **do me a favour** ▷ FAVOUR; **don't give me that** ▷ GIVE; **don't make me laugh** ▷ LAUGH; **tell that to the marines** ▷ MARINES

come 'out

A homosexual person **comes out** when they tell everyone the truth about their sexuality: *Whether you come out or not must be your own decision, so don't be pressurized by other people.*

'out someone: *The gay rights campaigners outed a number of public figures as part of their protest.*

◇ SEE ALSO **come out of the closet** ▷ CLOSET

come to 'that or **if it comes to 'that**

1 You say '**come to that**', or '**if it comes to that**', to indicate that you are making a new statement which adds to, and strengthens, something you have already said: *I don't want you to see him again. Or any of his friends, come to that.* **2** If you hope a situation does not have the result that you have just mentioned, you say you hope it does not **come to that**: *If I lose my job, we'll have to sell the house. But with a bit of luck, it may never come to that.*

◇ SEE ALSO **for that matter** ▷ MATTER

don't come it with 'me (*informal*)

When someone says to another person '**don't come it with me**', they are telling that person to stop lying and to tell the truth: *Don't come it with me, son. I'm not in the mood for silly games.*

get your come-'uppance

You **get your come-uppance** if something bad happens to you after you have done something bad yourself: *The picture of the late President was simply one of a celebrated political monster who got his come-uppance.*

how 'come? (*informal*)

How come? means 'why?' or 'why not?': *So, how come you always get lots of letters and I never get any?* □ *'I'm not taking a holiday this year.' 'How come?'*

to 'come

Something which is **to come** is in the future: *Still to come tonight are 'The Flames', the best dance band in town.* □ *the shape of things to come* [= what will happen in the future].

comes

when it comes to 'such-and-such

You use '**when it comes to** a certain thing' to introduce the subject which you are going to talk about next: *When it comes to sailing, Clive is the man you should ask. He knows everything.* □ *When it came to discipline, our parents were never very strict with us.* □ *When it comes to bad language, you should just listen to Matt. He even makes me blush.*

comfort

cold 'comfort

You call something a **cold comfort** if it should make you feel less unhappy, but it does not: *He had upset me a lot, and it was a cold comfort to know that I had upset him, too.*

too close for 'comfort

If someone or something is **too close for comfort**, it is so close in space or time that it makes you feel nervous: *He was getting a bit close for comfort, so she edged away along the bench.* □ *These exams are getting a bit too close for comfort. I'd better start my revision.*

coming

have it 'coming to you (*informal*)

If you say that someone **has it coming to them**, you mean that they deserve something bad: *I'm sorry for him, failing the course, but I'm afraid he had it coming to him. He didn't do any work.*

◇ SEE ALSO **deserve whatever** or **anything you get** ▷ DESERVE

command

have something at your 'command (*formal*)

You have skills or abilities **at your command** if you possess them: *You must have all the key techniques at your command if you want to interview people effectively.*

comment

no 'comment

People say '**no comment**' as a way of refusing to answer a question: *'Mrs Smith, what did you think when you discovered the truth about your husband?' 'No comment.'* □ *Mr Westmancoat gave a 'no comment' when contacted about the issue this week.*

commentary

a running 'commentary

Someone who is giving **a running commentary**, or **a running commentary on something**, is talking continually about what they are seeing or doing: *Will you stop your running commentary on the film and let me work out what's going on for myself?*

In sport, the **commentary** is the report of what is happening which starts at the beginning, and continues without stopping to the end, of a game or a race.

commission

out of com'mission

Something which is **out of commission** is not in a usable, working condition: *My old car's out of commission at the moment.*

In the navy, a ship which is out of commission is out of use or being repaired.

common

common as 'dirt or common as 'muck (*informal*)

1 Something that is as **common as dirt** is very easy to find or obtain: *All those birds are as common as dirt around here.* **2** If someone says that a person is as **common as dirt**, or as **common as muck**, they mean that they do not approve of their badly-educated and unrefined behaviour: *That Sue's as common as dirt.*

common-or-garden

A **common-or-garden** person or thing is an ordinary or unexceptional person or thing: *He lived in a normal common-or-garden 'caravan, the type people stay in on holiday.*

have something in 'common

Two or more people who **have something in common** have a particular characteristic which makes them similar to each other: *I get on really well with her, but we don't have much in common.*

◇ SEE ALSO **tarred with the same brush** ▷ BRUSH; **a chip off the old block** ▷ CHIP; **cut from the same cloth** ▷ CLOTH; **in the same mould as someone** ▷ MOULD

company

in good 'company

If someone has a problem which you have also experienced, you can tell them that they are **in good company**, in order to make the problem seem less important: *None of us passed our driving test first time either, so you're in good company.*

keep someone 'company

You **keep someone company** when you stay with them so that they do not feel alone: *Why don't I come and keep you company this evening?*

keep 'company with someone

If you **keep company with someone**, you are friendly towards them and regularly spend time with them: *Don't keep company with gambling men like him.*

part 'company

People **part company** when they separate from each other and go in different directions: *He finds that his soul in sleep can part company with his body and roam the forests.* □ *In November it was announced that Sangster and Dickinson were to part company, and the trainer took his skills to the USA.*

two's company, three's a 'crowd

If someone says '**two's company, three's a crowd**', they mean that, in their opinion, two people are more likely to be happy together than a group of three: *No, sorry, I'd rather you didn't come with us. Two's company.*

This expression can also refer to a couple of lovers who do not want to be disturbed by another person.

your own 'company

If you are in **your own company**, you are alone: *I tend to prefer my own company to that of other people.*

compare

beyond com'pare (*old*)

Something which is **beyond compare** is almost unbelievable because it is so much better than any other thing of the same type: *Her beauty was beyond compare.*

comparison

by com'parison or in com'parison

When you use '**by comparison**' or '**in comparison**' you are emphasizing the difference between the two things mentioned: *His life had been such a success that my little achievements seemed pathetic in comparison.* □ *He has always been very healthy. His sister, by comparison, has been troubled by illness since birth.*

complement

the full 'complement

The full complement of a group is achieved when all the members of that group are present: *I'm afraid we don't have the full complement today because Sally is off sick.*

complete

complete with 'such-and-such

Something that comes **complete with** a certain thing has that thing included automatically: *Order your Christmas turkey, complete with all the trimmings, from us.*

complexion

put a different com'plexion on something

An incident or piece of information **puts a different complexion on something** if it changes the nature of that thing, or your opinion of it: *What they had told me put quite a different complexion on the mystery.*

compliment

backhanded 'compliment

A **backhanded compliment** is a remark which is intended to be, or seems like, a compliment, but in fact is not: *She said that I was dressed much more tastefully than usual, which was rather a backhanded compliment, to say the least.*

compliments

compliments of the 'season (*formal*)

You write or say '**compliments of the season**' as a way of giving someone your good wishes at a time of year such as Christmas: *With compliments of the season to all our customers.*

fish for 'compliments

You **are fishing for compliments** if you try, probably by asking questions, to persuade someone to make a positive comment about you: *'You're pushing me in the direction of flattery again,' he said softly. 'I was not fishing for compliments!'*

conception

Immaculate Con'ception

The expression '**Immaculate Conception**' refers to the way that Jesus Christ, according to Christians, was created, with no sex taking place between his mother Mary and any man.

concern

a going con'cern

Something such as a business is **a going concern** if it is operating successfully and making money: *We will have to increase the profits before we can sell the business as a going concern.*

concerned

as far as 'I am concerned

You say '**as far as I am concerned**' to show that what you are saying is your personal opinion: *He can have the television, as far as I am concerned. I never watch it anyway.*

as far as 'so-and-so is concerned

If something is the case **as far as** a certain person **is concerned**, they are basing their judgement of a situation on the limited amount of information which is available to them: *As far as he's concerned, everything* *is fine so long as the rent comes in on time.* □ *Nothing terrible has happened as far as they are concerned, so let's just keep quiet about it.*

◇ SEE ALSO **for all so-and-so knows** ▷ KNOWS

as far as 'such-and-such is concerned or **where 'such-and-such is concerned**

You use **as far as**, or **where**, a certain person or thing **is concerned** to introduce a certain subject: *As far as insuring the equipment is concerned, this will be the responsibility of your employer.*

conclusion

a foregone con'clusion

If you think that a particular result is **a foregone conclusion**, it is obvious to you, basing your judgement on similar situations in the past, what that result will be: *The Board was trying to give the impression that the result of the enquiry was a foregone conclusion.*

conclusions

jump to con'clusions

You **jump to conclusions** when you form a judgement of a situation without knowing all the facts: *It may just be a coincidence, so let's not jump to any conclusions.*

concrete

concrete 'jungle

The **concrete jungle** is another name for the city, emphasizing the dangers and problems which are a part of living there: *Life isn't easy in the concrete jungle, and only the fittest survive.*

condition

in mint con'dition

Something that is **in mint condition** is in excellent condition, as if it had never been used: *A black and white £5 note, printed between 1920 and 1956, costs from £20. Those in mint condition have doubled in value over the last two years.* □ *Gibson, nylon strung solid guitar, wine red, mint condition, with case, £650.*

◇ SEE ALSO **in good nick** ▷ NICK; **in good repair** ▷ REPAIR; **sound as a bell** ▷ SOUND

on con'dition that

You use **on condition that** to introduce the circumstances which will be necessary for the other part of your statement to be true: *You can go to the party, on condition that you are back by midnight.*

on no con'dition

You use **on no condition** to introduce an event or action which will not or must not ever happen in any situation: *On no condition would I ever hitch-hike alone.*

on one con'dition

You use **on one condition** to introduce the single thing which must happen for the statement you have just made to be true: *You may take it home on one condition. I must have it back first thing tomorrow morning.*

out of con'dition

People or things which are **out of condition** are not in a good physical state: *Look at my hair – it's so out of condition.*

◇ SEE ALSO **out of shape** ▷ SHAPE

confess

I must con'fess or I have to con'fess

You say **I must confess** or **I have to confess** when you are admitting something about yourself or about how you are feeling: *I must confess that I was nervous and wary about meeting him.*

confidence

'confidence trick

If a person plays a **confidence trick**, they deceive someone they do not know with the aim of obtaining something, usually money: *This new taxation policy is little more than an elaborate confidence trick.*
'confidence trickster: *The view of the salesperson as being a slick fast-talking confidence trickster is unrealistic in a world where most sellers depend upon repeat business.*

in 'confidence

You tell someone something **in confidence** when you instruct them to keep it secret: *Why did you go spreading the things I told you in strictest confidence?*

take someone into your 'confidence

You **take someone into your confidence** when you tell them a secret because you trust them not to tell other people: *I hope I haven't made a mistake, taking him into my confidence.*

conscience

a guilty 'conscience

If someone has **a guilty conscience**, they realize that they have done something wrong, even though they do not admit it openly: *Her face was pale. 'I haven't been sleeping well, lately.' 'Guilty conscience?' asked Mrs Clancy unpleasantly. 'Bad dreams?'*

in all 'conscience or in good 'conscience

If you do or say something **in all conscience**, or **in good conscience**, you do or say it without feeling guilty: *How, in all conscience, can you continue living with your parents without paying any rent?*

prick someone's 'conscience

If certain thoughts are **pricking your conscience**, they are preventing you from forgetting guilty feelings: *All the signs which I saw and chose to ignore ... they've been pricking my conscience since he died.*

with a clear 'conscience

You do something **with a clear conscience** if you are sure that you have no reason to feel ashamed or guilty about doing it: *The clear conscience with which most people here avoid taxes if they can, is to do with their feeling of powerlessness in relation to government.*

consequence

in 'consequence

One thing happens **in consequence** of another if it happens as the result of it: *He had no teaching commitments and in consequence had much free time for research.*

consequences

take the 'consequences or suffer the 'consequences

You **take**, or **suffer, the consequences** of your actions if you accept the bad things which happen to you as a result: *If you do something illegal, you must be prepared to take the consequences.*

◇ SEE ALSO **get your just deserts** ▷ DESERTS

considered

all things con'sidered

You say that something is the case, **all things considered**, when you are giving a general opinion after thinking about the whole situation: *It rained all the time, but all things considered, we had a good weekend.*

◇ SEE ALSO **at the end of the day** ▷ END

consideration

take something into conside'ration

You **take something into consideration** if you think about it, and how your actions will affect it, before making a decision: *You've got to take his feelings into consideration.*

under conside'ration

Something that is **under consideration** is being considered by someone before they decide whether to accept or reject it: *Proposals for a new visitors' centre are currently under consideration.*

conspiracy

conspiracy of 'silence

A **conspiracy of silence** is an apparent agreement between a number of people not to say anything about a certain subject, in order to prevent a very important secret from becoming known: *There is a conspiracy of silence about what is happening. Nobody likes to admit that they entertain very little, or that they rarely enjoy it when they do.* □ *So there is a conspiracy of silence against me in my household.*

constitution

have the constitution of an 'ox

Someone who **has the constitution of an ox** is very strong and healthy: *Don't worry, she never gets tired. She's got the constitution of an ox.*

contempt

hold in con'tempt

If you **hold** someone or something **in contempt**, you have no respect at all for them: *He holds all violence in the utmost contempt.*

contention

in con'tention

In competitions, if a person or team is **in contention** for something, their performance has been good enough to give them the possibility of achieving that thing: *Rangers' 3-0 win puts them back in contention for the Cup.*

out of con'tention

In competitions, if a person or team is **out of contention** for something, their performance has not been good enough to give them any possibility of achieving that thing: *And I'm afraid that Robert Smith's disastrous last round puts him out of contention for a placing.*

contradiction

contradiction in 'terms

If you call a combination of words a **contradiction in terms**, you are saying that it does not make sense because the two elements from which it is formed contradict each other: *The most important instrument is subsidy, even though subsidy in a free market is a contradiction in terms.*

contrary

'contrary to something

Something which is **contrary to something** else is against or opposite to that thing: *Why do you persist in doing things which are contrary to my wishes?*

on the 'contrary (*formal*)

You use '**on the contrary**' to tell the previous speaker that you think what they have just said is incorrect: *'Anyway, we have no power to change things.' 'On the contrary, I think we have a lot of power.'*

convenience

to the 'contrary (*formal*)
To the contrary means 'stating or suggesting that the opposite is true': *As I haven't heard anything to the contrary, I presume that the work was satisfactory.*

convenience

at your earliest con'venience (*formal*)
In a formal letter, people sometimes use '**at your earliest convenience**' to show that they want their correspondent to act as soon as possible: *Please contact us at your earliest convenience.*

conversation

conver'sation piece
A **conversation piece** is something, probably an unusual object, which provides a subject for people to talk about: *The elephant foot table? Well, however disgusting it is, it's an effective conversation piece.*

In art, a **conversation piece** is an informal painting of a group of people. The modern meaning may have come from a wrong use of the expression, or from a joke.

cookie

tough 'cookie (*informal, disrespectful*)
If you call someone, usually a woman, a **tough cookie**, you mean that they are hard, independent, and unlikely to worry about the feelings of others: *She was also winning something of a reputation as a tough cookie, a determined career girl refusing to be deflected from her dreams.*

cooking

what's 'cooking? (*old, informal*)
If you ask '**what's cooking?**' you think something is happening or about to happen and you want to know what it is: *Okay, Linda. Tell me what's cooking.*

cooks

too many cooks spoil the 'broth
In a situation where so many people are trying to help with a job that they are all getting in each other's way, you can say '**too many cooks spoil the broth**': *Thanks for offering, but we've got lots of volunteers. We don't want a case of too many cooks.*

Notice the common short form: '**too many cooks**'.

cool

cool as a 'cucumber (*informal*)
Someone who is as **cool as a cucumber** is very calm: *He arrived at the church half an hour late and cool as a cucumber.*

'cool it (*informal*)
If you want someone to behave more calmly, you can tell them to **cool it**: *Appeals from the Democratic Party leaders for the candidates to cool it have apparently been ignored.* □ *He was shouting 'Hey! Cool it! Let's hear what the preacher has to say.'*

keep your 'cool (*informal*)
Someone who **is keeping their cool** is remaining calm in a difficult situation: *He kept his cool and worked at the lock until he had finally broken through.*

lose your 'cool (*informal*)
When someone **loses their cool**, they fail to remain calm in a difficult situation: *The only time I've ever seen him lose his cool was when he ran out of cigarettes before a meeting.*

cop

'cop it (*informal*)
To **cop it** is to be punished: *You'll cop it if your mum finds out.*
◇ SEE ALSO **get it** ▷ GET

'cop-out (*informal*)
A **cop-out** is something which is easy, chosen as an alternative to something which is more difficult because it does not involve so much work or effort: *Teaching is hard work – as a career, it's certainly not a cop-out.*
◇ SEE ALSO **anything for a quiet life** ▷ LIFE; **the soft option** ▷ OPTION; **take the easy way out** ▷ WAY

it's a fair 'cop (*informal*)
If a person says '**it's a fair cop**' when they are accused of doing something wrong, they are admitting their crime or error and saying that they are prepared to accept punishment for it; if other people say '**it's a fair cop**', they mean that, in their opinion, the person has committed a crime or error and should accept punishment for it: *You've pleaded guilty to the charge anyhow, it's a fair cop!*

not much 'cop (*informal*)
Something which you describe as **not much cop** is not very good: *The film wasn't much cop in the end, so we just went to bed.*

copper

copper-'bottomed
If something such as an agreement or a promise is **copper-bottomed**, it is safe and you can trust it: *a copper-bottomed guarantee of quality..*

copy

carbon 'copy

If two people or things are so similar that it is not easy to tell which one is which, you can say they are **carbon copies** of each other: *That particular trip was more or less a carbon copy of the previous one.* □ *They help the half-child, half adult-teenager to find a place in the world, without becoming a carbon copy of his parents.*

A **carbon copy** is a copy of the document you are typing or writing, made by a piece of carbon paper placed between the original and a plain sheet of white paper.

copybook

blot your 'copybook

If you **blot your copybook**, or **blot your copybook with someone**, you do something which changes that person's favourable opinion of you: *Langford made some thundering tackles, but then blotted his copybook with a stupid kick which might have cost his side the match.*

core

'hard core

The **hard core** of a group of people who take part in a particular activity are the small number at the centre of that group who are most enthusiastic about the activity: *Although many have given up, a hard core of protesters continue the fight.*
'hard-core: *a hard-core anarchist.*

corner (*see also* **corners**)

box someone into a 'corner

You **box someone into a corner** when you force them into a place or a situation where they are no longer in control of things; someone who feels **boxed into a corner** is unable to think of a way out of the difficult situation in which they find themselves: *He had me boxed into a corner, and I knew that if I refused, he would not return my money.*

every corner of the 'earth or every corner of the 'world or every corner of the 'globe

You say that people or things come from **every corner of the earth**, or **world**, or **globe**, if they come from many different countries: *This exotic dish combines ingredients from every corner of the world.*
◇ SEE ALSO **the four corners of the earth** or **world** or **globe** ▷ CORNERS

fight your 'corner

You **fight your corner** when you argue strongly in defence of your own opinion: *I know she's in the minority, but she's certainly capable of fighting her corner, isn't she?*

just round the 'corner or just around the 'corner

An event which is **just round**, or **around, the corner** is going to happen very soon: *Spring is just round the corner.*

out of the corner of your 'eye

When you see something **out of the corner of your eye**, you notice it without looking straight at it: *I saw something move out of the corner of my eye, but when I turned round it had disappeared.*

turn the 'corner

You say that you **have turned the corner** if the worst part of a bad period is finished and things are starting to get better: *The general message is that Kent have turned the corner and are confident that improvements on the field will be matched by overall prosperity.*

corners

cut 'corners

You **cut corners** when you try to do something in a way which involves less effort, money or time than if you had used the more usual method, probably giving you a result which is not so good: *Constructing equipment of this nature is is a time-consuming occupation although there are a few that try to cut corners to maximize profits.*

the four corners of the 'earth or the four corners of the 'world or the four corners of the 'globe

You say that people or things come from **the four corners of the earth**, or **world**, or **globe**, if they come from many different countries: *People came from all four corners of the world to attend the royal wedding.*
◇ SEE ALSO **every corner of the earth** or **world** or **globe** ▷ CORNER

correct

correct me if I'm 'wrong

You say **'correct me if I'm wrong'** when you are about to make a statement which you are almost, but not quite, sure is true: *Correct me if I'm wrong, but I think Sally is allergic to eggs.*

corridors

the corridors of 'power

The **corridors of power** are the higher levels of government where people in authority make important decisions: *He notes a shifting from protesting outside nuclear bases towards well-mannered lobbying in the corridors of power.*

cost (*see also* **costs**)

at 'any cost
If you want something **at any cost**, you want it very much and will do anything you can to get it: *I was determined to see him at any cost.*

cost someone 'dear
Something which **costs someone dear** gives them a lot of problems: *Warwickshire were bowled out and lost by 66 runs, and it could well cost them dear in their championship ambitions.*

count the 'cost
1 You **count the cost** when you consider the disadvantages for yourself before deciding to do something: *Are you capable of loving someone without counting the cost?* **2** You also **count the cost** when you consider the financial and other problems which a bad event has caused: *Insurers were yesterday starting to count the cost of the storms.*

to someone's 'cost
You know about something **to your cost** if you learned it through having a bad experience: *He found to his cost that people are not always as honest as they appear.*
◇ SEE ALSO **learn something the hard way** ▷ WAY

costs

at 'all costs
Something which must happen **at all costs** is so important that everything possible must be done to make sure it happens: *This letter must reach him by this afternoon at all costs.*

couch

couch po'tato (*informal, disrespectful*)
If you call someone a **couch potato**, you mean that they are very lazy and never do anything physically active: *Leisure studies, interests and hobbies will keep you on your toes, so if you're a couch potato or telly addict, you'd better change your ways.*

counsel

keep your 'counsel (*old*)
You **are keeping your counsel** if you are keeping quiet and taking care not to tell a secret: *She kept her council as she had promised, refusing to tell them what she knew.*
◇ SEE ALSO **keep something to yourself** ▷ KEEP; **keep it under your hat** ▷ HAT; **mum's the word** ▷ MUM

count

count me 'in
If you say to a person or a group of people '**count me in**', you mean that you want to be

involved in something they are planning: *I can't come on Thursday, but you can count me in for the trip to London next week.*

count me 'out
If you say to a person or a group of people '**count me out**', you mean that you do not want to be involved in something that they are planning: *You can count me out if this is going to mean doing anything illegal.*

don't 'count on it
If someone says '**don't count on it**', they mean that you should not be too sure that something good you have just mentioned is going to happen: *You might cover your costs but don't count on it.*
◇ SEE ALSO **I wouldn't bank on it** ▷ BANK **don't bet on it** ▷ BET **don't count your chickens before they are hatched** ▷ CHICKENS

keep 'count
You **are keeping count**, or **keeping count of something**, if you are aware at all times of the total number of things there are or have been: *Are you keeping count of how many beers they've had?*

lose 'count
You **lose count**, or **lose count of something**, if you cannot remember the total number of things there are or have been: *I've had so many interviews that I have lost count.*

out for the 'count (*informal*)
Somebody who is **out for the count** is sleeping so deeply that it would be very difficult to wake them up: *I knew the children were tired. Look at them. They're both out for the count.*

> In boxing, **out for the count** refers to a boxer who is lying on the floor and who fails to get up while the referee counts to ten.

counter

under the 'counter
Something that is sold **under the counter** is sold secretly and illegally: *He sometimes used to slip me some cigarettes under the counter for wholesale prices.*

country

country 'cousin
If you call someone a **country cousin**, you consider them to have simpler tastes and less culture than you, because they live in the country and you live in the town: *With her hair swept up into a sophisticated style, the older woman made Lucy feel like a country cousin.*

country 'pancake (*informal*)
Country pancake is a children's name for a cowpat: *Mummy, look at Sam! He just fell in a country pancake!*

courage

go to the 'country

The political party in power **goes to the country** when they hold a general election to find out if public opinion supports or rejects their decisions: *The Tories were forced to go to the country over the affair.*

the 'old country

The **old country** is the place where you were born or where your family comes from: *It had all the greens and blues and purples of the old country, but more so.*

up and down the 'country

If people **up and down the country** are doing something, people from places all over the country are doing it: *Voluntary organizations up and down the country, from the Samaritans to the Women's Royal Voluntary Service, were standing by to help bereaved families.*

courage

Dutch 'courage

You get **Dutch courage** when you drink alcohol to make you feel braver than usual: *Then, with slightly more than a little Dutch courage inside him, he suddenly took it into his head that he wanted to sing.*

have the courage of your con'victions

You **have the courage of your convictions** if you act on what you think or decide, without wondering whether you may be wrong: *You should have had the courage of your convictions and told me we were going the wrong way!*

pluck up your 'courage or screw up your 'courage

You **pluck**, or **screw, up your courage** when you get yourself ready to do something unpleasant or risky: *I noticed an advert for an evening class, 'cookery for men', and I finally plucked up courage to enrol. I needn't have worried.*

course

in due 'course (formal)

Something which will happen **in due course** will happen at some suitable time in the future rather than immediately: *Your application has been received and we will contact you in due course.*

par for the 'course

Something unpleasant is **par for the course** if it is to be expected as a usual part of the situation: *Long hours and tough working conditions are often par for the course in catering.*

run its 'course or take its 'course

You let a situation **run**, or **take, its course** when you let it develop naturally without trying to change or prevent it: *He just had to let things run their normal course.* □ *We must wait for the illness to take its natural course.*

stay the 'course

If you **stay the course**, you manage to continue with something difficult or challenging until you have achieved your aim: *The question is often asked when a firm is taking people on for training: how many will stay the course?*

steer a middle 'course

You **steer a middle course** between two options when you choose to do something which is neither one nor the other, but halfway between them: *Not knowing whether to be gentle or more fierce, I decided to steer a middle course between the two.*

court

laughed out of 'court

If an idea, or the person who suggested it, is **laughed out of court**, it is so ridiculous that nobody takes it seriously: *Of the ideas for fundraising, many were laughed out of court.*

rule out of 'court

You **rule** someone or something **out of court** when you refuse to allow them to be considered, to take place, or to be involved in something: *The offer of a 3% pay rise has been ruled out of court by the nurses.*

Coventry

send someone to 'Coventry

If people **send someone to Coventry**, they agree together to ignore and not to speak to that person, as a form of unofficial punishment: *To disregard such a challenge was unthinkable. I would be sent to Coventry and be considered a coward for the rest of my schooldays.*

cover

blow someone's 'cover

To **blow someone's cover** is to reveal their secret identity: *She was posing as a health visitor, but a complaint to the Department of Health blew her cover.*

break 'cover

When someone or something **breaks cover**, they stop hiding from those who are chasing them, and start running away: *She took several deep breaths, then broke cover and sprinted in a zig-zag weave across the open ground.*

In hunting, the fox breaks cover when it comes out from where it is hiding.

under cover of 'darkness or under cover of 'night

If you do something **under cover of darkness** or **night**, you are doing it at night-time in an effort to prevent people from noticing you: *We left the city under cover of darkness, and reached the frontier by dawn.*

covers

under the 'covers

Somebody who is **under the covers** is in bed, rather than on it, for example: *I crawled under the covers and went to sleep*

cow

sacred 'cow

A **sacred cow** is a basic belief which all the members of a certain group share and are not supposed to question: *'Sustainable growth', for years a sacred cow of industrialized societies, is a practical impossibility.*

cows

till the 'cows come home

If you say that a certain activity could continue **till the cows come home**, you mean that you think it could go on forever: *People are able to go on reasoning till the cows come home, but nothing ever gets done.*

crack

crack of 'dawn

Crack of dawn is the time, very early in the morning, when the sun comes up: *We got up at crack of dawn.*

a fair crack of the 'whip

You have had **a fair crack of the whip** if you have had a good length of time doing a certain activity and it is the end of your turn: *Okay, you've had a fair crack of the whip now. Who's next?*

have a 'crack (*informal*)

You **have a crack** at a new activity when you try to do it: *I don't mind having a crack at water-skiing, but I probably won't be much good.*

◇ SEE ALSO **have a bash** ▷ BASH; **have a go** or **give something a go** ▷ GO

cracked

not what it's cracked 'up to be or not all it's cracked 'up to be (*informal*)

Something which is **not what**, or **not all, it's cracked up to be** is not as good as its reputation suggests: *Life as a rock star is not all it's cracked up to be. There are many bands who are barely making a living.*

cracking

get 'cracking (*informal*)

You tell someone to **get cracking** if you want them to start doing something immediately, and as fast as they can: *We'd better get cracking if we want to finish cleaning before your parents arrive.*

◇ SEE ALSO **put your shoulder to the wheel** ▷ SHOULDER

cracks

paper over the 'cracks

Someone who is **papering over the cracks** is trying to hide the fact that they have done a job badly or made a mistake: *That tax policy was a disaster, and the Government have been papering over the cracks ever since.*

cradle

'cradle-snatcher (*disrespectful*)

Cradle-snatcher is a name for a person who is having a relationship with someone a lot younger than themselves: *She's going out with a fourteen-year old? What a cradle-snatcher.* □ *Call me a cradle-snatcher but I love him, and age doesn't matter when you're in love.*

> **'Cradle-snatcher'** literally means 'someone who steals babies from their beds'.

from the cradle to the 'grave

Something which lasts **from the cradle to the grave** lasts for a person's life from the day they are born to the day they die: *The aim of the National Health Service was to provide free medical care from the cradle to the grave.*

crap

cut the 'crap! (*offensive, vulgar*)

If someone says '**cut the crap!**' to another person, they are rudely telling that person to stop delaying by making important-sounding statements which mean nothing: *He handed him the film, preceding it with a string of apologies. 'For Christ's sake, just cut the crap and show it,' thought the sergeant.*

full of 'crap (*vulgar*)

If you say that someone is '**full of crap**', you are saying rudely that you think most of what they say is worthless: *Oh, don't worry about what Jim said. He's full of crap.*

crazy

like 'crazy (*informal*)

If you do something **like crazy**, you put all your energy into it for a period of time: *The boy was kicking like crazy to get free of him but Philip held on.*

crease

'crease yourself or 'crease up (informal)

To **crease yourself**, or **crease up**, is to laugh so much that it hurts: *I have never seen such a ridiculous haircut. I was creasing myself all night looking at him.* □ *I nearly creased up and fell off the chair.* □ *We were creased up.*

◇ SEE ALSO **kill yourself laughing** ▷ KILL

creature

creature 'comforts

If you talk about a person's **creature comforts**, you mean the luxuries which they consider to be necessary for their happiness, such as good food, warmth, and a comfortable place to sleep: *George won't go camping. He likes his creature comforts too much.*

creature of 'habit

A **creature of habit** is someone who likes their life to include actions or processes which they repeat every day: *I like to think I haven't changed much as a person. I'm a creature of habit – in the way I have my hair cut, the suits I wear.*

◇ SEE ALSO **set in your ways** ▷ WAYS

credit

all credit to 'someone

If you say '**all credit to someone**', you are expressing your admiration for something which they have done: *All credit to Tranmere – their finishing was superb.*

be a 'credit to someone or do someone 'credit

You **are a credit to someone** who has had an influence on your life, or you are **doing them credit**, if you make them very proud of you: *In the meantime you must work hard and be a credit to your dad.*

credit where credit's 'due

You are giving **credit where credit's due** when you admit that a person has done something much better than you had expected: *I expected her to make a mess of the painting. But, credit where credit's due, she did a great job.*

give someone 'credit for or 'credit someone with

When you **give someone credit for**, or **credit them with**, a particular quality, you believe that they have that quality, even if you cannot prove it: *Give me credit for a bit of common sense, will you?* □ *We do not credit a parrot with meaning what it says.*

to someone's 'credit

If a certain action or way of dealing with a situation is **to someone's credit**, you admire them for it: *It is to her credit that she remained calm in a situation where most people would have panicked.*

creek

up the creek without a 'paddle or up the 'creek (informal)

Someone is **up the creek without a paddle**, or **up the creek** if their situation is so bad that they do not know how to get out of it: *We're up the creek because we don't know where to go from here.*

◇ SEE ALSO **out of your depth** ▷ DEPTH; **in the shit** ▷ SHIT; **up shit creek** ▷ SHIT; **in the soup** ▷ SOUP; **in a tight spot** ▷ SPOT; **in trouble** ▷ TROUBLE; **in deep water** ▷ WATER; **in hot water** ▷ WATER

creeps

give someone the 'creeps

1 If someone **gives you the creeps**, you have strong negative feelings about them, because they seem strange and possibly dangerous: *Just standing there like big kids. Saying nothing. Great red faces, not smiling. They used to give us the creeps.* **2** A place **gives you the creeps** if it makes you feel strangely uncomfortable or afraid: *I look round uneasily. This place really gives me the creeps. I can't stand the smell.*

crème

crème de la 'crème

The **crème de la crème** of a certain group are the very best members of that group: *dog shows where you can see the crème de la crème of all the famous breeds.*

Crème de la crème is French for 'cream of the cream'.

cricket

not 'cricket (old)

People sometimes say that a certain way of behaving or doing something is **not cricket** if they consider that it is unfair, or not honourable: *It was a filthy trick, totally unsporting and certainly not cricket.*

crock

crock of 'shit (informal)

If you describe an idea, or something that someone has said, as **a crock of shit**, you mean that it is nonsense: *Isn't that the biggest crock of shit you ever heard?* □ *To me it's a crock of shit to go out and 'harmonize with nature' on a resin polyurethane surfboard.*

crocodile

'crocodile tears

When someone is pretending to cry, or claiming to feel sad, because that is what people expect, or in order to obtain something for themselves, you say they are crying **crocodile tears**: *They weep crocodile tears for the the poor and disadvantaged, but are basically happy with things the way they are.*

There are stories which tell of crocodiles crying, either to attract the attention of their victims, or while eating them.

cropper

come a 'cropper

Somebody **comes a cropper** when, probably as a result of becoming too confident, they have a piece of bad luck: *He came a cropper last night when he punched that man. It turned out he was a judo teacher.*

◇ SEE ALSO **come to grief** ▷ GRIEF

In hunting, you **come a cropper** when you have a serious fall from your horse.

cross

at cross-'purposes

When people are talking **at cross-purposes**, they are under the impression that they are talking about the same thing, when in fact each person is talking about something different: *Sometimes they talked at cross-purposes – it was not just their vocabulary that differed – the culture gap was their greatest obstacle.*

◇ SEE ALSO **get your lines crossed** ▷ LINES

have a 'cross to bear

You **have a cross to bear** if you have a problem which you must accept: *Look – you've got your cross to bear, all right, I've got mine.*

crossfire

get caught in the 'crossfire

If two or more people are having a disagreement or a fight and you become involved without wanting to, you can say that you **got caught in the crossfire**: *Major sponsors of the Renault-Williams team, caught in the crossfire of the battle between the world champion and his boss, are in a panic.*

crossroads

at a 'crossroads

A person or activity which is **at a crossroads** has come to a point when an important choice or decision must be made: *My career has come to a bit of a crossroads and I don't know what to do next.*

crow

as the 'crow flies

When you state a distance **as the crow flies**, you are talking about the distance as a straight line between two points, not the distance by road: *You can see the monastery from here. It's about 12 miles away as the crow flies.*

crowd

far from the madding 'crowd

A place which is **far from the madding crowd** is quiet and peaceful, and a long way from any big towns or cities: *I'd love to live in a secluded cottage, far from the madding crowd.*

go with the 'crowd

You **go with the crowd** when you do the same as everyone else, or accept the opinions held by most people, because it would be more difficult to do something different or to disagree: *It may be better to go with the crowd on small issues, and keep your arguments for the big issues.*

◇ SEE ALSO **go** or **drift** or **swim with the current** ▷ CURRENT **go with the flow** ▷ FLOW **go with the stream** ▷ STREAM **go, drift,** or **swim, with the tide** ▷ TIDE

crown

to crown it 'all

You use **'to crown it all'** to add one last misfortune to a list of unfortunate events: *To this, the French contributed their own mistakes, which soon lost them any advantage they may have enjoyed. To crown it all their king, John, was captured in battle.*

◇ SEE ALSO **to cap it all** ▷ CAP **to make matters worse** ▷ MATTERS; **to top it all** ▷ TOP **what is more** ▷ WHAT

crows

stone the 'crows! (*old or humorous*)

You exclaim **'stone the crows!'** as an expression of surprise: *Well, stone the crows, if it isn't good old Jim! We used to play together when we were children.*

◇ SEE ALSO **stone me!** ▷ STONE

cruel

cruel to be 'kind

You are being **cruel to be kind** when you do something which makes someone unhappy at the time, but which you know will benefit them in the future: *You will have to be a little cruel to be kind or she'll never regain her stability or independence.*

crunch

come to the 'crunch (*informal*)

You say that it **has come to the crunch** at the moment when an important decision or action is urgently needed: *If it came to the crunch, how many of us would sacrifice our lives for what we believe?*

◇ SEE ALSO **when the chips are down** ▷ CHIPS
when push comes to shove ▷ PUSH

crush

have a 'crush on someone

Someone who **has a crush on a** certain
person, has fallen in love with that person, who is probably older than themselves, in a rather childish and temporary
way: *When I was fourteen, I had this huge
crush on my chemistry teacher.*
◇ SEE ALSO **hold a candle for someone**
▷ CANDLE; **have a soft spot for someone**
▷ SPOT

crust

upper 'crust (*informal*)

If you describe a person as **upper crust**, you
consider them to be upper class: *All his
relatives are terribly upper crust. I wonder
what they thought of me?*

cry

a far cry from

Something which is **a far cry from** another
thing is not at all similar to that thing:
*Labour's lead over the SNP was 30 percen-
tage points, a far cry from the four-point gap
which separated them in 'January.*

in full 'cry

You are **in full cry** if you are enthusiastically chasing someone or something: *She
left the airport followed by the newspaper
reporters in full cry.*

> In hunting, you say that the hounds [=
> hunting dogs] are **in full cry** if they can
> smell an animal and they are running
> after it in a big group, barking with
> excitement.

crying

for crying out 'loud!

You exclaim **'for crying out loud!'** to express
a sudden, strong feeling of anger or annoyance: *Oh, for crying out loud, child! Stop
moaning, will you?*

crystal

crystal 'clear

1 If something such as water is **crystal clear**
it is transparent and clean: *The pool was
very deep and crystal clear, so you could see
the bottom.* **2** If something such as an
instruction is **crystal clear**, it is easy to
understand: *I hope I have made myself
crystal clear.*

cud

chew the 'cud

Someone who **is chewing the cud** is thinking
deeply about something: *Ten minutes later,
I could see she was still chewing the cud
about what I had said.*

> Cows often look as if they are thinking
> deep thoughts when they **chew the cud**
> [= chew for a second time on grass
> which they have already swallowed
> once before].

cue

on 'cue

Something happens **on cue** if it happens at
just the right moment: *Right on cue, a
Brazilian goal arrived in the 54th minute.*
□ *As if on cue, a cistern flushed and the door
of the cubicle opened to reveal the emerging
figure of George Prendergast, the Personnel
Director.*

> The second example: 'as if on cue ...'
> refers to the way an actor arrives on a
> scene at precisely the right time, to create
> the best dramatic effect.

take your cue from 'so-and-so

You **take your cue from someone** if, encouraged by the fact that they have done something first, you then do something similar:
*Britain should take its cue from the Scandi-
navian countries and start cleaning up the air
we breathe.*
◇ SEE ALSO **take a leaf out of someone's book**
▷ LEAF **follow suit** ▷ SUIT

cuff

off the 'cuff

You do something **off the cuff** when you do
it with no previous preparation: *I wish I
could speak off the cuff like he does.*
□ *brilliant off-the-cuff remarks.*

culture

'culture shock

A **culture shock** is a feeling of confusion
which is the result of a sudden change
in your social environment: *Being at
home with small babies is an instant
culture shock to the young woman of
the world.*

'culture vulture (*disrespectful*)

A **culture vulture** is a lover of the arts
(music, painting, drama, etc), who tries
to go to as many cultural events as
possible: *The clientele ranges from young
revellers to local residents, cuture vultures
to sober-suited lawyers reluctant to go
home.*

Using this term can sometimes give the impression that you think that the 'culture vulture' considers it more important to be seen at these events, and to be heard talking about them, than it is for them to actually appreciate the art itself.

cup

not your cup of 'tea

If something is **not your cup of tea**, it is not the type of thing which interests you: *No, I'm afraid an Anne Summers party is not really my cup of tea.*

◊ SEE ALSO **not go a bundle on something** ▷ BUNDLE

cupboard

'cupboard love

Cupboard love is the affection that a person or animal shows for someone who can provide them with food or other material things: *'I think your dog likes me.' 'Only when you've got a sandwich in your hand. It's just cupboard love.'*

curate

a curate's 'egg or like the curate's 'egg – good in parts

If you describe something as **a curate's egg**, or **like the curate's egg – good in parts**, you are saying that the quality of that thing is variable, with some good and some bad bits: *I am sorry to say that many aspects of the book are disappointing. Of course – like the curate's egg – parts of it are excellent.* □ *Her empire, like the curate's egg, was only good in parts.*

An old story tells of a curate [= a priest, or vicar] who was served a boiled egg which was rotten. When his host asked him how the egg was, he replied, in an effort to be polite, 'Parts of it are excellent!'

curiosity

curiosity killed the 'cat

You tell someone that **curiosity killed the cat** to advise them not to ask any more questions: *She was curious, but it would be stupid to forget that curiosity had killed the cat.*

curl

curl up and 'die (*informal*)

People sometimes say they want to **curl up and die** if they are very embarrassed, uncomfortable, or ill: *When I realized he was there at the party, I just wanted to curl up and die.*

current

go against the 'current or drift against the 'current or swim against the 'current

When you **go**, or **drift**, or **swim**, **against the current**, you refuse to accept the situation as it is, and act differently from others.

◊ SEE ALSO **go against the flow** ▷ FLOW **go against the stream** ▷ STREAM **go** or **swim against the tide** ▷ TIDE

go with the 'current or drift with the 'current or swim with the 'current

When you **go**, or **drift**, or **swim**, **with the current**, you accept the situation as it is, and try to act in a way which makes it easy for you to fit into that situation: *As far as computers are concerned, you have to go with the current or get left behind.*

◊ SEE ALSO **go with the crowd** ▷ CROWD **go with the flow** ▷ FLOW **go with the stream** ▷ STREAM **go**, or **drift**, or **swim**, **with the tide** ▷ TIDE

curtain

bring down the 'curtain

You **bring down the curtain** on something when you end it: *Now I think we should bring down the curtain on this little episode, and go to bed.*

'curtain raiser

A **curtain raiser** is a first subject for discussion, or the first action in an activity, which is not the most important one planned, but which is useful for getting things started or for showing how things are likely to continue: *As a curtain raiser for today's discussion, has anybody here ever experienced racial harrassment?*

ring down the 'curtain on something

A certain event **rings down the curtain on something** when it marks the end of that thing: *With the demolition of the wall, Germany rang down the curtain on an era in European history.*

curtains

curtains for

It is **curtains for** someone or something if the time of their end or death has come: *If that happens, it's curtains for the European organi'zation.*

◊ SEE ALSO **have had your chips** ▷ CHIPS

customer

cool 'customer (*disrespectful*)

Cool customer is a name for someone who seems unfriendly and unwilling to express their feelings openly: *He was a young, cool customer, dark and striking. I met him at a cocktail party in the prestigious Monomatapa Hotel.*

slippery 'customer (*disrespectful*)

If you call someone a **slippery customer**, you mean that you do not trust them: *I'd watch out for that landlord of yours. He strikes me as a bit of a slippery customer.*

cut

a cut a'bove or **a cut above the 'rest**

If you consider that someone or something is **a cut above**, or **a cut above the rest**, you think that they are of a better standard than the average, or than the people or things you are comparing them with: *The Café Noir is a cut above the other restaurants in town.*

◇ SEE ALSO **not fit to hold a candle to** ▷ CANDLE **in a class of your own** ▷ CLASS **in a different league** ▷ LEAGUE

cut-and-'dried

An opinion or an answer that is **cut-and-dried** is definite, and not dependent on any conditions: *They have very cut-and-dried views on many issues. For example, they take the view that 'all criminals should be severely punished'.* □ *I cannot possibly give you a cut-and-dried answer to such a complex question.*

cut and 'run

To **cut and run** is to escape from a difficult situation while there is still enough time to do so: *Have a bit of sense! Better cut and run before the coppers* [= police] *arrive.* □ *You will be greeted by a receptionist who asks you for embarrassing personal details in a loud voice. The temptation to cut and run may be overwhelming.*

◇ SEE ALSO **break free** or **break loose** ▷ BREAK; **make a break** ▷ BREAK; **give someone the slip** ▷ SLIP

cut and 'thrust

The **cut and thrust** of a certain activity is the fierce competition which it involves: *She enjoys the cut and thrust of international marketing.*

> In sword-fighting, **cut and thrust** describes the motions made with the sword.

cut someone 'dead

If someone **cuts you dead**, they pretend not to see you, or they refuse to greet you, as a way of showing their dislike or anger towards you: *I knew it was her. I approached. 'Sophie,' I said. And she cut me dead. My own child cut me dead.*

cut it 'fine

You **are cutting it fine** when you give yourself only just enough time to be able to achieve your aim: *He began the two-mile journey from the hotel in a courtesy car at 9.25am. Even with normal traffic, it was cutting it fine.*

cut it 'out

If you tell someone to '**cut it out**', you are telling them angrily to stop doing something: *Cut it out Ma, I'm warning you.*

cut 'out for something

Someone who is **cut out for something** is perfectly suited for it: *I tried my best, but I'm afraid I'm just not cut out for teaching.*

cut someone 'short

If someone **cuts you short** when you are saying something, they interrupt you rather aggressively: *Rose chatted on about some interesting gossip she'd picked up there, but Anna cut her short, saying she was busy and would see her later.*

cut 'up (*informal*)

If you are **cut up**, or **cut up about something**, you are very upset about it: *She's just lost her job, and I think she's pretty cut up about it.*

cut up 'rough or **cut up 'nasty**

If someone **cuts up rough**, or **nasty**, they react badly to something, becoming angry or violent: *You can get round him if you go the right way about it. But he can cut up rough and turn a bit nasty if he's got a mind to.*

half 'cut

Someone who is described as **half cut** is drunk: *Smith also told the police the three men were half cut; they'd lost their sense of safety.*

◇ SEE ALSO **drunk as a lord** ▷ DRUNK; **well-oiled** ▷ OILED; **one over the eight** ▷ ONE

'short cut

A **short cut** is a way of getting somewhere which involves a shorter distance than the normal or most obvious way: *This is the short cut to the station.*

cylinders

fire on all 'cylinders

Someone or something that **is firing on all cylinders** is working at full strength or perfectly: *A lot of people have been off sick recently, but we'll be firing on all cylinders again on Monday.*

d

daggers

at daggers 'drawn

Two people or countries are **at daggers drawn** if the situation between them is not friendly, and they are in a state very close to confrontation: *The prospect of an interesting friendship had been destroyed and now they were at daggers drawn.*

◇ SEE ALSO **cross swords** or **have crossed swords with someone** ▷ SWORDS

A **dagger** is a weapon, like a knife, with a sharp, pointed end. In the past, people used to **draw daggers** when they took them out in preparation for a fight.

look 'daggers (*informal*)

You **look daggers** at someone if you look at them in a way that shows that you hate them, or that you are extremely angry with them for something they have done: *'Anyway, it wasn't my fault.' He looked daggers at me.*

daisy

'oops-a-daisy!(*informal*)

People say **'oops-a-daisy!'** to show that the situation is not very serious when someone, especially a child, falls or drops something.

daisies

pushing up the 'daisies (*humorous*)

Someone who **is pushing up the daisies** is dead: *I should think I'll be pushing up the daisies before they decide to do anything about modernizing the computing system in this office.* □ *They were fighting over the head of my son, as if his parents were already pushing up daisies.*

◇ SEE ALSO **dead as a doornail** or **dodo** ▷ DOORNAIL; **six feet under** ▷ FEET

A **daisy** is a kind of flower that often grows on graves.

damage

the damage is 'done

The damage is done means that it is too late now to change the results of an action that you regret: *And so that Ven should know how truly sorry she was, she held on to him*

with both arms and tried to pull him to her. But – the damage was done, and he resisted.

what's the 'damage?(*informal, humorous*)

You ask **'what's the damage?'** as a humorous way of asking for a bill, or asking how much you have to pay.

damn

'damn it (*informal*)

Damn it! is an expression of annoyance: *Damn it! I've gone wrong again!*

◇ SEE ALSO **fuck it** ▷ FUCK **sod it** ▷ SOD

not give a 'damn or not care a 'damn (*informal*)

If you say that you **don't give**, or **care**, **a damn**, you mean that you don't care about something at all: *She doesn't give a damn whether she passes her exams or not.*

◇ SEE ALSO **not care a fig** or **two figs** ▷ FIG, FIGS **not care** or **give a hoot** or **two hoots** ▷ HOOT, HOOTS **not give a monkey's** ▷ MONKEY **not give a shit** ▷ SHIT; **not care a sod** ▷ SOD; **not give a tinker's cuss** ▷ TINKER; **not give** or **care a toss** ▷ TOSS **not care** or **give tuppence** ▷ TUPPENCE

damned

I'll be 'damned! (*informal*)

I'll be damned! is an expression of great surprise: *'Did you know Tim and Carol are finally getting married after all these years?' 'Well I'll be damned; are they really?'*

I'm 'damned if (*informal*)

You can say **'I'm damned if'** as a way of refusing to do something very strongly: *I'm damned if I'm going to help him!*

damper,

dampers

put a 'damper on something or put the 'dampers on something

You **put a damper**, or **the dampers**, **on something** when you do or say something that spoils other people's enjoyment of it: *However, if you are with a group and everyone is laughing, it might put a damper on things if you remained tight-lipped and poker-faced.*

◇ SEE ALSO **pour cold water on** ▷ WATER

A **damper** is a device which reduces vibrations, for example, in a piano.

dance

lead someone a 'dance or lead someone a merry 'dance

Someone **leads you a dance**, or **a merry dance**,when they cause problems for you, making you do a lot of unnecessary things: *She could have any man she fancied. None of them seemed to last very long. She led them all a merry dance, including me.*

dare

don't you 'dare(*informal*)

You say '**don't you dare**' or '**don't you dare do such-and-such**' to someone who is threatening to do something which will harm you, or make you look stupid: *Don't you dare make fun of me. □ Don't you dare try and tell me what to do!*

how 'dare you? (*informal*)

You say '**how dare you?**' to someone who has made you angry by humiliating you: *How dare you, you little monster! □ Her chest was tight and her throat hurt. She refused to cry. 'How dare you talk to me like that! How dare you?'*

dark

in the 'dark

You are **in the dark** about something if you do not know about it: *They've been keeping us in the dark about the plans to restructure the company.*

dash

cut a 'dash

Someone who **cuts a dash** dresses with style in order to impress others, or acts in a way that suggests that they want to be noticed: *Harvey really cut a dash in his new suit and white silk scarf.*

date

blind 'date

A **blind date** is an arranged romantic meeting between two people who do not know each other: *Daryl Hannah fell in love with John F Kennedy Junior on a blind date set up by step-dad Jerry Wexler, friends have revealed.*

make it a 'date

You might say 'why don't we **make it a date**?' if you want to agree on a particular day for doing something: *Okay, I'll come over to see you; shall we make it a date for next Wednesday?*

out of 'date

Something that is **out of date** is old-fashioned, or no longer useful or appropriate; someone who is **out of date** is not aware of all the information which has been made available up to the present time: *Don't those wide ties look out of date now? □ Don't use that list; it's out of date. I've got the new one here. □ You're a bit out of date, actually. Haven't you read the last article she wrote?*

to 'date

To date means 'up to and including now': *How much of your project have you written to date?*

up to 'date

Something that is **up to date** is modern or recent; someone who is **up to date** knows all the information which has been made available up to the present time: *That dictionary's pretty up to date; you might find what you're looking for in there. □ It's not always easy keeping up to date with all the new developments in the computer world.*

Davy

Davy Jones' 'locker

Davy Jones' locker is the bottom of the sea.

People sometimes say that someone has gone to **Davy Jones' locker** when that person has died at sea.

dawn

dawn 'chorus

The **dawn chorus** is the sound of birds singing at sunrise: *We finally went to bed just as the dawn chorus was starting up.*

day (*see also* **days**)

all in a day's 'work

You can say that something is **all in a day's work** if it forms part of your everyday activities, and must be accepted as normal, even if you find it unpleasant or difficult in some way: *Controlling a class of excitable seven year olds is all in a day's work if you are a teacher on a placement scheme.*

◇ SEE ALSO **a necessary evil** ▷ EVIL; **a fact of life** ▷ FACT

any day 'now

You can say that something could happen **any day now** if you are expecting it to happen very soon: *The baby's due any day now.*

big 'day

Someone's **big day** is a day on which they do something or are planning to do something very important, such as getting married: *Far from being influenced by superstitions about* *her groom seeing her wedding dress before the big day, Erika enlisted Trevor's help in making it.* □ *It's going to be a big day for me; my first international match.*

call it a 'day
You **call it a day** when you decide to stop working on something: *At 11pm we finally decided to call it a day and went home to get some sleep.*

carry the 'day
Someone or something **carries the day** if they are responsible for an event's success: *Thank you so much for providing the food; it really helped to carry the day.*

> This was originally a military expression, which meant 'to win the battle'.

curse the 'day
You **curse the day** that something happened when you angrily wish that that thing had never happened: *He silently cursed the day he had got involved with her. He'd misjudged Paula, he realized.*

day after 'day
Something that happens **day after day** happens repeatedly or continuously in either a determined, or a tiresome way: *I keep telling him that we're not happy with the system, but day after day it's the same thing.* □ *Day after day she tirelessly pursued her duties, never complaining.*

> You can change this idiom to talk about things that happen over different periods of time, for example, **month after month, year after year, night after night**.

day by 'day
Day by day means gradually, as the days pass: *Day by day her health improved, until she was finally able to walk again.*

day in day 'out
Something that happens **day in day out** happens repeatedly and unchangingly: *I couldn't live there; it rained day in day out when I went there on holiday.*

> **Year in year out** is also used to describe things that happen unchangingly over very long periods of time.

the day of 'reckoning
The day of reckoning is the day on which an important decision or judgement will take place: *As the day of reckoning grew nearer, the athletes trained harder than ever.* □ *The day of reckoning, in the form of a three hour written exam.*

> **The day of reckoning** is another way of referring to The Day of Judgement, which is often mentioned in the Bible as the time when God will judge 'all men'.

from one day to the 'next
Someone or something that changes **from one day to the next** changes very suddenly, and without warning: *You never know what sort of mood he'll be in from one day to the next.* □ *The weather can change from one day to the next, so make sure you take an umbrella.*

give me such-and-such 'any day (*informal*)
You can say '**give me** a certain thing **any day**' if you like it best, even though it may not be the most modern or sophisticated of its kind: *Give me one of those old mechanical cameras any day; at least you can mend them when they go wrong.*

the happy 'day
People sometimes refer to a planned wedding as **the happy day**: *So, you're getting married! When's the happy day then?*

have a 'field day (*informal*)
You **have a field day** when you take good advantage of, and really enjoy, a situation: *The newspapers had a field day, as the case caught the imagination of the country.*

haven't got all 'day (*informal*)
If you say that you **haven't got all day**, you are impatiently saying that you think someone is taking too long, and you have more important things to do than wait for them: *Come on, I haven't got all day you know; what have you lost now?*

in 'my day
People say '**in my day**' to introduce a description of how people behaved when they were younger: *So you two are living together now? In my day that would never have been acceptable.*

in 'this day and age
'**In this day and age**' means nowadays, these days, or in these times: *I can't believe they still treat children like that in this day and age.*

late in the 'day (*informal*)
You say that it's a bit **late in the day** to do something if you think it is probably too late for your actions to have a positive effect: *I think it's a bit late in the day to start making fundamental changes to the text; I mean, the project's supposed to be finished by the end of the month.*

live for the 'day
Someone who **lives for the day** believes in enjoying the present, rather than worrying about what the future will bring: *He and Maureen decided to live for the day and not worry about what the future would bring for them, good or bad.*

◊ SEE ALSO **seize the day** ▷ DAY; **you're only young once** ▷ YOUNG

day

live to fight another 'day

You **live to fight another day** if you are still feeling strong and ready to try something again, despite a failure or defeat: *The Welsh team lost this one, but they live to fight another day.* □ *His excellent performance in the elections ensures that he lives to fight another day.*

make a 'day of it

You **make a day of it** if you decide to take advantage of a visit or event by spending the whole day in the place: *Well look, if we both have to go over there, why don't we make a day of it and stay for lunch, and maybe a walk in the afternoon?* □ *Imagine how lovely it would be – you could take the whole family and make a day of it!*

make someone's 'day

You **make someone's day** if you do something which makes them very happy: *The news that they'd decided to come home at last really made my day.*

name the 'day

You **name the day** when you decide on a date for an event or meeting to take place: *Why are they so reluctant to name the day for the wedding?*

nine day 'wonder

You can describe someone or something as a **nine day wonder** if they enjoy only a very short-lived period of great popularity: *Most of her boyfriends tend to be nine day wonders.* □ *Perhaps it would just blow over – a nine day wonder.*

◇ SEE ALSO **flash in the pan** ▷ FLASH

This idiom comes from an old saying which states that 'there is no wonder so great that it lasts more than nine days'.

not be someone's 'day

It **is not your day** if things seem to be going wrong for you all the time: *Oh no! It's not my day today; what a mess!*

◇ SEE ALSO **get out of bed on the wrong side** ▷ BED; **one of those days** ▷ DAYS; **get up on the wrong side of the bed** ▷ SIDE

the other day

The other day means at some time in the recent past: *Guess who I saw the other day.*

a rainy 'day

You save something, for example money, for **a rainy day** if you save it for a time when you might unexpectedly need it: *I spent half the money, and put the rest away for a rainy day.*

rue the 'day

You **rue the day** that something happened if you deeply regret it: *I rue the day I bought that car; it's brought me nothing but trouble.* □ *You embarrassed him, and he said you'd rue the day* [= he would take his revenge]. □ *He rued the day he'd sold those shares.*

save the 'day

Someone **saves the day** if they do something which makes a disastrous situation successful again: *The concert was quite atrocious, but once again, James saved the day with a beautiful rendition of 'Ave Maria'.*

seize the 'day

If someone tells you to **seize the day** they mean that you should take every opportunity to learn and experience new things now, rather than waiting until a later date. ◇ SEE ALSO **live for the day** ▷ DAY; **you're only young once** ▷ YOUNG

'that'll be the day

You can say **'that'll be the day'** if you think that it is very unlikely that something you would like to happen will happen: *'If we can get some more staff in, things will be much easier.' 'Huh! that'll be the day.'*

daylight

in broad 'daylight

Something which happens **in broad daylight** happens during the day, when you would normally expect it to happen at night: *They walked into the house and carried off the television, the computer, and all my jewellery; in broad daylight.*

daylights

beat the living 'daylights out of someone or **knock the living 'daylights out of someone** (*informal*)

People say that they will, or that they want to, **beat**, or **knock, the living daylights out of someone** when they are threatening to attack them physically: *If I ever catch the person who did this to you, I'll beat the living daylights out of them.*

Daylights here means 'eyes'. The idiom may mean that the person is beaten until they can no longer see.

scare the living 'daylights out of someone (*informal*)

Something **scares the living daylights out of you** if it terrifies you or makes you jump: *I don't find him funny at all. Quite the contrary, he scares the living daylights out of me.*

days

the best days of your 'life

People sometimes refer to the time they spent at school as **the best days of their life**: *And tell me about your schooldays. Were they the best days of your life?*

someone's days are 'numbered or **something's days are 'numbered**

You can say that **someone's**, or **something's, days are numbered** if they will soon no longer be useful, successful or alive: *If you ask me, his days are numbered; the company just doesn't need people with his skills any more.* □ *It was when the sales figures dropped below 400 a year that we knew the product's days were numbered.*

early 'days

It is **early days** in a situation, when you are near the beginning, and there is still plenty of time for improvements and changes to be made: *Don't worry too much; it's early days yet. I'm sure you'll settle down and make friends soon.*

the 'good old days (*informal*)

The good old days are the times in the past that, when remembered, seem to have been simple, enjoyable, and not stressful: *The crowd went home quietly via the 300 pubs that were to be found in the East End of Glasgow in the good old days.* □ *I wish you'd stop harking back to 'the good old days', and start enjoying the present.*

halcyon 'days

Halcyon days are calm, happy and successful times in the past: *It's hard for youngsters to get the job they want these days; not like those halcyon days of our youth.* □ *the halcyon days of British industry.*

> Traditionally, according to legend, the **halcyon**, or kingfisher, had power to calm the sea.

have seen better 'days (*informal*)

Something that **has seen better days** in not in very good condition: *Well, the furniture's nice, but the carpet's seen better days.*
◇ SEE ALSO **in bad repair** ▷ REPAIR; **the worse for wear** ▷ WEAR

in all my born 'days (*informal*)

You say that you have never seen or heard something so amazing **in all your born days** as a way of emphasizing how surprised or shocked you are: *Well, I've never heard anything so stupid in all my born days.*

one of these fine 'days (*informal*)

You say that something will happen **one of these fine days**, as a warning that it will happen soon: *One of these fine days you're going to get yourself into trouble if you carry on behaving like that.*

one of those days (*informal*)

You say that it's **one of those days** if everything seems to be going wrong for you on a particular day: *Sorry, I'm afraid it's just one of those days; I think I should go home and start afresh tomorrow.*
◇ SEE ALSO **get out of bed on the wrong side** ▷ BED; **not be someone's day** ▷ DAY; **get up on the wrong side of the bed** ▷ SIDE

those were the 'days (*informal*)

People say '**those were the days!**' when they are thinking about times in the past which were pleasant in some way when compared to the present: *'I remember when a pint of Guinness cost 15p.' 'Mm, those were the days, eh?'*

dead

dead as a 'doornail or as dead as a 'dodo (*informal*)

Someone or something that is as **dead as a doornail** or as **dead as a dodo** is dead without any doubt at all: *It's not surprising he doesn't answer his fans' letters; he's been dead as a doornail for 30 years now.* □ *The plants are all dead as a dodo; she hasn't been in to water them.* □ *No wonder it doesn't work; the batteries are dead as a dodo.*
◇ SEE ALSO **pushing up the daisies** ▷ DAISIES; **six feet under** ▷ FEET

> A **dodo** was a large bird, which was unable to fly, and which no longer exists.

deaf

deaf as a 'post (*informal*)

Someone who is as **deaf as a post** is completely, or almost completely, deaf: *He sat there smiling and laughing at my jokes; I felt quite pleased with myself, until someone told me that he was actually deaf as a post.*

deal

big 'deal (*informal*)

You can say '**big deal**' as a way of showing that you are not at all impressed by something that someone has just told you: *'They've finally agreed to give the nurses a 1% pay rise.' 'Big deal.'*

a raw 'deal

You get **a raw deal** if you do not benefit as greatly from a situation as someone else: *They see this as a way of helping to ensure that their employees do not get a raw deal – for example, when candidates for promotion are being compared.*

dear

oh 'dear

People say '**oh dear**' as a way of showing sympathy or concern about something which has gone wrong: *Oh dear, I'm going to be late again.* □ *'I got a really bad mark for my essay.' 'Oh dear, what went wrong?'*

death

at death's 'door

Someone who is **at death's door** is very ill and in danger of dying: *Even when he was at death's door he was still cracking the same old jokes.*
◇ SEE ALSO **not long for this world** ▷ WORLD

catch your 'death or **catch your death of 'cold**

You can tell someone that they will **catch their death**, or **catch their death of cold**, if they are going outside without enough clothes on: *The grass here is quite damp you know, and in those silly slippers, you'll catch your death.*

the 'death of someone

You can say that someone or something **will be the death of you** if they continually cause problems for you: *He always said that his job would be the death of him. □ That Garry will be the death of me!*

◊ SEE ALSO **the end of someone** ▷ END; **to an early grave** ▷ GRAVE

dice with 'death

You **are dicing with death** if you are taking a great risk, possibly with your life: *all those youths who might have experimented with the drug, not knowing that they were dicing with death. □ Agassi was dicing with death with that last shot, but the ball was just in.*

◊ SEE ALSO **court disaster** ▷ DISASTER; **risk your neck** ▷ NECK

die a 'death

Something **dies a death** if it stops being popular or if it stops operating, often because it was not founded on very solid grounds in the first place: *What happened to all his big plans to start up a business? They died a death, didn't they? □ Do you remember when plastic clothes became fashionable? They soon died a death, didn't they?*

do to 'death (*informal*)

You **do something to death** if you use, say or do it so often that all its originality is lost: *We can't do that sketch; it's been done to death; it's not funny any more.*

◊ SEE ALSO **flog to death** ▷ DEATH

flog to 'death

You **flog something to death** when you do it, discuss it or work on it so much that it no longer has a positive effect: *I quite enjoyed 'Madame Bovary' the first time round, but we've flogged it to death in our French course this year and I'm sick of it now. □ The trainer should recognize that the team should not be flogged to death during the days leading up to a match.*

◊ SEE ALSO **do to death** ▷ DEATH

If you **flog** an animal, you beat it very hard with a whip or stick.

hang on like grim 'death or **hold on like grim 'death** (*informal*)

You **hang on**, or **hold on** to something **like grim death** if you hold on to it very tightly: *We hung on to the boat like grim death as it*

rose and then crashed down again into the stormy seas.

◊ SEE ALSO **for dear life** ▷ LIFE

look like death warmed 'up or **feel like death warmed 'up** (*informal*)

You **look**, or **feel**, **like death warmed up** if you look or feel very tired or ill: *I wish I'd been a bit more sensible last night; I feel like death warmed up. □ You definitely need a holiday – you look like death warmed up.*

◊ SEE ALSO **off-colour** ▷ COLOUR; **pale** or **green about the gills** ▷ GILLS

sign your own 'death warrant

Someone **signs their own death warrant** if they do something which ensures their own failure: *No industrialist can think in terms of a single market. If he does, he is signing his own death warrant.*

◊ SEE ALSO **burn your boats** ▷ BOATS; **blow your chance** ▷ CHANCE

sound the 'death knell

A situation **sounds the death knell of, for,** or **on,** something if it leads to its downfall: *These further problems sounded the death knell on their marriage, which was already going through difficulties. □ The superstores' plans to open on Sundays could sound the death knell for some of the smaller shops in the area.*

The **death knell** is the sound of a bell rung slowly for a funeral.

worried to 'death

You are **worried to death** if you are extremely worried: *Where have you been? I've been worried to death.*

◊ SEE ALSO **at the end of your tether** ▷ END; **at your wits' end** ▷ WITS

debt

in someone's 'debt

You are **in someone's debt** if they have done something very important to help you, and you feel extremely grateful to them: *I'm forever in your debt for saving my life.*

decks

clear the 'decks (*informal*)

You **clear the decks** when you tidy up: *We'd better clear the decks a bit before they arrive; the place looks such a mess.*

A **deck** is a flat area for walking on, on a boat. Marines **clear the decks** when they get a ship ready for battle.

deep

deep 'down

You feel something **deep down** when you know that something is true, even if it is hard to accept: *Deep down I knew that I didn't really love him.* □ *Deep down, I knew what she was saying was true.*

degree

to a de'gree
Something is the case **to a degree** if it is not completely the case: *I agree with you to a degree, but there are some things in your argument that I just can't accept.*
◇ SEE ALSO **to a certain extent** ▷ EXTENT

to the nth de'gree
You do something, or something is the case, **to the nth degree** if you do it, or if it is the case, to the extreme, or as much as is possible: *The electorate's credulity was tested to the nth degree, with promises of lower taxes, higher pensions and better financial aid for those in need.* □ *In his style of writing there is a predictability beyond the nth degree. His new book is, however, extremely entertaining.*

degrees

by 'degrees
Something that happens **by degrees** happens gradually: *By degrees it became obvious to me that something had to be done about it.*
◇ SEE ALSO **slowly but surely** ▷ SLOWLY

déjà

déjà 'vu
You have a feeling or sense of **déjà vu** when you go somewhere and you suddenly feel as if you have been there before: *I experienced a strange feeling of déjà vu when I walked into that house; funny since I know I've never been there before in my life.*

Déjà vu is a French expression, which means literally 'already seen'.

delusions

delusions of 'grandeur
Someone who has **delusions of grandeur** makes themselves look ridiculous by imagining that they are more important than they really are: *He was a major, a middle-aged man, and non-combatant, who had delusions of grandeur. He'd been given a position in prison administration in Paris.*

demands

make de'mands on someone
Someone **makes demands on you** when they continually put pressure on you to do what they want: *Don't make too many demands on her at the moment; she's overworked as it is.*

den

a den of i'niquity
You humorously describe a place as **a den of iniquity** if people do things there which are generally considered to be immoral; people with very strict or old-fashioned morals might use this expression seriously: *As far as my father was concerned, the theatre was a den of iniquity, and no daughter of his would be seen following a career there.*

depth

out of your 'depth
You are **out of your depth** if you are in a situation which is too difficult for you to cope with, or where you do not understand what is happening: *I was completely out of my depth at the dinner; I mean, I know nothing about stocks and shares and futures markets.* □ *Broderick, who plays Clark Kellog, a smalltown college boy out of his depth in big, bad New York, is excellent.*
◇ SEE ALSO **up the creek without a paddle** or **up the creek** ▷ CREEK; **in the shit** ▷ SHIT; **up shit creek** ▷ SHIT; **in the soup** ▷ SOUP; **in a tight spot** ▷ SPOT; **in trouble** ▷ TROUBLE; **in deep water** ▷ WATER; **in hot water** ▷ WATER

You are **out of your depth** if you are in deep water where you cannot touch the bottom with your feet.

depths

in the depths of
You are **in the depths of** despair or depression when you feel very desperate or depressed: *When he came to me, he was in the depths of des'pair. It's difficult to believe that he's the same person now.*

sink to such 'depths
You wonder how someone could **sink to such depths** when you are shocked that they could act in such an immoral or degrading way: *I find it quite incredible that any authority or any member of an authority has to sink to such depths in order to try to make a case.*

deserts

get your just de'serts
Someone **gets their just deserts** when they get what they deserve for something bad they have done: *It is like turning to the end of the story before you begin reading it, to find out if the bad guys got their just deserts, if the good guys won.*
◇ SEE ALSO **take** or **suffer the consequences** ▷ CONSEQUENCES

deserve

deserve whatever you 'get or deserve everything you 'get

You might say, angrily, that someone **deserves whatever**, or **everything, they get** if you think that they have acted badly and irresponsibly, and that you will not feel any sympathy for them if their actions have unpleasant results for them: *I know it sounds harsh, but he deserves whatever he gets.*

◇ SEE ALSO **have it coming to you** ▷ COMING

designs

have de'signs on

You **have designs on** someone or something when you want them, and you plan to get them: *If he did have designs on her, and planned to marry her, why was he saying all the things that would irritate and upset her?* □ *I know Jeremy has got designs on that Alfa Romeo that Roger's selling, but we really can't afford it.*

dent

make a dent in

Something **makes a dent in** something else when it has the effect of reducing it: *That made a dent in his 'pride.* □ *Getting these repairs done is going to make a huge dent in our 'savings.*

desired

leave a lot to be de'sired *(informal)*

Something that **leaves a lot to be desired** is not of a very high quality, or not satisfactory: *It is not user-friendly and leaves a lot to be desired for a software support product.*

devil

be a 'devil *(informal)*

You might tell someone to **be a devil** if you want to encourage them to do something unusual, daring or indulgent, that they would not normally do: *Go on, be a devil! Nobody's watching.*

better the devil you 'know

If you say **'better the devil you know'**, you mean that it is preferable to continue in a situation which is not perfect but satisfactory, than it is to take the risk of changing to a new and unknown situation: *Fenton said, 'Better the devil you know, and we know Neil Webb. We had good times when he was here before.'*

> This idiom is the shortened form of the saying 'Better the devil you know than the devil you don't know'.

between the devil and the deep blue 'sea

You find yourself **between the devil and the deep blue sea** if you have to make a choice between two alternatives, both of which are unpleasant: *On this question regarding EC membership, the Government finds itself between the devil and the deep blue sea.*

cheeky 'devil *(informal, humorous)*

You call someone a **cheeky devil** if they have said something rude or disrespectful, but in a way that you find charming or amusing: *'Haven't you put on a bit of weight since I last saw you?' 'No I have not, you cheeky devil.'*

◇ SEE ALSO **cheeky monkey** ▷ MONKEY

the devil makes work for idle 'hands

'The devil makes work for idle hands' is an expression which means that if people find themselves with nothing to do, they are more likely to cause trouble: *There remains truth in the adage, 'the devil makes work for idle hands', and I assert that lack of hope is the greatest recruiting officer for all criminal activity.*

the 'devil to pay

If you say that there'll be **the devil to pay**, you mean that there is going to be a lot of trouble when someone find out what has happened: *I fell in the muddy water and spoilt my dress, and there was the devil to pay when we got home that night.*

> In some legends, people bargain with the devil, offering their soul in return for immediate success.

give the devil his 'due

You say **'give the devil his due'** when you want to remember someone's good points, especially when they have just done something wrong: *'I can't believe it! Peter's late again!' 'I know, but give the devil his due – he's such a lovely guy, he's just a bit disorganized.'*

◇ SEE ALSO **give so-and-so their due** ▷ DUE

go to the 'devil *(offensive)*

You might tell someone to **go to the devil** if you are angry with them and you do not want to talk to them any more: *Oh, go to the devil! That's complete nonsense, anyway!*

◇ SEE ALSO **go to hell** ▷ HELL

like the 'devil *(informal)*

You do something **like the devil** if you do it with great energy, very strongly, very well or very much: *I've missed you like the devil!* □ *He played the violin like the devil.*

the luck of the 'devil

Someone who has **the luck of the devil** is very lucky, sometimes when you think they do not necessarily deserve to be: *'He revised only three subjects out of ten and they all* *came up in the exam.' 'I don't know; that boy has the luck of the devil.'*

play the devil's 'advocate

You **play the devil's advocate** when you support an opposing or unpopular point of view in an argument, either in order to make the debate more interesting, or to question the most widely-held opinion: *To tell you the truth, I was just playing the devil's advocate – I actually agree with everything you said.*

This expression comes from the Latin 'Advocatus Diaboli', referring to a person who was appointed by the Church to state the case against someone who was being considered for a high position in the clergy.

speak of the 'devil or talk of the 'devil (*informal*)

People often say '**speak**,or **talk, of the devil!**' when they have just been talking about someone and then that person arrives: *'Huh! Talk of the devil.' 'Why? What were you saying about me?'*

People used to believe that talking about evil gave it power to happen.

who the 'devil or what the 'devil or where the 'devil (*informal*)

You ask **who** or **what** or **where**, etc, **the devil** something is, for example, when you are intrigued or have difficulty believing what is happening: *What the devil are you talking about? I didn't say that!* □ *What the devil do you want at this time of night?* □ *Why the devil didn't you say so before?*

devices

leave someone to their own de'vices

You **leave someone to their own devices** if you let them do as they please, without interfering or trying to help: *Most gliding clubs have a system of re-checking pilots during the first few hours of solo flying, but then pilots are left very much to their own devices.*

diamond

rough 'diamond

A **rough diamond** is someone who is maybe not very polite, but who is in fact kinder and more pleasant than they seem to be: *He may sometimes be a rough diamond, he may swear and complain, but he shrewdly weighs up the people he meets.*

diarrhoea

verbal diar'rhoea (*informal, humorous*)

Someone who has **verbal diarrhoea** talks too much: *There's nothing worse than having to spend all evening at dinner with someone who's got verbal diarrhoea.*

dick

'clever dick (*informal, rather offensive*)

A **clever dick** is someone who has a very high opinion of themselves, and who has an answer to everything: *Come on then, clever dick, seeing as you know everything – what's the longest word in the English language?*
◇ SEE ALSO **smart aleck or alec** ▷ ALECK; **clever clogs** ▷ CLOGS; **know-all** or **know-it-all** ▷ KNOW

die

die 'hard

People's attitudes and habits **die hard** when they do not change over long periods of time: *Old habits die hard, and even the most progressive-thinking members found that it didn't always come naturally to use the new politically correct terms.*
die-hard: *die-hard supporters of the 'king.* □ *die-hard con'servatives.* □ *You old die-hard!*

the die is 'cast

If you say '**the die is cast**', you mean that a decision has been taken and it must be followed through: *In any case, the die was cast, she had made up her mind.* □ *Now that the die was cast, he felt a certain calm.*

Die is the singular of **dice** [= the small cube-shaped objects that you throw to see how many moves forward you may make in a game]. The idiom refers to the fact that once the die is cast [= thrown], you must accept the number that is shown on it.

I'd rather 'die (*informal*)

People say '**I'd rather die**' when they are imagining having to do something which they would find extremely embarrassing or humiliating: *Sing a solo in front of the whole school? I'd rather die.* □ *The British would rather die than cause a scene by complaining. Very little food was ever sent back at Jolly Griddles.*
◇ SEE ALSO **wouldn't dream of** ▷ DREAM; **wouldn't be seen dead** ▷ SEEN

difference

for all the 'difference it makes

For all the difference it makes means 'but it will not make any difference' or 'because it will not make any difference': *I told her to come home before midnight, for all the difference it makes; you know she just doesn't listen to me any more.* □ *But for all the difference it is going to make to your life and to mine, I might as well not bother.*

make a world of 'difference or make all the 'difference

A change **makes a world of difference**, or **makes all the difference**, if it greatly improves a situation: *After all, the right software can make a world of difference to your business.* □ *It's incredible; the new wallpaper makes all the difference.*

same 'difference (*informal*)

You say **'same difference'** when you accept a correction that someone has made, but you think that the difference is unimportant: *Two thousand or twenty hundred, same difference.*

split the 'difference

You **split the difference** if you agree on an amount or number that is exactly between two stated amounts: *He refused to accept that he'd overcharged me, so in the end we decided to compromise and split the difference.*

with a 'difference (*informal*)

You describe something as being **with a difference** if it has something unexpected about it that makes it unusual, original or interesting: *Enjoy a holiday with a difference on this 'Action Break' organized by the Scottish Conservation Projects group.* □ *If you're looking for a hobby with a difference, why not take up groundhopping?*

dig

dig 'in (*informal*)

You say **'dig in'** as a way of telling people to start eating: *Okay, dig in then, or it'll get cold.*

dignity

beneath someone's 'dignity

People, sometimes ironically, say that something is **beneath** a person's **dignity** if they think that the person considers themselves to be too important to do it: *Oh, no! that would be beneath her dignity. She had always said she had never been a shop-girl and she wasn't going to start now.*

dime

a dime a 'dozen (*informal*)

Something is **a dime a dozen** if it is very common: *British ski champions are not exactly a dime a dozen, which is why everyone was so amazed at his performance.*

dine

dine 'out on something (*informal*)

You **dine out on something**, for example, an event, if you repeatedly use a funny or shocking story about something that has happened to you or someone you know, in order to get people's attention in social situations: *Wow, this was an event on which one could dine out for many months back in one's home town!*

ding

'ding-dong (*informal*)

A **ding-dong** is a noisy disagreement or fuss and commotion: *They had a bit of a ding-dong and one of the kids knocked a dish off a cooker.* □ *There was a right old ding-dong when half the managers lost their jobs, and were replaced by young graduates.*

dinners

have had more of such-and-such than so-and-so has had hot 'dinners (*informal*)

If you say that you **have had more of** a certain thing **than** a particular person **has had hot dinners**, you mean that that person should not question your knowledge on the subject, because you have much more experience of it than they have: *Eddie Futch, 80, who's probably seen more fights than even most men of his age have had hot dinners, expects it to be one of the best he's been involved with.*

dint

by dint of 'such-and-such

By dint of a certain thing means 'because of', 'thanks to', or 'as a result of' that thing: *He's got to where he is today by dint of sheer hard work.*

◇ SEE ALSO **by virtue of** ▷ VIRTUE

dirt

dirt 'cheap (*informal*)

Something is **dirt cheap** if it is very cheap: *It keeps the rain out, it lets a certain amount of light in and it's dirt cheap.*

treat like 'dirt or treat like a piece of 'dirt (*informal*)

Someone **treats you like dirt** or **like a piece of dirt** when they treat you badly, and without respect: *I know his sort. Thinks he can treat people like dirt. Well, she'll make him sorry. She'll find a way.*

disaster

court di'saster

You **court disaster** when you take a great risk: *To make fun of these little men was to court disaster, for they made formidable enemies.*

◇ SEE ALSO **dice with death** ▷ DEATH; **risk your neck** ▷ NECK

distance

go the 'distance

Someone or something **goes the distance** when they succeed or prove their worth: *That song had so many lyrics and different types of music in there, that I didn't think it'd go the distance.*

ditch

in 'spitting distance or within 'spitting distance (*informal, humorous*)

You are **in**, or **within**, **spitting distance** of something, or of doing something, if you are very close to it: *Once the house must have been very much on its own, but now there are modern houses within spitting distance.* □ *There is nothing worse than playing two superb shots to get within spitting distance of the green, then going to pieces on the last putt.*

◇ SEE ALSO **on your doorstep** ▷ DOORSTEP; **a stone's throw** ▷ STONE

> **Spitting distance** means how far you can spit [= project the contents of your mouth, especially the saliva].

keep your 'distance

You **keep your distance** when you avoid going too near to someone or something: *Harry was gripped by a sneezing fit which dissolved into painful coughing. 'I really am sorry about this, Alan. You'd better keep your distance.'*

◇ SEE ALSO **at arm's length** ARM; **give a wide berth to** ▷ BERTH; **steer** or **stay clear of** ▷ CLEAR

ditch

last-ditch at'tempt

A **last-ditch attempt** is a final effort made without much hope of success: *As a last-ditch attempt to acquire some proper qualifications, she had enrolled as a student teacher with a woman who ran dancing classes for children.*

> The **last ditch** refers to the trenches in which soldiers defended a military position, making every effort to defend something, up to the last moment.

do

can do with'out something

You **can do without something** 1 if you do not need it: *I usually have a cigarette after dinner, but I can do without if I have to.* 2 (*informal*) if it causes you more problems than you already have: *I could do without this extra work with all these guests staying at the moment.*

could do with 'such-and-such

You say that you **could do with** a certain thing if you feel that you would like it or that you need it: *I could do with a cold drink after all that running.* □ *You look as if you could do with a holiday.*

do a 'so-and-so (*informal*)

You **do a so-and-so** if you do something annoying which is typical of someone else's behaviour: *Oh no, you're not going to do a Joe on us and change your mind at the last minute, are you?*

do as I say, not as I 'do (*informal*)

If someone says to you '**do as I say, not as I do**', they mean that you should follow their advice, rather than copy their behaviour, because they do not want you to make the same mistakes as them.

do's and 'don'ts

Do's and don'ts are things that you should and should not do: *a list of do's and don'ts.*

doctor

just what the doctor 'ordered

Someone or something that is described as **just what the doctor ordered** is exactly what was required: *A lovely cold beer. Just what the doctor ordered.* □ *I suppose maybe because he has that kind of style he might be just what the doctor ordered for the nineties.*

does

that 'does it

You can say '**that does it**' if something happens that makes you decide that you will not tolerate the situation any longer: *Right, that does it. I'm going over there now to speak to his parents.*

◇ SEE ALSO **enough is enough** or **that's enough** ▷ ENOUGH

dog (*see also* **dogs**)

the dog's 'bollocks (*vulgar, humorous*)

If you describe something as **the dog's bollocks**, you mean that it is great, or the best of its kind: *New high taste, low alcohol lager – it's the dog's bollocks.*

'dog days

Dog days are the hottest days of the summer: *The dog days drove most people indoors to keep cool, and some adventurous spirits down to the coast.*

> There is traditionally supposed to be a hot period in summer when the Dog Star can be seen.

a 'dog's life

Someone's life is described as **a dog's life** if they have to work very hard in order to survive, and they have very few pleasures: *It's a dog's life, working on those farms up north; no-one around and complete darkness for half a year.*

dog eat 'dog

A situation is described as a case of **dog eat dog** if everyone is acting in a way that will benefit themselves the most, without worrying about what happens to anyone else: *The dog eat dog brand of free market capitalism.*

dog-'tired (*informal*)

You are **dog-tired** if you are very tired: *'I'm dog-tired and hungry too,' he told her. 'And that's when I'm likely to make a major mistake.'*

done up like a dog's 'dinner or dressed up like a dog's 'dinner or got up like a dog's 'dinner (*offensive*)

Someone, especially a woman, who is **done up**, or **dressed up**, or **got up**, **like a dog's dinner** is dressed in a vulgar, and sexually provocative way: *Go on, ask her where she's been all afternoon, dressed up like a dog's dinner and missing for hours.*

give a dog a bad 'name

If you say **'give a dog a bad name'**, you mean that once someone has had their reputation damaged, it is difficult for them to regain people's respect: *Picking on Woodhouse Close is perhaps predictable* (give a dog a bad name, and all that) *but Coundon?*

> This is a short form of the expression **'give a dog a bad name and hang him'**, meaning that if a dog bites, for example, it will have to be killed, because it cannot be trusted.

shaggy 'dog story

A **shaggy dog story** is a long joke which has a deliberately silly or disappointing ending: *Certain kinds of jokes are preferred by men: the 'shaggy dog' kind or narrative type that begins with formulas like 'Have you heard the one about ...?'*

top 'dog

A person, group or country that is described as **top dog** is better or more powerful than others of its kind: *He was determined to prove that he, Simon Cooper, was top dog.* □ *He liked being a top dog in his own little way, and he was very satisfied with the small business he operated.*

work like a 'dog

You **work like a dog** when you work very hard: *I've been working like a dog to get this job finished.*

◇ SEE ALSO **work your fingers to the bone** ▷ FINGERS

you can't teach an old dog new 'tricks

If you say **'you can't teach an old dog new tricks'**, you mean that it is very difficult to change old people's opinions, habits and behaviour: *It's a nice thing to learn. They say you can't teach an old dog new tricks, but I'm living proof.*

◇ SEE ALSO **a leopard never changes its spots** ▷ LEOPARD

doggy

'doggy bag (*informal*)

A **doggy bag** is a bag that a restaurant or host at a party provides, in which you can put food that you have not finished, and take it home to eat later: *Fortunately, he was allowed to take a doggy bag. A big slice was wrapped up, to be devoured later on in the plane.*

doghouse

in the 'doghouse (*informal*)

You are **in the doghouse** if someone is not pleased with you, and is not being friendly towards you, or not talking to you: *'Oh, what a relief! I was beginning to think I must be in the doghouse for some reason.' He spoke as though they knew each other well.*

> **Doghouse** is a less common word for 'kennel'; a small, wooden shelter, where a dog sleeps. This expression suggests that the person in question has been sent outside in disgrace.

dogs

go to the 'dogs (*informal*)

A person or thing **has gone to the dogs** if they have changed from being respectable to being worthless: *I'm sick and tired of reading the news. The country's going to the dogs – people out of work everywhere – there's no money about.*

◇ SEE ALSO **go downhill** ▷ DOWNHILL

> Something that you give to the dogs is worthless, and not wanted by anyone.

let sleeping dogs 'lie

When people say **'let sleeping dogs lie'**, they mean that you should not try to improve a person or situation that is not making trouble at the moment, because they might start making trouble if you do: *If the child is behaving well or playing quietly the typical parental attitude is 'let sleeping dogs lie'. They do not want to disturb their child by commenting on how good he or she is in case the child starts to demand attention again.*

doldrums

in the 'doldrums

Someone who is **in the doldrums** is depressed or sad: *I'm feeling a bit in the doldrums today; sorry if I'm rather quiet.*

◇ SEE ALSO **down in the dumps** ▷ DUMPS

> **The doldrums** is a part of the sea where there is no wind, making it difficult for sailing boats to make progress.

done

'done for
You are **done for** if you no longer have any chance of escaping a very dangerous situation: *That's it now, we're done for. I can't see any way of getting out of here before the tide comes in.*

done 'in (*informal*)
You are **done in** if you are very tired: *I'm done in; let's not go out tonight.*
◇ SEE ALSO **all in** ▷ ALL

not the done 'thing
An activty is **not the done thing** if it is not considered appropriate or polite by a particular group or society: *Dad, don't haggle with the traders; it's just not the done thing over here.* □ *Is it the done thing to give tips in pubs?*

dollar

bet your bottom 'dollar
You **bet your bottom dollar** that something is the case if you are certain that it is so: *Michael is looking for ways to make people take out private insurance. Poverty in old age is one target. Health care must be another on his list. You can bet your bottom dollar.*

'dollar signs in your eyes
Someone who has **dollar signs in their eyes** is only doing something because they know that they will get money through doing it: *You could almost see the dollar signs in her eyes as she walked along arm in arm with that old brute, McNorton.*

sixty-four-thousand dollar 'question
The **sixty-four-thousand dollar question** is the question that everyone is asking, but to which no-one knows the answer: *Ah, now that's the sixty four thousand dollar question. I'm very confident that if we have the best first class facilities, people will come to watch.*

dollars

look like a million 'dollars or feel like a million 'dollars
Someone who **looks**, or **feels**, **like a million dollars** looks or feels very well and attractive: *I left the hairdresser's feeling like a million dollars.* □ *Darling, you look like a million dollars in that outfit.*

donkey

the 'donkey work
The **donkey work** is the hard, tiring, physical work involved in a task: *The direction of research within a department is under the control of the supervisors in that department, for whom the PhD student does the donkey work.*

The donkey is an animal traditionally used for carrying heavy loads.

'donkey's years
Donkey's years means 'a very long time': *Chris Hunter, for donkey's years or so it seemed, had a sweet shop between our house and the football ground in Shildon.*

This is a play on words with 'donkey's ears', which are very long.

door

by the back 'door or through the back 'door
Someone enters a place, especially with regard to getting a job, **by**, or **through**, **the back door** when they enter by unconventional or unofficial means: *He called these environmental controls 'socialism by the back door'.*

door to 'door
1 A journey takes a certain length of time **door to door**, if it takes that length of time between leaving one building and arriving at the final destination: *The actual train journey takes four hours, but door to door it's more like five.* **2** Someone who goes from **door to door** moves from one house or flat to the next: *a door-to-door salesman.*

never darken someone's door a'gain
Someone tells you **never to darken their door again** if they never want to see you again: *Don't you dare ever darken my door again.*

show someone the 'door
You **show someone the door** when you tell them you want them to leave, usually because you are annoyed with them: *I would have gone further though. I'd have shown him the door, told him to go elsewhere.*

doors

behind closed 'doors
Something takes place **behind closed doors** when it takes place in secret, or when it is hidden from the public: *It is said that a lot of the peace agreement discussions went on behind closed doors.*

doorstep

on your 'doorstep
Something that is **on your doorstep** is conveniently close to your home: *It's a great little neighbourhood; you've got everything you need on your doorstep.*
◇ SEE ALSO **in** or **within spitting distance** ▷ DISTANCE; **a stone's throw** ▷ STONE

dose

like a dose of 'salts
You do something **like a dose of salts** if you do it very quickly.
◇ SEE ALSO **like a shot** ▷ SHOT

Salts, here refers to a laxative, which relieves constipation.

doses

in small 'doses

You say you can tolerate someone or something **in small doses** if you can tolerate them only for short periods of time: *Babies are fine – in small doses.*

dot

dot your i's and cross your 't's

You **dot your i's and cross your t's** when you pay great attention to small details, especially when you are putting the finishing touches to a piece of work: *'Those conditions still stand,' she told MPs, 'but no one is suggesting that we dot every 'i' and cross every 't' before we look at it.'* □ *The pair will meet again today and Mr Taylor said: 'We want to dot the i's and cross the t's on a whole range of issues – and we want to do it sooner rather than later.'*

on the 'dot

You do something **on the dot** when you do it precisely at a specified time: *She arrived at six o'clock on the dot.* □ *He always pays his bills on the dot.*

double

on the 'double or at the 'double

You tell someone to do something **on,** or **at, the double** if you want them to do it immediately: *Okay, that's enough; out of here. On the double!*

doubt

beyond all 'doubt

Something which is proven to be true **beyond all doubt** is shown to be definitely true: *Do not give your conclusions until you have established the verdict beyond all doubt.*
◇ SEE ALSO **for certain** ▷ CERTAIN; **without a doubt** ▷ DOUBT; **without question** ▷ QUESTION; **beyond any shadow of doubt** or **without any shadow of doubt** ▷ SHADOW; **sure as eggs is eggs** ▷ SURE

cast 'doubt on something

You **cast doubt on something** when you cause people to ask themselves if they are really as sure about something as they thought they were: *The empirical evidence is such as to cast doubt on conventional wisdom.*
◇ SEE ALSO **call into question** ▷ QUESTION

no 'doubt

You say that something is **no doubt** the case if you think that it is very probably the case: *No doubt they'll be late, as usual.* □ *As they no doubt told you, I shall be leaving at the end of the year.*

without a 'doubt

You say that something is the case **without a doubt** if you know, or you are sure that what you are saying is true: *She is, without a doubt, one of the most influential writers of the twentieth century.*
◇ SEE ALSO **for certain** ▷ CERTAIN; **beyond all doubt** ▷ DOUBT; **without question** ▷ QUESTION; **beyond any shadow of doubt** or **without any shadow of doubt** ▷ SHADOW; **sure as eggs is eggs** ▷ SURE

down

down and 'out

Someone who is **down and out** is homeless, and lives on the streets: *Would you believe that there was a time when this man was down and out on the streets of London?*
down-and-'out: *a soup kitchen for down-and-outs.*

down to 'so-and-so

You say that a situation is all **down to** a certain person if they are responsible for it: *Don't thank me, thank Peter – the whole thing's down to him.*

down to the last 'such-and-such

You are **down to the last** of a particular thing if you have very little of it left: *We're down to the last bottle of that wine we bought in France last year; we'll have to get some more.*

Down 'Under

People sometimes refer to Australia or New Zealand as **Down Under**: *the best beers from Down Under.* □ *These regulations are interpreted differently Down Under – especially in New Zealand.*

Australia and New Zealand are traditionally presented on a globe as being 'underneath', that is on the opposite side of the world to Britain.

down with 'so-and-so! or down with 'such-and-such!

People shout **'down with'** a certain person or thing when they are in a big group, protesting noisily in public: *Down with council tax!*

get 'such-and-such down you (*informal*)

Someone tells you to **get** food, or drink, **down you** when they want you to eat or drink something: *Get that down you – you'll feel much better.*

downhill

go down'hill

You say that something **is going,** or **has gone, downhill** if it is not as good as it used to be: *The service here has gone right downhill since the last time I came.* □ *Ralph's not* much of a businessman. Between ourselves, he's gone downhill recently in more ways than one.

◇ SEE ALSO **go to the dogs** ▷ DOGS

dozen

six of one and half a dozen of the 'other

1 If you describe an unfortunate situation as **six of one and half a dozen of the other**, you mean that neither of the two parties mentioned is more to blame for it than the other: *You blame me, I blame you. It was six of one and half a dozen of the other.* **2** You also say '**it's six of one and half a dozen of the other**' if you see no difference between two things or solutions: *'Do you mind if we have our main meal tonight, rather than at lunchtime?' 'Not at all – it's six of one and half a dozen of the other for me.'*

drag

in 'drag

A man who is **in drag** is dressed as a woman: *Boy George was nothing less than a man in drag, who flounced his sexuality in the face of the outraged media and ecstatic teenagers.*

dragon

chase the 'dragon (*slang*)

Someone who **is chasing the dragon** is smoking heroin by heating it and inhaling the fumes.

drain

down the 'drain (*informal*)

Something, such as a plan is, or goes, **down the drain** if it is no longer useful or valid, or if it has been wasted: *There are fears of family life going down the drain, as staff may get only two complete weekends off in seven.*
◇ SEE ALSO **down the pan** ▷ PAN **down the plughole** ▷ PLUGHOLE; **down the toilet** ▷ TOILET **down the tubes** ▷ TUBES

dread

dread to 'think

You say you **dread to think** what will or would happen if you feel very anxious when you think about a very unpleasant possibility in the future: *I dread to think what would happen if I lost my job. □ I dread to think how we would have managed without all their help.*

dream

the American 'Dream

The **American Dream** is the belief that everyone in the United States can be rich and successful if they work hard enough: *the myth of the American Dream. □ He* represents the American Dream boy; he's young, beautiful, he's got the future ahead of him.

dream 'on (*informal*)

You say to someone '**dream on**' if you think that something which they hope for, or that they believe, will probably never happen, or is not the case: *'It would be nice if we could completely update the computer system in this office.' 'Huh, dream on; who's going to pay for it?' □ Bright, yes. Motivated, yes. But tough? Dream on. Young Jack thought he was hard, but underneath it all he was soft.*

like a 'dream

Something that goes **like a dream** is very successful: *The whole day went like a dream. □ 'How's the car going now?' 'Like a dream, thanks.'*

wouldn't 'dream of

You say that you **wouldn't dream of** doing something if you are sure you would never do it, because you think it is rude, immoral or ridiculous: *I can't believe they're accusing Harry; he wouldn't dream of hurting anybody.*
◇ SEE ALSO **wouldn't be seen dead** ▷ SEEN; **I'd rather die** ▷ DIE

dreams

your wildest 'dreams

Things that exist **in your wildest dreams** are things that you never dared believe were possible: *Performing on stage in Hollywood, with world famous stars in the audience, was beyond my wildest dreams. □ For a moment he thought his wildest dreams were about to come true.*

dribs

in dribs and 'drabs

People or things arrive **in dribs and drabs** when they arrive slowly, and in small quantities or numbers, rather than all at the same time: *Up until now they've been let out in dribs and drabs. They're talking here about a kind of mass release aren't they? □ They use methods of giving chemotherapy in gentle dribs rather than massive doses.*

drift

if you catch my 'drift or if you get my 'drift (*informal*)

You add **if you catch**, or **get, my drift** to something you have just said, to let the listener know that you are trying to say something indirectly: *The company 'let him go', if you get my drift. □ Give somebody a lift and take cash for it and we've got you, so you might have to be very careful who you travel with, if you catch my drift.*

drink (*see also* **drunk**)

cannot hold your 'drink

A person who **cannot hold their drink** easily loses control of their behaviour when they drink alcohol: *I can't think what suddenly got into him. He's not usually like that. He can normally hold his drink.*

the demon 'drink

You refer to alcohol as **the demon drink** if you want to refer to the fact that it is responsible for a lot of unpleasant things which happen to people: *Since he came out of the clinic, he hasn't allowed one drop of the demon drink to pass his lips.*

drink to

People **drink to** someone or something when they raise their glasses and express wishes that good things will happen in the future: *He bought two large whiskies and, sitting Kate in the corner, they drank to their daughter's 'health.*

drive someone to 'drink

Someone or something **drives someone to drink** if it makes them so anxious that they start drinking alcohol regularly to calm their nerves; you say that someone or something **will drive you to drink** if they constantly cause you to feel frustrated, angry, or upset: *It was his job that drove him to drink.* □ *That child will drive me to drink one day.*

the worse for 'drink

Someone who is **the worse for drink** is drunk: *He was walking unsteadily along the road, obviously the worse for drink.*
◇ SEE ALSO **have had a few** or **have had a few too many** ▷ FEW; **under the influence** ▷ INFLUENCE

drive

drive someone 'mad or drive someone 'crazy or drive someone in'sane

Someone **drives you mad**, or **crazy**, or **insane** when they annoy you intensely: *That noise outside is driving me mad; are they allowed to do that all day?* □ *I simply could not understand the boys' sense of humour. And the noise they made – it was driving me crazy.*
◇ SEE ALSO **make someone's blood boil** ▷ BLOOD

drop

drop 'dead (*offensive*)

You tell someone to **'drop dead'** if you are very angry with them, or if you think that what they have said is nonsense: *'Drop dead, yer silly old bugger,' said a woman.*

'drop everything

You **drop everything** when you stop whatever you are doing in order to do something else which someone considers to be more important: *This very moment is the most important point of my career. I can't just drop everything.*

a drop in the 'ocean

You describe something as **a drop in the ocean** if it seems a very small amount in relation to something else, or in relation to what is needed: *We munched our way through an average 18 pasta meals per head last year, a drop in the ocean compared to the Italians, who managed to swallow a massive 300 meals each.*

fit to 'drop

You are **fit to drop** if you are exhausted: *Just when we were fit to drop, they would tell us that we were going to spend the night on a mountainside, keeping watch for 'enemy advances'.*
◇ SEE ALSO **dead on your feet** ▷ FEET

drum

beat the 'drum

You **beat the drum** for someone or something when you try to attract public attention to it: *We don't preach or beat the drum. We get out and raise money to build things.*

> In the past, people used to beat a drum to call people together before making a public announcement.

drunk

drunk as a 'lord

Someone who is as **drunk as a lord** is very drunk: *He spends what little money he has on drink, coming home at all hours of the night from the pubs in the village, drunk as a lord.*
◇ SEE ALSO **half cut** ▷ CUT; **well-oiled** ▷ OILED; **one over the eight** ▷ ONE

dry

dry as a 'bone

Someone or something that is as **dry as a bone** is completely dry: *I've been out in the rain in these all day and my feet are dry as a bone.*

dry as 'dust

Someone or something that is as **dry as dust** is **1** completely dry. **2** very boring: *His throat was dry as dust.* □ *What the students learned was 'dry as dust', one young man told me about his studies.*

duck

lame 'duck

A **lame duck** is a person or organization that is in serious difficulties, and that needs help in order to survive: *Heseltine warned rebels they would be left with a lame duck administration if they did not ratify Maastricht.* □ *'He's adopted another lame duck, and he's coming to live here with us,' she groaned.*

sitting 'duck

A **sitting duck** is someone or something that people find it easy to criticize or attack, because they are the most obvious target: *Visiting soccer bosses are sitting duck targets for verbal and, sometimes, physical abuse.*

◇ SEE ALSO **sitting target** ▷ TARGET

take to something like a duck to 'water

Someone **takes to something like a duck to water** if they learn it very easily, or feel comfortable with a new situation very quickly: *Anna moved from Christine's school, and took to the new one 'like a duck to water'.*

duckling

an ugly 'duckling

You describe someone or something as an **ugly duckling** if they begin their life by being dull and ordinary; people usually use this expression to talk about someone or something that ends up being very beautiful, successful or popular: *And it was your grandmother who convinced you that you weren't an ugly duckling, that you would grow up to be a swan?* □ *Just like the fairy tale about the ugly duckling turning into a lovely white swan, butterflies have a similar story.*

From a story by Hans Christian Andersen, about an ugly young duck that grew into a beautiful swan [= a large, white water bird with a long neck].

due

give so-and-so their 'due

You say '**give** a certain person **their due**' when you think that, although they have done something wrong or disappointing, it is important to remember the good things they have done: *To give him his due, he never involved anyone else in his problems.*

◇ SEE ALSO **give the devil his due** ▷ DEVIL; **do justice to** or **in justice to** ▷ JUSTICE

duff

up the 'duff (*vulgar*)

A woman who is **up the duff** is pregnant.

◇ SEE ALSO **up the spout** ▷ SPOUT **in the family way** ▷ FAMILY **have a bun in the oven** ▷ BUN **in the pudding club** ▷ PUDDING **in the club** ▷ CLUB

dumps

down in the 'dumps

You are feeling **down in the dumps** if you are depressed or sad: *She's a bit down in the dumps today; she didn't get that job she wanted.*

◇ SEE ALSO **in the doldrums** ▷ DOLDRUMS

duration

for the du'ration

You say that something unpleasant lasts **for the duration** if it seems to be continuing for an unlimited length of time: *We've been sitting here for the duration; when do you think we'll be able to see a doctor?*

The duration originally referred to the length of time of the Second World War, when certain business activities had to be stopped 'for the duration'.

dust

allow the 'dust to settle or let the 'dust settle

You **allow the dust to settle** or **let the dust settle** when you let someone calm down before you try to do anything else about a situation: *If I were you I'd let the dust settle before you go and ask her for your money back.*

bite the 'dust

Someone or something **bites the dust** when they finish, no longer have any use, or die: *Another coal mine bit the dust today.*

◇ SEE ALSO **breathe your last** ▷ LAST; **kick the bucket** ▷ BUCKET; **cash in your chips** ▷ CHIPS; **pop your clogs** ▷ CLOGS; **shuffle off this mortal coil** ▷ COIL; **give up the ghost** ▷ GHOST; **depart this life** ▷ LIFE; **snuff it** ▷ SNUFF; **go the way of all flesh** ▷ WAY

When men are killed in battle, they fall to the ground with their face in the dust.

gather 'dust

You say that something **is gathering dust** if it is not being used: *There have also been reports of piles of school books gathering dust in shops, because people cannot afford to buy them.*

not see someone for 'dust

You **do not see someone for dust** when they leave very quickly: *We're leaving on Friday, from Dover. First ferry and you won't see us for dust.*

When a horse and carriage moved away quickly and suddenly, it would make a cloud of dust behind it.

Dutch

double 'Dutch

You say that something is **double Dutch** if you do not understand it at all: *That quantum mechanics stuff she reads is all double Dutch to me.*

◇ SEE ALSO **it's all Greek to me** ▷ GREEK **can't get your head round something** ▷ HEAD

go 'Dutch (*old*)

People **go Dutch**, especially at a restaurant, when they share the bill between them equally: *Once a fortnight she and a group of friends would go Dutch at one of their three favourite restaurants.*

◇ SEE ALSO **go halves** ▷ HALVES

This idiom was originally an American expression, from the tradition of a 'Dutch lunch', where the guests are expected to contribute something to the meal.

duty

duty 'bound

You feel **duty bound** to do something if you feel that you should do it for moral reasons or politeness: *An employer is not duty bound to provide a reference when an employee leaves.* □ *In a pub, he felt duty bound to drink beer, although a good strong vodka would have suited him far better.*

duty 'calls

If you say '**duty calls**', you mean that you have got to stop doing something pleasant because you have some work to do: *And now, if you'll excuse us, duty calls, I'm afraid.*

dying

be 'dying for something or be dying to 'do something (*informal*)

You **are dying for something** if you want or need it badly; you **are dying to do something** if you are very excited about doing it: *I'm dying for a drink.* □ *I'm dying to see you all again.*

be 'dying of something (*informal*)

If you say you **are dying of something**, for example hunger, you mean that the feeling you mention is very strong: *I'm dying of 'thirst; is there any coke in the fridge?*

e

eagle

the eagle eye of 'so-and-so

You are under **the eagle eye** of a certain person if they are watching you very carefully to make sure that you do not do anything wrong: *Nothing ever escaped the eagle eye of our 'maths teacher.*

legal 'eagle

If you describe a lawyer as a **legal eagle**, you mean that they are well-known for being exceptionally good at, and enthusiastic about, their job: *Leigh Lawson, alias TV legal eagle Kinsey.*

ear *(see also* **ears***)*

bend someone's 'ear *(informal)*

You **bend someone's ear** when you force them to listen while you talk to them for a long time about something: *Whenever I meet her, she bends my ear about how things have changed since the good old days.*

catch someone's 'ear

When a sound **catches your ear**, you suddenly notice it for some reason: *A noise on the pavement behind me caught my ear and I turned round.*

◇ SEE ALSO **catch someone's eye** ▷ EYE

'ear-bashing *(informal)*

Someone gives you an **ear-bashing** if they tell you, forcefully and without listening to your comments, how much they disapprove of something: *I picked up the phone and gave him an ear-bashing.* ▢ *Evelyn was inclined to appease Samuel rather than endure his ear-bashing tantrums.*

easy on the 'ear

Something which is **easy on the ear** is pleasant to listen to, and does not require much concentration: *Country and western music is usually relaxing and easy on the ear.*

◇ SEE ALSO **easy on the eye** ▷ EYE

go in one ear and out the 'other

When something that you tell someone **goes in one ear and out the other**, they do not listen to it carefully enough to remember it later: *I told her what I thought she should do, but my advice went in one ear and out the other.*

grin from ear to 'ear or beam from ear to 'ear

Someone who **is grinning from ear to ear** is smiling broadly, probably because they are pleased about something: *Mr Crangle was grinning from ear to ear. How could he not be happy at the news?* ▢ *When she finally left him to go upstairs her heart was overflowing, and she was beaming from ear to ear.*

◇ SEE ALSO **grin like a Cheshire cat** ▷ CHESHIRE

have your 'ear to the ground or keep your 'ear to the ground

You **have**, or **are keeping**, **your ear to the ground** if you are taking care to be well-informed about what is happening around you: *You must keep your ear to the ground and contact me if you discover anything suspicious.*

> Native Americans used the method of listening with an ear next to the ground to help them discover the position of other people or animals.

lend an 'ear

When you **lend an ear** to someone or something, you listen to them: *She is incapable of lending a sympathetic ear to anyone else's problems.*

listen with half an 'ear

If you **are listening with half an ear**, you are aware of what you are hearing, but you are not giving it your full attention: *Wycliffe felt stolid and dull; he listened with only half an ear and his thoughts wandered.*

out on your 'ear *(informal)*

If you are **out on your ear**, you have been ordered to leave your job or the place where you were living, probably because of your bad behaviour: *We'll give it one more try, but if you come home drunk again, you'll be out on your ear.*

play something by 'ear

When you **play music by ear**, you are able to play a tune which you have heard, without seeing it written down.

play it by 'ear

If you deal with a situation in a way which is not fixed, but can change in response to changes and new demands in that situation, you **are playing it by ear**: *I don't know how often we'll want you to come into the office. We'll have to play it by ear.*

thick 'ear (*humorous, informal*)

If someone threatens to give you a **thick ear**, they mean they are going to hit you: *Stop that, or you'll get a thick ear.*

◊ SEE ALSO **give someone a bunch of fives** ▷ BUNCH; **give someone a knuckle sandwich** ▷ KNUCKLE

If someone hits you hard on the ear, it may become swollen and 'thick'.

turn a deaf 'ear

You **turn a deaf ear** to something when you decide to ignore it, and to pretend you cannot hear it: *He refused to promise anything, just as he turned a deaf ear to their demands for his resignation.*

◊ SEE ALSO **turn a blind eye** ▷ EYES

earnest

in 'earnest

You are doing something **in earnest** if you are putting all your effort into making it a success: *I had other things to finish, so I've only been working in earnest on this project for a few weeks.*

ears

all 'ears (*informal*)

You say you are **all ears** if you are listening very carefully: *Okay, so tell me what's bothering you. I'm all ears.*

◊ SEE ALSO **all eyes** ▷ EYE

believe your 'ears

You say that you cannot **believe your ears** if you hear something which is so surprising or ridiculous that it is difficult to believe: *She couldn't believe her ears when the doctor told her she was pregnant.*

◊ SEE ALSO **believe your eyes** ▷ EYES

so-and-so's 'ears are burning

You say that a certain person's **ears are**, or **must be, burning** if people are talking about them a lot: *Some people's ears must've been burning yesterday afternoon when that personnel meeting was taking place.*

As long ago as Roman times, people used to say that your ears grew hot when someone was talking about you.

fall about so-and-so's 'ears

If you say that things **are falling about** a certain person's **ears**, you mean that everything is going wrong for that person: *I do feel sorry for her. It seems as if her whole life's falling about her ears.*

fall on deaf 'ears

If the things you say **fall on deaf ears**, they are being ignored by the person you are talking to: *She wept and cried, but her protests fell on deaf ears.*

give your 'ears

If you say you would **give your ears** for something, you mean that you desire it and would give a lot to possess it: *Most of them would give their ears to be on the stage.*

◊ SEE ALSO **give your right arm** ▷ ARM; **give your eyeteeth** ▷ EYETEETH; **give your right hand** ▷ HAND; **give the world** ▷ WORLD

have something coming out of your 'ears (*informal*)

If you have so much of something that you do not know what to do with it all, you say you **have it coming out of your ears**: *We've got information coming out of our ears and what we need now is some way to make sense of it.*

keep your 'ears pinned back

Someone who **is keeping their ears pinned back** is listening carefully and paying attention: *I must watch my step and keep my ears pinned back.*

prick up your 'ears

Someone **pricks up their ears** when they suddenly look interested in what they are hearing: *She said she'd seen pupils doing something that might give a wrong impression of the school. We pricked up our ears.*

A lot of animals prick up [= raise] their ears when they are listening to something.

set someone by the 'ears

If something **sets** the members of a group of people **by the ears**, it causes trouble for, or between, those people: *revolutionary designs that would set competitors like Cartier by the ears.*

up to your 'ears (*informal*)

If you have so much of something to deal with that you cannot see how you are going to manage, you say that you are **up to your ears** in it: *I've been up to my ears in work these past few weeks.*

◊ SEE ALSO **up to your eyes** ▷ EYES; **up to your eyeballs** ▷ EYEBALLS; **up to your neck** ▷ NECK

wet behind the 'ears (*disrespectful*)

If you say that someone is **wet behind the ears**, you mean that they are not very experienced in life: *Japan's Prime Minister may still be a little wet behind the ears but, not for the first time, he has confounded his more experienced rivals.*

earth

bring someone back down to 'earth

You **bring someone back down to earth** when you make them understand that they are not thinking or behaving in a realistic way; you **come**, or **are brought, back down to earth** when you understand that you have not been thinking or behaving in a realistic way: *The news brought me back down to earth with a bump.*

cost the 'earth (*informal*)

You say that something **costs the earth** when you think it is too expensive; you **pay the earth for something** when you pay a lot of money for it: *A good joint of beef costs the earth these days.*

◇ SEE ALSO **cost a bomb** ▷ BOMB; **cost a packet** ▷ PACKET

'earth mother (*humorous*)

If you describe a woman as an **earth mother**, you mean that she gives the impression of being natural and sensitive, and that she is the kind of person who enjoys having and looking after children: *Delia Smith, with her earth mother image, has been Britain's favourite TV cook since the 1970s.*

the 'earth moved (*humorous*)

If a person, usually a woman, says after having sex that **the earth moved**, they are saying that the experience was enjoyable and special; if you ask a person **'did the earth move for you?'** after they have had sex, you are asking if the experience was enjoyable or special: *A friend rang up asking, 'Did you feel the earth move?' She was surprised, but replied, 'It wasn't that good.'*

◇ SEE ALSO **how was it for you?** ▷ YOU

> This idiom is usually only used in jokes.

Earth to 'so-and so or Earth calling 'so-and-so (*humorous*)

If you are speaking to a person who does not seem to be listening, you sometimes say **'Earth to**, or **Earth calling**, so-and-so', to attract their attention: *'This is Earth calling Starship Bob,' I said. 'Please respond.'*

> In science fiction, this phrase is used by the people at a base on Earth when they are trying to make contact with someone in a spaceship.

go to 'earth

When someone **goes to earth**, they disappear into a secret hiding-place, so that they cannot be found by the police: *The prime suspect in the murder case has gone to earth.*

◇ SEE ALSO **go to ground** ▷ GROUND

> In hunting, the fox goes to earth when it escapes into its hole.

like nothing on 'earth (*humorous, informal*)

If you say that you feel or look **like nothing on earth**, you are saying that you feel or look very ill, unattractive or untidy; something that looks, tastes, sounds, etc, like nothing on earth is awful: *I wish I hadn't met him after being at the dentist's. I must have looked like nothing on earth.* □ *It looks like smoked salmon and tastes like nothing on earth.*

on 'earth

You use **on earth** to give a strong emphasis to the question-words who, what, when, where, why and how, especially if you are surprised or angry: *Where on earth have you been?* □ *What on earth have you been doing?* □ *How on earth did you get your essay done on time?*

run to 'earth

You **run** someone or something **to earth** when you find them after a long search: *I finally ran my uncle to earth in an antique shop on the King's Road.*

◇ SEE ALSO **run to ground** ▷ GROUND

> In hunting, the hounds run a fox to earth when they chase it into its hole.

earthly

not have an 'earthly or not stand an 'earthly (*informal*)

1 You say you do **not have an earthly** when you do not know something: *I haven't an earthly where he's gone.* **2** You also say you do **not have**, or **stand, an earthly** when you do not have even the slightest chance of success: *I haven't an earthly of winning this game.* □ *He didn't stand an earthly.*

◇ SEE ALSO **not have a clue** ▷ CLUE; **not have the foggiest** ▷ FOGGIEST; **not have the faintest** ▷ FAINTEST

ease

at 'ease

1 You feel **at ease** when you are relaxed and happy in a situation; you put someone **at their ease** when you make them feel relaxed and happy: *He was at ease in her company.* □ *I was nervous when I arrived, but the interviewer put me at my ease.* **2** Soldiers stand **at ease** when they are standing in a relaxed position with their feet apart.

◇ SEE ALSO **to attention** ▷ ATTENTION

ill at 'ease

You feel **ill at ease** when you are nervous or unable to relax in a situation: *She was ill at ease sitting next to her boss at the dinner party.*

easy

easy as AB'C or **easy as 'anything** or **easy as falling off a 'log** or **easy as 'pie** or **easy as 'winking**
Something which is as **easy as ABC**, or **anything**, or **falling off a log**, or **pie**, or **winking**, is very easy: *She patted me on the back. 'Easy as pie, wasn't it?' she said.*
◇ SEE ALSO **child's play** ▷ CHILD; **kids' stuff** ▷ KIDS; **a piece of cake** or **a piece of piss** ▷ PIECE; **nothing to it** ▷ NOTHING

easy come, easy 'go
If you say '**easy come, easy go**', you mean that because someting was easy to obtain, you are not too bothered about losing it; '**easy come, easy go**' also refers to an easy-going attitude in general, often one that is disapproved of: *But my attitude to money is slightly easy come, easy go. That is to say, I earn a lot, but I also give quite a lot away in different ways.* □ *No easy come, easy go, in this house! I was brought up in a hard school, Mrs Willow, and I don't forget it.*

easy-'going
An **easy-going** person is usually relaxed and reasonable about things which would make other people angry or worried: *I wish my mum was as easy-going as yours.*

go 'easy on someone
You **go easy on someone** when you do not punish or criticize them as severely as you could do: *I know he was wrong, but go easy on him. He's still very young.*

go 'easy with something or **go easy on something**
You **go easy with**, or **on, something** if you do not take too much of it: *You can take whatever you like for your picnic, but go easy on the pizza. I want some left.*

I'm 'easy (*informal*)
If someone asks you what you want and you reply '**I'm easy**', you mean that you do not mind and that you want them to choose: *'Do you want lunch now or later?' 'I'm easy.'*

take it 'easy or **take things 'easy**
You **are taking it easy** or **taking things easy** if you are relaxing or being careful not to work too hard: *The doctor told me to take it easy for a couple of weeks.*
◇ SEE ALSO **put your feet up** ▷ FEET

eating

what's eating 'so-and-so (*informal*)
If you seem unusually anxious or unhappy, people sometimes ask '**what's eating so-and-so?**': *What's eating him this morning? He's usually so bright and cheerful.*
◇ SEE ALSO **rattle someone's cage** ▷ CAGE

ebb

at a low 'ebb
You say that someone or something is **at a low ebb** if they are not as strong or in such a good state as usual: *Enthusiasm among the volunteers has been at a low ebb since the funding for the project was cut.*

When the tide is **at a low ebb**, the level of the sea is very low.

ebb and 'flow
The **ebb and flow** of somethingis the pattern of change which affects it all the time: *the ebb and flow of public support for the Prime 'Minister.*
◇ SEE ALSO **ups and downs** ▷ UPS

The **ebb and flow** of the sea describes the way the tides affect it, with the level of the water falling during the ebb tide and rising during the flow.

economy

false e'conomy
A **false economy** is an action which seems to save you money, but which will end up costing you more, or at least causing you not to gain anything: *Economy in lighting is always false economy. Have several light points and keep a good general level of lighting at all times.*

ecstasies

go into 'ecstasies (*slightly disrespectful*)
If someone **is going into ecstasies** about something, they are praising or admiring it in an exaggerated way: *They loved everything. The heather, purple now, they went into ecstasies over. It was like but not like Scotland.*
◇ SEE ALSO **wax lyrical** ▷ LYRICAL; **go into raptures** ▷ RAPTURES

edge

the cutting 'edge or **the leading 'edge**
When you talk about **the cutting edge** or **the leading** edge, you mean the most modern and advanced level in the stated activity: *He's at the cutting edge of research into renewable 'energy sources.*

The **cutting edge** of a blade is the sharp edge which starts the cutting process.

have the 'edge on someone or **have the 'edge over someone**
You **have the edge on**, or **over, someone** if you have a slight advantage over them: *Musically, we are of a similar standard, though his better sense of rhythm gives him the edge.*

on 'edge

If you are **on edge** you are in a nervous state, and anything unexpected is likely to give you a shock: *No wonder he had seemed a bit on edge. It must have been a shock, her turning up out of the blue like that.*

take the 'edge off something

Something that **takes the edge off** a feeling or taste, for example, makes it less harsh: *This not only took the edge off the bitter taste, but also gave the drink a warm, attractive colour. □ The sun was warm on my back, but the south-easterly wind took the edge off the stifling heat.*

teeter on the 'edge

A person or thing that **is teetering on the edge** of some disaster is so dangerously close to that disaster that any small event is likely to cause it to happen: *It is a dangerous moment, teetering on the edge of despair. □ Many believed that the country was teetering on the precipice of political anarchy and economic collapse.*

◇ SEE ALSO **on the brink of something** ▷ BRINK

> To **teeter** is to stand unsteadily like a person who is drunk, giving the impression that you are about to fall.

eff

effing and 'blinding

Effing and blinding means swearing, involving a lot of rude words, probably spoken in a loud voice: *The action is set in a south London council flat, and it begins with a young man effing and blinding in a crescendo of inarticulate fury.*

◇ SEE ALSO **swear like a trooper** ▷ TROOPER

> The word **eff** in this expression represents the way we pronounce the letter F, which is an abbreviation for 'fuck'. Therefore, **effing** refers to the use of the word 'fuck', or other, equally strong, swearwords. **Blinding** probably comes from an exclamation of anger which is not commonly used today, 'blind me!'

effect

come into ef'fect or be put into ef'fect (*formal*)

Something such as a law **comes into effect**, or **is put into effect** at the moment when it starts being used or comes into operation: *The new alcohol limits for drivers come into effect on the first of next month.*

for ef'fect

Someone who is doing something **for effect** is doing it in a conscious way, because they want to make a certain impression: *Oh, she just says things like that for effect. She doesn't really mean them. □ She lowered her voice for dramatic effect.*

in ef'fect (*formal*)

You use **'in effect'** when you are speaking about what you consider to be the truth or reality of a situation: *In effect, this new tax means that every household in Britain will be £10 a week poorer.*

take ef'fect

1 When something such as a drug **takes effect**, it starts to work: *Give antibiotics 36 hours to take effect. If no improvement is observed, seek medical advice.* **2** (*formal*) You say a new arrangement **takes effect** from a particular date or time if that is when it starts or comes into operation: *Your new job description takes effect from next Monday morning.*

to best ef'fect (*formal*)

Something is seen **to best effect** when it is likely to impress you because its good qualities are particularly evident: *The city is seen to best effect at night.*

◇ SEE ALSO **to best advantage** ▷ ADVANTAGE; **in a good light** ▷ LIGHT

to this ef'fect or to the ef'fect that or to that ef'fect (*formal*)

You use **'to this effect'**, or **'to the effect that'**, or **'to that effect'**, when you are going to report the general meaning of what has been said or written; you use **to that effect** to refer back to your report of what has been said or written: *He made a statement to this effect: that he would not leave his job unless requested to do so. □ I've heard rumours to the effect that she's applied for a post in the States. □ I think she probably told them to mind their own business, or something to that effect.*

egg

bad 'egg (*old, informal, disrespectful*)

In the past, people used **'bad egg'** to refer to a completely worthless person: *The chairman, who sacked Fry last week, said, 'I will never, ever sell the company to anyone who will employ Barry Fry. He's a bad egg.*

◇ SEE ALSO **bad news** ▷ NEWS

can't boil an 'egg

If you say that you **can't boil an egg**, you mean that you do not know how to cook: *I took one of those cordon bleu cookery courses. Useful. I couldn't boil an egg before.*

have 'egg on your face

You say someone **has egg on their face** if their unwise actions result in a situation where they look foolish: *I didn't follow his advice, and I ended up with egg on my face.*

eggs

put all your eggs in one 'basket or **have all your eggs in one 'basket**
People sometimes tell you not to **put, or have, all your eggs in one basket** if they think that you are in danger of losing everything by depending on just one plan: *City wisdom suggests that you shouldn't put all your eggs in one basket, so for most people, a general distribution of investment is the wiser choice.* □ *This means that the risk is spread – 'we haven't got all our eggs in one basket,' she says.*

eggshells

walk on 'eggshells or **tread on 'eggshells**
You **are walking**, or **treading, on eggshells** if you are being careful in what you do and say because you are afraid of upsetting someone: *He was treading on eggshells when he met the unions this week for the second in a series of talks concerning the reform of the post office.* □ *I started to walk on eggshells for fear of setting him off.*
◇ SEE ALSO **handle with kid gloves** ▷ KID

> The shells of eggs are so delicate that you would find it difficult to walk on them without breaking them.

ego

'ego trip
An **ego trip** is a feeling of exaggerated self worth that someone gets when they realize that other people like or admire them: *It was the biggest ego trip I'd ever had. Seeing all those people coming out of the pub to watch me was fantastic.*

elbow

'elbow-grease (*informal*)
When you talk about **elbow-grease**, you mean the hard physical work or effort needed to do a certain task well: *No polishing is needed. This will save many householders a great deal of elbow grease.* □ *With the right ideological tools and political elbow-grease, racism can be dealt with once and for all.*

'elbow-room
You say that you need some **elbow-room** if you want people to move away and give you enough space to move or do something: *Stringed instruments always raised difficulties, because they had less power than the wind section, and their operators needed more 'elbow-room'.*

give someone the 'elbow (*informal*)
If someone **gives you the elbow**, they get rid of you or take away your job; if you **get the elbow**, you are not wanted any more, or

you lose your job: *I hear she's given that boyfriend the elbow at last.* □ *He got the elbow from his last job for being rude to the customers.*
◇ SEE ALSO **give someone the boot** ▷ BOOT; **give someone the heave-ho** ▷ HEAVE; **give someone the push** ▷ PUSH

element

in your 'element
You say you are **in your element** if the situation you are in gives you confidence and allows you to perform at your best: *He was in his element here. Every few minutes, it seemed, men came up to him, sometimes just to greet him, often to ask advice.*

> According to medieval science, every creature belonged to one of the four elements: earth, fire, air and water. The signs of the Zodiac are still arranged under these elements.

elephant

an elephant never for'gets (*humorous*)
If you say '**an elephant never forgets**', you mean that a certain person is going to remember something, probably something bad, such as an insult, for a very long time.
◇ SEE ALSO **memory like an elephant** ▷ MEMORY

> People say that elephants have good memories, although there is no evidence for this.

white 'elephant
1 A **white elephant** is something which has no practical use, and which causes a lot of trouble without doing any good: *The highly expensive Trident has become a complete white elephant.* **2** The **white elephant** stall at a sale is the stall where a general assortment of other people's unwanted items are sold: *The afternoon will feature a tombola, a raffle, a white elephant stall and home baking, and doors will open at 1.30pm.*

> There is a story that in Thailand, where the king's white elephants were traditionally treated like royalty, the king would give any person who had displeased him an elephant to look after, because he knew that the great expense would make them poor.

elephants

pink 'elephants (*humorous*)
People are supposed to see **pink elephants** when they are drunk: *Take more water with it in future, or you'll be seeing pink elephants next time.*

else

or 'else

1 You use '**or else**' to mean 'or' when you are introducing the second of two possibilities: *Would you like to come home for supper? Or else, if you prefer, we could go to the pub.* **2** You use **or else** to introduce the bad things which will happen if the person you are speaking to does not do what you have just said; **or else** can also be a general threat if you say it after telling someone to do something: *I've got to do better next year, or else I'm out.* □ *That'd better be finished tonight, or else!*

embryo

in 'embryo

Something that is planned is **in embryo** when it is in its earliest stages, and not yet properly formed: *Plans for renovating London's South Bank exist in embryo, but the project will take years to complete.*

The **embryo** is a person or animal in the stages of its development which take place inside the mother's womb or the egg.

emperor

the emperor's new 'clothes

1 If you compare something to **the emperor's new clothes**, you are saying that you must be careful not to be deceived by it, because it may seem to be desirable or of a good quality when in fact it is not: *Remember that buying software is like buying the emperor's new clothes.* **2** If someone is dressed in **the emperor's new clothes**, they are naked: *The emperor's new clothes: Milan's new costume museum without garments.*

The story of 'The Emperor's New Clothes' by Hans Christian Andersen tells of an emperor who is deceived into appearing naked in public, a situation which everyone accepts because they believe that he is wearing clothes which can only be seen by special, or superior, people. It is only when a child shouts, 'But the Emperor has nothing on at all!' that everyone realizes the truth.

end (*see also* **ends**)

at an 'end (*formal*)

Something which is **at an end** is finished: *Our holiday was nearly at an end.*

at the end of the 'day

At the end of the day means 'when you look at the whole situation': *At the end of the day, it doesn't matter how many hours you work. It's what you get done that counts.*
◇ SEE ALSO **all things considered** ▷ CONSIDERED

at the end of your 'tether

You are **at the end of your tether** if you have been worried or angry for so long that you cannot bear it any more; you are **at the end of your tether with** someone or something if you have lost patience with them: *My moody boss is driving me to the end of my tether. I am fed up with being put down and made to feel stupid by him.*
◇ SEE ALSO **worried to death** ▷ DEATH; **at your wits' end** ▷ WITS

An animal kept on a **tether** [= a rope attached to a central post] can only eat the grass growing inside the circle, whose size depends on the length of the rope. When the animal reaches the end of its tether, it is very hungry and trying to reach more grass.

at a loose 'end

You are **at a loose end** if you have some spare time, but no ideas of what to do with it: *So then, are we to suppose that being at a loose end leads to drunkenness and murder?*
◇ SEE ALSO **twiddle your thumbs** ▷ THUMBS

can't see beyond the end of your 'nose or can't see past the end of your 'nose or can't see further than the end of your 'nose (*informal, disrespectful*)

You say that someone **can't see beyond**, or **can't see past**, or **can't see further than**, **the end of their nose** if they only notice the most obvious things, or the things that they themselves are doing: *If he thinks redundancies will help the business, he obviously can't see beyond the end of his nose.*

come to an 'end or draw to an 'end

When something **comes to an end**, it finishes; if something **is drawing to an end**, it is about to finish: *The Great War came to an end on 11 November 1918.* □ *Now it was five o'clock, the working day was drawing to an end, his desk almost free of questions needing answers.*
◇ SEE ALSO **come** or **draw to a close** ▷ CLOSE

come to a sticky 'end or come to a bad 'end (*informal*)

When you say that a person will **come to a sticky end** or **come to a bad end**, you mean that, in your opinion, they are so bad that their life will end in an unpleasant way: *His point made – a kind of 'behave yourself young lad, or you'll come to a sticky end' – he stood up and wandered back to the bar.*

dead' end

1 A **dead end** is a road which does not go anywhere; a situation that does not lead anywhere is also called a **dead end**: *We came* *to a dead end and had to turn back.* □ *What he really wants is a relationship, not a dead end.* **2** The adjective **dead-end** describes an activity in which it is impossible to make any progress: *He was stuck doing a dead-end job in the local warehouse.*

don't know one end of a such-and-such from the 'other or can't tell one end of a such-and-such from the 'other

You say that you **don't know**, or **can't tell**, **one end of a** certain thing **from the other** if you have no knowledge about, or skill with, that thing: *Don't ask me if it looks ill. I don't know one end of a horse from the other.*

an end in it'self

If you describe a certain activity as **an end in itself**, you mean that the process of doing it is at least as satisfying and important as what you will gain from it: *Learning a language not only improves your prospects; the learning process is an end in itself.*

'end it all

To **end it all** is to kill yourself: *Sometimes things were so bad that I wanted to end it all.*
◇ SEE ALSO **blow your brains out** ▷ BRAINS

the end justifies the 'means

If you believe that **the end justifies the means**, you think that any action, however bad it may be, is acceptable if the final result which it produces is a good one: *How can you support the claim that the end justifies the means when so many people are suffering?*

This phrase is often used to express the ideas of the philosopher Machiavelli, who suggested in his work *The Prince* that all political actions, however bad, were acceptable if they strengthened the power of the State.

the 'end of someone (*informal*)

When you say that someone or something will be **the end of you**, you mean that they are causing you a lot of problems: *That child will be the end of me.*
◇ SEE ALSO **the death of someone** ▷ DEATH; **to an early grave** ▷ GRAVE

The end of someone really means 'the cause of that person's death', but it is not usually used seriously.

the end of the 'road or the end of the 'line (*informal*)

You have reached **the end of the road** or **the end of the line** when you realize that you cannot continue or survive any longer: *I told him we had reached the end of the road, and that I wanted a divorce.*

end of 'story (*informal*)

When you say **'end of story'**, you mean that a certain decision has been made, and that the subject is no longer open for discussion: *But as soon as he heard about the latest strike, that was it. End of story. He instructed Mueller to phase out vehicle manufacture in the UK.*
◇ SEE ALSO **no two ways about it** ▷ WAYS; **that's that** ▷ THAT; **that's flat** ▷ FLAT

get your 'end away or have your 'end away (*vulgar*)

If a man says he **got**, or **had, his end away**, he means that he managed to meet, and have sex with, someone: *The long nights he spent in coffee bars discussing Jack Kerouac and René Magritte over cold cups of espresso, the night-school fine arts courses. But he never got his end away.*
◇ SEE ALSO **have it away with someone** ▷ AWAY; **get laid** ▷ LAID; **have it off with someone** ▷ OFF

'End' is an informal name for a man's penis.

get hold of the wrong end of the 'stick or get the wrong end of the 'stick (*informal*)

When you **get hold of**, or **get, the wrong end of the stick**, you misunderstand a situation or the sense of what someone has said: *People who think the song is about ecstasy have got the wrong end of the stick.*

go off the 'deep end (*informal*)

When someone **goes off the deep end**, they lose their temper: *I knew he'd be angry, but I had no idea he was going to go off the deep end like that.*
◇ SEE ALSO **blow a fuse** ▷ FUSE; **blow a gasket** ▷ GASKET; **let fly** ▷ LET; **blow** or **flip your lid** ▷ LID; **do your nut** ▷ NUT; **lose your rag** ▷ RAG; **fly into a rage** ▷ RAGE; **hit the roof** ▷ ROOF; **blow your stack** ▷ STACK; **lose your temper** ▷ TEMPER; **blow your top** ▷ TOP; **throw a wobbly** ▷ WOBBLY

hear the 'end of something

If you say that you will never **hear the end of something**, you mean that you are sure that people will keep reminding you of something you have done which you are possibly ashamed of, or embarrassed about: *If she marched out, it was going to turn into a major incident. She'd never hear the end of it when she got home.*

in at the 'deep end

When you are thrown **in at the deep end** of a situation, you are given something very difficult to do, with very little help from anyone: *I'd only been there a week when they threw me in at the deep end and asked me to chair a meeting.* □ *Finniston admits* *that having been plunged into the deep end of commercial decisions he inevitably made mistakes in the early stages.*

◇ SEE ALSO **sink or swim** ▷ SINK

Notice the variant '**into the deep end**'.

in the 'end

You use '**in the end**' to talk about the final result, following a period of consideration or activity: *I was worried about the exams, but they went all right in the end.*

keep your 'end up (*informal*)

You **are keeping your end up** if you are being brave and managing in a difficult situation, or performing your part in something equally as well as all the others who are involved: *Michael still had to keep his end up against attacks on his beliefs.*

◇ SEE ALSO **put a brave face on it** ▷ FACE

In cricket, you keep your end up if you do not lose your wicket.

no 'end

No end means 'a lot': *I'm enjoying this TV series no end.* □ *There was no end of delicious food to eat at the party.*

not the end of the 'world

If you tell someone that something is **not the end of the world**, you are trying to comfort them by saying that it is not as bad as it seems: *Hey, come on, it's not the end of the world. We'll do something else instead.*

on 'end

You use '**for days, for weeks, or for months, on end**' when referring to a long and continuous period during which something was happening: *On many occasions, I have sat on a cold river bank, watching him fish for hours on end.* □ *We were left for weeks on end with no news.*

put an 'end to something

When a person **puts an end to something** they prevent it from happening any more: *Better policing might help put an end to racist attacks and insults.*

◇ SEE ALSO **put paid to** ▷ PUT

the re'ceiving end

If you are on **the receiving end** of something unpleasant, that unpleasant thing is directed towards you, even though you may not have done anything to deserve it: *'Imagine how you would feel if you were on the receiving end of your criticism,' she suggests.*

thin end of the 'wedge

When you describe something as the **thin end of the wedge**, you mean that it may be the first sign of something bad which is to come in the future: *The new policy is seen by many as the thin end of the wedge, where*

payment will be demanded for access to land which was previously open to the public.

A **wedge** is a triangular block of wood which you use for opening a narrow gap. People sometimes put one under a door to hold it open.

to the bitter 'end

You continue with something unpleasant **to the bitter end** if you continue doing it to the very end, despite all the problems and difficulties involved: *Andrew Neil, editor of The Sunday Times, welcomed the decision and said his newspaper would pursue the case to the bitter end.*

endowed

well-en'dowed (*humorous*)

If you describe a woman as **well-endowed**, you mean that she has big breasts: *Now there's lots of choice, both for the well-endowed and smaller busted. Wider bra straps are another new feature.*

ends

all's well that 'ends well

You say '**all's well that ends well**' after someone has escaped unharmed from a situation which could have had bad results: *'So all's well that ends well, to quote Shakespeare,' she said cheerfully when Luce had finished. 'What will you be doing now?'*

make ends 'meet

You **are making ends meet** if you are managing to survive with very little money: *It was the time of their lives when they found it hardest to make ends meet. It could not have happened unless the Church had helped to pay for the heating.*

enemy

the enemy with'in

The **enemy within** something, or **the enemy within**, is a problem or threat which comes from inside the group that is attacking, often in the form of a person or people who are acting against the interests of the group they belong to: *Britain seemed to be close to open class war; Mrs Thatcher denounced 'the enemy within'.*

wouldn't wish such-and-such on your worst 'enemy

If you want to express how unpleasant something or someone is, you sometimes say that you **wouldn't wish them on your worst enemy**: *She's treated you badly. I wouldn't wish a friend like that on my worst enemy.*

your own worst 'enemy

If someone creates severe problems for themselves by the way they behave, you

enfant

enfant ter'rible

An **enfant terrible** is a person or organization whose new ideas and lack of respect shock and embarrass older and more traditional people: *Cantona – the enfant terrible of English football.*

> **Enfant terrible** means 'terrible child' in French, and the expression in English comes from *Les Enfants Terribles*, the title of a series of prints by the 19th-century caricaturist Gavarni.

English

English as she is 'spoke (*humorous*)

English as she is spoke is a phrase referring to a form of the language which is not grammatically correct, spoken by people who are either badly educated or whose first language is not English: *In a sense, he is supporting the case for the language as she is spoke. 'I'm not so young as I used to was' is wrong, except that when Somerset Maugham makes a Cockney landlady say it, it makes perfectly good sense.*

Englishman

an Englishman's home is his 'castle

If someone says '**an Englishman's home is his castle**', they mean that it is natural to be proud of your home, and to want to defend your right to privacy there: *If an Englishman's home is his castle it has typically become, since the war, a castle which lacks character, individuality and substance.*

enough

enough is e'nough or that's e'nough

You say '**enough is enough**' or '**that's enough**' when you are telling someone firmly to stop doing something: *That's enough now. Stop talking and settle down to sleep.*
◇ SEE ALSO **that does it** ▷ DOES

have had e'nough

When you **have had enough**, you are bored or have lost patience with a certain activity and you want to stop doing it: *I've had enough and I'm going home.*
◇ SEE ALSO **up to here** ▷ UP

envy

be the 'envy of someone

Something that **is the envy of someone** is greatly admired by someone who wishes it

belonged to them: *His prize-winning garden is the envy of all his neighbours.*

errands

run 'errands

You **run errands** for someone when you do a number of small jobs for them, usually involving the delivery or collection of items in different places: *Clean his boots, run errands, lay out his clothes, prepare hot water for him to shave, serve the dishes of tea and coffee and the table dishes of food.*

error

see the error of your 'ways

You say you have **seen the error of your ways** when you realize that you have been behaving badly and you decide to change: *'Leave the boy with me.' He chuckled, 'Perhaps I can make him see the error of his ways.'*

escape

narrow es'cape

You have a **narrow escape** when you are lucky to escape unharmed from a dangerous situation: *Mr Greenwald helped Chrysler revive after the firm's narrow escape from bankruptcy in 1979. □ A woman and a child had a narrow escape yesterday when their car left the road.*
◇ SEE ALSO **close call** ▷ CALL; **close shave** ▷ SHAVE; **narrow squeak** ▷ SQUEAK; **close** or **near thing** ▷ THING

escort

under 'escort

If a person or vehicle is **under escort**, it is moving along with, and being guarded by, a number of other people or vehicles: *The accused left court under police escort.*

essence

in 'essence (*formal*)

You refer to something **in essence** when you are talking about its true or basic quality or nature: *I'm a bit confused. What, in essence, is your argument? □ We are talking, in essence, about a housing problem, not a people problem.*

of the 'essence

You say that something is **of the essence** if it is of the greatest importance: *We only have three hours of daylight left, so time is of the essence.*

esteem

hold someone in high e'steem

If you **hold someone in high esteem**, you respect them: *The findings have tended to support the view that the police are held in* *relatively high esteem, although those polled have invariably had little or no contact with the police in any capacity.*

even
get 'even
You **get even**, or **get even** with someone, when you do something to hurt or harm them, in return for something they have done to hurt or harm you in the past: *I had been waiting for years to get even with him, and now I saw my chance.*
◇ SEE ALSO **get your own back** ▷ OWN

evening
make an 'evening of it
A group of people decide to **make an evening of it** when they agree to spend the whole, or the rest, of the evening together: *The theatre finished late, so we decided to make an evening of it and go to the pub for a drink.*

event
the happy e'vent (*humorous*)
People sometimes refer to the birth of an expected baby as **the happy event**: *The news of the happy event was of special interest to all in the sales-admin office as it is where both mother and father work.*
◇ SEE ALSO **the patter of tiny feet** ▷ PATTER

in 'any event (*formal*)
In any event means 'in any case', but is especially likely to be found in official or legal texts: *I'll send you my new address so we can keep in touch. In any event, I'll see you before I leave.* □ *Maintenance work should be carried out on a permanent basis or, in any event, without a foreseeable limit to its duration.* □ *They seem to argue less about housework. A routine, in any event, has certainly established itself.*
◇ SEE ALSO **in any case** ▷ CASE; **at all events** ▷ EVENTS; **at any rate** ▷ RATE

in the e'vent (*formal*)
You use **in the event** of something, or **in the event** that something happens, to introduce the action which should be taken if a certain situation develops; you also use **in the event** on its own to talk about which one of a number of possible situations finally did develop: *In the event of fire, leave the building by the closest exit.* □ *In the event that fire breaks out, leave the building by the closest exit.* □ *Police were standing by, ready to contain the crowd, but in the event they were not needed.*

non-e'vent (*informal*)
A **non-event** is a social occasion which is not as good or exciting as you had hoped: *The party was a bit of a non-event, so we left early.*

wise after the e'vent
You are **wise after the event** when you realize how you should have behaved in a particular situation: *Lord Justice Slade said that it was all too easy to be wise after the event.*

events
at 'all events (*formal*)
At all events means 'in any case', but is more formal and is used less often: *What a lot of changes in his life. At all events, he seems to be settling in quite well at the moment.* □ *His theory was for years considered to be incomprehensible, at all events in mathematical terms.* □ *Maybe a second building programme would have done more harm than good: at all events, nothing more was attempted.*
◇ SEE ALSO **in any case** ▷ CASE; **in any event** ▷ EVENT; **at any rate** ▷ RATE

turn of e'vents
A **turn of events** is a change in the situation, often an unexpected one: *This unexpected turn of events has resulted in Celtic pulling out of the Coca-Cola Cup.*

ever
as 'ever
You use **'as ever'** when you are referring to a certain quality which never seems to change: *Considerate as ever, he sent me a beautiful bunch of flowers the next day.* □ *Pat Cash, looking as confident as ever, is just warming up on Wimbledon's centre court.*

ever 'more
If a certain thing or person grows **ever more** a particular way, they are becoming more and more full of that quality: *The work grew ever more frustrating as time progressed.*

'ever so (*informal*)
You use **'ever so'** to add emphasis to an adjective or an adverb: *'Oh yes,' added Polly. 'It's ever so good of you to pop in.'*

'ever such (*informal*)
You use **'ever such'** to add emphasis to a noun: *He was in ever such a panic this morning.* □ *She was gone for ever such a long time.*

Yours 'ever
People write **'Yours ever'**, followed by their signature, as an affectionate ending to an informal letter.
◇ SEE ALSO **yours faithfully** ▷ FAITHFULLY; **yours sincerely** ▷ SINCERELY; **yours truly** ▷ TRULY

everything

and 'everything (*informal*)

You use '**and everything**' when you want to emphasize that you are just giving examples, and that there may be other things which you have not mentioned: *What with all the shopping and the washing and everything, I haven't had a moment to relax today.*

◇ SEE ALSO **and so on** ▷ SO

evil

a necessary 'evil

You say that something unpleasant is **a necessary evil** if you do not like it, but you have to accept it as a normal part of things: *Negotiation is a necessary evil. It is the antithesis of open, honest communication.*

◇ SEE ALSO **all in a day's work** ▷ DAY; **a fact of life** ▷ FACT

ewe

ewe 'lamb

If you call something or someone your **ewe lamb**, you are talking in a humorous way about your dearest possession: *Wryly he added, 'I couldn't allow my ewe lamb to be torn to pieces by those talons.'*

In the Bible (2 Samuel 12:3), there is a poor man who had nothing except 'a little ewe lamb', which he loved as much as if it had been a child.

exactly

not ex'actly

1 You use '**not exactly**' to show that something is almost, but not completely, true: *'Is she a feminist?' 'Not exactly. But she's certainly very involved in equal opportunities issues.'* **2** You also use '**not exactly**' to show that something is the opposite of being true: *I know they're not millionaires, but they're not exactly poor, are they?*

example

make an ex'ample of someone

You **make an example of someone** when you punish them for something they have done in an obvious and severe way, to discourage others from doing the same thing: *The School Board came to the decision that they should make an example of the two boys.*

set someone an ex'ample

You **are setting someone an example** if you are careful to behave in a responsible way, because you are older or more experienced than they are, and you know they are likely to copy what you do: *It's not exactly setting a good example to be fiddling your taxes when you're supposed to be running the*

country. □ *Try not to set a bad example by smoking in front of your child.*

shining ex'ample or glowing ex'ample

If something or someone is so good that everyone admires and wants to copy them, you say they are a **shining example**, or a **glowing example**: *His life's work in setting up homes for people with disabilities was 'a shining example' of what a person could achieve, she said.*

exception

the exception that proves the 'rule

If you believe that something is always the case, and then you find an example where the theory does not work, people sometimes say that you have found **the exception that proves the rule**: *Not many business executives or lawyers write satirical novels or plays about their own profession. John Mortimer may be the exception that proves the rule.*

This idiom depends on the idea that all rules have exceptions. The 'logic' of it is that if you find an exception, then your rule is a typical one.

take ex'ception to something

When you say that you **take exception to something**, you are expressing your anger at being treated in a certain way: *Mr Jones, 43, who runs the café in Ross-on-Wye, said: 'I took exception to the fact that she was selling teas outside our door without informing me first.'*

◇ SEE ALSO **not take kindly to something** ▷ KINDLY

excess

in ex'cess of (*formal*)

In excess of means 'greater than': *The bank reported profits in excess of £70 million last year.*

to ex'cess (*formal*)

If you do something **to excess**, you do it more than is good for you: *A woman who regularly drinks more than 14 units of alcohol per week may be drinking to excess.*

exchange

in ex'change

You give something **in exchange** for something else when you give it to someone because you have received something from them: *Hoffman has sold a US company to Amersham in exchange for shares.*

excuse

ex'cuse me

You say '**excuse me**' as an apology **1** when you want to attract someone's attention in a polite way: *Excuse me. Could you pass the salt, please?* **2** when someone is in your way and you are politely asking them to move: *Excuse me. Can I get through please?* **3** after burping, for example, in public. **4** when you are asking permission to leave a group of people: *Excuse me everyone, I'm afraid I have to leave, or I'll miss my plane.* **5** when you are about to interrupt someone: *Excuse me Simon, Mrs Henderson has arrived. Shall I show her in?* **6** when you have made a mistake, or you want someone to repeat what they just said: *Do you like living in England, excuse me, Scotland?*

◇ SEE ALSO **I beg your pardon** ▷ PARDON

exhibition

make an exhi'bition of yourself

You say someone **is making an exhibition of themselves** if they are behaving in such a foolish way that they are attracting attention: *He used to come in here ranting and raving and making an exhibition of himself.*
◇ SEE ALSO **make a fool of yourself** ▷ FOOL; **make a spectacle of yourself** ▷ SPECTACLE

expense

at the ex'pense of

1 You do something **at the expense of** someone if that person is **a** paying for, or being financially disadvantaged by, it: *Current tax policy tends to benefit the very rich at the expense of those in the middle wage bracket.* **b** being made to look ridiculous because of your actions: *I don't mind them having a joke, but not at my expense.* **2** You do something **at the expense of** a particular thing if you do it even though it means that you harm or destroy that thing: *He decided on a career in acting, at the expense of his marriage.*

experience

chalk it up to ex'perience or put it down to ex'perience

If you say you **are chalking up**, or **putting down, to experience** a mistake you have made, you mean that you have decided to learn a lesson from the experience, rather than complain about it: *And if it ends up being rejected by the board, we simply put it down to experience, and start again.*
◇ SEE ALSO **just one of those things** ▷ THINGS

extreme

in the ex'treme

You use 'in the extreme' to mean 'extremely', usually when you are making a strong criticism of something: *I checked my job description. It was vague in the*

extreme. '*To undertake Special Projects,*' *it read.*

extremes

go to ex'tremes

When you describe behaviour as **going to extremes**, you mean that you consider it to be unreasonable or unacceptable: *Don't be tempted to go to extremes. Go for a fairly formal and conservative outfit, probably a suit, and keep your hair under control.*
◇ SEE ALSO **over the top** ▷ TOP

eye *(see also* **eyes***)*

all my eye and Betty 'Martin *(old)*

The exclamation '**all my eye and Betty Martin!**' means 'nonsense!': *'That's all my eye and Betty Martin,' said the Colonel.*

cast an 'eye over something or run an 'eye over something

When you **cast**, or **run, an eye over something**, you look at it very quickly to get a general impression: *That evening, Scott took his place at the news desk and ran an eye over his script.*
◇ SEE ALSO **cast a glance at** or **over something** ▷ GLANCE

catch someone's 'eye

When you see something which **catches your eye**, you suddenly notice it for some reason: *I waded out in the direction of the area where I had seen the fish, when a glint of white under the water caught my eye.*
◇ SEE ALSO **catch someone's ear** ▷ EAR

easy on the 'eye

Something which is **easy on the eye** is pleasant to look at, and does not require much concentration: *'What wallpaper do you think would be nice for the living-room?' 'Something fresh and easy on the eye.'*
◇ SEE ALSO **easy on the ear** ▷ EAR

the evil 'eye

People who believe in the magical power to cause harm by looking at someone, call this power **the evil eye**: *The symbol was regarded as a powerful protection against evil forces, especially that of the evil eye.*

an 'eye for something

If someone has **an eye for something**, they have a natural appreciation of and ability to use that thing in a skilful way: *Ernest had an eye for detail.* □ *You have to develop an eye for spotting possibilities.*

an eye for an eye and a tooth for a 'tooth

When people talk about **an eye for an eye and a tooth for a tooth**, they are referring to the idea that, if someone does something bad to you, you have the right to do something equally bad to them: *I'll get* *my revenge, just wait and see. An eye for an eye, that's my philosophy.*

This is a Biblical reference, from Exodus 21:24, often considered to express, in its simplest form, the severe moral teaching of the Old Testament.

'eye-opener

An **eye-opener** is an event or experience which makes you aware of something you did not know before: *It was an eye-opener for me to see how much domestic refuse is recycled in poorer countries.*

◊ SEE ALSO **open someone's eyes** ▷ EYES

get your 'eye in

In a game which involves hitting a ball, you say you **are getting your eye in** when you start to hit more accurately, following a period at the beginning of the game when you were not doing so: *She was missing a lot of shots at first, but soon she began to get her eye in and play better.*

◊ SEE ALSO **get** or **keep your hand in** ▷ HAND

go into something with your 'eyes open or walk into something with your 'eyes open

You **go**, or **walk**, **into something with your eyes open** when you put yourself in a certain situation despite knowing the possible dangers which that situation holds: *He has entered into the contract with his eyes open to the true facts; this comes as no surprise to him.*

have your 'eye on

If you **have your eye on** someone or something, you are interested in them and would like to have them for yourself: *Charlie had his eye on Sonia. She was a dark, broad-faced girl with Slavic eyes.* □ *She was delighted to find that she only needed to borrow 60% of the purchase price of a three-bedroom flat she had her eye on.*

in the public 'eye

Someone who is **in the public eye** is well-known, or often seen in public: *She underestimated the effects that being constantly in the public eye would have on her life.* □ *He was getting more and more embarrassed as the public eye focused on him.*

keep an 'eye out for

You **are keeping an eye out for** someone or something if you are not actively searching for them, but you are watching, in case they appear, while you are doing other things: *According to this we've to keep an eye out for anything – or anybody – suspicious.*

keep an 'eye on

You **are keeping an eye on** something or someone if you are watching them to make sure they are all right, or that they do not do anything wrong: *I'll keep an eye on the kids if you want to pop out to the shops.*

look someone in the 'eye

When you **look someone in the eye**, you look straight at their eyes; doing this is often thought to be a sign that you are telling the truth: *Look me in the eye and tell me you love me.*

the naked 'eye

You talk about **the naked eye** in reference to what you can see without any special equipment, such as a microscope, or a telescope: *The mite is just visible to the naked eye and feeds on honey bees and their grubs by sucking their body fluids.*

not see eye to 'eye

If you and another person **do not see eye to eye**, you never agree at all; if you **do not see eye to eye** with someone over, or about something, you cannot agree with them on a certain subject: *I'm afraid I can't come to the meeting if Bruce is going to be there. We just don't see eye to eye.* □ *It was an extremely popular programme and we always saw eye to eye about it.*

one in the 'eye for

You say a certain action is **one in the eye for** someone or something if it is understood as a direct refusal or criticism of that person or thing: *The surprise victory of the Labour candidate at the by-election was one in the eye for the Tories.*

private 'eye (*informal*)

A **private eye** is someone whose job is to do secret searches for people or information, for which they are paid by the member of the public who is employing them.

roving 'eye (*informal, insulting*)

You say someone has a **roving eye** if they are always looking at, and trying to get sexually involved with, members of the opposite sex: *If Rachel wasn't around, he had a roving eye, and sometimes more than an eye, although at that stage he was technically faithful, I think.*

see something with half an 'eye

If you say that you can **see something with half an eye**, you mean that it is very obvious: *Anyone with half an eye could see Susan's antagonism towards her. It was in every action, every glance.*

there's more to such-and-such than meets the 'eye

If you say that **there is more to** a certain thing or person **than meets the eye**, you mean that they are more complicated or interesting than they seemed at first: *I always thought that windsurfing looked easy, but there is more to it than meets the eye.*

turn a blind 'eye

You **turn a blind eye**, or **turn a blind eye** to something, if you decide to ignore it, or to pretend you cannot see it: *I usually turn a blind eye to staff arriving a couple of minutes late.*

◇ SEE ALSO **turn a deaf ear** ▷ EAR

what the eye doesn't see, the heart doesn't 'grieve over

If you say '**what the eye doesn't see, the heart doesn't grieve over**', you mean that if the truth is hidden, it cannot make people upset: *Unless you are looking for it, you don't notice it. This means that the authorities have been able to work on the assumption that what the eye doesn't see the heart won't grieve over.*

◇ SEE ALSO **ignorance is bliss** ▷ IGNORANCE

with an 'eye to something

If your actions are done **with an eye to something**, they have that thing as their aim: *Like most shows which are produced with an eye to commercial success, this one will probably fail.*

with an eye to the main 'chance (*informal*)

If your actions are done **with an eye to the main chance**, you are acting in a way which will improve your own chances of getting a profit or an advantage out of something: *This able and likeable man was admirably adaptable to circumstances and had something of an eye to the main chance.*

In the game of hazard, **the main chance** was the highest score you could get.

eyeball

eyeball to 'eyeball (*informal*)

You are **eyeball to eyeball** with someone when you are close to them and facing them directly, for example in a fight: *Both tall men, they were eyeball to eyeball. 'This is your fault. One way or another you caused this, and I'm going to make you pay for it.'*

eyeballs

up to your 'eyeballs (*informal*)

If you have so much of something to deal with that you cannot see how you are going to manage, you can say that you are **up to your eyeballs** in it: *I'll come over to see you next week. I'm up to my eyeballs in work till then.*

◇ SEE ALSO **up to your ears** ▷EARS; **up to your eyes** ▷ EYES; **up to your neck** ▷ NECK

eyebrows

raise 'eyebrows

Something which **raises eyebrows** causes people to express restrained surprise or disapproval: *She certainly raised a few eyebrows by getting married in a black dress.* ◻ *The state-owned bank's involvement has raised eyebrows among French politicians.*

raised 'eyebrows: *He caused a few raised eyebrows among physicists and astronomers*

with his calculations that a working time machine could be built.

eyelashes

flutter your 'eyelashes at someone

A person, usually a woman, **flutters her eyelashes at someone**, usually a man, when she opens and closes her eyes several times very quickly while looking at him in a seductive way: *'Did Sally say you might be able to squeeze me into your car?' she asked, fluttering her eyelashes.* ◻ *He was doing his charming act, almost fluttering his eyelashes at her.*

eyelid

not bat an 'eyelid (*informal*)

You **don't bat an eyelid** when you show no surprise or emotion: *They're quite relaxed about clothes. No-one batted an eyelid when I came in to the office wearing jeans.*

The verb **bat** in this expression is from the Old French 'batre', meaning 'to blink'.

eyes

all 'eyes (*informal*)

You say you are **all eyes** if you are watching very carefully: *'Now, you won't see anything unless you pay attention.' 'Go ahead. I'm all eyes.'*

◇ SEE ALSO **all ears** ▷ EARS

before someone's 'eyes

Something happens **before your eyes** if you are watching while it is happening: *It was a miracle happening before our very eyes.*

believe your 'eyes

You say that you cannot **believe your eyes** if you see something which is so surprising or ridiculous that it is difficult to believe: *I sat up late watching the election results and could hardly believe my eyes.*

◇ SEE ALSO **believe your ears** ▷ EARS

can't take your 'eyes off someone or something or **can't keep your 'eyes off someone or something**

You say you **can't take**, or **keep, your eyes off someone or something** if you keep looking at them because they are so interesting or beautiful: *'I can't keep my eyes off you,' he whispered in my ear as he got up from the table.*

close your 'eyes to something or **shut your 'eyes to something**

If you **close**, or **shut, your eyes to something**, you ignore something bad because you wish it did not exist: *You can't just close your eyes to the facts. It's a dangerous hobby.*

cry your 'eyes out (*informal*)
Someone who **is crying their eyes out** is crying hard and for a long time, with great sadness: *He's heartbroken. He's so upset. He came back to the house crying his eyes out.*
◇ SEE ALSO **weep buckets** ▷ BUCKETS; **cry** or **sob your heart out** ▷ HEART

your eyes are bigger than your 'belly (*informal*)
You say that your **eyes are bigger than your belly** if you have asked for, or served yourself with, more food than you can eat: *We ordered so much we couldn't eat the last dish. Vivienne got really angry. 'You're just being greedy,' she said. 'Your eyes are bigger than your bellies.'*

eyes in the back of so-and-so's 'head
You say someone has **eyes in the back of their head** if they always notice exactly what is happening, even when they do not seem to be paying much attention: *You need eyes in the back of your head to see what the children are getting up to in the back of the car.*

your eyes nearly popped out of your 'head (*informal*)
You say that someone's **eyes nearly popped out of their head** when they react with great surprise or shock to something: *Her eyes nearly popped out of her head when I told her I'd got a job in Barbados.*

eyes out on 'stalks (*informal*)
You say that someone's **eyes** are **out on stalks** if they are looking with great surprise or interest at something: *When I first read a small paragraph about him being arrested I remember my eyes popping out on stalks like a cartoon character.*

feast your 'eyes
When you **feast your eyes** on someone or something, you look at them with desire: *He feasted his eyes on her, slender and seductive.*

hit someone between the 'eyes
Something **hits you between the eyes** when you suddenly realize or understand it for the first time: *Only when his sister actually moved to Australia did it hit him between the eyes how much he relied on her.*

keep your 'eyes peeled or **keep your 'eyes skinned** (*informal*)
You **keep your eyes peeled** or **keep your eyes skinned** when you watch for something

with all your attention and concentration: *The sky's so clear tonight. If we keep our eyes peeled, we'll probably see a shooting star.* □ *He pedalled along the canal bank quite slowly, keeping his eyes skinned for signs of human activity.*

lay 'eyes on or **set 'eyes on** or **clap 'eyes on** (*informal*)
When you **lay**, or **set**, or **clap**, **eyes on** someone or something, you see them for the first time: *I don't know who you are, lass, never clapped eyes on you.*

make 'eyes at someone (*informal*)
You **make eyes at someone** when you look at them with sexual interest, in a way which you hope they will find attractive: *Bodie was making eyes at the girl, and had been doing so for some time.*

open someone's 'eyes
An event or experience **opens your eyes**, or **opens your eyes** to something, if it makes you aware of something you did not know before: *This weekend has really opened my eyes. Without knowing it I have been living in poverty for the last 14 years.*
◇ SEE ALSO **eye-opener** ▷ EYE

'square-eyes (*disrespectful*)
Square-eyes is a name for someone who watches a lot of television: *Come on square eyes! Never mind the television.*

up to your 'eyes (*informal*)
If you have so much of something to deal with that you cannot see how you are going to manage, you can say that you are **up to your eyes** in it: *I'm up to my eyes in washing just now.*
◇ SEE ALSO **up to your ears** ▷ EARS; **up to your eyeballs** ▷ EYEBALLS; **up to your neck** ▷ NECK

eyeteeth

give your eye'teeth for something
If you say you would **give your eyeteeth for something**, you mean that you desire it and would give a lot to possess it, but that in reality you understand that it will probably never be yours: *I would give my eyeteeth to be a soprano, and to be able to get that high.*
◇ SEE ALSO **give your right arm** ▷ ARM; **give your ears** ▷ EARS; **give your right hand** ▷ HAND; **give the world** ▷ WORLD

f

face (*see also* faces)

disappear off the face of the 'earth
You say that someone or something **has disappeared off the face of the earth** if you have no idea where they are.

your 'face fits
If **your face fits**, you look like the right sort of person for a particular job, or to be accepted by a certain group: *It's fine while you're young and attractive, but when your face doesn't fit any more, you have to go.*

a face like the back of a 'bus or a face like the backend of a 'bus
You say, rudely, but humorously, that someone has **a face like the back**, or **backend, of a bus** if you think that they are very ugly: *Poor old Miss Evans – she was a dreadful teacher, and she did have a face like the back of a bus, didn't she?*
◇ SEE ALSO **ugly as sin** ▷ UGLY

face to face with someone
You are **face to face** with someone if you are looking at them and they are looking at you: *What would you do if you found yourself face to face with a 'burglar in your own home?*
◇ SEE ALSO **in person** ▷ PERSON; **in the flesh** ▷ FLESH

fly in the face of 'such-and-such
You **fly in the face of** an accepted norm or belief when you go against it: *He would deliberately fly in the face of convention in order to attract media attention.* □ *The proposal appeared to fly in the face of all logic.*

get out of my 'face (*informal, offensive*)
You say to someone '**get out of my face**' if you want them to stop annoying you.

give something a 'face-lift
You **give something**, such as a room or a place, **a face-lift** when you change and improve its appearance: *The whole town was given a face-lift in preparation for the royal visit.*

A **face-lift** is a medical operation, where the patient's skin is tightened in order to make them look younger.

in-your-'face (*very informal*)
Someone or something that is described as **in-your-face** is direct, provocative and very confident: *an in-your-face film.* □ *This band has an upfront and in-your-face approach.*

let's 'face it
You say '**let's face it**' as a way of introducing a fact which describes the reality of a situation, which must be accepted, even if it is not what people would like: *We might as well stop work and go home now; I mean, let's face it, we're not going to be able to finish it tonight, are we?*

long 'face
Someone who has a **long face** is looking sad and gloomy: *What's wrong with her? She's been walking round with a long face all morning.*

look someone in the 'face
If you can't **look someone in the face**, you are ashamed of something you have done to them: *It's awful, I just haven't been able to look her in the face ever since she heard me talking about her.*

lose 'face
You **lose face** when you lose other people's respect: *If they publicly disagree with her, they'll lose face as a united party.*

on the 'face of it
You introduce a statement with '**on the face of it**', when you want to show that what you are going to say describes the way a situation appears, rather than how it really is: *On the face of it, it would seem that unemployment has been greatly reduced; in actual fact, the situation is worse than ever before.*

pull a 'face or make a 'face
You **pull**, or **make**, **a face** when you **1** make an unusual expression with your face to make people laugh: *He wandered round the room, looking at himself in the mirrors and pulling faces and laughing.* **2** make a disgusted or displeased expression with your face, to show that you do not like something: *She made a face; 'I hate long walks,' she said.*
◇ SEE ALSO **turn your nose up at something** ▷ NOSE

put a brave 'face on it

You **put a brave face on it** when you try to show courage, even though you are feeling worried or afraid: *There was nothing I could do but put a brave face on it and hope things would work out all right in the end.*

◇ SEE ALSO **keep your end up** ▷ END

save 'face

You **save face** when you do something to prevent yourself, or someone else, from being humiliated: *They are trying to save face for John Major, President Mitterrand and Chancellor Kohl. Instead, they should be trying to save their nations' economies.*

show your 'face

You dare to **show your face** somewhere when you go to a place where people do not expect to see you because you have done something that you should be ashamed of: *How dare you show your face in here after what you've done?*

shut your 'face (*offensive or humorous*)

If someone tells you to **shut your face**, they mean, rudely, that they want you to be quiet.

◇ SEE ALSO **shut your gob** ▷ GOB; **shut your mouth** ▷ MOUTH; **shut it** or **shut up** ▷ SHUT

staring you in the 'face

Something, such as the answer to a problem **is staring you in the face** if it should have been obvious to you, but you didn't see it: *It has been staring us in the face for months and we never even realized!*

take at face 'value

You **take** someone or something **at face value** when you accept it for what it appears to be, rather than paying attention to detail: *Taken at face value, their evidence was powerful; on closer examination, certain important flaws became apparent.*

the unacceptable face of 'such-and-such

The **unacceptable face of** a system is the part of it which you believe is immoral or bad in some way: *the unacceptable face of capitalism.*

throw something back in someone's 'face

Someone **throws something back in your face** when they remember something you told them in confidence, and use it against you in an argument: *I told her I was having trouble working to deadlines and she threw it back in my face at the management meeting.*

until you are blue in the 'face (*informal*)

Someone does something **until**, or **till**, **they are blue in the face** when they keep doing it without being successful: *She realized that she could deny his accusation until she was blue in the face, but he wasn't going to believe her.*

written all over someone's 'face

Something which is supposed to be a secret is **written all over someone's face** when you can see it, just by looking at them: *He's lying; it's written all over his face.*

faces

the same old 'faces

If you say that you saw **the same old faces** at a certain place, you mean that there was no-one new or interesting to meet there: *It was an obvious choice, because the public was fed up with the same old faces; here was someone fresh at last.*

fact (*see also* **facts**)

in actual 'fact

You say '**in actual fact**' in order to introduce a statement which contradicts what the listener appears to believe to be the case: *In actual fact, he was a very vulnerable guy, a very kind guy; but he tended to put up a front to disguise it.*

◇ SEE ALSO **in point of fact** ▷ POINT; **as a matter of fact** ▷ MATTER

fact of 'life

A **fact of life** is something you must accept, however unpleasant, since it is not likely to change: *There was very little anyone could do; poverty was a fact of life in places like World's End.*

◇ SEE ALSO **all in a day's work** ▷ DAY; **a necessary evil** ▷ EVIL

the fact re'mains

You introduce a statement with **the fact remains** when you want to show that despite what you have just said, something that was true before is still true now: *Still, the fact remains that few women in television are seen as suitable to handle the major political interviews.* □ *It may be true that reviewers regard this poem as too trivial for discussion, but the fact remains that it is much liked.*

there's no escaping the fact that

You introduce a statement with **there's no escaping the fact that** something is true, when you do not want people to ignore of forget something important: *There's no escaping the fact that he's a very good 'athlete, and that he has every chance of winning this race.*

factor

the deciding 'factor

The **deciding factor** in a situation is something which enables you to make a decision: *I know it was hard for you to leave a career that meant a lot to you. What was the deciding factor?*

facts

face the 'facts

You say that you have to **face the facts** if you think that it is difficult, but necessary, to accept the truth: *They often don't have the strength of character to face the facts when these are presented to them.*

the facts of 'life

The facts of life are the basic facts about sex: *Should children learn about the facts of life at school, or is it the parents' responsibility?*

◊ SEE ALSO **the birds and the bees** ▷ BIRDS

fade

fading 'fast

1 You are **fading fast** if you are suddenly feeling very tired, and think that you will have to go to sleep or stop what you are doing soon: *'How are you?' 'Fading fast I'm afraid; I think I'd better go home.'* **2** Hopes or memories **are fading fast**, if they are getting weaker: *Swindon Town football team's hopes of promotion are fading fast, after another defeat last night.*

fag

'fag hag (*offensive*)

Fag hag is an offensive name for a woman who particularly likes to socialize with homosexual men.

fail

if all else 'fails

You say **'if all else fails'** to introduce a statement about a possible way of solving a problem if none of your other proposed solutions work: *We'll try and persuade him over the phone, but if all else fails, we'll have to drive over there and talk to him.*

faintest

not have the 'faintest

You say that you **haven't got the faintest** when you have no idea of something: *'What's the difference between defining and non-defining relative clauses?' 'I haven't got the faintest.'*

◊ SEE ALSO **not have the foggiest** ▷ FOGGIEST; **not have an earthly** ▷ EARTHLY; **not have a clue** ▷ CLUE

fair

fair and 'square

Everything is **fair and square** if you no longer owe someone any money and they no longer owe you any: *Right, I think we're all fair and square now, aren't we?*

◊ SEE ALSO **be quits with someone** ▷ QUITS

fair e'nough (*informal*)

You say **'fair enough'** if you are prepared to accept what someone has done or said: *All right, fair enough, you've done that, but what about all the other things you were supposed to do?*

fair's 'fair (*informal*)

Fair's fair means 'let's be fair': *Come on, fair's fair; you've had your turn, now let someone else have a go.*

fair to 'middling (*informal*)

You describe something as **fair to middling** if it is not very good, but not very bad either: *'How are you feeling?' 'Fair to middling; I still haven't got over this cold.'*

it's only 'fair

You say **'it's only fair'** if you want to emphasize that something should happen for the situation to be fair: *Well, as you contributed so much, it's only fair that you should enjoy the benefits.*

fait

fait accom'pli

A **fait accompli** is an action that has already been done and that cannot be changed: *They were worried that the decision would be made without them and that they would be confronted with a fait accompli.*

> **Fait accompli** means 'accomplished fact' in French.

faith

break 'faith with

You **break faith with** someone or something when you do not remain loyal to them: *We refuse to break faith with our customers by cutting costs in this way.*

in bad 'faith

You act **in bad faith** when you act dishonestly: *She acted in bad faith, telling them she was ill when she was out enjoying herself.*

in good 'faith

You act **in good faith** when your intentions are good, even if the result hurts someone: *I promise you, I acted in good faith when I told you that; I felt you should know the truth.*

faithfully

yours 'faithfully

You write **'yours faithfully'** before signing your name at the end of a formal letter which you have begun 'Dear Sir' or 'Dear Madam'.

◊ SEE ALSO **yours ever** ▷ EVER; **yours sincerely** ▷ SINCERELY; **yours truly** ▷ TRULY

fall

fall 'flat

An event **falls flat** when it is not as successful or entertaining as you hoped or expected: *Those jokes fell a bit flat, didn't they?* □ *'How was the party?' 'Well, it fell flat; hardly anyone turned up.'*

◇ SEE ALSO **go down like a lead balloon**
▷ BALLOON

family

in the 'family way (*informal, humorous*)

A woman who is **in the family way** is pregnant: *Looks like the O'Connells' daughter's in the family way again, eh?*

run in the 'family

A characteristic **runs in the family** if it is shared by two or more members of a family: *His father was just the same; looks like it runs in the family.*

familiarity

familiarity breeds con'tempt

When people say **'familiarity breeds contempt'**, they mean that the better you know someone, the more you become aware of their faults.

fancy

fancy 'that

Fancy that is an expression of surprise; it is often used ironically, and with exaggerated intonation to suggest that the speaker is not surprised by an unpleasant event, because it has happened so many times before: *'He let me down again.' 'Well fancy that! I warned you, didn't I?'*

◇ SEE ALSO **bless my soul** ▷ SOUL

take your 'fancy or tickle your 'fancy (*informal*)

Something **takes**, or **tickles, your fancy** when you like it a lot: *If you see anything that takes your fancy, I'll treat you.* □ *There are, however, many different massage methods, creams and gadgets on the market, so to help you find one that tickles your fancy, read our guide.*

fanny

sweet fanny 'adams or sweet F'A (*informal*)

Sweet fanny adams or **sweet FA** means 'nothing': *Are you going to sit around here doing sweet fanny adams all day?* □ *We are aware that a number of incidents have been reported but sweet FA seems to have been done about it.*

> **Sweet FA** is also an abbreviation for the much more vulgar expression 'sweet fuck all'. People say **sweet fanny adams** as a humorous way of avoiding using the more vulgar expression.

far

as far as 'I'm concerned

As far as I'm concerned means 'to the extent that the situation relates to me': *As far as I'm concerned you can go there, but I don't know what your mother would say.*

far be it from me to 'such-and-such

You say **'far be it from me to such-and-such'**, often ironically, when you say you are going to do something that you would not normally do: *Far be it from me to criticize, but isn't this piece of work a bit below standard?*

far 'from it

'Far from it' means 'not at all': *He had not calmed down at all as he had grown older – far from it – and could not now be still for a single moment.*

from far and 'wide

People or things come **from far and wide** when they come from distant places: *His professional musical friends who took part in the concert came from far and wide and gave their services as a gift to him in gratitude for his work.*

not go as far as to

You say that you would **not go as far as to** say, or **do**, such-and-such, if you would not go to that extreme: *'He's one of the best actors this century.' 'Oh I wouldn't go as far as to say 'that.'* □ *I don't think they'd go as far as to 'sack him, but he might be suspended for a while.*

so far so 'good

If you say **'so far so good'**, you mean that a specified activity seems to be working out successfully: *'How's the new job?' 'So far so good.'*

farm

'funny farm (*humorous, offensive*)

The funny farm is a humorous or offensive term for a mental hospital: *Old Frank next door was carted off to the funny farm again last night; you should've heard the noise.*

fashion

after a 'fashion

You do something **after a fashion** if you do it, but not very well: *'Can you speak German?' 'Well, after a fashion.'*

'fashion victim

A **fashion victim** is someone who is always buying new clothes in order to keep up with the current fashion: *You can be sure that no fashion victim will be seen without one of these designs on their back in the coming months.*

fast

fast and 'furious

Fast and furious means 'with great energy or speed': *The match started at a fast and furious pace.* □ *There was a fast and furious movement in the woods.*

fat

chew the 'fat

You **chew the fat** when you talk to someone in an informal, friendly way: *We were chewing the fat, telling stories about peculiar things that had happened to us.*
◇ SEE ALSO **shoot the breeze** ▷ BREEZE

the fat is in the 'fire

If you say that **the fat is in the fire** you mean that someone has done something that is likely to cause trouble: *It only needs one person to find out about this and the fat will be in the fire.*

the fat of the 'land

Someone who is living off **the fat of the land** is rich enough to enjoy everything they want: *Landlords and merchants lived off the fat of the land, and labourers worked that land.*

fate

a fate worse than 'death *(informal, humorous)*

A **fate worse than death** is something terrible which could happen to you: *He saved me from a fate worse than death, and it was all over so quick I never did get the chance to thank him properly.*

This expression was originally used as a way of avoiding direct reference to seduction or rape.

tempt 'fate

If you say that someone **is tempting fate**, you mean that they are taking a big risk, or, superstitiously, that they are encouraging something bad to happen by being over-optimistic: *Opening the parachute at just 250 feet would have been tempting fate.* □ *Buying the champagne before getting the results was tempting fate a bit, wasn't it?*
◇ SEE ALSO **tempt the gods** ▷ GODS; **tempt providence** ▷ PROVIDENCE; **speak too soon** ▷ SPEAK

to a 'fault

You describe someone as having a certain characteristic **to a fault** if they have it more than is necessary or expected: *He was scrupulous to a fault.*

faux

faux 'pas

A **faux pas** is an embarrassing social mistake made in public: *I think I made a bit of a faux pas when I introduced her as 'Mrs', rather than 'Lady', Saville-Hamilton.*

Faux pas means 'false step' in French.

favour

curry 'favour

You **curry favour** with someone when you win their approval by praise or flattery: *Mr Lamont conceded that the Budget was 'not designed to curry favour or popularity' but was intended to meet the needs of the country.*

do me a 'favour *(informal)*

You say to someone '**do me a favour**' 1 when you are asking them, informally, to do something for you: *Do me a favour; would you close the door, please?* 2 when you want to show that you don't believe or accept what someone has just said to you: *'What about £2 an hour?' 'Do me a favour, will you?'*
◇ SEE ALSO **come off it** ▷ COME; **don't give me that** ▷ GIVE; **don't make me laugh** ▷ LAUGH; **tell that to the marines** ▷ MARINES

fear

in fear of your 'life

You are **in fear of your life** when you are afraid that you might die: *He had evidently been in fear of his life and had purchased the weapon for that reason.* □ *'If you are in a situation where you are in immediate fear of your life, you may take whatever defensive measures are necessary,' said a senior detective.*

never 'fear

Never fear means 'don't worry': *Never fear; I'll make sure you get there in time.*

'**Never fear**' is most frequently used before a statement that begins with 'I'll', in order to reassure someone that you will take charge of a situation.

no 'fear *(informal)*

No fear means 'I have absolutely no intention of doing that': *'Are you going to give a paper at the conference?' 'No fear.'*

put the fear of 'God into someone

Someone or something **puts the fear of God into you** if they terrify you: *It puts the fear of God into me when I think about the children being offered drugs in the playground.*

feat

no mean 'feat
Something that is described as **no mean feat** is difficult: *It's no mean feat, getting five children ready in time for school in the morning.*

feather

'feather in your cap
A **feather in your cap** is an achievement that you can be proud of: *Cambridge will be led by John Wilson, who was last year's Oxford chief coach. It will be quite a feather in his cap if Cambridge win today.*

American Indians had a tradition of presenting a feather to someone who had been very brave.

feathers

ruffle someone's 'feathers
You **ruffle someone's feathers** when you upset or annoy someone slightly: *She was determined that she would make sure he didn't ruffle her feathers again. She would be distant but polite.*
◇ SEE ALSO **rattle someone's cage** ▷ CAGE

feel

get the 'feel of something
You **get the feel of something** when you start to understand it better: *They give you a couple of days to get the feel of it, then they really start to expect results.*

not feel your'self
You **don't feel yourself** if you feel ill or uneasy: *Ruth, though deadly tired, was curiously wakeful; not quite feeling herself but not able to put a finger on what was wrong.*

feelers

put out 'feelers
You **put out feelers** when you suggest something in an informal way, in order to see how someone reacts to it: *He had already put out feelers with local employers but they hadn't been too keen on employing a well-known trouble-maker.*

An insect's **feelers** are the two stalks on its head that it uses to sense things around it.

feeling

have a nasty 'feeling
You **have a nasty feeling** about something when you suspect that something unpleasant may happen or may have happened: *I've got a nasty feeling I left the oven on.*

'sinking feeling
You get a **sinking feeling** when you suddenly realize something unpleasant: *You know that sinking feeling you get when you suddenly realize you haven't done enough work for an exam?*

feelings

no hard 'feelings
You say '**no hard feelings**' to someone who has treated you badly or upset you, when you want them to know that you do not feel angry with them: *I was deeply upset, but not in any resentful way. Once it was done, it was done and there were no hard feelings on my part.*

have mixed 'feelings
You **have mixed feelings** about something when you can see its good side, but you also have reservations about it: *She parted from him at her gate with very mixed feelings. Part of her trusted him still, but the voice of reason whispered that he could not be the frank and open person he appeared.*

feet

dead on your 'feet
You are **dead on your feet** when you are very tired: *I'm dead on my feet; just couldn't get to sleep last night.*
◇ SEE ALSO **fit to drop** ▷ DROP

drag your 'feet
You **are dragging your feet** if you are taking an unnecessarily long time over something: *The management have been dragging their feet over this; I think it's about time they made a decision.* □ *The authorities have dragged their feet in taking on their responsibilities.*

fall on your 'feet or land on your 'feet
You **fall**, or **land**, **on your feet** when you are successful or lucky, especially after a period of bad luck: *I wouldn't worry too much about James; he always falls on his feet.*

feet of 'clay
A person or organization that is described as having **feet of clay** has a hidden weakness, and is therefore not as perfect as people originally believed them to be: *It can be hard to discover that your greatest sports idol has feet of clay.*

In the Bible, there is a story about Nebuchadnezzar's dream, when he saw an image with a head of gold and feet of clay.

find your 'feet
You **find your feet** when you start to feel confident and at ease in a new place: *She lacked assertiveness for a while as she found*

her feet, but she is remembered mainly for her obvious concern to do the best in every situation.

get cold 'feet

You **get cold feet** when you decide not to do something you had planned to do because you suddenly feel afraid: *We were going to take part in the dancing competition, but my partner got cold feet at the last minute.*

have your 'feet on the ground

Someone who **has their feet on the ground** is realistic: *In Paula, he's found a woman who helps him keep his feet on the ground. 'Our favourite times are Sunday afternoons, cooking, watching television and going for long walks.'*

have itchy 'feet

You **have itchy feet** if you feel that you need a change: *I have permanently itchy feet – an affliction which I attribute to having spent most of my childhood abroad.*

have two left 'feet

Someone who **has two left feet** cannot dance very well: *Perhaps with two left feet I should never have volunteered to take part in the display, but going to the classes has done wonders for me.*

in your stockinged 'feet

You are **in your stockinged feet** when you are not wearing shoes: *I measure 1m 60cm in my stockinged feet.*

put your 'feet up

You **put your feet up** when you sit or lie down and rest for a while: *I'm just going to put my feet up for a bit before I start on the next job.*

◇ SEE ALSO **take it easy** or **take things easy** ▷ EASY

rushed off your 'feet

You are **rushed off your feet** if you are very busy: *We need more staff over the holiday period; we're rushed off our feet the way it is at the moment.*

six feet 'under

Someone who is **six feet under** is dead and buried: *I should think I'll be six feet under by the time they finally get a law like that through parliament.*

◇ SEE ALSO **pushing up the daisies** ▷ DAISIES; **dead as a doornail** or **dead as a dodo** ▷ DEAD

stand on your own two 'feet

You **stand on your own two feet** when you are independent, and do not need help from other people: *Yes, we'll encourage people to stand on their own two feet, but we'll also seek to aid those who for a variety of reasons need a bit of extra help.*

sweep someone off their 'feet

Someone **sweeps you off your feet** when they cause you to fall suddenly in love

with them: *So when Dawson came on the scene and swept me off my feet, I half jumped into his arms.*

think on your 'feet

You **think on your feet** when you have to make quick decisions: *You have to be able to think on your feet if you want to work in stocks and shares.*

throw yourself at someone's 'feet

You **throw yourself at someone's feet** when you humbly ask them for forgiveness: *He threw himself at her feet and pleaded with her.*

under someone's 'feet

You are **under someone's feet** if you are in their way all the time, and making demands on them: *They've been terribly nice, and they don't seem to mind having me under their feet all the time.*

vote with your 'feet

You **vote with your feet** when you stop going to a place or buying a particular product in order to protest against something: *House-buyers are voting with their feet and looking outside city centres, as house prices continue to soar.*

fence

sit on the 'fence

You **sit on the fence** when you avoid making a decision or committing yourself to something because you understand and have sympathy for both sides of the argument: *Many MPs have certainly supported him in the first round. He is the obvious choice for those who wish to sit on the fence.*

fever

at 'fever pitch

A situation is **at fever pitch** if it causes wild excitement: *The computer craze started by the Nintendo character reached fever pitch as more than 15,000 people waited for up to three hours to get into the exhibition.*

run a 'fever

You **are running a fever** if you are very hot because you are ill.

few

few and far be'tween

People or things that are **few and far between** are very rare: *Tramway accidents are fortunately few and far between, and a tram is a very safe vehicle indeed.* □ *People like her are few and far between; treasure her as a friend.*

have 'had a few or have had a few too 'many

Someone who **has had a few**, or **a few too many**, has had too much to drink: *Trouble* *is, when he's had a few, he starts to get aggressive.*

◇ SEE ALSO **the worse for drink** ▷ DRINK; **under the influence** ▷ INFLUENCE

fibre

every fibre of your 'being

Something that affects **every fibre of your being** affects you very deeply: *Every fibre of your being is affected in some way, as you struggle to reach beyond the confines of your first language and culture, into a new one.* □ *Every fibre of her being was vibrantly aware of his magnetic presence.*

fiddle

on the 'fiddle (*informal*)

Someone who is **on the fiddle** is trying to get money dishonestly, for example, by falsifying company accounts or tax declarations: *They knew he was on the fiddle, but they just couldn't catch him at it.*

play second 'fiddle

You **play second fiddle** to someone if they are more important than you: *Throughout her married life she had to play second fiddle to the interests of her husband.*

field

lead the 'field

Someone who **leads the field** in their subject is the best at it: *We led the field for years, but competition is so fierce now that we're starting to lose our grip.*

play the 'field

You **play the field** when you get involved with several people or things at the same time, in order to increase your opportunities: *'And you don't want to get married?' he asked. 'Only play the field?'* □ *We suggest you play the field a bit, rather than concentrating all your resources on one customer.*

fields

fresh fields and pastures 'new

Someone who goes to **fresh fields and pastures new** moves into a different field of work, or tries a new kind of activity: *Are they ever sacked, or disciplined for their blunders? Or do they just move on, looking for fresh fields and pastures new?*

◇ SEE ALSO **pastures new** ▷ PASTURES

fifty

fifty-'fifty

Fifty-fifty means 'in two halves' or 'half and half': *Let's split the winnings fifty-fifty.* □ *The operation has a fifty-fifty chance of succeeding.*

fig

not care a 'fig or not care two 'figs

You say that you **do not care a fig** or **two figs**, when you do not care at all about something: *I do not care a fig if I never have to see him again.*

◇ SEE ALSO **not give a damn** ▷ DAMN; **not care** or **give a hoot** or **two hoots** ▷ HOOT, HOOTS; **not give a monkey's** ▷ MONKEY; **not give a shit** ▷ SHIT; **not care a sod** ▷ SOD; **not give a tinker's cuss** ▷ TINKER; **not give** or **care a toss** ▷ TOSS; **not care** or **give tuppence** ▷ TUPPENCE

fight

pick a 'fight

You **pick a fight** with someone if you deliberately try to start a fight: *We used to go round the town, picking fights with the boys from the other school.*

put up a good 'fight

You say that someone **has put up a good fight** when they have acted courageously, without giving in, even if they have not won in the end: *Never mind; you put up a good fight, that's what counts.*

figment

figment of your imagi'nation

A thought or feeling is described as a **figment of your imagination** if it relates to something that does not exist or is impossible: *All this nonsense about ghosts is just a figment of her imagination.*

figure

figure of 'fun

A **figure of fun** is someone who people laugh at unkindly: *The real reason was that he felt at ease; he was no longer a figure of fun or an eyesore, he had a place.*

figures

round 'figures

You tell someone a price, for example, in **round figures** when you give it to the nearest number ending in zero: *How much is it going to cost in round figures?*

that 'figures

You say **'that figures'** when you think that what someone has just said makes sense, based on what you already know.

fill

eat your 'fill or drink your 'fill

You **eat**, or **drink, your fill** when you eat or drink until you are completely satisfied: *After he had eaten his fill, he sat back, sighed loudly, and took out a pipe and a small leather tobacco pouch.*

finger

cannot put your 'finger on something
You say that you **cannot put your finger on something** if you have a feeling about something, but you can't say exactly what it is: *There's something strange about her, but I can't quite put my finger on what it is.*

a finger in every 'pie
Someone who has **a finger in every pie** is involved in a lot of different activities: *He has a finger in every pie, and is well-known to all the shop-owners in the area.* □ *When we started up in business, we had a finger in every pie, but we soon realized we had to narrow things down a bit.*

◇ SEE ALSO **irons in the fire** ▷ IRONS

finger on the 'pulse
You have your **finger on the pulse** of something if you are aware of all the new developments in a particular area as they are happening: *As a doctor, it's very important to have your finger on the pulse of new developments in your field.*

not lay a 'finger on someone
If you say that you would **not lay a finger on someone**, you mean that you would not harm them physically: *Don't you dare lay a finger on her!* □ *I don't know what you're talking about; I never laid a finger on him.*

not lift a 'finger
Someone who **does not lift a finger** does not make any effort to help: *I couldn't believe it; she could see that we were late, and she didn't lift a finger to help.*

point the 'finger at someone
You **point the finger at someone** when you blame them for something: *Her devastated husband Robin, an engineer, said: 'If her work was a factor, it was only one among others. I don't want to point the finger at anyone.'*

pull your 'finger out or get your 'finger out
(*informal*)
If you tell someone to **pull their finger out**, you mean that they should stop being lazy or slow, and start working harder: *I'd better pull my finger out if I'm going to get this finished by the end of the week.* □ *Come on, pull your finger out; I want this work finished by this afternoon, not next year!*

put your 'finger on it
You say that someone **has put their finger on it** if they have described or identified something precisely or accurately: *He put his finger on it when he said recently that the crisis in farming is a cultural crisis. It concerns the very identity of farming.*

◇ SEE ALSO **hit the nail on the head** ▷ NAIL

wrap someone round your little 'finger
You **wrap someone round your finger**, or **your little finger**, when you cause them to agree to anything you want; you **have someone wrapped round your finger** when they will do anything to please you: *She wraps him round her little finger; I mean, would you sleep outside rather than ring the bell and wake someone up?* □ *That little girl's got her Dad wrapped round her finger all right.*

◇ SEE ALSO **have someone right where you want them** ▷ WANT; **have someone eating out of the palm of your hand** ▷ PALM; **have someone eating out of your hand** ▷ HAND; **have someone in your pocket** ▷ POCKET

fingers

all fingers and 'thumbs
You are **all fingers and thumbs** if you are using your hands in an awkward or clumsy way: *I can't tie this thing; I'm all fingers and thumbs today.*

count on the fingers of one 'hand
You say that you could **count something on the fingers of one hand** if there are not many of them: *I think I can count on the fingers of one hand the men I know who were desperate to experience fatherhood.*

fingers 'crossed
You say '**fingers crossed**' to someone to show them that you are hoping they will be successful.

◇ SEE ALSO **have your fingers crossed for someone** ▷ FINGERS; **good luck** ▷ LUCK

get your 'fingers burnt
You **get your fingers burnt** when you suffer from a bad decision or foolish action: *They've had their fingers burnt on a few occasions already this year, and they're not likely to be taking any more risks.*

give someone two 'fingers or stick two 'fingers up at someone
You **give someone two fingers** or **stick two fingers up at someone** when you show in a very offensive way that you are angry with them, by turning the back of your hand to face them, and raising your first two fingers in a V-shape: *I couldn't believe it; he drove past, sticking two fingers up at me.* □ *If he makes any more sexist comments like that, just give him two fingers.*

green 'fingers
Someone who has **green fingers** is a successful gardener.

have your 'fingers crossed for someone
You tell someone that you **have got your fingers crossed for them** if you want them to be successful; '**fingers crossed**' means 'let's hope for success': *We'll have our fingers*

crossed for you tomorrow afternoon; I'm sure you'll do well anyway.

◇ SEE ALSO **fingers crossed** ▷ FINGERS

have your 'fingers in the till

Someone who **has their fingers in the till** is stealing small amounts of money from the shop or organization they work for: *'What was he sacked for?' 'Fingers in the till.'*

◇ SEE ALSO **cook the books** ▷ BOOKS

have light 'fingers

Someone who is described as **having light fingers** has a tendency to steal things: *I wouldn't like to accuse him of being a criminal, but, well, let's just say he's got light fingers.*

light-'fingered: *Having rid himself of a somewhat light-fingered shop assistant, he was able to start making a small profit again.*

slip through your 'fingers

Something **slips through your fingers** when you do not quite manage to obtain it or hold on to it: *And that gold medal has slipped through his fingers again!* □ *He felt that time was slipping through his fingers.*

work your fingers to the 'bone

You **work your fingers to the bone** if you work extremely hard over a long period of time: *Granny worked her fingers to the bone to pay for Mum's education.*

◇ SEE ALSO **work like a dog** ▷ DOG

fingertips

have something at your 'fingertips

You have information about something **at your fingertips** if you are able to give people facts easily, without having to refer to books: *The more facts you've got at your fingertips the more easy it is to persuade people.*

fire

fight fire with 'fire

You **fight fire with fire** when you use the same methods as someone else to defeat them: *Spain, clearly fearing Ireland's physical strength, have decided to fight fire with fire in this match.*

fire someone with something

Something **fires you with** a feeling, such as enthusiasm, when it makes you feel it very strongly: *I left university, fired with en'thusiasm to go and live in Moscow to practise the language.* □ *Just thinking about her fired him with 'passion.*

This idiom is most frequently used in the passive form.

play with 'fire

You **are playing with fire** if you are doing

something very dangerous: *She tried to warn Maurice he was playing with fire. But he wouldn't listen. He didn't take her seriously.*

first

first and 'foremost

First and foremost means 'more than anything else': *She has many talents, but she is, first and foremost, a writer.*

first and 'last

A characteristic is described as **first and last** the case if it is the most important characteristic: *She was first and last a singer.*

big 'fish

A **big fish** is an important or influential person; someone who is described as **a big fish in a small pool** feels important within their small organization, but would not command much respect in a larger one: *When you were at drama school you were a big fish – now you're a tiddler* [= a small, 'unimportant' fish]. □ *The club made you 'someone' in the town, a big fish in a small pool.*

◇ SEE ALSO **big cheese** ▷ CHEESE; **fat cat** ▷ CAT; **big noise** ▷ NOISE

cold 'fish

You describe someone as a **cold fish** if they do not show any emotion or warmth towards other people.

drink like a 'fish

Someone who **drinks like a fish** drinks a lot of alcohol.

have bigger fish to 'fry or have other fish to 'fry

If you say that you **have bigger**, or **other**, **fish to fry**, you mean that you have more important things to do: *How come? I thought you'd have bigger fish to fry with clients like Krantz and Marsh and so on.* □ *I don't see why I should sit around here listening to this nonsense; I've got other fish to fry.*

like a fish out of 'water

You are **like a fish out of water** if you feel very uncomfortable or look very unusual because you are in a situation that you are not used to: *'In the city, we were fish out of water,' said one of the villagers.*

plenty more fish in the 'sea

You tell someone who has been deserted by a lover that there are **plenty more fish in the sea**, as a way of reassuring them that there are a lot of other people in the world who could make them happy: *She closed her eyes, and decided that really, if she tried hard enough, she might just be able to convince herself that Piers Morrison wasn't the only fish in the sea.*

fist

with an iron 'fist

Something that is done **with an iron fist** is done firmly and strictly: *My father ruled our household with an iron fist.*

fit

fit as a 'fiddle

You are as **fit as a fiddle** if you are strong and very healthy: *The doctor seems to think I'm fit as a fiddle so I suppose there can't be anything wrong with me.*

◇ SEE ALSO **hale and hearty** ▷ HALE; **right as rain** ▷ RIGHT

have a blue 'fit (informal)

You **have a blue fit** when you are very angry: *She's going to have a blue fit when she finds out about the car.*

◇ SEE ALSO **go off at the deep end** ▷ END; **blow a fuse** ▷ FUSE; **blow a gasket** ▷ GASKET; **let fly** ▷ LET; **blow** or **flip your lid** ▷ LID; **do your nut** ▷ NUT; **lose your rag** ▷ RAG; **fly into a rage** ▷ RAGE; **hit the roof** ▷ ROOF; **blow your stack** ▷ STACK; **lose your temper** ▷ TEMPER; **blow your top** ▷ TOP; **throw a wobbly** ▷ WOBBLY

fits

in fits and 'starts

Something that happens **in fits and starts** is irregular or occurs in small groups: *People arrived in fits and starts.* □ *He was only able to sleep in fits and starts, the pain was so bad.*

flag

fly the 'flag

You **fly the flag** for a country or organization when you publicly promote it: *Ian Rowlands will fly the flag for North Wales golf in Europe next month.*

keep the 'flag flying

You **keep the flag flying** when you act or speak for a country or organization: *A small team of sales reps keeps the company flag flying in Singapore.*

flame

old 'flame

An **old flame** is someone who you used to be romantically involved with: *Do you think it's right to invite an old flame to one's wedding?*

flames

fan the 'flames

Something that **fans the flames** of a conflict makes it even worse: *His comments only served to fan the flames of the hostility between the two countries.*

flash

flash in the 'pan

You describe something as a **flash in the pan** if it is the object of great popularity or enthusiasm for only a very short period of time: *Everything she does is a flash in the pan; it was saxophone lessons last month, now it's aerobics.*

◇ SEE ALSO **nine day wonder** ▷ DAY

flat

flat as a 'pancake

Something that is as **flat as a pancake** is very flat: *I wouldn't go there if you like mountains; it's as flat as a pancake.*

that's 'flat

You say **that's flat** when you have forbidden someone to do something and you want to show that you will not be persuaded to change your mind: *You're not going by yourself and that's flat.*

◇ SEE ALSO **end of story** ▷ END; **no two ways about it** ▷ WAYS; **that's that** ▷ THAT

flatter

flatter to de'ceive

Something that **flatters to deceive** does not give a true account of a situation: *These unemployment figures flatter to deceive; it's amazing the way they can distort them.*

flavour

flavour of the 'month

Someone or something that is described as **flavour of the month** is the most popular person or thing of the moment: *But Portillo is fast becoming flavour of the month and will increasingly find himself in the public eye.* □ *We've never considered it right to sponsor a project, or support a charity because it happened to be the flavour of the month.*

flea

send someone away with a 'flea in their ear

You **send someone away with a flea in their ear** when you make an angry remark and tell them to go away: *I sent him away with a flea in his ear; I don't think he'll do it again.*

◇ SEE ALSO **give someone hell** ▷ HELL; **give someone a piece of your mind** ▷ PIECE; **read the riot act** ▷ RIOT; **give someone the rough side of your tongue** ▷ SIDE; **tear someone off a strip** ▷ STRIP

flesh

add 'flesh to your argument or put 'flesh on your argument

A point **adds flesh to your argument** or **puts flesh on your argument** if it makes your argument stronger: *If you say you'll do a course when you're over there, that might put a bit of flesh on your argument.*

in the 'flesh

You see someone **in the flesh** when you actually meet or see them, rather that just seeing them on television, for example: *It's funny; he's much smaller when you see him in the flesh.*

◇ SEE ALSO **face to face with someone** ▷ FACE; **in person** ▷ PERSON

make someone's 'flesh crawl or make someone's 'flesh creep

Something that **makes your flesh crawl**, or **creep**, disgusts or horrifies you: *I just can't touch it; the thought of it makes my flesh crawl.* □ *His slow smile made her flesh creep.*

own flesh and 'blood

You refer to people who are related to you as your **own flesh and blood**: *One day they would be sorry that they had abandoned their own flesh and blood.*

flies

drop like 'flies

People **drop like flies** when they fall ill or give in to exhaustion in great numbers: *The heat was unbearable; people were dropping like flies.*

flight

flight of 'fancy

A **flight of fancy** is a dream or idea that is unrealistic, and probably impossible to realize: *Some of these desires might be adolescent flights of fancy, which you never honestly wanted to happen. But other desires will be impulses which you should act upon.*

floodgates

open the 'floodgates

You **open the floodgates** when you remove restrictions or controls that have been repressing thoughts, feelings or actions: *Durkheim opened the floodgates, offering a radically new way of making sense of social institutions.* □ *She was too confused and unhappy to speak, knowing that if she did, the floodgates on her feelings would open, and there would be no stopping the tears.*

> **Floodgates** are barriers that prevent an area from flooding during periods of heavy rain.

floods

in floods of 'tears

Someone who is **in floods of tears** is crying a lot: *'She was in floods of tears when I went*

round there.' 'Not surprising really; she'd had that dog since it was a little puppy.'

floor

take the 'floor

You **take the floor** when you stand up to speak in public, for example, to address a meeting: *Don't take the floor until you've been introduced.*

wipe the 'floor with (*informal*)

You **wipe the floor with** someone when you beat them easily in a competition or match: *'Did you win?' 'No way, they wiped the floor with us.'*

◇ SEE ALSO **give someone a hammering** ▷ HAMMERING; **make mincemeat of** ▷ MINCEMEAT

flotsam

flotsam and 'jetsam

The **flotsam and jetsam** of a place, group or society are the people, things or ideas that are left behind, because they have no use: *His theory is that we improvise our culture from the flotsam and jetsam of other civilizations.* □ *The place became quiet, and, like flotsam and jetsam, Richard and Philippa were left alone.*

> **Flotsam and jetsam** literally refers to the assorted objects and pieces of debris that are washed up on a beach by the sea.

flow

go against the 'flow

You **go against the flow** when you do not follow the ideas or actions of the majority: *Fortunately, he's not afraid to go against the flow; he's the only one who seems to really care about the staff here.*

◇ SEE ALSO **go** or **drift** or **swim against the current** ▷ CURRENT; **go against the stream** ▷ STREAM; **go** or **swim against the tide** ▷ TIDE

go with the 'flow

You **go with the flow** when you do the same as everyone else, or accept the opinions held by most people, because it would be more difficult to do something different or to disagree.

◇ SEE ALSO **go with the crowd** ▷ CROWD; **go** or **drift** or **swim with the current** ▷ CURRENT; **go with the stream** ▷ STREAM; **go**, or **drift**, or **swim, with the tide** ▷ TIDE

in full 'flow

You are **in full flow** when you are in the middle of explaining or describing something: *It's hard to cut people off when they're in full flow, but we have to respect time constraints.*

fluff

'fluff it (*informal*)

You **fluff it** when you fail at something or when you do something very badly: *'How was the exam?' 'I reckon I've fluffed it.'*

◇ SEE ALSO **blow it** ▷ BLOW

flush

in the first flush of

You are **in the first flush of** a particular state if you are in the early stages of it, when you feel the effects of it most strongly: *He's not in the first flush of 'youth, but he's tall and well-built, which does help.* □ *The famous kiss on the balcony of Buckingham Palace on their wedding day showed Charles and Diana in the first flush of ro'mance.*

fly (*see also* **flies**)

a fly on the 'wall

If you say you would love to be, or to have been, **a fly on the wall**, you mean that you would like to be able, or to have been able, to observe or hear something without being noticed: *I'd love to have been a fly on the wall when she said that to him; can you imagine his face?*

fly-on-the-wall: *a fly-on-the-wall documentary.*

> A **fly** is a kind of insect.

'fly in the ointment

You describe something as a **fly in the ointment** if it spoils a situation which could otherwise be pleasant: *The only fly in the ointment was that I still had to study for my maths exam, which was scheduled to take place after the summer break.*

flying 'low

You tell someone, humorously, that they are **flying low**, if their trousers are unfastened at the front.

wouldn't harm a 'fly or wouldn't hurt a 'fly

Someone who **wouldn't harm**, or **hurt, a fly** is gentle and kind-hearted, and would not intentionally make anyone suffer: *What? Liam? He wouldn't hurt a fly; no, it can't have been him.*

foggiest

not have the 'foggiest

You say that you **haven't got the foggiest** when you have no idea of something: *'What's the population of the USA?' 'I haven't got the foggiest.'*

◇ SEE ALSO **not have the faintest** ▷ FAINTEST; **not have an earthly** ▷ EARTHLY; **not have a clue** ▷ CLUE

> This idiom is the short form of the expression 'I haven't the foggiest idea'.

food

food for 'thought

Something that provides **food for thought** makes you think because it is particularly important or interesting: *Thanks for your suggestions; they certainly provide food for thought.*

fool (*see also* **fools**)

act the 'fool or play the 'fool

You **act**, or **play, the fool** when you behave in a playful, childish way, often in order to make other people laugh: *Stop acting the fool and listen to me; I've got something important to ask you.*

◇ SEE ALSO **act the goat** or **play the goat** ▷ GOAT

a fool and his money are soon 'parted

'A **fool and his money are soon parted**' means that you are foolish if you spend money too quickly, rather than saving it.

a fool's 'errand

A **fool's errand** is a wasted effort: *He said it would be a fool's errand, so he didn't bother going at all.*

a fool's 'paradise

You are living in **a fool's paradise** if you are enjoying life without paying attention to the inevitable, unpleasant long-term consequences: *If you think you can have two girlfriends and keep them both happy, you're living in a fool's paradise.*

make a 'fool of yourself

You **make a fool of yourself** when you do something that makes you appear ridiculous: *I can't believe I made such a fool of myself; why didn't someone tell me to be quiet?*

◇ SEE ALSO **make an exhibition of yourself** ▷ EXHIBITION; **make a spectacle of yourself** ▷ SPECTACLE

more fool 'you (*informal*)

If you say '**more fool you**' to someone, you mean, unkindly, that they were foolish not to take advantage of a situation: *'I decided not to go on that course in the States because it would mean leaving my boyfriend for two months.' 'More fool you.'*

no 'fool or nobody's 'fool

Someone who is **no fool** or **nobody's fool** is not easily deceived: *Come on, she's no fool; of course she can see what her son is up to.*

fooled

you could have fooled 'me (*informal*)

'**You could have fooled me**' means, rather rudely, 'that's not the conclusion I came to from what I know': *'He's a nice guy, really.' 'You could've fooled me; look at the way he treats his staff.'*

fools

fools rush 'in

If you say '**fools rush in**', you mean that foolish people attempt to do things that wiser people would avoid: '*He offered to take a class of 35 kids camping; talk about fools rush in!*

This idiom is the shortened form of the saying '**fools rush in where angels fear to tread**'.

not suffer fools 'gladly

Someone who **does not suffer fools gladly** is impatient and unsympathetic towards foolish people: *She's a good manager, but watch out; she doesn't suffer fools gladly.*

foot (*see also* **feet**)

a foot in both 'camps

You have **a foot in both camps** if you have links with people in two groups, each with opposing opinions: *It helps to have a foot in both camps if you can; that way you are sure of understanding both sides.*

a 'foot in the door

You have **a foot in the door** if you have already completed one stage towards achieving an aim, especially one that involves being accepted by a group or organization: '*They've agreed to give me a month's work experience.*' '*Great, well that's a foot in the door at least, isn't it?*'

If you put your foot in a doorway, the door cannot be shut.

get off on the wrong 'foot

You **get off on the wrong foot** when you start something badly: '*How did you get on with his parents?*' '*Well, I got off on the wrong foot by using their first names.*'

When soldiers are marching, they all have to start on the same foot.

hardly put one foot in front of the 'other

You can **hardly put one foot in front of the other** if you are so tired that you are almost unable to walk any further.

◇ SEE ALSO **be on your last legs** ▷ LEGS

have one foot in the 'grave (*informal*)

If you say that someone **has one foot in the grave**, you mean, humorously, that they are very old: *These holidays aren't only for people with one foot in the grave; they can provide a relaxing break for people of any age.*

A grave is a place where a person's body is buried when they are dead.

put a foot 'wrong

1 You **put a foot wrong** when you make a mistake or do something that someone disapproves of: *I realized that I should not put a foot wrong; if I did, we might never get the offer accepted.* **2** You say that a person **cannot put a foot wrong** if someone likes or loves them so much that they cannot see that person's faults: *I'm sure you cannot put a foot wrong where she's concerned.*

put your best foot 'forward

You **put your best foot forward** when you start working with firm purpose: *Right, if we're going to get this job done, we'll have to put our best foot forward.*

put your 'foot down

You **put your foot down** when you decide very firmly not to allow something: *You're just going to have to put your foot down this time; you can't have the children walking round the streets on their own at night.*

put your 'foot in it or put your foot in your 'mouth (*informal*)

You **put your foot in it** or **put your foot in your mouth** when you unintentionally say something that embarrasses or upsets someone: *Oh no, I really put my foot in it there; why didn't you tell me they'd split up?*
◇ SEE ALSO **drop a brick** ▷ BRICK; **drop a clanger** ▷ CLANGER

footloose

footloose and fancy-'free or fancy-'free

You are **footloose and fancy-free** or **fancy-free** if you can do whatever you want, perhaps because you are not romantically attached to anyone: *Largely thanks to the fact that I am footloose and fancy-free, I can follow my job where it takes me.* □ *I'm not sure I like the idea of him going away with his fancy-free brother.*

footsie

play 'footsie

You **play footsie** when you touch someone's legs or feet with your own feet under the table, in order to show sexual interest: *Well, he started playing footsie with me, but I think he must have mistaken my foot for Karen's.*

footsteps

follow in someone's 'footsteps

You **follow in someone's**, usually a member of the family's, **footsteps** when you do the same job, or lead a similar life to them: *The oldest daughter will probably follow in her father's footsteps, and take over the family business when she's old enough.*

force

bring something into 'force

You **bring** a law, for example, **into force** when you cause it to take effect; a law **comes into force** when it takes effect: *They've finally decided to bring that 'stop and check' law into force.*

the driving 'force

The **driving force** behind a project, for example, is the person or thing that makes it possible: *We have to thank Catherine, who has been the driving force behind all this.*

force of 'circumstance

You do something through **force of circumstance** when you do it because other factors that are beyond your control force you to act in this way: *We form relationships with particular individuals for a period of time and then, often through force of circumstance, move away from them.*

force of 'habit

You do something through **force of habit** when you do it because you have always done it, rather than for any practical reason: *She was about to leave the room when she caught sight of the unmade bed. Force of habit compelled her to stop and straighten the quilt.*

a force to be 'reckoned with

Something that is described as **a force to be reckoned with** is very powerful and has a lot of influence: *Their accumulated experience, together with their local knowledge, means that they are a force to be reckoned with.* □ *The senior team's rebuilding period was over, and they once again look a force to be reckoned with.*

in 'force

People are present **in force** when there are large numbers of them: *The police were out in force this morning; is there a state visit or something?*

forewarned

forewarned is fore'armed

'**Forewarned is forearmed**' means that it is easier to deal with something unpleasant if you are told about it beforehand: *I don't like having to tell you this, but I think it's best that I tell you about it now; forewarned is forearmed.*

forgive

forgive and for'get

You suggest that two people who have had an argument **forgive and forget** if you think they should become friends again: *My goodness, you are bitter. Obviously you don't know the meaning of the words 'forgive and forget'.*

form

bad 'form

Bad form is inappropriate or unacceptable behaviour: *That was pretty bad form I thought, him being late after lecturing us on punctuality.*

good 'form

Good form is the right and acceptable way to behave: *Apparently, it's good form to arrive a bit late when you go to a dinner party.*

on top 'form

You are **on top form** if you are healthy and in good condition: *Leconte is back on top form after his injury earlier in the season.*

true to 'form

Someone's behaviour is **true to form** if it is typical of them: *They acted true to form, by refusing to shoulder any responsibility for the situation.* □ *True to form, her talk was practical and to the point.*

fort

hold the 'fort

You **hold the fort** when you temporarily take over the running of an organization: *'Where's Mrs McLeod?' 'She's on holiday at the moment; I'm holding the fort.'*

fortune

a small 'fortune

Something that costs **a small fortune** is very expensive: *It'll cost you a small fortune if you want to provide all the food and drink for the party yourself.*

fortune smiles on 'so-and-so

You say that **fortune smiles on** a certain person when they have been successful or lucky: *Fortune smiled on us, for the rain kept off until we boarded our coach for home.*

make a 'fortune

You **make a fortune** when you make a lot of money: *He made a fortune buying and selling other people's rubbish.*

◇ SEE ALSO **make a bomb** ▷ BOMB; **make a bundle** ▷ BUNDLE; **coin it** or **coin it in** ▷ COIN; **make a killing** ▷ KILLING; **make your pile** ▷ PILE

tell someone's 'fortune

Someone **tells your fortune** when they tell you, usually by means of an aid such as special cards, what they believe will happen to you in the future: *'Have you ever had your fortune told?' 'No, I don't believe in all that stuff.'*

four

'four-eyes (*disrespectful*)

Four-eyes is a name, used especially by children, for someone who wears glasses:

*I just went past these fellows and one of them
shouted, 'Hey, speccy four-eyes,' and I ignored them like you told me.*

frazzle

burnt to a 'frazzle

Something, especially food, that is **burnt to
a frazzle** is so badly burnt that it is black
and unrecognizable: *The Christmas dinner
was burnt to a frazzle, Grandpa was drunk,
and the children were running around the
house screaming.*

◊ SEE ALSO **burnt to a cinder** ▷ CINDER

free

free as a 'bird

You are, or you feel, as **free as a bird** if you
are, or you feel, completely free: *I feel free
as a bird now I don't have to do that awful
job any more.*

French

excuse my 'French or pardon my 'French
(*humorous*)

People say **'excuse, or pardon, my French'** as
a humorous way of apologizing for swearing: *If you'll pardon my French, I think he's a
bit of an arsehole.* □ *Shit! Excuse my French.*

fresh

fresh as a 'daisy

You are as **fresh as a daisy** if you are bright
and clean, even when it is very hot: *She's
just won the 1500m and look, she's as fresh
as a daisy.*

friend

fair-weather 'friend

A **fair-weather friend** is someone who is
friendly with you when you are enjoying
good times, but who abandons you when
you need help: *This is a time when you will
find out who your fair-weather friends are.*

feathered 'friend

Feathered friends are birds, especially those
found in people's gardens: *Don't feed your
feathered friends very dry bread, or salty
food.*

a friend in need is a friend in'deed

'**A friend in need is a friend indeed**' means
that a friend who helps you when you have
problems is a real friend.

friends

have friends in high 'places

Someone who **has friends in high places**
knows people who are important and influential, and who may be able to help
them: *She had friends in high places everywhere, contacts in embassies.*

with friends like that, who needs 'enemies?
If someone says '**with friends like that, who
needs enemies?**' they mean that they disapprove of the way in which someone's friend
or friends have behaved towards that person.

fright

the fright of your 'life

You get **the fright of your life** when you
suddenly get a severe shock: *I got the fright
of my life when they said he was in hospital;
in fact he'd only cut his finger.*

frog

a 'frog in your throat

You say you've got **a frog in your throat** if
your voice is not clear, and you feel you
need to cough: *Excuse me, I've got a bit of a
frog in my throat.*

A **frog** is a small animal that lives in
water, and makes a croaking sound.

front

put on a false 'front

You **put on a false front** when you act in an
unnatural way, in order to give the impression of being different from the way you
really are: *They always put on a false front
when they invite people round for dinner; I
wish they'd just be themselves.*

fruit

bear 'fruit

Efforts **bear fruit** when they are successful:
*It's good to see that all that work finally bore
fruit.*

forbidden 'fruit

You refer to someone or something as
forbidden fruit when they become more
attractive due to the fact that you are
not supposed to have them: *That forbidden
fruit, his best friend's wife.*

From the forbidden apple in the Bible
story of Adam and Eve.

fry

'small fry

'**Small fry**' refers to people or things that
are not very important: *Those people she's
so proud to know are just small fry; the
really influential ones are too busy for all
that socializing.*

frying

out of the frying pan into the 'fire

A situation is described as **out of the frying
pan into the fire**, when it gets even more
difficult than it was before.

fuck

for fuck's 'sake (*vulgar*)

'For fuck's sake' is an exclamation of great anger or annoyance: *For fuck's sake, what's the matter with this stupid machine?*

◇ SEE ALSO **for Christ's sake** ▷ CHRIST; **for Pete's sake** ▷ PETE; **for God's sake** ▷ GOD; **for goodness sake** ▷ GOODNESS; **for heaven's sake** ▷ HEAVEN; **for Pete's sake** ▷ PETE; **for pity's sake** ▷ PITY

fuck 'all (*vulgar*)

Fuck all means, usually angrily, 'nothing at all': *They've done fuck all about the repairs we asked for.*

'fuck it (*vulgar*)

Fuck it! is an expression 1 of anger: *Fuck it! The car won't start again.* 2 of a decision that something is unimportant: *Oh fuck it, just do it, I don't care.*

◇ SEE ALSO **damn it** ▷ DAMN; **sod it** ▷ SOD

fullness

in the fullness of 'time

You say that something will happen **in the fullness of time** if you think it will happen when the right time arrives, or eventually: *Don't worry if your child is not speaking much yet; she will do so, in the fullness of time.*

fun

for the 'fun of it

You do something **for the fun of it** when you do it for amusement, rather than for any practical purpose: *When asked why they had taken the car and driven the wrong way down the motorway, the youths said they had done it 'for the fun of it'.*

fun and 'games (*informal*)

You describe something as **fun and games** when it causes you difficulty: *We had fun and games finding the place.*

poke 'fun at or make 'fun of

You **poke fun at**, or **make fun of**, someone when you make jokes about their looks or behaviour in public: *comedians who poke fun at politicians.*

◇ SEE ALSO **take the mickey** ▷ MICKEY; **take the piss out of** ▷ PISS

funnily

funnily e'nough

You say **'funnily enough'** to introduce a statement of a fact that will surprise someone who has just stated an opposite opinion: *'I thought I'd feel nervous, but funnily enough I didn't.*

funny

funny ha-'ha

Funny ha-ha means 'funny', in reference to something that makes you laugh, rather than to something that is strange: *'That film was really funny.' 'You mean funny ha-ha?'*

funny pe'culiar

Funny peculiar means 'funny', in reference to something that is strange, rather than to something that makes you laugh: *'He's funny.' 'Funny ha-ha or funny peculiar?'*

fuse

blow a 'fuse

You **blow a fuse** when you become extremely angry: *When I told her about the car, she blew a fuse.*

◇ SEE ALSO **go off at the deep end** ▷ END; **have a blue fit** ▷ FIT; **blow a gasket** ▷ GASKET; **let fly** ▷ LET; **blow** or **flip your lid** ▷ LID; **do your nut** ▷ NUT; **lose your rag** ▷ RAG; **fly into a rage** ▷ RAGE; **hit the roof** ▷ ROOF; **blow your stack** ▷ STACK; **lose your temper** ▷ TEMPER; **blow your top** ▷ TOP; **throw a wobbly** ▷ WOBBLY

fuss

kick up a 'fuss or make a 'fuss

Someone **kicks up**, or **makes**, **a fuss** when they react angrily to something, especially when their anger does not appear to be justified: *The neighbours kicked up a terrible fuss when we told them we were planning to have a small party.*

make a fuss of someone

You **make a fuss of someone** when you pay a lot of attention to them, and make sure they have everything they need and want: *You'll like my Mum; she always makes a fuss of my 'friends.*

g

gaff

blow the 'gaff (*informal*)
You **blow the gaff** when you reveal a secret: *If I tell you, what guarantee do I have that you won't blow the gaff?*
◇ SEE ALSO **let the cat out of the bag** ▷ BAG; **spill the beans** ▷ BEANS; **give the game away** ▷ GAME

gaga

go 'gaga (*informal*)
You **go gaga 1** when you are very enthusiastic about something: *Thousands of teenagers have gone gaga over these three blonds from Newcastle.* **2** when you go mad: *He's been more or less gaga since the car crash.*
◇ SEE ALSO **lose your marbles** ▷ MARBLES

gallery

play to the 'gallery
Someone who **is playing to the gallery** is acting in an amusing or showy way intended to appeal to the masses: *He tried to explain that what he had said was not entirely true; he's just been playing to the gallery.*

The **gallery** is the part of a theatre where the cheapest seats can be found.

game

easy 'game
Someone who is described as **easy game** is easily deceived, attacked or made fun of: *The southern states have always been regarded as backward, and therefore easy game.*

fair 'game
If you describe someone as **fair game**, you mean that it is reasonable to criticize or attack them in some way: *But when it came to practical jokes, he regarded anybody as fair game, from people he hardly knew to his dearest friends.*

give the 'game away
You **give the game away** when you reveal a secret: *If I tell you, will you promise not to give the game away?*
◇ SEE ALSO **let the cat out of the bag** ▷ CAT; **spill the beans** ▷ BEANS; **blow the gaff** ▷ GAFF

on the 'game (*informal*)
Someone who is **on the game** is working as a prostitute: *She had been on the game for three years, and in two more she intended to retire in luxury somewhere far away.*

play the 'game
You tell someone to **play the game** when you want them to behave fairly.

play a 'waiting game
You **play a waiting game** when you make someone wait for something, such as your decision, in order to be in a stronger position: *Had she forgotten their date or was she playing a waiting game?*

'two can play at that game
You tell someone that **two can play at that game** when you think they have behaved unfairly towards you and you want to suggest that you could do the same thing to them: *So, I hear you've been talking about me behind my back; well two can play at that game.*

what's your 'game? (*informal*)
You say to someone **'what's your game?'** when you want to know their intentions, and you suspect that they are not good.

gander

have a 'gander or **take a 'gander** (*informal*)
You **have**, or **take, a gander** at something when you have a look at it: *It's a great piece of architecture, and well worth a gander.* □ *While he was out of the room, I took a gander at some of the stuff on his desk.*

gap

bridge the 'gap
You **bridge the gap** when you make it easier to move from one stage of a process to another: *The book is designed to bridge the gap between the very simple descriptions of homoeopathy and the much larger texts.*

gene'ration gap
The **generation gap** refers to the difference in attitudes and behaviour between people of different generations, and the problems caused by this: *Despite the generation gap, we found we had a surprising amount in common.*

garden

everything in the garden is 'rosy

You say that someone thinks **everything in the garden is rosy** when they appear to be very contented with life, but in fact they are ignoring something unpleasant: *The politicians' attitude is that everything in the garden is rosy.* □ *It would appear that everything in the garden is not as rosy as might have been suspected.*

lead someone up the garden 'path

You **lead someone up the garden path** when you deceive them: *The writer of the crime story has to plot carefully to achieve the surprise at the end. The reader has to be led up the garden path.*

◇ SEE ALSO **take someone for a ride** ▷ RIDE

gasket

blow a 'gasket (*informal*)

Someone **blows a gasket** when they become extremely angry.

◇ SEE ALSO **go off at the deep end** ▷ END; **have a blue fit** ▷ FIT; **blow a fuse** ▷ FUSE; **let fly** ▷ LET; **blow** or **flip your lid** ▷ LID; **do your nut** ▷ NUT; **lose your rag** ▷ RAG; **fly into a rage** ▷ RAGE; **hit the roof** ▷ ROOF; **blow your stack** ▷ STACK; **lose your temper** ▷ TEMPER; **blow your top** ▷ TOP; **throw a wobbly** ▷ WOBBLY

gatepost

between you, me and the 'gatepost

You say '**between you, me and the gatepost**' when you are going to tell someone something secret: *Between you, me and the gatepost, I think she's having an affair.*

◇ SEE ALSO **between you, me and the bedpost** ▷ BEDPOST

gates

the pearly 'gates (*humorous*)

The **pearly gates** are the imaginary entrance to heaven: *He wondered if Huxley and Kennedy had shared a fiery chariot to the pearly gates, since Huxley had also died on the previous day.*

gathering

gathering of the 'clans

A **gathering of the clans** is a meeting of a group of people with similar interests, in order to enjoy themselves: *This annual gathering of clans has, in the past, been associated with magnificent weather, allowing executive members to combine business with pleasure.*

gauntlet

pick up the 'gauntlet or take up the 'gauntlet

You **pick**, or **take up, the gauntlet** when you agree to fight or compete with someone: *He*

took up the gauntlet he saw set before him and entered a career in boxing.

See note at **throw down the gauntlet**.

run the 'gauntlet

You **run the gauntlet** when you are attacked or criticized by a lot of people together: *Greeted with shouts of 'traitor!' he had to run the gauntlet of 3000 anti-fascists in Gateshead and 5000 in Newcastle.*

This idiom comes from an old Swedish military punishment – running the 'gatlopp', where the person who had done something wrong would have to run between two lines of men who would hit him.

throw down the 'gauntlet

You **throw down the gauntlet** when you challenge someone to a fight, or to compete with you in some way: *Mr Clarke threw down the gauntlet to a trio of Cabinet colleagues yesterday.* □ *Fresh from their success, they have thrown down the gauntlet to the rest of the group.*

This idiom comes from a medieval tradition where someone would throw down a gauntlet (a long protective glove), as a sign that they wished to fight.

gear

step 'up a gear or move 'up a gear

You **step up**, or **move up, a gear** when you improve your performance: *It seems that Leeds decided to step up a gear and put Swindon to the test.* □ *We now have to build on the satisfaction our clients have expressed and move up a gear to create delight in their view of us.*

gender

'gender-bender (*informal*)

A **gender-bender** is someone whose appearance and behaviour are sexually ambiguous: *Boy George was nothing less than a man in drag, a gender-bender who flounced his sexuality in the face of the outraged media and ecstatic teenagers.*

gentlemen

gentlemen's a'greement

A **gentlemen's agreement** is an agreement made by people who do not sign any legal documents, but instead trust each other to keep to the terms in an honest way: *The company has a gentlemen's agreement with its staff that they will not speak about current projects with outsiders.*

get

can't get 'over (*informal*)
You say you **can't get over** something when you are amazed by it: *I can't get over how much you've grown!*

'get it (*informal*)
You say that someone will **get it** when you think that they will be punished: *You'll get it when Mum comes home.*
◇ SEE ALSO **cop it** ▷ COP

get nowhere 'fast or not get 'anywhere
You say you **are getting nowhere fast** or **not getting anywhere** when you are not making any progress: *We seem to be getting nowhere fast with this decorating.*

'get somewhere
You say you **are getting somewhere** when you are making progress.

get-up-and-'go (*informal*)
Someone who has a lot of **get-up-and-go** is very lively and is always finding new and interesting things to do: *You, with all your chat about your full social life, your glamorous lifestyle, the get-up-and-go philosophy that you're always talking about?*

ghost

give up the 'ghost (*informal*)
Someone **gives up the ghost** when they die; a machine **gives up the ghost** when it stops working: *What if she should die before I got home, give up the ghost and pass on, alone in the dark?* □ *I'm a bit worried the car's going to give up the ghost in the middle of nowhere.*
◇ SEE ALSO **breathe your last** ▷ LAST; **kick the bucket** ▷ BUCKET; **cash in your chips** ▷ CHIPS; **pop your clogs** ▷ CLOGS; **shuffle off this mortal coil** ▷ COIL; **bite the dust** ▷ DUST; **depart this life** ▷ LIFE; **snuff it** ▷ SNUFF; **go the way of all flesh** ▷ WAY

lay the ghost of something to 'rest
You **lay the ghost of something to rest** when you stop being worried by it: *Art helps me to lay the ghost of the past to rest.*

not a 'ghost of a chance
Someone **does not have**, or **stand**, **a ghost of a chance** of succeeding when there is almost no possibility that they will succeed: *You would have thought that the play wouldn't have stood a ghost of a chance with just two actors and such a simple set.*

gift

gift from the 'gods or a gift from 'God
You describe something as **a gift from the gods**, or **from God**, if it is very special, and you feel lucky to have it: *I felt my baby was a gift from God.*

the gift of the 'gab
Someone who has **the gift of the gab** is able to manipulate people by talking to them very confidently and easily: *Fortunately, one of my friends had the gift of the gab and was able to defuse the situation.*

gills

pale about the 'gills or green about the 'gills
Someone who is looking **pale**, or **green**, **about the gills** is not looking very well.
◇ SEE ALSO **off-colour** ▷ COLOUR; **look like death warmed up** ▷ DEATH

gilt

take the gilt off the 'gingerbread
Something that **takes the gilt off the gingerbread** spoils an experience which could otherwise be enjoyable: *I find it rather takes the gilt off the gingerbread if you have to stay behind after a party to clear up.*

Until the middle of the nineteenth century, gingerbread was often sold decorated with gold leaf.

girl

a big girl's 'blouse (*very informal, humorous, slightly offensive*)
You call someone **a big girl's blouse** when they are behaving in a weak or cowardly way: *I choked, and, big daft girl's blouse that I am, burst into tears.*

give

don't give me 'that (*informal*)
You say to someone '**don't give me that**' when you are sure they are not telling you the truth: *'I didn't know what time it was, honest.' 'Don't give me that; you've got a watch, haven't you?'*
◇ SEE ALSO **come off it** ▷ COME; **do me a favour** ▷ FAVOUR; **don't make me laugh** ▷ LAUGH; **tell that to the marines** ▷ MARINES

give and 'take
Give and take refers to the idea that in order to form good relationships, we must give support, love, etc, as well as receiving these things from others: *A bit of give and take would do wonders for their relationship.*

give or 'take
You say '**give or take** a certain number or quantity' to show that the amount you have said is not precise: *It should take about two hours, give or take a few minutes.*

glance

cast a 'glance
You **cast a glance** at, or over, something when you look at it very quickly to get a general impression.

◇ SEE ALSO **cast** or **run an eye over** ▷ EYE

glory

'glory days
Someone's **glory days** are a period of time when they enjoyed great success: *The sales results cannot compare with those of the glory days of 1989, but nobody was complaining.*

gloves

treat someone with kid 'gloves
You **treat someone with kid gloves** when you treat them very gently, being careful not to do or say anything which could cause offence: *There was no point in treating him with kid gloves; he'd have to know sooner or later.*

◇ SEE ALSO **walk** or **tread on eggshells** ▷ EGGSHELLS

Kid gloves are made from the very soft leather of a baby goat's skin.

glutton

glutton for 'punishment
You describe someone as a **glutton for punishment** if they seem to enjoy being in stressful or difficult situations: *Being gluttons for punishment, we decided to carry tents with us, rather than stay in youth hostels.*

go

give something a 'go or have a 'go
You **give something a go**, or **have a go**, if you try something in order to see if you can do it, or to see if you like it: *Why don't you just give it a go? You can always leave if you don't like it.* □ *I'll have a go at anything, as long as I'm not risking my life.*

◇ SEE ALSO **have a bash** ▷ BASH; **have a crack** ▷ CRACK

'go for it (*informal*)
You tell someone to **go for it, 1** to encourage them to try something new and challenging: *'I don't know whether to take the risk or not.' 'Go for it, I would.'* **2** to encourage them to perform well: *Go for it! We'll be cheering for you!*

it goes without 'saying
You say that something **goes without saying** when you think that people know a particular fact, but you are going to tell them it anyway because it is very important: *And of course it goes without saying that you have to be here on time in the mornings.*

goalposts

move the 'goalposts
You **move the goalposts** when you change the conditions of an agreement: *He was always moving the goalposts so that we could never anticipate what he wanted.*

goat

act the 'goat or play the 'goat
You **act**, or **play**, **the goat** when you behave in a foolish way, usually in order to make people laugh: *Will you stop acting the goat and listen to me for a moment?*

◇ SEE ALSO **act the fool** or **play the fool** ▷ FOOL

get someone's 'goat (*informal*)
Someone **gets your goat** if they annoy you: *I hope I didn't say anything rude to Sandy. She gets my goat sometimes with her loud voice and self-assertion.*

◇ SEE ALSO **drive someone round the bend** ▷ BEND; **make someone's hackles rise** or **raise someone's hackles** ▷ HACKLES; **get on someone's nerves** ▷ NERVES; **get up someone's nose** ▷ NOSE; **rub someone up the wrong way** ▷ WAY; **get on someone's wick** ▷ WICK

gob

shut your 'gob (*offensive*)
Shut your gob is a very offensive way of telling someone to be quiet.

◇ SEE ALSO **shut your face** ▷ FACE; **shut your mouth** ▷ MOUTH; **shut it** or **shut up** ▷ SHUT

God

for God's 'sake (*informal*)
You introduce a request with **for God's sake** when you are angry, or when you feel that you cannot tolerate a situation any more: *For God's sake, you lot; can you be quiet?*

◇ SEE ALSO **for Christ's sake** ▷ CHRIST, **for goodness sake** ▷ GOODNESS; **for heaven's sake** ▷ HEAVEN; **for Pete's sake** ▷ PETE; **for pity's sake** ▷ PITY

God Al'mighty (*very informal*)
God Almighty! is an expression of amazement, horror or surprise.

◇ SEE ALSO **Christ Almighty** ▷ CHRIST

'god-awful (*informal*)
You describe something as **god-awful** if it is very bad or unpleasant: *Have you heard that god-awful music they play while you're waiting to be put through?*

God for'bid
You add '**God forbid**' to something you have said could happen as a way of saying

that you sincerely hope it will not: *If the Government are re-elected, God forbid, is it not a fact that privatization would be put into effect across the board?*

◇ SEE ALSO **heaven forbid** ▷ HEAVEN

'god-forsaken

A **god-forsaken** place is lonely and empty, with nothing interesting about it: *The last thing we need is having to spend any longer in this god-forsaken place than we have to.*

God 'help someone

1 You say '**God help you, him** or **her**' to warn someone that something unpleasant will happen if someone does not do a particular thing: *God help you if you don't take proper care of her.* **2** You also say '**God help him, her** or **them**' if you feel sorry for someone: *God help him, the poor man, he didn't even know how to boil an egg.* **3** You say '**God help us**' if you do not like the thought of what you are suggesting: *God help us all, he thought, there's enough pain and suffering ahead; let's not worry about the details.*

'God knows or God alone knows (*informal*)

God knows, or **God alone knows** means 'I have no idea': *We're still looking, but God knows how long it's going to take.*

◇ SEE ALSO **Christ knows** ▷ CHRIST; **goodness knows** or **goodness only knows** ▷ GOODNESS; **heaven knows** or **heaven alone knows** ▷ HEAVEN; **Lord knows** ▷ LORD

God 'willing

God willing means 'if everything happens as I hope it will': *God willing, we'll have an answer to our mystery in the morning.*

God's gift to 'such-and-such

Someone who thinks they are **God's gift to** a particular thing has a very high opinion of themselves with regard to that thing: *I can't bear him; he thinks he's God's gift to 'women.*

God's 'truth

You say that something you have said is the **God's truth,** as a way of insisting that it is true, and that you are not lying: *God's truth, that's what he said.*

in God's 'name or in the name of 'God

You ask what, where, why, etc, **in God's name** or **in the name of God** something is the case when you are angry, or when you are amazed that it is the case: *How in God's name do you manage to put up with your job?* □ *What in the name of God do you think you're doing?*

◇ SEE ALSO **in heaven's name** ▷ HEAVEN

My 'God (*informal*)

My God! is an exclamation of amazement, anger, disgust, fear or excitement: *My God! How are you going to eat all that?* □ *My God! Look at this mess!*

'please God

You say '**please God**'when you desperately want something to happen: *Please God, let me live.*

thank 'God (*informal*)

You say '**thank God**' or '**thank God for** a certain thing' when you are very relieved: *Thank God for that.* □ *Thank God he still had his wallet.*

◇ SEE ALSO **thank goodness** ▷ GOODNESS; **thank heaven** ▷ HEAVEN

gods

tempt the 'gods

If you say that someone **is tempting the gods,** you mean, superstitiously, that they are encouraging something bad to happen by being over-optimistic: *Few cultures have been so willing to tempt the gods. That we should do so says a great deal about the arrogance of our cultural values.*

◇ SEE ALSO **tempt fate** ▷ FATE; **tempt providence** ▷ PROVIDENCE; **speak too soon** ▷ SPEAK

going

while the going is 'good

You do something **while the going is 'good** when you take advantage of the circumstances: *Let's get out of here while the going's good.*

gold

strike 'gold

You say that you **have struck gold** when you find wealth, happiness or exactly what you need: *I think we've struck gold; he's just the man for the job.*

good (*see also* goods)

as good as 'gold

A child who is **as good as gold** is very well-behaved: *It's no trouble looking after him, I assure you; he's as good as gold.*

be so good as to (*formal*)

You ask someone if they would **be so good as to** do something as a polite way of asking them to do something: *Would you be so good as to bring us some 'coffee please, Jean?*

for the common 'good

Something that is done **for the common good** is done to help everyone: *I felt happy to know honourable people who were fighting for the common good.*

give as good as you 'get

You **give as good as you get** when you fight, argue or joke with other people as well as they fight, argue or joke with you: *Don't worry about Kate; she can give as good as* *she gets.* □ *The result gives a false impression of the match, as United gave as good as they got.*

no good to man nor 'beast

You say that something is **no good to man nor beast** if it is not at all useful: *'No good to man nor beast since Chernobyl. They're still radioactive,' he explained. 'We still can't eat their mutton.'*

◇ SEE ALSO **no use to man nor beast** ▷ USE

too good to be 'true

If you say that something is **too good to be true**, you mean that it is so good that you can hardly believe it: *It was like a dream, too good to be true and never likely to be recaptured.*

up to no 'good

Someone who is **up to no good** is secretly doing something dishonest or illegal: *If you ask me, he's up to no good.*

goodbye

kiss something good'bye or say goodbye to something

You **kiss something goodbye** or **say goodbye to something** you wanted when you have to accept that you will not have it or get it any more: *Well we can kiss that pay rise goodbye.* □ *It was then that I finally said goodbye to any hope of being able to 'walk again.*

goodness

for goodness 'sake

You introduce a request with **for goodness sake** when you are annoyed or impatient: *For goodness sake, just make up your mind and stick to it.*

◇ SEE ALSO **for Christ's sake** ▷ CHRIST; **for God's sake** ▷ GOD; **for heaven's sake** ▷ HEAVEN; **for Pete's sake** ▷ PETE; **for pity's sake** ▷ PITY

goodness 'knows

1 People say **'goodness knows'**, or **'goodness only knows'**, if they have no idea about something **2** You also use **'goodness knows'** to emphasize something you are about to say: *Apparently there are some awful traffic jams between here and London, so goodness only knows what time they'll arrive.* □ *He just won't try to learn. Goodness knows we've tried to help him.*

◇ SEE ALSO **Christ knows** ▷ CHRIST; **God knows** or **God alone knows** ▷ GOD; **heaven knows** or **heaven alone knows** ▷ HEAVEN; **Lord knows** ▷ LORD

thank 'goodness

You say **'thank goodness'** or **'thank goodness for such-and-such'** when you are relieved: *Thank goodness you woke me up!* □ *Thank goodness for that.*

◇ SEE ALSO **thank god** ▷ GOD; **thank heaven** ▷ HEAVEN

goods

come up with the 'goods or deliver the goods

Someone **comes up with**, or **delivers, the goods** when they do what they have promised they will do, or when they do a job well: *She's got a lot of qualifications, but do you think she can deliver the goods?*

goods and 'chattels

In law, someone's **goods and chattels** are their personal possessions, other than any land and buildings they own: *We've got plenty of things, goods and chattels and land, but very little money because we can't sell anything.*

'Goods and chattels' is an old legal term.

'goody-goody (*offensive*)

A **goody-goody** is someone who tries to please people in authority by never breaking rules: *I was such a goody-goody at school. I would never have dared miss a class.*

goose

cook someone's 'goose

Something that **cooks your goose** spoils your chances of success: *This fall in share prices will cook Arthur's goose.*

golden 'goose

A **golden goose** is something that is to your advantage, especially financially: *Monstrous concrete high-rise blocks were built before the authorities realized they were killing the golden goose of tourism.*

the goose that lays the golden 'egg

The goose that lays the golden egg is something that brings you good things: *Life was hard now that the goose who laid the golden egg had died.*

wouldn't say boo to a 'goose

Someone who **wouldn't say boo to a goose** is reserved or shy, and would never attack or criticize anybody.

gooseberry

play 'gooseberry (*informal*)

You **are playing gooseberry** when you are invading the privacy of a couple who are romantically involved with each other: *All right, I'll come, if you really don't mind my playing gooseberry.*

gospel

take something as 'gospel

You **take something**, such as a statement, **as gospel**, when you believe it without questioning it: *Rather than taking as gospel what* *the manufacturers told us, we decided to visit one of their factories ourselves.*

grabs

up for 'grabs (*informal*)

Something that is **up for grabs** is for sale or available in some way: *A £3 million jackpot will be up for grabs every week for that one person who picks the right six numbers.* □ *The famous Ritz hotel is up for grabs for a mere £1 million.*

grace

by the grace of 'God

You say that something happened **by the grace of God**, when you are very relieved that it happened: *It was only by the grace of God that I had enough money to pay the bill.*

fall from 'grace

You **fall from grace** when you lose your reputation by doing something immoral: *But he fell from grace for the first time in 1983 when he was convicted of drink-driving.*

saving 'grace

Someone's or something's **saving grace** is a characteristic it has that makes it acceptable or desirable, despite other less pleasant characteristics it has: *Whatever her political views, her sense of humour has to be her saving grace, especially when she is not afraid to laugh at herself.*

there but for the grace of God go 'I

People say '**there but for the grace of God go I**' when they learn of someone's misfortune, and realize that it might have happened to them.

with bad 'grace

You do or accept something **with bad grace** when you do or accept it unwillingly, and in a bad-tempered way: *She felt in her pocket and handed the key over with bad grace.*

with good 'grace

You do or accept something unpleasant **with good grace** when you do or accept it without complaining: *If you've changed your mind and the shop won't give you your money back, I think you have to accept that with good grace.*

grade

make the 'grade

You **make the grade** when you reach the required standard, in an exam, for example: *Determination and resilience are two of the most important qualities needed to make the grade as a sportsperson.*

In the US, a train that could **make the grade** was one that could climb a steep section of the track.

grain

go against the 'grain

Something **goes against the grain** when you find it difficult to accept, or do, it because it opposes a belief or principle that you hold: *A lie went against the grain, but it was necessary.*

On a piece of wood, the **grain** is the natural patterns and lines on its surface. It is easier to cut with the grain than against it.

grandmother

teach your grandmother to suck 'eggs

You **are teaching your grandmother to suck eggs** if you are trying to give advice to someone who already has a lot of experience or knowledge about the subject: *There's nothing worse than going in to the classroom and thinking, 'they may already know this, I might be teaching my grandmother to suck eggs here.'*

grapes

sour 'grapes

Sour grapes means 'jealousy': *It may sound like sour grapes, but I assure you I feel no bitterness, just disappointment.*

From Aesop's fable about the fox who, being unable to reach a bunch of grapes, went away saying, 'I see they are sour' [= not sweet].

grapevine

hear something on the 'grapevine

You **hear** a piece of information **on the grapevine** when you hear it through gossip, rather than directly from the person who is affected: *We were amazed at the number of people who had found out on the grapevine.*

grass

the grass is always greener on the other side of the 'fence

If you say that **the grass is 'greener**, or **the grass is always 'greener**, or **the grass is always greener on the other side of the 'fence**, you mean that things that you do not, or cannot, have always seem more attractive than the things you do have: *The other man's grass is always greener, and I had the opportunity when I was younger to work abroad.* □ *He was very happy with us, but wanted to see if the grass was greener elsewhere.*

◊ SEE ALSO **the best of both worlds** ▷ WORLDS; **have your cake and eat it** ▷ CAKE

'grass on someone (*informal*)

You **grass on someone** when you inform the authorities of something wrong or illegal that the person has done: *'You don't grass on a 'mate,' he said, and fell silent.*

not let the grass grow under your 'feet

You **don't let the grass grow under your feet** when you do not delay, or waste time: *Travis was not the kind to let the grass grow under his feet.* □ *Get on with it you lot, don't let the grass grow under your feet.*

put someone out to 'grass or **turn someone out to 'grass** or **send someone out to 'grass**

You **put someone out to grass** when you cause them to give up work or retire, usually because they are too old to be effective: *David James is a young man with a mission to put England's number one goalkeeper out to grass.* □ *At the ripe old age of fifty five I've been turned out to grass, so to speak.*

◊ SEE ALSO **be put out to pasture** ▷ PASTURE

Farm animals that are no longer strong enough to work are left out in the fields.

grasshopper

knee-high to a 'grasshopper

You describe someone as **knee-high to a grasshopper** if they are very small: *My father told me that story when I was knee-high to a grasshopper.*

A **grasshopper** is a small jumping insect that makes a harsh noise by rubbing its back legs against its wings.

grave

beyond the 'grave

'**Beyond the grave**' refers to what happens to us after we die: *Her late husband's most recent visit from beyond the grave, Mrs Palko said, came as she was praying.* □ *those unbelieving of a world beyond the grave.*

dig your own 'grave

You **dig your own grave** when you are responsible for harming yourself, or for your own failure: *These are women who dig their own grave by doing all the housework themselves out of resignation.* □ *I heard the whirr of the back wheel as the car dug its own grave.*

so-and-so must be turning in their 'grave (*humorous*)

You say that someone who is already dead **must be turning in their grave** if people are doing or saying something that they would not have approved of: *Your poor mother will be turning in her grave to think of you going out on your own like this.*

to an early 'grave

Someone goes **to an early grave** when they die young: *He didn't need to be a doctor to see that his mother was drinking herself to an early grave.*

◊ SEE ALSO **the death of someone** ▷ DEATH; **the end of someone** ▷ END

greedy

'greedy-guts (*informal*)

You call someone **greedy-guts** if they eat a lot, even when they are no longer hungry.

Greek

it's all Greek to 'me

You say '**it's all Greek to me**', if you do not understand something at all: *I read an article about it in the 'New Scientist', but it's all Greek to me.*

◊ SEE ALSO **double Dutch** ▷ DUTCH; **can't get your head round something** ▷ HEAD

From Shakespeare's *Julius Caesar* I. ii.

grief

come to 'grief

You **come to grief** when you fail, have an accident, or suffer the unpleasant results of something you have been doing: *Candidates who come to grief in exams often lack practice in structuring their thoughts into an effective exam answer.* □ *This was not the first vehicle that had come to grief on that stretch of road.*

◊ SEE ALSO **come a cropper** ▷ CROPPER

grin

grin and 'bear it

You have to **grin and bear it** when you have to tolerate an unpleasant situation because you have no choice: *I'm in a dead-end job, but for the moment I'm just going to have to grin and bear it.*

grip

get a 'grip on yourself or **get a 'grip**

You **get a grip on yourself** when you manage to regain control of your emotions: *Come on, get a grip on yourself; panicking won't get you anywhere.* □ *Jessica breathed deeply, trying to get a grip.*

grips

get to 'grips with

You **get to grips with** a subject, for example, when you start understanding it: *I've never really been into that kind of poetry; I couldn't really get to grips with it.*

grist

grist to someone's 'mill

Something that is described as **grist to your mill** is anything that can be used to your advantage: *All this free publicity was grist to his mill.*

> **Grist** means 'corn for grinding'. A supply of grist keeps a mill operating profitably.

ground

break new 'ground

You **break new ground** when you discover or invent something new: *Far from breaking new ground, most of the work that goes through design offices bears a strong relation to that which has gone before.*

get something off the 'ground

You **get something off the ground** when you cause it to start happening or operating; something **gets off the ground** when it starts happening or operating: *The chances are that he will never get the business off the ground, and he'll never be able to repay the money.* □ *The economic recession of that year forced the Conservative Government to change its policies before they had got off the ground.*

go to 'ground

Someone **goes to ground** when they hide in order to escape from someone or something that is following them: *He went to ground and wasn't heard of again until 1975 when word reached the CIA that he was in Angola.*

hold your 'ground

You **hold your ground** when you argue for something you believe without being intimidated or easily persuaded by other people's arguments: *But Richard held his ground, his fixed look showing that he would not give way.*

◇ SEE ALSO **stick to your guns** ▷ GUNS

the moral 'high ground

Someone who claims, takes, or occupies, **the moral high ground** claims that they are morally superior to someone else: *In film-making terms, South Africa is one of those subjects on which it is fairly easy to occupy the moral high ground.*

on dangerous 'ground

You are **on dangerous ground** when you are talking about a subject that you feel uncomfortable with, and that is likely to offend your listeners: *She realized she was on dangerous ground; she had no option though now, but to continue.*

on safe 'ground

You are **on safe ground** when you are talking about a subject that you feel comfortable with, and that does not offend your listeners: *He had thought he would be on safe ground with this, but the audience seemed bored and restless.*

run to 'ground

You **run** someone or something **to ground** when you find them after a long and difficult search: *That was the police squad who last year ran to ground the fake Giacommetis.*

suit down to the 'ground

Something **suits you down to the ground** when it suits you well, and you are happy with it: *The climate there would probably suit you down to the ground.*

thin on the 'ground

Something that is **thin on the ground** does not exist in large quantities: *Public transport is pretty thin on the ground there, so it's advisable to hire a car.*

guard

catch someone off 'guard

You **catch someone off guard**, or **off their guard**, when you surprise them by doing something that they are not expecting, or that they are not ready for: *He looked up suddenly, catching Emily off her guard.*

◇ SEE ALSO **catch someone napping** ▷ CATCH

off your 'guard

You are **off your guard** when you are not prepared for unexpected events: *The detectives were never off their guard.*

on your 'guard

You are **on your guard** when you are prepared for something to happen and ready to prevent it: *Police are warning residents to be on their guard after two men tricked a pensioner out of £200 yesterday.*

guardian

guardian 'angel

Your **guardian angel** is a spirit who is believed to look after you: *'How on earth did you survive the crash?' 'I don't know; I must have a guardian angel.'*

guess

'anybody's guess

You say that the answer to a question is **anybody's**, or **anyone's, guess** if you think it is impossible to know the answer: *What really happened is anyone's guess, but afterwards each accused the other of cheating.*

an educated 'guess

An **educated guess** is a guess based on all the evidence and knowledge you have available to you: *A little logic mixed with an educated guess or two provided the other figures and the project was complete.*

your guess is as good as 'mine

You say 'your guess is as good as mine' when you have no idea about something: *We sent out a distress signal, but your guess is as good as mine if anyone heard it.*
◇ SEE ALSO **how should I know** or **I wouldn't know** ▷ KNOW

guess 'what

You say to someone **'guess what'** when you are about to tell them something that you think will please or surprise them: *Guess what! I got the job!*

guessing

no prizes for 'guessing

You say **'no prizes for guessing'** if the answer to something is obvious: *Here's his picture; no prizes for guessing his nationality!*

guest

be my 'guest

Be my guest means 'please do', and is used in response to a request.

guinea

'guinea pig

A **guinea pig** is a person used as a subject for an experiment: *I've got a new teaching method I'd like to try out, and you're to be the guinea pig.*

gum

up a 'gum tree (*informal*)

You are **up a gum tree** if you are in a very difficult position: *If all this leaves you up a gum tree, you would be well advised to seek the help of a good lawyer.*

> In Australia, the possum commonly hides up a gum tree when it is being chased.

gun

jump the 'gun

You **jump the gun** when you try to start something before the time is right: *If we jump the gun and put the blame on Werner, we could get ourselves into trouble later on.*

> In a race, you have to wait for the gun to be fired before you can start running.

guns

go great 'guns

You **are going great guns** if you are doing something with energy and vigour: *The company is going great guns at the end of its first year.*

spike someone's 'guns

You **spike someone's guns** when you try to spoil someone's plans because you do not want them to succeed: *So she had concocted this marvellous plan to spike Jenny's guns.*
◇ SEE ALSO **put a spanner in the works** ▷ SPANNER; **put a spoke in someone's wheel** ▷ SPOKE

> In the past, in order to make enemy guns useless, soldiers used to hammer a spike into them.

stick to your 'guns

You **stick to your guns** when you hold your position in an argument: *And there was great admiration for his honesty, his modesty, and determination to stick to his guns.*
◇ SEE ALSO **hold your ground** ▷ GROUND

> A soldier who **sticks to his guns** continues to fire at the enemy and does not run away.

with guns 'blazing

You do something **with guns blazing** when you do it in a determined and angry way: *She would go storming in with all guns blazing, never stopping to think of the possible consequences.*

gut

bust a 'gut (*informal*)

You **bust a gut** when you make a big effort to do something: *Here, let me do that before you bust a gut.*
◇ SEE ALSO **break your back** ▷ BACK; **sweat blood** ▷ BLOOD; **work your guts out** ▷ GUTS

gut 'feeling

You have a **gut feeling** about something when you are quite sure of it, although you have no concrete evidence to prove it: *I had a gut feeling Eric was the right man for us.*

> Your **gut** is your stomach.

guts

have someone's guts for 'garters (*informal, humorous*)

If you say that you will **have someone's guts for garters**, you mean that you will be very angry with them, or that you will punish them: *If you breathe a word to anyone I'll have your guts for garters.*

have the guts to do something

If you **have the guts to do something**, you are not afraid to do it: *He was the only one who had the guts to say what he really 'thought.*

work your 'guts out or slog your 'guts out (*informal*)

You **work,** or **slog, your guts out** when you work very hard: *I worked my guts out getting*

my doctorate, and look where it's got me.
◇ SEE ALSO **break your back** ▷ BACK; **sweat blood** ▷ BLOOD; **bust a gut** ▷ GUT

gutter

'gutter press (*informal*)
The **gutter press** is the name given to the lower quality newspapers that pay more attention to scandals, rather than to more serious matters: *The gutter press particularly enjoyed the story, especially as the artefacts had belonged to a man who had been murdered.*

A **gutter** is a channel at the side of a road, which carries away rain and dirt.

h

habit

kick the 'habit
You **kick the habit** when you give up a bad habit, such as smoking: *Please don't offer me one; I'm trying to kick the habit.*

hackles

make someone's 'hackles rise or raise someone's 'hackles
You **make someone's hackles rise** or **raise their hackles** when you say or do something that annoys them intensely.

◇ SEE ALSO **drive someone round the bend** ▷ BEND; **get someone's goat** ▷ GOAT; **get on someone's nerves** ▷ NERVES; **get up someone's nose** ▷ NOSE; **rub someone up the wrong way** ▷ WAY; **get on someone's wick** ▷ WICK

> When a dog is angry, the hairs on the back of its neck [= the hackles] stand up.

hair (*see also* **hairs**)

get in someone's 'hair
Someone **gets in your hair** when they annoy you by being present all the time when you wish they would go away: *Are the kids getting in your hair over the long summer break?*

keep your 'hair on
'**Keep your hair on**' means 'calm down': *All right, all right! Keep your hair on!*

let your 'hair down
You **let your hair down** when you relax and enjoy yourself without worrying about what other people think about you: *Visitors young and old let their hair down and enjoyed the entertainment.*

◇ SEE ALSO **enter into the spirit** ▷ SPIRIT; **get into the swing of things** ▷ SWING

> In the past, women always used to put their hair up when they went out, only letting it down when they were in private.

make your 'hair curl
Something that would **make your hair curl** would horrify you: *I could tell you tales about her that would make your hair curl.*

make someone's 'hair stand on end
Something that **makes your hair stand on end** terrifies or horrifies you: *His language makes my hair stand on end.*

not turn a 'hair
Someone who does **not turn a hair** is not surprised or shocked: *Nick wouldn't be embarrassed, he could say things like that without turning a hair.*

not a hair out of 'place
Someone who **never has a hair out of place** is always extremely smart and tidy: *He seemed austere and I never saw him with a hair out of place, or a button undone.*

tear your 'hair out over something
You **are tearing your hair out over something** if you are worrying about it or having great difficulties with it: *Anyone else would be tearing their hair out, but you're so calm!*

the hair of the 'dog
The **hair of the dog** is an alcoholic drink taken as a cure after having drunk too much the night before: *It's not that the hair of the dog remedy actually works, it just makes you forget how bad you feel for a while.*

> This idiom comes from the expression 'the hair of the dog that bit you'. People used to believe that if you were bitten by a mad dog you could be cured by putting some hairs from the dog's tail on the wound.

a hair's 'breadth
A **hair's breadth** is a very small distance or amount: *You escaped death by a hair's breadth.*

◇ SEE ALSO **within a whisker** ▷ WHISKER

haircut

pudding basin 'haircut
A **pudding basin haircut** is an unfashionable hairstyle that looks as if it has been created by placing a round bowl on your head and cutting round the edge of it.

hairs

have someone by the short 'hairs (*slang*)
You say that someone **has you by the short hairs** when they have you in their power.

The **short hairs** here refer to a person's pubic hairs [= the hair found around the sexual organs].

split 'hairs

You **split hairs** when you pay too much attention to small details, or make unnecessary distinctions between things which are basically the same.

'that'll put hairs on your chest (informal, humorous)

You say **'that'll put hairs on your chest'** to someone who is about to eat or drink something that is very strong or filling: *A pint of Guinness? That'll put hairs on your chest!*

hale

hale and 'hearty

Hale and hearty is a rather old-fashioned way of saying 'fit and strong': *He was only just sixty, hale and hearty, and still practising as a highly reputed solicitor.*

◊ SEE ALSO **fit as a fiddle** ▷ FIT; **right as rain** ▷ RIGHT

half (see also **halves**)

a such-and-such and a 'half

You describe something as **a such-and-such and a half** if you want to emphasize its size, value, importance, etc: *Breakfast was a meal and a half – porridge with cream, bacon and eggs, thick fresh toast with farm butter, and mugs of sweet tea.*

don't know the 'half of it or haven't heard the 'half of it

You tell someone that they **don't know the half of it** or **haven't heard the half of it** if the situation is even worse than they think it is.

half and 'half

Half and half means 'in two equal amounts': *They decided to split the work half and half. □ He's half and half, in fact a little bit more English if you weigh it up.*

half-'arsed (slang)

A **half-arsed** attempt or plan is one that is weak, or that has not been considered carefully enough: *Have you seen their half-arsed attempt at improving conditions?*

◊ SEE ALSO **half-baked** ▷ HALF

half-'baked

A **half-baked** attempt or plan is one that is weak, or that has not been considered carefully enough: *It is better to report that you had insufficient time to collect certain data than to produce half-baked results.*

◊ SEE ALSO **half-arsed** ▷ HALF

how the other half 'lives

You see **how the other half lives** or **live** when you see how people who are much richer than you or much poorer than you live:

Tomorrow, Katie Wood will be showing us how the other half live when she mixes with guests on a country house weekend in Oxfordshire.

other 'half or better 'half (humorous)

People sometimes refer to their husband, wife, or partner, as their **better half**: *I've checked with my other half and it's fine, we can come. □ My better half's always maintained that if they don't want to go to church, then we won't force them.*

too such-and-such by 'half

You describe someone or something as being **too** clever, for example, **by half** if you think that they are much too clever, for example: *Your trouble, my girl, is that you're too independent by half.*

hallmarks

have all the hallmarks of

Something, such as a crime, that **has**, or **bears**, **all the hallmarks** of the activities of a particular person or group, shows all their typical characteristics: *These policies bear all the hallmarks of 'Thatcherism.*

halt

grind to a 'halt

Someone or something **grinds to a halt** if they finally stop after gradually slowing down: *The engine spluttered and the car slowly ground to a halt.*

halves

go 'halves

You **go halves** with someone on something when you both pay equal amounts for it: *Come on, I insist we go halves this time.*

◊ SEE ALSO **go Dutch** ▷ DUTCH

not do things by 'halves

Someone who does **not do things by halves** always puts all their energy and enthusiasm into the things they do: *She never did anything by halves. She gave one hundred and one per cent of herself to whatever was important at the time.*

hammer

come under the 'hammer

Something that **comes under the hammer** is offered for sale at an auction: *Forty modern Russian paintings and forty designs by Dutch jewellers and silversmiths came under the hammer at Sotheby's yesterday.*

In an auction, the auctioneer uses a hammer to indicate that a sale has been made.

go at it hammer and 'tongs

You **go at it hammer and tongs 1** when you do something with a lot of energy: *I always* *go hammer and tongs at my running.* **2** when you argue or fight violently: *You two fought hammer and tongs to marry her mother.*

hammering

give someone a 'hammering

You **give someone a hammering** when you beat them easily in a football match, for example.

◇ SEE ALSO **wipe the floor with** ▷ FLOOR; **make mincemeat of** ▷ MINCEMEAT

hand *(see also* **hands***)*

a heavy 'hand

You do something with **a heavy hand** when you do it with an unnecessary amount of force: *The real power should be with the people; not with the heavy hand of the government.*

at first 'hand

You experience something **at first hand** when you experience it yourself, and in reality, rather than on television, for example: *His organization has, in fact, collected all the information at first hand from the people themselves.*

at second 'hand

You learn about something **at second hand** when you hear about it from another person, rather than experiencing it yourself: *You may feel safer watching nature at second hand, on television.*

bite the hand that 'feeds you

You **bite the hand that feeds you** when you criticize or attack the person or thing that helps and supports you: *In an organization which stresses the importance of loyalty, employees may feel guilty about biting the hand that feeds them by revealing their dissatisfaction.*

by 'hand

You do something **by hand** when you do it without using machinery: *I still prefer to write personal letters by hand.* □ *All the jewellery sold here is made by hand.*

dab 'hand

If you say that someone is a **dab hand** at something, you mean that they are very skilled at doing it: *Well, I'm a dab hand with the old hammer and nails. Why don't I come up and help you?*

get out of 'hand

An activity **gets out of hand** when it becomes uncontrollable: *They never faced the situation realistically; inflation got out of hand and contributed even more to their downfall.*

give a 'hand or lend a 'hand

1 You **give**, or **lend**, **someone a hand** when you help them: *Could you give me a hand*

with this box, please? **2** An audience **gives someone a hand** or a **big hand** when they clap to show that they appreciate something they have done, or to welcome them on to the stage before a performance: *Let's have a big hand for Oasis!*

give someone a free 'hand

You **give someone a free hand** when you let them organize something in their own way, rather than supervising them yourself: *They had good reason to fear that Sutton, given a free hand, would get rid of them.*

give your right 'hand

You say that you would **give your right hand** for something if you would like to have it very much: *I'd give my right hand to make things different for you here.*

◇ SEE ALSO **give your right arm** ▷ ARM; **give your ears** ▷ EARS; **give your eyeteeth** ▷ EYE-TEETH; **give the world** ▷ WORLD

go hand in 'hand

Two things **go hand in hand** when they always happen or are found together: *Youth and experience do not normally go hand in hand.*

hand in 'glove

You are **hand in glove** with someone when you are very closely associated with them: *This cure for inflation went hand in glove with a rise in unemployment.*

hand in 'hand

Two people are **hand in hand** when they are holding each other's hand as a sign that they like each other: *Michael and Katy ran up, hand in hand.*

'hand-me-down

A **hand-me-down** is an article of clothing that is passed from one child to another: *One of the problems of being the youngest is that you always get to wear hand-me-downs that are three years out-of-date.*

hand over 'fist

You make, or lose, money **hand over fist** when you make, or lose, a lot of money: *Since he started up this business, he's been losing money hand over fist.*

have someone eating out of your 'hand

You **have someone eating out of your hand** if you can persuade them to do anything you want them to do: *I bet you he'll be eating out of your hand by the second beer.*

◇ SEE ALSO **have someone wrapped round your little finger** ▷ FINGER; **have someone right where you want them** ▷ WANT; **have someone eating out of the palm of your hand** ▷ PALM; **have someone in your pocket** ▷ POCKET

keep your 'hand in

You do an activity to **keep your hand in** when you do it so that you do not forget how to do it: *He left journalism, but managed to keep his hand in by writing the staff newspaper.*

◊ SEE ALSO **get your eye in** ▷ EYE

the left hand doesn't know what the right hand is 'doing

You say that **the left hand doesn't know what the right hand is doing** in an organization, for example, when there does not seem to be sufficient communication between two parts of it: *An accord was signed yesterday aiming to shake off local government's image of the left hand not knowing what the right hand is doing.*

near at 'hand or close at 'hand

Someone or something that is **near**, or **close, at hand** is in a place where you can reach them easily if you need them: *She hated walking into a room full of strangers, and hoped Bridget would be near at hand.* □ *The catalogues are easy to use, but if there are any problems, the library staff are always close at hand.*

old 'hand

You describe someone as an **old hand** at something if they have been doing it for a long time and know how to do it well: *I was becoming an old hand; I wasn't nearly as nervous, even though the audience was twice the size.*

on 'hand

You have someone **on hand** if they are present in case they are needed: *John is always on hand if you have trouble with your computer.*

on 'one hand ... on the 'other hand

You use **on (the) one hand ... on the other (hand)** to show two sides of an argument: *Such confusion has, on one hand, led many doctors to reject acupuncture as a superstition, while on the other it has led a large number of people to react by rejecting traditional medicine.*

put your hand in your 'pocket

Someone **puts their hand in their pocket** when they spend money: *Johnny was always a little slow about putting his hand in his pocket* [= he was a bit mean].

take someone in 'hand

You **take someone in hand** when you start trying to restrain and improve their behaviour: *Someone needs to take that child in hand. He's being spoilt rotten.*

try your hand at something

You **try your hand at something** when you do it in order to see if you like it, or to see if you are good at it: *We had run out of bread again, so I tried my hand at 'making some.*

turn your hand to 'anything

Someone who can **turn their hand to any-**thing learns new skills easily and quickly: *Valuable experience can be gained in small agencies because you have to learn to turn your hand to any job that needs doing.*

the upper 'hand

You have **the upper hand** if you are in a more powerful position than someone else; you gain **the upper hand** when you become more powerful than someone else: *The 'just-in-time' manufacturing method quickly led to the Japanese gaining the upper hand.*

wait on someone hand and 'foot

You **wait on someone hand and foot** when you bring them everything they need, so that they do not have to do anything for themselves: *They expect to be waited on hand and foot; they've got no consideration for others.*

with your hand on your 'heart

You say something **with your hand on your heart** when you mean it sincerely: *Can anyone put their hand on their heart and say that they are looking forward to very old age?*

with an iron 'hand

You do something **with an iron hand** when you do it firmly and severely: *He was a dictator and monopolist, ruling with an iron hand in military and civil life.*

with your own fair 'hand (*humorous*)

You say that you have done something **with your own fair hand** when you have made it yourself, rather than buying it in a shop, for example.

handcuffs

golden 'handcuffs

Golden handcuffs are payments made by a company to its more senior employees, in order to persuade them not to leave: *Company pensions were the golden handcuffs which chained staff to a company.*

> **Handcuffs** are two metal rings which are joined together, and which can be fixed around the wrists, usually by the police when they make an arrest.

handle

fly off the 'handle

You **fly off the handle** when you suddenly become very angry: *She flies off the handle without any warning.*

get a 'handle on something

You **get a handle on something** when you become familiar with it so that you can understand it better: *I think I'm starting to get a handle on the situation now, but thanks for your help.*

too hot to 'handle

A subject that is described as **too hot to handle** is one that people try to avoid because it causes difficulty, embarrassment or argument: *Homosexuality was a subject which was too hot to handle at my school.*

hands

beat someone hands 'down

You **beat someone hands down** when you beat them easily.

◊ SEE ALSO **beat someone hollow** ▷ BEAT

get into the wrong 'hands or fall into the wrong 'hands

Something that **has got**, or **fallen, into the wrong hands** has been acquired by someone who is dishonest: *If such advanced technology were to get into the wrong hands, it could change the history of this planet.* □ *A crossed cheque gives some protection against fraud if it falls into the wrong hands.*

have your 'hands full

You say that you **have your hands full** if you are very busy: *And Mother had her hands full coping with the housework and looking after four old people.*

in the hands of 'such-and-such or in 'so-and-so's hands

Something that is **in the hands of** a particular person is in their possession: *Within society, power is in the hands of a small number of individuals and groups who may be prominent in industry, in financial, or in political circles.* □ *Unsold copies of his book are in the hands of the receiver.*

◊ SEE ALSO **in someone's charge** ▷ CHARGE

in safe 'hands

You say that something is **in safe hands** if it is being looked after by someone who can be trusted: *You can step on board close to home, know your luggage is in safe hands, and travel in carefree comfort to your hotel near Paris.*

sit on your 'hands

You **sit on your hands** when you do nothing, when people expect you to do something: *The Government cannot remain complacently sitting on its hands in the face of an economic crisis which is damaging all our communities.*

throw up your 'hands

You **throw up your hands** in horror or despair, for example, when you show great horror, anger, or despair: *Of course everyone threw up their hands and said it was impossible.*

◊ SEE ALSO **throw up your arms** ▷ ARMS

wash your hands of

You say that you have **washed your hands of** someone or something when you no longer want to have anything to do with them: *The Government seems to be washing its hands of all its 'industry, as it hands it over to the free market.* □ *They decided to wash their hands of the whole af'fair.* □ *I'm washing my hands of that 'man, he's caused me nothing but trouble.*

win hands 'down

You **win hands down** when you beat someone very easily: *When we had a quiz, Ken always won hands down.*

with your bare 'hands

You fight, or defend yourself, **with your bare hands** when you do so without any weapons: *A court was told yesterday that the victim of a knife attack fought off his assailant with his bare hands.*

hang

get the 'hang of

You **get the hang of** something when you start understanding how to do it, or how it works: *I think I'm starting to get the hang of this new software at last.*

hanky-panky

hanky-'panky(*humorous*)

Hanky-panky is a humorous way of referring to sex, especially when it is illicit: *She checked to make sure that no hanky-panky was going on under the table between Piers and her daughter.*

ha'pennies

not have two ha'pennies to rub to'gether

Someone who **does not have two ha'pennies to rub together** is very poor.

◊ SEE ALSO **not have a red cent** ▷ CENT; **not have two pennies to rub together** ▷ PENNIES; **not have a penny to your name** ▷ PENNY

happy

happy as a 'sandboy

Someone who is **happy as a sandboy** is very pleased about something, or in a good mood: *I persuaded poor old Ed to take some of this stuff for his back, and it's done him a power of good. He's as happy as a sandboy now.*

◊ SEE ALSO **pleased as Punch** ▷ PLEASED

happy-go-'lucky

A **happy-go-lucky** person enjoys life and does not worry about things too much: *He found that he couldn't go out with the lads anymore, and he felt he'd lost his happy-go-lucky side.*

hard

hard and 'fast

A **hard and fast** rule is one which cannot easily be changed: *The rules aren't hard and fast – they're just supposed to be a guide.*

hard-'done-by

You feel **hard-done-by** when you feel sorry for yourself because you think you have been treated unfairly.

hark

hark at 'so-and-so

You say **'hark at so-and-so!'** when you hear someone criticizing someone else for doing something that they too are guilty of, or when you think someone has too high an opinion of themselves: *'Ooh, just hark at you, speaking all lah-de-dah!' Gloria giggled. 'You've got yourself a posh accent, just like Mrs H.'*

◇ SEE ALSO **you're a fine one to talk** or **you can talk** or **you can't talk** ▷ TALK; **look who's talking** ▷ LOOK

> **Hark** is an old-fashioned word which means 'listen'.

harm

out of harm's 'way

You say that you are putting something **out of harm's way** when you tidy it away in a safe place.

harness

back in 'harness

You are **back in harness** when you come back to work after a period of absence.

hassle

no 'hassle

You say **'no hassle'** to show that what you are doing for someone is not a problem for you.

◇ SEE ALSO **no bother** ▷ BOTHER; **no problem** ▷ PROBLEM; **no probs** ▷ PROBS

hat

'hat trick

A **hat trick** is a group of three wins or successes, one after the other: *Team captain Peter Blyth will be going for a hat trick of wins as captain – all with different teams.*

> In cricket, if a player got three players out in a row, he used to be entitled to a new hat from his club.

keep something under your 'hat

You **keep something under your hat** when you do not tell anyone about it: *He said that somebody or other discovered America before Columbus, but decided it was best to keep it under his hat.*

◇ SEE ALSO **keep your counsel** ▷ COUNSEL; **keep something to yourself** ▷ KEEP; **mum's the word** ▷ MUM

pass the 'hat round

You **pass the hat round** when you try to collect money from people: *We're going to pass the hat round later, buy some beer and go back to their place.*

take your 'hat off to so-and-so

You say that you **take your hat off to** a certain person when you admire something they have done: *I take my hat off to her – she did all that by herself with two kids and a full-time job to hold down.*

talk through your 'hat

Someone who **is talking through their hat** is speaking without having sufficient knowledge of the subject in question.

have

have someone 'on

You **are having someone on** if you are teasing them by trying to make them believe something that isn't true: *Oh come on, you're having me on.*

have it 'out with someone

You **have it out with someone** when you finally talk to them about something they have done that makes you angry: *I finally decided to have it out with him; I couldn't bear all that suspicion.*

◇ SEE ALSO **have a bone to pick with someone** ▷ BONE

have someone 'over or have someone 'round

You **have someone over** or **round** when they come to visit you in your home after having been invited by you: *We're thinking of having a few people over tomorrow evening; do you fancy coming?*

hay

hit the 'hay

You **hit the hay** when you go to bed: *Time I hit the hay. Good night everyone.*

> **Hay** is grass that has been cut and dried so that it can be used to feed animals. People sometimes use it for sleeping on outdoors.

make hay while the 'sun shines

If you tell someone to **make hay while the sun shines**, you mean that they should take advantage of the current favourable circumstances. *The price is right. Make hay while the sun shines, you know.*

◇ SEE ALSO **strike while the iron is hot** ▷ IRON

head

an old head on young 'shoulders

A child who is described as having **an old head on young shoulders** is very wise, or carries a lot of responsibility in comparison with other children of his or her age.

bang your 'head against the wall

You say that you **are**, or that you feel like you **are, banging your head against the wall** when you have the impression that something you are doing or saying is having no effect at all: *If you get into a situation where you're banging your head against a brick wall, then you get out of the situation and move on to something else.*

bring to a 'head

You **bring** a situation **to a head** when you feel that it has reached a point where something must be done about it; a situation **comes to a head** when someone finally does something about a difficult situation: *The Rachman affair brought matters to a head, and new legislation had to be brought in.* □ *The strained relationship between staff and management came to a head in the form of widespread industrial action in 1978.*

bury your head in the 'sand

You **bury your head in the sand** when you try to ignore a problem, in the hope that it will go away: *If you can't afford to repay your debts, don't bury your head in the sand.*

can't get your 'head around something

You say that you **can't get your head round something**, such as a new concept, when you have tried very hard, but you still can't understand it: *I just can't seem to get my head around this post-modernism stuff.*
◇ SEE ALSO **double Dutch** ▷ DUTCH; **it's all Greek to me** ▷ GREEK

can't make head or 'tail of

You say that you **can't make head or tail of** something, such as a piece of information, when you can't understand it: *I can't make head or tail of these instructions.*

from head to 'foot or from head to 'toe

Someone or something affects you **from head to foot** or **toe** if it affects your whole body: *He was trembling from head to toe.* □ *There she was, Poppy, dressed from head to foot in black.*

go to someone's 'head

1 Success **goes to your head** if it makes you over-confident: *All the publicity she's been getting has gone to her head.* **2** An alcoholic drink **goes to your head** if it makes you feel drunk: *He was suddenly tired and the beer was going to his head.*

have your 'head screwed on

Someone **has their head screwed on** if they make wise decisions, and do not easily let people deceive them: *Oh, she's got her head screwed on all right, despite what she leads people to believe.*

head and shoulders above

Someone who is **head and shoulders above** everyone else is **1** very tall: *Towering head and shoulders above the 'customs officer, the man strode in, his face as dark as an impending storm.* **2** much better than them at something: *This success had given him the confidence to stand head and shoulders above the 'rest.*

'head butt

A **head butt** is a way of attacking someone by forcefully hitting them on the head with the front of the head: *The judge said: 'There are ways of calming an aggressive drinker more acceptable than a head butt.'*

'head case

If you call someone a **head case**, you mean that they are mad or very foolish.
◇ SEE ALSO **basket case** ▷ BASKET; **nut-case** ▷ NUT

'head in the clouds

You have your **head in the clouds** if you do not consider the realities of a situation: *He seemed to have his head in the clouds, to be living in a dream world.*

head over heels in 'love

You are, or you fall, **head over heels in love** if you are so in love that everything else in your life loses importance: *We met, fell head over heels in love in a shockingly short time, and were still in love 30 years later when he died.*

head to 'head

A **head to head** is a competition between two people or teams who are very close to each other in ability: *It's going to be a head to head between Mansell and Senna this weekend.*

hold your 'head up high

You can **hold your head up high** if you do not have any feelings of guilt or shame: *I was told by my mother always to hold my head up high, and remember that I was a MacLeod.*

'hole in your head

You say that you need something like a **hole in the head** when you do not want it at all because it causes so much trouble: *Oh please, not now, I need this conversation like a hole in the head.*

keep a cool 'head or keep your 'head

You **keep a cool head** or **keep your head** when you stay calm in a stressful situation: *Campbell kept a cool head and handled things perfectly.* □ *As a former BBC war correspondent, he knew how to keep his head.*

laugh your 'head off

You **laugh your head off** when you laugh a lot about something: *Just because I don't go round laughing my head off all the time, doesn't mean I'm annoyed.*

lose your 'head

You **lose your head** when you lose control of yourself and do not stay calm: *As soon as I saw the photographers, I lost my temper, lost my head.*

not right in the 'head

Someone who is **not right in the head** is mentally ill, or behaves in a strange, disturbing way: *To tell you the truth, I don't think she's right in the head, poor thing.*

out of your 'head (*informal*)

Someone who is **out of their head** is very drunk.

◇ SEE ALSO **pissed as a fart** or **newt** ▷ PISSED; **rat-arsed** ▷ RAT

over your 'head

Something goes **over your head** when you do not pay enough attention to it, or when it is too complicated for you to understand: *Some of what you said went straight over my head, but on the whole it was interesting.*

◇ SEE ALSO **beyond you** ▷ BEYOND

stand something on its 'head

You **stand something on its head** when you cause people to doubt something that they have long believed to be true: *Pollock had stood the art of painting on its head, reversed it, negated it.*

take something into your 'head or get something into your 'head

You **take**, or **get, something into your head** when you decide that something is the case, and you refuse to change your mind: *For some reason, she's got it into her head that I don't care about her.*

use your 'head

You say to someone '**use your head**' when you think that thay are not trying hard enough to find a solution to something: *Well why don't you use your head and go and do it yourself?*

hear

not hear yourself 'think or hardly hear yourself 'think

You say that you **cannot**, or that you **can hardly, hear yourself think** if you are disturbed by a lot of noise.

heart

after your own 'heart

You say that a certain person is a man, woman, etc, **after your own heart** if they appreciate something that you also appreciate very much: *You like good malt whisky? Ah, there's a man after my own heart.*

bless so-and-so's 'heart (*informal*)

1 You say '**bless so-and-so's heart**' about someone when they have done something very sweet or funny, or when you are talking about, or remembering, them fondly: *And this is a photo of my old Mum, bless her heart; she died last year.* **2** You say '**bless your heart**' to someone when they have done something kind for you: *Oh bless your heart, that's great.*

by 'heart

You know something **by heart** if you know it so well that you can repeat it from memory with no mistakes: *In his day, he said, students were grounded in spelling and had learned poetry and the Bible by heart.*

◇ SEE ALSO **off pat** ▷ PAT

cry your 'heart out or sob your 'heart out

Someone who **is crying**, or **sobbing**, **their heart out**, is crying hard and for a long time, with great sadness.

◇ SEE ALSO **weep buckets** ▷ BUCKETS; **cry your eyes out** ▷ EYES

eat your 'heart out (*informal*)

If you say '**eat your heart out** so-and-so', or 'so-and-so **eat your heart out**', you jokingly mean that you have done something even better than that person, who is already famous for being good at it: *Nice guitar playing; hey, Jimi Hendrix, eat your heart out.*

find it in your 'heart

You **find it in your heart** to feel a certain way if you make yourself feel that way: *I may find it in my heart to forgive her.* □ *He could not find it in his heart to condemn his brother for what he had done.*

harden your 'heart

You **harden your heart** when you show or feel less emotion than before: *Hardening his heart, he turned his back on her.*

have a heavy 'heart

You **have a heavy heart** when you are upset or unhappy about something: *She gave the letter to the postman with a heavy heart, wondering if she would ever see her sister again.*

◇ SEE ALSO **heart in your boots** ▷ HEART

heart and 'soul

You do, or feel, something **heart and soul** when you do or feel it completely: *They committed themselves heart and soul to what they were doing.* □ *She loved him with all her heart and soul.*

heart 'bleeds for

You say that your **heart bleeds for** so-and-so when you feel deeply sorry for them; people sometimes use this idiom sarcastically to mean that they have no sympathy for a certain person: *Her heart bled for Cowdrey, for he looked desperate, panic-stricken.*

heart in your 'boots

Your **heart is in your boots** if you are upset or unhappy about something: *I had no alternative but to follow her, my heart in my boots.*

◇ SEE ALSO **have a heavy heart** ▷ HEART

heart in your 'mouth

Your **heart is in your mouth** when you feel very nervous or afraid about what is about to happen: *Hesitantly she followed, her heart in her mouth, creeping nervously down the dark, damp pathway.*

'heart in the right place

You say that someone's **heart is in the right place** when you are recognizing that their intentions are kind, even if the results of their actions do not help anyone: *He's a bit mixed up, but his heart's in the right place.*

heart of 'gold

Someone who has a **heart of gold** is very kind and generous.

heart of 'stone

Someone who has a **heart of stone** is unemotional and uncaring: *It needs a heart of stone not to sympathize with someone in this predicament.*

your 'heart sinks

Your heart sinks when you are suddenly very disappointed about something: *My heart sank when I saw Richard's car outside the house. I wasn't looking forward to telling him about the secrets I'd been keeping.*

heart skips a 'beat or heart misses a 'beat

Your **heart skips**, or **misses, a beat** when you are momentarily very excited: *You see him across the room. Your heart skips a beat.*

heart-to-'heart

Two people have a **heart-to-heart** when they talk to each other honestly about their feelings.

in your heart of 'hearts

You know, or feel, something **in your heart of hearts** when you know or feel it, even though you do not really want to admit it: *Can you really say, in your heart of hearts, that you are looking forward to old age?*

lose your 'heart

You **lose your heart** to someone when you fall in love with them: *Nicholas lost his heart and knew for certain that at last, without doubt or question, he had fallen in love.*

open your 'heart

You **open your heart** when you let down any emotional barriers you may have, and allow yourself to feel compassion: *Open your heart to find room for these children.*

put heart and 'soul into

You **put heart and soul into** an activity when you do it with all your energy and enthusiasm.

set your 'heart on something

You say that someone **has set their heart on something** when they have decided that they want something very much: *To help him over his ordeal she has bought him the mountain bike he had set his heart on.*

◇ SEE ALSO **set your sights on** ▷ SIGHTS

strike at the 'heart of

You **strike at the heart of** a problem when you attempt to solve it directly: *This decision struck at the heart of problems that have existed here for years.*

wear your heart on your 'sleeve

Someone who **wears their heart on their sleeve** does not, or cannot hide their emotions.

young at 'heart

Someone who is described as **young at heart** is old in years, but still thinks, and sometimes acts, in a young and lively way: *Holidays for the young and young at heart!*

hearts

lonely 'hearts

The **lonely hearts** column in a newspaper is the section in which people place advertisements for finding new friends or lovers: *He opened the paper at the lonely hearts section. When would he find someone to call his own?*

Heath

Heath 'Robinson

You humorously describe a piece of machinery or other equipment as **Heath Robinson** if it seems to have a lot of working parts that together perform a relatively minor task: *the unnecessary complexity of the car's bizarre, Heath Robinson, clap-hands windscreen wipers.*

heave

give someone the heave-'ho

If someone **gives you the heave-ho**, they get rid of you or take away your job; if you **get the heave-ho**, you are not wanted any more: *The majority thought differently, however, and voted to give him the heave-ho in Labour's favour by a margin of 9%.*

◇ SEE ALSO **give someone the boot** ▷ BOOT; **give someone the elbow** ▷ ELBOW; **give someone the push** ▷ PUSH

heaven

for heaven's 'sake
You introduce a request with **for heaven's sake** when you want someone to stop doing something that is annoying you: *For heaven's sake can you be quiet?*

heaven for'bid
You add **heaven forbid** to something you have said could happen as a way of saying that you sincerely hope it will not.
◊ SEE ALSO **God forbid** ▷ GOD

heaven 'help
1 You say '**heaven help you, him,** or **her,**'to warn someone that something unpleasant will happen if someone does not do a particular thing: *Heaven help you if you don't take proper care of her.* **2** You also say '**heaven help him, her,**or **them,**' if you feel sorry for someone: *Heaven help him, the poor man, he didn't even know how to boil an egg.* **3** You say **heaven help us** if you do not like the thought of what he is suggesting: *Heaven help us, what's he going to do now?*

heaven 'knows or heaven alone knows
Heaven knows or **heaven alone knows** means 'I have no idea': *Heaven knows how many calls we've already missed.*
◊ SEE ALSO **Christ knows** ▷ CHRIST; **God knows** or **God alone knows** ▷ GOD; **goodness knows** or **goodness only knows** ▷ GOODNESS; **Lord knows** ▷ LORD

heaven-'sent
You describe something as **heaven sent** when you are very relieved and happy that it has happened, or that you have received it: *As we start afresh to build a new church, we have a heaven sent opportunity to try again for this possibility of godly unity.*

in heaven's 'name
You ask why, what, how, etc **in heaven's name** something is the case when you are amazed that it is so: *Why in heaven's name are you dressed up like that?*
◊ SEE ALSO **in God's name** ▷ GOD

in seventh 'heaven
You are **in seventh heaven** when you are very happy about something, or enjoying yourself immensely: *Gloria was in seventh heaven as she wandered around the shops knowing she could buy whatever she liked.*
◊ SEE ALSO **walk on air** ▷ AIR; **thrilled to bits** ▷ BITS; **on cloud nine** ▷ CLOUD; **over the moon** ▷ MOON; **on top of the world** ▷ TOP

move heaven and 'earth
You **move heaven and earth** to achieve something when you do everything possible to make sure it happens: *You shake, you sweat, you're pale and weak. We've all experienced it and most of us would move heaven and earth to avoid it.*

thank 'heaven or thank 'heavens
You say '**thank heaven** or **heavens**', or '**thank heaven** or **heavens** for such-and-such',when you are very relieved or grateful for it.

heavens

the heavens 'open
The heavens open when it suddenly starts raining very hard.

heebie-jeebies

heebie-'jeebies
Something that gives you the **heebie-jeebies** makes you feel afraid or anxious: *Doesn't it give you the heebie-jeebies when you see him up there, hanging on by his finger-tips?*

heels

close on someone's 'heels or hard on someone's 'heels or hot on someone's 'heels
You are **close,** or **hard,** or **hot, on someone's heels** if you are chasing them and you have almost caught them: *They're close on our heels now – come on, we must get away.*

dig your 'heels in
You **dig your heels in** when you stubbornly refuse to change your mind about something: *You can try and persuade her, but she's likely to dig her heels in on this one.*

take to your 'heels
You **take to your heels** when you start running as fast as you can, usually in order to escape from someone or something.

hell

all 'hell breaks loose
All hell breaks loose when people suddenly panic, or when there is sudden great activity and noise: *As the news of the President's resignation reached the Stock Exchange, all hell broke loose.*

In some religions, **Hell** is the place where bad people are believed to go after their death. It is imagined as being under the ground and full of flames.

bloody 'hell (*vulgar*)
Bloody hell is a vulgar expression of annoyance: *Bloody hell. I can't get anything right today.* □ *Why the bloody hell did you marry him if you want to be on your own?*

come hell or high 'water
You say that you will do something **come hell or high water** if you are determined to do it, even if you have to fight for it: *I'll do it tomorrow, I promise. Come hell or high water.*

get the hell 'out of (*informal*)

You **get the hell out of** a place when you leave it very quickly: *Okay, let's get the hell out of here.* □ *Get the hell out of here!*

give someone 'hell

You **give someone hell** when you shout at them, criticize them, or cause them pain or suffering: *They've been giving me hell about employing you, but I'm sure I've chosen the right person for the job.*

◇ SEE ALSO **send someone away with a flea in their ear** ▷ FLEA; **give someone a piece of your mind** ▷ PIECE; **read the riot act** ▷ RIOT; **give someone the rough side of your tongue** ▷ SIDE; **tear someone off a strip** ▷ STRIP

go to 'hell (*offensive*)

You tell someone to **go to hell** if you are very angry or upset because of something they have done or said, and you want them to go away: *I don't give a damn. You can go to hell.*

◇ SEE ALSO **go to the devil** ▷ DEVIL

go to 'hell and back

You say that you **have been to hell and back** when you have been through a period of extreme emotional suffering: *We have been to hell and back, but our love for this little boy has kept us going.*

hell's 'bells

Hell's bells is an expression of surprise, anger or fear.

hell bent on

You are **hell bent on** doing or achieving something when you are determined to achieve it, and you will not let anyone stop you: *And I was speeding into the darkness with a man who seemed to be hell bent on risking our lives for no apparent 'reason.*

'hell freezes over

You say that **hell will freeze over** before something happens if you believe that it will never happen: *Their last win was 22 years ago, and it looks like hell will freeze over before they manage to do it again.* □ *You're right, you'll wait. You'll wait till hell freezes over.*

> Hell is usually imagined to be an unbearably hot place.

hell on 'earth

You describe a place or situation as **hell on earth** if you find it unbearable: *The party was hell on earth, with everybody awkward and self-conscious.*

'hell to pay

You tell someone that there will be **hell to pay** if they do a certain thing, as a warning that someone will be very angry with them if they do it: *There'll be hell to pay when the officers hear about this in the morning.*

the 'hell you do or **the 'hell you are** or **like 'hell** (*informal*)

You answer someone with **the hell you do**, or **are**, or **can**, etc, or **like hell**, to show that you don't believe them or that you don't agree with them: *'I generally do quite a lot of work around the house.' 'The hell you do.'*

play 'hell with or **play merry 'hell with**

Someone or something **plays hell**, or **plays merry hell with**, something when they cause confusion: *The band have been playing merry hell with their distributors, delaying the launch of their new album by yet another three months.*

raise 'hell

You **raise hell** when you cause a noisy disturbance: *Write to your local MP, support the rallies, and generally raise hell until they are forced to react.*

◇ SEE ALSO **raise Cain** ▷ CAIN; **kick up a stink** ▷ STINK

see someone in 'hell

You say that you will **see someone in hell** before you do something if you are determined not to do it: *She stared out of the window. She'd see him in hell before she spoke to him again, she fumed.*

hello

hello 'stranger

You say **'hello stranger'** as an informal way of greeting someone whom you haven't seen for some time.

help

beyond 'help

Someone who is **beyond help** is too stupid, incompetent or ill to be worth trying to help: *Some of the animals were beyond help and had to be put to sleep, which was upsetting.*

hen

'hen night or **'hen party**

A **hen night** or **party** is a party organized by a woman who is about to get married, to which she invites her female friends only: *We all thought we were going out for a quiet night with the girls, but it suddenly transpired that we'd been invited to a raucous hen night, at the local striptease club.*

herd

'herd instinct

The **herd instinct** is the tendency which many people have to go with the majority, rather than against it, or to meet in places where there are many other people: *What makes people go to these gatherings? In my view it's the herd instinct.*

> A **herd** is a group of certain kinds of animal, such as sheep or cows.

hero

'hero worship

Hero worship is the adoration of, and admiration for, someone that you do not know personally, usually a famous person: *Even as an adult his hero worship of the man did not fade.*

hide

not see hide nor 'hair of

You say that you **have not seen hide nor hair of** someone when you have not seen them at all: *Nobody has seen hide nor hair of him since he was here last month.*

save your 'own hide

You do something to **save your own hide** when you do it so that you personally will not have to suffer some kind of disaster: *He'll say anything in court, just to save his own hide.*

tan someone's 'hide

To **tan someone's hide** means to beat them physically: *If I find you out of bed again I'll tan your hide, boy.*

higgledy-piggledy

higgledy-'piggledy

Things that are described as **higgledy-piggledy** are not tidy, straight or well-ordered: *Small higgledy-piggledy streets run back up the hill from the main beach, and here you'll find an assortment of small shady bars.*

high

high and 'mighty

A person is described as **high and mighty** if they act as if they think they are more important than other people: *Don't get all high and mighty with me. Why don't you just admit it?*

◇ SEE ALSO **full of your own importance** ▷ IMPORTANCE

hill

over the 'hill

Someone who is **over the hill** is considered to be too old to perform a particular activity: *Isn't he a bit over the hill to be taking up a job like that?*

◇ SEE ALSO **past it** ▷ PAST; **no spring chicken** ▷ SPRING; **long in the tooth** ▷ TOOTH; **not getting any younger** ▷ YOUNGER

hit

hit it 'off

You **hit it off** with someone you have just met when you like each other and quickly form a good relationship: *She was a gentle quiet girl, deeply thoughtful, and we hit it off from the start.*

hit-and-'miss

A situation that is described as **hit-and-miss** depends more on chance than on good planning or organization: *The system at present is far too hit-and-miss. Can't we have a more controlled system of payment?*

hit someone when they're 'down

If someone **hits you when you are down**, they criticize or attack you when you are already suffering from unpleasant circumstances: *He was a big and unfair bully who believed in kicking a man when he was down.*

hive

hive of ac'tivity or hive of 'industry

You describe a place as a **hive of activity** or **industry** if everyone there is very busy: *The Market House was a hive of activity, with the selling of corn and other farming commodities.*

hobby-horse

'hobby-horse

Your **hobby-horse** is a subject that you feel strongly about, and keep talking about, often to the point where people get bored with you: *Once he was on his hobby-horse, Philippe became an unbearable bore.*

hockey

jolly 'hockey sticks

'**Jolly hockey sticks**' refers to the characteristic behaviour and attitudes of some girls and women from British private girls' schools who exhibit great enthusiasm, especially for sports, and a loud, confident manner: *I got to know the house officer quite well eventually, very 'jolly hockey sticks' and friendly.*

hocus-pocus

hocus-'pocus

You describe something such as a theory or explanation as **hocus-pocus** when you consider it to be deliberately deceptive, or unclear in order to deceive people: *If you ask me, that's all a load of hocus-pocus designed to make you forget about the real problems.*

◇ SEE ALSO **a load of rubbish** ▷ LOAD

hog

go the whole 'hog

You **go the whole hog** when you do something as completely as possible: *In the end we decided to go the whole hog and get a professional photographer in to do the job.*

holds

no holds 'barred

No holds barred means that nothing is omitted or forbidden: *He was under immense pressure to support no holds barred military action from UN forces.*

hole

burn a 'hole in your pocket

Something, especially money, **burns a hole in your pocket** when you have the tendency to use it as long as you have it, rather than saving it: *If you find that money burns a hole in your pocket, why not come in and have a chat with one of our finance advisors?*

dig yourself into a 'hole

You **dig yourself into a hole** when you make a situation even worse for yourself, especially when you are desperately trying to improve it: *Don't try and make any more excuses; you're just digging yourself deeper into a hole.*

need such-and-such like you need a 'hole in the head

You say that you **need such-and-such like you need a hole in the head** if it will cause you a lot of problems and trouble: *At that time, just before an election, the Government needed a scandal like they needed a hole in the head.*

holes

pick 'holes in

You **pick holes in** someone or something if you criticize them, especially for insignificant faults: *If you pick too many holes in your students' work, they may lose motivation.*

◇ SEE ALSO **pull to bits** ▷ BITS; **pull or tear to pieces** ▷ PIECES; **tear or rip to shreds** ▷ SHREDS

home

feel at 'home

You **feel at home** in a place if you feel comfortable and at ease there: *It's funny, I felt at home as soon as I walked into this place.*

hit 'home

Something **hits home** when you suddenly realize its implications: *Frankly, I'm surprised the message hasn't hit home yet; there just isn't adequate medical care in the area.*

hoo-ha

'hoo-ha *(informal)*

A **hoo-ha** is a big fuss: *After a considerable hoo-ha, girls were recognized as fit to be young explorers and the first mixed expedition went to Arctic Norway in 1980.*

hook

hook line and 'sinker

You fall for a joke **hook line and sinker** when someone tells you something that is not true and you believe them: *I fell for that one hook line and sinker; they had me running around in a terrible panic for a while.*

> **Hook**, **line** and **sinker** are all fishing terms.

let someone off the 'hook

You **let someone off the hook** when you decide not to punish them for something wrong they have done: *I tell you, they will not be let off the hook for this; discrimination will not be tolerated here.*

sling your 'hook

You tell someone to **sling their hook** if you think they are being rude to you and you want them to go away.

hooks

get your 'hooks into

Someone **has got their hooks into** you if they hold or influence you strongly: *It never makes sense to borrow from backstreet money lenders. Once they've got their hooks into you, they will never let go.*

hoot

not care a 'hoot or not give a 'hoot, or not care two 'hoots or not give two 'hoots

You do **not care** or **give**, **a hoot**, or **two hoots** if you do not care about something at all: *She doesn't give two hoots about other people, as long as she's okay.*

◇ SEE ALSO **not give a damn** ▷ DAMN; **not care a fig** or **two figs**; ▷ FIG, FIGS; **not give a monkey's** ▷ MONKEY; **not give a shit** ▷ SHIT; **not care a sod** ▷ SOD; **not give a tinker's cuss** ▷ TINKER; **not give** or **care a toss** ▷ TOSS; **not care** or **give tuppence** ▷ TUPPENCE

hop

catch on the 'hop

You **catch someone on the hop** when they are not ready for, or expecting, you: *British tourists were caught on the hop yesterday as storms spread across southern Europe.*

'hop it

You tell someone to **hop it** if they are doing something they shouldn't, and you want them to go away.

◇ SEE ALSO **beat it** ▷ BEAT

hope

hope against 'hope

You **hope against hope** that something is the case when you very much want it to be the case, although you know that it is unlikely: *And so she would return, to watch and listen, and to hope against hope that all would come well for both Richard and Beth.*

not have a hope in 'hell
Someone who **hasn't got a hope in hell** of achieving something will not be able to achieve it under any circumstances: *They've been training hard all season, but if you ask me, they haven't got a hope in hell against this lot.*

◊ SEE ALSO **not have** or **stand a cat in hell's chance** ▷ CAT; **not a snowball's chance in hell** ▷ SNOWBALL

hopes

pin your 'hopes on
You **pin your hopes on** a particular person or thing when you depend on their success for your own happiness or satisfaction: *'Don't pin your hopes on it,' warned David. 'I don't want to see you hurt.'*

hornet

'hornet's nest
A **hornet's nest** is an unpleasant situation where a lot of people are dissatisfied or angry: *'Forbes has stirred up a hornet's nest. He intends to get other unions to lobby the Government for some sort of taxation on the hotel industry.'*

A **hornet** is a large wasp with a powerful sting.

horns

draw in your 'horns or **pull in your 'horns**
You **draw,** or **pull in your horns** when you start spending less money or going out less often than before: *A busy social life could cost a packet, so you might have to pull in your horns a wee bit.*

horse

flog a dead 'horse
You say that you **are flogging a dead horse** if you feel that what you are doing is no longer having any effect: *You'll be flogging a dead horse if you try to make him change his ways; I gave up years ago.*

'horse sense
Horse sense is knowledge about what the wisest thing to do in a situation would be: *These homeless kids know what to do, they get whatever they can whenever they can. It's plain horse sense.*

I'm so hungry I could eat a 'horse
You say that you **are so hungry you could eat a horse** if you are very hungry.

on your high 'horse
Someone who is **on their high horse** is forcefully telling people how they think things should be done: *Well there were one or two who got on their high horse, you know, saying, 'It's disgusting', but I never did because I wouldn't condemn people.*

horses

hold your 'horses
You say to someone **'hold your horses!'** in order to tell them to stop and think before they go ahead and do something: *She could be heard walking to the front door, grumbling to herself, 'Hold your horses, I'm coming, I'm coming.'*

wild 'horses
You say that **wild horses** wouldn't, or couldn't, make something happen, if you feel that nothing could make it happen: *Wild horses would not have dragged that secret out of me.*

hot

hot and 'bothered
You feel **hot and bothered** when you are hot and uncomfortable, because you are embarrassed or you are in a place that is not properly ventilated: *Pickerage, already flushed, looked down at the sheets, hot and bothered.*

hots

have the 'hots for someone
If someone **has the hots** for someone else, they find that person attractive, and would like to form a romantic or sexual relationship with them: *Do you think he's got the hots for this fabulous brown-eyed career woman he's met in London?*

hour

your hour has 'come
You think **your hour has come** if you think you are going to die: *I caught a glimpse of her, eyes red with fury, and I wondered if my last hour had come.*

in your hour of 'need
Someone who helps or abandons you **in your hour of need**, does so at a time when you need emotional or financial support: *How could he abandon his father now, in his hour of need?*

hours

till 'all hours
You stay out **till all hours** when you come home in the early hours of the morning: *Better not wake her, she worked till all hours last night, she deserves a bit of a lie-in.*

house

eat someone out of house and 'home

You say that someone **has eaten you out of house and home** when you are rather surprised because they have come to stay at your home, and eaten a surprisingly large amount of your food: *Dr Neil would eat them out of house and home if he continued to run through biscuits at his present rate.*

get on like a 'house on fire

Two or more people **get on like a house on fire** when they greatly enjoy each other's company: *She asked specifically to be seated next to him. They got on like a house on fire and didn't stop talking afterwards.*

set your 'own house in order or put your 'own house in order

You tell someone to **set**, or **put, their own house in order** when you think that they should solve their own problems before they start trying to advise you on yours: *The Government would do well to put its own house in order before it starts attacking the Opposition.*

hows

the hows and the 'whys

The hows and the whys of a situation are the reasons and explanations for its existence: *And we want to know the hows and whys, the purposes of this project.*

hue

hue and 'cry

There is, or people raise, a **hue and cry** when they protest angrily about something: *If I don't clean the place up there'll be a hue and cry.*

huff

huff and 'puff

You **huff and puff** when you draw people's attention to the fact that you are having to use a lot of mental or physical energy to complete a task: *After much huffing and puffing, the Government backed down from implementing most of these proposals.*

hump

have the 'hump or get the 'hump

Someone who **has**, or **gets, the hump** is sulking because they could not get someone to agree with them about something, or to let them do something: *He was gentle enough about it, but of course Lisabeth got the hump.* □ *John started acting very oddly. Either because he had the hump or because he thought it would make for a good show he started smashing the footlights one by one.*
◇ SEE ALSO **stew in your own juice** ▷ JUICE

i

ice

break the 'ice
You **break the ice** when you do something that makes people feel more at ease with each other, usually at the beginning of a social occasion: *Hudson broke the ice, fixing both girls with his smile, buying them drinks, and listening intently to them as though he was fascinated by life in the trade department of the Norwegian Embassy.*

cut no 'ice
You say that someone's behaviour or attitude **cuts no ice** with you if it does not impress you: *So what was this with his new sharp suit? It cut no ice with me.*

put something on 'ice
You **put something on ice** when you decide not to do anything about it for a while: *The whole project may have to be put on ice until the end of the next decade.*

If you want to save food, you can stop it from going bad by putting it on ice.

skate on thin 'ice
You say that someone **is skating on thin ice** when they are doing something risky or dangerous: *He was a political outcast who skated on thin ice deliberately to keep himself in the public eye.*

icing

the icing on the 'cake
You describe something as **the icing on the cake** if it makes a very good situation even better: *And he really put the icing on the cake of this remarkable recovery story by winning the 400 metres at last year's Olympic Games.*

Icing is the white or coloured sugary coating that sometimes covers cakes.

idea

get the i'dea
You **get the idea** when you understand someone's explanation, or you know what they mean: *When I left he was gazing about disconsolately, still trying to get the idea.*

have no i'dea
You say you **have no idea** when you cannot even guess the answer to someone's question: *'What time did he leave?' 'I've no idea.'*
◇ SEE ALSO **not have the remotest idea** ▷ IDEA

not have the remotest i'dea
You say that you **do not have the remotest idea** when you want to emphasize the fact that you cannot even guess the answer to someone's question: *When I joined the organization, it was more than apparent that the other women did not have the remotest idea about women's liberation.*
◇ SEE ALSO **have no idea** ▷ IDEA

run away with the idea that
You **run away with the idea that** something is the case when you draw a conclusion too soon: *No one should run away with the idea bonuses will be easily ob'tained.*

the very i'dea
The very idea of doing something unpleasant is the thought of it alone: *The very idea of taking drugs disgusted me.*

what's the big i'dea?
You ask '**what's the big idea?**' if you are annoyed by someone's behaviour and do not understand why they are acting in such a way.

ideas

get i'deas
You tell someone not to **get ideas** if you do not want them to start imagining the possibility of having something that they are unlikely to be allowed to, or able to, have: *Don't get ideas. The apartment is exquisite, but small; there's only enough room here for one.*

give someone i'deas or put ideas into someone's 'head
Someone or something **gives you ideas** or **puts ideas into your head 1** when they encourage you to think you can have something that may in fact be very difficult or impossible to acquire. **2** when they make you start thinking about new, possibly radical, concepts: *That new teacher has been putting ideas into your head again, I'll bet.*

ifs

ifs and 'buts or ifs or 'buts

Ifs and buts, or **ifs or buts**, are points for consideration or discussion, which are, or are not taken into account before action is taken, or a request is carried out: *The public is entitled to know what has been paid for from public assets; there can be no ifs or buts about that.*

ignorance

ignorance is 'bliss

Ignorance is bliss means, often ironically, that you will be much happier, at least in the short term, if you are unaware of unpleasant things: *This is the stage where ignorance is bliss, when it looks easy and you don't realize how much there is to it.*

◇ SEE ALSO **what the eye doesn't see the heart doesn't grieve over** ▷ EYE

image

the spitting 'image of someone

Someone who is **the spitting image of** another person resembles them very closely: *And they would all say how he was the spitting image of his mother, which was strange, since she was not his mother.*

◇ SEE ALSO **like as two peas in a pod** ▷ LIKE

imitation

a pale imi'tation

Someone or something is described as **a pale imitation** of someone or something else if they are not nearly as good as that person or thing: *Mention UK hip hop and he immediately denounces it as a pale imitation of the 'real thing'.*

◇ SEE ALSO **no match for** ▷ MATCH

importance

be full of your own im'portance

Someone is **full of their own importance** if they act as if they are much more important than other people: *He was a gentleman who was full of his own importance and not usually given to conversing with the lower servants.*

◇ SEE ALSO **high and mighty** ▷ HIGH

impression

under the im'pression that

You are **under the impression that** something is the case if you think, perhaps wrongly, that it is the case: *I'm sorry, I was under the impression that you'd nearly finished.*

improvement

room for im'provement

You say that there is **room for improvement** if you think that something could be made better: *I started to evaluate my performance, to see mistakes and room for improvement.*

in (see also **ins**)

in for 'such-and-such

You predict that you are **in for** a particular event when you are quite sure that it is going to happen: *Looks like we're in for a storm.*

'in on something

You are **in on something** if you are one of a number of people carrying out the same activity, or sharing a secret: *Everyone wants to be in on this project now that it looks as if we're going to make some money out of it.*

'in with someone

You are **in with** a particular famous or influential person if you have some kind of connection with them that can benefit you: *If you're in with the band, you should be able to get in for free.*

what's in it for 'so-and-so?

You ask '**what's in it for me?**' when you want to know if there are any advantages for you in a situation.

inch

give 'em an inch and they'll take a 'mile

Give 'em an inch and they'll take a mile means that if you do a small favour for a particular person or group of people, they will take advantage of your kindness and demand more.

inch by 'inch

Someone or something progresses **inch by inch** when they do so very slowly, but steadily: *Inch by inch, he dragged himself along the dark tunnel, toward the small circle of light in the distance.*

> An **inch** is a small unit of length, equal to about 2.5cm.

not budge an 'inch or not give an 'inch or not move an 'inch

1 Something that will **not budge**, or **give**, or **move, an inch** cannot be moved at all: *We've been trying to open this old box here, but it won't give an inch.* **2** Someone who will **not budge**, or **give, an inch** refuses absolutely to change their mind: *I lay in bed and ranted at Richard; explaining, arguing, weeping with frustration. He would not budge an inch.*

initiative

on your own i'nitiative

You do something **on your own initiative** when you do it without being asked to do so: *But he is also intelligent and responsible, a player who on his own initiative has made a series of public anti-violence appeals.*

take the i'nitiative

You **take the initiative** when you take a decision to do something without being asked to do so: *It might have been difficult to prove that librarians themselves took the initiative for the censorship, although many would have been pleased to make that claim.*

influence

under the 'influence

You are **under the influence** of something, such as alcohol or drugs, if it has some control over you: *In an interview to promote his book, Morgan acknowledged that he had spent years under the influence of cocaine.*
◇ SEE ALSO **the worse for drink** ▷ DRINK; **have had a few** or **have had a few too many** ▷ FEW

innings

have had a good 'innings

You say that someone **has had a good innings** if they have had a good, and long life: *He's not afraid of dying; says he's had a good innings and he's ready to move on to the next life.*

> In cricket, an **innings** is the period of time that a player is batting, before they are out.

inroads

make 'inroads into something

You **make inroads into** a task, for example, when you do enough work to have a noticeable effect: *All the combined scientific efforts have still only made comparatively small inroads into the accumulating list of unsolved questions.*

ins

the ins and 'outs of something

The **ins and outs** of something are the detailed facts about it: *For the purposes of our argument here, it is not necessary to understand all the ins and outs of these various schemes.*

inside

inside 'out

Something, such as an item of clothing, is **inside out** if the surface that is usually on the outside is facing inwards, and the surface that is usually on the inside is facing out: *You've got your pullover on inside out.*

on the 'inside

Someone who is **on the inside** has access to information that others do not because they are a member of a particular organi-

zation: *We've got someone on the inside who's prepared to let us see the documents.*

insignificance

pale into insig'nificance

Something **pales into insignificance** when it no longer seems to have any importance in comparison with something else: *Even the initial cost of buying the animal pales into insignificance when you start to add up vets' bills, insurance, transport.*

instant

for one 'instant

You experience something **for one instant** when you experience it for a very short time: *She saw a flicker of murderous rage in his eye for one instant.*

insult

add insult to 'injury

Someone or something **adds insult to injury** when they make a bad situation even worse: *Then, to add insult to injury, it started to rain.*

intents

to all intents and 'purposes

Something is the case **to all intents and purposes** when it may be considered to be the case, even if it is not officially so: *These professional consultations are to all intents and purposes interviews, and should be treated as such.*

interest

pay something back with 'interest

You **pay something back with interest** when you react to some harm that someone has done you by doing something even worse to them: *Those who offended the girls in some way were paid back with interest.*
◇ SEE ALSO **pay someone back in their own coin** ▷ COIN; **give someone a taste of their own medicine** ▷ TASTE

vested 'interest

You have a **vested interest** in a project when you are likely to gain financially from it if it is successful: *Young fans found a new 'hooligan' identity created for them by journalists with a vested interest in whipping up public indignation.*

iron

a cast iron 'such-and-such

You have **a cast iron** stomach, or constitution, for example, if that part of you is very strong, and not easily affected by adverse conditions: *You'll need a cast iron stomach to survive one of her curries.*

> **Iron** is a very hard metal.

the Iron 'Curtain

'The Iron Curtain' is the term given to the barrier that used to exist between western and eastern Europe, which prevented free communication and trading: *The moment Hungary began to dismantle its part of the Iron Curtain, hundreds began to leave.*

strike while the iron is 'hot

You **strike while the iron is hot** when you take advantage of favourable circumstances to get something done.
◇ SEE ALSO **make hay while the sun shines** ▷ HAY

> An **iron** is an electrical device with a flat metal base. You heat it up and pass it over clothes to remove creases.

with an iron 'hand or with an iron 'fist

You control someone or something **with an iron hand** or **fist** when you control them very strictly and severely: *'My father ruled us with an iron fist,' Joe recalls. 'But he loved us and he worked himself to death for us.'*

irons

irons in the 'fire

You have several **irons in the fire** when you are involved in several projects at the same time; you have too many **irons in the fire,** when you are involved in so many projects that you cannot do any of them successfully: *He did have a few other economic irons in the fire: among them a share in the tobacco monopoly.*
◇ SEE ALSO **a finger in every pie** ▷ FINGER

issue

at 'issue

The point or question **at issue** is the point or question that it is important to discuss: *At issue is one small, but key part of the European Commission's plan for an alignment of Value Added Tax (VAT), which it considers essential.*

cloud the 'issue

You **cloud the issue** when you give unclear information to support an argument, making people believe something that is not correct: *Our objective is to examine the nature of doubt, clarifying three common misconceptions which cloud the issue today.*

make an 'issue of something

You **make an issue of something** when you make something the subject of an argument: *But Christine was relaxed and didn't make an issue of it.*

take 'issue with

You **take issue with** someone when you state that you disagree with something they have said: *Mr Eduard Shevardnadze, the Foreign Minister, and other senior Soviet spokesmen took issue with Chancellor Helmut Kohl's 10-point plan for German reunification.*
◇ SEE ALSO **argue the toss** ▷ TOSS

ivories

tinkle the 'ivories or tickle the 'ivories

You **tinkle,** or **tickle,** the ivories when you play the piano: *It is not clear where Sir Trevor learned to tickle the ivories, but he went down a treat at the annual summer conference of the Institute of Chartered Accountants in England and Wales.*

> '**The ivories**' refers to the white keys of a piano, which were traditionally made of ivory.

j

Jack

I'm all 'right, Jack or I'm al'right Jack
'I'm all right, Jack' is a phrase which expresses the attitude held by some people that the problems of others should be no concern of theirs, and that everyone should look after themselves: *It's the same old I'm alright Jack mentality. I can do it, I can afford it, I'm gonna go ahead and I'm gonna get it for me.*

jack of all trades, master of 'none
A person who is a **jack of all trades, master of none** knows how to do a lot of things, but is not skilled at any of them: *Pilots were expected to be jacks of all trades. If the cooling system broke down pilots had to land and mend the pipe with chewing gum and tape.*

jackpot

hit the 'jackpot
You say you **have hit the jackpot** when you win or obtain a lot of money or success: *Unemployed roadsweeper Mickey Reid hit the jackpot yesterday when his £4 lottery ticket won him £1.8 million.*

Jack Robinson

before you can say Jack 'Robinson
Something that happens **before you can say Jack Robinson** happens very soon or immediately: *If you don't keep a close eye on her she'll be in trouble again before you can say Jack Robinson.*
◇ SEE ALSO **in the blink of an eye** ▷ BLINK; **quick as a wink** or **a flash** ▷ QUICK; **in the wink of an eye** ▷ WINK

jam

jam to'day
Jam today describes a situation where you get something good immediately, rather than a promise that you will have it in the future: *The economic climate makes jam today worth more than jam tomorrow, with the emphasis on immediate profits.*

In Lewis Carroll's *Alice through the Looking Glass*, the White Queen offers Alice a job. The payment is to be 'Twopence a week, and jam every other day ... jam tomorrow and jam yesterday – but never jam today.'

jam to'morrow
Jam tomorrow describes the situation where you are promised something good in the future, but you do not believe that you will ever really get it: *For years the public has had to content itself with the politicians' promises of jam tomorrow.*

See note at **jam today**.

want 'jam on it
If you say that someone **wants jam on it**, you mean that they are dissatisfied with the situation although it is full of advantages for them: *Most people know that we give great value for money, but there are always some who want jam on it.*

Jane

plain 'Jane (*disrespectful*)
If you call a girl or woman a **plain Jane**, you mean that they are not at all good-looking: *The President's plain Jane wife didn't do much for the dynamic image he tried to portray.*

jaw

so-and-so's 'jaw dropped
If it was obvious from the expression on a certain person's face that they were surprised by something, you say that **their jaw dropped**: *When she realized she had won first prize, her jaw dropped.*

jazz

and all that 'jazz (*informal*)
And all that jazz means 'and other similar things', and you use it after giving an example: *I'd like to join the local hockey team, but I can't be bothered with training and all that jazz.*

Jekyll

Jekyll and 'Hyde
A **Jekyll and Hyde**, or a **Jekyll and Hyde** character, is a person who seems to have two sides to their personality, usually one

good and one bad; anything that is described as **Jekyll and Hyde** changes unexpectedly, or has two opposing characters: *As he spoke, his language grew rougher and rougher, as if a Jekyll and Hyde transformation were taking effect.*

> **Dr Jekyll and Mr Hyde** is a story by Robert Louis Stevenson about a man whose character had two separate parts; Dr Jekyll was the good side, and Mr Hyde was the bad side.

je

je ne sais 'quoi

A **je ne sais quoi** is a quality which makes something special, although you cannot describe that quality in words: *He has a certain je ne sais quoi about him, that's all. A touch of class.*

> **Je ne sais quoi** means 'I do not know what' in French.

jelly

shake like a 'jelly

You say you **are shaking like a jelly** if you are shaking a lot, usually because something has made you afraid: *'I was shaking like jelly,' said Bessie. 'I was disappointed the police didn't turn up sooner.'*

◇ SEE ALSO **shake like a leaf** ▷ LEAF

turn to 'jelly

You say that a part of your body **has turned to jelly** if it feels weak and shaky, usually because you are nervous, afraid, or tired: *She had to lean against him in order to remain upright. Her limbs trembled, the muscles turned to jelly.*

jest

in 'jest

You say something **in jest** when you say it in order to be amusing, and do not mean it to be taken seriously: *I'd rather you didn't make racist comments, even in jest.*

jet

'jet set

The **jet set** are the type of rich, fashionable people who regularly make short trips by plane to different countries, either for business or for pleasure: *Visit the beautiful island of Formentera where you can see the yachts and speedboats of the jet set.*
'jet-setter: *They were apparently all jet-setters. Always flying from one business deal to another.*
'jet-setting: *Week after week her face is splashed across fashion magazines, alongside tales of her jet-setting travels and stun-*

ning performances at fashion shows.

jewel

jewel in the 'crown

The **jewel in the crown** of something is the most valuable or the most important part of it: *The Victorians sometimes referred to India as the 'jewel in the crown of the British Empire'.*

job, Job (*see also* jobs)

'blow job

If someone gives their male sexual partner a **blow job**, they suck his penis to give him sexual pleasure.

do the 'job

Something, usually an object, that **does the job** solves a practical problem: *It's difficult to get rid of rats, but a good brand of rat poison should probably do the job.*

◇ SEE ALSO **do the trick** ▷ TRICK

do a good 'job

You say that someone **is doing a good job** if they are doing something well: *I'm surprised that you are so critical. I think she's doing a very good job as councillor.*

give something up as a bad 'job

You **give something up as a bad job** when you decide that there is no point in continuing with it, as there are too many problems involved: *At around six o'clock Pooley gave the whole thing up as a bad job, put on an overcoat, and went home.*

a good job well 'done

When you say something is **a good job well done**, you mean that you have, or someone else has, worked hard on it, and that you are pleased with the results: *Many craftsmen take pride in a good job well done and often friendly rivalry develops between them to achieve objectives.*

have a 'job (*informal*)

You **have a job** doing something if it is difficult to do: *You can try and get her to come, but you'll have a job persuading her.*

it's a good 'job (*informal*)

You say **'it's a good job'** if you think it is lucky that something is the case: *It's a good job you've come round today, because I'm going on holiday tomorrow.* □ *She never saw him when he was ill, and a good job too. She'd have been very upset.*

◇ SEE ALSO **a good thing** ▷ THING; **just as well** ▷ WELL

Job's 'comforter

A **Job's comforter** is a person who tries to comfort someone who is upset, but ends up making them feel even worse: *The last thing you need is to be surrounded by a load of Job's comforters* *telling you their troubles and explaining how hard life can be.*

In the Bible, Job calls his friends 'miserable comforters'.

a job 'lot

A **job lot** is a large quantity of similar items which have been bought together, probably at a reduced price per item: *Even kitchen utensils are being sold along with a job lot of washing machines, dryers and ironing machines for £200.*

just the 'job

Something that is **just the job** is exactly what you need: *This screwdriver with the short handle is just the job for getting into tight little corners.*

◇ SEE ALSO **just the ticket** ▷ TICKET

make the best of a bad 'job

You **make the best of a bad job** when you do your best to make an unpleasant situation as pleasant or as tolerable as possible: *Look, why don't we just make the best of a bad job and book into a nice hotel for the night?*

make a good 'job of something

You **make a good job of something** if you do it well: *She's made such a good job of that decorating, I think I'll pay her a bit extra.*

on the 'job

1 If somebody is doing something which is not permitted while they are supposed to be working, they are doing it **on the job**: *The control room staff were found to be falling asleep on the job.* **2** You learn how to do something **on the job** when you learn it by experiencing the reality of the workplace, rather than through theoretical lessons in a college, for example: *They will be spending 80% of their time in schools learning on the job, instead of listening to lectures on education theory.*

'put-up job

A **put-up job** is a plan or action which is designed to trick or deceive people: *Maybe there had been no accident. Maybe his disappearance had been a put-up job.*

jobs

jobs for the 'boys

If you talk about **jobs for the boys**, you are referring to a situation in which you think people are getting jobs because they are friends or relatives of the people in charge, rather than because they are the best people to do those jobs: *Jobs for the boys and misspent funds ... it seems that the company is rotten with corruption.*

Joe

Joe 'Public or Joe 'Bloggs

When you talk about **Joe Public**, or **Joe Bloggs**, you mean no particular person, just an ordinary member of the public: *While Joe Public wants fast food shops, he does not want them near him, and he is prepared to fight to stop anyone opening one near his house.*

◇ SEE ALSO **man on the Clapham omnibus** or **man on the street** ▷ MAN

joie

joie de 'vivre

When you talk about someone's **joie de vivre**, you mean the obvious pleasure which they get from everything in life: *She has such optimism and such joie de vivre. A few minutes in her presence are so refreshing.*

Joie de vivre means 'joy from living' in French.

joint

case the 'joint

You say someone **is casing the joint** if they are examining a place with the intention of committing a burglary there: *The burglar hung around for a couple of minutes, casing the joint.*

out of 'joint

When you put a part of your body such as your shoulder or your knee **out of joint**, you suffer an injury when the bones move suddenly out of their normal position: *I've put my shoulder out of joint.*

joke (*see also* **joking**)

beyond a 'joke

Something is **beyond a joke** when it has become unacceptable: *The noise coming from the flat next door is getting beyond a joke. What are we going to do about it?*

crack a 'joke

To **crack a joke** is to make an amusing or witty comment: *All the boys were laughing and cracking jokes.*

dirty 'joke

A **dirty joke** is a joke about sex: *They liked me because I told them dirty jokes, made good after-dinner speeches and did a reasonable job for them.*

no 'joke (*informal*)

Something that is **no joke** is unpleasant or difficult: *It's no joke getting up at five in the morning if you've had too much to drink the night before.*

practical 'joke

A **practical joke** is a trick which you use

against someone so that you can laugh at their reaction when they discover their mistake: *At school, he demonstrated a liking for practical jokes, and also a socially unpopular talent for manufacturing explosives.*

see the 'joke
You **see the joke** when you realize that something, especially an awkward or unpleasant situation that you are in, is quite funny: *The other men laughed too. Plummer didn't see the joke and glanced round irritably, waiting until they calmed down.*

◇ SEE ALSO **see the funny side** ▷ SIDE

standing 'joke
A **standing joke** is a subject of amusement between people who know each other, based on their mutual knowledge of one another's behaviour or actions in the past: *It has become a standing joke; he always disappears when it's his turn to buy the drinks.*

take a 'joke
Someone who can **take a joke** is able to laugh at jokes that other people make about them: *Oh, come on. You know I didn't mean it when I said you were fat. Can't you take a joke?*

joking

joking a'side or joking a'part
If you want to stop being funny and talk about something seriously, you say '**joking aside**', or '**joking apart**': *Yes, I just sit in front of the fire in my rocking chair all day, knitting for my grandchildren! No, joking apart, I have found it hard to adjust to being retired.*

you're 'joking or you must be 'joking
1 '**You're joking**' or '**you must be joking**' are expressions of surprise or disbelief: *'The President died this morning.' 'You're joking.' 'No, really. It's true.'* 2 You also say '**you must be joking**' to someone when you are opposing, or refusing to do, something they have suggested because you consider it to be unreasonable: *'I'll invite them to dinner.' 'You must be joking. They stayed till three in the morning the last time.'*

◇ SEE ALSO **you're kidding** or **you must be kidding** ▷ KIDDING

jolly

jolly well (*informal*)
You use '**jolly well**' for emphasis: *I've worked for it, I deserve it and I'm jolly well going to do it.*

Joneses

keep up with the 'Joneses
When people try to **keep up with the Jon-**eses, their competitive nature makes them try to do the same things that their neighbours or friends have done, only better: *Poorer families who see the superior goods being consumed by their richer neighbours may attempt to 'keep up with the Joneses'.*

◇ SEE ALSO **go one better** ▷ BETTER

> The **Joneses** here, refers to a hypothetical family whose surname is 'Jones'.

journey

break your 'journey
You **break your journey** somewhere when you stop there for a rest: *We decided to break our journey north at Aviemore.*

joy

no 'joy
You say '**no joy**' to report that you have not had the luck, news or information which you were hoping for: *'Did you find one?' 'No joy. Everything's closed.'*

judge

to judge from 'something or to judge by 'something
You say '**to judge from something**' or '**to judge by something**' when you are giving a reason for your opinion: *To judge from the position of the sun in the sky, I'd say it was about three o'clock.*

judgement

against your better 'judgement
When you agree to something **against your better judgement**, you agree to it although you are not sure that it is wise: *She knew it had been against his better judgement; that all his own instincts had told him to wait, to take it more slowly.*

'judgement day
Judgement day, according to Christians, is the day on which God will sort out the good people from the bad people, and make a final decision on who will be allowed into heaven.

pass 'judgement
1 A judge or court of law **passes judgement** on a case or on an accused person when they make their decision: *The court had passed its judgement, and the young man was executed a few days later.* 2 You **pass judgement** on someone or something when you express your opinion of them or criticize them: *I don't know what gives you the right to pass judgement on the way I live my life.*

reserve 'judgement
You **reserve judgement** when you wait till you know more about something before

giving your opinion on it: *I'd advise you to reserve judgement on him till you get to know him a little better.*

sit in 'judgement on someone

If someone **sits in judgement on you**, they have decided that they are in a position to be able to criticize you: *What right do you have to sit in judgement on somebody you hardly know?*

juice

stew in your own 'juice

A person who **is stewing in their own juice** is being forced to spend some time alone, giving them an opportunity to realize that their bad situtation is the result of their own actions: *She was still standing there now, waiting impatiently. She suspected he was enjoying letting her stew in her own juice.*

◇ SEE ALSO **have** or **get the hump** ▷ HUMP

jump

for the 'high jump

You say that someone is **for the high jump** if they are going to be punished or get into serious trouble for something they have done: *You'll be for the high jump when mum finds out.*

'jump to it

If you tell someone to **jump to it**, you are ordering them to hurry up and do what they have been told: *Come on, lads, jump to it. We don't have time to sit about chatting all day.*

one jump a'head

You keep **one jump ahead** of the person or people you are competing with when you guess what they will do next and prepare yourself to deal with it: *The trick of dealing with trouble-makers in your class is always to be one jump ahead of them.*

take a running 'jump *(offensive)*

If you tell someone to **take a running jump**, you are telling them rudely to go away and leave you alone: *'Can you be quiet?' 'Oh, take a running jump.'*

◇ SEE ALSO **go jump in the lake** ▷ LAKE

jumped

jumped-'up

If you describe someone as **jumped-up**, you mean that they are over-confident for their age or situation: *He wasn't going to take orders from a jumped-up sixth-former.*

just

just a'bout

You use **'just about'** when the state or level of something is almost exactly that men-

tioned: *Okay, everyone, don't give up. We're just about there now.* □ *They must be just about the same age as each other.*

just 'so

1 You have everything **just so** when you have arranged everything exactly as you want it: *He's such a neat and tidy person. Everything has to be just so.* **2** *(formal, old)* You say **'just so'** if you want to express your agreement with the thing that someone has just said: *'In my opinion, there is no advantage to be gained from rushing into a decision.' 'Just so, just so.'*

◇ SEE ALSO **that's just it** ▷ JUST; **quite so** ▷ QUITE; **too right** ▷ RIGHT

that's just 'it

You say **'that's just it'** when someone makes a statement which you **1** agree with completely: *'She's growing up.' 'That's just it. She's much more mature.'* **2** disagree with completely: *'I understand what you're going through.' 'That's just it. You don't understand.'*

◇ SEE ALSO **just so** ▷ JUST; **quite so** ▷ QUITE; **too right** ▷ RIGHT

justice

bring someone to 'justice

Criminals **are brought to justice** when they go through the legal system and are finally punished for their crime: *MPs are not special, and an MP who has committed a crime must expect to be brought to justice.*

do justice to or in justice to

1 In law, to **do justice**, or to **do justice to someone** or **something**, is to use the legal system to obtain fair treatment for someone: *He doubted whether this type of taxation would have done justice to the contractual right of the mortgagee.* **2** To **do justice to someone** or **something**, or to **do them justice**, is to present them in the best or the clearest way, or to fulfil the demands that they make: *Your photograph doesn't do you justice.* □ *a 12V CD player and a selection of discs that would do justice to a small radio station.* □ *Only an organization of this kind was capable of doing justice to the cause of the deaf and dumb and of representing it properly.* **3** You **do yourself justice** in a competition or performance when you do it well enough to be pleased with yourself: *Come on, people, you're not doing yourselves justice.* **4** You say **'to do so-and-so** or **such-and-such justice'**, or **'in justice to so-and-so** or **such-and-such'**, when you try to change a person's unreasonably critical opinion of someone or something, by giving that person more facts: *To do her justice, she would not, I think, have missed the meeting.* **5** You **do justice to** a meal, or you **do** it **justice**, when you are hungry enough to appreciate it properly: *I'm so sorry I didn't do your lovely meal justice. I haven't been feeling well all day.*

◊ SEE ALSO **give so-and-so their due** ▷ DUE

poetic 'justice

If a certain person does not get the punishment which you feel they deserve for something bad they have done, but then they suffer a misfortune of some kind, you say there is **poetic justice** in the situation: *Would it not be poetic justice if he who had devised the weapon, eventually died by it?*

rough 'justice

1 If a decision, usually an official one, is supposed to be fair, but in fact is not fair at all, you say that the victim of the decision has had **rough justice**: *She was injured at work and she's going to lose her job now. Seems like rough justice to me.* **2** If the treatment that someone gets is approximately fair, you say that they have had **rough justice**: *As it happens, there'd be a certain rough justice if I got a wage from it.* **3** Rough justice is also a harsh act of revenge or a deserved punishment: *They became vigilantes or revolutionaries: machines for dispensing rough justice and revenge.*

Notice that senses 1 and 2 virtually contradict each other. Only the context can tell you which meaning is intended.

k

keel

on an even 'keel

Someone or something is **on an even keel** if they are in a normal, calm state: *The right politician must be put in charge of the Treasury to bring the economy back to an even keel.*

> When the **keel** of a boat is even, it is level or horizontal in the water, allowing the boat to move forward in a steady way.

keen

keen as 'mustard (*old*)

Someone who is as **keen as mustard** is full of enthusiasm and energy.

keep (*see also* **keeping** *and* **keeps**)

keep a'breast of something

You **keep abreast of** a situation which is changing if you keep yourself properly informed of any developments in that situation: *Representative staff will keep abreast of national developments by attending conferences and by visiting other schools.*
◇ SEE ALSO **keep pace with** ▷ PACE

keep 'at it

You **keep at it** if you continue doing something, especially working at something, until you finish the activity or succeed: *Even if it sometimes seems you are getting nowhere with this treatment, you should keep at it.*
◇ SEE ALSO **stay** or **take the pace** ▷ PACE; **never say die** ▷ SAY

keep it 'up

You **are keeping it up** if you manage to continue doing something at the same speed or as regularly as you are doing it at present: *This exercise will help if you do it regularly and keep it up for several months.*

keep to your'self or keep yourself to your'self

You **keep to yourself**, or **keep yourself to yourself**, when you avoid other people and spend most of your time alone: *He was a studious boy, with no friends, who kept himself to himself.*

keep something to your'self

You **keep something to yourself** when you do not tell anyone about it: *Even if you are sure you are pregnant, you should try to keep it to yourself for the first month.*
◇ SEE ALSO **keep your counsel** ▷ COUNSEL; **keep it under your hat** ▷ HAT; **mum's the word** ▷ MUM

keeping

in 'keeping with something

One thing is **in keeping with another** if it is suitable for it or fits in with it: *They've been asked to design something in keeping with the existing architecture of the building.*

out of 'keeping with something

Something that is **out of keeping with something else** is not suitable for it or does not fit in with it: *His remarks seemed strangely out of keeping with what he had said earlier.*

keeps

for 'keeps (*informal*)

You give something to someone **for keeps** when you intend them to keep it permanently: *'Here, you can have it.' 'What? For keeps?'*

ken

beyond someone's 'ken

Something which is **beyond your ken** is not possible for you to understand, because you have no knowledge or experience of it: *Even she, who had never been afraid of anyone, felt that he was sometimes beyond her ken.* □ *But why they attacked in such numbers and with such determination is beyond my ken.*

> Originally, the word **ken** was a measure of distance, equal to the range of ordinary vision at sea, which is about 32 kilometres.

kerb

'kerb-crawling

Kerb-crawling is the activity of driving a car slowly along a street, with the intention of choosing a prostitute: *You can be arrested for kerb-crawling.*

kettle

kettle of 'fish

1 A pretty, or a fine, **kettle of fish** is a complicated and awkward situation: *As if to herself, she added: 'This is a fine kettle of fish.' And turning back to me: 'You'll do something, eh? Arrange something?'* **2** If you say 'that's a different **kettle of fish**', you mean 'that changes the situation completely'; a person who is described as a different **kettle of fish** is very different from others, or from someone else who they are being compared to: *But Kate, she was a different kettle of fish altogether. They discussed everything under the sun.*

◇ SEE ALSO **a whole new** or **a completely different ball game** or **a different ball game altogether** ▷ BALL

keyed

keyed 'up

You say someone **is keyed up** if they are excited and nervous: *He had been keyed up, expecting just such a confrontation.*

kibosh

put the 'kibosh on something

An event which **puts the kibosh on something** prevents that thing from taking place or being successful: *Well, the rain has put the kibosh on my plans for a barbecue.*

You pronounce the first syllable of **ki-bosh** to rhyme with the word 'my'.

kick (see also **kicking** and **kicks**)

better than a kick up the backside (*informal*) or **better than a kick up the 'arse** (*vulgar*)

If you say that something is **better than a kick up the backside** or **arse**, you mean, humorously, that it is better than nothing: *It's not much of a wage increase but I suppose it's better than a kick up the backside.*

◇ SEE ALSO **better than a poke in the eye** ▷ POKE

for a 'kick-off (*informal*)

You say '**for a kick-off**' to emphasize that what you are saying is just the first in a list of arguments or complaints: *'What's wrong?' 'Well, I don't feel great for a kick-off ... and I had a bit of bad news this morning.'*

◇ SEE ALSO **for starters** ▷ STARTERS

kick someone up'stairs

An organization **kicks someone upstairs** when they give that person a job or a position which seems better than the job they had before, but which, in fact, reduces the amount of responsibility which that person has: *In theory he was promoted, but in practice he was kicked upstairs to manage a smaller project.*

kick-'start something

An action or event **kick-starts something** if it suddenly gives that thing extra energy to help it recover from certain problems: *The Chancellor's new policy was designed to kick-start the economy.*

You **kick-start** a motorbike by jumping with a lot of force on a pedal which starts the motor.

a kick up the 'backside or a kick up the 'arse (*vulgar*)

You can say that someone needs **a kick up the backside** or **a kick up the arse** if you think that they are lazy or not taking their responsibilities seriously, and that they need to be told forcefully to improve their behaviour: *If you ask me, that boy needs a kick up the backside or he'll never pass those exams.*

'kick yourself

You say you are **kicking yourself** if you are annoyed with yourself for making a mistake or doing something stupid: *I'm never careful enough about the details, and then I end up kicking myself.*

kicks

for 'kicks

You are doing something, usually something bad, **for kicks** if you are doing it for fun and the feeling of excitement which it gives you: *I believe they are more ethical – at least they're stealing for a practical reason, not just for kicks.*

kid (see also **kidding** and **kids**)

I kid you 'not

You say '**I kid you not**' when you want to emphasize that what you are telling someone is true, even though it may be difficult to believe: *She always sent me Californian poppy bath salts for Christmas. I kid you not, each year.*

kidding

no 'kidding?

You say '**no kidding?**' to someone when they have just said something surprising, and you are checking that it is true: *'My dad knew Elvis Presley before he was famous.' 'No kidding?'*

you're 'kidding or you must be 'kidding

1 You say '**you're kidding**' or '**you must be kidding**' to someone when they have just said something surprising: *'Gerry told me last night he wants a divorce.' 'You're kid-*

ding.' 'No. He says he's met someone else.' 2
You say **'you must be kidding'** to someone
when you are opposing, or refusing to do,
the thing which they suggest because you
consider it to be unreasonable: *'Get on my
back and I'll carry you across.' 'You've got
to be kidding. I'd rather get wet feet, thanks.'*
◇ SEE ALSO **you're joking** or **you must be
joking** ▷ JOKING

kids

'kids' stuff

Something which is **kids' stuff** is so easy
that it is almost not worth doing: *'Come
on,' he said, winking at me. 'Burglaries are
kids' stuff.'*

◇ SEE ALSO **child's play** ▷ CHILD; **easy as ABC**
or **anything** or **falling off a log** or **pie** or
winking ▷ EASY; **a piece of cake** or **a piece of
piss** ▷ PIECE; **nothing to it** ▷ NOTHING

kill

in at the 'kill

You are **in at the kill** if you are present at,
and therefore able to enjoy, the exciting
moment when someone or something is
defeated: *Can I be there when you confront
him? I want to be in at the kill.*

kill or cure

You describe an action as **kill or cure** if it
has a chance of solving a problem, but
could do a lot of harm if it fails: *The
Chancellor is proposing the kill or cure
measure of drastically increasing taxes for
a limited period of time.*

kill yourself 'laughing (*informal*)

To **kill yourself laughing** is to laugh so much
that it hurts: *I felt really embarrassed,
especially as they were all killing themselves
laughing.*

◇ SEE ALSO **crease yourself** or **crease up**
▷ CREASE

killing

make a 'killing

You **make a killing** when you make a lot of
money quickly: *We can make an absolute
killing by taking a percentage of the profits,
and charging them rent.*

◇ SEE ALSO **make a bomb** ▷ BOMB; **make a
bundle** ▷ BUNDLE; **make a fortune** ▷ FOR-
TUNE; **make your pile** ▷ PILE

kin

next of 'kin

Your **next of kin** are the people who are
considered to be your closest relatives, for
legal purposes: *The victim's next of kin must
be informed in the event of an accident.*

kind

in 'kind

1 If you pay someone **in kind**, you give them
something other than money in exchange
for their goods or services: *Will you accept
rent-free accommodation as payment in kind
for the work you do?* **2** You repay someone
who has treated you badly **in kind** if you
react by treating them badly too.

'kind of (*informal*)

1 **Kind of** (or **kinda**) means 'rather' or 'a
bit': *I'd like to come, but I feel kind of tired
tonight.* **2** You use **'a kind of'** when giving a
rough description or idea of something:
*The pudding was a kind of cheesecakey
thing, but without a cheesecake base.*

◇ SEE ALSO **sort of** ▷ SORT

nothing of the 'kind

Nothing of the kind means 'not at all the
thing just mentioned': *'You said you would
be willing to stand down as Prime Minister.'
'I said nothing of the kind.'*

◇ SEE ALSO **nothing of the sort** ▷ SORT

of a 'kind

1 You say that a small number of people
or objects are two, three, etc, **of a kind** if
they are the same as, or similar to, one
another: *In the card game cribbage, three
of a kind* (three kings, for example) gives
you six points. □ *The reason they fight so
much is because they are so similar.
They're two of a kind.* **2** Something described as a thing **of a kind** is not a very
good one: *The Prime Minister has given
us a statement of a kind, but he still hasn't
answered our questions.*

◇ SEE ALSO **of sorts** ▷ SORTS

so kind as to or kind enough to

You use **'so kind as to'**, and **'kind enough to'**
when you ask someone politely to do something: *Would you be kind enough to follow
me, Sir?*

kindly

not take 'kindly to something

When you say that you **do not take kindly to
something**, you are saying that you find that
thing hard to accept because you dislike or
feel insulted by it: *He doesn't take kindly to
being told he's put on weight.* □ *They don't
take kindly to strangers.*

◇ SEE ALSO **take exception to something**
▷ EXCEPTION

kindness

kill someone with 'kindness

You **are killing someone with kindness** if
you are trying too hard to be good to them,
with the final result that you cause them
harm: *He spends hundreds of pounds on me.*

He'd kill me with kindness. With chocolates and food and flowers.

king

for king and 'country
When you do things **for king and country**, your actions come from a desire to do what is good for your country: *With the war over, people had to stop living for king and country and live for their families again.*

the king of the 'castle
A child who is standing on a raised object, making them higher than everyone else, sometimes shouts **'I'm the king of the castle'**; someone who is described as **the king of the castle** is the person who has most influence or power in an organization or relationship: *'There can only be one king of the castle, as far as male Leos are concerned,'* Julie had told her.

> The whole expression is, in fact, a rhyme: 'I'm the king of the castle, and you're the dirty rascal'.

king's 'ransom
A **king's ransom** is a large sum of money: *I don't care if the painting's expensive. I'd pay a king's ransom for it.*

turn King's 'evidence
A criminal who **turns King's evidence** makes a statement against their partner or partners in crime, and in return receives a less severe punishment for their part in the crime: *Each prisoner, in his separate cell, is invited to betray his colleague by turning King's evidence against him.*
◇ SEE ALSO **turn Queen's evidence** ▷ QUEEN

kingdom

till kingdom 'come
You are doing something **till kingdom come** if you continue with it for a long time or forever, without getting the results you hope for: *At this rate we could be waiting till kingdom come for a pay rise.*

> In the Lord's Prayer, Christians look forward to the future with the words 'thy kingdom come'.

to kingdom 'come
Someone goes, or is sent, **to kingdom come** if they are killed violently, especially by an explosion of some kind: *He'd started to forget things, see. Left the gas on, things like that. He nearly blew us all to kingdom come once.*

kiss

kiss and 'tell
To **kiss and tell** means to have a sexual relationship with a famous person who has

an important reputation, and then sell the story to a newspaper: *'One thing I can promise you, Dr Blake,' she said softly, 'I never kiss and tell.'*

kiss-and-'tell: *She pioneered 'kiss-and-tell' journalism, closely following the lives of the rich and famous.*

kiss good'bye to something
To **kiss goodbye to something** is to accept that a change in the situation means you can no longer have or do something which you had been hoping for: *With this latest scandal, the Labour Party can kiss goodbye to their chances of taking power.*

kiss of 'death
A **kiss of death** is an action which is meant to be helpful to someone, but which in fact does them a lot of harm: *A reference from your boss would be the kiss of death. I mean it. Everyone in the business hates him.*

kiss of 'life
You give someone who has stopped breathing the **kiss of life** when you breathe into their mouth to try and make them start breathing again: *I'm sure she would have died without the kiss of life and I would have been devastated to lose her. She is a great companion.*

kit

get your 'kit off! (*very offensive or humorous*)
'**Get your kit off!**' literally means 'take your clothes off!'; people sometimes shout it at someone they find physically attractive: *Cor, that girl has a fantastic pair of legs ... Oy! Get your kit off, love!*

kith

kith and 'kin (*old*)
Your **kith and kin** are all the people who are related to you: *She is a widow now without kith or kin.* □ *It's so nice to see you, hearing all your bits of news about your kith and kin.*

kittens

have 'kittens
You say someone **is having kittens** if they are very nervous, upset or angry: *Where have you been all night? Your dad was having kittens.*

knee

on bended 'knee or on your bended 'knee
You ask for something **on**, or **on your**, **bended knee** if you ask for it in a humble way: *I beg you, on bended knee, to forgive me for this.*
◇ SEE ALSO **cap in hand** ▷ CAP

> The past participle of the verb 'bend' is normally 'bent', not 'bended'. 'Bended' is an old form.

knees

bring someone to their 'knees

A situation **brings someone to their knees** if it weakens, defeats or destroys them: *The loss of its biggest contract finally brought the company to its knees.*

go weak at the 'knees

When you suddenly feel nervous or slightly afraid in a certain situation, especially when it involves communication with a person that you admire greatly or feel attracted towards, you say you **have gone weak at the knees**: *There was something about his voice that moved her, made her go weak at the knees.*

'knees-up

A **knees-up** is a lively party or celebration: *We had a bit of a knees-up last night. I think we'll be staying in and taking it easy this evening.*

on your 'knees

You are **on your knees** when you are kneeling, or when you are desperately asking someone to do something: *'What are you doing down there on your knees?' 'I've dropped my contact lens.'* □ *I fell on my knees and asked them not to punish the child any more. They seemed to understand.*

knickers

get your 'knickers in a twist

You **get your knickers in a twist** when you are unable to relax and behave in a sensible way because you are so worried or upset: *I've been getting my knickers in a twist about work. It's stupid of me, because it's not that important.*

knife

get the 'knife in

You **get the knife in** when you make an aggressive verbal attack on someone in the knowledge that they will not be able to defend themselves properly: *He spotted a flaw in her argument, and did not hesitate to get the knife in.*

go under the 'knife

You say that someone **is going under the knife** when they are going to have an operation: *'I go into hospital on Monday, but I won't be going under the knife till Friday.'*

have your knife into someone

Someone who **has got their knife into you** is always trying or hoping to harm or upset you: *The only reason she's got her knife into 'me is because she's so jealous.*

twist the 'knife in the wound or turn the 'knife in the wound

If somebody has already made you feel upset by saying or doing something, and then, instead of stopping or saying sorry, they add something which makes you even more upset, you say they **are twisting**, or **turning, the knife in the wound**: *She went on brutally, turning the knife in the wound, watching the pain intensify. It gave her a feeling of vindictive pleasure.*

knight

knight in shining 'armour (*humorous*)

Your **knight in shining armour** is someone who saves you from a situation which you had thought was hopeless: *The police became knights in shining armour yesterday as they went to the rescue of a young German woman injured on a mountain top.*

In traditional folk tales, handsome knights saved young women from terrible and dangerous situations.

knobs

with brass 'knobs on

If a person, especially a child, says 'same to you **with brass knobs on**', they are returning an insult or criticism: *'You look like a pig.' 'Same to you with brass knobs on.'* □ *Fat and lazy yourself with brass knobs on.*

◇ SEE ALSO **with bells on** ▷ BELLS

This expression is used to return an insult when the speaker cannot think of a better one.

knock

knock 'em 'dead (*informal*)

You say '**knock 'em dead!**' to someone who is about to give a performance, as a way of encouraging them to perform as well as possible.

◇ SEE ALSO **break a leg!** ▷ LEG

knock someone for 'six

Something which **knocks you for six** surprises or shocks you so much that you are unable to think clearly: *It knocked me for six when she told me she was pregnant. I didn't know what to say.*

knock it 'off (*informal*)

You say '**knock it off!**' to someone if you want them to stop doing something which is annoying you: *Knock it off, will you? Some people are trying to sleep round here.*

◇ SEE ALSO **give me a break** ▷ BREAK; **give it a rest** ▷ REST

take a 'knock

You say something **has taken a knock** if it has been badly affected by an unpleasant event or experience: *His confidence took quite a knock when he had that accident last year.*

knot (see also **knots** and **knotted**)

tie the 'knot

You say you **are tying the knot** when you get married: *We met four years ago, and we tied the knot last June.*

knots

tie yourself in 'knots

You **are tying yourself in knots** when the harder you try to express yourself, the more difficult it becomes to do so: *He's been tying himself in knots all day, working out how he would tell you about the accident.*

knotted

get 'knotted (offensive)

When you say '**get knotted!**' to someone who is annoying you a lot, you are telling them to shut up and go away: *'Now, don't let me catch you smoking again.' 'Oh, get knotted.'*

◇ SEE ALSO **get stuffed** ▷ STUFFED

know

as far as so-and-so 'knows

Something you are saying is true **as far as you know** if it is true according to what you know or have been told: *'Has your daughter ever had any serious problems at school?' 'Not as far as I know.'*

◇ SEE ALSO **to your knowledge** ▷ KNOWLEDGE

before you know where you 'are

Something happens **before you know where you are** if it happens so quickly that you do not have time to understand the problem or situation properly: *Imagine you won the national lottery. Suddenly, before you knew where you were, you'd be rich.*

◇ SEE ALSO **before you can turn round** ▷ TURN

for all 'so-and-so knows

You say '**for all** a certain person **knows**' when that person has so little information that they cannot even reject the extreme or ridiculous possibility which has just been mentioned: *I haven't heard from my sister for such a long time now. For all I know, she may be dead.* □ *'What kind of car does he drive?' 'I've no interest in cars. For all I know, it might be a Rolls.'* □ *My parents have no idea where we are. We could be in Outer Mongolia for all they know.*

◇ SEE ALSO **as far as someone is concerned** ▷ CONCERNED

get to 'know

1 If two or more people **get to know each other**, they start to spend time together and to learn more about each other: *I got to know Karen and Sue through my evening classes.* **2** When you **get to know of something**, you discover that it exists or is

happening: *The redundancies were announced today, but I got to know of them a month ago from private sources.*

'I don't know

You use '**I don't know**' as an exclamation of annoyance or resignation: *Oh, I don't know, this is ridiculous. How much longer are they going to make us wait?* □ *I don't know. What will they do next?*

in the 'know

A person who is **in the know** about something is one of the few people who have information about it: *Those in the know say that she had good reasons for resigning.*

'know-all or 'know-it-all

If you call someone a **know-all** or a **know-it-all**, you mean that they seem to consider themselves so wise that they can give people their unwanted advice or opinions all the time: *'All right, know-all,' he said acidly to Evans, 'tell me something: if this thing we're looking for is radiation, why can't they find it with detectors?'*

◇ SEE ALSO **smart aleck or alec** ▷ ALECK; **clever clogs** ▷ CLOGS; **clever dick** ▷ DICK

I wouldn't 'know or how should 'I know?

If you say '**I wouldn't know**', or '**how should I know?**' when someone asks you a question, you are saying in rather an unfriendly way that you are not in a position to know the answer: *'When will she be back?' 'I wouldn't know.'*

◇ SEE ALSO **your guess is as good as mine** ▷ GUESS

'How should I know?' is ruder than 'I wouldn't know'.

know something 'backwards

You **know something backwards** when you know it well and in great detail: *We'd studied the novel till we knew it backwards.*

know 'best

You say a particular person **knows best** if they are the person most likely to understand what should be done: *If your doctor has told you to stay in bed, that's what you should do. I'm sure he knows best.*

know 'better

1 You **know better**, or **know better than to do something** if you realize you should not do it: *Billy's not a bad dog. His previous owner let him sit on the furniture, so he doesn't know any better.* □ *He knows better than to allow a confrontation to develop between himself and his predecessor.* **2** Someone who **knows better** than others has information that they do not have, and therefore can judge the situation better: *Everyone else thought he was ill in bed, but I knew better.*

know

... or two about something if
... ot of skill and experience in
...ea or activity: *I don't know if she can
...lue the vase for you, but she certainly
knows a thing or two about antiques.*

◇ SEE ALSO **teach someone a thing or two**
▷ TEACH

'know-how

You have the **know-how** if you have the
practical knowledge and skill to deal with
something: *Trust us with your catering
needs. We've got the know-how which
comes from years of experience.*

know what's 'what

Someone who **knows what's what** is an
expert in a certain area, or just generally
well-informed: *He knows what's what when
it comes to race-horses.* □ *If I'm ever unsure
about things, I usually check with Tommy.
He knows what's what.*

◇ SEE ALSO **know your onions** ▷ ONIONS

let someone 'know

You **let someone know**, or **let someone know
something** when you inform them about it:
*We'll let you know when we've come to a
decision.*

**not know whether you are coming or
'going**

You say you do **not know whether you are
coming or going** when you are feeling completely confused.

what do you 'know? or **waddaya 'know?**
(*informal, humorous*)

You say **'what do you know?'** or **'waddaya
know?'** either when you are pleasantly
surprised by something, or when you are
pretending to be surprised by something
which, in fact, does not surprise you at all:
*Well, what do you know? Here comes Billy,
late as usual.*

you 'know

You say **'you know' 1** to introduce a person
or thing that you are just going to say
something about: *You know that old toilet
which used to sit outside our house? Well, I
just sold it for £50.* **2** to add information
that helps to identify something: *What's the
name of that woman? You know, the one
with the smart clothes who does the lottery.* **3**
for emphasis, for example, when you are
giving advice or an opinion: *You shouldn't
smoke all that marijuana, you know. It can't
be good for you.* **4** with no real meaning at
all, when you are speaking informally, to
help the flow of what you are saying, and to
hold your listener's attention: *I was walking
along the street, you know, minding my own
business, when out jumped this big dog.*

you never 'know

1 You say **'you never know'** if you are acting to
avoid a possible danger or problem: *I always
use condoms. Well, you never know, do you?* **2**
You say **'you never know'** if you consider that
the event just mentioned is not impossible:
*'Will you have time to visit us this summer?' 'I
might just manage, you never know.'*

◇ SEE ALSO **better safe than sorry** ▷ BETTER;
you can't be too careful ▷ CAREFUL; **err on
the side of such-and-such** ▷ SIDE

knowledge

have carnal 'knowledge of someone

In legal terms, if you **have carnal knowledge
of someone,** you have had sex with them on
at least one occasion: *Is it true to say that
you have carnal knowledge of the deceased,
Mr Nicolas Smith?*

common 'knowledge

You say that something is **common knowledge**
if it is information which everyone knows:
*Didn't you know about his daughter in Aus-
tralia? I thought it was common knowledge.*

have a 'reading knowledge of something

You **have a reading knowledge of something**
such as a language if you can read it but are
not confident enough to produce it yourself: *As well as being fluent in French, I have
a reading knowledge of Italian.*

have a 'working knowledge of something

You **have a working knowledge of something**
if you know enough about it to be able to
use it, without being an expert on it: *I have
a working knowledge of several wordproces-
sing packages.*

to the best of your 'knowledge

You say that something is true **to the best of
your knowledge** if you are almost but not
completely sure that it is true: *These facts
were, to the best of my knowledge, true when
I made the speech a week ago.*

◇ SEE ALSO **to the best of your belief** ▷ BELIEF

to your 'knowledge (*rather formal*)

The thing you are saying is true **to your
knowledge** if it is true according to what
you know or have been told: *'Have you ever
had sex with a person in one of these high-
risk groups?' 'Not to my knowledge.'*

◇ SEE ALSO **as far as I know** ▷ KNOW

knuckle

give someone a knuckle 'sandwich (*humorous, informal*)

A person **gives someone a knuckle sandwich**
when they punch them: *What did you just
call me? Do you want a knuckle sandwich,
mate?*

◇ SEE ALSO **give someone a bunch of fives**
▷ BUNCH; **thick ear** ▷ EAR

l

labour

labour of 'love
You describe a piece of work as a **labour of love** when you have devoted all your time and energy to making it a success: *He bought an old 1965 Sunbeam Tiger and spent eight years rebuilding it – a labour of love.*

lack

not for lack of
Something fails **not for lack of** trying, for example, when the reason for its failure is not laziness or indifference: *The Government's initial failure to hold spending down in the early 1980s was not for lack of 'trying. The recession was much deeper than forecast.*

ladies

'ladies' man
A **ladies' man** is a man who enjoys entertaining and flattering women, especially in extravagant and lavish ways: *Oh, he's a ladies' man all right! And from what I've seen the ladies seem glad of it.*
◇ SEE ALSO **lady-killer** ▷ LADY; **Latin lover** ▷ LOVER

'ladies' room
The **ladies' room** is a polite term for the women's toilets in a public place: *She excused herself when halfway through the meal, and made for the ladies' room.*

lady

'lady-killer
A **lady-killer** is a man who is aware of his sexual attractiveness, and who uses his charm to form many relationships with women: *When he'd had a few drinks he thought himself a bit of a lady-killer.*
◇ SEE ALSO **ladies' man** ▷ LADIES; **Latin lover** ▷ LOVER

lady 'muck
Lady muck is an insulting name for a woman who thinks she is more important than everyone else: *Look, it's Lady Muck herself; who does she think she is?*

lady of 'leisure
A **lady of leisure** is a woman who does not have to do much, or any, work: *Emily Grenfell was no weak-kneed lady of leisure, but a strong, hard businesswoman.*

lads

one of the 'lads
A man, or sometimes a woman, who is described as being **one of the lads**, tends to be lively and sociable, and likes being with men with whom they share the same age and interests: *No. I don't think it's a good idea to promote one of the workers. Charlie is too much one of the lads and won't hold their respect.*

lager

'lager lout
A **lager lout** is a young man who, usually as part of a group of other young men, spends his time in pubs, on the streets, and at football matches, making a noise, drinking beer, and trying to start fights with other young men: *The police risk losing control of the streets to lager louts, vandals and drug dealers, the Police Federation conference was warned.*

Lager is a light-coloured beer.

laid

get 'laid (*vulgar*)
Someone **gets laid** when they have sex with someone with whom they are not already in an established relationship.
◇ SEE ALSO **have it away with someone** ▷ AWAY; **get** or **have your end away** ▷ END; **have it off with someone** ▷ OFF

laissez-faire

laissez-'faire
Laissez-faire attitudes are characterized by an unwillingness to get involved in or influence other people's actions; a government with **laissez-faire** policies does not attempt to control the buying and selling of goods: *the passing of laissez-faire and the coming of the welfare state.*

Laissez-faire means 'allow to do' in French.

lake

go jump in the 'lake
You rudely tell someone to **go jump in the lake** if you are very angry with them and want them to go away.

◇ SEE ALSO **take a running jump** ▷ JUMP

lamb

like a lamb to the 'slaughter
Someone goes to a place **like a lamb to the slaughter** when they go there calmly and without protesting because they do not know that they will find something extremely unpleasant there, or because there is nothing they can do to avoid it: *The night before the wedding I was very calm, deathly calm. I felt I was the lamb to the slaughter. I knew it and I couldn't do anything about it.*

This idiom comes from the Bible: Isaiah 53:8.

land

find out how the 'land lies
You **find out**, or **see**, **how the land lies** when you make sure you know all the necessary details about a situation before taking any action: *And that's what I hope the Treasurer will do – find out just how the land lies, what the best position is, and what interest rates we might be able to get.*

◇ SEE ALSO **spy out the land** ▷ LAND

land someone 'in it
You **land someone in it** when you reveal something about them that was supposed to be kept a secret, or if you get them into a difficult situation: *Why did you go and land me in it? I'll never be able to get myself out of this one.*

'land-lubber (old or humorous)
Land-lubber is a humorous or old-fashioned name for someone who does not have much experience of boats or travelling by sea.

the land of the 'living
You are in **the land of the living** if you are alive, when you may be expected to be otherwise: *Only the odd bouts of involuntary twitching in his sleep reassured his owner that Jess was still safe and sound in the land of the living.*

land of milk and 'honey
A **land of milk and honey** is a country that has good living conditions, and where there are opportunities for making a lot of money: *There was a lot of talk of emigration, possibly to Canada but more usually to England, the land of milk and honey and opportunity.*

the land of 'nod
You go to **the land of nod** when you go to sleep: *You'll need earplugs, a light where it disturbs nobody and a good book till the warm drink you've made for consolation lulls you back to the land of nod.*

'land someone one
You **land someone one** when you hit them.

never-'never land
Never-never land is an imaginary place where life is perfect to an extent that is impossible in real life: *I am not making promises of a vague future, a never-never land that exists only in dreams; these are the tangible developments that will take place.*

◇ SEE ALSO **cloud cuckoo land** ▷ CLOUD

'promised land
A **promised land** is a place where people expect to acquire wealth, health and happiness: *Italy, the promised land for any musician, particularly a potential opera composer, beckoned.*

The **Promised Land** in the Bible was Canaan, the land that was promised to the Jews by God.

spy out the 'land
You **spy out the land** when you obtain information about something in advance: *In the spring of 1705 Colonel Nathaniel Hooke was sent to Scotland to spy out the land.*

◇ SEE ALSO **find out how the land lies** ▷ LAND

landslide

landslide 'victory
A **landslide victory** is a situation in an election where the winning candidate gets a very large proportion of the votes: *A year before their landslide victory in the election of June 1987 the Conservatives lagged behind Labour in the opinion polls.*

lane

the 'fast lane
Someone who lives their life in **the fast lane** has a very busy, competitive and risky lifestyle: *His face was beginning to show the strain of a life lived in the fast lane.*

On a motorway, the **fast lane** is the section of the road designated for fast drivers.

language

bad 'language
Bad language is language that may offend or shock people: *They were not allowed to*

smoke or 'be guilty of noisy behaviour or bad language' on or off the golf course.

◇ SEE ALSO **strong language** ▷ LANGUAGE

speak the same 'language or talk the same 'language

Two people **speak**, or **talk**, **the same language** when they understand and relate to each other very well: *Like any hobby or job, it's vital that we speak the same language, understand the same terms.*

strong 'language

Strong language is language that states ideas forcefully, and that may involve swearing: *It was a sign of their anxiety that no-one noticed this strong language despite the presence of ladies.*

◇ SEE ALSO **bad language** ▷ LANGUAGE

lap

drop into someone's 'lap

Something **drops into your lap** when it comes to you or arrives without you having to make any effort to get it: *This chance of a lifetime, he appreciated, had dropped miraculously into his lap.*

Your **lap** is formed by the upper parts of your legs which are horizontal when you are sitting on a chair.

in the lap of the 'gods

You say that the result of a particular situation is **in the lap of the gods** if it depends entirely on luck, or on circumstances outside your control: *The result of tomorrow's match is in the lap of the gods.*

in the lap of 'luxury

You live **in the lap of luxury** if you live in great comfort, especially when it is provided by expensive, beautiful surroundings and objects: *There will always be a need for socialism, so long as there are millionaires living in the lap of luxury and other people living in cardboard boxes.*

'lap it up (*informal*)

You **lap it up** when you enjoy hearing praise, gossip or information, and accept it eagerly: *He was tall, very fair, reasonably attractive, and when he made with the charm at hospital parties they lapped it up.*

An animal **laps up** liquid when it noisily drinks it, using its tongue to scoop it up.

large

at 'large

1 If you refer to people **at large**, you mean most people or people in general: *A prime minister who was the subject of such a massive loss of confidence among both the political élite and the public at large should*

have been removed from office. **2** A dangerous person or animal that is **at large** has escaped from prison or captivity and has not yet been recaptured: *'You don't think that fellow Burrows could have done it?' asked Frobisher. 'From what I gather, he's still at large.'*

by and 'large

Something that is so **by and large** is so in a general way: *By and large we don't have too many problems with absence in our office.*

lark

up with the 'lark

You are **up with the lark** when you get up very early in the morning: *Tomorrow we start to clean through the house, top to bottom. So it's up with the lark, my girl!*

A **lark** is a bird that is known for its beautiful song.

last

last but not 'least

Last but not least is used before mentioning a person or thing that is last in a list, in order to emphasize that they are as important as those mentioned before: *Manifestos and artists' statements, interviews, catalogues, biographies, chronologies, memoirs, and, last but not least, exhibition catalogues and survey books abound.*

see the 'last of

You **see the last of** someone or something that you don't like when you see them for the last time: *I heard the outer door shut. It was a relief to see the last of them.*

too good to 'last

You say that a favourable situation is **too good to last** when you feel, pessimistically, that it cannot continue because someone will want to spoil it: *She wept and said she had always known it was too good to last, and went off back home to her mother.*

lather

in a 'lather

You are **in a lather** when you are very excited or upset: *'And where do you think you've been till now?' Dad was in a right lather.*

laugh

don't make me 'laugh

You say, rudely, **'don't make me laugh'** to someone when they have suggested something that you cannot take seriously: *Your old man a hero? Don't make me laugh!*

◇ SEE ALSO **come off it** ▷ COME; **do me a favour** ▷ FAVOUR; **don't give me that** ▷ GIVE; **tell that to the marines** ▷ MARINES

for a 'laugh
You do something **for a laugh** when you do it for fun or as a joke: *When asked their reasons for stealing the car, the boys said they just did it for a laugh.*

have the last 'laugh
You **have the last laugh** when you are finally proved right or succeed in the end: *Yet women drivers have the last laugh. They get cheaper insurance rates because their accident records are better.*

you've got to 'laugh
People say '**you've got to laugh**' when something unfortunate but rather comical happens to them: *The unfortunate Julie said yesterday at her home in Swansea: 'You've got to laugh – otherwise you'd go under.'*

laurels

look to your 'laurels
If you tell someone to **look to their laurels**, you mean that they should be careful not to lose a position or reputation because of better performances by others: *I feel sure their new white wines will soon be making the French look to their laurels.*

> In ancient Greece the winner of a competition received a crown made of laurel leaves.

rest on your 'laurels
Someone who has been successful is said to **be resting on their laurels** if they are relying on their reputation rather than trying to progress further: *In her famed speech on election night 1987, she encouraged her party troops not to rest on their laurels, but to continue the fight.*

law

be a law unto your'self
Someone who is described as **a law unto themselves** does not follow conventional rules and ways of behaving: *Conventions didn't exist for her. She was a law unto herself and did what she wanted to do.*

law and 'order
Law and order is a term used to talk about the law being obeyed, and maintained by the police or the army: *In February this year, the Minister of Law and Order declared that the Government would not repeal its most notorious detention law.*

the law of 'averages
The **law of averages** is a rule which states that if something is done often enough, for example, tossing a coin, the result will become regular: *The law of averages suggests it is Arsenal's turn to beat their neighbours this afternoon.*

the law of the 'jungle
The **law of the jungle** is the idea that the strongest and most selfish people in a society are most likely to succeed: *The assassination of seven students by death squads in 1988 showed that the country was living by the 'law of the jungle' despite the supposed democratization of political life.*

lay down the 'law
Someone **lays down the law** when they state something in a way that indicates that they expect their opinion and orders to be accepted without argument: *I am not attempting to lay down the law, but simply wish to voice my opinion that ethics should be the first guideline of those dealing with public resources.*

take the law into your own 'hands
Someone **takes the law into their own hands** when they decide to punish someone themselves, rather than following official legal procedures: *Donna, you can't take the law into your own hands. This isn't some bloody film where the heroine takes out a gun and blows away the bad guys.*

lay

an easy 'lay
Someone, especially a woman, who is described as **an easy lay** has many sexual partners, and does not always form established relationships before having sex with them: *To loads of people, wearing short skirts means you are an 'easy lay'.*

lay it on 'thick
You **lay it on thick** when you **1** try to gain people's sympathy by exaggerating your misfortune. **2** praise someone or something highly in order to obtain something from them: *'How well you look!' she exclaimed, determined to lay it on thick to please him.*

lay someone 'low
An illness **lays someone low** when it stops them from being able to do what they usually do: *Gooch had his infamous encounter with a poisonous prawn that laid him low for several days.*

lay someone 'open to something
A circumstance **lays you open to** criticism or attack if it puts you in danger of being criticized or attacked: *This decision would lay him open to accusations of favouritism or vindictiveness.*

lead

lead a'stray

You **lead someone astray** when you teach them bad habits, or are responsible for making them do something wrong: *Teenagers are fiercely independent, but the risks of being led astray are also much greater at this age.*

swing the 'lead

Someone **swings the lead** when they try to avoid working, or invent excuses to hide the fact that they have neglected their work: *I'm not swinging the lead, my doctor sent me here. He has assured me that there really is something wrong with me.*

take the 'lead

You **take the lead** when you do things before other people do them: *They took the lead with a fine goal, then conceded two.*

leaf

shake like a 'leaf

You **are shaking like a leaf** if your body is trembling, usually because you are afraid, shocked or cold: *You're shaking like a leaf. It's no doubt the shock. Come along with me – you need a brandy.*

◊ SEE ALSO **shake like a jelly** ▷ JELLY

take a leaf out of 'so-and-so's book

You **take a leaf out of** a certain person's **book** when you use them as a good example, and try to copy something that they do: *Take a leaf out of my book. Give up smoking.*

◊ SEE ALSO **take your cue from someone** ▷ CUE; **follow suit** ▷ SUIT

Leaf is an old-fashioned word for a page.

turn over a new 'leaf

You **turn over a new leaf** when you begin a new and better way of behaving or working: *Seems he's decided to turn over a new leaf – let's hope it lasts.*

◊ SEE ALSO **change your ways** ▷ WAYS

league

in a different 'league or not in the same 'league as someone

Someone or something that is **in a different league from**, or **not in the same league as**, someone or something else, does not reach that thing's or person's standard: *Their clothes are cheaper, but then they're not in the same league as Armani and Gaultier.*

◊ SEE ALSO **in a class of your own** ▷ CLASS; **a cut above** or **a cut above the rest** ▷ CUT; **not fit to hold a candle to** ▷ CANDLE

in 'league with someone

You are **in league with someone** when you agree to work with them, usually in secret or for some bad purpose: *Was it really reasonable to think that they were all in league against him? Maybe he was just imagining it.*

leak

take a 'leak (*informal or vulgar*)

You **take a leak** when you urinate.

◊ SEE ALSO **go for a slash** ▷ SLASH

lean

lean over 'backwards

You **lean over backwards** to help someone when you do everything you can to help them: *We had support, people helping us and advising us; they leant over backwards to help us.*

◊ SEE ALSO **bend over backwards** ▷ BEND

leap

a leap in the 'dark

You take **a leap in the dark** when you act or decide something without knowing what the consequence may be: *Health ministers were accused of a massive 'leap in the dark' yesterday as they prepared another shake-up of the NHS.*

A **leap** is a sudden or quick jump.

leaps

in leaps and 'bounds or by leaps and 'bounds

Someone or something progresses **in**, or **by**, **leaps and bounds**, when they move forward quickly and successfully: *It was a great learning experience, but I wasn't moving in leaps and bounds; I wanted to really progress.*

learning

a little learning is a dangerous 'thing

If you say '**a little learning is a dangerous thing**', you mean that you are more likely to make serious errors if you have only a little knowledge on a subject than if you have none: *'Maybe you don't know as much about me as you think. A little knowledge can be a dangerous thing. You should always be sure of your facts.*

lease

a new lease of 'life

You get **a new lease of life** when you suddenly feel more energetic or enthusiastic again after a period of tiredness or boredom: *Ironically, since the accident, their marriage has gained a new lease of life.*

least

in the 'least
You use 'in the least' to emphasize a statement in the negative: *She wasn't in the least surprised to hear the news.*

least of 'all
Least of all emphasizes a particular person or thing to which a negative statement applies: *'You see dears,' said the old lady, 'no-one, least of all a great detective, believes what they read in the newspapers.'*

the 'least someone can do
The least someone can do is the minimum they can do, even if they do not do anything more: *The least he can do is respond to such a complaint immediately with a carefully worded personal letter.*

to say the 'least
If something is so to say the least, the situation is actually more extreme than that: *The instructions are confusing, to say the least.*

leave

French 'leave
You take French leave when you are absent or on holiday from your duties without permission: *Children had been left with matches to light the gas, and the girls' caretaker and the needlewoman had both taken 'French leave'.*

> The British used to believe that it was a French custom to leave an occasion without saying goodbye to the host, while the French believed that it was a British custom.

leave 'be or leave well a'lone
You leave someone or something be, or leave them well alone, when you do not get involved with them, or allow the situation to remain as it is, so as not to make it worse: *'Leave him be, for the moment,' Madeleine advised, 'and he'll be all right.'* □ *If you had left well alone and let me carry on my business I wouldn't be in this trouble now.*
◇ SEE ALSO **let be** ▷ LET

leave a lot to be de'sired or leave something to be de'sired
Something that leaves a lot, or something, to be desired does not reach the standard you would like or expect it to reach: *It is not user-friendly and leaves a lot to be desired for a software support product.* □ *He explained they had all been up late the night before and that their performance might leave something to be desired. It did.*
◇ SEE ALSO **no great shakes** ▷ SHAKES

leave of 'absence
You are given leave of absence when you are given permission to be away from your duties for a certain period of time: *In 1928 he took leave of absence from a lectureship at a college in Birmingham to go to India.*

leave someone a'lone
You leave someone alone when you stop disturbing or annoying them: *She won't leave me alone, talking to me all the time, distracting me.*

leave someone 'standing
You leave someone standing when you are much better than them at something.

take leave of your 'senses
You say that someone has taken leave of their senses if they have done something which makes you think they must have gone mad: *Her daughter had taken leave of her senses and her husband was never at home when he was needed. The world had gone completely mad.*

leg (*see also* **legs**)

break a 'leg!
You say 'break a leg!' to someone who is about to perform in public, as a way of wishing them good luck.
◇ SEE ALSO **knock 'em dead** ▷ KNOCK

> According to superstition, you should not say the words 'good luck!' to an actor as this may tempt the gods.

get your 'leg over (*vulgar*)
A man gets his leg over when he seduces a woman and has sex with her: *In the Oxford of the late Sixties, anyone who didn't get his leg over and smoke a few joints wasn't regarded as a normal human being.*

give someone a 'leg-up
You give someone a leg-up when you 1 help them to climb over something 2 help them to improve their situation at work, for example: *This offers the opportunity to develop a range of skills, as well as giving some a leg-up into an acting career.*

'leg it (*informal*)
You leg it when you run very fast, usually to escape from someone or something: *Saunders was arrested later and told police he 'legged it' after someone shouted at him from a car.*
◇ SEE ALSO **run for it** ▷ RUN

not have a leg to 'stand on
You say that someone does not have a leg to stand on if you think that their behaviour or opinions cannot be supported by facts or evidence.

legend

pull someone's 'leg
You **pull someone's leg** when you try to make them believe something which is not true, as a joke: *'You're pulling my leg!' Did he really expect her to believe such nonsense?*

shake a 'leg
You tell someone to **shake a leg** when you want them to hurry up.

talk the hind leg off a 'donkey
Someone who can, could, or would, **talk the hind leg off a donkey** talks a lot: *That man would talk the hind leg off a donkey, does he never stop?*

◇ SEE ALSO **talk a blue streak** ▷ STREAK

legend

be a legend in your own 'lifetime
Someone who is described as **a legend in their own lifetime** has become famous and highly respected while they are still alive.

legs

be on your last 'legs
You are **on your last legs** when you are so tired or old that you can hardly continue what you are doing: *Anyone reading the papers would think I was on my last legs. Where did these journalists get their information?*

◇ SEE ALSO **hardly put one foot in front of the other** ▷ FOOT

as fast as your legs can 'carry you
You run **as fast as your legs can carry you** when you run as fast as possible.

◇ SEE ALSO **run like the wind** ▷ WIND

'sea legs
You get your **sea legs** when you get used to the motion of a ship: *And now those with a sense of adventure and sometimes a good pair of sea legs can join in the fun on board the former lifeboat.*

stretch your 'legs
You **stretch your legs** when you walk around and get some exercise and fresh air after having spent a long time in the same position: *We pulled over at a roadside café to have a cup of coffee and to stretch our legs.*

leisure

at 'leisure
You do something **at leisure** when you take your time and enjoy it: *You are escorted to your hotel in Salzburg. The rest of the day is spent at leisure.*

lend

'lend itself to
Something **lends itself to** being used or dealt with in a particular way if it can easily be

used or dealt with in that way: *Negotiating is an art, not a science. But it does lend itself to careful analysis and preparation too.*

length

at 'length
1 You describe something **at length** when you describe it in great detail. **2** You speak **at length** when you speak for a long time.

the length and breadth of
Something that happens throughout **the length and breadth of** an area happens everywhere in it: *Covering the length and breadth of 'Ireland, the programme will focus on a wide variety of gardens, both large and small.*

lengths

go to great 'lengths or go to any 'lengths
You **go to great lengths** to do or achieve something when you take a lot of trouble over it; someone who is prepared to **go to any lengths** to achieve something is determined to achieve it by whatever means may be necessary: *To fulfil his ambition he was prepared to go to any lengths, no matter how underhand or devious they might be.* □ *Given the information and access, responsible suppliers will go to great lengths to solve a real problem up to and even including commissioning full scale research projects.*

◇ SEE ALSO **push the boat out** ▷ BOAT; **go to town on something** ▷ TOWN; **go to a lot of trouble** ▷ TROUBLE; **go out of your way** ▷ WAY

leopard

a leopard never changes its 'spots
A leopard never changes its spots means that people's characters are unlikely to change: *'A leopard can't change his spots' and other maxims take an essentially pessimistic view about people's ability to change their behaviour.*

◇ SEE ALSO **you can't teach an old dog new tricks** ▷ DOG

less

no 'less
You add **'no less'** after mentioning someone or something in order to emphasize their importance: *When you get to my age, you get a telegram from the Queen, no less.*

This expression is often used ironically, for humorous effect.

lesser

the lesser of the two 'evils
The lesser of the two evils is the less unpleasant or harmful of two unpleasant or

harmful things: *Suddenly she felt that being with safe, secure Peter was by far the lesser of the two evils.*

lesson

learn your 'lesson

You **learn your lesson** when you realize that you should not have done something, probably because it has harmed you or someone else, and you decide not to do it again: *I've learnt my lesson. I realize what a fool I was, throwing myself at you the way I did.*

teach someone a 'lesson

You **teach someone a lesson** when you try to make sure they will not do something bad or wrong again by punishing them: *She had let me down one too many times, and I decided to teach her a lesson.*

let

let a'lone such-and-such

If one thing is not so, **let alone** another, the second thing cannot be so, since it is the less likely or possible of the two: *We can put our heart into the work without worrying about whether or not it will sell, let alone whether it will sell at an 'economic price.*

let 'be

You **let** someone or something **be** when you do not get involved with them, or allow the situation to remain as it is, so as not to make it worse: *If I were you, I'd just let things be for a while.*

◊ SEE ALSO **leave be** ▷ LEAVE

let 'fly

You **let fly** at someone when you suddenly become very angry with them: *He had a tendency to let fly for seemingly no reason at all.*

◊ SEE ALSO **go off at the deep end** ▷ END; **have a blue fit** ▷ FIT; **blow a fuse** ▷ FUSE; **blow a gasket** ▷ GASKET; **blow** or **flip your lid** ▷ LID; **do your nut** ▷ NUT; **lose your rag** ▷ RAG; **fly into a rage** ▷ RAGE; **hit the roof** ▷ ROOF; **blow your stack** ▷ STACK; **lose your temper** ▷ TEMPER; **blow your top** ▷ TOP; **throw a wobbly** ▷ WOBBLY

let it all hang 'out

If you **let it all hang out**, you relax and behave as you wish, without worrying about what other people think of you: *Go on. Let it all hang out. Just this once.*

let it 'drop

You **let it drop** when you stop talking about something because it is not having any effect: *But don't think I'm going to let it drop. I'll find out your reasons, one way or another.*

let it 'lie or let things 'lie

You **let it lie**, or **let things lie**, when you do not try to interfere with a situation for a while, in the hope that it will improve: *We'll let it lie for now, and if we do get a good response we can think about planning another programme.*

let it 'pass or let it 'go

If someone makes a mistake and you **let it go**, or **pass**, you do not pay attention to it or mention it to them: *I'll let it pass this time, but please try to make more of an effort in future.*

let 'loose

1 You **let** an animal **loose** when you allow it to run around freely after it has been restrained in some way. **2** You **let** people **loose** on a place when you allow them to go there, even though they are likely to do something foolish or irresponsible: *Sixty journalists were let loose on the pop group this morning as they left their hotel for rehearsals.*

let 'me

You use '**let me**' when you are offering to do something, or saying that you are going to do it.

let 'rip

You **let rip** when you do something as loudly or as fast as possible: *She turned to the keyboard and let rip: the noise nearly blew me off the balcony.*

let's 'see or let me 'see

You say '**let's see**' or '**let me see**' when you are thinking or trying to remember something: *There must have been, let me see, at least 200 people there.*

let someone 'have it

If you **let someone have it**, you suddenly attack them, physically, or with words: *Both were found guilty of murder after an Old Bailey jury heard that Bentley shouted: 'Let him have it, Chris'.*

let someone 'know

If you tell someone you will **let them know**, you mean that you will give them the information they want later: *I'm afraid I haven't got my diary with me – can I let you know tomorrow?*

let something 'slide

You **let something slide** when you neglect it and cause its standard to drop: *I noticed he's been letting things slide recently, but I didn't realize he was so depressed.*

let something 'ride

You **let something ride** when you do not take any action to stop it: *So, you don't agree with the idea, but if it happened to be found elsewhere, other than your home town, you'd let it ride?*

let something 'slip

If you **let** a piece of secret information **slip**, you tell someone about it unintentionally: *Try not to let it slip that we're organizing something – I'd really like it to be a surprise.*

to 'let

A building which is **to let** is available to be rented.

letter

four-letter 'word

A **four-letter word** is a swear word: *Over-reacting with shock and dismay when the child first comes out with a four-letter word will only encourage him or her to use it again.*
◇ SEE ALSO **the F word** ▷ WORD

French 'letter (*old or humorous*)

French letter is an old-fashioned or humorous word for 'condom': *A sheath* (condom, French letter) *plus a spermicide provides good protection for both partners against both unwanted disease and unwanted pregnancies.*

the letter of the 'law

If you follow **the letter of the law**, you act according to its exact words, rather than its general meaning: *What the Leeds manager appeared to be saying was that he was glad to see a referee not sticking rigidly to the letter of the law.*

red-'letter day

A **red-letter day** is a day that you will always remember because something pleasant or important happened on it: *Whether you are celebrating a birthday, a wedding anniversary or some other red-letter day, these candles will provide the right atmosphere.*

to the 'letter

You follow instructions, for example, **to the letter** when you follow them exactly, paying attention to every detail: *I don't understand it – I followed your guidelines to the letter, and it still doesn't work.*

level

find your 'level

You **find your level** when you find the place on a scale where you naturally belong: *Once you've found your level, you'll feel much happier.*

level-'headed

Someone who is described as **level-headed** is calm and in control in situations where other people might panic: *Martha soon came back, visibly distressed. Our supervisor, the level-headed Mrs Long, was called.*

on the 'level (*informal*)

Someone or something that is **on the level** is honest or genuine: *Are you sure this deal is on the level? I don't know if I can trust Holt.*

sink to 'such-and-such a level

Someone **sinks to** a certain **level** when they do something shameful: *Don't sink to their level. If that's the way they behave, it doesn't mean you have to do the same.*

liberty

at 'liberty

You are **at liberty** to do something if you are free, or allowed, to do it: *After lunch, you are at liberty to do whatever you want, as long as you are back before 6pm.*

Liberty 'Hall

You refer to a place as **Liberty Hall** if people there can come and go as they please: *Come and go as it suits you. Liberty Hall, that's what you've made of my home!*

take the liberty of

You **take the liberty of** doing something when you do it without permission: *We took the liberty of asking our friend Percy 'Hoskins to join us for dinner. I hope it doesn't put you out.*

liberties

take 'liberties

Someone who **takes liberties** expects too much freedom, or does not treat other people or their possessions with enough respect: *I didn't mind at first, but he's started taking liberties now that he knows I'm easy-going.*

licence

artistic 'licence

You use **artistic licence** in painting, for example, when you allow yourself to diverge from reality, rather than representing it exactly, in order to produce a particular effect: *A little artistic licence may be necessary. Try to create a picture that gives the feeling of the wedding flowers without reproducing them exactly.*

licence to print 'money

You are given a **licence to print money** when you are enabled to do something that will make you very rich: *When we were privatized, there were those I'm sure who thought, It's a licence to print money. Which it would be of course if you weren't a regulated body.*

poetic 'licence

You use **poetic licence** when you allow yourself to diverge from the usual rules of grammar or meaning, in order to produce a particular effect: *He presents a glowing idea of a prosperous countryside, although how much of this is poetic licence is difficult to judge.*

lick

a lick and a 'promise
A **lick and a promise** is a quick and careless attempt to do something, such as to wash yourself: *The children were out of the house with not much more than a lick and a promise:*

a lick of 'paint
Something that needs **a lick of paint** needs to be painted: *The door could do with a lick of paint, but apart from that there's not much that needs doing.*

lid

blow the 'lid off something or take the 'lid off something
You **blow**, or **take**, **the lid off**, a scandal, for example, when you expose it to the public.

blow your 'lid or flip your 'lid
You **blow**, or **flip**, **your lid** when you suddenly become very angry: *This was his moment of weakness, the point at which he'd flipped his lid for the first and last time in his career.*

◇ SEE ALSO **go off at the deep end** ▷ END; **have a blue fit** ▷ FIT; **blow a fuse** ▷ FUSE; **blow a gasket** ▷ GASKET; **let fly** ▷ LET; **do your nut** ▷ NUT; **lose your rag** ▷ RAG; **fly into a rage** ▷ RAGE; **hit the roof** ▷ ROOF; **blow your stack** ▷ STACK; **lose your temper** ▷ TEMPER; **blow your top** ▷ TOP; **throw a wobbly** ▷ WOBBLY

keep the 'lid on something
You **keep the lid on something** when you try to ensure that people do not find out about it or that they do not do something undesirable: *In fact, the Princess of Wales must wish she was able to keep the lid on her private life as tightly as Selina has.* □ *The Government in 1989 had to appoint a special transport minister to keep the lid on the widespread anger of developers about the lack of transport to Docklands.*

put the 'lid on something
You **put the lid on** a certain activity when you stop people from doing it: *His new responsibilities have put the lid on all those late nights and parties.*

lie

give the 'lie to something
A fact which **gives the lie to something** proves that something you originally believed to be true is actually false: *Tombs found near the pyramids, which were constructed from about 2,550BC, also give the lie to the theory that the men who built them were slaves.*

I tell a 'lie (*informal*)
You say **'I tell a lie'** when you are about to correct something you have just said: *I got home at 6 o'clock, no, I tell a lie, 7 o'clock.*

lie 'doggo
You **lie doggo** when you keep very still, usually in order to hide from someone: *As they entered the building, they were surrounded by a dozen officers who had been lying doggo nearby for many hours.*

lie 'heavy on someone
A feeling, such as guilt, **lies heavy on you** if it makes you feel depressed and unable to think about anything else: *It was the loss of human life that lay heavy on him.*

lie 'low
You **lie low** when you hide from someone in order to avoid getting caught: *At the time of the murder he appears to have been lying low in a barn near Gainsborough.*

the lie of the 'land
You investigate **the lie of the land** when you try to find out the details of a situation before taking action.

live a 'lie
Someone who **is living a lie** is deceiving everyone about who they are or what they are doing: *It was the guilt of living a lie for 50 years that forced moral adviser Marge Proops into confessing her secret love affair.*

a white 'lie
You tell **a white lie** when you say something that is not entirely true because you do not want to upset or offend someone, or just because it makes things easier: *'I did hold down a responsible job before,' she said. Which wasn't strictly true. But her self-confidence needed the support of that little white lie.*

life

anything for a quiet 'life
You say **'anything for a quiet life'** when you do something that would normally go against your principles, but you do it anyway, because it is the easiest option: *Do you always give way to your children, perhaps because it's the easiest thing to do?* (Anything for a quiet life!)

◇ SEE ALSO **cop-out** ▷ COP; **the soft option** ▷ OPTION; **take the easy way out** ▷ WAY

breathe 'life into something or bring something to 'life
Someone **breathes life into something**, or **brings something to life**, when they make it more lively, interesting or attractive; something **comes to life** when it is caused to become more lively, interesting or attractive: *Bogart was just the type of actor needed to breathe life into this kind of story.* □ *The road was screened by another brick wall, topped with trellis, brought to life by a mass of climbers and a large purple flowered lilac.*

can't do such-and-such to save your 'life

You say that you **can't do such-and-such to save your life** if you cannot do it at all, or if you do it very badly: *I can't sing to save my life.*

a charmed 'life

Someone who leads **a charmed life** has lot of good luck: *By his own admission he has led a charmed life. He survived a train crash at Allendale between Newcastle and Edinburgh in the Sixties.*

depart this 'life

You **depart this life** when you die: *To the memory of Leopold Thomas Rice Dersingham who departed this life 12 July 1942 in the 18th year of his life.*

◊ SEE ALSO **breathe your last** ▷ LAST; **kick the bucket** ▷ BUCKET; **cash in your chips** ▷ CHIPS; **pop your clogs** ▷ CLOGS; **shuffle off this mortal coil** ▷ COIL; **bite the dust** ▷ DUST; **give up the ghost** ▷ GHOST; **snuff it** ▷ SNUFF; **go the way of all flesh** ▷ WAY

People use this expression in order to avoid offending people by saying 'die'.

for dear 'life

You do something **for dear life** when you do it as forcefully or as firmly as you can: *In the mountains of Greece the passengers cling on for dear life and make the sign of the cross at every bend in the road.*

◊ SEE ALSO **hang** or **hold on like grim death** ▷ DEATH

for the 'life of me

You say you cannot remember, or understand something **for the life of you** to emphasize the difficulty you are having remembering or understanding it: *To that vile city of yours! I can't for the life of me understand what it is you see in it. It's filthy!*

get a 'life *(informal)*

If you tell someone to **'get a life'**, you mean that they should stop behaving in a ridiculous, pathetic or foolish way, because you have no respect or patience for them.

give your 'life for or lay down your 'life for

A person **gives**, or **lays down**, **their life** for something when they die for something they believe in very strongly: *I mean to lay down my life that men like you can live in freedom to fight for what is right in the world.*

'high life

High life is a style of living that is characterized by extravagant social occasions and luxurious living conditions: *Elegant young ladies appear who talk of nothing but high life, and high-lived company; with other fashionable topics, such as pictures, taste and Shakespeare.*

how's 'life? or how's life 'treating you? *(informal)*

You use **'how's life?'** or **'how's life treating you?'** after saying hello to a friend you have not seen for a while.

larger than 'life

You describe someone as **larger than life** if they have a strong, vibrant personality; something that is **larger than life** makes a very strong impression on you: *She was larger than life, she had seen the world, she was game for anything, she was jolly and vibrant, spoke her mind; all in all, she was fun to be with.*

the life and 'soul

You describe someone as **the life and soul** of a party, for example, if they are the most lively and enthusiastic person there, and their good mood makes other people feel the same way: *She appeared laughing with the other women, toasting Alex in lemonade, her hair flying, her eyes glinting, the life and soul of the party.*

life begins at 'forty

Life begins at forty is a saying which means that after the age of forty, you can really start enjoying life: *In some ways, life does begin at forty, I suppose, for many women; for children are beginning to grow independent and women can resume their careers.*

life goes 'on

Life goes on means that people go on living their daily lives, despite problems that individuals may be facing: *Ah well, life goes on I suppose. Can't be depressed for ever.*

◊ SEE ALSO **that's the way the cookie crumbles** ▷ WAY; **such is life** ▷ LIFE; **that's life** ▷ LIFE

life is a bowl of 'cherries

If you say that someone's **life is a bowl of cherries**, you mean that everything about it is pleasant; people often use the expression **life is no bowl of cherries** to express the idea that life is not always easy: *Life here is no bowl of cherries; discipline is strict, and the work is hard.*

life is for 'living

If you tell someone **life is for living**, you mean that they should start enjoying themselves, rather than worrying too much about the future: *Life is for living, do your own thing sometimes. Do not just exist.*

◊ SEE ALSO **you only live once** ▷ LIVE

the life of 'Riley

Someone who lives the **life of Riley** doesn't do any work, and spends their time enjoying themselves in expensive ways: *I hear that all the older boys are driving big expensive cars and living the life of Riley.*

When people use this expression, it usually means that they disapprove of the person's lifestyle.

a 'life-saver
You call someone or something **a life-saver** when they help you out of a very difficult situation: *Why not get a hanging shoe rack with multi-purpose compartments? Machine washable, this little life-saver can be found at Argos for £6.90.*

life's rich 'tapestry
Life's rich tapestry is the good and bad experiences that happen in life: *This was all new to her, part of life's rich tapestry which she had discussed with her girlfriends through endless long nights.*

lose your 'life
Someone **loses their life** when they are killed, usually in an accident or a war: *They had a memorial to those employees who lost their lives in the two world wars displayed on the outside wall of their social club.*

low 'life
Low life refers to the lives of people who exist through crime, possibly take drugs, and generally live in a way that other people disapprove of: *Then comes the train journey to Chicago, the low life amid the bright lights.*

make someone's life 'hell
Someone who **makes your life hell** causes you severe emotional suffering: *In Central News tonight – 'They've made my life hell', a dying man's anger over threat to evict his family.*

not on your 'life
Not on your life means 'certainly not': *Oh, no! I ain't going there. Not on your life.*
◊ SEE ALSO **not on your nellie** or **nelly** ▷ NELLIE

see 'life
Someone who **has seen life**, or **seen a bit of life**, has often travelled widely, is experienced and confident in social affairs, and is not easily deceived: *She knew her way around and had seen a bit of life. She told us often that she belonged to the theatre and knew all the tricks that some of them got up to.*

such is 'life
You say **'such is life'** when you are accepting that problems are inevitable in life: *Ah. Oh dear. Such is life. I feel so tired yet I've done nothing.*
◊ SEE ALSO **that's the way the cookie crumbles** ▷ WAY; **life goes on** ▷ LIFE; **that's life** ▷ LIFE

take your life in your 'hands
You **take your life in your hands** when you take the risk of being killed or attacked: *I knew every driver in that race was taking his life in his hands to the most ludicrous degree.*

that's 'life
That's life means 'this kind of thing happens in life and is to be expected'.
◊ SEE ALSO **that's the way the cookie crumbles** ▷ WAY; **life goes on** ▷ LIFE; **such is life** ▷ LIFE

there's life in the old dog 'yet (*humorous*)
You say **'there's life in the old dog yet'** to express surprise that although someone or something is old, they still have a lot of energy or strength left in them; old people sometimes say it about themselves when other people doubt their abilities: *In Britain, Italy and Greece, the left tops the opinion polls. There's life in the old dog yet.*

to the 'life
If you can imitate someone or something **to the life**, you can do it so well that it is impossible to hear or see the difference between the imitation and the real thing: *Bird notes, not songs, he could emulate to the life, and had made use of this faculty in trapping birds.*

true to 'life
Something such as a painting or story that is described as **true to life** closely resembles reality: *These portraits appear to modern eyes reassuringly true to life and easy to understand.* □ *His book is well written and easy to read, its charm further enhanced by many true-to-life sketches made in the field by John Busby.*

lifetime

the such-and-such of a 'lifetime
Something that is described as **the such-and-such of a lifetime** is the best one you will ever experience: *Go on, it's the chance of a lifetime – you won't regret it.*

once in a 'lifetime
If you say that something happens **once in a lifetime**, you mean that it happens very rarely; a **once-in-a-lifetime** experience is one that you may never get the chance to experience again: *Tempting, too, to join one of the numerous excursions to see the once-in-a-lifetime sights of the Sahara.*

light (*see also* **lights**)

bring something to 'light
If facts **are brought to light**, or if they **come to light**, they become known: *Part of the scandal only came to light when an observant bank clerk spotted changes made to the information on an authorized cheque.*

cast 'light on something or shed 'light on something or throw 'light on something

Someone or something that **casts**, or **sheds**, or **throws**, **light on** a situation provides information which makes it easier to understand: *Are there elements in your upbringing which help to explain or cast light on who you are and how you behave and respond?*

first 'light

First light is the time in the morning when the sun has just come up: *In the first light of morning he had got up to see what the village might have looked like before.*

give the green 'light to

You **give the green light to** someone when you allow them to do something: *At this Annual General Meeting in May 1983, the green light for change was finally given.*

go out like a 'light

You **go out like a light** when you go to sleep as soon as you get into bed: *Either it was the brandy or it was the heat, but she went out like a light.*

guiding 'light

A **guiding light** is someone whom you admire, or follow, and who shows you how things can be achieved: *Bradshaw became apprenticed to Eddie Aikau. Eddie was his hero, his guiding light.*

hide your light under a 'bushel

Someone who **hides their light under a bushel** does not reveal their talents to other people because they are modest: *And how has she achieved all this? 'Joan hides her light under a bushel' says one who knows her well.*

in a bad 'light

A report or story about someone or something shows them **in a bad light** if it gives the impression that they are bad.

in the cold light of 'day

You consider something **in the cold light of day** when you consider it calmly and logically, especially after having first considered it while in a state of excitement: *In the cold light of day it seems incredible that I fell to my knees in such a manner.*

in a good 'light

Someone or something is seen **in a good light** if their good qualities are made to be particularly evident.

◇ SEE ALSO **to best advantage** ▷ ADVANTAGE; **to best effect** ▷ EFFECT

in the light of 'such-and-such

You make a decision **in the light of** a particular fact, when you base your decision on that knowledge: *In the light of what we have just heard, I think it would be wise to reassess our decision.*

leading 'light

A **leading light** is an important or respected member of a group: *The leading light of the animal welfare revival was Jeremy Bentham.*

light as a 'feather

Someone or something that is as **light as a feather** is not at all heavy: *I know it looks heavy, but it's light as a feather – great for travelling with.*

the light at the end of the 'tunnel

Someone who is carrying out a long or difficult task can see **the light at the end of the tunnel** when they start to see the possibility of success, or of an end to their suffering: *This is definitely the worst recession I have seen in 42 years in the industry. Few see light at the end of the tunnel, whatever the election result.*

the light of someone's 'life *(humorous)*

If you describe someone as **the light of your life**, you mean, humorously, that they are the person you love and care for most: *Oh yes, he was the light of my life, Walter Machin. I used to watch his every movement.*

make 'light of something

You **make light of** a problem or a mistake that someone has made when you show, or give the impression, that you do not think it is important: *But Kendall's men made light of any suggestion of a crisis with an irresistible first-half display.*

red-'light district

The **red-light district** is the part of a town where you can find sex shops, striptease shows and prostitutes, etc: *Her house had always been spotless, and was considered to be one of the most exclusive brothels in the red-light district.*

see the 'light

You **see the light 1** when you suddenly understand or accept something: *It took him a while, but he's finally seen the light and started doing some work.* **2** when you suddenly change your beliefs as a result of a religious experience: *She told me she saw the light after the tragic death of her husband.*

lightly

get off 'lightly

You say that someone who has done something wrong **has got off lightly** when they have **1** not been given the punishment that you think they deserve: *'Either Fairbank's punishment is disproportionate, or Whitehead got off lightly,' Brook said.* **2** not been as severely affected by something as you might expect: *Unlike last year, most insurers have got off lightly. Commercial Union is an exception, with probable losses of more than £15m.*

lightning

like greased 'lightning

You move **like greased lightning** when you move very fast: *He leaped over the tailboard of the lorry like greased lightning, and he was gone.*

lights

the bright 'lights

If you refer to the city, as opposed to the countryside, as **the bright lights**, you are considering it as a centre of excitement and entertainment: *As soon as you have had enough take a return flight to the bright lights of Reykjavik.*

like

and the 'like

And the like means 'and other things of this type': *Citrus fruits – lemons. oranges, grape-fruit and the like.*

compare like with 'like

You **compare like with like** when you compare one thing with another of the same kind: *We have to be careful to compare like with like when comparing different elements of the media.*

like as two peas in a 'pod

Two people are described as **like as two peas in a pod** if they resemble each other very closely.

◇ SEE ALSO **the spitting image of someone** ▷ IMAGE

like it or 'lump it or if you don't like it you can 'lump it (*informal*)

If you tell someone that they can **like it or lump it**, or say that **if they don't like it they can lump it**, you mean that they will have to accept what has been offered to them, because they have no choice: *They've been told: take the lower interest rate – or lump it.*

nothing 'like

A person or thing that is **nothing like** another is completely different from them: *It's nothing like as hot here as it is down south.*

likely

not 'likely! (*informal*) or not bloody 'likely! (*vulgar*)

Not likely! or **not bloody likely!** means 'definitely not', and is used as a strong refusal to a request, or as a denial: *When Sean Connery discovered he was to be filmed with eight-foot sharks for 'Thunderball' his reaction was: 'You must be joking – not bloody likely.'*

likes

the likes of 'such-and-such

The likes of me, or **you**, or **us**, etc. means 'people like me, or you, or us', etc: *I've often wished that I had stayed on and tried for university, but my family wasn't the sort to encourage it. 'Not for the likes of us,' was the philosophy.*

liking

to so-and-so's 'liking (*formal*)

When something is **to your liking** you are pleased or satisfied with it: *Is the wine to your liking, Sir?*

too such-and-such for 'your liking

Something that is, for example, too big, **for your liking** is bigger than you want it to be.

lily

gild the 'lily

If you **gild the lily**, you add unnecessary decoration or exaggeration to something: *Councillor Arthur Collinge condemned the 'competitive status seeking' of colleges that are seeking to gild the lily by changing their names.*

'lily-livered

Someone who is described as **lily-livered** is not courageous: *If any were against the proposal, they must have been too lily-livered to protest.*

limb

out on a 'limb

Someone who is **out on a limb** is in a dangerous and isolated position, usually because they have ideas or opinions that are not accepted by other people.

limbo

in 'limbo

You are **in limbo** when you are in a state of uncertainty and confusion about what is going to happen next: *She's in limbo between university and working life at the moment – I think a vocational course would do her good.*

limelight

in the 'limelight

Someone who is **in the limelight** is getting a lot of public attention, either because they are famous, or because they have done something remarkable: *At first, we really enjoyed being in the limelight, but now all we want is a bit of peace and quiet.*

limit

the 'limit

You say that someone or something is **the limit** when you are annoyed with them: *He really is the limit, isn't he. What on earth will he do next?*

limits

within 'limits
You say '**within limits**' when something you have said applies to a certain extent or with a moderate degree of freedom only: *We're allowed to do what we want, within limits of course.*

line (*see also* **lines**)

all along the 'line or down the 'line
Something that happens **all along the line** or **down the line** happens at every stage of a process: *There is a commitment within the company to develop workers' skills right down the line, and this has been done through training and education schemes.*

the bottom 'line
The **bottom line** is the final result, or the most important consideration of a situation, activity or discussion: *Okay, enough of all that; what's the bottom line?*

bring into 'line
You **bring** rules, for example, **into line** with a particular policy, when you change them so that they follow or obey it: *Britain needs to be brought into line with the rest of Europe on this issue.*

'chat-up line (*humorous*)
A **chat-up line** is a phrase, usually used by a man, when he wants to engage a woman in conversation because he finds her attractive.

> Most women do not respond very well to chat-up lines. The most common include:'Do you come here often?' 'Haven't I seen you somewhere before?' and 'What's a nice girl like you doing in a place like this?' This kind of chat-up line is not considered original and therefore makes the man appear boring and undesirable.

draw the line at 'such-and-such
You **draw the line** at something when you refuse to do or accept it: *'Anyway,' said Graham, 'I do draw the line at being described as 'militant'.*

drop someone a 'line
You **drop someone a line** when you write them a letter: *I'll drop him a line and tell him we're coming over to Oxford.*

fall into 'line or fall in 'line
You **fall into**, or **in, line** when you start to follow the rules and behave in a way that is expected of you: *You must show yourself to be a strong leader. Once you've done that, Europe will fall into line.*

feed someone a 'line or shoot someone a 'line
If you **feed**, or **shoot, someone a line**, you give them a false explanation or tell a lie: *He fed me some line about the bus breaking down. □ The man did nothing, after all, except shoot a line to you, and that's not a crime in itself.*
◇ SEE ALSO **tell porkies** ▷ PORKIES

get out of 'line or step out of 'line
You **get**, or **step, out of line** when you start behaving in a way that is not allowed or expected of you: *You'd better not step out of line for a while – we need them on our side at the moment.*

hold the 'line
You ask someone, on the telephone, to **hold the line** when you want them to wait while you try to find the person they want to speak to: *Hold the line please, I'll put you through.*

a 'hot line
A **hot line** is a line of quick communication between people, especially for use in emergencies: *Phone our 24-hour hotline for all emergency electrical work.*

in the 'firing line
You are **in the firing line** if you are in a position where you are most likely to be affected by attack or criticism: *Cities are likely to find themselves very much in the firing line, as a series of radical measures are implemented concerning education, social security and local taxation.*

in the front 'line
Someone who is **in the front line** is in a position where they can have direct experience of, or influence on, an activity: *Organizations like ACET who are in the front line giving practical care and support to AIDS sufferers.*

in line for 'such-and-such
You are **in line for something** if you are likely to get it: *I'd stay there if I were you – I think you're in line for promotion.*

keep someone in 'line
You **keep someone in line** when you make them behave as they ought to: *He had a middle-aged secretary who used to follow him about with his diary and try to keep him in line.*

lay it on the 'line
You **lay it on the line** when you say very clearly that something is the case: *But soon – perhaps very soon – I am going to have to lay it on the line, tell them what really has been happening.*
◇ SEE ALSO **lay** or **put your cards on the table** ▷ CARDS

the line of least re'sistance
The **line of least resistance** is a course of action that will cause the least trouble, argument or difficulty: *If you take the line of least resistance where children are concerned, you will actually make things worse.*

on the 'line

Something such as your job or reputation is **on the line** if you are in danger of losing it.

out of 'line with something

One person or group is **out of line with** others when they disagree with the others, or act differently from them: *His work philosophy is out of line with the rest of the company.*

sign on the dotted 'line

You **sign on the dotted line** when you write your signature at the bottom of an agreement in order to legally confirm it: *Before you sign on the dotted line, check to see if the company is a member of the Kitchen Specialists Association.*

somewhere along the 'line

Somewhere along the line means 'at some point in a procedure': *I realized then that somewhere along the line I must have gone wrong.*

take a hard 'line

You **take a hard line** when you take strong actions, or hold firmly to decisions or policies that have been made: *The Government has decided to take a hard line on Europe in the period leading up to the election.*

toe the 'line

You **toe the line** when you behave as you ought to: *On the one hand, they are being urged to make decisions about their future while, on the other, they are expected to toe the line both at home and at school.*

linen

wash your dirty linen in 'public

You **are washing your dirty linen in public** if you are having an argument about something private, while in the company of others: *They are concerned it should stay in the community, in the house. You shouldn't wash dirty linen in public.*

Linen is a formal or old-fashioned word for underwear.

lines

get your 'lines crossed

Two people **get their lines crossed** when they misunderstand each other: *I think we got our lines crossed – I thought we were invited for the weekend, but in fact it was just for dinner.*
◇ SEE ALSO **at cross-purposes** ▷ CROSS

hard 'lines

Hard lines means 'bad luck', and is used to sympathize with someone; **hard lines** is sometimes used to show lack of sympathy.

on the lines of 'such-and-such or along the lines of 'such-and-such

You describe something as being **on**, or **along, the lines of** something else if that is what it is roughly like: *We would then organize the party along the lines of other large events such as pop concerts or sports meetings, in co-operation with the police.*

on the right 'lines

You are **on the right lines** if you are acting or working in a way that is likely to bring successful results: *He said I'm on the right lines, but I've still got a lot of work to do.*

read between the 'lines

You **read between the lines** when you understand what is implied by what someone says, although they do not express it openly: *Those who took time to read between the lines would have realized that things were not going as well as they may have first appeared.*

lion

beard the lion in his 'den

You **beard the lion in his den** when you bravely face or confront someone in authority, in their own surroundings: *You couldn't beard the lion in his den if you let your fears get the better of you.*

the 'lion's share

The **lion's share** is the largest part of something: *The dozen strong mixed team also secured the lion's share of individual medals.*

lions

feed someone to the 'lions or throw someone to the 'lions

You **feed**, or **throw, someone to the lions** when you put them in a position where they will be attacked: *His philosophy of management was neatly summed up in his reply when asked what he would do if he were a referee, a prospect he compared to being 'thrown to the lions'.*

lip

bite your 'lip

You **bite your lip** when you stop yourself from saying something that will show how distressed or angry you are feeling: *And that was that. I bit my lip. If they hadn't been there I would have had to say something.*
◇ SEE ALSO **bite your tongue** ▷ TONGUE

give someone 'lip (*informal*)

If you **give someone lip**, you are rude and disrespectful towards them: *Don't you give me that lip, boy.*

pay 'lip service to something

Someone who **pays lip service to** an idea or principle pretends to support or uphold it without really doing so: *The Government pays lip-service to the official declarations that no such deals should be made, but in reality they seem to be inevitable.*

a stiff upper 'lip

You keep **a stiff upper lip** if you hide your feelings when you are upset or worried: *The message being sent to the hostages was that they had to keep a stiff upper lip and hope that, one day, the kidnappers might let them go.* □ *Many Englishmen conceal their feelings so effectively beneath a stiff upper lip that it's fair to ask whether they're really human at all.*

lips

my lips are 'sealed

If you say that **your lips are sealed**, you mean that you will not reveal a secret that someone has told you: *'You can keep a secret?' Benjamin asked sharply. The fellow nodded, round-eyed. 'Of course. My lips are sealed.'*

on everyone's 'lips

Something is **on everyone's lips** when a lot of people are talking about it: *The question on everyone's lips is, will there be a Jurassic Park II?*

list

someone's 'hit list

Someone's **hit list** is a list of people or things that they want to kill, attack or dispose of: *Some banks also have a hit list of people whom they threaten to sue for damages.* □ *They spoke of a national British Rail hit list of lines which would close under privatization.*

lists

enter the 'lists (*formal*)

Someone **enters the lists** when they join in a contest or argument: *He decided not to enter the lists. He calculated that he could not beat either Heath or Maudling, and he preferred to avoid the contest.*

litmus

the 'litmus test

A **litmus test** is an event or statement that suggests something about how things really are, or about how things are on a wider scale: *The litmus test between the great mind and the clever mind is that the former is always conscious of how little he knows, and the latter of how much he knows.*

Litmus is a powder which is used as a test for finding out if a substance contains acid.

little

little by 'little

Something that happens **little by little** happens gradually: *Little by little, her memory was coming back.*

make 'little of something

You **make little of something** when you treat it as unimportant: *Subsequent generations made little of their royal connection. Behind this change lay a more business-like attitude.*

too little too 'late

An action is described as **too little too late** if it has not happened early enough and in a strong enough way to be effective: *Today's protest is designed to draw attention to hundreds of cases of supposed miscarriages of justice. As far as we are concerned it's too little too late.*

live

live and 'breathe something

If you **live and breathe** something, it foms a very important part of your life: *Because we ourselves are Italian we live and breathe Italy and all things Italian.*

live and 'learn

If you say that people have to **live and learn**, you mean that they must learn by their mistakes or experience; **live and learn** is also an expression you use when you have just learnt something that you did not know before, and that surprises you. *'Never mind,' Anne consoled her. 'We've got to live and learn.'*

live and let 'live

If you say **'live and let live'**, you mean that people should tolerate each other's actions: *If people are biased about one thing they are very often biased about other things and I think people should adopt an attitude of live and let live!*

live it 'up

You **live it up** when you have an enjoyable time, especially with an exciting social life: *He was an individualist who liked to do things his own way, like living it up at West End night clubs until the early hours.*

◇ SEE ALSO **have a ball** ▷ BALL; **rave it up** ▷ RAVE; **have the time of your life** ▷ TIME

you only live 'once

If you say **'you only live once'**, you mean that people should take advantage of every opportunity for enjoying themselves now, because life is short, and they may not get a second chance: *You only live once. Live your life how you want. Before you know it you'll be old. Old as me.*

◇ SEE ALSO **life is for living** ▷ LIFE

lo

lo and be'hold

You say '**lo and behold**'when telling a story, to dramatically introduce the unexpected appearance of someone, or an unexpected occurrence: *And lo and behold, who should walk in the door but Bill, the man himself!*

load

get a load of 'this (*slang*)

You say '**get a load of this**' in order to get someone's attention when you are about to tell them something interesting or scandalous.

lighten someone's 'load

Something that **lightens your load** makes a difficult situation easier to manage: *Ironing is probably one of the least favourite household chores so lighten the load with one of the latest irons from Philips.*

a load of 'rubbish

Something that is described as **a load of rubbish** is worthless, untrue or nonsensical: *'These reports are a load of rubbish,' she said. 'I have no idea where the journalists got this information from.'*

◊ SEE ALSO **hocus pocus** ▷ HOCUS

a load off your 'mind

You say that something is **a load off your mind** if it makes you feel relieved after a period of worry: *Providing the income you will need after you stop work can take a load off your mind.*

◊ SEE ALSO **a weight off your mind** ▷ WEIGHT

loaf

half a loaf is better than no 'bread

If someone says '**half a loaf is better than no bread**', they mean that you should be grateful for what you have, since it is better to have something than nothing at all.

◊ SEE ALSO **count your blessings** ▷ BLESSINGS; **thankful for small mercies** ▷ MERCIES; **look on the bright side** ▷ SIDE

use your 'loaf

Use your loaf means 'use your intelligence'.

Loaf of bread is Cockney rhyming slang for 'head'.

lock

lock, stock and 'barrel

If you win or lose something **lock, stock and barrel**, you win or lose all of it: *He may even try to buy the club lock, stock and barrel.*

A lock, a stock, and a barrel are the three main parts of a gun.

under lock and 'key

You have something **under lock and key** when you have it securely locked up: *All*

medicines should be kept out of reach of children and, where appropriate, under lock and key.

log

sleep like a 'log

You **sleep like a log** when you sleep very deeply: *He won't have heard anything, he sleeps like a log.*

◊ SEE ALSO **sleep like a top** ▷ TOP; **sleep like a baby** ▷ BABY

loggerheads

at 'loggerheads

You are **at loggerheads** with someone if you disagree with them violently: *For Mrs Thatcher, at loggerheads with many of her own party over European issues, this summit was crucial.*

A **loggerhead** was a long iron bar with a ball at the end, used, when heated, for melting tar [= a thick, black, sticky substance, used in making roads]. It probably served as a weapon among workers who used it.

loins

gird up your 'loins (*old or humorous*)

You **gird up your loins** when you prepare yourself for energetic activity: *There are some seats still going. But be quick: pick up your phone or gird up your loins, they won't wait for you.*

This is a phrase from the Bible. In ancient times, Hebrews wore loose, flowing robes which were impractical for working or travelling in, unless they were fastened up with a girdle.

lonesome

be on your 'lonesome (*informal*)

You are **on your lonesome** if you are not with other people: *Let's spend a couple of hours together all on our lonesome.*

long

at long 'last

You say **at long last** when something you have been waiting for finally happens: *'I've passed my driving test!' 'At long last!'*

before 'long

Something that happens, or will happen, **before long**, happens, or will happen, soon: *The sky turned grey and a cool wind began to blow. Before long it started to rain.* □ *It should be finished before long.*

the long and the 'short of it (*informal*)

You say '**the long and the short of it**',when you are summarizing a story in a few words: *She hadn't known what to expect. She'd expected too much: that was the long and the short of it.*

long as your 'arm

A list that is as **long as your arm** is a very long list: *I have a list of vices as long as your arm but I am not mean.*

so 'long

So long means 'goodbye'.

longer

before much 'longer

Something that happens **before much longer** happens quite soon: *Before much longer, she'll be off to university, and then we won't see much of her.*

look

a black 'look

If someone gives you **a black look**, they look at you angrily, without speaking to you: *I gave him such a black look, however, that the smile froze on his face.*

◇ SEE ALSO **look like thunder** ▷ THUNDER

by the 'look of something

By the look of something means 'judging by the appearance of something': *By the look of him, he must have been up all night.*

a dirty 'look

If someone gives you **a dirty look**, they look at you in a way that shows that they disapprove of, or are angry with, you.

look a'skance at

You **look askance at** someone or something when you disapprove of them: *Despite their theoretical commitment to sexual equality, they looked askance at any woman who aspired to be more than a middle manager.*

look before you 'leap

If someone tells you to **look before you leap**, they mean that you should consider something more carefully before deciding to do it: *Each was given a free booklet called 'Look Before You Leap', an introduction to time management for the professional photographer.*

look your 'best

You **look your best** when you have made yourself look as tidy and well-dressed as possible: *Try to look your best for the interview – first impressions are important.*

look 'here!

You say '**look here!**' to someone when you are angry with them and you are about to tell them so: *Look here! I've just about had enough of this nonsense.*

look 'kindly on

You **look kindly** on someone or something if you like them and have a good opinion of them, because their behaviour pleases you:

Penry was unlikely to look kindly on someone who landed on his island uninvited twice in a row.

look 'lively! or look 'sharp! or look 'snappy! (*informal*)

If you tell someone to **look lively!** or **look sharp!** or **look snappy!** you mean that they should hurry up: *'You boys are supposed to be helping with the washing up,' said Mrs Crumwallis. 'Look lively. Wattling, bring me those saucers there.'*

look 'small

If someone makes you **look small**, they humiliate you: *He had never quite forgiven her for making him look small in front of his colleagues.*

look who's 'talking

You say '**look who's talking!**' to someone who has just criticized someone else for a fault of which they themselves are guilty: *'You can be a bit selfish sometimes though, can't you?' 'Huh! Look who's talking! You're the one who always has to have her own way.'*

◇ SEE ALSO **you're a fine one to talk** or **you can talk** or **you can't talk** ▷ TALK; **hark at so-and-so** ▷ HARK

never look 'back

Someone who **has never looked back** has had a very successful career: *She launched her own company, Betty Jackson Ltd, in October 1981 and has never looked back.*

not get a 'look-in or not have a 'look-in

Someone who **doesn't get**, or **have, a look-in** does not get a chance to participate, or has no chance of winning a race, match, etc: *The selection process prevents the eccentric and the too-individualistic getting a look-in.* □ *Yorke scored 17 goals for Atkinson last season but hasn't had a look-in this year.*

not look your'self

You **are not looking yourself** if you look ill, or anxious about something.

not much to 'look at

Someone or something that is **not much to look at** is not particularly attractive: *You should see the garden, although it's not much to look at at this time of the year.*

◇ SEE ALSO **no oil painting** ▷ OIL

lookout

on the lookout for

You are **on the lookout for** someone or something when you are watching to make sure you see them when they appear: *Eager Hollywood producers, always on the lookout for real-life 'drama, are sending hard currency their way.*

looks

good 'looks
Someone who has **good looks** is attractive: *He is universally popular in all circles being blessed with great charm, a ready wit and good looks.*

if looks could 'kill
You say '**if looks could kill**'when someone looks at you, or at someone else, in a way which shows that they are very angry with them, or that they hate them: *O'Hara shot her a hostile, challenging glance. If looks could kill, she thought.*

When you use this expression you imply that if it were possible to kill someone just by looking at them, the victim of the look would certainly be dead now.

loom

loom 'large
Something that **looms large** is a strong possibility, especially one that is likely to cause a problem or danger: *At the same time, family disruption by separation and divorce looms large among the reasons for social work intervention.*

loose

on the 'loose
A dangerous person or criminal is **on the loose** when they have escaped from prison or control.
◇ SEE ALSO **on the run** ▷ RUN

lord

live like a 'lord
Someone who **lives like a lord** lives in a very rich and luxurious manner: *We can live like lords, we can feast off the fat of the land!*

A **lord** is a man who has a high position in the nobility.

Lord! or **Good 'Lord!** or **Oh 'Lord!** (*informal*)
People use **Lord!**, or **Good Lord!** or **Oh Lord!** as expressions of surprise or dismay.

In the Christian church, people refer to God or Jesus Christ as the **Lord**.

'lord it over someone
Someone **lords it over you** when they behave towards you as if they were more important than you: *The officer's clerk sat drinking tea and lording it over the candidates.*
◇ SEE ALSO **queen it over someone** ▷ QUEEN

'Lord knows
Lord knows means 'I have no idea': *Lord knows when I'll get this thesis finished.*
◇ SEE ALSO **Christ knows** ▷ CHRIST; **God**

knows or **God alone knows** ▷ GOD; **goodness knows** or **goodness only knows** ▷ GOODNESS; **heaven knows** or **heaven alone knows** ▷ HEAVEN

lorry

fall off a 'lorry or be off the back of a 'lorry
If you say that something **fell off a lorry**, or that it's **off the back of a lorry**, you mean that it was stolen: *It's a lovely present, but I can't help wondering if it fell off the back of a lorry.*

lose

have nothing to 'lose
You **have nothing to lose** by acting in a certain way if it cannot harm you to do so: *Look, you've got nothing to lose. They can only say no if they don't want you.*

'lose it
Someone who **is losing it** is losing control of themselves or of their surroundings, and allowing the quality of their work to deteriorate.

'lose yourself in something
You **lose yourself in something** when all your attention is taken up by it: *I very much wanted to be a character actress, to be able to lose myself in various parts.*

loss

at a 'loss
You are **at a loss** when you are puzzled or shocked and do not know what to do or say: *I'm at a loss for words.*

a dead 'loss
You describe someone or something as **a dead loss** if you think they are hopelessly bad, boring or ineffective: *That course is a dead loss – not worth the money at all.*

losses

cut your 'losses
You **cut your losses** when you stop doing something that is making a situation worse: *The first principle of success in any walk of life is to know when to cut your losses.*

lost

get 'lost (*offensive*)
If you tell someone to **get lost**, you mean, rudely, that you want them to go away.
◇ SEE ALSO **bugger off** ▷ BUGGER; **sod off** ▷ SOD

'lost on someone
You say that something is **lost on someone** when they do not use, appreciate, or understand it properly: *Her sweetly ironic tone seemed lost on him.*

loud

loud and 'clear
Something that is stated **loud and clear** is stated so that it can be easily understood: *The message was loud and clear, and it was attended.*

loud and 'long
People complain **loud and long** about something when they complain bitterly about it: *He grumbled loud and long about the money he had paid out that morning.*

out 'loud
You say something **out loud** when you speak it, as distinct from thinking it, or when you say it so that other people can hear you, rather than to yourself: *One morning, Marie got this letter and she sort of read it quickly. Not out loud like she normally does.*

lounge

'lounge lizard (*informal*)
A **lounge lizard** is a man who does not work, and who spends his time in places where he is likely to meet the rich and famous: *The Latin moustache is the kind worn by the lounge lizard in the movies – Clark Gable, Errol Flynn, Adolph Menjou.*

love

for the love of 'God or for the love of 'Mike (*informal*)
You introduce a statement or a request with **for the love of God**, or **for the love of Mike**, when you feel annoyed, impatient or disappointed: *Sit down, this bank's quite dry. And for the love of Mike take off those shoes!* □ *Virginia, for the love of God, will you just talk to me? Tell me what's happened to you!*

> People use **Mike** or another name, instead of **God**, because they do not want to use God's name disrespectfully.

'love child (*old-fashioned*)
A **love child** is a child whose parents are not married to each other: *Was William a love child, kept in the background because of the embarrassment? We shall never know.*

> The term **'love child'** is considered old-fashioned now, but is still used by journalists writing for sensationalist newspapers.

'love handles (*informal*)
Love handles are the areas of fat around a person's waist: *You'd better try and get rid of those love handles if you're going to be out on the beach.*

love is 'blind
If you say **love is blind**, you mean that when someone is in love they do not always see the faults of the person whom they love: *I don't know why they say that love is blind – I was always very aware of all your father's little defects.*

'love nest
A **love nest** is a place where two people who are having a love affair meet in order to make love: *We have spent these last few days in a very secluded country house. The kind of place that the newspapers like to describe as a love nest.*

> The term **love nest** is mostly used by journalists writing for sensationalist newspapers.

make 'love
When two people **make love** they have sex: *They have such small beds here to stop undergraduates making love.*

no 'love lost between
If you say that there is **no love lost between** two people you mean that they dislike each other.

not for love nor 'money
If you say that you will **not** do something **for love nor money**, you mean that you absolutely refuse to do it: *You wouldn't find me in a place like that for love nor money. Why don't you get respectable premises somewhere more suitable?*
◊ SEE ALSO **not for all the tea in China** ▷ TEA

there's a 'love (*informal*)
People sometimes follow a kindly request to a child with **there's a love**: *Pass me my glasses, would you darling? There's a love.*

lover

Latin 'lover
A **Latin lover** is a dark, attractive man who is experienced in love and sexual relationships, and who probably comes from Italy, Spain, or southern France: *Garlic is one of the most widely used aphrodisiacs around the world, and its popularity in Mediterranean food may have something to do with the reputation of the Latin Lover.*
◊ SEE ALSO **ladies' man** ▷ LADIES; **lady-killer** ▷ LADY

live-in 'lover
A person's **live-in lover** is someone with whom they are having a sexual relationship, and who is living with them during this time: *She took no new live-in lover, and as far as she was aware, neither did Charles.*

low

the 'low-down

You give someone **the low-down** on something when you bring them up to date on what has been happening with regard to a given situation.

low on something

You are **low on something** when you do not have much of it: *We're a bit low on 'milk – shall I get some when I'm out?*

luck

bad 'luck or hard 'luck or tough 'luck

You say '**bad luck**', or '**hard luck**', or '**tough luck**' to someone when something unfortunate has happened to them, either to show sympathy, or ironically, as a way of saying that the person will have to accept the situation: *'We lost.' 'Bad luck.'*

◇ SEE ALSO **hard cheese** ▷ cheese; **tough** ▷ TOUGH

be down on your 'luck

If you **are down on your luck**, you are having problems and things are not going well for you: *I met her in Paris three years ago, a bit down on my luck because the circus I'd been with had gone bankrupt.*

better luck 'next time

You say '**better luck next time**'as a way of encouraging someone who has had some bad luck, or who has failed in something: *Thanks to all of you who wrote in. And if you didn't win, better luck next time.*

for 'luck

If you do something **for luck**, you do it in the hope that it will bring you good luck: *Have one more try, for luck.*

good 'luck or the best of 'luck

You wish someone **good luck**, or **the best of luck**, when you want them to be successful.

a hard-'luck story

A **hard-luck story** is a story of someone's bad luck or suffering which they tell you because they want your sympathy or your money, for example: *He went on looking at me sympathetically as if I'd been telling him a hard-luck story.*

in 'luck

You are **in luck** when you are lucky or fortunate, especially about a particular thing: *We were in luck – they were at home, and they had a full can of petrol in the garage.*

just so-and-so's 'luck

You say that something which has happened is **just your luck** if it is typically bad luck: *No tickets left – just my luck.*

the luck of the 'devil or the luck of the 'Irish

Someone who has the **luck of the devil** or the **luck of the Irish** enjoys more than a reasonable or usual amount of good luck: *It was the luck of the Irish that saved him. Martin survived an unsurvivable accident.*

the luck of the 'draw

You describe something that happens as **the luck of the draw** if it depends purely on chance, rather than on any kind of planning or skill: *It's the luck of the draw whether you get a nice room or not – they all cost the same.*

A **draw** is a kind of competition where you buy a ticket with a number on it. If your number is chosen, you win a prize.

more by luck than 'judgement

You achieve something **more by luck than judgement** when it happens more through chance than because of any skill: *The only goal came more by luck than judgement but McGinlay's flick was good enough to win it.*

◇ SEE ALSO **more by accident than design** ▷ ACCIDENT

no such 'luck (*informal*)

No such luck means 'unfortunately not': *'Are you going abroad this year?' 'No such luck.'*

not believe your 'luck

You say that you **cannot believe your luck** if you are very happy and surprised about something that has happened to you: *'I could not believe my luck,' she said. 'I have no idea why they chose me, but when I got the call, I screamed with delight.*

out of 'luck

You are **out of luck** if you are unlucky, especially about a particular thing: *We were out of luck. No-one seemed to be able to help us.*

push your 'luck

Someone **is pushing their luck** if they are risking disappointment or failure by trying to gain too much: *Trying to fit the walk into a two-week holiday is pushing your luck – you must make allowances for delays.*

try your 'luck

You **try your luck** at something when you try it, hoping that you will succeed: *There's golfing and tennis, scintillating nightclubs and even a casino in which to try your luck.*

with 'luck or with any 'luck

You can add **with luck** or **with any luck** to a statement that you hope will be true: *With any luck, they'll be here before ten.*

worse 'luck

Worse luck means 'unfortunately': *'Have you got any homework for tonight?' 'Yes, worse luck.'*

lucky

'I should be so lucky

If you say '**I should be so lucky**', you mean that it is very unlikely that the thing mentioned would ever happen to you: *'Are they paying for your trip to the States?' 'Huh, I should be so lucky!'*

'you'll be lucky

You say '**you'll be lucky**' to someone when you think it is very unlikely that they will get something: *'I'm going to ask if I can borrow the car.' 'You'll be lucky.'*

lull

the lull before the 'storm

The lull before the storm is a period of quiet and peace before something unpleasant begins, or before a very busy period: *Have a nice cup of tea and enjoy the lull before the storm, before the children come home from school.*

lumbered

be lumbered with or get lumbered with

You **are**, or you **get**, lumbered with a job or task, when you are given one you do not want: *Why do I always get lumbered with 'organizing these things?*

lump

have a 'lump in your throat

If you **have a lump in your throat**, you are emotionally moved, you get a tightening feeling in your throat, and feel as if you are going to cry: *I hate it when people cry – it makes me want to do the same thing. I get this lump in my throat and then my eyes start to sting.*

'lump it *(informal)*

You say that someone will have to **lump it** if they must accept a bad situation without complaining: *If I were you I'd tell them if they don't like it, lump it.*

lunch

out to 'lunch *(informal)*

Someone who is **out to lunch** is crazy: *He looked out to lunch – his deep-set eyes flashed about behind the long, sweaty strands of hair.*

◇ SEE ALSO **have a screw loose** ▷ SCREW

there's no such thing as a free 'lunch

If you say '**there's no such thing as a free lunch**', you mean that it is not possible to enjoy any kind of pleasure without paying for it in some way later: *There's no such thing as a free lunch where the environment's concerned – somebody somewhere must foot the bill.*

lurch

leave someone in the 'lurch *(informal)*

You **leave someone in the lurch** if you withdraw your help or support and leave them in a difficult situation: *TV fashion queen Selina Scott has left BBC bosses in the lurch by quitting the Clothes Show days before a new series.*

◇ SEE ALSO **leave someone holding the baby** ▷ BABY

lurgy

the dreaded 'lurgy *(informal, humorous)*

Someone who has got **the lurgy**, or **the dreaded lurgy**, has got an illness which is not very serious, but which it is easy to catch: *There's nothing more frustrating than having to waste a couple of days – or more – of your precious summer break recovering from some kind of lurgy.*

lying

take something lying 'down

You **take something lying down** if you accept something which is unfair, without complaining or protesting: *Don't take it lying down. Fight to the end.*

m

mad

barking 'mad
If you describe someone as **barking mad** you mean they are completely mad: *There are so many visuals, wild lights and other bizarre things grabbing your attention, it's enough to drive you barking mad.*

hopping 'mad
Someone who is **hopping mad** is very angry: *That really infuriated Henry! Good Lord, he was hopping mad!*
◇ SEE ALSO **in a temper** ▷ TEMPER

like 'mad
You are doing something **like mad** if you are doing it with great energy or enthusiasm: *I've been working like mad to get this stuff finished.*

mad as a 'hatter or mad as a March 'hare
Someone who is as **mad as a hatter**, or as **mad as a March hare**, acts in an unpredictable, eccentric or mad way.
◇ SEE ALSO **nutty as a fruit-cake** ▷ NUTTY

The **Hatter** and the **March Hare** are two characters at the 'Mad Tea-Party' in Lewis Carroll's *Alice in Wonderland*, but these two expressions existed before Lewis Carroll's book. **Mad as a hatter** refers to the fact that, in the past, people whose job was to make hats often went mad as a result of contact with a certain chemical (nitrate of mercury) which was used in hat-making. **Mad as a March hare** refers to the strange and amusing behaviour of hares in the spring, when the males are looking for a mate.

made

'made for someone
You say that a person or thing was **made for someone** if it fits or suits them perfectly: *John and Sue are so happy. I think they were made for each other. □ You got that coat second hand? It suits you so well it could have been made for you.*

madness

midsummer 'madness (*old*)
If people talk about **midsummer madness**, they mean a state of mind caused by hot weather in the summer, which makes you behave in a strange or mad way: *People don't always have logical reasons for the things they do! Put it down to midsummer madness.*

In the past, it was believed that hot weather caused people to go mad.

magic

work like 'magic
If something **works like magic**, it works effectively and fast: *I got this new carpet cleaner from Tesco's – look, it works like magic.*

magnitude

of the first 'magnitude
Something such as a quality is **of the first magnitude** if it is strong or extreme: *We are in the presence of a disaster of the first magnitude.*

maid

old 'maid (*disrespectful*)
People sometimes call an old woman who has never been married an **old maid**: *She sighed. 'I'm destined to die an old maid, I am.' □ Constance viewed Miss Hatherby as an old maid, unworldly, afraid of emotions and inexperienced in life.*

Maid is an old word which means 'young woman' or 'virgin'.

maiden

maiden 'lady
A **maiden lady** is an older woman who has never been married: *Mother served her time as a dressmaker with a maiden lady who had a business in Kirkby Stephen.*

maiden 'speech
A **maiden speech** is the first speech which a politician makes after becoming a Member of Parliament: *David Laing MP, in his*

maiden speech, urged married women to give up their jobs.

The word **maiden** is only used with this general sense of 'first' in a few specific cases. In the past, it referred to a woman who had never had sex before, but now its ordinary sense is simply an old-fashioned way of saying 'young woman'.

maiden 'voyage

The **maiden voyage** of a new ship, aeroplane, or other vehicle, is the first journey which it makes: *On her maiden voyage, on 14 April 1912, the Titanic struck an iceberg in the North Atlantic and sank.*

See note at **maiden speech.**

main

in the 'main

In the main means 'mostly' or 'generally': *Though journalists are well-mannered and thoughtful in the main, some of them are intrusive.*

majority

the silent ma'jority

If you speak about **the silent majority**, you mean the large number of people who may have strong opinions, especially on political matters, but who do not make any special effort to express these opinions publicly: *A few people feel strongly enough to campaign, but how does the silent majority view the fur trade?*

make *(see also* **made** *and* **making***)*

make as 'if to

You **make as if to** do something when you give the impression by your actions that you are just about to do it: *The phone rang. She made as if to answer it, but then sat down again and waited till it stopped.*

make 'do

You **make do**, or **make do with something**, when you accept it or make the best use of it, even though it is not exactly what you wanted, because nothing better is available: *If we can't get butter, we'll just have to make do with margarine.*

'make it

You **make it** when **1** you are successful in doing or being something: *I never hear from him any more, now that he's made it as a pop singer.* **2** you manage to come out of a dangerous situation alive: *My climbing partner broke his leg, falling from the rock face, and I began to wonder if we'd make it.* **3** you manage to reach a place: *Even if you drive at top speed, we'll never make it in time.* **4** you manage to be present at an

event that you have been invited to: *I'd like to come, but I'm not sure if I can make it.* ◊ SEE ALSO **make it big** ▷ BIG; **make a name for yourself** or **make your name** ▷ NAME

make it 'up

You **make it up** to someone you have disappointed when you do something for them as a way of apologizing: *I can't be home for your birthday, but I'll make it up to you. I promise.*

on the 'make *(informal)*

1 You say that someone is **on the make** if you are suspicious of them because you think that they are only concerned with getting money: *He's always on the make, and he doesn't care what rubbish he sells you.* **2** You also say that someone is **on the make** if they are obviously flirting with people and encouraging their sexual interest: *She looks like she's on the make this evening.*

maker

meet your 'maker

To **meet your maker** means 'to die': *Finally he fell down on to the pavement completely exhausted and convinced he was going to meet his maker there and then.*

This expression refers to the belief that you will meet God when you die and go to heaven.

making

in the 'making

In the making describes a person or thing that is developing into something: *Here is a talented musician in the making.*

the 'making of someone

An experience or event that will be **the making of** a person or thing will be the most important influence in bringing about their success: *What you regard at the time as being your downfall often turns out to be the making of you.*

of someone's own 'making

Something, especially a problem or failure, is **of your own making** if you have caused it by your own actions: *I have no sympathy for her. Any problems she has are of her own making.*

makings

have the 'makings of something

A person or thing that **has the makings of something** has the qualities or abilities needed to develop into that thing: *This boy has the makings of a world-class yachtsman.*

man (see also **men**)

be your own 'man

A man who **is his own man** is independent in his thinking and behaviour and does not have to obey any other person: *If you run your own cab, you're your own man, you can choose your own hours, plan your holidays.*

dirty old 'man (*disrespectful*)

A **dirty old man** is a man who has a lot of sexual desires, usually towards girls and women who are much younger than himself, which he expresses in ways which are socially unacceptable: *'Peep-shows and pornography are just for dirty old men with nothing better to do,' she argues.* □ *My friend was followed home from work by a dirty old man yesterday.*

every man has his 'price

If someone says **'every man has his price'**, they mean that, if the temptation or reward is great enough, most people will act in a way which they believe is morally wrong: *They are all honourable men. But common sense tells me that every man has his price.*

every man 'jack

Every man jack means every single person, with no exceptions: *Every man jack has to work ten days each year for nothing as a kind of tax.* □ *Every man jack of them is sick of the way you treat them.*

go to see a man about a 'dog

If you ask someone where they are going, and they reply that they **are going to see a man about a dog**, they mean that they have no intention of answering your question.

the grand old man of 'such-and-such

You call someone **the grand old man of** a particular thing if they are old now, but have in the past been a great champion in that field: *Red Rum, the grand old man of British horseracing, still appears at the Grand National every year.*

'hit man

A **hit man** is a man who commits murders in exchange for payment: *One man who did give evidence claimed a hit man had been paid twenty thousand pounds to kill him.*

hit a man when he is 'down or **kick a man when he is 'down**

You say that someone **is hitting**, or **kicking**, **a man when he is down** if they are attacking a person who has already been put in a weak position: *The 'don't kick a man when he is down' doctrine meant nothing to Wigg – he believed in gaining the upper hand and keeping it.*

kept 'man

A **kept man** is a man who does not work, and who relies on his wife or partner to provide the money which they both live on:

He had been learning this work from his father-in-law since three weeks after his wedding, and he hated it. He felt like a kept man.

man-about-'town

A **man-about-town** is a man who spends a lot of time in fashionable places, meeting a lot of people and enjoying their company in a relaxed way: *He was leaning against the car, smoking a cigarette and looking more than ever the dashing young man-about-town.*

man and 'boy

If a man does something **man and boy**, he starts doing it in his early childhood and continues all his life: *In many rural areas it has always been the case for local farm workers to work on the land man and boy.*

man's best 'friend

If people talk about **man's best friend**, they mean dogs.

man cannot live by bread a'lone (old)

If someone says **'man cannot live by bread alone'**, they mean that people have basic emotional needs which are at least as important for the quality of their lives as their basic physical needs: *Man cannot live by bread alone! Madam, when you put bread into these children's mouths, you feed their bodies, but you are starving their souls!*

'man-eater

If people describe a woman as a **man-eater**, they mean that she has a habit of tempting men, one after another, into sexual relationships with her: *He obviously imagined she was some kind of flighty, sex-starved man-eater.*

In its scientific sense, a **man-eater** is an animal that eats people.

'man enough

A person who is **man enough** to do something is brave enough to do it: *'Our baby is without a father because he has not been man enough to face up to his responsibility,' she said.*

a Man 'Friday

A **Man Friday** is a general male servant or employee who does all kinds of jobs: *He's the group assistant, a kind of Man Friday who does all the things no-one else has time for.*

In Daniel Defoe's novel Robinson Crusoe, Robinson meets a native inhabitant of the desert island, whom he names **Man Friday** (because the day he met him was a Friday) and trains to be his servant.

a man for all 'seasons

A man for all seasons is a man who has the ability to operate successfully in a wide range of situations: *If there ever was a man for all seasons it is John Jackson, whose posts include a board seat at Philips and the vice chairmanship of Ladbroke.*

The English politician and scholar Thomas More (1478-1535) was described during his own lifetime as **a man for all seasons**. In 1960, this description was used as the title of a play about More by Robert Bolt, and became a popular expression.

a man of his 'word

You describe a man as **a man of his word** if he always keeps his promises: *I'm a man of my word, and if I say I'll be there, I will.*

a man of many 'parts

A man of many parts is a man who has a lot of different abilities or who has achieved a lot of different things: *Edouard was a man of many parts. He passed from opera box to ski slope with equal elegance and aplomb.*

the man of the 'match

You describe someone as **the man of the match** if he is the sportsman who performed better than everyone else in a game that has just finished: *So, victory for England, but Hastings has to be the man of the match, with those three amazing tries.*

the man of the 'moment

You describe someone as **the man of the moment** if he is the person who is dealing with, or is best able to deal with, the present situation, especially when this is a political situation: *With his skilful statesmanship and tact, he has yet again proven himself to be the man of the moment.*

a man of 'straw

1 A man of straw is a man that you consider to be weak or worthless: *He is accused of being a man of straw, even by certain members of his own party.* **2 A man of straw** is also a person who does not exist, but who has been invented as a cover for some dishonest or illegal activity: *The creation of hundreds of votes by men of straw enabled the party to alter the election results.* **3** In a discussion, **a man of straw** is an argument which neither side really supports, but which has been invented by one side so that they can accuse the opposing side of supporting it: *Their argument is a man of straw. The pressure group knows that tests have shown it may be the most environmentally friendly option.*

a man of the 'world

You describe someone as **a man of the world** if he has had a lot of experience of life, giving him a realistic attitude and an ability to look after himself: *I'm surprised that a man of the world like him should have fallen for a trick like that.*

man on the Clapham 'omnibus or man on the 'street

When you talk about the **man on the Clapham omnibus**, or the **man on the street**, you mean no particular person, just an ordinary member of the public: *You ask the man on the street where he thinks the lottery money goes and he'll say, 'To charity.'*

◇ SEE ALSO **Joe Public** or **Joe Bloggs** ▷ JOE

a man or a 'mouse

If you ask someone whether they are **a man or a mouse**, you are telling them that they should try to be braver: *What are you, a man or a mouse? Just go and ask for one.*

a man's gotta do what a man's gotta 'do

If someone says **'a man's gotta do what a man's gotta do'**, they mean that, although a certain activity may be unpleasant, either they themselves, or the person they are referring to, is going to do it: *I'd better see if I can unblock that toilet. A man's gotta do what a man's gotta do, eh?*

◇ SEE ALSO **needs must when the devil drives** ▷ NEEDS

This is a phrase from Westerns, and is sometimes said with an American accent.

a 'man's man

If you describe a man as **a man's man**, you mean that they prefer the company of, and fit in better with, other men rather than women: *He's your typical man's man, never happier than when he's watching football with his mates.*

man to 'man

When two men talk **man to man**, or have a **man-to-man** discussion, they discuss something, especially something personal, honestly together: *Young Michael and I have had a proper man-to-man talk and I think he understands now. Eh, Michael?*

marked 'man

A marked man is a man who is in danger from some enemy who is chasing or trying to harm him: *Although he is receiving full protection from the British Government, Rushdie is still a marked man.* □ *He's been a marked man ever since he questioned his boss's competence.*

may the best man 'win

If someone says **'may the best man win'** at the beginning of a race or other competitive event, they mean that they want the event to be fair, and that they hope the strongest, fastest, etc competitor will win.

◇ SEE ALSO **may the best person win** ▷ PERSON

need a man like a fish needs a 'bicycle

If a woman says she **needs a man like**, or **as much as**, **a fish needs a bicycle**, she means that she neither needs, nor wants, to be in a relationship with a man: *You assume a woman like me can't feel complete without a man, but a woman needs a man as much as a fish needs a bicycle.*

This expression comes from the feminist movement.

a 'no-man's land

You are in **a no-man's land** if you are in a situation which is not clear, and you do not know what action you should take: *After my girlfriend left me, I was in an emotional no-man's land for weeks.* □ *The 'chronically unemployed' are in a no-man's land, unemployable because they have never worked.*

No-man's land is the neutral area which no-one owns, especially between two armies which are fighting each other.

odd man 'out

The **odd man out** in a group of things or people is the one that is different from all the rest: *Once again at Maastricht, Britain appeared as the odd man out.*
◇ SEE ALSO **odd one out** ▷ ODD

so-and-so's old 'man (*informal*)

If you talk about a certain person's **old man**, you mean that person's father: *Sandra's old man was a lighthouse keeper before he retired.*

one-man 'band

A **one-man band** is an organization which is directed and run by a single person: *An impressive variety of practices is featured in the exhibition, from the one-man band to the big, quoted companies.*

The original meaning of **a one-man band** is a particular type of musician who has learned to play a lot of different instruments, attached to his body, all at the same time, and who plays his music alone, often outside or at a circus.

one man's meat is another man's 'poison

If someone says '**one man's meat is another man's poison**', they mean that, just because one person likes something, it is not certain that everyone will like it: *If you don't like it, just say. Don't be afraid. One man's meat is another man's poison, as they say.*

poor man's 'such-and-such

You describe something as the, or a, **poor man's such-and-such** if it is considered to be a substitute for something more luxurious and expensive: *This fizzy wine is a poor man's champagne.* □ *lumpfish eggs – the poor man's caviare.*

to a 'man

When a group of people do something **to a man**, they all do that thing: *They all agreed to a man that the mission should be abandoned.*

you can't keep a good man 'down

If someone says '**you can't keep a good man down**', they mean that it is impossible to defeat or discourage the person they are referring to for long, because that person has so much strength and determination: *He's back playing rugby, after being told he might never walk again. You can't keep a good man down.*

manna

manna from 'heaven

You say that a good thing is like **manna from heaven** if it comes as a pleasant surprise to you when you are in difficult circumstances: *Tea dances with cakes; it all sounds rather dull now, but to us, in wartime Britain, the cakes were manna from heaven.*

This is a reference to the story in the Bible in which delicious bread called **manna** fell from heaven as a gift from God to the Israelites when they were starving (Exodus, chapter 16).

manner

by no manner of 'means or not by any manner of 'means

By no manner of means and **not by any manner of means** both mean 'not at all': *We have all worked hard, but by no manner of means can we afford to sit back and relax yet.*

in a manner of 'speaking or as a manner of 'speaking

You add '**in a manner of speaking**' to what you are saying to show that a word or phrase you have used gives a good description of what you mean, but is not intended to be exact or accurate; you say something **as a manner of speaking** if the words you say are not intended to be exact or accurate, only to express some basic idea: *'And I, in a manner of speaking, am a plane without a pilot,' Dwayne says.* □ *He later admitted that he had merely said between seventeen and eighteen as a manner of speaking.*

to the manner 'born

You say that someone is **to the manner born** if they seem comfortable and natural doing something, as if they have been doing it since the day they were born: *McGrath's companion is also a welcome guest at the dinner, and sits on a chair as if to the manner born with a serviette tucked into his collar.*

This expression often refers to accomplished social behaviour by someone who is not experienced in such matters.

manners

manners maketh 'man
If someone says 'manners maketh man', they mean that it is important to have good manners, because it is by your manners that people often judge you.

mind your 'manners
If you tell someone, especially a child, to **mind their manners**, you are telling them to be more polite: *I gave him a frown and told him to mind his manners because I wasn't sure what the old lady's reaction would be.*

map

put such-and-such on the 'map
If something **puts** a certain place **on the map**, it causes that place to be important: *The aeroplane exploded over Lockerbie, putting an otherwise unexceptional town on the map.*

marbles

lose your 'marbles
If you say that someone **is losing their marbles**, you mean that they are going mad, or becoming forgetful and confused: *As one of her oldest friends affectionately put it to me on her 100th birthday, she has lost her marbles.*
◇ SEE ALSO **go gaga** ▷ GAGA

march

steal a 'march on someone
If you **steal a march on someone**, you secretly gain an advantage, especially an advantage in time, over them: *We tried to steal a march on the other teams by setting off a day early.*

This is a military term, meaning to move an army unexpectedly while the enemy is resting.

mare

a 'mare's-nest
A **mare's-nest** is a discovery of something which turns out to be imaginary: *He occupied himself with finding mare's-nests in the form of non-existent errors in the arrangement of my plans.*

marines

tell that to the ma'rines
If someone says '**tell that to the marines**', they mean that they do not believe what has just been said: *Sir G. Howe seemed to*

declare that a nation with its own currency could not survive in the days of the ecu. Tell that to the marines.
◇ SEE ALSO **come off it** ▷ COME; **do me a favour** ▷ FAVOUR; **don't give me that** ▷ GIVE; **don't make me laugh** ▷ LAUGH

This expression comes from the fact that, in the past, sailors were the only ordinary people who were able to travel the world. For this reason they were more experienced in worldly matters than other people, and less likely to believe anything they were told.

mark

a black 'mark against someone
When someone has **a black mark against them**, they are disliked by someone in authority for having done something in the past which made that person angry: *She got a very stern reprimand and a black mark against her name for the rest of her career.*

In the past, teachers used to put a **black mark** in the class register beside the name of a pupil who had been particularly badly behaved. If the pupil got three black marks, he or she was then punished.

close to the 'mark or **near to the 'mark**
If something such as a guess is **close**, or **near to, the mark**, it is nearly correct or accurate, and sometimes closer to the truth than some people would like: *I think she was pretty near to the mark when she said the whole thing was a publicity stunt.* □ *The question was uncomfortably close to the mark.*

In archery, the **mark** was an old name for the target which you try to hit with your arrows.

hit the 'mark
Something which you attempt **hits the mark** if it achieves what it is intended to achieve: *T2 follows this trend but somehow fails to hit the mark due to poorly designed sequences.* □ *It was a guess, though scarcely a wild one, and Cunningham's reaction confirmed it had hit the mark.*

See note at **close** or **near to the mark**.

leave your 'mark
You **leave your mark** if you are remembered for the influence you have had on something: *She died many years ago, but the words she said have left their mark on me.* □ *Many civilisations have left their mark on this part of Ulster – Celts, Danes, Normans.*

make your 'mark

You **make your mark** when you first become successful or influential in a particular field: *As a poet, he made his mark first in 1712 with the publication of 'Nereides'.*

miss the 'mark

Something which you attempt **misses the mark** if it fails to achieve what it is intended to achieve: *She's usually quite funny, but her most recent comedy show seemed to miss the mark.*

See note at **close** or **near to the mark**.

off the 'mark or **wide of the 'mark**

A guess is **off**, or **wide of**, **the mark** if it is not at all correct or accurate: *We can't give a pass to an exam paper like that. He's way off the mark with over half his answers.* □ *All the opinion polls were seriously wide of the mark.*

See note at **close** or **near to the mark**.

overstep the 'mark

A person **oversteps the mark** when they go beyond what are accepted as the permitted limits: *The regulators obviously feel that he has overstepped the mark with his comments this time.*

quick off the 'mark

You are **quick off the mark** if your mind works quickly or you have quick reactions in a situation: *Michael was very good at improvising. He was very bright and quick off the mark.* □ *But UK firms will have to be quick off the mark to benefit from the scheme.*

In track athletics, the **mark** is the line from which a race starts.

slow off the 'mark

You are **slow off the mark** if your mind does not work quickly or you have slow reactions in a situation: *You can't accuse her of being slow off the mark. She's a mathematical genius.* □ *The Financial Times was slow off the mark in exposing Labour's tax plans.*

See note at **quick off the mark**.

up to the 'mark

Someone or something is **up to the mark** if it is of the good standard that you expect: *I don't think the service here is quite up to the mark.*

market

in the 'market for something

If you are **in the market for something**, you are interested in buying that thing: *I wish I had known that he was in the market for the painting before the auction began.*

on the 'market

Something is **on the market** if it is on sale and available for people to buy: *Their house has been on the market for ages.*

price something out of the 'market or **price yourself out of the 'market**

If a person or company **has priced something**, such as one of their products, **out of the market**, they have raised the price of that product so high that no-one is willing to buy it; if they **have priced themselves out of the market**, they have raised the price of their services so high that no-one is willing to pay for them: *I know they are high quality products, but don't make the mistake of pricing them out of the market.* □ *They realized that they had priced themselves out of the market and had little to offer except kudos and tradition.*

marrow

chilled to the 'marrow or **frozen to the 'marrow**

You are **chilled**, or **frozen**, **to the marrow**, if you are very cold.

◇ SEE ALSO **chilled to the bone** ▷ BONE; **cold as ice**▷ COLD

The **marrow** is the soft substance in the centre of your bones.

mask

someone's 'mask has slipped

You say that someone's **mask has slipped** if they have been unable to continue with their false behaviour, and have started doing things which show who they really are, or what they are really like: *Recently the movement's mask has begun to slip as they become more desperate for political success.*

If a mask which you are wearing to hide your face slips down, your face will no longer be covered and people will see what you really look like.

mass

in the 'mass

When you think about a group **in the mass**, you are considering it as a whole, not as a number of separate individuals: *Her mother had a genuine affection for humanity in the mass.*

masses

'masses of something

Masses of something is a large quantity of it: *There's masses of time before the concert starts.* □ *'Have you got enough chicken?' 'Yes thanks. Masses.'*

mast

at half-'mast

You say that someone's socks are **at half-mast** if they are falling down; you say that someone's tie is **at half-mast** if it has been loosened so that it is not tight around the neck: *He always was an untidy-looking boy, with his shirt untucked and his socks at half-mast.* □ *He was ambling towards them, his shirtsleeves rolled to the elbows, tie at half-mast.*

If a flag is flying **at half-mast**, it has only been raised to the half-way point on a mast or flagpole, often as a sign that there has been a recent death.

before the 'mast (*old*)

Someone who works **before the mast** on a ship works there as an ordinary sailor, not as an officer or in a position of responsibility: *Life before the mast in one of His Majesty's ships was not likely to be easily forgotten.*

master

old 'master

An **old master** is any great painter or painting from a period before the 19th century, especially from the 15th and 16th centuries: *We spent a pleasant day in the National Gallery, looking at all the old masters.* □ *This term we will be looking at the Italian old masters: among others, Leonardo, Titian and Botticelli.*

a past 'master

A **past master** is someone who has developed a skill in a particular activity, as a result of years spent practising it: *He considers himself a past master in the art of seduction.*

masters

serve two 'masters

You say that a person **serves two masters** if their life or the way they think is influenced by two completely different things which are probably opposed to each other: *Conflicts of interest occurred in trying to serve two masters (the patient and the system).* □ *They were not allowed to serve two masters. They were to choose their stance and they were to live with the consequences of their choice.*

match

a 'match for

Someone or something is **a match for** another person or thing if they can equal that person or thing in some skill or quality: *This is a high quality horse, madam, and to be frank, I'm not sure your son will be a match for him.*

meet your 'match

You say that someone **has met their match** when they meet someone who is their equal in some skill or quality: *He finally met his match in one Major Faulks in 1905 who stayed with the firm as a consultant until 1965 when he finally retired – at the age of 90.*

no 'match for

Someone or something is **no match for** another person or thing if they cannot equal that person or thing in some skill or quality: *In the final analysis students do not have power and are no match for the military.*

◇ SEE ALSO **a pale imitation** ▷ IMITATION

a 'slanging match or a 'slagging match

When two or more people are shouting insults at each other, you say they are having **a slanging match**, or **a slagging match**: *Why can't any of us talk without it turning into a slanging match?*

matter

as a matter of 'course

Something which happens **as a matter of course** happens automatically without any need for special instructions or arrangements: *Do I have to re-apply for funding every year? I thought I would get it as a matter of course.*

as a matter of 'fact

You use the phrase **as a matter of fact** to introduce an unexpected piece of information related to what has just been said, or to correct somebody when you think they have got the wrong impression about something: *So you like hill-walking, do you? I used to do a bit myself, as a matter of fact.* □ *'You don't mind my smoking, do you?' 'As a matter of fact, I do.'*

a different 'matter or another 'matter

If you say that something is **a different matter** or **another matter**, you mean it is a completely different thing: *It's easy enough to buy a house, but selling it again may be a different matter.*

for 'that matter

For that matter draws attention to a second statement, usually a short one, which extends the first: *My wife didn't enjoy the film much. For that matter, neither did I. Too much sex and violence.*

◇ SEE ALSO **come to that** ▷ COME

'grey matter

If you talk about your **grey matter**, you mean your brain or your powers of thought and reasoning: *Of course, I've never thought her dizzy; I've always admired her, and I wish I had a little of her grey matter.*

Grey matter is a scientific term for the greyish material containing brain cells which the most complex parts of the brain are made from.

a matter of 'such-and-such

1 Something that can be done in **a matter of** seconds, minutes, hours, days, or weeks only takes that amount of time to do: *Oh, give it to me. I'll get it typed in a matter of seconds.* □ *It will only be a matter of a few weeks until you start to notice the difference in how you feel.* **2** You use the expression 'just **a matter of** something' when you are talking about a simple way of dealing with something: *It's simply a matter of taking a few basic precautions when cooking chicken.*

a matter of life and 'death

You say that something is **a matter of life and death** if it is of the greatest importance, or so urgent that it must be dealt with immediately: *So insistent was the man, saying his message was a matter of life and death, that she finally agreed to go to his room to see if he would listen to what the messenger had to say.*

a matter of o'pinion

If you say that something is **a matter of opinion**, you mean that it is something that is not clearly proven and is therefore a matter of personal judgement: *Her beauty was, of course, a matter of opinion, as these things often are.* □ *Whether this new scheme is desirable or not is a matter of opinion.*

no laughing 'matter

If you say that something is **no laughing matter**, you mean that it is a serious matter, or that it is an unpleasant experience: *Having to wait for a bus at 5am on a chilly winter morning is no laughing matter.*

no 'matter

1 You use **no matter** before **what, how, where, when**, and so on, to give them the same meaning as 'whatever', 'however', 'wherever', 'whenever' and so on, to emphasize that what you are saying will remain true, independent of all possible conditions: *No matter where I go, my dog always goes with me.* □ *Give us a call when you arrive, no matter what time it is.* **2** You say that something is **no matter** if you do not consider it to be important: *'Did you get the margarine?' 'What margarine?' 'Oh, no matter. I'll go shopping and get some later.'*

what's the 'matter?

You say '**what's the matter?**' when you are asking what is wrong, or what the problem is: *What's the matter? You look so sad.*

matters

to make matters 'worse

If you are talking about a bad situation and you want to mention something which makes that situation even worse, you can introduce it with the expression '**to make matters worse**': *I've got a horribly busy weekend, and to make matters worse, the car's out of action.*
◇ SEE ALSO **to cap it all** ▷ CAP; **to crown it all** ▷ CROWN; **to top it all** ▷ TOP; **what is more** ▷ WHAT

May

May and De'cember

If people talk about **May and December**, they mean a marriage or relationship between a young person and a much older person: *I know some people would say it was May and December, but I thought it was a lovely relationship.*

meal

make a 'meal of something

You say that someone is **making a meal of something** if they are taking more than the necessary amount of time or trouble over it, or making it seem more complicated than it really is: *Get it done as quickly as you can – don't make a meal of it.*
◇ SEE ALSO **make a rod for your own back** ▷ ROD; **your own worst enemy** ▷ ENEMY

a 'meal ticket

You say that someone treats a person or organization as **a meal ticket** if they seem happy to take all the support or help that that person or organization offers, without showing any gratitude or offering anything in return: *There were times when he suspected he was just a meal ticket to his wife.*

a square 'meal

A **square meal** is a nutritious, filling meal: *You've got so thin. You look as if you could do with a good square meal.*

mean

'mean well (*disrespectful*)

You say that someone **means well** if you think their intentions are good or kind, even if their actions often annoy or upset people: *I know she talks too much, but she means well.*

no mean 'such-and-such (*informal*)

1 You describe a person as **no mean such-and-such** if they have a particular ability in the activity you are referring to: *No mean performer on the rugby field, he has now developed a taste for academia.* **2** You describe something as **no mean such-and-such** if it is impressive: *an estate, which, although small, was of no mean value.*

means

beyond your 'means
A price to be paid for something is **beyond your means** if you do not have enough money to pay it; someone is living **beyond their means** if they spend more money than they earn: *I'm afraid that the house is a bit beyond our means at the moment.* □ *Credit cards just encourage people to live beyond their means.*

by 'all means
You say '**by all means**' as a polite way of giving permission: *'May I look at your garden?' 'By all means.'*

by fair means or 'foul
If a person is determined to do or obtain something **by fair means or foul**, they want it so badly that they are prepared to do anything, even very bad things, to achieve this: *They were determined to do whatever lay in their power to ensure victory for themselves, by fair means or foul.*
◇ SEE ALSO **at any price** ▷ PRICE; **stop at nothing** ▷ STOP

by 'no means or not by 'any means
By no means and **not by any means** mean 'not at all': *She has given me a bit of money back, but by no means all that she owed me.* □ *'May I go now, sir?' 'Certainly not. I haven't finished with you yet, not by any means.'*

a means to an 'end
Something that is **a means to an end** is something that people do not for enjoyment but to achieve something: *Think of discipline as a means to an end, not an end in itself.*

within your 'means
A price to be paid for something is **within your means** if you have enough money to buy it; someone is living **within their means** if they do not spend more money than they earn: *A hundred and fifty pounds? Yes, I suppose that's just within our means.* □ *It's hard to live within your means when the only money you have coming in is Income Support.*

measure

for good 'measure
You do or have something extra **for good measure** when you do or have it, even though it may not really be necessary, in order to make sure that the situation is complete: *I filled the cake with cream, and dolloped some more round the sides for good measure.*

have the 'measure of someone or get the 'measure of someone
You **have the measure of** a person or animal if you understand them and are able to deal with them effectively; you **get the measure of** them when you start to understand them and to deal with them effectively: *You should have made sure you had the measure of your horse before riding on the roads.* □ *It's taken me months, but I think I've finally got the measure of that boy in my class.*

meat

dead 'meat
You say that someone is **dead meat** if they have no chance of escaping from a situation alive: *'You are dead meat, Sheikh!' Mafouz yelled.*

> This expression is often used as a threat, as in the above example.

easy 'meat
If a certain person or group is **easy meat**, it is easy to defeat or take advantage of them: *They showed they will be far from easy meat for England in Saturday week's Twickenham Test.*

meat and 'drink to someone
Something such as a favourite activity is **meat and drink to someone** if it gives that person so much pleasure that you wonder if they could manage without it: *These corporate executives are people to whom the Conservative party is meat and drink.*

> In the past, **meat** meant 'food' in general.

meat and two 'veg
If people talk about **meat and two veg**, they mean the main dish of a traditional meal, consisting of meat, potatoes and some other vegetable: *A good balanced meal is traditional meat and two veg, and not tonics and pep pills.*

medicine

take your medicine like a 'man
You say that someone is **taking their medicine like a man** if they do or accept something unpleasant bravely and without complaining: *I thought he might object to doing Community Service, but he is taking his medicine like a man.*

medium

happy 'medium
A **happy medium** is a way of dealing with a situation which comes between two extreme methods: *'You have to strike a happy medium between looking like royalty and looking like a housewife,' Mrs Tony Newton, wife of the Leader of the Commons, explained.*

meet

meet someone half'way

You **meet someone halfway** if you refuse to do exactly what they want, but agree to change some of your plans or demands to fit in with theirs: *We'll never find a solution unless the unions are willing to meet us halfway.*

meeting

fancy meeting 'you here!

You exclaim **'fancy meeting you here!'** if you are surprised to see someone in a place where you did not expect them to be: *Well, fancy meeting you here! I thought I was coming to Australia to get away from my neighbours.*

> This expression is often used in a humorous way when the person being spoken to is in exactly the place the speaker expects them to be.

memory

commit something to 'memory

You **commit something to memory** when you make a mental note of that thing with the intention of remembering it: *I committed the number to memory and threw the paper slip on to the fire.*

◊ SEE ALSO **commit something to paper** ▷ PAPER

in living 'memory or within living 'memory

Something which has happened **in**, or **within, living memory** can be remembered by people who are still alive: *In 1946-47, Britain saw what was probably the heaviest snow-fall in living memory.*

in memory of 'so-and-so

People do something **in memory of** a dead person if they do it as a way of remembering that person: *Let us drink a toast in memory of our departed friends.*

memory 'lane

A person goes down **memory lane** when they remind themselves of a time when they were younger, by doing or experiencing again the things they used to do in the past: *And at six o'clock on BBC1, there's a trip down memory lane with some of your old favourites in 'Those were the Days'.*

a memory like an 'elephant or the memory of an 'elephant

You say that someone has **a memory like**, or **the memory of, an elephant** if they have an excellent memory: *If you want to know about the day the Government was elected, speak to Anne. She's got the memory of an elephant.*

◊ SEE ALSO **an elephant never forgets** ▷ ELEPHANT

> People say that elephants have good memories, although there is no evidence for this.

a memory like a 'sieve

You say that someone has **a memory like a sieve** if they forget things easily: *Oh dear. Now where did I put my glasses? I've got a memory like a sieve.*

> A **sieve** is a piece of kitchen equipment with a lot of small holes in it to let liquid and small particles through. The idea is that a bad memory lets information escape from it in the same way.

men

dead men can't 'talk

If someone says **'dead men can't talk'**, they mean that a certain secret will only be safe if the person or people who know it are dead: *'What a good thing hanging is!' he murmured. 'Dead men can never talk, or betray old friends!'*

dead men's 'shoes

If you achieve something by filling, or stepping into, **dead men's shoes**, you do it by taking the job or position of someone who has recently died: *Here was this obscure relation who had fallen into the estate by a series of dead men's shoes.*

men in grey 'suits

The **men in grey suits** are the powerful businessmen and officials who make the most important decisions in politics and business, although the public are often not aware of their existence: *The Tories are the most ruthless party in the democratic world. If the men in grey suits do not think Mr Major can win the next election for them, he'll be dumped.* □ *The Beatles had to start taking responsibility for their world instead of being acted upon by a panoply of 'men in grey suits'.*

the men in white 'coats (*humorous*)

If people talk about **the men in white coats**, they mean doctors, especially doctors who treat mental illnesses: *You'll have the men in white coats coming to get you if you carry on talking to yourself like that.*

separate the men from the 'boys or sort out the men from the 'boys

You say that a certain activity **will separate**, or **sort out, the men from the boys** if it will allow people to see who is really able to excel under tough conditions: *John McEnroe goes into today's US Open final with world No.1 Jim Courier insisting: 'This will separate the men from the boys. It will be an unbelievably tough match.'*

◇ SEE ALSO **separate** or **sort out the sheep from the goats** ▷ SHEEP; **separate** or **sort out the wheat from the chaff** ▷ WHEAT

mend

on the 'mend
Someone who has been ill is **on the mend** if they are getting better: *He's maybe not a hundred per cent better yet, but he's certainly on the mend.*

mention

don't 'mention it
You say '**don't mention it**' as a polite way of accepting a person's thanks: *'Thanks for all your help.' 'Don't mention it.'*

honourable 'mention
1 An entry in a competition gets an **honourable mention** when it is selected as one of the best, but not given a prize: *Both projects were shortlisted and received an honourable mention in the 1991 awards.* **2** You say, especially in a humorous way, that someone deserves an **honourable mention** if you think that they have done something admirable: *He also deserves an honourable mention for working with Graham Knight and Carlton Brown, and retaining a sense of humour.*

not to 'mention
People say '**not to mention**' before they add something else to what they have already said: *They've got everything in that house. Fitted kitchen, new carpets. Not to mention the spa bath.*

mercies

leave someone to the tender 'mercies of so-and-so (*humorous*)
If you **leave someone to the tender mercies of** a certain unpleasant person, you leave them in the care of that person: *I can hardly imagine anything worse than being left to the tender mercies of that dreadful woman.*

thankful for small 'mercies
If you say that someone should be **thankful for small mercies**, you are remarking that they should take courage from the few positive things which make their situation less difficult: *She died suddenly, so at least she didn't suffer. I suppose we should be thankful for small mercies.*

◇ SEE ALSO **count your blessings** ▷ BLESSINGS; **half a loaf is better than no bread** ▷ LOAF; **look on the bright side** ▷ SIDE

mercy

at the 'mercy of
If you are **at the mercy of** someone or something, they have complete control

over you and can treat you as badly or unfairly as they wish: *You camp if you want, but I don't fancy a night outside at the mercy of the elements.*

merrier

the more the 'merrier
If someone says '**the more the merrier**', they mean that the more people or things there are, the better: *'Have you got room in the car for us?' 'Pile in. The more the merrier.'*

merry (*see also* **merrier**)

make 'merry (*old*)
People in a group or at a party **make merry** when they enjoy themselves together: *While you are eating and generally making merry, spare a thought for the poor and the hungry.*
'**merry-making**: *Christmas, traditionally a time for merry-making, is also the most stressful day of the year for most people.*

mess

make a 'mess of something
You say that someone **has made a mess of something** if they have done it badly: *I'm surprised they offered me the job. I made a horrible mess of the interview, I thought.* □ *Get down off that ladder and give me the brush. I can't bear to see you making a mess of that painting.*

a mess of 'pottage
If people talk about **a mess of pottage**, they mean something that someone has received in exchange for something more valuable: *Do we really want to go down in history as the generation which sold for a mess of pottage the finest British companies?*

In the Bible (Genesis, chapter 25) Esau is so hungry that he sells his birthright to his brother Jacob for a meal of lentil **pottage** [= thick stew] and some bread.

message

get the 'message
You **get the message** when you understand what someone has been suggesting, especially if they have been doing it in an indirect way: *Was he stupid or was he lying? He had a feeling he'd never get rid of the boy. He'd never get the message.*

message received and under'stood
If you say '**message received and understood**', you mean that you have understood the situation: *'OK,' she sighed, swinging her legs over the side of the bed and standing up. 'Message received and understood.'*

This phrase was the official way of replying to a radio message, used by the military services in the Second World War.

metaphor

mixed 'metaphor

A **mixed metaphor** is an expression or image which is produced by combining two images which are not normally used together, often having an amusing effect: *If a mixed metaphor can be forgiven: John Major has opened a Pandora's box of worms.*

method

there is method in so-and-so's 'madness

You say that **there is method in** a certain person's **madness** if, although that person seems to be doing things in the wrong way, they do in fact have a purpose in doing them that way: *We have imagined him as absolutely, and monstrously, evil. But is he a primitive and irrational alien? Might there not be method in his madness?*

In Shakespeare's Hamlet, II ii, Polonius realizes that Hamlet's words make some kind of sense although he seems to be mad, and makes the remark 'Though this be madness, yet there is method in it'.

mettle

put someone on their 'mettle

If something **puts someone on their mettle**, it makes them anxious to do their best and perform well: *Her near defeat in the first set has put the defending champion on her mettle, and she's fighting hard.*

mickey

a Mickey 'Finn

1 A **Mickey Finn** is a drug which has been put into someone's drink without their knowledge: *She poured champagne and slipped a Mickey Finn into Kattina's glass.* **2** A **Mickey Finn** is also a drink which has been drugged in this way.

take the 'mickey

You **take the mickey** when you make jokes or try to play tricks on someone; you **take the mickey**, or **take the mickey out of** something or someone when you make fun of them: *'I found a puppy in the street, so I brought it home.' 'Are you taking the mickey?'* □ *When other people are taking the mickey out of someone else, try to imagine how they feel about it. Don't join in if it is getting hurtful.*

◊ SEE ALSO **make fun of** or **poke fun at** ▷ FUN; **take the piss** ▷ PISS

Midas

the 'Midas touch

You say that someone has **the Midas touch** if everything they do seems to produce a lot of money: *It was clear that Anita had the Midas touch. Her business was doing well in Britain and abroad.*

In Greek myth, the god Dionysus gives **King Midas** the power to turn everything he touches into gold.

middle

in the 'middle of

You are **in the middle of** something, or of doing something, when you are busy with that thing: *Don't interrupt when I'm in the middle of a conversation.*

in the middle of 'nowhere

You are **in the middle of nowhere** if you are in a place which is a long distance from any towns and houses, often with a feeling of being lost: *Eventually, we stopped. We were in the middle of nowhere, and it was beginning to get dark.*

◊ SEE ALSO **the back of beyond** ▷ BACK; **out in the sticks** ▷ STICKS; **off the beaten track** ▷ TRACK; **out of the way** ▷ WAY

middle-of-the-'road (*disrespectful*)

You describe something as **middle-of-the-road** if it does not involve extreme ideas, tries to be reasonable in all ways, and so appeals to popular taste: *Many people shy away from voting Lib Dem because it seems to be a middle-of-the-road option.* □ *He was committed to middle-of-the-road filmmaking, which he defined as 'escapist entertainment of pleasant people in pleasant surroundings doing pleasant things'.*

in mid'stream

You stop **in midstream** when you suddenly pause while doing something busily, especially talking: *'Will,' he said breathlessly, and stopped in midstream. 'I say, what's going on here? Is this a party?'*

might

do something with all your 'might

You are **doing something with all your might** when you are putting all your energy and strength into doing it: *I tugged on the rope with all my might, but I just wasn't strong enough.*

with might and 'main (*old*)

You are doing something **with might and main** when you are putting a lot of energy and strength into doing that thing: *We* *battled on with all our might and main through the stormy seas.*

mildly

to put it 'mildly
You use 'to put it mildly' to show that you are not expressing yourself as strongly as you could do, considering the situation: *I was a bit annoyed, to put it mildly.*

mile

run a 'mile
You say that a certain situation would make someone run a mile if you think that person would be afraid of, and try to escape from, it: *Oh, I think she likes me. But she'd run a mile if I suggested we got married.*

see something a 'mile off or spot something a 'mile off
You say that you can see, or spot, something a mile off if you notice it easily: *You mean you didn't even notice she'd been crying? But you could spot it a mile off.*

stand out a 'mile or stick out a 'mile
You say that something stands, or sticks, out a mile if you think it is obvious: *Oh, come on. You can tell how posh he is from his accent. It sticks out a mile.*

miles

'miles away
You say that someone is miles away when they are having such deep thoughts about something else that they are not aware of what is happening around them or what someone is saying to them: *'Carrie,' I said. She looked up dreamily. 'Sorry, I was miles away.'*

milk

cry over spilt 'milk
Someone who is crying over spilt milk is regretting something which cannot be changed: *It's no good crying over spilt milk. It's the question of what happens from now on that's very important.* □ *Nora Simpson didn't believe in crying over spilt milk. What had happened had happened, and there was nothing she could do about it now.*

milk and 'water (*disrespectful*)
You say that someone is made of milk and water if they have a weak character: *He was all milk and water. He lacked the fire to take a firm hand with the woman.*

the milk of human 'kindness
If people talk about the milk of human kindness, they mean natural kindness towards other people: *Dear old Martha had much of the milk of human kindness about her; she never begrudged sharing whatever she had.*

From Shakespeare's Macbeth, I v.

mill (*see also* **mills**)

go through the 'mill or be put through the 'mill
You say that someone has gone, or been put, through the mill when they have undergone a series of difficult tests or experiences: *You poor thing. Sounds like you were put through the mill at your interview, then?*

millpond

like a 'millpond
An area of water that is described as being like a millpond, or a millpond, is very flat, and not disturbed by any wind and waves: *May sunshine and a temperature of seventy degrees. The sea was a brilliant blue millpond.*

mills

the mills of God grind slowly but they grind exceedingly 'small
If someone says 'the mills of God grind slowly but they grind exceedingly small', they mean that people always get the punishment or reward which they deserve, even if it takes a long time to happen.

millstone

a millstone round someone's 'neck
You describe an unpleasant duty or responsibility that prevents you from doing what you would like as a millstone round your neck: *Mr Smith said that unemployment at this 'tragic level' was an economic millstone round the country's neck costing £27 billion a year.*

mincemeat

make 'mincemeat of someone
To make mincemeat of someone is to defeat them completely: *We got through to the final round of the quiz, but the champions made mincemeat of us.*

◇ SEE ALSO wipe the floor with ▷ FLOOR; give someone a hammering ▷ HAMMERING

mind (*see also* **minded** *and* **minds**)

all in the 'mind
You say that a situation is all in the mind if you consider it to be wholly produced by your attitudes towards something: *If you believe you're beautiful, you'll look beautiful. It's all in the mind.*

bear something in 'mind or keep something in 'mind
You bear, or keep, something in mind when you remember it or take it into consideration: *Bear in mind that it could rain every day, even in the middle of the summer.*

blow someone's 'mind (*informal*)
Something which **blows someone's mind** surprises or excites them greatly: *It blows your mind to think that people built these monuments over five thousand years ago.*

This expression was originally used to describe the effect of mind-altering drugs such as LSD.

bring something to 'mind
If a thing or an event **brings something to mind**, it causes you to remember or think of that thing: *The sound of the waves on the shore brought to mind the sunny summers of her childhood.*

cast your 'mind back
You **cast your mind back** to a certain period or event when you try to remember it: *Cast your mind back to the first time you drove a car. Remember how difficult it seemed?*

change your 'mind
You **change your mind** when you change your opinion, or change a decision or choice that you have made: *I thought she was quite nice at first, but I've changed my mind about her.* □ *'But I thought you said you were coming?' 'Well, I've changed my mind.'*

come to 'mind or **spring to 'mind**
An idea or memory **comes**, or **springs, to mind** when you suddenly think of it: *'What shall I make for dessert? Something light and not too expensive.' 'Fruit salad springs to mind.'*

cross someone's 'mind
If a thought **crosses your mind**, you think about it for a moment: *It crossed my mind recently that I hadn't heard from her for some time.* □ *I didn't claim benefits while I was ill. It never even crossed my mind that I might get any.*

a dirty 'mind
Someone who has **a dirty mind** is always thinking about sex: *'I can't look at a peach without thinking of naked bottoms.' 'You've just got a dirty mind.'*

do you 'mind? or **do you mind not ...?**
You say '**do you mind?**' or '**do you mind not...?**' to someone to express annoyance at what they are doing: *Do you mind? It's very rude to interrupt when two people are having a conversation.* □ *Hey! Do you mind not making so much 'noise? People are trying to get some sleep round here.*

go out of your 'mind
Someone who **is out of their mind** is mad; you say that someone is **going out of their mind** if they are behaving irrationally, often because they are worried or upset: *You gave the police a false name and address? You*

must be out of your mind. □ *And what time do you call this to be coming home? Your mother was going out of her mind.*

have something in 'mind
If you **have something in mind**, you want or intend to have or do that thing: *'What exactly did you have in mind?' 'Something nice. It's for my girlfriend.'*

have a mind of your 'own
1 You talk about a person or animal **having a mind of their own** if they are able to think for themselves, and do not accept other people's instructions or opinions without question: *Their baby is only six months old, but she's already got a mind of her own.* **2** You say that an object **has a mind of its own** if it behaves in a way that suggests it is thinking and making its own decisions, although you know this is not really the case: *I can't make your bike go in a straight line. It's got a mind of its own.*

have your 'mind on something
You **have your mind on something** when you are thinking about it or paying attention to it: *It's difficult to work when you've got your mind on other things.*

have a mind to or **have a good mind to** or **have half a mind to**
You say you **have a mind to**, or **have a good mind to**, or **have half a mind to** do something if you are seriously considering doing it, especially if you think it should be done and you think no-one else is going to do it: *He's been putting poisonous chemicals down the drains. I've a good mind to report him to the 'council.*

in your mind's 'eye
You see something **in your mind's eye** when you have a mental picture of it: *I wondered what his girlfriend was like. In my mind's eye, she was tall, with long, dark hair.*

in your right 'mind
A person is **in their right mind** if they are in their normal mental state: *I know she said some terrible things, but she wasn't in her right mind. She was ill.* □ *After all, who in their right mind would reject enthusiastic and cost-free labour?*

This expression is most often used in the negative and interrogative forms.

keep your 'mind on something
If you **are keeping your mind on something** which you are doing, you are giving all your attention to it: *If you keep your mind on the job you won't have time to speculate about me and my problems.*

keep an open 'mind
You **keep an open mind** about something if you are willing to consider new ideas about

it and change your own: *So now three people believed in the ghost. Noreen said she was keeping an open mind on the subject.*

make up your 'mind

You **make up your mind** when you make a decision or form an opinion: *I'd like to come, but I may not have time. Can I phone you back when I've made up my mind? □ I've only heard this song once before, and I can't make up my mind whether I like it or not.*

the mind 'boggles

If you say '**the mind boggles**', you mean that you find it difficult or impossible to imagine the thing that is being discussed, because it is so surprising or ridiculous: *British international players should soon be able to charge £1,500 for a solitary interview. The mind boggles.*

mind how you 'go!

You say '**mind how you go!**' to someone who is leaving, as a friendly way of saying goodbye and of wishing them good luck: *Send me a postcard, won't you? Bye now. Mind how you go.*

mind over 'matter

If people talk about **mind over matter**, they mean the power that determination can give you to succeed in something which you may have thought you were physically unable to do: *It was just a question of mind over matter, I thought, and tried to prepare myself for the physical effects of a rough ride.*

mind 'you

People say '**mind you**' as a way of emphasizing a point, especially a new point which has not previously or recently been mentioned: *The food at the café is very good. Mind you, it isn't cheap. □ I'm surprised he did so well at university. He always was a clever little boy, mind you.*

never 'mind

You say **never mind** to someone **1** to comfort them when they are unhappy or disappointed: *Never mind. You can have a party when you get better.* **2** to say that you have forgiven them for something: *Never mind. I probably deserved half the things you said.* **3** to tell them not to do something, either because it is unnecessary, or because you intend to do it yourself: *'I thought you wanted me to do the washing up?' 'Oh, never mind. I'll do it myself.'*

on someone's 'mind

Something is **on your mind** if you are anxious about it: *You seem quite quiet today. Have you got something on your mind?*

prey on someone's 'mind

A worry **is preying on your mind** if it remains in your mind, however hard you

try to forget it: *I wish I hadn't gone to that fortune-teller. Those things she said have been preying on my mind. □ She was worried about her husband; it had been obvious for the past few days that something was preying on his mind.*

put someone in 'mind of something (*rather formal*)

If something **puts you in mind of** a certain thing, it reminds you of that thing: *The distant ringing of church bells puts me in mind of happier days.*

put someone's 'mind at rest or set someone's 'mind at rest

If something **puts**, or **sets**, **your mind at rest**, it releases you from anxiety or worry: *Why not phone the hospital if you're worried? It'll put your mind at rest.*

put your 'mind to something

You **put your mind to something**, or to doing something, when you determinedly start deciding how you are going to do it: *You can do anything if you put your mind to it.*

slip someone's 'mind

Something **slips your mind** when you forget to do it, or forget to deal with it: *'Have you phoned the travel agent yet?' 'Oh, I'm sorry. It completely slipped my mind.'*

speak your 'mind

You **speak your mind** when you say what you really think: *I'm going to tell that nasty little man exactly what I think of him. I'm not afraid to speak my mind. □ She's a woman who speaks her mind.*

state of 'mind

Your **state of mind** is your mental and emotional state at any particular time: *She can't give you a response yet. She's in no state of mind to be making important decisions.*

take your 'mind off something

Something that **takes your mind off something** such as your problems makes you relax and forget them temporarily: *If your job is stressful, it's good to do something in the evenings to take your mind off your work.*

to 'my mind (*rather formal*)

Something that is the case **to your mind** is the case in your opinion: *To my mind, the Government will only get motorists to use their cars less by forcing them to do so.*
◇ SEE ALSO **to my way of thinking** ▷ WAY

wouldn't 'mind

You say that you **wouldn't mind** something if you would like that thing: *'What would you like for dinner, then?' 'Mmm... I wouldn't mind a nice stir-fry.'*

minded

like-'minded

You say that two people are **like-minded** if they consider the same things to be important: *If you care about the environment and want to meet like-minded people, come to our monthly meetings.*

narrow-'minded

A **narrow-minded** person is someone who finds it impossible to accept anything which is different from their own limited thoughts, ideas and values: *When I returned home from university, everyone in the village seemed terribly narrow-minded.*

minds

great minds think a'like (*humorous*)

If someone says '**great minds think alike**', they mean that clever people usually have the same ideas and opinions: *'I was just about to say that myself.' 'Great minds think alike, eh?'*

People usually say this when they discover that someone else shares their own ideas or opinions, as a way of flattering themselves and the other person. '**Fools seldom differ**' is a common reply which you can use as a humorous way of denying that these two people are as clever as they are suggesting.

in two 'minds

You say you are **in two minds** about something when you cannot decide whether or not you want it or want to do it: *I have been offered a place on a business course, but I'm in two minds whether to take it or not.*

◇ SEE ALSO **in a quandary** ▷ QUANDARY; **in a cleft stick** ▷ STICK

small things please small 'minds or simple things amuse simple 'minds (*disrespectful*)

If someone says '**small things please small minds**' or '**simple things amuse simple minds**', they mean that silly people are pleased or amused by silly subjects or achievements: *'Ha ha! You looked so funny when you fell over in front of everyone.' 'Ah well, simple things amuse simple minds, I suppose.'*

You can say this if you want to insult a person who is doing or saying something intended to annoy you.

mine

a mine of infor'mation

If you describe a person or thing as **a mine of information**, you mean that they are full of information: *Jimmy Webb, her seventeen-year-old assistant, was a mine of information about absolutely everything that was going on.* □ *This book is a mine of information on herbal remedies.*

minute

any minute 'now

You say that something which you have been waiting for is going to happen **any minute now** if it is just about to happen: *Any minute now, we expect to hear the official election result.*

at any 'minute

You say that something may happen **at any minute** if it is likely to happen in the present situation, although you do not know exactly when: *The bombing could start at any minute.*

at the last 'minute

You do something **at the last minute** when you do it just before it is too late: *The plans all came together at the last minute.*

last-'minute: *the last-minute Christmas rush.*

at the 'minute

You use **at the minute** when you are referring to the situation as it is at the moment when you are speaking, or around the time, as opposed to how it was before, or will be later: *I'm very busy just at the minute. Could you call back in half an hour?* □ *His hands shook and his friend prescribed a sedative. 'Is work a strain at the minute?' asked the doctor.*

every minute 'counts

You say that **every minute counts** if there is very little time to do what has to be done, and therefore that time must be used as effectively as possible: *Every minute counts in an exam, so get straight down to your answer.*

just a 'minute

1 You say '**just a minute**' to someone if you want them to wait for a short time: *'Can I come in?' 'Just a minute, I'm changing.'* **2** You say '**just a minute**' to express the fact that you have just noticed or thought of something: *Just a minute, what did you say your name was?*

◇ SEE ALSO **just a moment** ▷ MOMENT

not for one 'minute or never for one 'minute

If you say you do **not for one minute** believe a person or what they say, or that **never for one minute** did you believe them, you mean that you do not believe them at all: *He says he's going to study while he's on holiday, but I don't believe him. Not for one minute.* □ *She kept saying she was going to emigrate, but I never for one minute believed she would.*

◇ SEE ALSO **not** or **never for one moment** ▷ MOMENT

not have a minute to call your 'own

You say you do **not have a minute to call your own** if you are so busy working that you have almost no free time: *Would you care to have a look at it yourself? I'm so busy, I haven't a moment to call my own at present.*

not a minute to 'lose or not one minute to 'lose

You say that there is **not a**, or **not one, minute to lose** when the situation is so urgent that you will have to act immediately and as fast as possible: *The escaped prisoners must be stopped before they reach the border. There's not a minute to lose.*

there's one born every 'minute (*informal*)

If someone says '**there's one born every minute**', they mean that there is always someone around who is stupid enough to be easily deceived by other people: *Behind their backs, the dealer would call his clients 'suckers', saying: 'There's one born every minute' and, 'They just haven't got a chance!' This was his job.*

People use this expression as a comment on how silly they think someone has been to believe a lie or some kind of trick.

this 'minute

You say that something must be done **this minute** if it must be done immediately: *No, I can't wait, I need you here this minute.*

up-to-the-'minute

A person or thing is **up-to-the-minute** if they are modern, fashionable, or recent: *He took her to Vidal Sassoon's salon in Grosvenor House so that her hair could be cut in an up-to-the-minute style.* □ *Napoleon lacked up-to-the-minute information at the crucial moment.* □ *Of course, you'll keep my desk diary strictly up-to-the-minute.*

mischief

do someone a 'mischief or do yourself a 'mischief (*humorous*)

If you **do someone**, or **do yourself, a mischief**, you hurt that person or yourself, particularly on a part of your body that you are embarrassed to mention: *He had always used a lady's bike because he thought the middle bar on a man's one might do him a mischief if he cocked his leg over it carelessly.*

make 'mischief

Someone who **is making mischief** is causing trouble: *'Where are the kids?' 'Making mischief as usual, I should think.'* □ *The Conservatives, who are desperate because of the popularity of our policy, will do what they can to make mischief about it.*

misery

put someone out of their 'misery

You **put someone out of their misery** when you stop them from worrying or waiting anxiously, probably by giving them a piece of information: *Eventually someone put him out of his misery and told him, between guffaws, that he was in fact talking to an actor, not the Prime Minister at all.*

Originally, to **put** an animal **out of its misery** meant to kill it, because it was wounded and suffering great pain.

miss

give something a 'miss

You **give something a miss** when you decide not to do it, have it, or be present at it: *'Are you coming to the party?' 'No, I think I'll give it a miss.'* □ *I'll give dessert a miss, I think.*

a miss is as good as a 'mile

If someone says '**a miss is as good as a mile**', they mean that if you fail in something it makes no difference how close you came to succeeding.

a near 'miss

1 If you just fail to hit what you are aiming at, or if you almost, but do not quite, succeed in doing something, you call the result **a near miss**: *a 2–2 near miss at home to Switzerland* **2** **A near miss** is also an unpleasant event which almost happened: *An Aer Lingus BAe 1-11 airliner was involved in a near miss with a Trans World Airlines TriStar over Hertfordshire yesterday.*

mission

mission ac'complished

People sometimes say '**mission accomplished**' when they have completed the thing which they have been told to do: *Rex clapped his hands together. 'Mission accomplished. Let's go and have a drink.'*

This was originally a military expression used in World War II.

missionary

the 'missionary position

The missionary position is the most traditional position for a man and a woman to have sex, with both partners facing each other, and the man on top.

mistake

and 'no mistake (*old*)

You add '**and no mistake**' to a statement you have just made, to emphasize that statement: *She was a beautiful woman and no mistake. Tall, slim and dressed with an elegant simplicity.*

mistaking
there is no mistaking 'such-and-such
You say that **there is no mistaking** someone or something if they are perfectly obvious or easy to recognize: *She picked it up at the third ring. 'Yes?' 'Sam?' There was no mistaking the deep voice at the other end.*

mo
just a 'mo
You say '**just a mo**' to someone if you want them to wait for a short time: *'Aren't you ready yet?' 'Just a mo. I'm brushing my teeth.'*

Mo is short for 'moment'.

mockers
put the 'mockers on or have the 'mockers on
You **put**, or **have**, **the mockers on** a person or organization if you take away their power or destroy them, especially by threatening to bring bad luck to them if they continue with something they have planned: *The mob had the mockers on him because of evidence of his homosexuality.*

mockery
make a 'mockery of
You say that a certain thing **makes a mockery of** someone or something if it makes them seem silly or unimportant, either by treating them without any respect or by ignoring them altogether: *The sale of such industries makes a mockery of the Government's 'commitment to British consumers'.*

Mohicans
the last of the Mo'hicans
The **last of the Mohicans** is the last one of a group or set that is left after all the rest have gone or been used: *'You're the last one, Jack,' said Bodie with a thin smile. 'The last of the Mohicans.'*

This expression was the title of a film starring Daniel Day-Lewis, based on a novel by the American writer James Fenimore Cooper (1789-1851). It is a reference to one of the North American Indian tribes which was destroyed by the white men who settled in America.

moment
any moment 'now
You say that something which you have been waiting for is going to happen **any**

moment now if you think it is just about to happen: *Any moment now, the President's car will turn the corner and come into sight.*

at any 'moment
You say that something may happen **at any moment** if it is likely to happen in the present situation, although you do not know exactly when: *You've got to be careful, because the alarm could go off at any moment.*

at the last 'moment
You do something **at the last moment** when you do it just before it is too late: *He had paid for the holiday and everything, and at the last moment he said he couldn't come.*

at the 'moment
You use '**at the moment**'when you are referring to the situation as it is, as opposed to how it was in the past or will be later: *I've got my mum staying with me at the moment.*

for the 'moment
You use '**for the moment**'when referring to the situation as it is, and is likely to remain for some time, as opposed to how it will be later: *We've got all the volunteers we need for the moment, but I'll take your name and address anyway.*

in a weak 'moment
If you do something **in a weak moment**, you do it as the result of persuasion or temptation, even though you know it is not wise: *In a weak moment she almost relented. 'How dare he!' she suddenly thought. How dare he imagine he could charm his way back into her life.*

just a 'moment
1 You say '**just a moment**' to someone if you want them to wait for a short time: *Just a moment. I've just got to write one more sentence.* 2 You say '**just a moment**' to express the fact that you have just noticed or thought of something: *Just a moment. Haven't I met you somewhere before?*
◇ SEE ALSO **just a minute**▷ MINUTE

the moment of 'truth
The **moment of truth** is a time when you finally hear a piece of information that you have been anxiously waiting for, usually regarding success or failure: *The finalists were now gripped with the tension of the approaching moment of truth, like expectant fathers at a birth.*

This expression comes from the Spanish 'el momento de la verdad', which is the moment at the end of a bullfight when the matador kills the bull.

not for one 'moment or never for one 'moment

If you say you do **not for one moment** believe a person or what they say, or that **never for one moment** did you believe them, you mean that you do not believe them at all: *I don't believe for one moment that the Government will ever provide free pre-school education.*

◇ SEE ALSO **not** or **never for one minute**
▷ MINUTE

not a moment to 'lose or not one moment to 'lose

You say that there is **not a**, or **not one, moment to lose** when the situation is so urgent that you will have to act immediately and as fast as possible: *Don't move an inch. There's not a moment to lose. I'm going to spell out a warning to the pilot.*

moments

have its 'moments or have your 'moments

1 You say that someone or something **has their moments** if they have been successful or interesting on a few occasions at least: *'How did you enjoy your day in London?' 'It had its moments,' said Helen evasively.* **2** You say that someone, especially a small child, **has their moments** if they occasionally lose their temper or behave badly: *'I can see your father having his hard side, but your mum's too nice.' 'She has her moments. She's not as soft as you might think.'*

money

even 'money

You say that it is **even money** whether one thing or another thing happens if both of the two possibilities are equally likely: *It's even money whether we get it or not.* □ *Shouting above those damned engines, perhaps there was an even money chance of being heard.*

for 'my money

For my money means 'in my opinion' or 'if I were to choose': *For my money, I'd say you'd be better going for a reliable man than a good-looking one.*

◇ SEE ALSO **if you ask me** ▷ ASK

'funny money

Funny money is money which is either false or which has come from dishonest or illegal activities: *Coleman often wonders how many of Hurley's confidential informants in Lebanon were paid with funny money.*

get your 'money's worth

You **get your money's worth** if you get good use out of something, or full value for the money which you have spent: *If you're saving all year for your holidays, you want to get your money's worth when you're there.*

□ *I'm afraid this old coat is going in the bin. I've certainly had my money's worth out of it though.*

have money to 'burn

You say that someone **has money to burn** if they have enough money to be able to spend it in ways that you think are foolish: *Unless you've got money to burn these expensive guitars are probably not the instruments to get you started.*

◇ SEE ALSO **spend money like water** ▷ MONEY; **throw money around** ▷ MONEY

'hush money

You are paying a person **hush money** if you give them money in exchange for their promise to keep something a secret: *He had an affair with a former church secretary, using PTL funds to pay her hush money afterwards.*

in the 'money

If you say that someone is **in the money**, you mean that they have got a lot of money, especially at the moment, rather than all the time: *It looks as if we're in the money – I just got a bonus at work!*

◇ SEE ALSO **in clover** ▷ CLOVER; **quids in** ▷ QUIDS; **easy street** ▷ STREET

make 'money

You **are making money** when you earn money or make a profit: *It sounds as if he's making lots of money with that new business of his.* □ *The firm just wasn't making money any more.*

money doesn't grow on 'trees

If someone says '**money doesn't grow on trees**', they are reminding the person they are talking to that money is difficult to obtain or earn, especially if that person seems not to understand this fact: *Sayings of Dorothy's came to mind: 'It doesn't grow on trees, you know.' 'You've got to learn the value of money.'*

◇ SEE ALSO **not made of money** ▷ MONEY

money for 'jam or money for old 'rope

When you talk about **money for jam**, or **money for old rope**, you mean money which is obtained with little or no effort: *I don't fancy it in the winter, but it's a fantastic summer job. Money for jam.* □ *Commission and a client, without having had to prospect in the first place. It was money for old rope.*

money is no 'object

If you say that **money is no object**, you mean that you do not consider money to be important in the decision which you are about to make, as you can afford to spend whatever amount is necessary to obtain what you want: *She flitted from country to country as if money was no object, which, knowing Lori, it probably wasn't.* □

Eye level grill, Tricity Rotisserie, fully stocked freezer, oh Derek insisted on it. Money no object.

money is the root of all 'evil

If someone says 'money is the root of all evil', they mean that many of the world's troubles are caused by money or by people's desire for it.

> Money is the root of all evil is in fact a Biblical misquote, the original version being 'the love of money is the root of all evil' (I Timothy 6:10).

money 'talks

If someone says 'money talks', they mean that people are more likely to be persuaded to do something if you can offer them money for doing it: *'Our star players are simply not for sale.' But usually money talks in football, no matter what the club, and if United do raise their bid, a sale might still be likely.*

not 'made of money

You tell someone that you are **not made of money** when you want them to realize that you have a limited amount of money to spend: *Stop asking for sweets, because you're not getting any. I'm not made of money, you know.*

◇ SEE ALSO **money doesn't grow on trees** ▷ MONEY

put your money where your 'mouth is

If you say that a person or organization should **put their money where their mouth is**, you are telling them to supply money for a purpose which they claim to support: *We want the Government to put their money where their mouth is and fund this project.*

spend money like 'water or spend money like it was going out of 'fashion

You say that someone **spends money like water**, or **spends money like it was going out of fashion**, if they spend a lot of money all the time: *No wonder she's always short of cash. She spends money like water.*

◇ SEE ALSO **have money to burn** ▷ MONEY; **throw money around** ▷ MONEY

throw good money after 'bad

A person or organization is **throwing good money after bad** if they are spending money in an unsuccessful attempt to get back money they have already lost: *The company has decided to stop throwing good money after bad and cease using it until it either improves or disappears.*

throw 'money around

You say that someone is **throwing money around** if they are spending money in an obvious way, in order to show people that they are rich: *Mum and Dad started to throw money around like water. Mum went around the shops buying clothes, and Dad ordered the drink.*

◇ SEE ALSO **have money to burn** ▷ MONEY; **spend money like water** ▷ MONEY

throw 'money at something

A person or organization is **throwing money at something** such as a project if they are providing a large amount of money for it, especially if they are doing so without considering carefully whether that thing is worth the money they are spending: *Investment in transport is scheduled to exceed $7 billion. However, throwing money at problems does not in itself bring solutions.*

you pays your money and you takes your 'choice

If someone says 'you pays your money and you takes your choice', they mean that, in a situation where there is not much difference between the possibilities which are open to you, you might as well just trust to luck and choose one: *When it comes to the state of mental health services, you pays your money and you takes your choice.*

monkey

cheeky 'monkey (*humorous*)

You call someone a **cheeky monkey** if they are not showing you proper respect: *'Aunt Edie, I still think you've got good legs for your age.' 'Cheeky monkey,' said Aunt Edie.*

◇ SEE ALSO **cheeky devil** ▷ DEVIL

make a 'monkey out of someone

If you **are making a monkey out of someone**, you are making them appear stupid or ridiculous: *I don't mind admitting I'm wrong, but I won't have my own son making a monkey out of me.*

'monkey business

Monkey business is an attempt to trick someone, or to avoid doing certain things, which involves behaviour which is dishonest or illegal: *I want you out of this house by tomorrow morning. And no monkey business, or I'll call the police.*

◇ SEE ALSO **funny businss** ▷ BUSINESS; **foul play** ▷ PLAY; **sharp practice** ▷ PRACTICE

not give a 'monkey's (*informal*)

If someone says that they do **not give a monkey's** about something, they mean that they do not care at all about it: *Quite frankly, I don't give a monkey's what anyone else thinks.*

◇ SEE ALSO **not give a damn** ▷ DAMN; **not care a fig or two figs** ▷ FIG, FIGS; **not care or give a hoot or two hoots** ▷ HOOT, HOOTS; **not give a shit** ▷ SHIT; **not care a sod** ▷ SOD; **not give a tinker's cuss** ▷ TINKER; **not give or care a toss** ▷ TOSS; **not care or give tuppence** ▷ TUPPENCE

monogamy

serial mo'nogamy (*humorous*)

If people talk about **serial monogamy**, they mean a life in which the person in question only ever has one lover at a time, but never settles into a permanent relationship with anyone: *Poor Charles. He'd love to find the 'right woman', but so far the best he's managed is serial monogamy.*

month

a month of 'Sundays

If you talk about **a month of Sundays**, you mean a period that is so long that it seems to go on for ever; '**never in a month of Sundays**' emphasizes the speaker's feeling that something in particular will never happen: *It'll never get done in a month of Sundays if I wait for you to do it.* □ *No one will find them in a month of Sundays.*

moon

cry for the 'moon

A person who **is crying for the moon** wants or is asking for something which is impossible to get: *He had new responsibilities now, there must be no more self-pity, no more time wasted on crying for the moon. He must face up to life like the mature man he was.*

once in a blue 'moon

You do something **once in a blue moon** if you almost never do it: *We never go out for a meal, and it's only once in a blue moon that he takes me to the cinema.*

On rare occasions, the moon seems to be slightly blue in colour.

over the 'moon

You say that you are **over the moon** if you are delighted about something: *She's over the moon to be pregnant at last.*

◇ SEE ALSO **walk on air** ▷ AIR; **thrilled to bits** ▷ BITS; **on cloud nine** ▷ CLOUD; **in seventh heaven** ▷ HEAVEN; **on top of the world** ▷ TOP

moonlight

do a moonlight 'flit

You say that someone **has done a moonlight flit** if they have moved away suddenly, especially at night, and usually to avoid people to whom they owe money: *Didn't you hear? I had decided to go and live with him. Well, I did a moonlight flit and stole two silver candlesticks.*

◇ SEE ALSO **do a bunk** ▷ BUNK

more

more or 'less

More or less means 1 'almost': *I've more or less finished writing my book now.* 2 'about'

or 'approximately': *It was more or less this time last year that I first met you.*

what is 'more

What is more is used to introduce a second statement relating or adding to the first: *I've had enough of this stupid work, and what is more, I've had quite enough of you.*

morning

the morning after the night be'fore

If people talk about **the morning after the night before**, they are referring to a morning when you feel ill from drinking too much alcohol the previous night: *'My God, you look awful.' 'Yeah, I don't feel too great. Morning after the night before.'*

most

make the 'most of something

You are **making the most of something** such as an advantageous position when you use it to get as much benefit as possible from the situation: *Make the most of your holidays when you are a student. You'll never have so much free time again.*

mother

at your mother's 'knee

You learn something **at your mother's knee** if you learn it when you are still a baby or a small child: *All the little songs and rhymes that I learned at my mother's knee are fresh in my memory to this day.*

a 'mother's boy (*disrespectful*)

If you call a boy or man **a mother's boy**, you mean that they depend too much on their mother, or that they do not seem to have the strength and independence which you expect in a normal adult man: *He's very sweet, but a bit of a mother's boy.*

◇ SEE ALSO **mummy's boy** ▷ MUMMY

be 'mother

To **be mother** is to pour the tea out of a teapot into people's cups: *Who wants tea? Toby, will you be mother?*

old enough to be so-and-so's 'mother (*disrespectful*)

People sometimes say that a woman is **old enough to be a certain person's mother** as a way of criticizing her for being in a romantic relationship with someone who is so much younger than herself: *She can't possibly be interested in him. She's old enough to be his mother.*

motions

go through the 'motions

You say that someone **is going through the motions** when they are pretending to do something, or they are doing it without sincerity or enthusiasm: *They didn't seem to know what they were doing. I think they were just going through the motions of what had worked before.* □ *We don't believe in marriage, but we're going to go through the motions to keep the parents happy.*

motley

on with the 'motley

1 On with the motley is used when talking about a theatrical performance to mean 'let's get started!' **2** People also say '**on with the motley**' before starting to do something which they are not looking forward to, but which they know must be done: *Sing? Of course I shall sing. I'm a trooper, aren't I? On with the motley.* □ *Ah, well – on with the motley.*

'On with the motley' means 'put on the clown's jacket' and is a translation of the Italian phrase 'vesti la giubba'.

mould

break the 'mould

Something which **breaks the mould** is new and different from previous things of the same type: *Classical violinists had never appealed much to teenage audiences until he came along and broke the mould.*

You can use a **mould** if you want to make a number of objects, all of exactly the same shape and size.

cast in the same 'mould as someone

A person who is **cast in the same mould as someone** is similar to them: *In his wide-shouldered tallness, he looked to Mum as if he had been cast in the same mould as Joshua himself.*

◇ SEE ALSO **tarred with the same brush** ▷ BRUSH; **a chip off the old block** ▷ CHIP; **cut from the same cloth** ▷ CLOTH; **have something in common** ▷ COMMON

See note at **break the mould**.

mountain (*see also* mountains)

if the mountain will not come to Mohammed then Mohammed must go to the 'mountain

If someone says '**if the mountain will not come to Mohammed then Mohammed must go to the mountain**', they mean that you must make an effort yourself if you want a certain thing to happen, because it is unlikely that it will happen by itself or that you can rely on other people to make it happen: *'Come in, mum. It's a nice surprise to see you.' 'Yes, well, if the mountain will not come to Mohammed ...'*

This expression comes from a story about Mohammed in which he was asked to demonstrate his power by getting Mount Sofa to come to him. When this did not occur he is supposed to have said, 'If the hill will not come to Mahomet, Mahomet will go to the hill'. Note the two possible spellings – '**Mohammed**' or '**Mahomet**'.

make a mountain out of a 'molehill

You say that someone is **making a mountain out of a molehill** if they are treating something silly and unimportant as if it were serious or important: *People will often agree to principles because they are too embarrassed to argue or don't want to make a mountain out of a molehill.*

◇ SEE ALSO **a storm in a teacup** ▷ STORM

mountains

move 'mountains

You **move mountains** when you cause something to happen that people think is impossible or nearly impossible: *I have great faith in the power of love to move mountains. Things will turn out for the best.* □ *I'm not conceited enough to think that I can move mountains in the year ahead, but I promise you I will not let you down.*

mourning

in 'mourning

1 A person or community that is **in mourning** for someone who has died continues to feel or show deep sadness because of their death: *I can hardly believe the landlord would evict her while she was still in mourning for her husband.* □ *A town is in mourning after two people, one of them a nine year old boy, died in separate holiday accidents in the United States.* **2** You also say that someone is **in mourning** when they are wearing something, especially black clothes, as a formal sign that a member of their family has died: *The tabloid press have ignored Princess Diana's wish that she should not be photographed in mourning.*

mouth

all mouth and 'trousers

A person who is **all mouth and trousers** has a habit of talking a lot but never takes any action in connection with what they say: *He's a bit like Mallachy. All mouth and trousers.*

big 'mouth

You say that someone has a **big mouth** if they are in the habit of talking too loudly or too much, or of saying things they shouldn't: *Why can't you learn to keep* *your big mouth shut?* □ *I was so excited, I had to tell someone. Me and my big mouth.*

'big-mouth: *I get on quite well with him, but he's a bit of a big-mouth.*

down in the 'mouth
Someone who is **down in the mouth** is feeling sad: *He had never seen Karr looking so down in the mouth. 'Cheer up,' he said. 'It can't be that bad.'*

foam at the 'mouth
You say that someone **is foaming at the mouth** if they are mad with anger: *He scares me when he gets annoyed. One minute he's foaming at the mouth and the next he's laughing and joking.*

It is said that dogs which have rabies **foam at the mouth**.

hush my 'mouth
You say **'hush my mouth'** if you have just said something you shouldn't, especially if in fact you did so intentionally.

'motor-mouth (*informal*)
If you call someone, or describe them as having, a **motor-mouth**, you mean that they talk a lot: *He has the mind, the motor-mouth and the outrageously large ego to become a fine frontman.*

shoot your 'mouth off (*informal*)
A person who **is shooting their mouth off** is saying things proudly or in a loud voice, which they will probably regret later: *So you can't shoot your mouth off. You cannot say that you object, because you still have to get on with them at work.*

shut someone's 'mouth or stop someone's 'mouth (*rather old*)
If you **shut**, or **stop, someone's mouth**, you make them be quiet, especially about something secret: *I want his mouth shut. Permanently. If that means killing him, so be it.*

shut your 'mouth (*offensive*)
If you say **'shut your mouth'** to someone, you are telling them rudely to be quiet: *'What time do you call this? Mmm?' 'Oh shut your mouth. I don't need you to tell me what to do.'*
◇ SEE ALSO **shut your face** ▷ FACE; **shut your gob** ▷ GOB; **shut your mouth** ▷ MOUTH; **shut it** or **shut up** ▷ SHUT

mouthed

foul-'mouthed
A **foul-mouthed** person is someone who swears a lot: *Her foul-mouthed old mother was also to be seen at the school meetings, shouting abuse, while children hurled insults at one another.*

loud-'mouthed
A **loud-mouthed** person is someone who speaks too much and too loudly, and

who never has anything interesting to say: *loud-mouthed, lager-swilling football hooligans.*

'loud-mouth: *He's fine when he's sober, but he turns into an obnoxious loud-mouth when he's got a drink in him.*

mealy-'mouthed (*disrespectful*)
A **mealy-mouthed** person is someone who is not honest or sincere in what they say, because they are too cowardly to defend themselves or the things they believe in: *I've had enough of mealy-mouthed politicians and their mealy-mouthed promises.*

move

someone's every 'move
A person is watching **your every move** if they are watching everything you do: *It's difficult to behave normally when someone is watching your every move.*

get a 'move on
If someone tells you to **get a move on**, they want you to hurry up: *Come on, kids. Get a move on or you'll be late for school.*

make a 'move
1 Someone **makes a move** when they do something as a clear signal of their intentions: *It's no use sitting about waiting for someone else to make a move.* □ *In cases of mutual attraction, women often expect the man to make the first move.* 2 If you say it is time you **made a move**, you mean that it is time for you to go where you have to go, or for you to do what you have to do: *Right, we'd better make a move now, or we'll be here all night.*

In chess, each player **makes a move** and then has to wait and see how the opposing player will react.

on the 'move
1 You are **on the move** when you are busy doing things with no time for a rest: *No wonder you're exhausted if you've been on the move since nine o'clock yesterday evening.* 2 You are **on the move** when you are moving, advancing, or travelling from one place to another: *It's difficult for children to get a good education if they are constantly on the move.*

mover

prime 'mover
A **prime mover** is a person or organization with a lot of involvement in making a situation develop in a certain way: *Special thanks go to Jackie and Mike Cope who were the prime movers behind the setting up of the museum.*

movers

movers and 'shakers

Movers and shakers are people with the energy and power to make changes or get things done: *From Spike Lee to Reverend Jesse Jackson, Michael Jordan to Philip Michael Thomas, black movers and shakers now shape US opinion on more than just race.*

much

make 'much of

1 You are **making much of something** such as an achievement or a special feature when you try to give the impression that it is important and worth being proud of: *In fact, this hypothesis makes much of what are fairly small differences.* **2** When you **make much of** an animal or a child, you reward them for being good: *Pat your horse and make much of him after you have ridden him.*

much as

Much as is a strong way of saying 'although': *Much as I would like to support your 'cause, I'm afraid I have no spare time at the moment.*

much to

Something that happens **much to** your horror, amusement, disgust or delight greatly horrifies you, amuses you, disgusts you or delights you: *Then, much to the horror of his 'parents, the little boy burped loudly into the microphone.* □ *Our next-door neighbour was elected 'councillor, much to our disgust.*

not much of a 'such-and-such

You say that something is **not much of a** certain thing if you consider that it is not a good example of that thing, even though that is what it is meant to be: *It sounds as if it wasn't much of a holiday for you, with all that running around.*

muchness

much of a 'muchness

You say that two or more things are **much of a muchness** if they are all of roughly the same quality: *I don't bother buying expensive film for my camera now. They're all much of a muchness anyway.*

muck

make a 'muck of something

You say that you **have made a muck of something** if you have done it badly: *I've made a muck of it. I'll have to start again.*
◇ SEE ALSO **make a pig's ear of something**
▷ PIG

'muck-raking

Muck-raking is the activity of searching for and making public information which will damage the reputation of a certain person or group of people: *In an ill-advised piece of muck-raking the newspaper printed comments by two former Wolves players. 'Muck-raking guttersnipes,' he said. 'Showing those disgraceful dirty pictures.'*

'The man with a muck-rake in his hand' is a character in John Bunyan's Pilgrim's Progress, and was originally an image for greed. As the word **muck** began to be associated with bad moral behaviour, the image of **muck-raking** changed to mean what it does today.

where there's muck there's 'brass

If someone says '**where there's muck there's brass**', they mean that in an area where there is dirt and ugliness there is often a lot of industry and wealth: *After spending a day in Halifax with the town council's senior engineer, Gerald remarked to his wife, 'Where there's muck there's brass.'*

mud

here's 'mud in your eye! *(very informal, humorous)*

When two good friends raise their glasses to drink together, they sometimes say '**here's mud in your eye!**': *It's great to see you again. Anyway, here's mud in your eye, old boy.*

sling 'mud or throw 'mud

When one person or group **slings mud**, or **throws mud**, they say things in public which they hope will damage an opposing person's or group's reputation: *He confided to a journalist that he felt betrayed. 'They are trying to sling mud at me to cover up the defeat by Peru.'*
'**mud-slinging:** *As the shouting, mud-slinging and patriotic appeals die away, Americans face the moment when they have to decide who is to be their next President.*

'stick-in-the-mud

You call someone **a stick-in-the-mud** if they have annoyed you by refusing to take part in an activity which you think will be fun: *You'll enjoy yourself when you get there. Don't be an old stick-in-the-mud.*

If a person is stuck in mud, they are stuck in a certain position and are unable to move forward.

mug

a 'mug's game

A mug's game is an activity which is foolish and probably dangerous: *You don't want to get mixed up in drugs. It's a mug's game.*

multitude

cover a multitude of 'sins

Something which **covers a multitude of sins** hides a situation which you do not want people to be aware of, either by covering it physically, or, in the case of a phrase, by being so broad in what it refers to that it holds little real information: *The description 'natural spring water' often covers a multitude of sins.* □ *Baggy clothes can cover a multitude of sins.*

mum

mum's the 'word

'**Mum's the word**' means 'don't tell anyone – it's a secret': *'I've had to keep it quiet for good reasons, and if I say much to Marc he'll really go mad. So mum's the word, all right?' She nodded.*

◇ SEE ALSO **keep something to yourself** ▷ KEEP; **keep your counsel** ▷ COUNSEL; **keep it under your hat** ▷ HAT

mummy

a 'mummy's boy (*disrespectful*)

If you call a boy or man **a mummy's boy**, you mean that they depend too much on their mother, or that they do not seem to have the strength and independence which you expect in a normal adult man: *He's such a mummy's boy that he takes his washing home with him every weekend.*

◇ SEE ALSO **mother's boy** ▷ MOTHER

murder

get away with 'murder

Someone who **gets away with murder** is allowed to behave badly without being punished: *She lets her servants get away with murder, too. Look at the dust on that photograph frame.*

I could murder a 'such-and-such

If you say '**I could murder** a certain thing', you mean that you would love to eat or drink that thing: *I won't take a whisky, thanks. But I could murder a cup of tea.*

scream blue 'murder or shout blue 'murder

Someone who **is screaming**, or **shouting, blue murder** is screaming or shouting very loudly: *The frustration and worry she felt at the moment were enough to make her want to scream blue murder.*

Murphy

'Murphy's law

If people talk about **Murphy's law**, they mean the fact that if anything is able to go wrong in a situation, you can be sure

that it will: *Thanks to the operation of Murphy's Law relating to parents, they were coming downstairs hand-in-hand just as her mother walked in the door.*

muscles

flex your 'muscles

You say that a powerful person or organization is just **flexing their muscles** if you believe that they are doing certain small things at the moment in preparation for the big things they plan to do later: *The rebel forces may just have been flexing their muscles today, before launching a full-scale attack.*

music

face the 'music

You **face the music** when you put yourself into an unpleasant situation involving strong criticism of your past actions, where you will have to either admit that you were wrong, or to defend what you have done: *Candidates must stand and face the music as the returning officer reads out the results.*

music to someone's 'ears

If it gives you great pleasure to hear something, you can say that that thing is **music to your ears**: *Ah, the clink of ice-cubes in a glass. Music to my ears.* □ *'I'll do the washing-up, shall I?' 'Ah, music to my ears.'*

mustard

cut the 'mustard (*informal*)

You say that someone **cuts the mustard** if they are capable of achieving success in the activity which they are doing: *Other magazines have always tried to copy its style but have never quite cut the mustard.*

muster

pass 'muster

A person or thing that **passes muster** is of an acceptable standard: *Critically surveying her reflection, she told herself she would pass muster.*

mutton

mutton dressed as 'lamb

People describe an older woman as **mutton dressed as lamb** if they think she is trying without success to look much younger than she really is, probably by wearing clothes or make-up which are more suitable for young people: *'All leather and denim. She looks older than my mother.' 'Awful. Sounds a bit like mutton dressed as lamb.'*

n

nail

hit the nail on the 'head

You say that someone **has hit the nail on the head** if they have described or identified something precisely or accurately: *The moment she said it she knew she had hit the nail on the head. It was there in his expression.*
◇ SEE ALSO **put your finger on it** ▷ FINGER

'nail-biting

You describe a story, film, or competition as **nail-biting** if it makes you feel very excited or nervous because you do not know what is going to happen: *Her nail-biting drama about a woman CID officer tracking a serial killer, later won a British Academy award.*

People sometimes bite their nails when they feel anxious.

a nail in the 'coffin of

You describe an event as **a nail in the coffin** of something, or the **nail in such-and-such's coffin**, if it helps to contribute to the thing's failure: *His best-selling book 'Diana: Her True Story', is believed to have been the nail in the coffin of the royal marriage.*

A **coffin** is a wooden box that a dead person is buried or cremated in.

on the 'nail

You pay for something **on the nail** when you pay for it immediately: *Not paying on the nail could be extremely expensive, since interest rates were high.*

The pillars outside the Corn Exchange are called **Nails**, and merchants used to complete their financial deals on them before the Exchange was built.

name

clear someone's 'name

You **clear someone's name** when you prove that they are not guilty of doing something which people suspected them of having done: *I do not doubt your innocence but you must go and clear your name.*

give a bad 'name

You **give** someone or something **a bad name** when you harm their reputation by behav-

ing badly: *the sort of man-hating bitterness that has given feminism such a bad name.*

in the name of 'God

You follow a question with **in the name of God** as a way of expressing surprise or disbelief: *What in the name of God are you doing?*

in the name of 'such-and-such

You act **in the name of** a certain thing, such as justice, when you act with proper respect for it: *We urge, in the name of justice or fair play, that every facility should be provided for their employment.*

in name 'only or in name a'lone

Something is the case **in name only**, or **in name alone**, if it is the case only by title, and not really in practice: *Many of these mills remain in name alone, but there are two on the lower reaches that still contain much of interest.* □ *Commenting on this so-called friendly match, the coach explained: 'Games like this are friendly in name only.'*

make a 'name for yourself or make your 'name

You **make a name for yourself**, or **make your name**, when you become famous or get a good reputation: *He made a name for himself by touring the clubs, and doing Christmas shows.*
◇ SEE ALSO **make it big** ▷ BIG; **make it** ▷ MAKE

'name-dropping

Someone who is always **name-dropping** tries to impress people by mentioning the names of famous or influential people whom they know, or claim to know: *As I was telling the Queen the other night, I just hate name-dropping.*

so-and-so's name is 'mud

You say that a certain person's **name is mud** if people are very angry with them because of something they have done.

name 'names

You **name names** when you say the names of the people concerned or involved in a particular activity: *I can't name names, but the song concerns a series of people who'd recognize themselves in there if they examined the lyrics.*

the name of the 'game
The **name of the game** is the central or most important aspect of a certain activity: *Quality and value for money is the name of the game here!*

a name to 'conjure with
1 You say that someone's name is **a name to conjure with** if they are very respected and admired in their field: *Fraser Dawson – on the financial scene his is a name to conjure with.* **2** You say, humorously, that someone's or something's name is **a name to conjure with** if it is very difficult to pronounce: *Sachin Tendulkar. There is a name to conjure with and let slip easily off the tongue.*

take someone's name in 'vain
You **take someone's**, especially God's, **name in vain** when you use their name without showing proper respect for them: *'You dare to take God's name in vain?' His voice had an underlying note of hysteria.*

under a certain 'name
You do something **under a certain name** if you use that name while you do it: *Although he was operating under another name, rumours of his past caught up with him, and he escaped to America in the early 1880s.*

worthy of the 'name or worth the 'name
Someone who is **worthy of the name**, or **worth the name**, deserves to be called such: *These body oils are sold by any chemist worth the name.* □ *No composer was considered worthy of the name until he had written an opera.*

you 'name it
You name it means whatever you can think of or mention: *You name it, he's got it: courage, skill, pace, commitment, the lot.*

names

call someone 'names
You **call someone names** when you insult them with rude and unpleasant names: *'The man knocked on her door and started calling her names,' a spokesman for Greater Manchester Police said yesterday.*

no names, no 'pack-drill
If you say '**no names, no pack-drill**', you mean that if no names are mentioned, no-one will get into trouble: *I don't want to hear about it. No names, no pack drill.*

native

go 'native
You **go native** when you live according to the customs and manners of a foreign country in which you are staying: *A fantastic holiday, with the chance to eat the very best available in the shops, try out the local wines and generally go native!*

nature

back to 'nature
You go **back to nature** when you behave or live in a simple and inexpensive, but healthy way: *So get back to nature, try alternatives to conventional toiletries and techniques.*

nature abhors a 'vacuum
If someone says '**nature abhors a vacuum**', they mean that it is very unlikely that an unoccupied period of time will remain so for long: *Because nature abhors a vacuum, we have had to produce the second document for today's debate.*

second 'nature
Something that is **second nature** to you is very easy because you do it so often: *It takes practice and concentration at first, but it will soon become second nature.*

near

near as 'dammit or near e'nough (*informal*)
Near as dammit or **near enough** means so near in colour, quality, etc, to something, that it can be considered the same: *It may not be a perfect match, but from what I can gather, it's as near as dammit.*

nearest

your nearest and 'dearest
Your **nearest and dearest** are your closest family and friends: *By making a proper will, you will save your nearest and dearest from paying an unnecessary amount of inheritance tax.*

neat

neat as a new 'pin
Someone or something that is as **neat as a new pin** is very clean and tidy: *The low-beamed sitting room was neat as a new pin and showed no signs of the going-over it had suffered when Newman was last there.*

necessity

necessity is the mother of in'vention
If someone says '**necessity is the mother of invention**', they mean that if there is a need for something, people will be more likely to be able to find a way of fulfilling that need: *Necessity being the mother of invention, the foam mat from the back of my rucksack served as a seat for sliding down the snow.*

neck

break your 'neck

If you tell someone that they will **break their neck**, you mean that they are in danger of being seriously injured or killed in an accident: *'Come down off that! You'll break your neck!'*

breathe down someone's 'neck

Someone who **is breathing down your neck** is annoying you by watching you very carefully in case you make a mistake: *Decisions obviously have to go through the Director, but I don't have accountants breathing down my neck.*

dead from the neck 'up (*informal*)

If you describe someone as **dead from the neck up**, you mean that they are stupid, or uninterested in any kind of mental stimulation.

get it in the 'neck

You **get it in the neck** when you are punished or told off for doing something wrong: *I'd say that if we don't co-operate, we could all get it in the neck.*

neck and 'neck

Two or more competitors who are **neck and neck** are exactly level, with nobody clearly winning: *Yesterday's Sunday Telegraph put Labour and the Conservatives neck and neck on 37.5 per cent and the Liberal Democrats on 22.*

neck of the 'woods

Your **neck of the woods** is the area that you come from or live in: *His working life has been devoted, as one might expect from that neck of the woods, to the shoe trade.*

In the past, '**neck of the woods**' referred to a remote community in the woods of the early 19th century American frontier.

risk your 'neck

You **risk your neck** when what you do exposes you to some kind of danger: *It was interesting. It is years since I risked my neck. I am wet but utterly unharmed and I enjoyed it.*

◊ SEE ALSO **dice with death** ▷ DEATH; **court disaster** ▷ DISASTER

save your 'neck

You **save your neck** when you get out of a difficult or dangerous situation: *Don't use your brother's name to save your neck!*

stick your 'neck out

You **stick your neck out** when what you do puts you in a situation where you might fail, or might be criticized or attacked: *I wondered gloomily why I'd already stuck my neck out to protect Jett. He wasn't a friend.*

◊ SEE ALSO **go for broke** ▷ BROKE

up to your 'neck

You are **up to your neck** when you are very busy with something or deeply involved in something: *I'm up to my neck in work at the moment – can we make it next week?*

◊ SEE ALSO **up to your ears** ▷ EARS; **up to your eyes** ▷ EYES; **up to your eyeballs** ▷ EYEBALLS

need

if need 'be or if needs 'be

If need, or **needs, be** means if it is necessary: *Seek professional advice if needs be, rather than make a valiant attempt yourself and then regret it.*

that's 'all I need

That's all I need means 'I have too many problems already without having to cope with this one': *Kelly winced. 'That's all I need. Dinner with a tree surgeon.'*

needle

like looking for a needle in a 'haystack

If you are looking for something very small or insignificant, and you feel that the search is hopeless, you can say that it's **like looking for a needle in a haystack**: *I think you're wasting your time, to be honest. It will be like looking for a needle in a haystack. Far too many young people arrive from England every day.*

a 'needle match

A **needle match** is a competition in which both opponents are determined to win, especially because of strong local feelings: *Today's game is sure to be a needle match and the Aylesbury men will have a formidable task in trying to take three points from our rock-solid defence.*

needs

needs must when the devil 'drives

If you say '**needs must when the devil drives**', you mean that it is necessary to act in a certain way when it cannot be avoided, however unpleasant the task is: *Fred groaned again but sat up, quite good-humouredly, and put his boots on. 'Needs must when the old devil drives.'*

◊ SEE ALSO **a man's gotta do what a man's gotta do** ▷ MAN

neighbourhood

in the 'neighbourhood of

In the neighbourhood of means roughly, approximately, or about: *The average price at which shares sell during this period is somewhere in the neighbourhood of $55.*

nellie

not on your 'nellie or not on your 'nelly (informal)

Not on your nellie or nelly is an expression of strong refusal or denial: *My immediate reaction was to say 'Not on your nellie, not with all these people watching'.*

◇ SEE ALSO **not on your life** ▷ LIFE

> Nellie here, is short for 'Nellie Duff', Cockney rhyming slang for 'puff' [= life].

nerve

get on someone's 'nerves

Someone or something that **gets on your nerves** annoys or irritates you: *That dripping tap is getting on my nerves.*

◇ SEE ALSO **drive someone round the bend** ▷ BEND; **get someone's goat** ▷ GOAT; **make someone's hackles rise** or **raise someone's hackles** ▷ HACKLES; **get up someone's nose** ▷ NOSE; **rub someone up the wrong way** ▷ WAY; **get on someone's wick** ▷ WICK

have a 'nerve

Someone who **has got a nerve** is rude and disrespectful: *She's got a nerve, talking to me like that.*

lose your 'nerve

You **lose your nerve** when you lose your courage or calmness and you begin to be afraid or to panic: *Her voice trembled. 'Suddenly I've lost my nerve.' She tried to control her rising panic.*

nest

feather your own 'nest

You **feather your own nest** when you gain money for yourself, or make yourself rich, especially at other people's expense: *Two of the others, including the chairman, were using their positions to feather their own nests.*

◇ SEE ALSO **line your pockets** ▷ POCKETS

foul the 'nest

You **foul the nest** when you spoil things for people: *We all want basic comforts, but there are intelligent limits to impose on oneself in order not to foul the nest for everybody else.*

a 'nest-egg

A **nest-egg** is something, especially money, that you save up for the future: *His possessions and savings constituted quite a nice little nest-egg for his sons and his daughter.* □ *Winnie pressed his hand. 'I've a small nest-egg,' she told him. 'Enough to get us started.'*

net

cast your net 'wide

You **cast your net wide** when you make sure that you do not miss the opportunity of getting what you want by covering a wide area of supply in your search: *Casting the net wide, he pursued all branches of the creative arts, coming finally to music.*

> In fishing, the wider you cast your net, the more fish you are likely to catch.

surf the 'net

You **surf the net** when you use a computer to obtain information, using the electronic worldwide communication system called the Internet: *If you too are hooked on surfing the net, you'll know what a wealth of knowledge can be obtained from it.*

> When you surf on the sea, you follow the waves and the currents of the water, while standing on a surfboard. When you **surf the net**, you follow the information route that interests you, moving through the network by means of 'links'.

nettle

grasp the 'nettle

You **grasp the nettle** when you begin an unpleasant or difficult task in a firm, determined way: *However, the Council made it clear that it had no intention of grasping the nettle itself, and taking any decision.*

> Nettles are less likely to sting you if you grasp them firmly.

never

as never be'fore

Something is the case **as never before** if it is the most extreme case that has ever existed: *Party organizers want the conference to show that the party is united as never before.*

never 'ever (informal)

You say **never ever** to insist that something will never be, or has never before been the case: *I promise I'll never ever leave you again.*

on the never-'never

You buy something **on the never-never** when you buy it on credit: *They just let you go on buying on the never-never. This is just the kind of system that encourages crime.*

well I 'never! or well I never 'did!

Well I never! or **well I never did!** are expressions of astonishment, usually referring to something good: *'Well I never!' Bedelia said. 'You don't look that old.'*

new

a new one on 'you (*informal*)

You say **'that's a new one on me'** when you have just been told something that you didn't know before, and which you perhaps find difficult to believe: *However, what the honourable gentleman says is a new one on me, if I may put it as basically as that.*

◇ SEE ALSO **that's news to me** ▷ NEWS

news

bad 'news (*informal*)

If you describe someone as **bad news**, you mean that they should be avoided: *Don't get involved with him; he's bad news, from what I've heard.*

◇ SEE ALSO **bad egg** ▷ EGG

break the 'news

You **break the news** when you finally tell someone something that will cause them to feel some strong emotion: *They were all wondering how they were going to break the news to him that there'd been a terrible suicide.*

no news is 'good news

No news is good news means that if you haven't heard from someone, it probably means that they are happy and enjoying themselves, and that there is no need to worry: *It really is a case of no news is good news. There is no point in proceeding any further with your plans until you have proper confirmation.*

that's news to 'me

You say **'that's news to me'**, or that a certain thing **is news to** you, when someone tells you something you didn't know, especially something very surprising, or something you think others should have told you earlier: *British Waterways officer John Ellis said: 'The pollution is news to me. I shall have to investigate the matter further'.*

◇ SEE ALSO **a new one on me** ▷ NEW

nice

nice as 'pie

Someone who is acting as **nice as pie** is behaving in a very friendly, but probably insincere, manner: *As long as I'm useful to her she'll be as nice as pie. When I stop being useful, she'll ignore me.*

nick

in good 'nick (*informal*)

Something that is **in good nick** is in good condition: *But if you've kept the car in good nick you shouldn't have too much trouble selling it.*

◇ SEE ALSO **in mint condition** ▷ CONDITION; **in**

good repair ▷ REPAIR; **sound as a bell** ▷ SOUND

in the nick of 'time

You do something **in the nick of time** when you only just manage to do it before it is too late: *She was only just rescued in the nick of time.*

> 'Nick' here, refers to a notch on a stick, formerly used as a measurement of time.

night

make a 'night of it

You **make a night of it** when you decide to spend the evening by going out to enjoy yourself, for example to the theatre, pub, or a nightclub: *You've got to go out – that's part of entertaining the clients. Make a night of it, eh?*

a night on the 'town or **a night on the 'tiles**

A night on the town, or **on the tiles**, is an evening when you go out and enjoy yourself, dancing, eating, and drinking, for example: *Frequent nights on the tiles, punch-ups and eager girlfriends were clearly taking their toll on him.*

◇ SEE ALSO **paint the town red** ▷ TOWN

a night-'owl

A **night-owl** is someone who prefers to stay up at night: *She was a true night-owl. Any conference she'd been to, everyone ended up in her room long after midnight, playing poker.* □ *These late-night radio shows were inviting calls from night-owl listeners.*

one-night 'stand

A **one-night stand** is a sexual relationship that begins and ends on the same evening: *A 17-year-old pupil of mine got pregnant last year, the result of a one-night stand.*

spend the 'night with someone

People sometimes say **'spend the night with someone'** to avoid saying 'have sex': *'Let's Spend The Night Together' – by The Rolling Stones.*

turn night into 'day

You **turn night into day** when you stay up late, or all night: *The old man was demented, turning night into day, and persistently interrupting the sleep of neighbours.*

nines

dressed up to the 'nines or **dolled up to the 'nines**

Someone who is **dressed up**, or **dolled up, to the nines** is dressed in a very glamorous way, sometimes more so than necessary: *There I was, dressed up to the nines, trying to change the wheel of my car at the side of the motorway.*

nip

a 'nip in the air

If you say that there is **a nip in the air**, you mean that the weather is a bit cold: *There was a keen nip in the air; winter was only just round the corner.*

nit

'nit-picking

Nit-picking is the act of paying too much attention to small details, and criticizing others for unimportant errors: *a fiercely nit-picking bureaucracy.* □ *I refused to pander to this sort of nit-picking.*

A **nit** is the very small egg of an insect which is sometimes found sticking to people's hair.

nitty-gritty

get down to the nitty-'gritty

You **get down to the nitty-gritty** when you consider the basic facts of a situation: *There's an introductory talk; then we get down to the real nitty-gritty on Friday morning.*

nod

on the 'nod

A matter that is being decided on by a group of people goes through **on the nod** when it is concluded by general agreement, rather than by vote: *It must be debated properly – it's not something that should simply go through on the nod.*

You **nod your head** [= move it up and down] when you agree to something.

noise

big 'noise

A **big noise** is an important or influential person: *I recognized his face from the TV, but I didn't realize he was such a big noise.*
◇ SEE ALSO **fat cat** ▷ CAT; **big cheese** ▷ CHEESE; **big fish** ▷ FISH

none

none other than 'so-and-so

You use **none other than** when telling a story, for example, to dramatize a surprising piece of information about a particular person's or thing's presence: *The engine of the Royal Train failed near Cambridge. Inside was none other than the Queen.*

none too 'such-and-such

None too is used before adjectives and adverbs to mean their opposites: *The look in his eyes was none too friendly. 'What are you doing in here?' he demanded in a loud, bullying voice.*

nook

every nook and 'cranny

Every nook and cranny refers to every part of a place: *The full survey will ensure every nook and cranny is inspected. The surveyor will pull up carpets and crawl into the loft.*

Nook is an old word for 'corner' and **cranny** is an old word for 'crack'.

nose

cut off your nose to spite your 'face

You **cut off your nose to spite your face** when you do something because of pride or anger, in order to harm someone else, but which in fact harms your own interests: *The charity's director says that by reducing Third World aid to reduce public spending, the Government would be cutting off its nose to spite its face.*

follow your 'nose

You **follow your nose** when you **1** go straight on: *You follow your nose down to the bottom of there. Then you turn left.* **2** act according to your natural tendency: *You are on the right track so follow your nose.*

get a bloody 'nose

You **get a bloody nose** when your pride is hurt: *I got a bloody nose over that. I was told to mind my own business.*

get up someone's 'nose (*informal*)

Someone or something **gets up your nose** when they annoy or irritate you: *That fellow's preciseness gets up my nose.*
◇ SEE ALSO **drive someone round the bend** ▷ BEND; **get someone's goat** ▷ GOAT; **make someone's hackles rise** or **raise someone's hackles** ▷ HACKLES; **get on someone's nerves** ▷ NERVES; **rub someone up the wrong way** ▷ WAY; **get on someone's wick** ▷ WICK

have a 'nose for something

You **have a nose for something** when you are skilled at recognizing or identifying it: *That's lovely; you've got a nose for bargains, haven't you?*

keep your 'nose clean

You **keep your nose clean** when you behave well in order to avoid trouble from people in authority: *He could've got out of prison in a couple of months if he'd kept his nose clean.*

keep your nose to the 'grindstone

You **keep your nose to the grindstone** when you work hard, without a rest: *He keeps his nose to the grindstone and thinks everyone else should.*

A **grindstone** is a large round stone that is turned by a machine, and is used for making tools sharper.

lead someone by the 'nose

You **lead someone by the nose** when you persuade them to do whatever you want, or have control over them: *This does not mean that I like to be led by the nose, but only that I would appreciate a little extra guidance.*

Farm animals are sometimes led by a ring, fitted through their nose.

'nose-job

A **nose-job** is a medical operation which is done in order to change the shape of the patient's nose: *Apparently, she was so upset by his comments that she had a nose job.*

pay through the 'nose for something

You **pay through the nose for something** when you pay an unreasonably high price for it: *I am surprised that they continue to insist that we return to a system in which single people have to pay through the nose.*

poke your 'nose into something or stick your 'nose into something

You **poke**, or **stick, your nose into something** when you interfere with other people's business: *She didn't want this newsman poking his nose into her affairs.*

powder your 'nose

Some women say that they are going to **powder their nose** when they are going to the toilet.

◇ SEE ALSO **go to the bathroom** ▷ BATHROOM; **spend a penny** ▷ PENNY

put someone's 'nose out of joint

You **put someone's nose out of joint** when you offend them or hurt their pride: *'I'm afraid their noses are a little out of joint,' said Mrs Holliday. 'Never mind. They'll just have to learn.'*

rub someone's 'nose in it

You **rub someone's nose in it** when you constantly remind them of something they have done wrong: *'It's deliberate, isn't it?' Peter had said. 'Just rubbing my nose in it. As if I didn't feel bad enough already.'*

From a frequently recommended way of house-training animals.

thumb your 'nose at someone

You **thumb your nose at someone** when you refuse to obey them or show that you have no respect for them: *It is one thing to thumb your nose at Mr Gorbachev over the Kremlin wall. It is quite another to stand defiantly in front of the guns and hold your ground.*

◇ SEE ALSO **cock a snook** ▷ SNOOK

Putting your thumb on your nose with the rest of your fingers outstretched is a disrespectful (or humorous) gesture.

turn your 'nose up at something

If you **turn your nose up** at something, you are showing, rather rudely, that you do not like something, or that you think that it is not good enough for you: *The models too have a better attitude. They don't turn their nose up at a job for a lesser magazine if their last assignment was for 'Elle', for example.*

◇ SEE ALSO **pull** or **make a face** ▷ FACE

under someone's 'nose

Something happens **under your nose** when it happens in front of you or very close to you, so that you should notice it: *What I can't understand is how this all went on under my nose, without my noticing anything.*

with your 'nose in the air

If someone walks past you **with their nose in the air**, they make it obvious that they do not want to speak to you: *I said hello, but she just walked past me with her nose in the air.*

note

of 'note (*formal*)

Someone or something **of note** is influential or famous: *We hosted university seminars to which speakers of note could be invited to attend.*

on a 'lighter note

You introduce a statement with '**on a lighter note**' when you are changing the subject from a serious one to a pleasant or amusing one: *On a lighter note, but still on the animal theme, the Scottish rock band 'Eugenius' have rented a full-size cow to promote their debut album.*

on a more 'serious note

You introduce a statement with '**on a more serious note**' when you start to talk about a subject in a more serious way, or when you change the subject from a pleasant or amusing one to a more serious one: *On a more serious note, there are talks on the speed of expansion of the universe, fraud in the laboratory, and a seminar on how to protect your inventions with patents.*

strike the right 'note

You **strike the right note** when you do or say something that pleases people, or that they find appropriate: *Professor Noel Dilly struck precisely the right note of scepticism, receptivity and curiosity. And some illuminating principles emerged.*

take 'note

If you **take note** of something, you pay special attention to it: *Each month we take note of your letters and try to redress the balance, hoping that over the year we get it just about right.*

notes

compare 'notes

People **compare notes** when they informally discuss their opinion of someone or something: *A passport-size photograph will be a useful memory aid when you compare notes and come to a final decision after the interviews.*

nothing

count for 'nothing

If you say that something **counts for nothing**, you mean that it has no value or importance: *Having a degree counts for almost nothing when you are looking for a job these days.*

◇ SEE ALSO **not worth the paper it is written on** ▷ PAPER

make 'nothing of something

1 You **make nothing of something** such as an achievement when you try to give the impression that it is not important, or worth being proud of: *I think she got the highest score in the whole country in that exam, but she makes nothing of it.* **2** You **make nothing of something** bad which has happened when you treat it as if it were not important, or worth worrying about: *I told her I would pay for the vase I broke, but she made nothing of it.*

next to 'nothing

Next to nothing means almost nothing: *She came to the door wearing next to nothing.*

nothing but 'such-and-such

Nothing but a certain thing means 'that thing and only that thing': *I've had nothing but trouble with this car ever since the day I bought it.*

nothing 'doing

Nothing doing means that nothing is happening, or can be done; **nothing doing** is also a rude refusal to consider a request: *Yeah, but she's not working at the moment. She says that there's absolutely nothing doing just at the moment.* □ *Kisses, yes, but with these girls anything more and there's nothing doing, the shop's shut.*

nothing 'for it

If you say that **there's nothing for it** but to do a particular thing, you mean that it is the only possible thing to do, even though you would rather not do it: *There was nothing for it but to try to make their way on foot out of the town.* □ *There was nothing for it: I would have to run away.*

nothing if not 'such-and-such

You use '**nothing if not**' to emphasize a description: *The farmhouse was nothing if not practical.*

nothing 'in it

If you say, in reference to a story or report, that there's **nothing in it**, you mean that it isn't true.

nothing 'like

You say that someone or something is **nothing like** someone or something else if they are a long way from it in relationship: *There were very few major countries I didn't visit during that time and travel was nothing like as easy as it is now.*

◇ SEE ALSO **not anything like** ▷ ANYTHING; **not anywhere near** ▷ ANYWHERE

nothing short of

You use '**nothing short of** a certain thing', as a way of emphasizing that thing: *His behaviour has been nothing short of des'picable.*

nothing 'to it

If you say, in reference to a task, that there's **nothing to it**, you mean that it is very easy: *'Try not to worry,' he said inadequately. 'Both of us have done this kind of thing before. There's really nothing to it.'*

nothings

sweet 'nothings

When lovers whisper **sweet nothings** to each other, they privately say loving and intimate things to each other: *Ned appeared to be whispering sweet nothings in her ear but his attentions were being met with a stony silence.*

notice

at short 'notice

You do something **at short notice** when you do it without much warning, or without much time to prepare: *The French are masters at putting together something to eat at very short notice.* □ *Yes, it was the best I could do at short notice.*

sit up and take 'notice or sit up and take 'note

Someone or something that makes you **sit up and take notice** or **note** forces you to pay attention after a period of disinterest, perhaps because it shocks you, or because it affects your own interests: *Campaigning groups have drawn our attention to many of the world's diminishing rainforests and are making the guilty West sit up and take note.*

now

as of 'now

As of now means 'starting from now': *As of now all purchases must be paid for immediately.*

now and 'then or **now and a'gain** or **every now and 'then** or **every now and a'gain**

Something that happens **now and then**, or **now and again**, or **every now and then**, or **every now and again** happens occasionally: *We would stop every now and then to sit on our rucksacks in the snow and gaze in awe at the beauty of the scene.* □ *Every now and again it's jolly nice to go out and have an absolutely top-class meal in a super restaurant.*

now 'now

You say '**now now**' to people to calm them down or to try to stop them behaving in a certain way: *'Now now, none of that!' said Bedelia.*

'now then

You say '**now then**' in order to get someone's attention before explaining something to them, or telling them what to do: *Now then, what I'd like you to do is this.*

nowhere

get 'nowhere

You **are getting nowhere** if you are not making any progress: *He was unusually ambitious. But he was getting nowhere and felt frustrated.*

nude

in the 'nude

You are **in the nude** if you are not wearing any clothes: *But Modigliani insisted that he had painted several portraits of Madame in the nude that would be worth 'thousands' one day.*

nudge

nudge nudge, wink 'wink (*informal, humorous*)

People say '**nudge nudge, wink wink**' when they are suggesting that there is some sexual meaning in something they have just said: *His questions related to what I'd done for Jett in the past, nudge nudge, wink wink. I didn't like his innuendoes.*

> You **nudge** someone when you gently push them to show them that you are thinking about something improper, funny, or private, that you cannot say aloud. You **wink** when you look at someone and close one eye in a playful way.

number

little 'black number (*informal*)

A **little black number** is a short, stylish, black dress: *Get sexy! You can win this sensational little black number.*

your number is 'up

If you say that someone's **number is up**, you mean that they are about to die, or suffer something unpleasant: *That's what we used to say during the war. If your number was up there was absolutely nothing you could do about it.*

number 'one

1 Number one describes what is best, most important, the most popular, or the best: *Jimmy was number one in his mobility on the tennis court.* □ *After all, the voice is an actor's number one asset, and it will be in use all the time.* **2** If you say that you are looking after **number one**, you mean that you are making sure that you get what you want, rather than helping, or sharing with, others: *The prevailing attitude to life in the '80s seemed to be to look after number one, to get on, to make money, and not to bother about anyone else.*

someone's opposite 'number

Your **opposite number** is someone who does the same job as you, but in a different place or organization: *Nor was the speech by his Labour opposite number, Mr Robin Cook, that much more uplifting.*

> In team sports, a member of one team has the same number on their back as the person on the opposing team who has the same role.

nut

do your 'nut (*informal*)

You **do your nut** when you get very angry: *Your mum is going to do her nut! Look at your coat!*

◊ SEE ALSO **go off at the deep end** ▷ END; **have a blue fit** ▷ FIT; **blow a fuse** ▷ FUSE; **blow a gasket** ▷ GASKET; **let fly** ▷ LET; **blow** or **flip your lid** ▷ LID; **lose your rag** ▷ RAG; **fly into a rage** ▷ RAGE; **hit the roof** ▷ ROOF; **blow your stack** ▷ STACK; **lose your temper** ▷ TEMPER; **blow your top** ▷ TOP; **throw a wobbly** ▷ WOBBLY

a hard nut to 'crack or **a tough nut to 'crack**

If you describe a problem as **a hard**, or **a tough, nut to crack**, you mean that it is difficult to solve: *The enemy were determined to hold on to this position. It was a tough nut to crack.*

'nut-case (*informal*)

If you call someone a **nut-case**, you mean that they are mad or very foolish: *He sent his car for a Ministry of Transport Test with both headlights out of order and no brakes – a complete nut-case.*

◊ SEE ALSO **basket case** ▷ BASKET; **head case** ▷ HEAD

nuts

nuts about (*informal*)

If you are **nuts about** someone, you love them madly; if you are **nuts about** something, you are very enthusiastic about it: *I seek an Irish male, 19-25, as a penpal. I'm nuts about 'Ireland and everything to do with it.*

nuts and 'bolts

The **nuts and bolts** of a thing or situation are the basic facts or important practical details about it: *Whenever he had a promotional tour he would take Leonard along, acquaint him with the nuts and bolts of the business.*

nutshell

in a 'nutshell

You say '**in a 'nutshell**', when you are about to describe a situation very briefly, concentrating on the most important point: *'Were relations between himself and the ANC warm?' 'In a nutshell: Yes. But not only with the ANC.'*

nutty

nutty as a 'fruit-cake (*informal*)

If you say that someone is as **nutty as a fruit-cake**, you are saying, affectionately, that they are eccentric or a bit mad: *'You're going on your own? Then you really are nutty as a fruit cake,' Nick said with conviction.*

◇ SEE ALSO **mad as a hatter** or **March hare** ▷ MAD

O

oar

put your 'oar in or **shove your 'oar in** or **stick your 'oar in**

If you say that someone **puts**, **shoves**, or **sticks**, **their oar in**, you mean that they are trying to affect a situation, especially by offering their opinion, when their presence or ideas are not wanted: *We were sorting it out quite nicely until you stuck your oar in.*

oath

on 'oath or **under 'oath**

In a court of law, someone who is **on oath**, or **under oath**, has made an official promise to tell the truth: *We need some people to be made to testify under oath.* □ *The prosecution, brought forward several witnesses who stated under oath that they had heard Slatter encourage James to stab PC Hewett.*

oats

be off your 'oats

Someone who **is off their oats** is not well and therefore not eating much: *'You've only eaten a couple of mouthfuls. Didn't you like it?' 'No, I'm just a bit off my oats today.'*

> Horses usually like oats, and become lively and full of energy as a result of eating them.

get your 'oats (*informal*)

You say that a person, especially a man, is **getting their oats** if they are feeling satisfied as a result of having sex as often as they would like: *His wife's away for a fortnight, so he's not getting his oats.*

> See note at **be off your oats**.

sow your wild 'oats

You say that a person, usually a young man, is **sowing his wild oats** if he is living a life of wild enjoyment, especially involving having numerous romantic affairs and sexual experiences, before settling down to a quieter, more serious and respectable life: *The sowing of wild oats is not as threatening to the identity of a man as it is to women.*

object

such-and-such is no 'object

If you say that something such as money or expense **is no object**, you mean that you do not consider the price to be an important factor in the decision which you are about to make: *Just give me the best room you have. The price is no object.*

the object of the 'exercise

The object of the exercise is the aim of the activity you are referring to: *The management of properties will be reviewed. The object of the exercise is to ensure the efficient use of natural resources throughout the Trust.*

occasion

on oc'casion

If something happens **on occasion**, it happens from time to time but not often: *She's normally pretty irritable, but she can be utterly charming on occasion.*

rise to the oc'casion

You **rise to the occasion** when you manage, by making an extra effort, to deal in an admirable way with unusual demands: *Certainly it is a very poor play – but what a challenge for the actors and how well they rose to the occasion.*

◇ SEE ALSO **take the bull by the horns** ▷ HORNS; **rise to the challenge** ▷ CHALLENGE; **grasp the nettle** ▷ NETTLE; **pull out all the stops** ▷ STOPS

odd

odd one 'out

Someone or something that is the **odd one out** in any group is the one that is noticeably different from the rest: *Look at these objects and tell me which is the odd one out.*

◇ SEE ALSO **odd man out** ▷ MAN

odds

against all the 'odds or **against all 'odds**

Something happens or is done **against all the odds**, or **against all odds**, when it happens or is done despite great difficulty or disadvantage: *Against all odds, Greenpeace has brought the plight of the natural world to* *the attention of caring people.* □ *Against all odds, he regained his health, and Mary nursed him back to fitness.*

at 'odds with

You are **at odds with** someone when you are in disagreement with or in opposition to them; something, such as an idea or policy is **at odds with** something else, such as a person's actions, when they do not correspond to, or match, each other: *How can we ever agree when his views are at odds with everything I believe in?* □ *The Government's plans to double spending on roads were at odds with its proclaimed conversion to green issues.*

make no 'odds

You say it **makes no odds** when you want to make it clear that a fact or action will make no difference to a particular situation: *One three times a day, for seven days. You can take it with food, after food, between meals, makes no odds.*

odds and 'ends or odds and 'sods (*informal*)

Odds and ends, or **odds and sods**, are small objects of different shapes or kinds, and of little value or importance: *I have to be careful when I'm washing his clothes. His pockets are always full of odds and ends.* □ *'What have you brought?' He shrugged his shoulders. 'Stuff,' he said. 'What stuff?' 'Odds and sods that my dad didn't want.'*

over the 'odds

Over the odds means more than is necessary or expected, especially with regard to money: *While a collector may be happy to pay over the odds for such interesting issues, an investor would have to be confident of gold prices to show a profit on resale.*

odour

odour of 'sanctity

If something is done in the **odour of sanctity**, it is done in an atmosphere of extreme holiness or goodness: *She became Abbess of Ely and founded a great House, and was buried in the odour of sanctity.*

off

have it 'off with someone (*informal*)

If two people **have it off with** each other, they have sex together: *He stayed with us sometimes. He was having it off with my sister at one time. You know – just when they hadn't got anything better going.* □ *They've been having it off for months, but they've kept it secret till now.*

◇ SEE ALSO **get** or **have your end away** ▷ END; **have it away with someone** ▷ AWAY; **get laid** ▷ LAID

off and 'on

Something that is the case **off and on** is the case sometimes, but not all the time: *It's been raining off and on all day.*

offices

through the 'offices of (*formal*)

Something which is done **through the offices of** a certain person or thing is made possible because it has the official help of that person or thing: *He remained in touch with London through the offices of the American ambassador, Loy Henderson.* □ *I would urge that the Members of this Institute, through the offices of public relations, continue to provide platforms to promote the Science of Embalming.*

offence

give of'fence

Someone who **gives offence** does or says something that causes other people to feel annoyed, upset, or embarrassed: *The purpose of etiquette is to provide an easy set of rules which we can follow when we are in a hurry and want to make sure that we do not give offence to anybody.*

take of'fence

You **take offence** when you get annoyed or upset by something that someone has said or done: *Just watch what you say. She's very quick to take offence.*

offensive

on the of'fensive

If someone goes **on the offensive**, they make a strong attack, or prepare to make an attack, against someone or something: *In an effort to stamp out violence, the police have gone on the offensive.*

take the of'fensive

A person or organization **takes the offensive** when they attack first before the opposing person or organization can attack them: *UN forces took the offensive with a series of air strikes early this morning.*

offer

on 'offer

1 If something is **on offer**, it is available: *No, I'm not really hungry, thanks. But if there's a cup of coffee on offer, I'd love one.* **2** If a product is **on offer**, it is for sale, especially at a reduced price: *With all carpets on offer for a limited period only, you won't find a better time to buy.*

or nearest 'offer

Someone advertising something for sale at a certain price **or nearest offer** is willing to accept the highest offer they receive if no-one wants to give them the suggested price: *For sale. Fiat Uno, D reg, good condition, £1,100 or nearest offer.*

In advertisements, **or nearest offer** is frequently written: 'ono'.

offering

a burnt 'offering
If people talk about **a burnt offering**, they are referring in a humorous way to food which has been cooked for too long: *The roast beef came accompanied with little burnt offerings which I took to be Yorkshire puddings.*

offing

in the 'offing
Something that is **in the offing** is likely to come or to happen soon: *I heard that a new model was in the offing which would, the company told me, prove to be their most eye-catching to date.*

often

every so 'often
Something that happens **every so often** happens sometimes, but not frequently: *Every so often, he would come home with a bunch of flowers.*

often as 'not
Something that happens as **often as not** happens on at least half of the occasions that you are referring to, or in at least half of the cases; something that happens **more often than not** happens on most of the occasions, or in most of the cases, that you are referring to: *As often as not, if you apologize, people will forgive you and forget the whole thing.* □ *More often than not, lumps in the breast turn out to be harmless fibroids rather than cancers.*

oil

burn the midnight 'oil
You **burn the midnight oil** if you work or study until late at night: *Having only two weeks in which to complete the work, they burned more than the midnight oil to finish it in time.*

no 'oil painting
If you say that someone is **no oil painting**, you mean that they are not attractive to look at: *Nick Thomas admits he is no oil painting, so he was surprised to be asked to pose for a portrait.*
◇ SEE ALSO **not much to look at** ▷ LOOK

pour oil on troubled 'waters
A person who **is pouring oil on troubled waters** is trying to calm a person or to improve a difficult situation: *Ronnie smiled a light smile, seeking to pour oil on troubled waters. 'Please don't worry on my account. It doesn't matter.'*

strike 'oil
You say you **have struck oil** when you achieve success, especially financial success, or when you find what you are looking for: *If you, too, struck oil you could be as rich as Getty.*

oiled

well-'oiled
You say that a person is **well-oiled** if they are rather drunk: *By that time, well-oiled as we were, there were very few things wrong in the world for us.*
◇ SEE ALSO **drunk as a lord** ▷ DRUNK; **half cut** ▷ CUT; **one over the eight** ▷ ONE

old

any old 'such-and-such (*informal*)
Any old means 'any' or 'no matter what', emphasizing that the quality of the thing in question is not important, or not very good: *She was always in the shop. She would come up with any old excuse she could find to be in there.* □ *For her, the real issue is the second generation's right to education, but not any old education.*

'any old how
You do something **any old how** if you do it without taking any special care: *Could you fold the clothes properly, please? Don't just shove them in any old how.*

old as the 'hills
Someone or something that is as **old as the hills** is very old.

omelette

you can't make an omelette without breaking 'eggs
If someone says '**you can't make an omelette without breaking eggs**', they mean that it is often impossible to achieve a desirable aim without doing some kind of damage or harming someone in the process: *I take the view that one cannot make omelettes without breaking eggs. It is almost impossible to forge any sort of career associated with public life where you do not yourself become the object of hostility in some quarter.*

on

on and 'off
Something that is the case **on and off** is the case sometimes, but not all the time: *They've been seeing each other on and off since Christmas.*

'on to someone

If you get **on to someone**, you contact them: *Get on to your local Councillor if you are unhappy about the new parking restrictions.*

'on to something

If you say you are **on to something**, especially something wrong or illegal, you mean that you have become aware of it or have discovered it: *I'm on to your little game, and if you try it again I'll call the police.*

once

at 'once

1 Something that happens **at once** happens immediately: *Come here at once.* **2** You do a lot of things **at once** if you do them all at the same time, or all on one occasion: *Too many people are trying to use it at once. That's why it's crashed.*

just for 'once or just this 'once

You let something happen **just for once**, or **just this once**, if this is to be the only occasion on which it happens: *Just for once, I'd like you to cook the dinner.* □ *'Oh I shouldn't. I really shouldn't!' Miss Beard protested. 'Why not try it just this once?' Herbert said persuasively.*

once a'gain or once 'more

1 You do something **once again**, or **once more**, when you do it again: *He obviously hadn't heard me, so I asked once again, 'Shouldn't we leave the motorway here?'* **2** Something happens **once again**, or **once more**, when it happens again after an interval: *Once again, we see a demonstration of the Government's inefficient handling of public money.*

once and for 'all or once for 'all

You deal with something **once and for all**, or **once for all**, when you take an action which ends the matter, so that there is no need for any more discussion or action: *I hope this foot-spray will get rid of my athlete's foot once and for all.* □ *At this point it was proposed that the question be settled once for all by an amendment to the constitution.*

once or 'twice

Something that happens **once or twice** within a certain period happens a few times: *I visited London once or twice while I was living in Oxford.* □ *I've seen her once or twice, but I've never spoken to her.*

the 'once-over

If you give something **the once-over**, you examine it quickly: *Just days after the Ardtullagh mansion was put up for sale, at least a dozen prospective buyers have given its 13 rooms the once-over.*

once too 'often

Someone does something silly or annoying **once too often** when it finally has unpleasant results: *'I told you to double-bolt those doors.' 'I know. I forgot.' 'Well, you've forgotten once too often. Get out, you're fired.'*

one

all 'one

If, after considering two or more possibilities, you say that it is **all one** to you, you mean that you do not care which thing happens: *'So there are your options. What do you want to do?' 'Oh, you choose. It's all one to me.'*

at 'one

You are **at one** with someone or something if you are in agreement, or living peacefully, with them: *It's unusual to meet a couple who are so happy, so utterly at one with each other.* □ *Is it possible for mankind to be at one with nature?*

for 'one

You say 'I, **for one**' to introduce a personal opinion, or a statement concerning only yourself: *I for one will be approaching my MP to see what they can do to help end this appalling threat.*

one after the 'other

Things that happen **one after the other** follow each other quickly: *I picked up my cue and potted the balls that remained, one after the other.*

one and 'all *(old)*

One and all means 'everyone': *I wish a merry Christmas to one and all.*

the one and 'only

You use '**the one and only**' as a strong way of saying 'the only': *Ladies and gentlemen, please welcome the amazing, the one and only ... Cilla Black.* □ *He had won his one and only grand prix 10 years before.*

one by 'one

One by one means one after the other: *I lay watching the evening sky as, one by one, the stars came out.*

one in a 'million

You say that someone is **one in a million** if you want to show that you appreciate them and think they are special: *Oh darling, you shouldn't have. It's lovely. You know you really are one in a million.*

a one-'off

A **one-off** is **1** something which is made or happens on one occasion only: *'Maybe I'll get tickets for that play.' 'No, you won't. It was a one-off.'* **2** A **one-off** is also a person who is completely different from all other people: *The world will never see another* *guitarist like Jimi Hendrix. That guy was a one-off.*

one or 'two

One or two means 'a few': *I made one or two mistakes, but I think I did all right.*

one over the 'eight

Someone who has had **one over the eight** has drunk too much alcohol: *He was always accosting women whenever he'd had one over the eight.*

◇ SEE ALSO **drunk as a lord** ▷ DRUNK; **half cut** ▷ CUT; **well-oiled** ▷ OILED

> **The eight** in this expression refers to the eight pints that make a gallon (about 4.5 litres), and the idea is that a person can drink eight pints of beer without getting drunk, but will start getting drunk on the **one over the eight** (= the ninth). For driving purposes, however, a single pint is usually enough to take the average person to their legal limit.

the one that got a'way

If people talk about **the one that got away**, they mean **1** the large fish which a person claims to have almost caught: *'I lost a monster. It must have been at least six pounds.' 'Always the one that got away, eh Henry?'* **2** something that they wanted, and almost obtained: *That gold medal was the one that got away last year, but this time I'm not settling for anything less.*

one 'up on someone

You are, or get, **one up on someone** else if you have, or get, an advantage, especially an unimportant advantage, over them: *She knew she would regret it later, but the urge to get one up on him just once was far too strong to resist.*

one-'upmanship: *There is no doubt also that there is a peculiar element of one-upmanship among many gardeners in being able to boast of having the very latest rose in their gardens.*

onions

know your 'onions

If you say that someone **knows their onions**, you mean that they know their subject well or can do their job well: *I agree that he knows his onions, but that doesn't mean he'll be a good teacher.*

◇ SEE ALSO **know your stuff** ▷ STUFF

only

if 'only

If only is used **1** to express a wish or regret: *'So, what are your plans for the future?' 'If only I knew.'* □ *If I'd only known it was her birthday, I would have bought her a card.* **2** to introduce a reason or excuse for doing

something, especially if it is not a strong one: *I go to the shops when I can, if only to get out of the house for half an hour.*

only 'just

Something is **only just** the case if it is almost not the case: *'Is the spaghetti ready yet?' 'Yes, but only just. I think I'll let it cook another minute.'*

only 'too

Only too emphasizes that what you are saying is the case: *If you had asked me for money, I would have been only too 'willing to lend you some.* □ *I know only too 'well how it feels to be unemployed.*

open

in the 'open or out in the 'open

1 Something that is **in the open**, or **out in the open**, is out of doors, not inside a building: *Don't always exercise in an indoor school. Horses, like all animals, love to get out in the open.* **2** If something, especially something which might make you ashamed or upset, is **out in the open**, it is not hidden, ignored, or kept secret: *If you think he's seeing another woman, why not mention it? It's better to have it out in the open.*

operator

a smooth 'operator

You call a person **a smooth operator** if they are good at getting what they want without using obvious force, perhaps by using flattery or insincere friendliness: *For the instinctive smooth operator, for whom attention-seeking, money and excitement are more important than morals, dealing in shares is an easy job.*

option

the soft 'option

A person who has to decide between a number of possible actions takes **the soft option** when they choose the one which is easiest or involves the least effort: *Whoever thinks staying at home to look after the kids is a soft option should try it for themselves.*

◇ SEE ALSO **cop-out** ▷ COP; **anything for a quiet life** ▷ LIFE; **take the easy way out** ▷ WAY

options

keep your 'options open or leave your 'options open

If you **keep**, or **leave**, **your options open**, you avoid making a choice or decision now, so that you are free to do so at a later time when you have more information, or when you are forced to make a choice: *You need to keep your options open in order to be able to change courses at a moment's notice.*

order (*see also* **orders**)

by 'order of

Something that is to be done, or that is forbidden, **by order of** a person or group in authority has been ordered to be done, or forbidden, by that person or group: *Pub opening times have been restricted in Edinburgh, by order of the police.* □ *No dumping. By order of Strathclyde Regional Council.*

call to 'order

The person in charge of a meeting **calls** the people attending it **to order** when he or she asks them to behave according to the official rules: *The chairman called the meeting to order and introduced the first speaker.*

in 'order

Things are **in order 1** if they are tidy or correctly organized: *I won't be a minute, I'm just getting my papers in order.* **2** if they are arranged one after the other according to a system: *Arrange the objects in order of size, from the biggest to the smallest.* **3** if there is nothing wrong with them: *Make sure your passport is in order and that it is not going to expire during your holiday.*

in the order of or of the order of

An amount that is **in**, or **of**, **the order of** a certain total is approximately that: *It would probably cost in the order of a million 'pounds to do all the necessary repairs.*

in order to

You do something **in order to** achieve some result when you do it with that purpose: *I am phoning in order to a'pologize.*

in working 'order or in running 'order

A machine or vehicle is **in working order**, or **in running order**, if it is working satisfactorily and is ready for use: *Fifty pounds is very cheap for a microwave oven. Are you sure it's in proper working order?* □ *Even if it is in good running order when you buy it, an old car is likely to cost you a lot in repairs.*

keep someone in 'order

You **are keeping someone in order** when you are keeping control of their behaviour: *If you don't keep that boy of yours in order, he's going to get into trouble.*

keep 'order

You **are keeping order** when you are keeping control of a situation: *I am not strong on discipline, and find it difficult to keep order in the classroom.*

on 'order

Items which you have bought or are going to buy are **on order** when you have asked for them to be sent to you, but you have not received them yet: *I've got the book on order, but it's taking a long time to arrive.*

the order of the 'day

You say that something is **the order of the day** if it is considered to be necessary, normal, common or particularly fashionable at a certain time, or in a certain situation: *For Japan's high-tech industries, the order of the day is to maintain quality and cut prices.* □ *Unless we support innovative film-makers, the order of the day will soon be nothing but trash.*

In a political or formal meeting, **the order of the day** is the list of subjects which must be discussed.

out of 'order

1 Things are **out of order** if they are **a** not working properly: *Photocopier out of order. Please use photocopier in Finance Department.* **b** not arranged according to the correct system: *There is a file for every year. Don't let them get out of order.* **2** (*informal*) People are **out of order** if they are not behaving according to the rules of a certain situation: *He was way out of order last night, bossing everyone around like that.*

the 'pecking order

The **pecking order** is the system in which things or people find their natural place, depending on how powerful or influential they are in relation to one another: *Traditionally, Oxford and Cambridge come at the top of the pecking order of English universities.*

Pecking order is the translation of the German 'Hackordnung', first used in the 1920s to describe a social system which had been noticed in domestic hens. Apparently, each bird in a group is allowed to peck the bird next below it in rank and has to accept being pecked by the bird next above it.

a tall 'order

You call something that you are expected to do **a tall order** if it seems rather unreasonable, probably because it is too difficult: *They need to force both inflation and interest rates down in time for the next election – a tall order to say the least.*

to 'order

Something that is made **to order**, is only prepared if someone asks for it; taking into account any particular requests they may have: *You can have a sofa made to order in a choice of over 40 fabrics.*

orders

give someone their 'marching orders

Someone in authority **gives you your marching orders** if they make you leave the organization or group to which you belong, or activity in which you are taking part, usually because they think you have done something wrong: *Walsh received his marching orders 75 seconds into the second half after aiming a kick at another player.*

be in holy 'orders or **take holy 'orders**

A person who **is in holy orders** is a priest; when a person **takes holy orders**, they become a priest: *No person in holy orders in the Church of Rome shall be capable of being elected.* □ *He wanted to take holy orders, but his father prohibited such a step.*

orders is 'orders

You say **'orders is orders'** to explain that, although you may not want to do a certain thing, you have no choice because someone in authority has told you to do it: *'Sorry about this,' he said. 'But there you are. Orders is orders, as they say.'*

under 'orders

You are **under orders** to do something when you have been told by someone in authority to do it: *The soldiers were under strict orders to shoot anyone who tried to escape over the border.*

ordinary

out of the 'ordinary

Something is **out of the ordinary** if it is different, unusual or strange: *Did you notice anything out of the ordinary when you entered the house last night?*

other

or 'other

You add **or other** after words like 'someone', 'somewhere' and 'sometime' to show that the exact nature of that person, place or time is not at all certain, or not very important: *Don't worry. He's probably just been delayed by something or other at the office.* □ *Do you think John's enjoying himself? I expected him to have picked up some woman or other by now.*

out

have it 'out with someone

You **have it out with someone** when you have a discussion, usually an angry one, about something they have been doing which annoys you: *Her face registered gathering anger. 'I've a good mind to go and have it out with him here and now. I know where to find him.'*

out and a'bout

You get **out and about** when you get away from your house and lead a sociable life, for example after being ill: *It's great to see him out and about again.*

an out-and-out 'something

A person or thing is **an out-and-out something** if they are an extreme or complete

example of that thing: *If she told you that, then she's an out-and-out liar.* □ *I can hardly believe he said that to you. What out-and-out cheek.*

'out for something

You are **out for something** if your intention is to get it: *She's out for all she can 'get.*

'out of it

1 You feel **out of it** when you feel that you are unable to join in with other people's activities: *I still like the dancing, but I've been feeling a bit out of it since I've stopped going every week.* 2 (*informal*) You say that a person is **out of it** if they are not aware of what is happening around them, because they are tired, or as the result of drinking too much alcohol or taking drugs: *That guy is out of it. He can hardly stand up.*

out to 'do something

You are **out to do something** if your intention is to do it: *He's out to make money, and he doesn't care how he does it.*

'out with it

If you say **'out with it'** to someone, you mean that you want to hear what they have to say: *He was gripping her shoulder, saying, 'Where is she? Come on, out with it! Where is she?'*

take it 'out of someone

If something such as work **takes it out of you**, it makes you tired: *Even if I'm asleep for the whole journey, I still find that travelling takes it out of me.* □ *I'm exhausted. All this fresh air takes it out of you, doesn't it?*

take it 'out on someone

A person who is worried or upset is **taking it out on you** when they are unkind to you, not because of anything that you have done, but just because of the unhappy feelings which they themselves are having: *I know how disappointed you are, but there's no need to take it out on me.*

outset

at the 'outset

If something happens or is done **at the outset**, it happens or is done at the beginning or start of a period of time or a process; if it happens or is done **from the outset**, it happens or is done at the start of a period, and has an effect which continues until the end: *We agreed at the outset that we would share the work equally.* □ *It is important to establish the terms and conditions of your employment from the outset.*

outside

at the out'side

If you are guessing how much something will be and you decide on a certain number

at the outside, you mean that it cannot be more than that, and may be less: *It can't be more than three hours' drive at the very outside.*

ovation

a standing o'vation
An audience gives a performance **a standing ovation** when they stand up to clap their hands at the end, as a way of showing great appreciation: *The Chancellor of the Exchequer was given a two-minute standing ovation after he delivered an uncompromising defence of his policies yesterday.*

oven

like an 'oven
If you say that a room is **like an oven**, you mean that it is uncomfortably hot: *Phew, it's like an oven in here. Shall we open some windows?*

over

all 'over someone
Someone is **all over you** if they are being too friendly or trying hard to please you, usually so that you will do something that they want: *She found them too friendly and too knowing. 'They were all over me,' she told her friends.*

all over a'gain
You do something **all over again** when you repeat it, perhaps reluctantly, from the beginning: *I had to unpick my knitting and start all over again.*

get something 'over with or get something over and 'done with
You **get something over with**, or **get something over and done with**, if you do it satisfactorily, in order that it can be forgotten: *The longer you avoid apologizing, the harder it'll be. Better just to get it over and done with.*

over and a'bove
Things or amounts **over and above** something are in addition to it: *Remember, there will be tax and insurance to pay, over and above the price of the car itself.*

over and 'over or over and over a'gain
Something happens **over and over**, or **over and over again**, if it keeps happening: *I have asked him over and over to be a bit quieter, but he carries on just the same.* □ *I tried over and over again to start a conversation.*

◇ SEE ALSO **again and again** ▷ AGAIN; **time and time again** or **time and again** or **time after time** ▷ TIME

overboard

go 'overboard for or go 'overboard about (*informal*)
You **go overboard for**, or **go overboard about**, someone or something when you show a lot of, or too much, enthusiasm for that person or thing: *Avoid sexist language – learn to use 'he or she', rather than the male form of the pronoun, but don't go overboard – 'manpower' is still manpower.*

throw something 'overboard (*informal*)
You **throw something overboard** when you get rid of it or stop supporting it because you think it is no longer useful: *Almost all principles have been thrown overboard in the scramble to be elected.*

overdo

over'do it or over'do things
If someone says that you **have been overdoing it**, or **overdoing things**, they mean that you have been working too hard, or have been doing more than you can manage physically or mentally: *'You're not overdoing things?' 'Probably, but I want to make the most of every minute.'*

own

come into your 'own
You **come into your own** when you get the chance to show your good qualities, abilities, or intelligence: *She has always been a bit shy and nervous, but she comes into her own when she works with kids.*

get your 'own back
You **get your own back**, or **get your own back on someone** who has done you harm or played a trick on you, when you do something to harm or trick them in return: *She made you look a bit of a fool. Didn't it make you angry? Wouldn't you have liked to get your own back?*
◇ SEE ALSO **get even** ▷ EVEN

be on your 'own
You **are on your own** if **1** there is no-one else with you: *She's afraid to spend the night in that big house all on her own.* □ *Let's spend the evening together on our own.* **2** you are doing something without help from anyone: *It's not easy to bring up a child on your own.*

p

p

mind your p's and 'q's

When someone tells you to **mind your p's and q's**, they are telling you to take care to behave properly in a certain situation: *Three months' trial period, eh? You'd better mind your p's and q's.*

pace

keep pace with

1 You **keep pace with** someone or something that is moving if you move along at the same speed as them: *If she can just keep pace with the 'leaders, there may be a chance to pull ahead later in the race.* **2** You **keep pace with** changes in a situation if you change or develop in order to maintain your understanding of, or your effectiveness in, that situation: *At KLM, we're always improving to keep pace with your higher level of expec'tations.*

◇ SEE ALSO **keep abreast of** ▷ KEEP

set the 'pace

1 Someone **sets the pace** if they are in the lead at the start of a race, encouraging the other competitors to start at a good speed: *The lead runner is dropping behind now, having set the pace over the first few miles.* **2** Someone or something **sets the pace** if they start a process at a particular speed or rate which others have to compete with: *Britain must try not to get left behind, now that the pace has been set for economic recovery.*

stay the 'pace or take the 'pace

You **stay**, or **take**, **the pace** if you are able to work effectively in a situation which involves a lot of stress: *He's decided to retire. He says he just can't take the pace any longer.* □ *The small cellar bar was packed. Student Ken Payton, said: 'I hope to stay the pace and follow the election results through the night.'*

◇ SEE ALSO **keep at it** ▷ KEEP; **never say die** ▷ SAY

paces

put someone through their 'paces or put something through their 'paces

You **put someone**, or **something, through their paces** when you give them certain things to do, to test their abilities: *After this morning's written test, we'll be putting you through your paces in a real business situation.* □ *When you've put the new Rover 'K' series engine through its paces, and experienced the technically superior suspension, you'll agree too.*

> Horses have four paces: 'walk', 'trot', 'canter' and 'gallop'. Someone who is deciding whether to buy a horse puts it through all its paces, observing how it moves at different speeds.

show your 'paces

You **show your paces** when you perform an activity which shows the full range of your abilities: *I've given him a speech from Hamlet for the audition. That'll give him a chance to show his paces.*

> See note at **put someone** or **something through their paces**.

pack

pack it 'in (*informal*)

1 You **pack it in** when you stop doing a certain activity: *'Did you get the sack or did you just pack it in?' 'No, I got another job.'* **2** You say **'pack it in!'** (*rather old*) to someone when you want them to stop doing or saying something which is annoying you: *'Ow!' 'What did you do?' 'Susan just punched me!' 'Well pack it in both of you!'*

a pack of 'lies

Someone who is telling **a pack of lies** is saying a lot of things which are not true: *He admitted telling a pack of lies in court.*

packet

cost a 'packet

You say something **costs a packet** if it is expensive: *'I want an underwater camera.' 'Oh, that'll cost you a packet.'*

◇ SEE ALSO **cost a bomb** ▷ BOMB; **cost the earth** ▷ EARTH

pain

on pain of 'something or under pain of 'something

If you give someone an order **on**, or **under**, **pain of something**, you are threatening them with that thing as a punishment if they fail to do what you ask: *The dissidents were ordered to cease their activities immediately, under pain of imprisonment.* □ *I've told her to be back by midnight, under pain of death.*

This use of the word **pain** comes from the French 'peine', meaning 'punishment' or 'penalty'. The expression 'under pain of death' is more often used in a humorous way than literally, as in the second example.

a pain in the 'neck or 'bum or 'backside or 'arse or 'butt or 'ass

You call someone or something **a pain in the neck**, or **bum**, or **backside**, or **arse**, or **butt**, or **ass** if you find that person or thing annoying: *It's a real pain in the backside, I've got to work this Saturday.* □ *Her mother was a pain in the arse. Always wanting to know where she was and what she was doing, who she was with and what they had done.*

'**Bum**' is a very informal word. '**Arse**' is more vulgar. '**Butt**' is the American word for 'bum', and '**ass**' is the American equivalent of 'arse'.

pains

be at 'pains or take 'pains

If you **are at pains** or **taking pains** to do something, you are making a lot of effort to do it as well as possible: *I never felt at home with the host family, although they were at pains to make me comfortable.* □ *The minister had taken pains to find out as much as possible about the old lady before attending her funeral.*

for someone's 'pains

If someone gives you something **for your pains**, they give it to you because they are grateful for the effort that you have made, or that you are about to make: *I expect to be promptly and generously reimbursed for my pains.* □ *She worked a full day cleaning that house, and what did she get for her pains? Not even a thankyou.*

◇ SEE ALSO **worth someone's while** ▷ WHILE

pair

have only one pair of 'hands

You say you **have only got one pair of hands** if you are trying, or someone is asking you, to do more things at once than you consider to be possible: *It's all very well for you to ask me to do all these things, but I've only got one pair of hands, you know.*

show a clean pair of 'heels

You say that a person or thing **shows a clean pair of heels** if they run away, or if they move a long way ahead of their competitors: *He showed the other runners a clean pair of heels with an astounding sprint to the finish.* □ *With such adventurous marketing, the company is showing the rest of the industry a clean pair of heels.*

pairs

in 'pairs

1 If objects come **in pairs**, you can only obtain them as a set of two. **2** A group of people does an activity **in pairs** if each person works with a partner on the activity: *No, you can't buy the earrings singly. They are only sold in pairs.* □ *Right then. I want you to work in pairs for this next activity.*

pale

beyond the 'pale

You say that behaviour or a certain action is **beyond the pale** if you think it is so bad that it is unacceptable: *I like to think I am broad-minded, but the language my father used was beyond the pale, and all because he couldn't find his razor.*

pale as 'death

Someone who is as **pale as death** is very pale.

◇ SEE ALSO **white as a sheet** or **as death** or **as snow** or **as paper** or **as a ghost** ▷ WHITE

palm

cross someone's palm with 'silver *(old)*

If someone asks you to **cross their palm with silver**, they are asking for money: *Cross my palm with silver, and I shall tell you more.*

These are the words which fortune-tellers are said to use when they are asking you to pay for their services.

grease someone's 'palm *(informal)*

If you **grease someone's palm**, you give them money, usually for something that you would not normally expect to have to pay for: *He can tell you where they are hiding, but you'll have to grease his palm first.*

'**palm-greasing**: *Palm-greasing for just about anything from entry to a favoured school to obtaining a bank loan has always been considered a fact of life.*

have someone in the palm of your 'hand or have someone eating out of the palm of your 'hand

You **have someone in**, or **eating out of**, the **palm of your hand** if you have so much influence over that person that you can persuade them to do what you want: *They won't do anything without his permission. He's got all his employees in the palm of his hand.*

◇ SEE ALSO **have someone wrapped round your little finger** ▷ FINGER; **have someone eating out of your hand** ▷ HAND; **have someone right where you want them** ▷ WANT; **have someone in your pocket** ▷ POCKET

pan

down the 'pan

Something, usually a plan or an organization, which goes **down the pan** fails completely and ceases to exist: *Communities are crumbling, hospitals are shutting and the economy is going down the pan.*

◇ SEE ALSO **down the drain** ▷ DRAIN; **down the plughole** ▷ PLUGHOLE; **down the toilet** ▷ TOILET; **down the tubes** ▷ TUBES

out of the frying-pan into the 'fire

You say '**out of the frying-pan into the fire**' when you have just escaped from a difficult or dangerous situation, only to find yourself in a situation which is even worse: *To me they sound as if they're very similar – so be warned. Marry Doreen and you'll be stepping out of the frying pan into the fire.*

Pandora

Pandora's 'box

You say that someone has opened **Pandora's box** when they discover that they are doing something which involves or creates a large number of hidden or unexpected problems: *Deciding how to decommission old oil platforms was like opening Pandora's box.* ◻ *The policeman who finally trapped Lee said: 'We found a Pandora's box of evidence in his fraudster's den.'*

◇ SEE ALSO **can of worms** ▷ CAN; **poisoned chalice** ▷ CHALICE

pants

bore the 'pants off someone (*informal, humorous*)

If you say that someone or something **bores the pants off you**, you mean that you find them very boring: *You should plan a few jokes into your speech, to avoid boring the pants off your audience.*

catch someone with their 'pants down

When you **catch someone with their pants down**, you put them in an embarrassing situation by doing something which they do not expect, or discovering something which they would have preferred to keep a secret: *You really caught them with their pants down in the meeting with that question you asked.*

◇ SEE ALSO **catch someone at it** ▷ CATCH; **catch someone red-handed** ▷ CATCH; **catch someone with their trousers down** ▷ TROUSERS

fancy the 'pants off someone (*informal, may be offensive*)

You say you **fancy the pants off someone** if you find them sexy: *She says that she used to 'fancy the pants off him', but has lost interest since he grew a beard.*

paper

commit something to 'paper

You **commit something to paper** when you write it down to make a permanent record of it: *I decided to commit my thoughts to paper and see if I could get them published.*

◇ SEE ALSO **commit something to memory** ▷ MEMORY

not worth the paper it is 'written on

You say that a document or other text is **not worth the paper it is written on** if you consider that there are so many things wrong with it that it has no value or power: *'Without the money to pay for your promises, your manifesto is not worth the paper it is written on.'*

◇ SEE ALSO **count for nothing** ▷ NOTHING

on 'paper

1 When you talk about something as it appears **on paper**, you are talking about the information you get from official documents, often in contrast to what is really the case, or to an agreement which is made unofficially: *He looked so good on paper, but he performed very badly at the interview.* ◻ *The agreement is verbal. We don't have anything on paper, I'm afraid.* **2** You get your thoughts or ideas down **on paper** when you write them down: *If you have a complaint, it is important to get it down on paper and send it to the manager.*

paper 'tiger

A **paper tiger** is someone or something that has a position of power, but which, in fact, has no real power at all: *He argued that if the association failed to take disciplinary action against its members, the Code of Practice would be discredited – as a paper tiger.*

par

below 'par or not up to 'par

1 Someone or something that is **below par** or **not up to par** is not performing at its usual high standard: *Oh yes, he's still playing good tennis. But I still think he was not quite up to par this year.* ◻ *His eyesight was below par, which disqualified him from being a pilot.* **2** If you are feeling **below par**, you are not feeling as well as you usually do: *You might feel below par, your resistance to infection could well be affected; you will not have the zest for life that you should have.*

◇ SEE ALSO **out of sorts** ▷ SORTS; **under the weather** ▷ WEATHER

on a 'par with something

You describe two things as being **on a par with each other** if you consider them to be approximately equivalent in terms of degree or achievement: *For a canoeist, the challenge of paddling to the Pharoes is on a par with climbing Everest.*

pardon

I beg your 'pardon (*formal*)

You say '**I beg your pardon**' when **1** you have not heard what has been said, and you want the speaker to repeat themselves: *'Could I see your ticket please, madam?' 'I beg your pardon?' 'Your ticket, please.'* **2** you consider that the person you are speaking to has just said something silly or rude, and you want to express your disagreement or annoyance: *'That watch is a very good imitation.' 'I beg your pardon. It's a genuine Cartier and it cost £1000.'* **3** you want to make a general apology for doing something wrong or making a mistake: *'We've been waiting for half an hour and we're in a hurry.' 'Oh, I do beg your pardon.'*

◇ SEE ALSO **excuse me** ▷ EXCUSE

pardon 'me

You say '**pardon me**' as an apology **1** when you want to show that you are angry, and your apology is not really sincere: *Pardon me if I don't break down in tears at the plight of the parents who are having to take their children out of private schools because they cannot afford the fees.* **2** after burping in public: *Mr Braithwaite belched loudly: 'Pardon me, ladies,' he bellowed.*

◇ SEE ALSO **excuse me** ▷ EXCUSE

> **Pardon me** is also an old fashioned way of making a sincere apology. American English uses 'pardon me?' as a way of asking a speaker to repeat themselves.

parker

a nosey 'parker (*disrespectful*)

You call someone **a nosey parker** if they always want to know things about other people's private affairs: *'Laura's a bit of a nosey parker,' Gloria continued, 'She was cleaning his room one evening and had a peek inside his cupboard, and what do you think she found?'*

parrot

'parrot-fashion

You learn something **parrot-fashion** if you learn it by memory, without making any attempt to understand it: *Some students were reduced to learning their work parrot-fashion, while lacking any real understanding of what they were taught.*

> Parrots can learn to speak, but they just copy the sounds that they hear, without understanding them.

part

the best part of 'such-and-such

The **best part of** a certain quantity is almost all of it: *He just disappeared, leaving behind him the best part of a million pounds' worth of unpaid 'debts.*

for 'my part

For my part means 'if you want to know my preference': *Some people like the city, and others the country. For my part, I prefer the country.*

for the 'most part

If you make a statement and say that it is true **for the most part**, you mean that there may be a few exceptions, but that, as a general statement, it is true: *The children were very well-behaved, at least for the most part. Charlie could have been less noisy.*

have no 'part in something or take no 'part in something

You decide to **have**, or **take**, **no part in something** if you decide not to get involved in that thing, probably because you do not approve of it: *He believed social segregation in education to be totally wrong and he could have no part in perpetuating it.*

look the 'part

Somebody who **looks the part** is wearing the proper clothes and behaving in the proper way for the situation which they are in, although it may not be natural to them: *Pietro looked at first sight like an English tourist. From his tweed jacket to his patterned brogues he looked the part perfectly.*

part and 'parcel

Something is **part and parcel** of a certain thing if it is a necessary, and probably rather unpleasant, part of that thing: *Infuriating it may be, but you may as well accept that these things are part and parcel of travel overseas.*

part of the 'furniture

You say that someone or something is like **part of the furniture** if you are used to them, and even feel some affection for them, just because they have been present for such a long time: *He was a drunken old fool, but we'll miss him here at the pub. He was like part of the furniture.*

play a 'part

A person or thing **plays a part** when they help to cause a certain event: *Whatever the official reasons may be, falling petrol sales certainly played a part in Shell's decision.* □ *By donating as little as £3, you can be sure that you have played a part in improving a child's life.*

take something in good 'part

You **take something**, such as a criticism directed at you, **in good part** if you are able to accept it with good humour and not get upset about it: *Well, I thought he took all those jokes about the Irish in remarkably good part.*

take 'part

You **are taking part**, or **taking part in something**, if you are doing an activity together with a number of other people: *I love silly party games, but my boyfriend always refuses to take part.*

take someone's 'part

When you **take someone's part**, you support them or their opinion against other people: *I thought I could rely on you to take my part. After all, you are my husband.*

parting

the parting of the 'ways

The parting of the ways is the moment when one or more members of a group start on some new activity or way of life which means that they can no longer be part of that group, after a period of time spent together: *We both knew this was the parting of the ways, and our farewells had an air of finality.*

parts

good in 'parts

If you describe something as **good in parts**, you are saying that the quality of that thing is variable, with some good and some bad bits: *'How's that book you're reading?' 'Oh, good in parts, I suppose. I skip all the boring bits.'*

◇ SEE ALSO **a curate's egg** or **like the curate's egg – good in parts** ▷ CURATE

private 'parts

People sometimes say **private parts** when they want to avoid using the word 'genitals': *In the cell there is a man with long dishevelled hair. His clothes are in rags, and do not even cover his private parts.*

party

be 'party to something

A person **is party to something** if they participate in it: *Just how that's going to be accomplished we don't know – we're not party to the discussions.*

a 'party piece

A person's **party piece** is a small piece of entertainment which that person often does to entertain a group of friends: *We all did a party piece. I did my usual bird impression – 'a vulture'.*

'party-pooper

You call someone a **party-pooper** if you think that they are being boring or spoiling other people's fun by refusing to go to a party or to take part in some kind of social activity: *Self-consciousness is a common party-pooper. When I go to a party I feel there's an expectation for me to be witty, so I become shy and nervous.*

the party's 'over

You say that **the party's over** when an activity which certain people were enjoying, especially one which you disapprove of, comes to an end: *The party was well and truly over for the business tycoons of the '80s and money was getting scarce.* □ *Okay, everyone. The party's over. Drop your guns and raise your hands slowly above your head.*

toe the party 'line

A person **toes the party line** when they show obedience and loyalty to the group they belong to, in their behaviour and the opinions they express: *Those MPs who have refused to toe the party line must expect to lose their places in the Cabinet.*

pass

come to 'pass

If something **comes to pass**, this is an old-fashioned literary way of saying that it happens: *And it shall come to pass, some bright summer's day, that he will return for his only son.*

come to a 'pass or come to a pretty 'pass

You say that things have **come to a pass** or **come to a pretty pass** if you feel shocked by how bad the situation has become: *Things have come to a pretty pass if we can't afford to feed a few visitors! It's disgraceful!*

make a 'pass at someone

If you **make a pass at someone** whom you find sexually attractive, you do or say something which makes your attraction obvious, to see whether they are interested in you too: *'My tutor made a pass at me today.' 'I would report it to the students' council if I were you.'*

'pass as something or **'pass for something**
You say that a certain person or thing **passes as something** or **passes for something** if they can be accepted as that thing, even though, in actual fact, they are not: *The plates don't actually match, but they will pass for a set, unless you look very closely.* □ *You'll never pass for eighteen unless you put on a bit of make-up.*

passing

in 'passing
You say something **in passing** if you mention it briefly, but it is not the main subject of what you are saying: *Now let us examine the text, but in passing, I want to give you a few details about the author's life.*

past

'past it (*informal, disrespectful*)
You say someone is **past it** if you consider that they are old, or too old to do certain things: *Don't you think he's getting a bit past it to be going on a skiing holiday?*
◇ SEE ALSO **over the hill** ▷ HILL; **no spring chicken** ▷ SPRING; **long in the tooth** ▷ TOOTH; **not getting any younger** ▷ YOUNGER

a thing of the 'past
A thing of the past is something which no longer exists, or which is no longer considered important: *Dandruff can be a thing of the past with our new medicated range of shampoos.*

pasture

be put out to 'pasture or **be turned out to 'pasture**
Someone who **is put out to pasture** loses their job because their employer considers that they are too old to be working: *You'll end up like poor old Eddy Moulton, put out to pasture in some quiet department where nobody bothers to talk to you.*
◇ SEE ALSO **put** or **turn** or **send someone out to grass** ▷ GRASS

pastures

pastures 'new
Someone who goes to **pastures new** moves into a different field of work, or tries a new kind of activity: *By moving to pastures new, successful managers can negotiate themselves a new package of highly desirable terms.*
◇ SEE ALSO **fresh fields and pastures new** ▷ FIELDS

pat

off 'pat
You know, or have, something **off pat** if you know it so well that you can repeat it from memory with no mistakes: *I haven't got all the lines off pat yet, but I should be all right in time for the dress rehearsal.*
◇ SEE ALSO **off by heart** ▷ HEART

a pat on the 'back
If you are praising someone for doing something well, you can say that they should give themselves, or that they deserve, **a pat on the back**: *First of all, you deserve a pat on the back for successfully completing the first four weeks of the diet.* □ *You've all worked very well today, so give yourselves a pat on the back.*
◇ SEE ALSO **a clap on the back** ▷ CLAP; **a slap on the back** ▷ SLAP

patch

go through a 'bad patch
You **are going through a bad patch** when you are having a lot of problems at a particular time in your life; a marriage or relationship **is going through a bad patch** if the two people involved are not getting on very well with each other: *When I was five my father hit a bad patch and he sold the house.* □ *'Tim and I,' said Louise heavily, 'are going through a bad patch. We get on each other's nerves, to put it bluntly.'*

not a 'patch on
You say that something or someone is **not a patch on** the thing or person you are comparing them with if they are much less good than that thing or person: *The barbecue was good, but it wasn't a patch on last year's.*
◇ SEE ALSO **not fit to hold a candle to** ▷ CANDLE; **in a class of your own** ▷ CLASS; **a cut above** or **a cut above the rest** ▷ CUT; **in a different league** ▷ LEAGUE

a 'purple patch
A purple patch is a period of time when someone has a lot of good luck or success: *He will want to know if I cope as well during a bad spell as I did when I was enjoying a purple patch and scored 11 goals in 14 games earlier in the season.* □ *You recently announced a series of multi-million pound contracts. Were they a coincidence or are you going through a purple patch at the moment?*

path

beat a path to someone's 'door
You say that someone **beats a path to your door** if they compete with others for your services: *Naomi no longer had to look for work; she soon had all the agencies beating a path to her door.*

cross someone's 'path
You **cross someone's path** when you meet that person or your life briefly becomes linked with theirs in some way, usually

by chance: *He has brought me nothing but bad luck. I never wish to cross his path again.* □ *She turned and went away with a look on her face which boded ill for anyone who crossed her path that day.*

paths

paths 'cross

Two people's **paths cross** when they meet each other or their lives briefly become linked in some way, usually by chance: *I hope our paths may cross again some day.*

patience

try the patience of a 'saint

You say that a person would **try the patience of a saint** if they are so annoying that you think they could make even the most patient people angry: *Hell, this machine would try the patience of a saint.*

patter

the patter of tiny 'feet

If people talk about **the patter of tiny feet**, they are referring to the possibility of children being born: *I'm not saying it's going to be easy, giving all this up, but I quite fancy hearing the patter of tiny feet.*
◇ SEE ALSO **the happy event** ▷ EVENT

pause

give someone 'pause or give someone pause for 'thought

Something **gives you pause** or **gives you pause for thought** if it makes you stop and think hard about something which you never usually consider: *'You should smile more often!' This gave me pause, and when I returned to the hut I tried out a few grins into a hand mirror.* □ *When they parted, he was sure that he had given Ludovico serious pause for thought. He was wrong.*

pay

in the 'pay of

Someone is **in the pay of** a person or organization if they are paid by that person or organization for their general loyalty, and probably for their involvement in certain secret activities: *Those purged were said to be in the pay of the CIA, and described as 'counter-revolutionary'.*

peace

at 'peace

1 Countries or people that are **at peace** or **at peace with** one another are not fighting: *Although the countries are officially at peace with one another, the fighting continues.* **2** You are **at peace with** yourself if you feel

happy and calm, with nothing to worry about or to blame yourself for: *The therapy served its purpose. I was much more at peace with myself and more accepting of the way that I looked.*

hold your 'peace (*old*)

If someone says '**hold your peace!**' to another person, they are telling that person to remain silent instead of starting to speak: *You will have your turn to speak, but now you must hold your peace, young man.*
◇ SEE ALSO **hold your tongue** ▷ TONGUE

keep the 'peace

1 The police or the army **keep the peace** when they are present in order to prevent violence, or to make sure the law is being obeyed: *The policeman said, 'I'm here to keep the peace, sir, and I'd appreciate your co-operation'.* **2** Someone is **keeping the peace** if they are managing to prevent a fight or disagreement from starting: *Provided we are able to exercise tact, the truth, spoken in love, will always achieve more than saying nothing in order to 'keep the peace'.*
'**peace-keeping**: *In past months, many have questioned the value and efficiency of UN peace-keeping.*

make 'peace

When countries that have been at war make an official agreement to stop fighting, you say they have **made peace**: *When the two countries finally made peace, they were both close to economic ruin.*

'**peace-making**: *The peace-making process will probably take years to complete.*

make your 'peace

You **make your peace** with someone when you decide to forgive each other and to stop fighting: *Life is so much more relaxed now that they have made their peace and are friends again.*

peace and 'quiet

Peace and quiet is the silence and lack of stress necessary for you to be able to rest or concentrate properly: *The hotels we've picked are a bit quieter, to offer just a little more privacy and peace and quiet for those that want it.*

peace of 'mind

If someone does something which cannot change the situation, but which helps them to stop worrying about it, you say they are doing it for their **peace of mind**: *Why don't you give them a call to check that your gift has arrived? Just for your own peace of mind.*

peanuts

for 'peanuts

1 If you do some work **for peanuts**, you are badly paid for it: *But I mean you don't want* to start working in the mines for peanuts or anything, you want a good job. **2** You say you cannot do something **for peanuts** if you cannot manage to do it, even when you try very hard: *I can't dance for peanuts.*

◇ SEE ALSO **for toffee** ▷ TOFFEE

pearl

a pearl of 'wisdom

If you call a remark **a pearl of wisdom**, you are saying humorously that it sounded, or was intended to sound, wise: *A small number of dedicated, respectful and conscientious students were eager to catch pearls of wisdom from their professor's lips.*

pearls

cast pearls before 'swine

You say that someone **is casting pearls before swine** if you think they are wasting themselves, or the things which they have to offer, on people who do not appreciate them: *'Television coverage of the arts is mainly a matter of casting pearls before swine,' she argued.*

pecker

keep your 'pecker up

If you tell someone to **keep their pecker up**, you mean that they should try not to be unhappy or to lose hope: *It's going to be a case of keeping your pecker up, looking on the best side of things.*

◇ SEE ALSO **keep your chin up** ▷ CHIN

pecking

the 'pecking order

The pecking order is the system in which things or people find their natural place, depending on how powerful or influential they are in relation to one another: *Traditionally, Oxford and Cambridge come at the top of the pecking order of English universities.*

> **Pecking order** is the translation of a German word, 'Hackordnung', first used in the 1920s to describe a social system which had been noticed in domestic hens. Apparently, each bird in a group is allowed to peck the bird next below it in rank and has to accept being pecked by the bird next above it.

pedestal

put someone on a 'pedestal

You **are putting someone on a pedestal** if your great admiration for them makes you imagine that they have no faults or weaknesses: *In the courtly love tradition, the woman was put on a pedestal – objectified.*

Such a conception of women has continued down the centuries.

peg

bring someone 'down a peg or two or take someone 'down a peg or two

If you think that someone is too sure of themselves, and you do or say something to reduce their confidence, you say you **are bringing**, or **taking, them down a peg or two**: *It would serve him right. Dared she? He deserved to be taken down a peg or two.*

off the 'peg

Clothes which are sold **off the peg** are in a shop, ready to be bought and worn, and there is no need to order them in advance: *He wore cream linen trousers and a pale yellow shirt that was definitely not off the peg.*

a square peg in a round 'hole

You feel like **a square peg in a round hole** if you feel uncomfortable because you do not understand or fit into the group of people or the environment which you are in: *Low self-esteem can be made worse by a sense of being a square peg in a round hole.*

pegging

level 'pegging

When two or more competitors have an equal number of points, you say that they are **level pegging**: *The match looked set to be a close affair when the two neighbours were level pegging after three heats.*

pelt

at full 'pelt

Someone or something is going **at full pelt** if they are running or travelling as fast as they can: *He broke his leg after running full pelt across a public road and hitting a car coming the other way.*

◇ SEE ALSO **hell for leather** ▷ HELL; **at full tilt** ▷ TILT

pen

put pen to 'paper (*formal*)

When someone **puts pen to paper**, they write a letter to someone: *Dear Sir, I feel I must put pen to paper, having just read your article on new European policies in the November issue of 'The Spectator'.*

pennies

look after or take care of the pennies and the pounds will take care of them'selves

People say '**look after**, or **take care of, the pennies and the pounds will take care of themselves**' if they believe that you should be careful about all the little things which you buy if you want to save money: *It's only a bit cheaper, but if you look after the pennies, the pounds will look after themselves.*

not have two pennies to rub to'gether

If you do **not have two pennies to rub together**, you have very little money: *Ever since they bought that house, they haven't had two pennies to rub together.*

◇ SEE ALSO **not have a red cent** ▷ CENT; **not have two ha'pennies to rub together** ▷ HA'PENNIES; **not have a penny to your name** ▷ PENNY

pennies from 'heaven

Pennies from heaven are unexpected financial benefits: *When I was overpaid, it just felt like pennies from heaven. I never thought to report it.*

penny (*see also* **pence** *and* **pennies**)

in for a penny, in for a 'pound

You say '**in for a penny, in for a pound**' if, after having taken a small risk, you decide to take a bigger one as well: *'Let's live together,' I said. In for a penny, in for a pound, I thought, and added, 'Will you marry me?'*

not cost a 'penny

Something which does **not cost a penny** costs nothing: *As an introductory offer, your first year of banking with us won't cost you a penny.*

◇ SEE ALSO **not cost a bean** ▷ BEAN

not have a penny to your 'name

If you do **not have a penny to your name**, you have no money or financial stability: *And look here, how do you think you're going to pay for it? You haven't a penny to your name.*

◇ SEE ALSO **not have a red cent** ▷ CENT; **not have two ha'pennies to rub together** ▷ HA'PENNIES; **not have two pennies to rub together** ▷ PENNIES

the penny 'dropped or the penny has 'dropped

You say '**the penny dropped**' or '**the penny has dropped**' to refer to the moment when someone understood or realized something that they had not understood or realized before: *She could only stare at him, completely at a loss as to what he meant. Then the penny dropped, and her eyes widened in horrified shock.*

a penny for your 'thoughts or a 'penny for them

You say '**a penny for your thoughts**', or '**a penny for them**', to someone if they seem to be thinking about something, and you want them to tell you what that thing is: *'A penny for them, Karen.' 'What?' 'A penny for your*

thoughts. You've gone all dreamy again.'

'penny-pinching (*disrespectful*)

You describe someone as **penny-pinching** if you think they are never willing to spend their money: *Some people would describe my mother as penny-pinching, but I prefer to say she is frugal.*

penny wise, pound 'foolish

You say someone is **penny wise, pound foolish** if they are careful with small amounts of money, but they have a tendency to buy large, expensive things which they may not really need: *He told the conference that the health service was being penny wise pound foolish in the use of medicines. Those in use may be cheap, but the side effects cause greater problems in the long term.*

a pretty 'penny

You say that something cost **a pretty penny** if it cost a large sum of money: *'That must have cost a pretty penny,' he declared, not really expecting to be told the price. To his surprise Max Klein announced: 'Two hundred and fifty pounds.'*

◇ SEE ALSO **an arm and a leg** ▷ ARM

spend a 'penny

If someone says they are going to **spend a penny**, they are saying in rather an old-fashioned way that they are going to the toilet: *Can you wait while I go and spend a penny? I won't be a moment.*

◇ SEE ALSO **go to the bathroom** ▷ BATHROOM; **powder your nose** ▷ NOSE; **take a leak** ▷ LEAK; **go for a slash** ▷ SLASH

> In the past, the doors on public toilets had a lock on them which only opened when you put a penny in.

turn up like a bad 'penny

You say that someone or something **turns up like a bad penny** if they are always arriving when they are not wanted: *'She's always turning up. Like a bad penny,' Constance thought viciously, saying nothing.*

> This expression comes from the idea that if you try to get rid of a false coin by spending it, that same coin may return to you some day, after passing through the hands of many people who all get rid of it in the same way.

two a 'penny or ten a 'penny

You say that things are **two**, or **ten, a penny** if they are common or easy to obtain: *Müllers are ten a penny in Germany, of course, but it might be the same one.*

pennyworth

put your 'pennyworth in
When you **put your pennyworth in**, you take part in a discussion by expressing your opinion: *The National Farmers' Union of Scotland put its pennyworth in when Alex Brown, the milk committee convener, said the union expected a reasoned decision.*

people

people who live in glass houses shouldn't throw 'stones
If someone says '**people who live in glass houses shouldn't throw stones**', they mean that a person who can be easily harmed or criticized should not criticize other people or draw attention to themselves: *One would have thought that the principle of people living in glass houses not throwing stones would have warned Ivan off a career as a journalist and gossip.*

peppercorn

peppercorn 'rent
A **peppercorn rent** is an almost ridiculously small amount of money which someone pays as rent: *If it hadn't been for the colonel letting me have this cottage for a peppercorn rent, God knows where I'd be.*

perch

knock someone off their 'perch
If you think that someone is too important or sure of themselves, and you do or say something to reduce their importance or confidence, you say you **are knocking them off their perch**: *Leo: You must anticipate some strange developments in the workplace – even a serious attempt to knock you off your perch.*

perfection

to per'fection
1 Something is done **to perfection** if it is done exactly as it should be and could not be done any better: *The meat was done to perfection.* 2 Something suits someone **to perfection** if it is exactly what they want or need: *Our new house is beautiful, and with three bedrooms, it suits us to perfection.*
◇ SEE ALSO **suit someone down to the ground** ▷ GROUND

peril

at your 'peril
If someone tells you that you do something **at your peril**, they are saying that you will be in great danger if you do it: *Neglect our advice at your peril.*

period

'period piece
A **period piece** is a person or thing such as a play, a piece of furniture, or a painting, that is typical of the time when they were born or made, especially if this is the main reason why they are interesting: *This clock is regarded as an excellent period piece from the late 18th century.*

perpetuity

in perpe'tuity
Something is to be done **in perpetuity** if it is intended to last for ever: *This land is to be held in perpetuity by a council of trustees who will ensure it is never sold.*

'**In perpetuity**' is a legal expression.

person

have something about your 'person or have something on your 'person (*formal* or *humorous*)
You **have something about**, or **have something on**, **your person** if you are carrying it in a pocket or somewhere else in your clothes: *At the time he died he was carrying the bomb on his person – concealed in the broad leather belt.* □ *How much money do you have about your person?*

in 'person
1 You do something **in person** if you actually go and do it yourself, instead of sending another person or a letter to represent you: *A written apology isn't enough. Tell him I want him to come and apologize to me in person.* 2 You meet, see, or hear someone famous or important **in person** when you manage to meet, see, or hear the real person instead of just seeing pictures or hearing recordings of them: *The protesters set out for London, determined to meet the Prime Minister in person.*
◇ SEE ALSO **face to face with someone** ▷ FACE; **in the flesh** ▷ FLESH

in the person of 'so-and-so
You use the expression **in the person of** before naming someone, to mean that they are the thing which you have just referred to: *The presence of royalty in the person of Princess Anne and her husband, kept up the social tone.*

the 'last person
If someone is **the last person** you would expect to do something, they are not at all the kind of person you would expect to do that thing: *He is the very last person you might expect to sympathize with a Greenpeace campaign.*

may the best person 'win

If the judge of a competition or someone equally important says '**may the best person win**' before the competition starts, he or she is encouraging everyone to try as hard as they can: *I wish everyone the best of luck, and may the best person win.*

◇ SEE ALSO **may the best man win** ▷ MAN

perspective

in per'spective

When someone sees something **in perspective**, they understand its real importance in relation to other things; when someone gets something **into perspective**, they begin to do this after a period of not doing so: *Outside advice is very important in helping you to see yourself in perspective.* □ *Okay, so it's a shame you failed your exams. But try to get it into perspective.*

out of per'spective

You say someone is getting something **out of perspective** if you think they are making it seem much more important than it really is: *The election results have been disappointing, but we must not get them out of perspective.*

◇ SEE ALSO **out of proportion** ▷ PROPORTION

petard

be hoist with your own pe'tard

You say that a person **is hoist with their own petard** if their plans have had the opposite result from that which they had intended, and they themselves end up in difficulty because of their own bad actions: *She found herself hoist with her own petard when the lie she had told turned out to be true.* □ *The Prime Minister's smile spread even further when he thought he had an opponent hoist with his own petard.*

Pete

for Pete's 'sake (*informal*)

For Pete's sake is an exclamation which people sometimes use to express great surprise, anger or annoyance, or to emphasize what they are saying: *For Pete's sake! Can't you just shut up for one minute and listen to me?*

◇ SEE ALSO **for Christ's sake** ▷ CHRIST; **for fuck's sake** ▷ FUCK; **for God's sake** ▷ GOD; **for goodness sake** ▷ GOODNESS; **for heaven's sake** ▷ HEAVEN; **for pity's sake** ▷ PITY

Peter

Peter 'Pan

A **Peter Pan** is a person or thing which never seems to grow up or get old: *We share a Peter Pan mentality, a lack of self-discipline and a strong lazy streak.* □ *Ian was boyish, athletic, charming, and, Clare suspected, terrified of his fortieth birthday: there was a bit of the Peter Pan in him.*

> The Scottish dramatist J M Barrie created the character of Peter Pan, the boy who never grows up, in 1904.

the 'Peter principle

The **Peter principle** is a theory which suggests that employees tend to be given jobs with more and more responsibility until they reach a level at which they can no longer work effectively: *In accord with the Peter principle, we promote the ego to its level of incompetence.*

rob Peter to pay 'Paul

You say that someone **is robbing Peter to pay Paul** when they obtain the money they need by taking it from an area where it is needed just as badly: *Britain's biggest bank has been robbing Peter to pay Paul through the recession. The cash it has taken from the public has gone to cover its losses caused by firms closing down because of the slump.*

petrel

a stormy 'petrel

A **stormy petrel** is someone whose presence suggests that there is likely to be some kind of trouble in the near future: *His career as a stormy petrel continued when he was given the education portfolio in 1987. He was quickly forced to resign after a long teachers' strike the following year.*

phoenix

rise like a phoenix from the 'ashes

Someone or something **rises like a phoenix from the ashes** if they become stronger or more admirable than ever before, after and maybe even as a result of having been almost completely destroyed: *Becker, after near defeat in the third set, rose like a phoenix from the ashes and triumphed in five sets.*

phone

on the 'phone

You are **on the phone** when 1 you are using the telephone: *Don't distract me when I'm on the phone, please.* 2 you have a telephone in your home, making it possible for people to phone you: *They are difficult to contact because they are not on the phone.*

phrase

to coin a 'phrase

You say '**to coin a phrase**' if you know that you are about to use, or have just used, either 1 a common phrase because you could not think of any better way of expressing your thoughts: *I had to find out the hard way – to coin a phrase.* **2** a new expression which you have just invented: *If the wearing of seat belts reduces accidents, it is also likely to reduce the number of kidneys available for transplant. It is an odd sidelight, to coin a phrase, on road accidents.*

phut

go 'phut

When something such as a piece of machinery **goes phut**, it stops working; when a performance or a film **goes phut**, it stops being interesting or entertaining: *We were motoring quite happily down the loch, and then the outboard went phut and cut out.* ☐ *Before it goes phut, the film manages to show us Streep at her best.*

pick

pick and 'choose

You **pick and choose** when you choose the thing or things you want with great care, and leave the rest: *You've got to earn a living, Dorothy. You can't pick and choose now. You've got to take whatever's going.*

picnic

no 'picnic

You say that something is **no picnic** if it involves a lot of problems and difficulty: *It's no picnic, trying to bring up a family on Income Support.* ☐ *I must have been very naive. I knew it would be no picnic, but I just didn't think they would treat human beings like that.*

picture

get the 'picture

You say that you **get the picture** to a person who has been describing or explaining something, to show that you understand or can see what they mean: *Fernie looked even more puzzled but Pascoe could see from Alice's face that she was beginning to get the picture.*

in the 'picture

1 You put someone **in the picture** when you give them enough information for them to know what is happening. *I'm not really supposed to tell anyone, but I thought I'd better put you in the picture.* **2** If you say that someone is **in the picture**, you mean that they are involved in the situation that you are discussing: *Are ICI still in the picture, or have they pulled out of the project now?*

out of the 'picture

If you say that someone is **out of the picture**, you mean that they are no longer involved

in the situation that you are discussing: *Are you still seeing Jeremy, or is he out of the picture altogether now?*

paint a black 'picture of

You **are painting a black picture of** something or someone if the way you are describing them makes them sound worse than they really are: *Why paint such a black picture of the economy when you know we are well on the way to recovery?*

pie

eat humble 'pie

If someone **eats humble pie**, they admit that they were wrong about something: *It could easily have been done after all. But they refused to eat humble pie, so we're stuck with the thing until the end of the next century.*
◊ SEE ALSO **eat your words** ▷ WORDS

pie in the 'sky

A promise, plan or hope for the future is **pie in the sky** if it is almost certainly never going to happen: *Some argue that while a coherent system may be desirable, it is not possible; it is pie in the sky, since it ignores reality.*

piece

all of a 'piece

A number of separate things, or a large thing made up of separate elements, is **all of a piece** if all the parts of it go to make up something which is whole and complete: *This is a city very much all of a piece, its chief delight for visitors lying in its completeness.* ☐ *It is sometimes argued that Freud's theories must be accepted or rejected all of a piece.*

give someone a piece of your 'mind

You **give someone a piece of your mind** when you tell them severely how much you disapprove of something they have done: *'He's treated his poor wife disgracefully.' 'I know. I'll give him a piece of my mind when I see him.'*
◊ SEE ALSO **send someone away with a flea in their ear** ▷ FLEA; **give someone hell** ▷ HELL; **read the riot act** ▷ RIOT; **give someone the rough side of your tongue** ▷ SIDE; **tear someone off a strip** ▷ STRIP

in one 'piece

You say that someone or something is **in one piece** if they are unhurt or undamaged after being in an accident or some other dangerous situation: *It was terrifying when the storm started out there. But we all got home in one piece.* ☐ *Did the parcel get to you in one piece?*

pieces

a nasty piece of 'work

If you say that someone is **a nasty piece of work**, you mean that they are an unpleasant, and possibly dangerous, person: *You'd best steer clear of him, Manderley, he's a nasty piece of work. Don't want you falling in with the wrong types, do we?*

a piece of the 'action

Someone who wants **a piece of the action** wants a share of another person's good luck, especially if this good luck is financial: *Will foreign firms get a piece of the action? American and European firms are unlikely to get much of a look in. Japanese contractors prefer to do business with their neighbours.*

◇ SEE ALSO **a slice of the action** ▷ SLICE; **a slice of the cake** ▷ SLICE

a piece of 'cake or a piece of 'piss (*vulgar*)

Something which is **a piece of cake** or a **piece of piss** is easy to do or to learn: *All you do is put some cement on the trowel and then throw it like this. It's a piece of cake.*

◇ SEE ALSO **child's play** ▷ CHILD; **easy as ABC** or **anything** or **falling off a log** or **pie** or **winking** ▷ EASY; **kids' stuff** ▷ KIDS; **nothing to it** ▷ NOTHING

say your 'piece

You **say your piece** when you say something that you think needs saying, for example in a discussion: *Cameron got up on a chair and said his piece. The scattered crowd drew closer together and listened quietly.*

a set 'piece

A **set piece** is some kind of performance which a person has prepared earlier, the purpose of which is to show that person's skills and ability: *I was impressed by her set piece, but her improvisation was a disaster.*

pieces

go to 'pieces

You **go to pieces** when you get so anxious or upset that you completely lose your ability to deal with things, or to perform as you usually do: *He had been managing well till then, but he went to pieces when someone mentioned his wife.*

pick up the 'pieces

You **pick up the pieces** when you try to get the situation back to normal again after something bad has happened, leaving everyone shocked and upset: *I just don't want you to get hurt, that's all. And if you do, it'll be me who has to pick up all the pieces.*

pull to 'pieces or tear to 'pieces

Someone **pulls** or **tears you to pieces** when they talk about, or to, you in a destructive

way; someone **pulls** or **tears something** such as your work **to pieces** when they criticize it in a cruel and severe way, or make it seem ridiculous: *Whatever he thinks of me, it doesn't give him the right to tear me to pieces in front of my friends.* □ *The committee considered and systematically pulled to pieces every one of her proposals.*

◇ SEE ALSO **pull to bits** ▷ BITS; **pick holes in** ▷ HOLES; **tear** or **rip to shreds** ▷ SHREDS

to 'pieces

Something falls, or comes, **to pieces** when it breaks, or separates, into several pieces.
◇ SEE ALSO **to bits** ▷ BITS

pig (*see also* **pigs**)

make a 'pig of yourself (*disrespectful*)

A person who **is making a pig of themselves** is being greedy and eating more food than they should: *Alyssia made a pig of herself. Starters, main course of gigot d'agneau, and a glutton's dessert of crème brûlée.*

◇ SEE ALSO **make a beast of yourself** ▷ BEAST

make a pig's 'ear of something

You say that someone **has made a pig's ear of something** if they have done it badly: *I'm afraid I'll have to unpick this sewing and start again. I've made a pig's ear of it.*

◇ SEE ALSO **make a muck of something** ▷ MUCK

pig-in-the-'middle or piggy-in-the-'middle

You say you feel like, or are playing, **pig-in-the-middle** or **piggy-in-the-middle** if you are under a lot of stress because you are the linking person between two people or groups of people who cannot agree: *There'd been so much friction of late, with herself acting as arbiter, conciliator, pig-in-the-middle.*

> **Pig-in-the-middle** is a game in which two people try to throw a ball to each other, and a third person (the 'pig' or 'piggy'), standing in between them, tries to catch the ball as it passes.

a pig in a 'poke

If someone tells you not to buy **a pig in a poke**, they mean that you should be careful to examine something properly before deciding to buy it: *Can you get your money back if the business you buy turns out to be a pig in a poke?*

> In the past, people were occasionally tricked into buying a poke [= a bag] with what they thought was a piglet inside, when in fact it was a cat.

sweat like a 'pig

Someone who **is sweating like a pig** is sweating a lot.

pigeon

not someone's 'pigeon

If a person says that something is **not their pigeon**, they mean that they are not interested in, or involved with, it: *'You weren't concerned about the conditions in which the servants lived?' 'Wasn't my pigeon, old boy. I can't say it worried me.'*

pigeon-'toed

A person or animal that is **pigeon-toed** turns the fronts of their feet inwards when they stand and walk.

pigs

pigs might 'fly

If someone replies **'pigs might fly'**, when you suggest that a certain event is just possible, though unlikely, that person is saying they do not believe it will happen: *'Someone who's not from the area could have been driving through and seen something.' 'Yeah, and pigs might fly.' Kate's voice was bitter.*

pile

make your 'pile

You **make your pile** when you earn a large amount of money: *Mr Cliburn, who was born in Shreveport, Louisiana, into a family that made its pile from oil, has been able to retire to a vast mansion.*

◇ SEE ALSO **make a bomb** ▷ BOMB; **make a bundle** ▷ BUNDLE; **coin it** or **coin it in** ▷ COIN; **make a fortune** ▷ FORTUNE; **make a killing** ▷ KILLING

pile it on 'thick

You say that a person **is piling it on thick** if they are expressing their feelings in such a strong way that you find it difficult to believe and slightly amusing: *Did you see that tribute to Margaret Thatcher on the telly? The guy was piling it on thick, wasn't he?*

piles

'piles of something

Piles of something is a large quantity of it: *I've got piles of work to do before tomorrow.* □ *There's piles of food left over from the party.*

pill

a bitter pill to 'swallow

You say that a fact is **a bitter pill to swallow** for someone if it is something that they do not want to know or believe, but which they have to accept: *To his surprise he found out that his friend had broken the agreement. It was a bit of a blow, a bitter pill to swallow. But I guess that's life!*

pillar

from pillar to 'post

You go, or are sent, **from pillar to post** when you go or are sent from one place to another without receiving the help you need at any one of them: *These migrants were pushed from pillar to post from the moment they left their homes in Europe.*

a pillar of 'such-and-such

You say that someone is **a pillar of** something such as society or the church, if they take part in a lot of useful activities and are greatly respected within it: *The vicar of St Peter's was there as a character witness to prove what a pillar of the community Menzies was.*

pillow

'pillow talk

Pillow talk describes private and frank conversations which take place between a husband and wife or between lovers when they are in bed together: *'Pillow talk!' Paula repeated, stunned. The notion was absurd. Nothing would ever make her give away confidential information.* □ *He decided that maybe later he'd be able to get the information during pillow talk.*

pin (*see also* **pins**)

like a new 'pin

Something such as a house or a room which is **like a new pin** is very clean and tidy.

'pin money

Pin money is a small sum of money which a woman earns, or which her husband gives to her, for items of personal use: *Elizabeth works two days a week in a friend's boutique which she enjoys, as it gives her a little pin money and some independent social contact.*

you could hear a 'pin drop

You say that **you could hear a pin drop** if no-one is making a sound and there is complete silence; you also say that **you could have heard a pin drop** when people are so shocked by something that no-one speaks for a moment: *I still think the great moments in acting are when you could hear a pin drop because you've got them totally captivated in the drama.* □ *Suddenly it was announced that the King had died. You could have heard a pin drop. I can still remember the feeling of intense shock.*

pinch

at a 'pinch or if it comes to the 'pinch

You say that something is possible or acceptable **at a pinch**, or **if it comes to the pinch**, if you consider it to be just possible or acceptable in a situation where there is

no other option: *The bus is full, but we can probably fit one more in at a pinch.*
◇ SEE ALSO **at a push** ▷ PUSH

feel the 'pinch
Someone who **is feeling the pinch** is having problems because of lack of money: *We've had VAT on domestic fuel for a while, but we will only feel the pinch with the first cold winter.*

take something with a pinch of 'salt
You **take something with a pinch of salt** when you do not take it too seriously: *Moira always has had a vivid imagination, you have to take what she says with a pinch of salt.*

pink

in the 'pink or in the pink of 'health
You say that you are **in the pink** or **in the pink of health** if you are very healthy: *You're sure you're all right now? In the pink, ready for action?* □ *Considering that the economy is not in the pink of health, it only makes sense to ask whether the cost will remain affordable.*

pins

for two 'pins
If you say that you would do something **for two pins**, you mean that it would not take much persuasion to make you do it: *For two pins I'd stand for election myself.* □ *Len looked as if for two pins he would cry.*

pins and 'needles
You get **pins and needles** when you feel sharp little pains in a part of your body, usually because the flow of blood is returning to it after being stopped or reduced for a time: *Her head spun and her left arm tingled painfully with pins and needles.*

pip

give someone the 'pip
Something which **gives you the pip** annoys, disgusts or upsets you: *It must give you the pip every time you think about those days.*

pipe *(see also* **piping***)*

a 'pipe dream
An idea or plan that someone has is **a pipe dream** if it is never going to happen or be carried out: *The organization of entire courses using the multi-media facilities of a school-based resource centre is still a pipe dream in most cases.*

put 'that in your pipe and smoke it
After insulting someone, or saying something that you know they are not going to like, you can add **'put that in your pipe and smoke it!'** to tell them rudely that you do

not care how they feel about it: *I'm going to the party whether you like it or not, so put that in your pipe and smoke it!*

pipeline

in the 'pipeline
You say that something is **in the pipeline** when it is being planned or prepared: *There are big changes in the pipeline, but no-one knows quite what they are yet.*

piper

he who pays the piper calls the 'tune
If somone says '**he who pays the piper calls the tune**', they mean that the person who provides the money for something usually has some control over it: *The relationship of artist to the public must be considered. How far should he who pays the piper call the tune?*

piping

piping 'hot
Food or water that is **piping hot** is very hot: *Be careful not to burn your tongue. It's piping hot.*

piss

couldn't organize a piss-up in a 'brewery
If you say that a certain person **couldn't organize a piss-up in a brewery**, you mean that anything which they try to organize always ends in failure: *They're trying to do me for burglary this time. Look at me. I couldn't organize a piss-up in a brewery let alone a burglary.*

'piss artist
A **piss artist** is a person who is often drunk.

'piss-up
A **piss-up** is a party or social gathering where people get drunk: *Let's organize a good old Christmas piss-up this year, shall we?*

take the 'piss
1 You **take the piss** when you make jokes or try to play tricks on someone: *'Did you know Nick's getting married?' 'You're taking the piss.' 'No, I'm serious.'* **2** You **take the piss**, or **take the piss out of something** or **someone** when you make fun of them: *I don't mind him, but he takes the piss out of my accent all the time.*
◇ SEE ALSO **take the mickey** ▷ MICKEY; **make fun of** or **poke fun at** ▷ FUN
a 'piss-take: *'I'm Too Sexy' is a great record, because it's a piss-take of people who fancy themselves sung by people who fancy themselves.*

pissed

pissed as a 'fart or **pissed as a 'newt**
(*informal, may be offensive*)
Someone who is as **pissed as a fart** or as **pissed as a newt** is very drunk.
◇ SEE ALSO **out of your head** ▷ HEAD; **rat-arsed** ▷ RAT

pistol

hold a 'pistol to someone's head

You say that someone **is holding a pistol to your head** if they are forcing you to do what they want, usually by using threats: *I tried to say no, but he was holding a pistol to my head. He said he'd go to the police if I refused.*

pistols

pistols at 'dawn

You talk about **pistols at dawn** when you are referring to a situation which may turn into a fight between two people: *I know it's all revenge and pistols at dawn just now, but he'll have forgiven you by tomorrow.* □ *He spoke the words 'sherry at six' with a hint of menace, rather as if he had said 'pistols at dawn'.*

pit (*see also* **pits**)

a bottomless 'pit

If you describe something as **a bottomless pit**, you mean that it can never be satisfied or exhausted: *But there is no bottomless pit of money, so certain players may end up being sold.*

pitch

queer the 'pitch or **queer someone's 'pitch**
You **queer the pitch** or **queer someone's pitch** if you do something which makes the situation difficult for someone: *Louise was to mind her own business and not queer the pitch.* □ *I know you better than to think you'd try to queer my pitch.*

pitchers

little pitchers have big 'ears

When people say '**little pitchers have big ears**', they mean that you should be careful when you talk in the presence of children, because they often understand more than you expect: *Even a toddler can be embarrassed, so mind what you say and remember, little pitchers have big ears.*

pits

the 'pits (*informal*)

When you say someone's behaviour, or a situation, is **the pits**, you are emphasizing that it is the worst possible behaviour or situation: *Mugging people is bad enough, but mugging defenceless old ladies? That's the pits.* □ *You mean you can't go out for a week? Man, that's the pits.*

pity

for pity's 'sake

For pity's sake is an exclamation which people sometimes use to make a request when the situation is making them so upset or impatient that they feel they cannot deal with it any more: *For pity's sake stop crying, will you?*
◇ SEE ALSO **for Christ's sake** ▷ CHRIST; **for God's sake** ▷ GOD; **for goodness sake** ▷ GOODNESS; **for heaven's sake** ▷ HEAVEN; **for Pete's sake** PETE

more's the 'pity

More's the pity means the same as 'I'm sorry to say', and you usually add it just after stating a fact which makes you unhappy: *They don't make them like him any more. They don't make films like his any more – more's the pity.*

pizza

'pizza face (*disrespectful*)

Pizza face is a name for someone whose face is covered in spots: *Hey pizza-face, what you need is medicated soap.*

place (*see also* **places**)

all 'over the place

1 Something that is **all over the place** is everywhere in the area you are referring to: *Doesn't the au pair do any housework? There were toys all over the place when I got home.* **2** Someone who is **all over the place** is disorganized in the way they behave or think: *I've got to get at least eight hours' sleep, otherwise I'm all over the place the next day.*

fall into 'place

1 Things **fall into place** when you begin to understand a particular situation: *I read the letter again, and then things started to fall into place.* **2** Things **fall into place** when your plans suddenly start to work after a time when things seemed uncertain: *Don't worry. Now that the church and the reception are booked, everything else will fall into place.*

give 'place to (*very formal*)

When one thing **gives place to** another, the first thing is followed and replaced by the second: *Over the past few weeks, her delusions have given place to something altogether more sinister.*

in the 'first place

You use '**in the first place**' and '**in the second place**' to introduce points or reasons in order of importance: *I'm not going home. In the first place it's too far, and anyway I can't afford it.*

in 'place

Something that is **in place** is 1 in the correct position: *Once the bow is in place, secure it with a pin to stop it slipping.* 2 ready or available for using: *All the systems are in place, but we can't start manufacturing without the official go-ahead.*

know your 'place

You say a person **knows their place** if they accept the authority that certain people have over them: *This new money, these upstarts, they don't know their place – they think they can tell me what to do.*

last 'resting-place

A person's **last resting-place** is the place where they are buried when they die: *This cemetery has been in existence since 1965 and is lovingly tended by regular visitors who often bring fresh flowers to mark the last resting place of a faithful friend.*

out of 'place

1 Something that is **out of place** is not in its correct position: *He is always smartly dressed, with never a hair out of place.* 2 A person or thing seems **out of place** if they seem not to belong to their environment: *I must say, I felt a bit out of place in among all those military men and their wives.*

a place in the 'sun

A **place in the sun** is a highly advantageous position: *The leader demanded that the farm worker be given his 'place in the sun', meaning not only better pay and conditions but more recognition.*

put someone in their 'place

You **put someone in their place** when you make them realize that they are not as important as they think they are, or that they cannot do everything they want: *If you don't put that kid in his place soon, he is going to become totally unmanageable.*

put yourself in such-and-such's 'place

1 You **are putting yourself in** a certain person's **place** when you think about how it must feel to be in the situation that they are in: *I know she is acting stupidly, but put yourself in her place. How would you feel?* 2 You say '**in your place**' before giving someone your advice: *Do you know what I would do in your place? I would go to the police and admit everything.*

◇ SEE ALSO **put yourself in such-and-such's shoes** ▷ SHOES

take 'place

Something **takes place** when it happens: *A motorbike scrambling competition is to take place at Westness Farm next Sunday.*

take the 'place of or take someone's 'place

A person or thing that **takes the place of** another person or thing is provided, or does something, instead of them: *There are plenty of people who would be happy to take her place if she got the sack.*

take second 'place

One person or thing has to **take second place** to another if they are treated as less important than the other: *She soon realized she would have to take second place to her mother-in-law in her husband's affections.* □ *It needed considerable refurbishment. And that cost money. Fun would have to take second place to the serious business of home-making and saving money.*

places

'go places

When you say that someone **is going places**, you mean that they are having a lot of success, especially in their job: *She's twenty-four, independent, and with a fairly flourishing career. In fact, she's a girl who's going places.*

plague

avoid like the 'plague

If you **are avoiding** someone or something **like the plague**, you are doing your best not to come into contact with or be involved with that person or thing: *That woman is poison. I'd avoid her like the plague if I were you.* □ *Charles was avoiding marriage like the plague.*

plain

make yourself 'plain

When you **make yourself plain**, you make your meaning clear and easy to understand: *If I find you've been withholding evidence, I'm going to come down on you so hard it'll make your eyes water. Do I make myself plain?*

plain as a 'pikestaff or plain as the nose on your 'face

Something which is as **plain as a pikestaff**, or as **plain as the nose on your face**, is very obvious. *None of us ever knew the whole story, even though it was as plain as a pikestaff when you came to think about it.*

plan

go according to 'plan

When things **go according to plan**, they happen exactly the way you had arranged

plate 257 **please**

or intended: *Everything went pretty much according to plan, although the weather could have been better.*

plate

hand something to someone on a 'plate
Something **is handed to you on a plate** when you have the chance to obtain it easily, without making much effort or doing anything special: *It was a win handed to him on a plate when rivals Prost and Schumacher were forced out of the race.*

on so-and-so's 'plate
The things you have **on your plate** are the things which you must do or attend to: *Now I fear we really must stop corresponding. I just have too much on my plate. Sincerely yours.*

play (*see also* **played**)

come into 'play or be brought into 'play
Something **comes**, or **is brought, into play** when it is introduced into a situation: *It is now that the side reins may be brought into play, encouraging your horse to lower his head.*

fair 'play
Fair play consists of honest behaviour and the absence of cheating between a number of people or groups who are in competition with one another: *I undertook work as a Justice of the Peace because I think I have a highly developed sense of fair play. I like to see the right thing being done.*

foul 'play
1 Foul play consists of dishonest behaviour or cheating between a number of people or groups who are in competition with one another: *The touch judge not only informs the referee of the act of foul play but will also advise the referee on the appropriate course of action.* **2 Foul play** also means 'murder', and is used especially by the police when investigating someone's death: *Gryschenko had been missing for more than two days. Police immediately began an investigation, but foul play was not suspected.*

◇ SEE ALSO **funny business** ▷ BUSINESS; **monkey business** ▷ MONKEY; **sharp practice** ▷ PRACTICE

make a 'play for ·
When you **make a play for** something or someone, you try to get them: *His eyes lingered on Lesley-Jane Decker. 'Who's that? Has Micky made a play for her yet?'*

make 'play of something
You **are making play of something** when you make it seem more important than it actually is, often as a way of getting people's attention: *They have made great play*

of their recent growth in profits. However, these have been due to large-scale redundancies.

play 'fair
Someone **is playing fair** when they behave honestly or do not cheat: *No one who witnessed these debates has ever suggested that Lewis played fair. And when he demolished his victims it was with evident relish.*

play fast and 'loose
You **are playing fast and loose**, or **playing fast and loose with** something or someone if you are doing what you want with them, or not acting in a responsible way with them: *Mr Alton said today: 'I am not prepared to play fast and loose with Britain's future in Europe.'*

play hard to 'get
Someone who **is playing hard to get** is trying to avoid someone else, or to avoid accepting an offer or invitation, often with the purpose of making themselves more desirable or wanted: *When he finally got her on the phone, she only asked him how he was then said she had to rush. She was obviously playing hard to get.* □ *The key to striking a good bargain is never to seem too eager. Play hard to get.*

play it 'cool
You say that someone **is playing it cool** when they deal with a situation or problem in a calm way: *If things go wrong, don't panic. Just play it cool and keep going.*

a play on 'words
A **play on words** is a joke made by playing with language, or a clever saying, based on similarities between words: *The play on words must now be obvious. Not only does it refer to developing in a photographic sense, but to the development of a group of young people.*

play 'safe or play it 'safe
You **are playing safe**, or **playing it safe**, when you take no risks: *Carry cash in a money-belt, and play it safe by leaving your passport at the hotel reception.*

played

played 'out
You say you are **played out** or **all played out** as a way of admitting defeat when you have no more energy or ideas left: *This change of tactics will come as a surprise to those who claimed the rebels were all played out.*

please

if you 'please
1 (*very formal, old*) People say '**if you please**' when asking for someone's attention, or making a request: *At the end of the first*

day Ruth presented herself to Mrs Carson. *'If you please, ma'am?' 'What is it, Ruth?'* □ *I'll take another look upstairs now, if you please, sir.* **2** People also say **'if you please'** when they are describing someone's attitude which they find pretentious or ridiculous: *The brick tower at Grimsby Docks was built by Wild, who modelled it – if you please – on the tower of the town hall in Siena.*

please your'self

You say **'please yourself'** to someone to show that you do not care or mind what they do: *'I don't want to come to the shops.' 'Please yourself. But I may be gone all day.'*

pleased

pleased as 'Punch

Someone who is as **pleased as Punch** is very happy or pleased.

◇ SEE ALSO **happy as a sandboy** ▷ HAPPY

> In Punch and Judy puppet shows, Punch (or Mr Punch) always seems to be pleased and excited, especially when he is doing something cruel to the other characters.

pleasure

have had the 'pleasure (*formal*)

You say that you **have had the pleasure** when you have met a certain person before: *'Mr Guest, have you met Miss Tulliver before?' 'I don't believe I have ever had the pleasure.'*

my 'pleasure or it's a 'pleasure

If you reply to an expression of thanks with the words **'my pleasure'**, or **'it's a pleasure'**, it means the same as 'you're welcome', 'not at all' or 'it's no trouble': *'Thank you for bringing her home safely.' 'My pleasure.'*

take 'pleasure in

Someone who **takes pleasure in** something enjoys it, especially when doing it gives them unfair power over others: *It's almost as if he takes pleasure in upsetting me.* □ *He seems to take pleasure in firing people.*

with 'pleasure (*formal*)

If you reply to a request or invitation by saying **'with pleasure'**, it means the same as 'willingly' or 'of course': *'Will you accept an invitation to dinner?' 'With pleasure.'*

plot

the plot 'thickens

You say **'the plot thickens'**, often in a humorous way, to show that the strange combination of recent events makes you suspect that something strange or mysterious is going on: *'The night I noticed my spectacles were missing, I found this note in*

my pocket.' 'Hmm. The plot thickens. What does it say?'

plug

pull the 'plug on something

You **pull the plug on something** when you suddenly make it impossible for that thing to continue or succeed: *The project was almost finished when the Government pulled the plug on it by withdrawing funding.*

plughole

down the 'plughole

Something, usually a plan or an organization, which goes **down the plughole** fails completely and ceases to exist: *'Bars all over the world acquired a fair percentage of my money,' Jimmy regrets. 'And the rest went down the plughole with various business ventures.'*

◇ SEE ALSO **down the drain** ▷ DRAIN; **down the pan** ▷ PAN; **down the toilet** ▷ TOILET; **down the tubes** ▷ TUBES

plum

have a 'plum in your mouth

If you say that someone **has a plum in their mouth**, you mean that they have a particular type of English accent and a way of talking which sounds as if they had a small, round object in their mouth, typical of the British upper class: *Daughters of good houses they were, still with a plum in their mouths. 'Tell me,' he'd said to the first. 'What made you give up your privileged life?'*

plumb

plumb the 'depths of something

If you say that someone or something **plumbs the depths of something** such as an unpleasant feeling or bad behaviour, you mean that they reach the lowest point of that feeling or behaviour: *All in the course of one day, I tasted glory, and then plumbed the depths of de'spair.*

plumb in the 'middle

When a certain thing is **plumb in the middle** of something, it is exactly in the middle of it: *It had to be worth a photo; a huge frog, sitting plumb in the middle of the lily pad.*

plunge

take the 'plunge

When you **take the plunge**, you decide to do something that is difficult, especially after stopping to think about it for some time: *'I am very pleased I finally took the plunge and started my own business,' he said.*

pocket

in 'pocket

You say you are **in pocket** if you have gained money as a result of something such as a business deal: *I was extremely lucky with the house sale, and ended up about ten thousand pounds in pocket.*

have someone in your 'pocket

If you **have someone in your pocket**, you have complete power or influence over them and you can make them do what you want: *During the years of the 'special relationship', critics claim Thatcher had Reagan in her pocket.*

◇ SEE ALSO **have someone wrapped round your little finger** ▷ FINGER; **have someone eating out of your hand** ▷ HAND; **have someone right where you want them** ▷ WANT; **have someone in the palm of your hand** or **eating out of the palm of your hand** ▷ PALM

out of 'pocket

You say you are **out of pocket** if you have lost money as a result of something, especially when you consider the situation to be unfair in some way: *If he stays in the house, he'll have to pay for the electricity. I don't want to end up out of pocket.*

pick someone's 'pocket

If someone **picks your pocket**, they steal something from the pocket of the clothes you are wearing: *A number of my friends have had their pockets picked on the Paris Metro.*

'pick-pocket: *Beware of pick-pockets operating in this area.*

pockets

be in each other's 'pockets

If you say that two people **are in each other's pockets**, you mean that they are together too much: *I know they're best friends, but it doesn't mean they have to live in each other's pockets, does it?*

line your 'pockets or line someone's 'pockets

Someone who is **lining their pockets** is making money dishonestly from their job; you **line someone's pockets** when the money you spend goes to someone dishonest, who is not providing the service you would expect: *It makes me mad to think of a man like him, lining his pockets from people's pension payments.* □ *They would do better to collaborate with the council to ensure the scheme's success, rather than lining the pockets of these so-called consultants.*

◇ SEE ALSO **feather your own nest** ▷ NEST

point (*see also* **points**)

beside the 'point

Something that someone says during a discussion is **beside the point** if it does not bear much or any relation to the main subject being discussed: *Whether he did it or not is beside the point. My question is, who is going to pay for the damage?*

at 'breaking point

Someone or something is **at breaking point** if they have reached a state in which they cannot bear something any longer: *By 1956, East-West tensions had reached breaking point.* □ *He was pale and his voice trembled as though he was at breaking point.*

An object is **at breaking point** when so much pressure is being applied to it that it breaks.

come to the 'point or get to the 'point

1 You **come**, or **get**, **to the point** of what you are saying when, following some introductory remarks, you finally make the comment or statement which is the main part of your message: *Could you stop wasting time and get to the point, please?* **2** If you say that someone is not able to do something when it **comes**, or **gets**, **to the point**, you mean that they cannot do it when the right time comes: *He had spent days rehearsing what he would say, but when it came to the point, he couldn't tell her.*

in point of 'fact (*formal*)

You use the phrase **in point of fact** to emphasize the truth or accuracy of what you are reporting, or to correct somebody when you think they have got the wrong idea about something: *Despite being branded a Eurosceptic, I am, in point of fact, more pro-European than my colleagues.*

◇ SEE ALSO **in actual fact** ▷ FACT; **as a matter of fact** ▷ MATTER

I take your 'point (*rather formal*) or point 'taken

If you say '**I take your point**', or '**point taken**' to someone you are discussing something with, you mean that you accept the fairness and truth of what they are saying: *I take your point Mr Blair, but surely you agree that a minimum wage will mean fewer jobs?* □ *'The problems experienced in the past won't recur.' 'Point taken, but are there no lessons to be learned?'*

make a 'point of or make it a 'point to

You **make a point of** doing something, or **make it a point to** do something, when you make a special effort to do it: *That woman is very kind. She made a special point of coming over to offer me her sympathy.* □ *You can rely on me. I shall make it a point to visit her regularly.*

make your 'point

You **have made your point** when you have clearly stated an opinion, or have done something that clearly shows what you think about something: *I will be quiet, but not until I have made my point.* □ *Okay, you've made your point. There's no need to go on about it.* □ *A public relations executive drove over the feet of a man wearing the boots. He certainly made his point!*

not to put too fine a 'point on it

You say '**not to put too fine a point on it**' to show someone that you are speaking honestly, and without trying to avoid shocking or upsetting the listener: *'Not to put too fine a point on it, your Emily is a liar,' said Chase.*

on the 'point of

You are **on the point of** doing something when you are just going to do it: *I was on the point of apologizing when she started insulting me again.*

the point of no re'turn

You reach **the point of no return** in some activity when you have to continue with it because it is too late to stop or give up: *Having reached the point of no return, the Government had no choice but to support the decision.*

point of 'view

Your **point of view** is your particular opinion or way of looking at something, based on your own experience or feelings: *I can appreciate your point of view, but the fact remains that squatters are acting illegally.*

score a 'point against someone

In a competitive situation, you try to **score a point against another person** when you attack them with a small or unimportant detail in the hope of establishing your own position of power, or impressing the other people who are present: *I can discuss things constructively with women, but men are always out to score a point against you.*
◇ SEE ALSO **score points** ▷ POINTS

a sore 'point

Something that is **a sore point** with someone is a subject which you should not raise when they are present, because, as a result of arguments they have had or criticism they have received about it in the past, they get easily upset or angry when people mention it: *It is still a sore point with both grandparents that neither Alice nor Henry have been baptized.*

stretch a 'point

You **are stretching a point** if you decide, as a special exception, to allow something which is not normally allowed: *We normal-*

ly prefer to have at least two weeks' notice, but I think we can stretch a point in this case.

someone's 'strong point

A person's **strong point** is a particular good quality that they have: *Woodwork was not his strong point. He found it impossible to hammer a nail in straight.*

to the 'point

Something such as a statement or a question that is **to the point** contains only the details which are useful and important: *A good interviewer will ask questions which are brief and to the point.* □ *Where is he, and more to the point, who is he?*

to the point of 'such-and-such

You talk about a person or thing being or doing something **to the point of** a certain state if you want to emphasize the extreme nature of the state which has been reached: *She drove me to the point of distraction with her constant questions.*

up to a 'point

Something that is the case **up to a point** is partly the case: *I certainly agree with socialist doctrine up to a point, but I would never call myself a communist.* □ *We can blame the crisis on negligence up to a point, but other factors do play a part.*

what's the 'point?

You say '**what's the point?**' when you believe that the action which you are considering is not worth doing, as it cannot have a useful result: *'You should write to your MP.' 'What's the point? He's already aware of the problem.'* □ *What's the point of worrying? You've sat your exams and you can't change the results now.*

when it comes to the 'point

You say '**when it comes to the point**' when you are inviting the person you are speaking with to think again about the thing you are discussing: *When it comes to the point, one of the clearest rights of a Prime Minister is that of choosing the date of an election.*

points

score 'points

In a competitive situation, you try to **score points**, or **score points off** another person, when you attack them with small or unimportant details in the hope of establishing your own position of power, or impressing the other people who are present: *Prime Minister's Question Time is dominated by MPs determined to score points off one another.*

◇ SEE ALSO **score a point against someone** ▷ POINT

poison

poison-'pen letter

A **poison-pen letter** is an unpleasant letter, sent by someone who keeps their name a secret, with the purpose of upsetting the person who receives it: *Most poison-pen letters can give rise to charges under the provisions of the Post Office Act 1953 or the Malicious Communication Act 1988.* □ *Roseanne Arnold has been sending poison-pen faxes to critics who criticized her husband Tom's new TV show.*

what's your 'poison? (*rather old*)

If someone says '**what's your poison?**', they are offering you a drink: *Frank, get Mr Newman a drink. What's your poison?*

poke

better than a poke in the 'eye

If you say that something is **better than a poke in the eye**, you mean, humorously, that it is better than nothing: *'I don't like it.' 'Well, it's better than a poke in the eye, so stop moaning.'*

◇ SEE ALSO **better than a kick up the arse** ▷ KICK

poker

poker 'face

You say that someone has a **poker face** if their facial expression never changes according to the emotions that they are feeling: *While the adoption of the inscrutable poker face has a role to play, the negotiator's chief weapon is sheer niceness.*

poker-'faced: *If you are with a group and everyone is laughing, it might spoil things if you remained tight-lipped and poker-faced.*

A poker player must learn the skill of showing no emotion during the game, as this can give the other players an idea of what cards he or she has.

pole

'pole position

Someone or something that is in **pole position** is in a position of advantage: *Elise, tall, red-haired and elegant, occupied pole position on the centre-page shot.* □ *The Portuguese escudo joined the European exchange rate mechanism on Friday and yesterday shot to pole position.*

up the 'pole

If you say that a person is **up the pole**, you mean that they are mad; you say that someone or something is driving you **up the pole** if they are annoying you very much: *I have had several letters saying that I am up the pole in carrying on about the*

method of charging recently mentioned in this column. □ *Taxes can be enough to drive you up the pole.*

poles

'poles apart

If you say that people or their opinions are **poles apart**, you mean that they are as different or as far apart as is possible: *We get on well together, but we have always been poles apart in matters of taste.*

◇ SEE ALSO **worlds apart** ▷ WORLDS

poor

like the 'poor

Something, especially a problem, which has always been present is sometimes described as being **like the poor**: *Like the poor themselves, the inner city has long been with us.*

poor as a church 'mouse

Someone who is as **poor as a church mouse** is very poor: *They'll take one look at my clothes and know I'm as poor as a church mouse.*

pops

be top of the 'pops

You say that someone or something **is top of the pops** if they are more popular and successful than anyone or anything else of their kind at that time: *Kingsley Amis seems to be top of the pops with English and American customers at the moment.*

porkies

tell 'porkies (*informal*)

You say that someone **is telling porkies** if they are telling lies: *She began telling us how rainbows were all an illusion caused by sunlight and raindrops. I told her she was telling porkies.*

◇ SEE ALSO **feed** or **shoot someone a line** ▷ LINE

Porkies is short for 'pork pies', which is Cockney rhyming slang for 'lies'.

port

any port in a 'storm

If someone says '**any port in a storm**', they mean that, if you are having difficulties, you must be prepared to accept any possible solution or help which is available: *I'll be changing doctors anyhow. I don't like that woman. It was just, you know, any port in a storm.*

pose

strike a 'pose

If you **strike a pose**, you take up a particular position which you hope will make people notice you or admire your body: *She struck a dramatic pose and waited for the click of the camera.*

position

in a po'sition to
If you say that someone is **in a position to** do something, you mean that they are able to do it: *Now that we've both got a job, we are probably in a position to consider buying a house.*

in no po'sition to
If you say that someone is **in no position to** do something, you mean that they are not able to do it, or have no right to do it: *We hardly have enough money to keep ourselves, and we're certainly in no position to have a baby.* □ *Until you stand where she is standing now you are in no position to pass any judgement on her attitudes.*

jockey for po'sition
When a number of people or organizations **are jockeying for position**, each one is trying to push their way into an advantageous position: *The knowledge that a general election was imminent saw all political parties jockeying for position during 1990.*

possessed

what pos'sessed so-and-so?
When you ask **what possessed someone** to do a certain bad or stupid thing, you are saying that you cannot understand why they did that thing: *Whatever possessed you to say that?*

possession

possession is nine tenths of the 'law or possession is nine points of the 'law
If someone says '**possession is nine tenths of the law**', or '**possession is nine points of the law**', they mean that, if there is a disagreement about who is the real owner of something, the person who has it at the time is in the strongest position: *Working on the principle that possession was nine tenths of the law, I made a bass in the woodwork shop at school, 'borrowing' the materials from a local carpenter's yard.*

possum

play 'possum
A person who **is playing possum** is pretending to be unavailable, to know nothing, or to have no interest in something, in order to protect themselves: *Hold 'em under your tongue and play possum.*

post

pip someone at the 'post
You **pip someone at the post** when you move ahead and beat them in the last stages of a competition; you **are pipped at the post** when you are beaten in this way: *She plans to launch her own designer clothes label but that is one area where her younger sister has pipped her at the post.* □ *And commiserations to our runner-up, who was just pipped at the post in the last round.*

In horse-racing, the horse that passes the winning-post first wins the race. In the past, the word 'pipped' meant 'defeated', and came from a system of voting in which votes were made by placing either a white ball (for) or a black ball (against) inside a box. The image of the pip comes from the black ball.

posted

keep someone 'posted
If you **keep someone posted**, you keep them informed about a situation by giving them the latest news or details of any developments: *Just to let you know, there is about to be a bit of a reshuffle in the department. Anyway, I'll keep you posted.*

pot

go to 'pot
If you say that something or someone **has gone to pot**, you mean that they have got into a bad state or been spoilt: *That used to be the best farm in the county, but since he started drinking, he's let it all go to pot.*

To **go to pot** originally meant 'to be made into a stew'.

a 'pot-boiler *(disrespectful)*
You say that a book or other artistic work is **a pot-boiler** if it has been produced with no other purpose than to make money: *This is a US pot-boiler set in the Old West of Oregon.*

the pot calling the kettle 'black
If someone criticizes you for some fault or bad characteristic which they also possess, you say it is a case of **the pot calling the kettle black**: *Both partners in the marriage consistently blame the other in the fights which ensue, the pot calls the kettle black.*

In the past, when cooking was done over a fire, pots, kettles and everything else which hung over the fire all got as black as one another.

take pot 'luck
You **are taking pot luck** when you choose something from among a group of similar

things without making a careful decision or worrying about getting the best one: *On the odd occasion when I bet on horses, I never bother with the racing tips. I just take pot luck.*

> To **take pot luck,** in its original sense, means 'to accept whatever is served to you from the cooking pot'.

take a 'pot-shot at something

You say that someone **takes a pot-shot at something** if they shoot at it in a relaxed way, not really caring if they hit it or not: *That old Willie, give him a gun and he'll take a pot-shot at anything.*

> Originally, this term was used in a rather disrespectful way to refer to the lack of skill of people who shot birds and animals for food, as opposed to the skill of people who shot for sport.

a tin-'pot such-and-such

You talk about **a tin-pot** person or organization when you consider them to be small and unimportant, although they may consider themselves to be the opposite: *a tin-pot dictatorship.*

a watched pot never 'boils

If you say '**a watched pot never boils**' to someone who is waiting anxiously for something, you mean that the more they think about that thing, the longer it will seem to take: *Go and do something else to occupy yourself – a watched pot ...*

> This expression is often shortened to '**a watched pot**' as in the example.

potato

a hot po'tato

A hot potato is a subject, or occasionally a person, that is difficult and dangerous to deal with: *The biggest political hot potato is the decision to put VAT on domestic fuel bills. □ The subject was dropped like a hot potato when they realized the amount of money involved.*

> If you try to hold a hot potato, you will burn your hands.

potatoes

small po'tatoes

If you call people or things **small potatoes**, you mean that they are small and unimportant: *Her business was very small potatoes beside his empire.*

pound

get your pound of 'flesh or have your pound of 'flesh

You say that someone **has got,** or **has had, their pound of flesh** if they have finally obtained something which is rightfully theirs, especially if this causes difficulties or unhappiness for another person: *The rail workers, determined to get their pound of flesh, have turned down the six per cent pay rise.*

> In Shakespeare's *The Merchant of Venice,* Shylock insists that Antonio give him a pound of his own flesh in exchange for a debt which he cannot repay, according to the terms of an agreement which they made earlier in the play.

powder

keep your 'powder dry

Someone who **is keeping their powder dry** has decided not to take immediate action, because they want to see how the situation will develop first: *Conservative critics decided to draw back from voting down the whole Budget, keeping their powder dry for future votes when the issue comes before the Commons in detail.*

> If gunpowder gets wet, it can no longer be used.

power

do someone a power of 'good

Something such as a drink or a holiday **does you a power of good** if you feel much better after it: *I'm sure that a few days away from the office will do him a power of good.*

more power to so-and-so's 'elbow

If you say '**more power to** a certain person's **elbow**', you mean that you wish them good luck: *If she could earn a few more pounds and give everyone a bit of fun, then more power to her elbow.*

the power behind the 'throne

You call someone **the power behind the throne** if they are the person who really runs an organization, while giving the impression that someone else is in charge: *Their patchwork assembly of troops were preparing to take on the real power behind the throne, the sinister drug baron who was using the organization as a front.*

powers

the powers that 'be

The powers that be are the people who have control or authority, for example the government of a country or the management of a business: *Research funding bodies are* *largely under the control of the powers that be in the medical profession.* □ *The product was deemed 'obscene' by the powers that be.*

practice

in 'practice
1 What happens **in practice** is what happens in reality, as opposed to what ought to happen in theory, or according to the rules: *While the system works in theory, in practice there are a number of other factors to be considered.* **2** If you keep **in practice**, you spend a lot of time practising an activity so that you maintain a certain level of skill at it: *I should play at least three games a week if I want to be in practice for the tournament this summer.*

make a 'practice of
You say that you **make a practice of** doing something if you do it often: *I don't make a practice of doing this, but, well, would you like to go for a drink tonight?*

out of 'practice
If you are **out of practice**, you cannot do an activity as well as you used to because you have not spent time practising it: *I used to be so good at this. But I'm a bit out of practice now, as you can see.*

practice makes 'perfect
If someone says 'practice makes perfect', they mean that the only way to develop a particular skill is by practising it: *Writing articles is a game, another area where practice makes perfect. The skills come through doing it again and again.*

put something into 'practice
You **are putting something** such as ideas or knowledge **into practice** when you use them to guide your actions in a real situation: *Now was the moment to put what she had learned into practice.* □ *The Council has promised to reduce city centre traffic. When will they put this into practice?*

sharp 'practice
If a person or business regularly cheats the people they deal with, you say that they are using **sharp practice**: *Any kind of sharp practice or dishonest dealing will ruin his career.*

◇ SEE ALSO **funny business** ▷ BUSINESS; **monkey business** ▷ MONKEY; **foul play** ▷ PLAY

practise

practise what you 'preach
If you **practise what you preach**, you never give advice to other people without following that advice yourself: *Practise what you preach: after all there's no logic in you telling her not to hit people if that's exactly what you're doing by smacking the child.*

praise

damn someone with faint 'praise
If you **damn someone with faint praise**, you say nothing particularly bad about them, but you express your disapproval by praising them in an unenthusiastic or insincere way: *He says she's a perfectly competent teacher ... Sounds a bit like he's damning her with faint praise.*

praises

sing the 'praises of
If you **sing the praises of** someone or something, you praise them enthusiastically: *I think I might try this new stain remover. My mum's always singing its praises.* □ *He never stopped singing her praises. I get the impression he takes far more than a professional interest in Alice.*

preach

preach to the 'converted
Someone who **is preaching to the converted** is wasting time and energy by speaking in a persuasive way to people who already agree with the things they are saying: *You've got to convince everybody. You're preaching to the converted in us – you've got to get at everyone else.*

precious

precious 'few
Precious few means 'not many': *There are precious few beautiful places left in Europe which are still unspoilt by tourism.*

precious 'little
Precious little means 'not much': *Unfortunately, there is precious little evidence that the government is trying to understand the protestors.*

prejudice

without 'prejudice to something
You do something **without prejudice to something**, for example someone's rights or position, when your actions do not affect or harm that thing: *The two countries could work together, on an equal and principled basis, without prejudice to the interests of other countries.*

premium

at a 'premium
Something is **at a premium** if it is much more valuable or expensive than usual because there is very little of it, or not enough of it: *Petrol could be obtained, all be it at a premium, throughout the crisis.* □ *Time is at a premium, so the quicker we get this job done the better.*

prepared

be pre'pared to

You **are prepared to** do something if you are willing to do it: *Of course I'll support you, but I'm not prepared to tell lies for you.*

presence

presence of 'mind

You have the **presence of mind** to do something when you do something sensible, or act quickly and sensibly in a difficult situation: *Mr Gair, 56, an airline pilot, said it was his grandson's presence of mind that saved Michael.* □ *Somehow I managed to have the presence of mind to photograph her going into the house.*

present

for the 'present

Conditions that exist **for the present** exist now, but are likely to change: *We'll leave things as they are for the present, but the rent will probably go up in the autumn.*

press

bad 'press

Someone or something gets a **bad press** when they are publicly criticized: *Personal pensions, despite the bad press they have received of late, are a good way to provide for your retirement.* □ *Divorced people, and therefore single parents, have had a bad press lately.*

good 'press

Someone or something gets a **good press** when they are publicly praised: *'Democracy', rule by the people, did not always have the good press it enjoys today.*

pressed

hard 'pressed

You say you would be **hard pressed** to do something if you would find it difficult or impossible to do: *'Well?' she demanded, hard pressed to conceal her anxiety as he put the phone down.*

'pressed for something

You **are pressed for something** such as time or money if you do not have enough of it: *It's good to see you, but I'm a bit pressed for time just now. Can we meet for coffee tomorrow?* □ *I'd buy it for you, but I'm pressed for cash at the moment.*

pressure

bring 'pressure to bear

You **bring pressure to bear** when you try to persuade someone to do what you want in a forceful way: *Workers have their own organizations which can bring pressure to bear on governments and make demands on the state.*

'pressure group

A **pressure group** is a number of people who join together to influence public opinion and government decisions in relation to a certain political matter: *environmental pressure groups such as Greenpeace and Friends of the Earth.*

pretences

under false pre'tences

You are doing something **under false pretences** if you have told lies, or allowed people to believe something which is not the case, in order to do it: *Is it morally permissible for a social scientist to get information through false pretences?*

pretty

pretty as a 'picture

Someone or something that is as **pretty as a picture** is very pretty.

pretty 'much (*informal*) or **pretty 'well** (*informal*) or **pretty 'nearly** (*informal*)

Pretty much, pretty well and **pretty nearly** all mean 'almost': *I think everything's under control now ... or pretty much, anyway.* □ *When we got there, it was past midnight and the party was pretty well over.* □ *'Have you finished yet?' 'Pretty nearly.'*

prevention

prevention is better than 'cure

If someone says '**prevention is better than cure**', they mean that, if you act immediately to prevent something bad from happening rather than trying to cure it after it has happened, you will probably save yourself a lot of time, energy, or money: *The message that prevention is better than cure applies just as much to dental problems as it applies to other health matters.*

prey

fall 'prey to or be 'prey to

If you **fall**, or **are**, **prey to** something or someone, you put yourself in a position where they harm or destroy you: *He said he suspected the birds had fallen prey to the same disease which hit the colony before.* □ *Police have warned old people to be on the alert after a woman fell prey to an intruder posing as a council worker.*

The **prey** of an animal which hunts for food are the creatures it kills and eats.

price

the 'asking price

The **asking price** of an item that is for sale is the price that the seller says they want for it: *It's been sold. It seems someone's offered* *more than the asking price and they've accepted it.*

at a 'price

1 Something which can be obtained **at a price** is very expensive: *The breast meat of the Muscovy duck comes at a price, but it is well worth the extra you pay.* 2 You achieve something **at a price** if you suffer while, or as a result of, achieving it: *Success in business often comes at a personal price, and family life often suffers as a result.*

at 'any price

A person who wants or demands something **at any price** is so determined to get it that they ignore the problems or the expense involved: *This man is out to win, and he'll do it at any price.* □ *I don't care how you do it, but I want that man captured and brought here alive, at any price.*

◇ SEE ALSO **by fair means or foul** ▷ MEANS; **stop at nothing** ▷ STOP

at what 'price?

You ask **at what price** some success has been achieved if you are afraid that it may have bad results in the future: *The Government has succeeded in authorizing the nuclear reprocessing plant, but at what price?*

beyond 'price

You say that something is **beyond price** if you consider that it has more value than anything that you could buy: *We had forty-eight days together in which he was serene, happy and free from pain, which I regard as beyond price.*

'cheap at the price or **cheap at 'half the price**

You say that something is **cheap at the price**, or **cheap at half the price**, if you think that it is not expensive, considering its quality: *A punnet of strawberries, madam? Cheap at the price of £1.25.* □ *I'll tell you, this is a quality car. It's a bargain, cheap at half the price.*

have a 'price on your head

If someone **has a price on their head**, a reward has been offered for the person who can catch or kill them: *The price on his head is high – higher than ever, currently at a cool three million dollars – and the hit squads are alert and patient.*

pay the 'price for something

You **are paying the price for something** such as a mistake or a crime if you are suffering or being punished for it; you **have paid the price for it** when you have been punished enough: *She didn't do much work at school, and she's paying the price now.* □ *I'll only play when I'm a hundred per cent better. I came back too quickly last time and paid the price.*

put a 'price on something

You **are putting a price on something** when you guess how much it is worth in money: *It certainly is a beautiful painting, but I wouldn't like to put a price on it.*

what price 'such-and-such?

1 You say **'what price** a certain thing?' to show that you think the person you are speaking about has forgotten the good values which used to be important to them: *You invest your extra cash in cigarette companies? What price ethics, then?* 2 You say **'what price** a certain thing?' when you are expressing an idea or a possibility and asking what someone thinks of it: *What price a back-to-back victory for Nick Price?*

This expression in its base sense means 'what price would you be willing to give if you were buying, or betting on, the thing in question?'

pricks

kick against the 'pricks

Someone who **is kicking against the pricks** is opposing, or protesting against, the people who are in control or who have power: *'Rebel Without a Cause', an exploitive title for a young actor who kicked against the pricks.*

When a person is making a cow move forward by poking it with a sharp stick, the cow may get angry and start kicking against the pricks, instead of obeying them.

pride

pride and 'joy

Your **pride and joy** is a person or thing that you are proud of and that is valuable to you: *The garden was my father's pride and joy, the real expression of his creativity.* □ *This car was his pride and joy – a Mark Ford Escort which he'd lovingly restored.*

◇ SEE ALSO **the apple of someone's eye** ▷ APPLE; **blue-eyed boy** ▷ BOY

pride comes before a 'fall or **pride goes before a 'fall**

If someone says **'pride comes before a fall'**, they are warning that a person who is too sure of themselves is likely to have some kind of failure or accident: *'She's convinced she's going to win.' 'I hate to say it, but pride often comes before a fall, you know.'*

the 'pride of something

The pride of something, usually a place, is the best and most famous thing that you can find there, or that comes from there: *The rose garden is the pride of the village,* *and in the summer people come from miles around to see it.* □ *Whisky, the pride of Scotland, is exported to every country in the world.*

pride of 'place

You give **pride of place** to something when the way you treat it shows that it is the most important thing in a group or collection: *But pride of place among their unique collection goes to the magnificent silver swan, which graces the entrance hall.*

swallow your 'pride

You **swallow your pride** when you do something which you know you must do, but that makes you feel ashamed: *If you're not very good at this sort of thing, swallow your pride and get somebody in to do it for you.*

take 'pride in something

1 You **take pride in something** if you are proud of it: *A bachelor friend of mine takes great pride in culinary art, which leaves him never short of admiring girlfriends.* **2** You **take pride in** doing something if you are always careful to work hard on it and do it as well as you can: *These are people who want no more than to earn an honest living and take pride in bringing up their families.*

prime

be cut off in your 'prime

1 A person **is cut off in their prime** if they die when they are still young, or during the most successful period of their life: *It's a tragedy that such a talented young man should be cut off in his prime.* **2** You can also say a person **has been cut off in their prime** if they have been stopped while they were in the middle of doing something with great enthusiasm or success: *Please keep an eye on the time – I don't want to have to cut anyone off in their prime, but I can't let you go over ten minutes.*

primrose

the primrose 'path

When people talk about **the primrose path**, they are referring to a way of life which is pleasant and easy, but which will eventually lead to destruction or some form of punishment from God: *We can't have you, of all people, sliding down the primrose path to the everlasting bonfire.*

In Shakespeare's *Macbeth*, II ii, the porter speaks of people who 'go the primrose way to the everlasting bonfire', meaning those who are on their way to hell.

principle

in 'principle

You agree with something **in principle** if you agree with it in general but not with all of its details: *I agree with the idea in principle, but I don't think it will be very easy to apply.*

on 'principle

You do something **on principle** if you have a particular religious or moral belief which causes you to do that thing: *I never eat veal on principle.*

print

in 'print

1 A book is **in print** if it is available from a publisher: *I'll order it for you, sir, if it's still in print.* **2** A speech or opinion is **in print** if it is published in an article, book or newspaper: *As an academic, he has produced a vast number of papers, most of which are in print.*

out of 'print

A book is **out of print** if it is no longer available from a publisher: *Specialized books of this type go out of print very quickly.*

the small 'print

The small print in a document are the sections of writing in small letters, where important information is given without being easily noticed: *More common is the seller who relies on his buyer not bothering to read (or not understanding) the small print.*

priorities

get your pri'orities right

You **get your priorities right** when you deal with things in the correct order, according to how important they are: *We need to get our priorities right. It is the villains we should be locking up.*

prisoner

take someone 'prisoner

You **take someone prisoner** when you catch them and make them your prisoner: *He tells the painful story of how rebel forces took him prisoner and brutally tortured him.*

private

in 'private

You do something **in private** if you do it secretly, or without other people there: *Could I see you in private for a moment please?*

probability

in all proba'bility

If you say that, **in all probability**, something is the case or is going to happen, you mean that it is likely to be the case or to happen: *In all probability, the Government will try to lower taxes again before the next election.* □ *The prisoners are, in all probability, still in hiding, somewhere on the Isle of Wight.*

probation

on pro'bation

1 A criminal is **on probation** if he or she is being allowed to stay out of prison, on condition that they behave well and go to regular meetings with a probation officer: *The Government is launching a scheme which will test electronic tagging of prisoners on probation.* **2** A new employee is **on probation** during the first few months of a new job if the employer is observing them during this period to check that they can do the job properly, and is able to dismiss them if this is not the case: *I'm on probation for the first two months, but it's a permanent job if they keep me on.*

problem

no 'problem (*informal*)

1 You say something is **no problem** if you can do it easily: *'Can you lend me your computer for a couple of days?' 'Yeah, no problem.'* **2** You say something was **no problem** as a way of accepting a person's thanks for doing it: *'How much do I owe you?' 'It was no problem, honestly. Buy me a drink sometime.'*

◇ SEE ALSO **no bother** ▷ BOTHER; **no hassle** ▷ HASSLE; **no probs** ▷ PROBS

what's your 'problem?

When you ask someone **'what's your problem?'** you are saying rudely that you think they are behaving in a way which is unreasonable: *Erlich did not understand the hostility of this man. 'What's your problem?' 'My problem? By Christ, I'll tell you what my problem is.'*

probs

no 'probs (*very informal*)

You say **'no probs'** to tell someone you are willing to do something for them, or as a way of accepting a person's thanks for something you have already done: *'Can you come in and work this afternoon?' 'Yeah, no probs.'* □ *'That's really very good of you. Thanks.' 'No probs, mate.'*

◇ SEE ALSO **no bother** ▷ BOTHER; **no hassle** ▷ HASSLE; **no problem** ▷ PROBLEM

process

in the 'process

1 If you are doing something, and you do something else **in the process**, you do the second thing while doing the first: *I've just*

been eating spaghetti, and somehow I managed to get sauce down my front in the process.* **2** You are **in the process** of doing something when you are still doing it: *Most of the house is finished, but I'm still in the process of decorating my bedroom.*

profession

the oldest pro'fession in the world or the oldest pro'fession

If people talk about **the oldest profession in the world**, or **the oldest profession**, they mean prostitution: *The 'oldest profession' probably didn't come into being until man had started settling into agricultural communities around 15,000 BC.*

profile

keep a low 'profile

You **are keeping a low profile** when you are behaving in such a way that people do not notice you: *Jackson, who has been keeping a low profile since the scandal, has just brought out a new single.* □ *He seems to have been keeping rather a low profile in political debates recently.*

progress

in 'progress

Something such as a meeting is **in progress** when it is taking place: *Could I ask you to write me a report of work in progress?* □ *Silence. Examinations in progress.*

proof

living 'proof of something

Someone or something is **living proof of** a particular theory if their existence, or the state they are in, gives support to, or proves, that theory: *Oprah is living proof of the diet's effectiveness.* □ *Fairport Convention – living proof that middle-age doesn't mean you're past it.*

the proof of the pudding is in the 'eating or the proof of the 'pudding

If someone says **'the proof of the pudding is in the eating'**, or **'the proof of the pudding'**, they mean that, even if something seems to be good, you can only judge how good it really is when you see how it performs: *Arguments of this kind are easy to invent, but difficult to settle. In the end, the proof of the pudding will be in the eating.* □ *Perhaps the proof of the pudding can be seen in public attitudes, for no such projects can succeed without support from the public.*

The only way of testing whether a pudding is as delicious as it looks is to taste it.

prophet

a prophet of 'doom
If you call someone **a prophet of doom**, you are saying, in a humorous way, that they have a negative attitude towards things, and that they always expect every situation to turn out badly: *It would be easy to be a prophet of doom and gloom in these difficult times but, in business, I sense a new spirit of optimism that better times are just around the corner.*

proportion

in pro'portion
1 Something is **in proportion** if the relationship between its separate parts is correct: *The model ship was skilfully made, with every detail in perfect proportion.* **2** One thing is small or large **in proportion to** another if it is small or large in relation to the second thing: *I hated my nose when I was a teenager. It seemed huge in proportion to the rest of my face.* **3** One thing grows **in proportion to** another if it grows at the same rate as the second thing: *The satisfaction you get from a hobby grows in proportion to the amount of effort you put in.*

out of pro'portion
You are letting things get **out of proportion** if you spend more time thinking or worrying about them than is necessary; one thing is **out of all proportion to** another if it seems larger, more important, or more serious than it needs to be, when you consider it in relation to the second thing: *I know money is important, but don't let it get out of proportion.* □ *Even if Cantona was provoked, his reaction was out of all proportion to the provocation.*

◇ SEE ALSO **out of perspective** ▷ PERSPECTIVE

pros

pros and 'cons
The **pros and cons** of something are the reasons in favour of and against it: *You need to see the situation clearly, evaluate the pros and cons of possible courses of action accurately, and to behave firmly and astutely.*

This phrase comes from the Latin words '**pro**' meaning 'for' and '**contra**' meaning 'against'.

prose

purple 'prose
Purple prose is writing which is bad, usually because it is too descriptive: *'Ten days on St Lucia, swimming around in the pellucid Caribbean waters – just quoting the purple prose of the travel brochures,' Lucy laughed.*

protest

under 'protest
You do something **under protest** if you do it unwillingly: *Eventually she agreed, albeit under protest, to see a marriage guidance councillor.*

proud

do someone 'proud
When someone has given you good treatment or entertainment, you say they **have done you proud**: *And special thanks to the catering staff who, once again, have done us proud.*

proud as a 'peacock
Someone who is as **proud as a peacock** is very proud.

providence

tempt 'providence
If you say that someone **is tempting providence**, you mean that they are taking a big risk, or, superstitiously, that they are encouraging something bad to happen by being over-optimistic: *John, having loved and lost, felt he would be tempting providence to allow himself to love again.*

◇ SEE ALSO **tempt fate** ▷ FATE; **tempt the gods** ▷ GODS; **speak too soon** ▷ SPEAK

prowl

on the 'prowl
A person is **on the prowl** if they are moving about and looking for something in a threatening way: *We'd better get a licence for our TV. The detector vans are on the prowl again.* □ *Mr Justice Jowitt told Anderson: 'I accept that you were not on the prowl looking for a victim.'*

An animal is **on the prowl** if it is hunting.

public

in 'public
You do something **in public** if you do it in the presence of other people: *The idea of standing up in public and giving a speech fills most people with horror.* □ *He has a nasty habit of taking all his clothes off in public when he gets drunk.*

pudding

in the 'pudding club (*informal, humorous, disrespectful*)
People occasionally use the expression '**in the pudding club**' to mean pregnant: *Cheer up, old boy. It's a shock to find your wife's in the pudding club, but things could be worse.*

◇ SEE ALSO **bun in the oven** ▷ BUN; **in the club**

▷CLUB; **up the duff** ▷DUFF; **in the family way**
▷FAMILY; **up the spout** ▷SPOUT

pull

pull a 'fast one

You say that someone **has pulled a fast one**,
or **pulled a fast one on** you, if they have
tricked or deceived you: *'You're trying to
pull a fast one, aren't you? You've been
playing around somewhere!' 'We haven't!
It was the train, truly it was!'*
◇ SEE ALSO **sell someone a pup** ▷PUP; **put one
over on someone** ▷PUT; **take someone for a
ride** ▷RIDE; **lie through your teeth** ▷TEETH

pull the 'other one

If you say **'pull the other one'** to someone,
you are telling them that you do not believe
what they say: *'I spend most of my evenings
at home.' Jake laughed. 'Pull the other one!
Don't tell me you've lost your taste for
nightclubs and fancy restaurants.'*
◇ SEE ALSO **tell me another** ▷TELL

A longer and more humorous version of
this expression is: 'pull the other one, it's
got bells on'. Both versions refer to the
core expression 'pull someone's leg'.

pull yourself to'gether

If you tell someone to **pull themselves
together,** you mean that they should take
control of themselves and stop behaving
foolishly: *If it had been any other soldier, he
would have told him sternly to pull himself
together and be a man.*
◇ SEE ALSO **snap out of it** ▷SNAP

punch

pack a 'punch

You say that someone or something **packs
a punch** if they have a strong effect on
people: *Switzerland may be small, but it
packs a powerful sightseeing punch.* □
*Though the hurricane packed a stronger
punch in the north-eastern states, it wreaked
greater havoc in the south.*

In its original meaning, **to pack a punch**
means 'to hit hard or powerfully with the
fist'.

'punch-drunk

Someone who is **punch-drunk** is behaving in
a confused way, as if they were drunk or
dizzy: *He's destroying his mind with all
those drugs. He's just punch-drunk all the
time now.*

In boxing, boxers who are **punch-drunk**
suffer from a type of temporary brain
damage after receiving blows to the
head, which makes them behave as if
they were drunk.

'punch-up

A **punch-up** is a fight in which people hit
one another: *The game does attract a minority of young men for whom a punch-up on a
Saturday afternoon is all part of it.*

punches

pull your 'punches

Someone who **is pulling their punches** is
using less force in attacking than they are
really capable of; someone who **does not
pull any punches** does not try to reduce the
strength of what they are saying or doing:
*Telling the man the simple truth could reduce
him to a wreck, so on the whole, she pulled
her punches and held her tongue.* □ *'I warn
you – I'm not going to pull any punches. It's
going to be straight revolutionary stuff.'*

In boxing, a boxer **is pulling his punches** if
he is not using his full strength to hit
with.

pup

sell someone a 'pup

If you have been **sold a pup**, someone has
cheated you: *They've been sold a pup with
these amendments.*
◇ SEE ALSO **pull a fast one** ▷PULL; **put one
over on someone** ▷PUT; **take someone for a
ride** ▷RIDE; **lie through your teeth** ▷TEETH

puppy

mucky 'puppy or mucky 'pup

You call a person, especially a child, a
mucky puppy or a **mucky pup**, if they have
got themselves dirty: *Come here, you mucky
pup, and let me wipe that chocolate off your
face.*

pure

pure and 'simple

Pure and simple means 'and nothing else':
*The man wants revenge, pure and simple,
and he's working logically through the family.*

pure as the driven 'snow

Someone, usually a young woman, who is
described as **pure as the driven snow** has no
evil thoughts, and probably not much sexual experience: *'Just my luck. Pure as the
driven snow!' 'My father would turn in his
grave if he knew I'd ever ...'* □ *Brown
claimed that Charlie was 'pure as the driven
snow'. An audible ripple of laughter went
round the court room.*

People often use this expression sarcastically, meaning the exact opposite of the
above definition.

purpose

accidentally on 'purpose

When someone does something **accidentally on purpose**, they do it intentionally, although they make it seem as if it is a mistake, or that it happened by chance: *It was surprising how 'accidentally on purpose' callers arrived whenever her car was parked outside.*

on 'purpose

You do something **on purpose** if you do it intentionally: *You got drunk on purpose to embarrass me!* □ *Did you do it on purpose or by accident?*

serve a 'purpose

Something or someone **serves a purpose** if it is useful; something **serves its purpose** if it does the thing it is designed to do: *Nobody likes traffic wardens, but they certainly serve a purpose.* □ *It's quite an ugly walking-stick, but it serves its purpose.*

to good 'purpose

You use something **to good purpose** if you find a good use for it: *I would leave him all my money if I thought he would use it to good purpose.*

to some 'purpose

You do something **to some purpose** if it produces some useful results; you do something **to no purpose**, or **to little purpose**, if it produces no useful results: *I don't mind doing years of hard work, as long as I know it's all to some purpose.* □ *We had a long chat the other day, but all to no purpose, it seems.*

purse

you can't make a silk purse out of a sow's 'ear

If someone says '**you can't make a silk purse out of a sow's ear**', they mean that, if the materials you are working with are bad, no amount of hard work will make a good quality final product: *It's a true case of trying to make an agricultural silk purse out of a sow's ear. If land is not suitable for efficient farming, the land should be used for more profitable purposes.* □ *Mocking his attempts to turn her into an Anglo-Irish lady, she said, 'You'll not make this particular sow's ear into a silk purse, young lad!'*

Certain types of pig have large ears which are similar in shape to purses, but everyone knows you cannot make a beautiful purse out of a sow's (= a female pig's) ear.

pursuit

in hot pur'suit

You are **in hot pursuit**, or **in hot pursuit of** someone or something, when you are chasing them and are determined to catch them: *The three killer dogs burst from the trees in hot pursuit, their gleaming white fangs bared for the attack.*

push (*see also* pushed *and* pushing)

at a 'push

You say that something is possible **at a push** if you consider it to be just possible, although a lot of extra effort would be needed to do it: *'Can you deliver the flowers today?' 'I could do it at a push, but it'll cost you extra.'*

◊ SEE ALSO **at a pinch** ▷ PINCH

give someone the 'push (*informal*)

1 If you **are given**, or **get**, **the push**, you are dismissed from your job: *It's not easy to mentally prepare yourself for getting another job after you've been given the push.* **2** If you **give** your boyfriend or girlfriend **the push**, you end your relationship with them: *I've given Sam the push, so there. I've got a new boyfriend now, Tom Parks is handsome and honest.*

◊ SEE ALSO **give someone the boot** ▷ BOOT; **give someone the heave-ho** ▷ HEAVE; **give someone the elbow** ▷ ELBOW

'push it

Someone **is pushing it** when they are making a certain person angry by putting pressure on them, or trying to insist that that person does something: *There's no harm in asking, but if he says no, don't push it.*

a 'pushover

1 You describe a job or activity as **a pushover** if it is easy to do: *This exam should be a pushover if you have revised properly.* **2** You also describe a person who can be easily persuaded or influenced as **a pushover**: *I'll ask if I can come to the party. My dad's a pushover, but it'll be harder to persuade my mum.*

when push comes to 'shove or if push comes to 'shove

You say **when**, or **if**, **push comes to shove** when **1** you are talking about what happens, or will happen, if the situation turns into an emergency, or becomes serious and important: *When push came to shove, the lad showed big-match composure.* **2** you are about to say what the reality of a situation is: *But when push came to shove, we knew that the government and the party would get their way.*

◊ SEE ALSO **when the chips are down** ▷ CHIPS; **come to the crunch** ▷ CRUNCH

pushed

pushed for 'something

You are **pushed for something** such as time or money if you do not have enough of it: *I'm a bit pushed for time, so I shall move quickly on to the last part of my talk.* □ *If you are pushed for cash, Christmas can become something of a nightmare.*

pushing

pushing such-and-such an 'age

You say that an adult **is pushing** a certain age if they are approaching that age, and you want to emphasize the fact that they are getting old, or at least, that they are not very young any more: *I had a look at him. Pushing forty but kind of athletic for his age.* □ *She must be pushing forty, he thought, but she's still a good looker.*

put

a 'put-down

A **put-down** is something that you say that makes someone appear foolish or stupid, or that criticizes them: *I remember asking John Lennon if those were his own teeth, and he answered, 'Yes. Are those your own spots?' – a good put-down.*

hard 'put

You say you would be **hard put** to do something if you would find it difficult or impossible to do: *I used to be good at maths, but I'd be hard put to solve a quadratic equation now.*

I wouldn't put it 'past so-and-so

You say that **you wouldn't put** a certain action, usually something bad, **past someone** if you think that they may have done it, considering the kind of person they are: *'I wonder if he stole the money that I left on my desk?' 'I certainly wouldn't put it past him.'*

'put it to someone that

You **put it to someone that** something is the case when you formally suggest a certain controversial fact or possibility to them: *I put it to the Prime Minister that Britain is becoming the dustbin of the Western hemisphere.*

put one 'over on someone

Someone **puts one over on you** when they tell you a lie or trick you: *Right, son. Tell me what happened, and don't try to put one over on me again.*

◇ SEE ALSO **pull a fast one** ▷ PULL; **sell someone a pup** ▷ PUP; **take someone for a ride** ▷ RIDE; **lie through your teeth** ▷ TEETH

put 'paid to something

When something **puts paid to** a certain thing, it prevents that thing from happening: *Our new procedures will soon put paid to any false claims for state benefits.*

◇ SEE ALSO **put an end to** ▷ END

put someone 'right

1 When you **put someone right**, you tell them the truth, in order to correct their false beliefs or ideas: *She'd imagined she would be heading for the summer sun. The girl in the travel agency had put her right about that!* □ *If I was in doubt about anything my sergeant would soon put me right.* **2** Something **puts you right** if it makes you feel well or healthy again: *'Are you ill, Herr Direktor?' 'A brandy and a short rest will put me right.'*

◇ SEE ALSO **set the record straight** ▷ RECORD

put something 'right

1 You **put something right** when you repair it or remove the faults in it: *My computer's crashed and there's no-one around to put it right.* **2** You **put something right** when you put an end to or change something that is wrong: *Be there at 6.30am. That way you have time to find problems – and put them right.*

putty

putty in someone's 'hands

You say that someone is **putty in** a certain person's **hands** if they are easily influenced by that person: *Her curls bounced enchantingly as she clung to her father's arm, 'Do say the blue.' 'Then the blue it is, my love,' said her father fondly, as putty in her hands.*

> **Putty** is a soft paste used for fixing glass panes into window frames. You can mould it easily into different shapes by squeezing it.

quandary

in a 'quandary
You are **in a quandary** about something when you cannot decide whether or not you should do it: *I think you must have some guidelines for them otherwise they're going to be in a quandary.*

◇ SEE ALSO **in two minds** ▷ MINDS; **in a cleft stick** ▷ STICK

> The word **quandary** comes from the Latin 'quam dare', meaning 'how to give?'

quantity

an unknown 'quantity
People describe a person or thing as **an unknown quantity** if they know nothing, or very little, about them: *After all, Luke was still something of an unknown quantity, and she had to be sure of her ground when the right moment came.*

quart

get a quart into a pint 'pot or put a quart into a pint 'pot
If you say that attempting something is like trying to **get**, or **put, a quart into a pint pot**, you mean that it is impossible, especially if you are trying to put a great quantity of something into another thing that cannot hold it: *The fundamental difficulty of all curriculum planning – how to get a quart into a pint pot – still remains to be addressed.*

> A **quart** is a measurement of liquid equal to two pints.

quarters

at close 'quarters
Someone or something is **at close quarters** when they are in a position very near you: *The soldier was skilled in all-round weaponry, able to fight at a distance and at close quarters.*

queen

'queen it over someone
A woman **queens it over you** when she behaves in a loud and commanding way: *You know, she has a similar set-up in Rome and also in Paris, a little place where she can go and queen it over everyone once a year.*

◇ SEE ALSO **lord it over someone** ▷ LORD

Queen's 'evidence
A criminal who **turns Queen's evidence** makes a statement against their partner or partners in crime, and in return receives a less severe punishment.

◇ SEE ALSO **turn King's evidence** ▷ KING

question

beg the 'question (*formal*)
An assumption **begs the question** which is asked, if it avoids dealing with a particular issue, or if it considers that certain matters are true, without evidence: *Asking if the government should pay of course begs the question, where does the government get the cash from if not from the consumer?*

beyond 'question
Something that is **beyond question** is absolutely certain, and there is no doubt about it: *Fiona Smith's win in the final of the English National Championships on Tuesday established her beyond question as the country's best woman player.*

the burning 'question
The burning question is the question that everyone is waiting to hear, or trying to find, the answer to: *But of course the burning question is: Who has been elected to lead the committee this year?*

call into 'question
You **call** something **into question** if you express doubts about it: *His judgement was called into question earlier this year when he sang on a chat show just hours after an IRA bomb killed eight building workers in County Tyrone.*

◇ SEE ALSO **cast doubt on something** ▷ DOUBT

it's a question of 'such-and-such
If you say about a situation that **it's a question of** a particular thing, you mean that the situation has to do with, or is about, that thing: *Just wait. It's all a question of being patient.*

it's only a question of 'time

If you say that **it's only a question of time**, you mean that a certain thing will definitely happen, even though it may not happen immediately: *It can only be a question of time before the party has to relinquish its leading role and allow political competition.*

no question of 'such-and-such

There is **no question of** your doing something, or of something happening, if you have no intention of doing it, or if there is no possibility of it happening: *He insisted last night that there was no question of him changing his mind and resuming his international career.*

open to 'question

Something that is **open to question** is not certain or agreed upon: *The Japanese launch was a success, although it is open to question how much of the success can be attributed to innovative marketing and how much to the technical qualities of the product.*

pop the 'question

You **pop the question** when you ask someone to marry you: *As their yacht, the Blue Doublet, bobbed about on the sea, Commander Tim Laurence finally found the courage to pop the question.*

a question mark hangs over 'such-and-such

If you say that **a question mark hangs over** a particular situation, you mean that people have doubts about it: *An even bigger question mark hangs over the proposed Channel Tunnel railway between St Pancras station and the coast.*

without 'question

Something is the case **without question** if there is absolutely no doubt about it: *Staffing levels and costs are, without question, too high and must be reduced.*

◇ SEE ALSO **for certain** ▷ CERTAIN; **beyond all doubt** ▷ DOUBT; **without a doubt** ▷ DOUBT; **beyond any shadow of doubt** or **without any shadow of doubt** ▷ SHADOW; **sure as eggs is eggs** ▷ SURE

questions

no questions 'asked

When something is done for you **no questions asked**, it is done immediately, without anyone asking you questions, or doubting your honesty: *If, after examining your first issue, you are not 100% satisfied, we'll send you a complete refund with no questions asked.*

queue

jump the 'queue

Someone **jumps the queue** when, rather than standing at the end of a line of people who are waiting for something [= a queue], they stand between two people who are already there; you also **jump the queue** when you are given help or allowed to do something before other people who have been waiting longer than you: *I don't want to have to wait until I'm homeless before I go for help; I don't want to jump the queue – it should be done on a fair system.*

The British have a reputation for standing politely in a queue when several people are waiting for something. It is considered very rude to take your place in the middle [= **jump the queue**] when you arrive, rather than standing at the end, behind the last person in the line.

quick

and be quick a'bout it

If you add **'and be quick about it'** to a request, you are telling someone, rudely, to hurry up: *Press that button there. That one – and be quick about it.*

cut to the 'quick

Someone who is **cut to the quick** is deeply offended: *There was a cruel taunt in his voice that cut her to the quick.*

The **quick** is the tender, sensitive area of skin under a finger nail.

quick as a 'flash

You do something, or something happens, as **quick as a flash** when you do it, or it happens, very quickly: *'All right, but I want five pounds for it,' said Henry, quick as a flash.*

a 'quick one (*informal*)

You go for **a quick one** when you go to a bar for a quick drink: *If he popped into the pub for a quick one that lunchtime, he would probably find Selwyn in there. □ Time for a quick one before the show starts?*

quids

quids 'in (*informal*)

You are **quids in** if you are in a very good or favourable position, especially financially: *But many borrowers choose a discount deal as the only criterion when they take out a loan. And yet this does not automatically mean they will be quids in.*

◇ SEE ALSO **in clover** ▷ CLOVER; **in the money** ▷ MONEY; **easy street** ▷ STREET

Quid is a slang term for the pound.

quiet

on the 'quiet
You do something **on the quiet** when you do it secretly: *He drinks at times; of course, on the quiet, after Gran's safely in bed.*

quiet as a 'mouse
You do something, or you are, as **quiet as a mouse** when you do it, or you are, very quiet: *I used to come in, in the early hours, quiet as a mouse; but Dad always knew what time I'd got in.*

quite

quite 'so (*formal*)
You use **quite so** to express agreement.
◇ SEE ALSO **that's just it** ▷ JUST; **just so** ▷ JUST; **too right** ▷ RIGHT

quits

be 'quits with someone
You **are quits with someone** when you do not owe them anything and they do not owe you anything any more: *If I pay for the drinks, we'll be quits, okay?*
◇ SEE ALSO **fair and square** ▷ FAIR

call it 'quits
You **call it quits** when you agree with someone that neither person owes the other anything: *'But the rest – forget it. Take this and we'll call it quits.' He handed me the cheque.*

quote

quote 'unquote
You say '**quote unquote**' after a word or phrase to show that you are using someone else's words, especially if you think they are not entirely suitable: *You had this broad approach, you had liberal, quote unquote, progressive, quote unquote, presidents, faced with conservative congresses.*

Quote here, is the short form of the term 'quotation mark'.

r

Rs

the three 'Rs

If people talk about **the three Rs**, they mean reading, writing and arithmetic, the three basic subjects which most people learn at primary school: *There is no evidence that earlier teaching of the three Rs leads to top marks and academic success for the child later on.*

The expression **the three Rs** is a kind of joke, because it is based on an uneducated spelling of two of the three words it refers to: 'Reading, Riting and 'Rithmetic'.

rabbits

breed like 'rabbits

You say that people or animals **are breeding like rabbits** if they are producing a lot of babies: *On a remote island with nothing to do, is it any wonder these people breed like rabbits?*

Rabbits are famous for their ability to reproduce fast and efficiently.

rabble

'rabble-rouser

A **rabble-rouser** is someone who encourages noisy disorder within a crowd of people: *His earlier image was that of a militant, a rabble-rouser, a fearless advocate of 'new unionism'.*

race

a race against 'time

You are involved in **a race against time** if you are hurrying to do something or finish something important in a limited period of time: *Three more were likely to explode. It was a race against time. There were thousands of people to alert and evacuate.*

rack

go to rack and 'ruin

1 A place **is going to rack and ruin** if it is getting into a bad state because no-one is looking after it or doing the repairs which are needed: *The house is much too big for her and it's been going steadily to rack and ruin for years.* **2** A person **is going to rack and ruin** if they are destroying their life or their health by behaving in a certain way: *He's gone to rack and ruin since he started drinking.*

rag (*see also* **rags**)

like a red rag to a 'bull

You say that something, such as a remark, is **like a red rag to a bull** if it is likely to make a certain person angry: *'Don't ever let me see you with her again,' she concluded. Saying this to me was like holding a red rag to a bull.*

lose your 'rag

You say that a person **has lost their rag** when they suddenly lose their patience and show how angry they are: *Last year he lost his rag in a pub down in Kent and started smashing glasses.*

◇ SEE ALSO **go off at the deep end** ▷ END; **have a blue fit** ▷ FIT; **blow a fuse** ▷ FUSE; **blow a gasket** ▷ GASKET; **let fly** ▷ LET; **blow or flip your lid** ▷ LID; **do your nut** ▷ NUT; **fly into a rage** ▷ RAGE; **hit the roof** ▷ ROOF; **blow your stack** ▷ STACK; **lose your temper** ▷ TEMPER; **blow your top** ▷ TOP; **throw a wobbly** ▷ WOBBLY

rage

all the 'rage (*rather old*)

Something that is **all the rage** is fashionable or popular, usually only for a short time: *Lost for gift ideas? All the rage in California: a fax machine for your car.*

fly into a 'rage

When a person **flies into a rage**, they suddenly lose control of themselves and become wild with anger: *She must be feeling guilty, because she flies into a rage every time I mention it.*

◇ SEE ALSO **go off at the deep end** ▷ END; **have a blue fit** ▷ FIT; **blow a fuse** ▷ FUSE; **blow a gasket** ▷ GASKET; **let fly** ▷ LET; **blow or flip your lid** ▷ LID; **do your nut** ▷ NUT; **lose your rag** ▷ RAG; **hit the roof** ▷ ROOF; **blow your stack** ▷ STACK; **lose your temper** ▷ TEMPER;

blow your top ▷ TOP; **throw a wobbly**
▷ WOBBLY

rags

rags to 'riches
You say that someone has gone from **rags to riches** if they started their life in poverty, but have managed to become wealthy, probably by working hard or using their special abilities: *James, who gained early fame from his ability to find valuable things in jumble sales, has written a book, 'Rags to Riches', giving advice on how to succeed in business.*

rails

go off the 'rails
You say that a person or organization **has gone off the rails** if they have stopped behaving sensibly, and have begun behaving in a wild, immoral, or slightly mad way: *I cannot stay within a party which I believe has ideologically gone off the rails.*

rain (*see also* rains)

bucket with 'rain or bucket 'rain
If it is **bucketing with rain**, or **bucketing rain**, it is raining very hard: *She kindly dropped me off home, which – as it was bucketing rain yet again – I appreciated.*
◇ SEE ALSO **rain buckets** ▷ BUCKETS; **rain cats and dogs** ▷ CATS; **chuck it down** ▷ CHUCK; **tip it down** ▷ TIP

come rain or 'shine
You do something regularly **come rain or shine** if nothing ever stops you from doing it: *Every morning at about 5am, come rain or shine, James Zarei leaves his South Croydon home on his morning run.*

take a 'rain check
You say that you will **take a rain check** on a certain activity if you are refusing an invitation to do it just now, but expressing a desire to do it some time in the future: *'Do you want to go to the beach?' 'I can't today, but can I take a rain check on it?'*

rainbows

chase 'rainbows
You say that someone **is chasing rainbows** if they are wishing or hoping for something that they will probably never get: *I had no ambition to become a 'star'. I certainly couldn't afford to waste petrol chasing rainbows as far as Leeds and back.*
◇ SEE ALSO **build castles in the air** ▷ CASTLES

rains

it never rains but it 'pours
If someone says '**it never rains but it pours**', they mean **1** that unlucky things often seem

to happen all at the same time: *My day was bad enough, and then poor old Gran broke her leg. It never rains but it pours.* **2** that it is common, after a long period of bad luck, for so many opportunities to present themselves at once, that you cannot possibly manage to take advantage of them all: *I'd have liked to have done more work with them, but, as ever, it never rains but it pours – I already had three sessions booked – and typically I had to say 'no' to that.*

rampage

on the 'rampage
People or animals go **on the rampage** when they run about in a wild, angry, violent way, causing damage and destruction: *Thousands went on the rampage, ripping up paving slabs, trees and street signs to hurl at riot police yesterday.*

rank

the rank and 'file
The lowest ranks within an organization are often referred to as **the rank and file**: *The strikes were sparked off by the rank and file, and most were unofficial.*
rank-and-'file: *Delegates to the party congress next July should be directly elected by rank-and-file members. This would deprive party bosses of control over the election.*

ranks

break 'ranks
You say that a person **breaks ranks** when they do something which is disloyal to the group which they belong to: *In order for the agreement to stick, no single firm must break ranks.*

close 'ranks
People in a group **close ranks** when they become more dependent on one another and less open to people who do not belong to their group, in order to defend themselves: *Scientists working on the project seem to have closed ranks, and no data is being made available.*

> When the soldiers in an army **close ranks**, they move closer together so that it is more difficult to get past them.

join the 'ranks of something
When you become part of a group, you can say that you **have joined its ranks**: *And if she decided not to renew her contract she would soon be joining the ranks of the unemployed.*

rise through the 'ranks
A person **rises through the ranks** of an organization if they start at a low level in that organization and move up over a period of time to reach a position of im-

portance: *Pavlov, 53, had started his career as a district auditor and had risen through the ranks of the Finance Ministry and the State Planning Committee.*

ransom

hold someone to 'ransom

To **hold someone to ransom** is **1** to keep them as a prisoner until money is paid in return for their release: *The terrorists demand ten million pounds for the release of the men they are holding to ransom.* **2** to force them to do something, using threats: *No longer did the miners have the power to hold the community to ransom by sheer industrial muscle.*

rant

rant and 'rave

A person who **is ranting and raving** is shouting or complaining about something, repeating the same things over and over again because they are so angry: *I don't care how much you rant and rave at me. I've made my decision and it's final.*

rap

give someone a rap over the 'knuckles

You **give someone a rap over the knuckles** when you criticize them sharply for doing something which you disapprove of: *They write as if totally familiar with raps over the knuckles and old-fashioned dictation.*
◇ SEE ALSO **haul someone over the coals** ▷ COALS; **give someone a rough time** ▷ TIME

take the 'rap

Someone **takes the rap**, or **takes the rap for** something, when they take the blame and are punished, often for something which they did not do: *I know it would save our reputation, but I'm sorry, I don't want him to take the rap for something he didn't do.*

raptures

in 'raptures about something or in 'raptures over something

You are **in raptures about** or **over something** if you are speaking about it with great enthusiasm or excitement; you **go into raptures about** or **over something** when you start speaking about it in this way: *She went into raptures about the climate, the food, the spring flowers, the language, the culture and the handsome men and women of her mother country.*

rat

a drowned 'rat

You say that someone looks like **a drowned rat** if they are very wet: *He had ridden his bike into the canal three times. Some said his*

wife didn't comment any more when Sammy was carried in like a drowned rat.

'rat-arsed (*informal, rather vulgar*)

Someone who is **rat-arsed** is very drunk: *You get rat-arsed on Friday and spend Saturday and Sunday recovering. Great weekend, eh?*
◇ SEE ALSO **out of your head** ▷ HEAD; **pissed as a fart** or **newt** ▷ PISSED

the 'rat race

If people talk about **the rat race**, they mean the fierce, endless competition for success or wealth which is a feature of the way people live in big towns and cities: *Nine out of ten people who move here from the city do so in order to get out of the rat race.*

smell a 'rat (*informal*)

You say you can **smell a rat** if you have a feeling that something is not as it should be, but is wrong or bad: *I smelt a rat when he said he was working late, so I went down to the office to check he was there.*

rate

at 'any rate

You use **at any rate 1** when you are adding something to correct what you have just said and to make it more accurate: *Teenagers, or at any rate the majority of them, are aware that it's important to get qualifications.* **2** when you are making a general statement containing the most important details of what you have just said: *I don't know if he's vegetarian or not. At any rate, he's coming, so you should reserve a place for him.*
◇ SEE ALSO **in any event** ▷ EVENT; **at all events** ▷ EVENTS; **in any case** ▷ CASE

at a rate of 'knots

You are doing something **at a rate of knots** if you are doing it quickly: *We're progressing at a great rate of knots at the moment.* □ *The landing – well now, your helicopter is approaching the ground at a great rate of knots with the engine idling and you have to land it – gently.*
◇ SEE ALSO **at breakneck speed** ▷ SPEED

The speed of a boat is measured in knots.

at 'this rate

At this rate means 'if what is happening now continues to happen for some time': *Where's he got to? At this rate we'll miss the train.*

first 'rate

A thing which is **first rate** is excellent: *He would not have bought the hat had he been by himself, but Maidstone assured him it was the right choice – 'Absolutely first rate, dear fellow.'*

rave

rave it 'up

People **rave it up** when they enjoy themselves in a loud, energetic way, for example at a party: *Mad Friday is just an opportunity for all the students to rave it up after their exams.*

a **'rave-up:** *There's always a lot of cleaning up to do after the annual rave-up to mark the end of the festival.*

◇ SEE ALSO **have a ball** ▷ BALL; **live it up** ▷ LIVE; **have the time of your life** ▷ TIME

raw

in the 'raw

You say that something is **in the raw** if it is in its natural state, with none of its ugliness or faults hidden: *It exposes capitalism in the raw: huge profits to be made from risking huge sums of money, while ordinary people wait for a verdict that will affect their jobs and lives.*

ray

a ray of 'hope

You say that there is **a ray of hope** when a situation is bad, but there is still a small chance that you will get the result you are hoping for: *Any ray of hope the prisoners had of escaping was lost when a plan of their escape route was found.* □ *There is one ray of hope, though. The Authority is talking about a new unit with 16 new beds.*

ray of 'sunshine

If someone or something is a **ray of sunshine** for a certain person, they make that person's life happier: *'Kim is like a ray of sunshine, a wonderful and beautiful girl who has changed my life,' he told a TV audience in Hollywood.*

rays

catch a few 'rays

You say that you are going to **catch a few rays** when you intend to go outside for a period of time because the sun is shining: *Do you fancy eating lunch outside? I'd like to catch a few rays before the sun goes in.*

razzle

go out on the 'razzle

You say that someone is **going out on the razzle** when they are going out, dressed in their party clothes, to enjoy themselves in a town at night: *Paul's arranged a romantic birthday dinner, but I'd far rather go out on the razzle with the girls.*

read

take something as 'read

You **take something as read** when you accept that it is the case, even though it has not been proven or checked, because you consider it to be certain or obvious: *We need to have it ratified by the Board. But you can take it as read that you have the contract.*

ready

at the 'ready

You have something **at the ready** when you are ready to use it if or when it becomes necessary: *Make sure you have a piece of paper and a pencil at the ready to note down the secret number.*

ready and 'waiting

You say that you are **ready and waiting** if you are well prepared to deal with something because you have been warned about it in advance: *When the smugglers reached the frontier, the drug squad was ready and waiting for them.*

ready, steady, 'go

You say **'ready, steady, go!'** at the beginning of a race, to make sure that all the competitors are prepared for the race, and that they start at the same time.

ready when 'you are

You say **'ready when you are'** to tell the person who is going to be your partner in a certain activity that you are ready and just waiting for their signal to start the activity: *'How are you getting on up there?' 'Ready when you are, mate.'*

real

for 'real

1 Something that happens **for real** is really happening, as opposed to being an idea or a practice situation: *Army drills are good training, but nothing can prepare you for combat when it's for real.* **2** Something that is **for real** is true or serious, and not a joke: *If you pretend to be ill all the time, nobody will believe you when you get sick for real.* □ *He said he was sorry, and I thought it was for real.*

reality

in re'ality

1 In reality means 'in real life', rather than in books or films, for example: *It would be nice if life were fair, but in reality it doesn't often work out that way.* **2** You also use **in reality** to show that you are going to make a true statement about a situation, in order to correct any false or inaccurate ideas that may have been formed: *He implied that most single mothers are teenagers, when in reality this is far from being the case.*

realms

within the realms of 'possibility or not beyond the realms of possi'bility

You say that something is **within**, or **not beyond, the realms of possibility** if it is certainly possible, although it may not be likely: *I suppose it is not beyond the realms of possibility that he was passively involved in the supposed robbery.* □ *It seems to me quite within the realms of possibility that charges for using motorways will eventually be introduced.*

reap

reap what you have 'sown

You say that a person **is reaping what they have sown** if something is happening to them as a result of something which they themselves did in the past: *He gave us the moral line about reaping what you have sown, then told us to go out there and get on with the rest of our lives.*

reaper

the grim 'reaper

If people talk about **the grim reaper**, they mean death.

The grim reaper is a skeleton holding a scythe [= a curved knife with a long handle for cutting grass], an image which was often used as a symbol of death.

rear

bring up the 'rear

The person who **is bringing up the rear** is the last one in a line of people moving together: *Right, can we have Jamie leading the way, please, and I'll bring up the rear.*

reason

it stands to 'reason

If someone says '**it stands to reason**', they mean that something is obviously the case: *It stands to reason that they should want a formal apology for the way they were treated.* □ *Of course he did it. He found his wife with her lover and murdered them both. Stands to reason.*

ours is not to reason 'why

If someone says '**ours is not to reason why**', they mean **1** that people who are not considered important enough to be asked their opinion are supposed to accept the strange or stupid decisions which influential people often make: *That new road bridge is just going to increase the amount of traffic in the city centre, but I suppose ours is not to reason why.* **2** that they would perhaps rather not know the answer to a particular question, or that it is not their business to know: *Curious – they don't usually dispense £20 notes. Still, mine not to reason why. It would pay the rent.*

Notice that '**ours**' may be replaced by '**mine**', '**yours**', '**hers**', etc.

within 'reason

Within reason means within the limits of what most people would consider sensible or acceptable: *I'll get you whatever you want for your birthday ... well, anything within reason.*

reasons

for reasons best known to them'selves

You say that someone is doing something **for reasons best known to themselves** if you cannot understand why they are doing it: *It's much cheaper to fly, but for reasons best known to herself, she's determined to take the train.*

rebound

on the 'rebound

A person who is **on the rebound** may be unusually willing to fall in love because they are feeling sad or lonely as a result of the breakdown of a previous relationship: *He began to take an interest in me just when I was on the rebound from a very unhappy love affair. I married for safety.*

recognition

change out of all 'recognition or change beyond all recog'nition

Something that **changes out of**, or **changes beyond, all recognition** changes so much that people can no longer recognize it: *I discovered that, during my ten-year absence, Glasgow had changed out of all recognition.* □ *The timid girl I had once known had changed out of all recognition.*

record

for the 'record or just for the 'record

You say you are telling people something **for the record** or **just for the record**, when you want people to know something, so there can be no misunderstanding about it: *Let me say for the record that I was at no point aware of the seriousness of my actions.* □ *If you would very kindly state your name and your organization, just for the record.*

off the 'record

If you tell someone that what you are saying is **off the record**, or **strictly off the record**, you mean that you do not want them to tell anyone else or make the information public: *Off the record, detectives refer to the growing number of burglaries as one of Britain's few growth industries.*

on 'record

You use **'on record' 1** as a way of talking about what someone has said publicly, so that others know about it and can prove that it was said: *He would never have made such remarks if he had realized they were going down on record.* **2** when you are talking about information that you keep, so you may look at it or refer to it in the future: *The original promise was to allow enough information to be placed on record for the public to know who was breaking the law.* **3** when you are talking about the highest or lowest standards or levels anyone has ever recorded: *Fort William had the hottest summer on record that year.*

set the 'record straight or put the 'record straight

You **set**, or **put, the record straight** when you tell the truth about something in order to correct people's false beliefs or ideas: *May I put the record straight on one point? I never claimed that nuclear power was safe, only that it was safer than the alternatives.*
◇ SEE ALSO **put someone right** ▷ PUT

red

in the 'red

Your bank account is **in the red** if you have spent more money than you have, and you therefore owe the bank money: *I was just a few pence in the red. A simple phone call from the bank to tell me about the problem would have saved me all this fuss and expense.*
◇ SEE ALSO **in the black** ▷ BLACK

> In accountancy, it is customary to write entries on the debit side of a ledger in red ink, and until recently, if you owed your bank a sum of money, that sum appeared in red on your bank statement.

reference

for future 'reference

You keep a note of something **for future reference** if you do not throw it away, because you know it may be useful in the future: *Here's a list of our opening times for future reference.*

in 'reference to or with 'reference to *(formal)*

1 When you are referring to something, you can say **'in**, or **with, reference to'** that thing: *I'm afraid I can't comment with reference to decisions that were made before I became chairman.* **2** You write **'with reference to'** in a formal letter, to show that you are replying to a particular letter or other communication which you have received: *With reference to your enquiry of 14 August,*

I regret to inform you that no places are available for the course mentioned.

reflection

a sad reflection on 'such-and-such or a poor reflection on 'such-and-such

You say that something is **a sad**, or **a poor**, **reflection on** a certain situation if it shows how bad that situation has become: *It is a sad reflection on relationships to'day that a group of strangers can have this kind of discussion, while lovers still cannot.*

refusal

first re'fusal

You give someone **first refusal** if you offer them the chance to buy a certain thing from you before you offer it to anyone else: *He's given me first refusal on that boat he's selling.*

regard

in this re'gard or in that re'gard *(formal)*

You use **'in this regard'**, or **'in that regard'**, to refer to a matter which has just been mentioned: *He is the most experienced candidate, and in that regard would seem to be well suited for the job.*

regards

as regards 'such-and-such *(formal)*

You use the expression **'as regards** a certain thing' to introduce or refer to the particular matter that you want to say something about: *As regards the 'comments he made earlier in your programme, I think he should get his facts right.*

send your re'gards

If you **send your regards**, or **send your regards to someone**, you send them your good wishes through someone else: *Your Aunt Susan sends her regards.*

region

in the 'region of

In the region of means 'approximately' or 'about': *The clean-up will cost somewhere in the region of £200 million.*

regular

regular as 'clockwork

Something which is as **regular as clockwork** happens with perfect regularity: *Miss Abberley used to give me these chocolates, you see, Christmas and Easter, regular as clockwork.*
◇ SEE ALSO **like clockwork** ▷ CLOCKWORK

rein

free 'rein or a free 'rein

You give someone **free rein** or **a free rein** when you allow them complete freedom to do what they want, or to make their own decisions: *I can't remember a time when he said, 'Don't play that; play this.' He'd always give you free rein.*

keep a tight 'rein on

You **are keeping a tight rein on** something or someone if you are controlling or limiting them firmly: *If we are to keep the level of taxation down, it is essential to maintain a tight rein on public spending.* □ *'How many wives have you got?' she asked with interest. 'One,' he replied. 'That is more than enough.' The woman cackled. 'She keeps you on a tight rein, does she?'*

reins

hold the 'reins

You say that someone **is holding the reins** in a situation if they are the person who is controlling that situation: *Despite 11 years of holding the reins of power and massive investment in the criminal justice system, the party had no long-term solutions to the problems.*

relation

poor re'lation

If people talk about the **poor relation**, they mean a person or thing that is similar in certain ways to, but generally considered to be of less importance or value than, another thing or group of things: *For many years radio has been the 'poor relation' of the media, attracting far less attention than, for instance, television or newspapers.*

in relation to 'such-and-such

You use '**in relation to**' when you are comparing things: *I think he spends a lot on food, but it's probably not much in relation to what he 'earns.* □ *You've got to look at the amount of alcohol you have drunk in relation to your 'body weight.*

remains

it remains to be 'seen

You say that **it remains to be seen** whether something will happen if you are avoiding making any judgement on the possibility of that thing happening: *I'm pretty certain her leg is broken, but how badly remains to be seen.* □ *It remains to be seen how far the structural changes will result in a 'cultural' change within the NHS.*

repair

beyond re'pair

1 A thing which is **beyond repair** is in such bad condition that it cannot possibly be repaired: *There was little furniture, for most was stored in Switzerland, and the few pieces that remained had been damaged beyond*

repair. **2** A situation or relationship is **beyond repair** if it is in such a bad state, as a result of recent events, that it can never become happy and stable again: *The friendship seems beyond repair. Suspicion is a soul-destroying evil. Trust, like respect, takes a long time to establish.*
◇ SEE ALSO **in bad repair** ▷ REPAIR; **the worse for wear** ▷ WEAR

in bad re'pair

Something that is **in bad repair** is in a bad or damaged condition and needs repairing: *In 1975, Lord Spencer inherited Althorp in a state of bad repair. Now Charles inherits a good, sound historic property.*
◇ SEE ALSO **have seen better days** ▷ DAYS; **the worse for wear** ▷ WEAR

in good re'pair

Something that is **in good repair** is in good condition: *In good repair, this watch would be worth well over £10,000.*
◇ SEE ALSO **in mint condition** ▷ CONDITION; **in good nick** ▷ NICK; **sound as a bell** ▷ SOUND

reputation

live up to your repu'tation

A person or thing **lives up to their reputation** if they are, or do, exactly as you would expect according to what people say about them: *We were told it was the most beautiful place on earth, and it certainly lived up to its reputation.* □ *Well, let's just say he didn't exactly live up to his reputation as the best lover in Hollywood.*

request

on re'quest

Something is done **on request** if it is done when people ask for it: *A full copy of the competition rules will be sent on request.*

resort

as a last re'sort

You do something **as a last resort** when you do it only because all other methods or approaches have failed: *As a last resort, I tried mouth-to-mouth again. Seconds later, Ben suddenly started spluttering and coughing – he was going to be all right!*

respect

with re'spect or with all due re'spect

You say '**with respect**' or '**with all due respect**' when you are politely disagreeing with someone: *With all due respect, I don't think your solution will work.*
◇ SEE ALSO **beg to differ** ▷ BEG

Ironically, '**with all due respect**' can sometimes seem rude, since it is so polite that it can sound insincere.

respects

with re'spect to (*formal*)
You use '**with respect to**' as a way of making clear what your remarks refer or relate to: *With respect to your 'last point, more money is being invested in the industry than ever before.*

respects

pay your last re'spects
If people talk about **paying their last respects** to someone who has recently died, they mean the act of going to their funeral or visiting the place where they are buried.

rest

come to 'rest
Something **comes to rest** when it stops moving: *The crow circled the house and came to rest on one of the chimney pots.* □ *The pebble slid across the ice and came to rest at my feet.*

give it a 'rest
You tell someone to **give it a rest** when you want them to stop doing or saying something which is annoying you: *'Why don't you buy some new clothes? You're such a mess.' 'Oh give it a rest, mum.'*

◊ SEE ALSO **give me a break** ▷ BREAK; **knock it off** ▷ KNOCK

lay someone to 'rest (*formal*)
You **are laying someone** who has died **to rest** when you respectfully bury their body: *John Smith was laid to rest on the holy island of Iona.*

lay something to 'rest
You **lay something** such as a problem or worry **to rest** when you are finally able to forget about it as a result of a certain change in the situation: *If we just received some compensation, we could lay the whole affair to rest.*

rest as'sured
You say that someone can **rest asssured of something**, or **rest assured** that something will happen, if you are promising them that thing will happen: *We know Italy as only Italians can, and you can rest assured that our staff are experts in their chosen field – Italian holidays.* □ *'Rest assured,' he said, 'your bicycle will be returned.'*

the rest is 'history
If someone says '**the rest is history**', they mean that they are not going to bother finishing the story which they have been telling, because everyone knows the story from that point on: *At the 1981 Festival, Sony, Philips, and the Polygram group joined to announce the imminent launch of the compact disc. The rest is history.*

retreat

beat a re'treat or beat a hasty re'treat
You **beat a retreat**, or **beat a hasty retreat**, when you run away from someone or something unpleasant: *He beat a hasty retreat when he spotted me approaching, but it was not hasty enough.*

sound the retreat
You **are sounding the retreat** when you show that you and the other people in your group have decided, perhaps unwillingly, to give up your plans for a certain activity: *Unless the country's dictator sounds the retreat in the next few days, he will soon be unable to meet the January 15th deadline.*

In battles, a soldier with a loud musical instrument **sounds the retreat** [= instructs his army to move backwards] by playing a particular combination of notes as a signal.

returns

many happy re'turns
You say '**many happy returns**' to someone on their birthday to wish them a happy birthday: *'It's my birthday on Monday.' 'Oh, is it?' 'Yeah, I'm not sure if it's twenty six or twenty seven.' 'Never mind, happy returns for Monday.'*

reverse

in re'verse
Things happen **in reverse** when they happen in the opposite order to the usual or expected way: *To stop the process, just go through the same operations in reverse.* □ *So you go to the door and you open the door and you walk backwards. It's like one of these films in reverse you know.*

rhyme

without rhyme or 'reason
Something that is **without rhyme or reason** does not make sense, or follow a logical pattern: *Three men attacked Joe – and we've been trying to figure out a motive. There's neither rhyme nor reason for it.* □ *At times, and briefly, they had seemed to be in sympathy, then without rhyme or reason his mood would change.*

ribbons

cut to 'ribbons or torn to 'ribbons
1 If a thin material of some kind has been **cut**, or **torn**, **to ribbons**, it has been badly damaged by cutting or tearing: *His knee was badly injured and his jeans were cut to ribbons.* **2** You say that people or things have been **cut**, or **torn, to ribbons** if they

have been badly damaged or destroyed: *'Don't move,' he ordered. 'There's glass everywhere. Fall and you'll cut yourself to ribbons.'* □ *Like fellow EEC members, the Republic has seen its economy torn to ribbons by recession.*

ribs

poke someone in the 'ribs or dig someone in the 'ribs

You **poke**, or **dig, someone in the ribs** when you give them a small, sharp push with your elbow, usually as a way of reminding them to say something or to remain silent: *'Have you seen him?' I poked Adrian in the ribs, and he responded, 'Actually, he gave us a message for you.'* □ *She asked us if we were hungry, but Sally dug me in the ribs and replied politely that we weren't.*

rich

get-rich-'quick (*disrespectful*)

A person or organization with a **get-rich-quick** attitude is only concerned with making the greatest possible amount of money in the shortest possible time: *The privatization of public companies is just a part of the get-rich-quick agenda of this Government.*

that's 'rich

You say **'that's rich'** when you are remarking how unreasonable you consider someone else's criticism or accusation to be, perhaps because you think that they are more guilty of that thing than you are: *Me nosey? That's rich coming from you!*

riddance

good 'riddance

You say **'good riddance'** when you are glad that you have got rid of something or someone: *In the end, we thought 'good riddance', you know, rather than have a few indecisive people, we might be better off without them.* □ *I've finally managed to sell that old car of mine, and good riddance to it.*

riddles

talk in 'riddles or speak in 'riddles

A person is **talking**, or **speaking, in riddles** when they are saying things in such a complicated or indirect way that it is impossible to understand them: *My brother liked to speak in riddles. He was a man who loved secrecy for secrecy's sake and hugged such secrets to his chest.*

ride

along for the 'ride

You say you are coming **along for the ride** when you join a person or group of people

simply out of interest, not to take part yourself in what they are doing: *Watching them line up, it was clear they wanted to win. They were not along for the ride.* □ *I didn't want to get involved with it at first, but it was interesting. I was along for the ride.*

> In its base sense, to go **along for the ride** means to travel with someone who is going somewhere, for no purpose other than to enjoy the journey and see somewhere new.

give someone a rough 'ride

You say that someone is **giving you a rough ride** if they are being unkind to you or making your life difficult: *John Major will be given a rough ride at the Tory conference in October over the Government's handling of the economy.*

let something 'ride

You **are letting something ride** when you decide not to do anything yet to change a certain situation: *David was making a conscious decision to become famous. He always did it for a while and then just let it ride to see what happened.*

take someone for a 'ride (*informal*)

You say that someone **has taken you for a ride** if they have cheated or deceived you in some way: *He told you this piece of junk was worth £100? Looks like you've been taken for a ride, mate.*

◇ SEE ALSO **pull a fast one** ▷ PULL; **sell someone a pup** ▷ PUP; **put one over on someone** ▷ PUT; **lie through your teeth** ▷ TEETH

> In American criminals' slang, to **take someone for a ride** used to mean to kill them, because murders were often committed in a moving car, in order to attract as little outside attention as possible.

riding

riding 'high

Someone is **riding high** when they are having a period of great success: *Aztec Camera, currently riding high in the charts with 'Good Morning Britain', will play a one-off date at London Brixton Academy on 20th December.*

> The moon is **riding high** when it is high up in the sky.

riff

'riff-raff (*disrespectful*)

'Riff-raff' is a term used to refer to people whom the speaker does not consider to be respectable: *I've heard about this new club. I* *heard a report about it. So the riff-raff can't get in, they say no jeans or something like that.*

right

do 'right by someone

You **do right by someone** if you manage to provide them with all the good things you think they deserve: *You mustn't get upset when I buy you things. I just want to do right by you, that's all.*

get something 'right

You **get something right** when you deal with it correctly: *Your wedding is a special day, and it's important to get your make-up just right.*

in the 'right

You are **in the right** if what you are doing is morally or legally right: *He has threatened to take me to court, but he won't because he knows I'm in the right.* □ *How can the Government be so sure they are in the right when so many people have criticized this policy?*

in your own 'right

You have a position or claim **in your own right** if it is yours because of your own ability or qualifications, independently of the ability or qualifications of the people you know: *Rodin's mistress Camille Claudel was an excellent sculptress in her own right.*

Mr 'Right

If people talk about **Mr Right**, they mean the imaginary ideal man that every woman is supposed to look for, or the real man that she has met, and decided she wants to stay with for the rest of her life: *It's no use sitting about waiting for Mr Right to come along.* □ *'It appears Steffi has finally found Mr Right,' said the report. The couple were introduced by Steffi's racing driver brother Michael.*

right as 'rain

Someone who is feeling as **right as rain** is feeling perfectly well again after a period when they were not so well.

◇ SEE ALSO **fit as a fiddle** ▷ FIT; **hale and hearty** ▷ HALE

right, left and 'centre

Things which are **right, left and centre** can be seen everywhere around you: *There were people screaming and panicking right, left and centre.*

In team games such as football and hockey, a team is divided into three sections, **right, left and centre**, so that the whole field can be covered effectively.

right 'on

People or ideas are **right on** if they are socially aware and express fashionable and broad-minded views: *But activists on the new right on issues, such as sexual and racial equality and low-level economic development, and ecology, had splintered into hundreds of smaller pressure groups.*

a 'right one

You say that someone is **a right one** if they are, or if you think they are going to be, difficult to cope with: *That kid's only six and he's already uncontrollable. He'll be a right one when he gets older.* □ *As soon as he walked into the shop, I said to myself, we've got a right one here.*

This expression is usually only said in private, when the person in question is absent, but sometimes people say it about someone who is present, as a joke.

right you 'are

People say **'right you are'** to show that they have heard and that they will do what someone has asked: *'Can you deliver my groceries to me?' 'Right you are, then. I'll drop them in this afternoon.'*

too 'right *(informal)*

You say **'too right'** when you completely agree with what someone has just said: *'You look a bit tired.' 'Too right. I've been up all night.'* □ *'Do you want a drink?' 'Too right I do.'*

◇ SEE ALSO **that's just it** ▷ JUST; **just so** ▷ JUST; **quite so** ▷ QUITE

rights

the rights and 'wrongs of

The rights and wrongs of a situation are the moral questions involved in it: *I am not going to get into a discussion on the rights and wrongs of a privatized water industry.*

within your 'rights

You are **within your rights** in doing something if you are not breaking the law by doing it: *He needs my permission to build a fence there. I would be well within my rights to have it removed.*

ring *(see also **rings**)*

have a familiar 'ring

If something you hear **has a familiar ring**, you think you recognize it but you are not sure from where: *Is he an actor or something? His name has a familiar ring.*

ringer

a dead 'ringer for someone

A person is **a dead ringer for someone** if they look exactly like them: *Their candidate is*

Peter Maughan, said to be a dead ringer for opera singer Luciano Pavarotti.

In American English, a **ringer** is a good horse which has been entered for a race under the name of another horse which looks similar but which is not so good. This sense of **ringer** probably comes from an earlier sense, meaning a person sent to vote illegally in a district where he or she is not allowed to vote.

rings

run 'rings round
You **run rings round** someone when you make them feel embarrassed by doing things which they have no power to prevent, by defeating them easily, or by showing that you are much better than them: *She has no discipline. The kids in her class run rings round her.* □ *'So tell me, are you nervous about the big fight?' 'No man. I reckon I can run rings round him.'*

riot

read the 'riot act
You **read the riot act**, or **read someone the riot act**, when you tell them angrily how much you disapprove of something they have done, and threaten them with punishments: *While he was in no position to read her the riot act, it was plain common sense to discourage her from her present ways.* □ *He then proceeded to read the riot act to his headstrong brother, asking him what on earth had possessed him to behave so grotesquely.*

◇ SEE ALSO **send someone away with a flea in their ear** ▷ FLEA; **give someone hell** ▷ HELL; **give someone a piece of your mind** ▷ PIECE; **give someone the rough side of your tongue** ▷ SIDE; **tear someone off a strip** ▷ STRIP

The **Riot Act** was a law passed in 1715, which said that if twelve or more people were together in a group and were considered to be causing a threat to the peace, the magistrates should read part of the Act to them, ordering them to break up their group and its activity, and threatening them with legal action if they did not obey within one hour.

run 'riot
To **run riot** is to behave in a wild and uncontrolled way: *Angry customers ran riot in a high street store after it ran out of mince pies, it was reported yesterday afternoon.* □ *Ruth felt as if he was trying to exert some power over her. Confusion ran riot in her heart.*

rise

get a 'rise out of someone
If someone is trying to **get a rise out of you**, they are trying to make you angry: *Ignore her. She's just trying to get a rise out of you.*

wakey-wakey rise and 'shine
You say **'wakey-wakey rise and shine'** to someone when you are telling them in a friendly way to get out of bed: *Come on, rise and shine. It's a beautiful day out there.* □ *Wakey-wakey rise and shine. We've got a busy day ahead of us.*

This expression uses the image of the sun rising and shining in the sky for a person getting up.

risk

at 'risk
Something is **at risk** if it is in a situation where it might be harmed, damaged or lost: *Women who smoke while they are pregnant may be putting their baby's life at risk.*

at the 'risk of
You say **'at the risk of** doing something' when you are aware that the thing you are about to say is likely to have an undesirable effect: *At the risk of sounding cruel, I reckon she got what she deserved.* □ *At the risk of being smug, I have to say I told you so.*

run the 'risk of
You **are running the risk of** some undesirable event when this event is likely to result from your actions: *Investing in shares can be very profitable, but of course you run the risk of losing the whole lot.*

rite

rite of 'passage
If people talk about a **rite of passage**, they mean a ceremony that must be participated in, or a thing that must be achieved, by a person who wants to develop from one stage of life to a stage of greater maturity, for example from childhood to adulthood: *Marriage is a rite of passage.* □ *Universities mark no mere rite of passage, now, between school and society.*

The word **passage** in this expression refers to the act of passing (from one state to another).

road

get out of my 'road or get out of the 'road (*informal*)
You say **'get out of my road'**, or **'get out of the road'**, when you are rudely telling someone to move because, in their present position they are blocking your way or

preventing you from doing something: *This box of vegetables is heavy and I'm about to drop it if you don't get out of my road.* □ *You'd better get out of the road, or you might get hit by a flying dart.*

◇ SEE ALSO **get out of my,** or **the, way** ▷ WAY

hit the 'road

You say it is time to **hit the road** when you have decided to leave the place you are in, and start travelling: *I'm not really a party-goer, so I just popped my head in to bid my good nights, and hit the road home about 1am.*

off the 'road

If your car is **off the road,** you cannot use it until it has been repaired: *My car's been off the road since April. I just can't afford to get it fixed.*

on the road to 'such-and-such

You are **on the road to** a certain thing if your situation is developing towards that thing: *Little Laura has responded positively to the treatment, and is well on the road to recovery.* □ *The company struggled to find a place in the market at first, but is finally on the road to success.*

one for the 'road

A person has **one for the road** when they take one last alcoholic drink before leaving the place they are in: *George Carter dipped his hand into his pocket and brought out some small silver. 'One for the road then, Jack?'*

the road to hell is paved with good in'tentions

If someone says '**the road to hell is paved with good intentions**', they mean that people who behave badly cannot expect to be forgiven just because they intended to behave well: *'I meant to phone.' 'Yes, well, the road to hell is paved with good intentions, and it's too late now.'*

robbery

daylight 'robbery

If you think that something costs too much, you can say it is **daylight robbery**: *Crab meat at six pounds a pound? That's daylight robbery.*

robin

round 'robin

A **round robin** is **1** a letter containing demands or complaints, signed by a lot of people and sent as a form of protest to the person or people in power: *Have you signed that round robin yet?* **2** a competition in which each player plays against every other player at least once: *'When you get the best eight players in the world together in a*

round robin tournament like this, there can be no favourites,' said world No. 1 Jim Courier.*

rock (*see also* **rocks**)

hit rock 'bottom

1 When something such as a quantity or value **hits rock bottom,** it reaches the lowest possible level: *Thousands of shop staff face the sack as sales hit rock bottom, bosses warned yesterday.* **2** When a person **hits rock bottom,** they have reached such a bad mental or physical state that they feel things could not get any worse: *I had been depressed for a while, but a few months after mother's death I hit rock bottom.*

rocker

off your 'rocker

You say that someone is **off their rocker** if you think that they are completely mad or stupid: *You agreed to babysit for him on your day off? You must be off your rocker.*
◇ SEE ALSO **be bananas** ▷ BANANAS; **off your chump** ▷ CHUMP; **off your trolley** ▷ TROLLEY

> The two curved pieces of wood on the bottom of a rocking chair are called the **rocker,** and if the chair comes **off its rocker,** it is broken.

rocks

get your 'rocks off (*vulgar*)

If people talk about **getting their rocks off,** they mean having sex.

on the 'rocks

1 A marriage or other relationship is **on the rocks** when the people involved are unhappy with each other and are maybe thinking about separating: *By this time, our marriage was on the rocks and Lorna had started drinking heavily.* **2** You serve a strong alcoholic drink **on the rocks** when you serve it poured into a glass on top of ice: *A Scotch on the rocks, please.* [= Scotch whisky with ice] **3** A business is **on the rocks** if it is in a state of great financial difficulty and will almost certainly have to stop trading if it cannot obtain money from somewhere: *The company looked to be on the rocks in late '91, but made a remarkable recovery the following year.*

run on to the 'rocks

When a ship **runs on to the rocks,** it gets stuck on rocks near the surface of the water: *Reports are coming in that an oil tanker has run on to the rocks near the south coast of Shetland.*

rod

make a rod for your own 'back

You say that someone **is making a rod for their own back** if, by their own actions, they are making unnecessary problems for themselves: *He believes the Corporation is making a rod for its own back. 'I think much of the pain and agony of change was avoidable.'*

◇ SEE ALSO **your own worst enemy** ▷ ENEMY; **make a meal of something** ▷ MEAL

> This expression comes from the medieval image of the person who provides a stick so that someone else can beat them with it.

spare the rod and spoil the 'child

If someone says '**spare the rod and spoil the child**', they mean that, unless children are punished when they behave badly, they will never learn to behave correctly: *His parents' doctrine was one of 'Spare the rod and spoil the child,' though in Leonard's case it was not 'the rod' but the dog-lead that reminded him of his responsibilities.* □ *He did not spare the rod as far as efficient administration was concerned – he was bad-tempered.*

> Notice that this idiom can be used to talk about situations other than those relating to children. The expression may also be shortened, as in the second example.

rogues

a rogues' 'gallery (*informal*)

1 A **rogues' gallery** is a police collection of photographs of known criminals. **2** A **rogues' gallery** is also any collection of people whom you consider to be dishonest or rebellious: *Like many of his fellow compatriots in the rogues' gallery of national football, he compulsively disliked authority.*

role

'role reversal

Role reversal happens when two people exchange their behaviour patterns and each one starts acting in the way that you would expect of the other: *In the week, if I'm busy, Martin can fix supper and do the ironing. It's good for the children to see some role reversal.*

roll

on a 'roll

1 You say you are **on a roll** if you are having a period of good luck: *The Meteors are on a roll – yesterday against the Solihull Dodgers they were looking for their fifth successive win.* □ *The brilliant new Twingo – Renault is*

on a roll. **2** You are also **on a roll** if you are doing something fast and enthusiastically, and may be unwilling to stop: *'Even if they really are fakes – synthetic fur,' (she was on a roll now) 'they're made from petrochemicals and they're non-biodegradable and therefore damaging to the environment.'*

roll up! roll 'up! (*rather old*)

If someone is trying to sell something, especially tickets, in a street or public area, it is traditional for them to attract people's attention by shouting '**roll up! roll up!**': *'Roll up, roll up for the Greatest Show on Earth,' Jack cried expansively, waving his arms around.*

rolling

'rolling in it

You say that someone is **rolling in it** if they have got a lot of money: *With five top 40 hits, you might think 'Take That' are rolling in it. Not so. According to Jason they just get a modest wage.*

Rome

fiddle while Rome 'burns

You say that someone **is fiddling while Rome burns** if they are doing nothing or spending time enjoying themselves, when they should be trying to help in a difficult or dangerous situation: *The Government, rather than address environmental issues, is content to fiddle while Rome burns.*

> The Roman Emperor Nero is said to have **fiddled** [= played the violin] while the city of Rome was burning. However, since the violin was only invented in the 16th century, the reference is more likely to be to an early instrument such as a lyre or a viol, if indeed the story is true at all.

Rome wasn't built in a 'day

If someone says '**Rome wasn't built in a day**', they mean that it takes time to change things or to make progress, and that you should not get discouraged just because it is taking longer than you had expected: *'The shop's been open six months and it still hasn't made a profit.' 'Rome wasn't built in a day, you know.'*

when in Rome, do as the 'Romans do

If someone says about a particular situation '**when in Rome, do as the Romans do**', they mean that it is better to adapt to the habits of the foreign culture you are in, rather than trying to hold on to your own familiar ways: *Gazza knows that when in Rome, do as the Romans do – so he got into the spirit with some impressive hand waving and high passion during a training match.* □ *The thought of eating sheep's eyes didn't* *exactly appeal. But then I thought, 'Oh, when in Rome ...', took a deep breath and stabbed one with my fork.*

It is common for journalists to use this idiom when they are writing about a subject relating to Rome, or Italy in general. But the expression can be used to refer to any foreign culture. People often just say 'when in Rome ...' as a way of resigning themselves to doing something that they would not normally do in their own country or environment.

roof

go through the 'roof

An amount that **goes through the roof** increases quickly to a high level: *The price of coffee has gone through the roof recently.*

have a 'roof over your head

A person **has got a roof over their head** if they have somewhere to live and do not have to live outside: *I worked in a hotel, in exchange for a small wage and a roof over my head.*

hit the 'roof

Someone **hits the roof** when they lose their temper and start shouting: *The foreman had naturally hit the roof over the loss of thirty minutes' production.*

◇ SEE ALSO **go off at the deep end** ▷ END; **have a blue fit** ▷ FIT; **blow a fuse** ▷ FUSE; **blow a gasket** ▷ GASKET; **let fly** ▷ LET; **blow** or **flip your lid** ▷ LID; **do your nut** ▷ NUT; **lose your rag** ▷ RAG; **fly into a rage** ▷ RAGE; **blow your stack** ▷ STACK; **lose your temper** ▷ TEMPER; **blow your top** ▷ TOP; **throw a wobbly** ▷ WOBBLY

under the same 'roof

1 People are **under the same roof** if they are living in the same house: *I was finding life under the same roof as my father almost impossible.* **2** Things are **under the same roof** if they can all be found in one building: *At the Scottish Careers Fair, you'll find over 500 company representatives all under the same roof.*

room

no room to swing a 'cat

You say that there is **no room to swing a cat** if there is not enough space to do things, or to feel comfortable, in the place you are referring to: *I would call it a cupboard, but they classed it as the bathroom. No room to swing a cat. Terrible.*

The word **cat** here refers to a cat-o'-nine-tails, a medieval type of whip with nine leather 'tails', each of which had a knot at the end.

room for im'provement

You say that there is **room for improvement** in something if it is not yet as good as you had expected or would wish: *Once there is a recognition that there is room for improvement there comes the task of developing a commitment and determination to bring about change.*

roost

rule the 'roost

The person who **rules the roost** is in charge and controls everyone else: *When their mother died in 1890, the eldest daughter was allowed to move to the first-floor bedroom, and from then on she ruled the roost.*

root

get to the 'root of something

You **get to the root of something** such as a problem or argument if you manage to discover what is causing it: *After hours of talking, we finally got to the root of why she had been so upset.*

the root 'cause of something

The **root cause of something** such as a problem or argument is the thing which is causing it: *In such a case the patient is quite unaware of the root cause of the problem, and is therefore unable to help the therapist consciously with the relevant case history.*

take 'root

Something such as an idea **takes root** when it establishes itself or starts to grow in strength: *If a negative thought is about to enter your mind, try to become aware of it before it has had time to take root in your unconscious.*

A plant **takes root** somewhere when its roots get strong and it starts to grow in that place.

roots

put down 'roots

You say you **are putting down roots** in a certain place if you have been living there for some time and are establishing a permanent life for yourself in that place: *Living the life of a nomad, travelling from city to city, never being able to put down roots in any one place, had taken its effect.*

A plant which has been moved to a new place has to **put down roots** in the earth around it before it can start to live and grow healthily.

rope

give someone enough rope to 'hang themselves

You **are giving someone enough rope to hang themselves** when, instead of accusing them of something immediately, you let them continue what they are doing in the hope that they will act even more foolishly and prove more obviously what you already know: *Kellard believes in the quiet approach: give enough rope. He would be the same in his interrogation room: no violence, no threats.*

> There are a lot of possible variants to this idiom. You can say, for example, 'Given enough rope, she would hang herself', or 'They'll give him just enough rope to hang himself'. Notice also, that you can shorten the idiom to 'give 'em enough rope' or 'give enough rope', as in the above example.

ropes

know the 'ropes

You **know the ropes** if you have a good idea, based on experience, of what needs to be done in a particular situation or for a particular job: *'He's got a good crew with him, hasn't he?' Carys said. 'George's lads know the ropes, they'll guide your Tom all right.'*

show someone the 'ropes

You **show someone the ropes** when you help them and show them what to do, because you are experienced in a situation or job which is new to them: *This is Laura. She'll be helping you out and showing you the ropes for your first month.*

roses

come up smelling of 'roses

People **come up smelling of roses** when, from luck rather than skill, they manage to deal with a situation in such a way that their reputations are improved rather than being damaged as was expected: *The affair could almost have bankrupted the firm. As it was, confidentiality was maintained and Smith managed to emerge smelling of roses.*

coming up 'roses

Things are **coming up roses** for a certain person when that person is having a period of good luck during which everything seems to be turning out perfectly for them: *She was going to marry a rising Minister, successful career, everything coming up roses.*

put the 'roses back in someone's cheeks

You say that something **puts the roses back in someone's cheeks** if it makes them look healthier and less pale than they looked before: *'You need good food, wine and sunshine to put the roses back into your cheeks. And love, of course,' she added.*

rot

the rot sets 'in

The moment when **the rot sets in** is the moment in a situation when things start to go so badly wrong that it is difficult or impossible to put them right: *The first proof that the rot had set in at the bank was the full disclosure of its profits and reserves in 1969.*

stop the 'rot

You do something to **stop the rot** when you attempt to stop a situation from getting worse: *Everyone has their own idea on how to stop the rot. The Engineering Careers Information service's answer was to spend £35,000 on a film to show school leavers.*

rough

rough and 'ready

1 A thing or situation which you describe as **rough and ready** has not been carefully made or prepared, but is probably good enough to do what you need it for: *Most of the huts have a table, chairs, some basic beds and even more basic mattresses, a kitchen and a rough-and-ready outside loo.* □ *a rough and ready performance.* □ *rough and ready guidelines.* **2** A person who is described as **rough and ready** is not well-educated or polite: *Her mother, who wished to distance her from the rough and ready children at the village school, arranged for her to have piano lessons.*

rough and 'tumble

Rough and tumble is play-fighting or, especially in sport or politics, any kind of behaviour which is friendly but competitive: *She would recall the boisterous rough and tumble of her younger brothers playing and fighting.* □ *After a lifetime in politics he knows all about the rough and tumble of public life.*

take the rough with the 'smooth

You **are taking the rough with the smooth** when you make yourself accept the bad things that happen by remembering that life cannot be easy all the time: *Relationships go up and down. You've got to learn to take the rough with the smooth.*

◇ SEE ALSO **take the bad with the good** ▷ BAD

rounds

do the 'rounds

1 You **do the rounds** when you spend a short period staying somewhere and visiting all the usual places, or going to see all the people you know there: *The duty* *corporal was doing the rounds of the barrack rooms, checking for cleanliness and tidiness.* □ *'What are your plans for Christmas?' 'We'll probably spend a few days doing the rounds back home.'* **2** You say that an illness **is doing the rounds** if a lot of people in a particular area are getting it: *'I think I've got some kind of stomach bug.' 'Yes. There's one doing the rounds just now.'* **3** A joke or a rumour **is doing the rounds** if a lot of people are telling it to each other at a particular time: *There was a rumour doing the rounds a few weeks ago that one of the big supermarket chains was on the point of phasing out its organic food lines.*

A doctor **does the rounds** when he or she goes to visit their patients in a hospital.

row

in a 'row
Several things happen **in a row** when they happen one after the other, with no breaks or changes in between: *I won six games in a row.*

rub

rub it 'in (*informal*)
You say that someone is **rubbing it in** when they keep reminding you of something that you find unpleasant or embarrassing, and are trying to forget: *'But how many of these wonderfully high-paid jobs have you been offered over the past eighteen months? None.' 'There's no need to rub it in. You don't know how difficult it is.'*

there lies the 'rub or there's the 'rub (*old*)
If someone says **'there lies the rub'** or **'there's the rub'**, they mean that the thing which has just been mentioned is the difficulty which is at the centre of a problem: *Finally, the reader will find chapters on finance and time-management. But there lies the rub. Will busy managers contemplate reading such a large amount of material?*

In the past, the word **'rub'** referred to any kind of hindrance or difficulty. Now, the word remains only in this idiom. In Shakespeare's *Hamlet*, III i, the hero considers killing himself, thinking being dead might be pleasant, just like sleeping. But he decides against suicide when he remembers what bad dreams people have when they are asleep, saying, 'To sleep! perchance to dream: – ay, **there's the rub**'.

Rubicon

cross the 'Rubicon
You **cross the Rubicon** when you do something which commits you to a particular course of action: *On the way to political union we are now crossing the Rubicon. There is no going back.*

The **Rubicon** is a small river in Italy which in ancient times was the boundary between Cisalpine Gaul and Italy. By crossing the river in 49BC, Caesar committed himself to a war with the Senate.

rule

as a 'rule
As a **rule** means 'generally' or 'usually': *I don't eat sweets as a rule.*

golden 'rule
A **golden rule** is a basic principle which should always be followed: *The golden rule when you are making Yorkshire puddings is to wait till the fat is extremely hot.*

make it a 'rule to do something
If you **make it a rule to do something**, you always try to do that thing: *I make it a rule never to miss breakfast.*

a rule of 'thumb
A **rule of thumb** is a measurement or general rule which is a good guide and easy to remember, although it may not be quite accurate: *You can expect to spend one third of your income on accommodation, as a general rule of thumb.* □ *As a rule of thumb, Dijon mustard ought to be presented with a pot au feu.*

In its original sense, **a rule of thumb** is a way of measuring using the width or length of your thumb as a guide.

rules

bend the 'rules or stretch the 'rules
You **bend**, or **stretch**, **the rules** when you do something that the rules do not totally allow: *You should be over sixteen to join the group, but we can bend the rules a bit in your case.*

run (*see also* **running**)

the general 'run of something or the usual 'run of something
The **general**, or **the usual**, **run of something** is the usual kind or mixture: *This happy pessimism is a far more compelling element than the cheerful man-gets-girl conclusion of the general run of romance-adventures.*

give someone a 'run for their money
You **give someone a run for their money** when you make it difficult for your com-

petitor or enemy to beat you, although you realize that you will probably have to admit defeat in the end: *'I don't pretend that this will ever be a Labour seat, but at least we can force the opposition to work harder, give them a run for their money,' he said.*

> In horse-racing, if a horse gives the people who have a bet on it **a run for their money**, it runs fast and tries hard to win the race, even though it does not manage to win in the end.

have a good 'run for your money

You say that someone **has had a good run for their money** if they can look back and be satisfied with what they have had or achieved, although it is now time for them to stop and let someone else take their place: *As company director for 30 years, I have had a good run for my money and plan to retire next spring.*

> See note at **give someone a run for their money**.

have a 'run-in with someone

You **have a run-in with someone** when you have an argument with them, usually about something practical such as bad behaviour or unsatisfactory work: *'We have had our run-ins in the past, but that's all behind us now. Barry has always been the best man for the job and we're going to continue our partnership.'*

◇ SEE ALSO **come to blows** ▷ BLOWS

in the 'long run

You think about something **in the long run** when you consider its more permanent effects: *You may not like the idea of studying for another year, but it'll be worth it in the long run.*

in the 'short run

You think about something **in the short run** when you consider its immediate effects: *In the short run we may see some improvement, but services will deteriorate in the longer term.*

on the 'run

A person who is **on the run** has escaped from an enemy, the authorities, or the police: *A prisoner was on the run last night after giving his guards the slip while he was visiting his dying mother in hospital.*

◇ SEE ALSO **on the loose** ▷ LOOSE

run a'mok

A person or group of people **run amok** when they start acting in a wild and violent way: *I forced an entry to find the raiders had ran amok inside, hurling bricks through the wooden huts and smashing window frames.*

run before you can 'walk

Someone who is trying to **run before they can walk** is trying to progress too quickly in a new skill or activity, moving on to the difficult stages before they are able to do the easy things correctly: *The first lesson was not to run before you can walk. 'It was a mistake to try to develop the business too fast,' says one of the founders.*

'run for it

You **run for it** when you try to escape: *Police had surrounded the house. Should he run for it, or give himself up without a fight?*

◇ SEE ALSO **leg it** ▷ LEG

run-of-the-'mill

Something that is described as **run-of-the-mill** is of an ordinary standard with nothing particularly good or interesting about it: *The menu looked fairly run-of-the-mill, so the excellent quality of the cooking came as a surprise.*

> **Run-of-the-mill** is originally an American term for the cut wood produced by a sawmill before it has been sorted for quality.

run 'short of something

You **are running short of something**, such as food, time, money or patience when you do not have much of it left: *He was running short of petrol and that route offered him the chance to find a petrol station along the way.* □ *He held onto the hat and hurried on. He was running short of time.*

runaround

give someone the 'runaround

1 A person or organization **gives you the runaround** when they keep sending you to someone else for help that they could have provided themselves: *A man living in Glasgow claims he has been 'given the runaround' by the legal system.*

runes

read the 'runes

You say that you **are reading the runes** when you understand what is going to happen in the future from the events which are happening in the present: *Scientists, quick to read the runes, predicted climate change as a result of using certain gases.*

rung

the lowest rung of the 'ladder or the bottom rung of the 'ladder

You are at **the lowest**, or **the bottom**, **rung of the ladder** when you are at the first stage in a certain system or organization, and it will take a long time or a lot of work for you to reach the more advanced stages: *When most people of her age are just setting their first steps on the bottom rung of life's ladder, she is already Radio One's most successful female disc jockey.*

the top rung of the 'ladder

You are at **the top rung of the ladder** when you have reached the most advanced level in a certain system or organization: *She can't work towards a promotion, because she's already at the top rung of the ladder.*

runner

do a 'runner

Someone **does a runner** when they leave a person or place without warning anyone, probably because they have done something illegal and do not want to be caught: *He still hasn't come back from the bank. You don't think he'd do a runner with my cash, do you?*

running

in the 'running

You say you are **in the running** when you have a chance of winning: *I didn't do well in the last round, but I'm still in the running for the cup.*

out of the 'running

You are **out of the running** when you have no chance of winning: *He only got a B-minus for his dissertation, which puts him out of the running for a distinction.*

running 'scared

You say that someone is **running scared** when they have become so afraid of something that they are starting to think and act foolishly: *For the moment Taylor isn't running scared of the barrage of hostile headlines.* □ *Labour are running scared that they will now lose their last remaining stronghold in Wear Valley.* □ *He sounds to me like a man who's running scared.*

up and 'running

An activity or process that is **up and running** is actually happening, as opposed to being in the planning stages: *We can start working out how to pay back our debts, now that the business is finally up and running.* □ *Many companies will only invest in the minimum training required to get the system up and running.*

rush

a rush of blood to the 'head

You experience **a rush of blood to the head** when you suddenly lose control of yourself and act in a fearless or foolish way as the result of excitement, nervousness, or some other emotion: *What lost us the match was a rush of blood to the head when they had the man sent off. It was terrible.*

rut

in a 'rut

You say you are **in a rut** when you are dissatisfied with your life because it has become boring and repetitive: *Apathy is a state of mind. It is the state of being in a rut, just carrying on with something without clear decisions or purpose.* □ *With a wardrobe comprising jeans and sweatshirts and a hairstyle that hadn't changed in ten years, Julia felt in a rut.*

S

sack

get the 'sack or **give someone the 'sack**
You **are given the sack**, or you **get the sack**, when your employer dismisses you from your job: *'I've been given the sack,' Leith told her shakily, and, over coffee, gave her a blow-by-blow account of his argument with the boss.*
◇ SEE ALSO **give someone the boot** ▷ BOOT

> The **sack** was the bag that workmen carried their tools in. When they were dismissed, they had to take their bag and go and look for work elsewhere.

hit the 'sack (*informal*)
You **hit the sack** when you go to bed: *Then he left and I hit the sack. Your English beer's a bit strong for me.*

sackcloth

sackcloth and 'ashes
Someone who is in, or who is wearing, **sackcloth and ashes** is very regretful, perhaps even more so than is necessary: *In ten seconds or so I would be either triumphant or in sackcloth and ashes.*

> Sackcloth and ashes were traditionally worn by the Jews for religious activities.

sadder

sadder but 'wiser or **sadder and 'wiser**
You are **sadder but wiser**, or **sadder and wiser** when you have lived through a painful experience which you have learnt something from: *Now sadder but wiser, we are prepared to admit that the implementation of curriculum change is a complicated business.*
□ *Now, as the couple face divorce, she is a sadder and wiser woman.*

saddle

in the 'saddle
Someone who is **in the saddle** is **1** on horseback. **2** in control or working effectively in a job or role: *He always had to be in the saddle, controlling everything within his reach with great brilliance and clarity of mind.*

> A **saddle** is a seat, made of leather, that you put on a horse's back so that you can ride it.

safe

safe and 'sound
If someone comes back **safe and sound**, they return from a journey or dangerous situation without having been injured or harmed: *It is his 42nd birthday on Monday. The greatest present we could wish for would be to see him safe and sound.*

safety

safety in 'numbers
If you say **'there's safety in numbers'**, you mean that it is fairly safe to do something, even if it seems to be dangerous, if a number of people are doing it together: *If either of you should get into difficulties, help will be at hand. Remember – there's safety in numbers.*

said (*see also* **say**)tsave

easier said than 'done
Something that is **easier said than done** is not as easy as it may seem, especially as it seems to the person who has suggested it: *Many books of advice assure people that once they start communicating properly, all their troubles will be over. This is easier said than done.*

enough 'said
Enough said, used after a statement, means 'and of course we all know about that': *Questioned on his views Lord White tried to backtrack. 'I'm beginning to sound like a right-wing lunatic.' Enough said.*

> This expression is often used when you are talking about something you find ridiculous or extreme in some way, but which you do not want to comment on directly.

least said, soonest 'mended
Least said, soonest mended means that it is better to say nothing than make a difficult situation worse by talking about it: *'Ah well,' he continued unhappily, having caught*

his wife's eye, 'least said soonest mended, I dare say.'

no sooner said than 'done

No sooner said than done emphasizes how quickly a particular task was carried out: *When asked what he wanted for his birthday, he said a visit to the lock factory. No sooner said than done.*

when all's said and 'done

You use when all's said and done to summarize a situation, having considered all the facts: *But when all's said and done, we've still got to work out how to pay for it.*

sailing

plain 'sailing

When you describe a task as plain sailing, you mean that it is straightforward and easy to do: *It is not always plain sailing. There are difficulties which may need to be overcome.*

◇ SEE ALSO **downhill all the way** ▷ WAY

sake

for the sake of 'argument

People assume something for the sake of argument when they treat it as true in order to discuss that depends on its being true: *Let us say, for the sake of argument, that the plotter and the assassin are one and the same person.*

salad

'salad days

Salad days refers to the time in your life when you were young and inexperienced: *Having concentrated on choral conducting during his salad days in the early 1970s, he found himself in something of a career rut by the age of 28.*

salt

rub salt into the 'wound

You rub salt into the wound when you do or say something that adds to the discomfort or distress that someone is already feeling: *The older painter was shocked by this reply and Pollock, sensing this, rubbed salt into the wound by adding: 'Your theories don't interest me!'*

Salt was traditionally used by sailors as an antiseptic. It caused great pain when applied to an already painful injury.

the salt of the 'earth

If you refer to other people or to another person as the salt of the earth, you consider them to be worthy of respect because you can always depend on them: *Most of the urban population see rural areas as being the backbone of society, the salt of the earth.*

take with a pinch of 'salt

You take something with a pinch of salt if you do not take it too seriosly because you have doubts about whether it is true: *She's got a very vivid imagination – take what she says with a pinch of salt.*

worth your 'salt

A person who is worth his or her salt is competent and worthy of respect: *Any lawyer worth his salt will tell the suspect in no uncertain terms to make no statement to the police under any circumstances.*

same

if it's all the same to 'you

You add 'if it's all the same to you' after a statement about what you intend to do, as a way of making sure that the other person doesn't mind you doing it: *I think I'd like just a small whisky now, Mr Dalgliesh, if it's all the same to you.*

much the 'same

Someone or something is much the same if they, or their condition, has altered very little: *'How's your husband – any better?' 'No, well much the same really.'*

never the same a'gain

If someone or something is never the same again, they are not, and never will be, as good as they were before: *'Fighters who have been in with Tyson are never the same again,' he said last week.*

same a'gain (*informal*)

People say 'same again' when they are requesting or ordering another drink of the kind they have just had: *'What're you having?' 'Same again please.'*

same as 'ever

Someone or something that is the same as ever has not changed over a certain period of time: *I hadn't seen him for a couple of years. But he was the same as ever.*

same to 'you

'Same to you' is a way of answering someone who has greeted you or insulted you, by wishing them the same thing: *'Sleep well, everybody.' She put her head into the kitchen. 'Same to you, sleep well. I'm off to bed.'*

sands

the sands of time are running 'out

If you say 'the sands of time are running out', you mean that there is not much time left before something fails or dies: *The sands of time are running out for a Yorkshire factory, unions said last night.*

sardines

packed like sar'dines

People are, or a place is, **packed like sardines**, if there are too many people in a place, and they are all crowded very closely together: *They offer us a form of transport where people are packed in like sardines, which is in danger of grinding to a halt at any moment.*

saturation

reach satu'ration point

Something **reaches saturation point** when no more can be added to it: *When the air at a particular temperature cannot hold any more moisture, it is said to have reached saturation point.*

sauce

what's sauce for the goose is sauce for the 'gander

If you say **'what's sauce for the goose is sauce for the gander'**, you mean that if something is good for one person, then it is also good enough for someone else, who may in fact believe themselves to be in a superior or more advantageous position: *And remember, what's sauce for the goose is sauce for the gander; if you've got a wife much richer than you, and you get divorced, you're the one who could benefit financially.*

sausage

not a 'sausage (*informal, humorous*)

Not a sausage means 'nothing at all': *'Did you manage to get any work done?' 'Not a sausage.'*

savoir

savoir-'faire

Savoir-faire is the ability to do and say the right thing in social situations: *Savoir-faire, good appearance and manners, were regarded as much more important than the ability to do well in examinations.*

Savoir-faire is a French term, meaning 'know how to do'.

say (*see also* **said**)

as they 'say

You use **'as they say'** before or after a saying or an idiom: *The new model simply isn't as much fun. But that, as they say, is the price of progress.*

have your 'say

You **have your say** when you take an opportunity to give your opinion: *I finally got a chance to have my say, but it was near the end of the meeting, and everyone wanted to get off for lunch.*

I'll say 'this for so-and-so or I'll say 'this for such-and-such

You say **'I'll say this for so-and-so'**, or **'I'll say this for such-and-such'** when you are about to state a quality you admire in someone, despite having just criticized them for something: *I did not agree one bit with his speech, but I will say this for him: at least he has political integrity.*

I'm sorry to 'say

You say **'I'm sorry to say'** to show that what you are about to announce causes regret or sadness: *He got in bad company, I'm sorry to say.*

I 'say (*old*)

People use **'I say!'** as a way of attracting someone's attention: *I say! You've dropped something.*

it's fair to 'say

You introduce a statement with **'it's fair to say'**, when you are about to say something that people might disagree with, but which, in your opinion, is true: *Of all the wonderful cricketers to come from the West Indies, it is fair to say that five have been of outstanding importance.*

needless to 'say or it goes without 'saying that

Needless to say means 'naturally' or 'of course': *We spent the rest of the weekend with my grandparents. Needless to say, we ate far too much.* □ *It goes without saying that you should study the contract with the utmost care.*

never say 'die

Never say die means 'don't give up or admit defeat': *Never say die, buddy. I've been in worse situations than this.* □ *Billy was an enthusiastic player, full of pep and fight, with the 'never say die' attitude that supporters love to see.*

◇ SEE ALSO **keep at it** ▷ KEEP; **stay** or **take the pace** ▷ PACE

say no 'more

People use **'say no more'** to show that it is not necessary to explain something any more because you already understand what they mean: *She said her husband's been late home every night this week. Say no more.*

say 'when (*informal*)

You tell someone to **say when** if you want them to tell you when to stop pouring them something to drink, or giving them something to eat.

what would you say to 'such-and-such? (*informal*)

You ask someone **what they would say to** a certain thing as a way of inviting them somewhere, or offering them something:

What would you say to another little drink before you go?

you can say 'that again! (*informal*)
You can say that again! means 'you're absolutely right!': *'Is he in trouble?' 'You can say that again!'*

you don't 'say! (*informal*)
You use '**you don't say!**' to express surprise, or mock surprise, at something you are told.

scales

tip the 'scales or **tilt the 'scales** or **turn the 'scales**
If a factor or circumstance **tips**, or **tilts**, or **turns**, **the scales** in favour of a certain decision, it is the one that causes that decision to be made: *When she hesitated, hardly knowing what to say, he tipped the scales by proposing briskly, 'Perhaps we should get down to business.'* □ *The conquest of the north decisively tilted the scales in Franco's favour.*

> Scales are a device for weighing things. Something that tips, tilts, or turns, the scales is slightly heavier than the weights on the other side.

says

what so-and-so says 'goes
If you say that **what** a certain person **says goes**, you mean that you have to do what they say: *If he says it's wrong, then of course it must be. I'm only the nurse. What he says goes.*

scarce

make yourself 'scarce
You **make yourself scarce** when you leave quickly, usually to avoid trouble or embarrassment: *If you know what's good for you, you'll make yourself scarce before you wake the whole house.*

scare

scare someone 'shitless (*informal, slang*)
Something that **scares you shitless** makes you feel very frightened: *Frightened? Sonny, I was scared out of my wits. Scared shitless, and that's the truth.*

scene

come on the 'scene or **arrive on the 'scene**
Someone or something **comes**, or **arrives**, **on the scene** when they become part of the current situation: *He came on the scene as a mild-mannered lawyer from Oregon with reasonable Republican credentials.*

create a 'scene or **make a 'scene**
If someone **makes**, or **creates**, **a scene**, they make an embarrassing display of emotion in public: *Please don't make a scene. Wait till we get home at least.*

not your 'scene (*informal*)
Something that you describe as **not your scene** is not the sort of thing that you like or enjoy: *I don't particularly want to go myself. Musicals aren't my scene.*

set the 'scene
You **set the scene** when you describe the situation in which an event took place: *Let's first set the scene. The sunset over a deserted beach. A single white sail on an azure-blue sea. A field of wild flowers.*

scenes

behind the 'scenes
If something happens, or is done, **behind the scenes**, it is done or happens out of the sight of the public so that they do not know about it: *Some people would do it in a very extrovert way. That's not my way of doing it. I prefer to work quietly behind the scenes.*

scent

throw someone off the 'scent
You **throw someone off the scent** when you give them wrong or confusing information, so that they will not find the person or thing that they are looking for: *He deliberately employed equations that nobody understood in order to put them off the scent and stop them contradicting him.*

> A scent is the natural smell that is given off by people and animals, which can be detected by other animals.

schedule

ahead of 'schedule
Something that happens or is completed **ahead of schedule** happens or is completed earlier than the time planned.

behind 'schedule
If something is **behind schedule**, it has not happened or been completed at the proper time according to a schedule.

on 'schedule or **according to 'schedule**
If something happens or is done **on schedule**, or **according to schedule**, it is done by, or happens at, the time planned: *Everything's going according to schedule.*

scheme

the 'scheme of things
When someone refers to **the scheme of things**, they are referring to the way the world seems to be organized: *Many are*

concerned with the Soviet Union's place in the scheme of things; with an intense probing of the values of nationhood and nationality.

school

of the 'old school
Someone who is described as being **of the old school** follows traditional customs and has old-fashioned habits: *Lord Carrington, an aristocrat of the old school whose experience of government went back to 1951, became Foreign Secretary.*

the old school 'tie
The **old school tie** refers to the habits of some upper class men, especially that of giving jobs to other men with similar backgrounds, or who went to the same school as them: *The old school tie network was a recipe for disaster. It just doesn't produce a rich enough mixture of ability needed in a political party.*

In Britain, many schools have their own uniform, which includes a tie of a particular colour and design. Some people, who went to very prestigious schools, continue to wear their **old school tie**, as a matter of pride, and also so that they may be recognized by others who went to the same school as them.

the school of hard 'knocks
If you say that you went to **the school of hard knocks**, you mean that a lot of what you have learnt about life has come from painful experience: *He certainly came from the school of hard knocks. But he wasn't bitter.*

◇ SEE ALSO **the school of life** ▷ SCHOOL

the school of 'life
If you say that you went to **the school of life**, you mean that a lot of what you have learnt about life has been through experience, rather than from studying: *Although I have no formal training, my experience is drawn from 'the school of life', having come through divorce, and the death of my son and partner.*

◇ SEE ALSO **the school of hard knocks** ▷ SCHOOL

schoolboy

as every schoolboy 'knows
If you say **'as every schoolboy knows'**, you mean **'as everyone knows (or should know)**, including young people': *They belong to the British Museum, which bought them in 1816 from Lord Elgin, as every schoolboy knows.*

science

blind someone with 'science
Someone **blinds you with science** when they use a lot of technical words to explain something, sometimes deliberately, so that you cannot understand their argument: *There is a technical difference between the two kinds of economy, but I don't want to blind you with science.*

score

on that 'score
On that score means 'concerning that' or 'with regard to that': *Don't worry on that score; everything's under control.*

settle a 'score or settle old 'scores
People **settle a score**, or **settle old scores**, when they take some action to settle grudges or grievances that they have had for a long time against the other people concerned.

scorn

pour 'scorn on
If you **pour scorn on** someone or something, you criticize them severely and contemptuously: *Did you ever have one of those teachers who would pour scorn on you if you made a spelling mistake?*

scot

scot-'free
If someone goes, escapes, or gets off, **scot-free**, they are unpunished or unharmed: *What I can't understand, is how the judge let them off scot-free.*

scrap

on the 'scrap heap
Someone or something is **on the scrap heap** when they are discarded or rejected because they are no longer useful: *As a result of these training schemes they would be better educated and would not be thrown on the scrap heap.*

scratch

from 'scratch
You start, or do, something **from scratch**, when you start it from the very beginning: *Students have the possibility of learning another language intensively from scratch in the first year.*

The **scratch** used to be the starting line which was scratched on the ground to show where a race would start.

up to 'scratch
If someone or something is, or comes, **up to scratch**, they meet or reach the required or

expected standard: *Our particular role in training is to make sure the standard of teaching in every centre is up to scratch.*

screen

the big 'screen
People sometimes refer to the cinema as **the big screen**: *Good and successful literature does not necessarily transfer easily to the big screen.*

screw

have a 'screw loose (*informal*)
Someone who **has got a screw loose** is a bit mad: *Normally I'd hesitate to believe her story because she does seem to have a screw loose, but it does correspond to the others.*
◇ SEE ALSO **out to lunch** ▷ LUNCH

screws

put the 'screws on someone
You **put the screws on** someone when you use force or pressure in dealing with them: *You see, you are a chauvinist. You put the screws on her and she submitted.*

> The **screws** or 'thumbscrews' used to be an instrument of torture.

scrounge

on the 'scrounge
You are **on the scrounge** if you are trying to get the things you want or need by begging or persuading other people to give them to you: *As she was always on the scrounge, it wasn't surprising that she didn't have any real friends.*

scruff

by the scruff of the 'neck
If someone holds a person or an animal, such as a cat, **by the scruff of the neck**, they hold them by the collar or by the skin on the back of their neck: *I got hold of him by the scruff of the neck and took him along to the police box and phoned for a car.*

scum

scum of the 'earth (*informal, insulting*)
If you refer to a person, or group of people, as **scum of the earth**, you think they are very bad, disgusting or worthless: *You drug dealers are the scum of the earth!*

> **Scum** is a frothy covering of dirt or unpleasant waste material.

sea

all at 'sea
If you are **all at sea**, you are in a completely disorganized state or have no idea what to

do next: *The next Lincoln attack swept United away. They were all at sea as Matthews took aim and fired in goal number two.*

seal

give your seal of ap'proval
If someone whose opinion is respected gives a plan or a project their **seal of approval**, they say or do something that shows that they are in favour of what is being proposed: *Mitterand was too clever a politician to put anything in writing but his seal of approval was clearly on the operation.*

set the 'seal on or put the 'seal on
Something that **sets**, or **puts**, **the seal on** something else, makes that thing definite, or confirms it in a formal or appropriate way: *He came out into the street to find that it had started to rain. It set the seal on his depression.*

seam

a rich 'seam
A **rich seam** of something is a high level of that thing: *Sunderland have a rich seam of experienced players.*

> The kind of seam that this idiom refers to, is a layer of minerals, such as coal, suitable for mining.

seams

bursting at the 'seams
A thing or a place that is **bursting at the seams** is very full, or so full that it appears to be, or actually is, about to break: *What with the festival and everything, all the hotels are bursting at the seams, but we'll do our best for you.*

> A **seam** here, is the join between two pieces of material, where they are sewn together.

fall apart at the 'seams or come apart at the 'seams
Someone or something **falls**, or **comes**, **apart at the seams** when they become useless, ruined, or unable to remain in control: *I fell apart at the seams – I was in tears all the time, and my doctor put me on pills.* □ *Sadly, in the second half, the play begins to fall apart at the seams as Harwood attempts to combine comedy with more serious themes.*

> See note above.

search

search 'me (*informal*)
Search me means 'I have no idea'.

season

Season's 'Greetings
The words **'Season's Greetings'** are often written on Christmas cards, as a way of wishing someone a happy Christmas.

seat

back-seat 'driver
A **back-seat driver** is a passenger in a car who annoys the driver by giving him or her instructions and advice regarding the best way to drive: *A driver with impaired hearing is observant and undistracted by chatting passengers, exciting radio programmes and back-seat drivers.*

flying by the seat of your 'pants
Someone who **is flying by the seat of their pants** is trying to achieve something by using instinct, luck, and not much skill: *What is the Government up to? Alas, it is flying by the seat of its pants. This student loans scheme has degenerated into open shambles.*

seat-of-the-pants: *seat-of-the-pants management.*

have a 'seat or take a 'seat
You say **'have a seat'**, or **'take a seat'** to someone when you are inviting them to sit down.

in the 'driving seat
Someone who is **in the driving seat** is running, or in control of something, such as a business: *It was the reappearance of Harold Wilson in the driving seat of government which prompted this.*

in the 'hot seat
You are **in the hot seat** if you are in a difficult position where you are responsible for dealing with awkward questions, criticisms, etc: *They will give the Prime Minister a warm welcome, but they will also put him in the hot seat because of mass unemployment, homelessness and general misery.*

on the edge of your 'seat
You are **on the edge of your seat** if you are excited, anxious or nervous about what might happen next: *This is a movie which insists you sit on the edge of your seat while skulls are cleaved and scalps lifted by the score.*

a ringside 'seat
If you have **a ringside seat**, you are in the best position to see something happen: *I'll try to get you a ringside seat for any special occasions, and generally help in any way I can.*

'Ringside' here refers to the area round the edge of a boxing ring.

take a back 'seat
You **take a back seat** when you take on a less important role than before: *He bowed out, dropping hints that in future he would be taking a back seat in politics.*

second

for a split 'second
You experience something **for a split second**, when you experience it in a very short period of time, probably in less than one second: *He passed by, and our eyes met for a split second.*

second 'only to
If one thing is **second only to** another, the other thing is the only one that is better than it: *A recent survey has shown that the microwave is America's favourite household appliance, second only to the smoke alarm in terms of its importance to the American lifestyle.*

secrecy

swear someone to 'secrecy
If you **swear someone to secrecy**, you make them promise that they will not tell anyone a particular piece of information: *Until it's all out in the open the examiners are all sworn to secrecy.*

see (see also **seeing, seen**)

as far as 'I can see
You use **as far as I can see** when expressing your own opinion about a situation: *As far as I can see they're just not interested in learning this stuff.*

could see it 'coming
If you say about some unpleasant event, that you **could see it coming**, you mean that it was clear to you that it was going to happen: *You know what conditions are like in there. He'll catch some illness or other, I can see it coming.*

I'll 'see or we'll 'see
You say **'I'll see'** or **'we'll see'** to avoid giving a definite answer to a request: *'So can we go and see Grandma tomorrow, Mum?' 'We'll see.'*

let's 'see
You say **'let's see'** when you are working something out: *Let's see, three fours are twelve, plus two more makes fourteen.*

see 'so-and-so coming (*informal*)
If you say that someone **saw you coming**, you mean that they took advantage of your trust in them: *I can't believe those kids managed to get my wallet like that – they saw me coming, all right.*

see 'red
If you say that something makes you **see red**, you mean that it makes you very

angry: *But she was not the only one who was losing her cool. Matilda was also beginning to see red.*

see to it that

If you say that you'll **see to it that** something happens, you mean that you will take the necessary steps to make sure that it happens: *Did she not understand that I would look after her, that I would see to it that she was safe and 'well?*

so I 'see

'**So I 'see**' means 'Yes I can see that, and I am not pleased about it': *'Er, we're having a party.' 'So I see.'*

seed

go to 'seed or run to 'seed

If a person has **gone**, or **run, to seed**, they have let themselves get untidy, fat or unhealthy because they have not paid enough attention to themselves: *She looked middle-aged, overdressed, a show-girl gone to seed.*

When a vegetable produces seeds after flowering, it is no longer possible to eat it.

sow the seeds of

You **sow the seeds of** a particular thing when you start a process that will develop into something important: *The scheme will overpay some lawyers and underpay others, and that may sow the seeds of mis'trust between client and solicitor.*

seeing

seeing is be'lieving

Seeing is believing is a saying which means that once you have seen something, you have no choice other than to believe in it: *If you're still not convinced, seeing is believing. Send for our full colour catalogue today.*

seen

have to be seen to be be'lieved

Something that **has to be seen to be believed** is incredible or ridiculous: *The amount of paperwork surrounding events such as this has to be seen to be believed.*
◇ SEE ALSO **beyond belief** ▷ BELIEF

seen one, seen 'em 'all (*informal*)

Seen one, seen 'em all means that if you have seen one of a certain type of thing, then it is not worth seeing any more of them, because they are all the same: *I can't be bothered to go and see that new horror film – you've seen one, seen 'em all.*

wouldn't be seen 'dead (*informal*)

You say that you **wouldn't be seen dead** doing something, or in a particular state, if you would never do it because you think it is stupid, ridiculous or embarrassing: *I wouldn't be seen dead in a hat like that. I'm not 19 any more, you know.*
◇ SEE ALSO **I'd rather die** ▷ DIE; **wouldn't dream of** ▷ DREAM

sense

in the 'biblical sense

You use '**in the biblical sense**' if you want to indicate that you are using the verb 'know' in its old-fashioned sense of 'have a sexual relationship with': *'Rachel, I'm a man of thirty-three, not an inexperienced boy. I've known a lot of women in my time, and -' 'In the biblical sense, no doubt!'*

in a 'sense

Something that is the case **in a sense** is partly so, or is the case in one way: *Well yes, I suppose in a sense you're right.*

knock some 'sense into someone (*informal*)

Someone **knocks some sense into you**, or **into your head**, when they use physical or persuasive force to make you understand something, or discipline yourself: *Let's hope the military prison knocked some sense into his head.*

a sense of oc'casion

A **sense of occasion** is a feeling caused by the excitement and organized social ceremony that goes with the act of celebrating something: *I never cease to wonder at the excitement, the sense of occasion, that these great musicians generate.* □ *If you want special dishes that still have a sense of occasion, then you should try out these recipes.*

a sixth 'sense

Someone who has **a sixth sense** knows or feels things, such as danger, and other people's thoughts, through intuition: *She is interested in the 'almost sixth sense that seems to exist between mothers and small babies'.*

talk 'sense

People **talk sense** when they speak wisely and sensibly: *Her father snapped, 'If you can't talk sense then be quiet.'*

there's no sense in

You say that **there's no sense in** doing something if there is no advantage or point in doing it: *There is no sense in training people to use fancy navi'gation aids when we would be unable to use them in 'wartime.*

senses

come to your 'senses

You **come to your senses** when you start behaving sensibly after a period of foolishness; someone or something **brings you to your senses** when they cause you to do this:

I had to lose a good woman before I came to my senses. But I did kick the drug.

take leave of your 'senses
People say that you **have taken leave of your senses** when you do something crazy: *She tugged his arm furiously. 'Let me go! This minute! Have you taken leave of your senses?'*

seriousness

in all 'seriousness
Someone does, or says, something **in all seriousness** when they do or say it without joking or speculating, especially when that is not what you would expect: *I met one of them at a party once and he told me they're going to be bigger than The Beatles – in all seriousness.*

serve

serve someone 'right
If you say, in reference to someone's misfortune, that it **serves them right**, you mean that they deserve it: *'He's been sick.' 'Serves him right for eating so much cake.'*

set

all 'set
People are **set**, or **all set**, to do something, when they are ready to do it or about to do it.

shade

put someone in the 'shade
You **put someone in the shade** if you are much better than them at doing something: *Her cooking really puts me in the shade.*
◇ SEE ALSO **knock spots off** ▷ SPOTS; **put to shame** ▷ SHAME

shadow

beyond any shadow of 'doubt or **without any shadow of 'doubt**
Something that is the case **beyond**, or **without**, **any shadow of doubt** is definitely the case, without any doubt at all: *Tonight, she knew without any shadow of doubt that he was lying to her.*
◇ SEE ALSO **for certain** ▷ CERTAIN; **beyond all doubt** ▷ DOUBT; **without a doubt** ▷ DOUBT; **beyond any shadow of doubt** or **without any shadow of doubt** ▷ SHADOW; **sure as eggs is eggs** ▷ SURE

shakes

in two 'shakes (*informal*)
In two shakes means 'immediately': *If I thought you'd gone telling the story all over town, I'd have you out of my house in two shakes.*

no great 'shakes (*informal*)
Something that is described as **no great shakes** is not very impressive or special: *It is a very simply made film, and no great shakes as a piece of cinema.*
◇ SEE ALSO **leave a lot** or **something to be desired** ▷ LEAVE

shame

a crying 'shame
If you describe something as **a crying shame** you mean that it is a very great shame: *I think it would be a crying shame if the country pub disappeared, but they need more customers.*

put to 'shame
A person or thing **puts** someone or something else **to shame** when they make them look less attractive or efficient than they appeared to be before: *She takes far better care of it than I ever did. She puts me to shame, she's so capable.*
◇ SEE ALSO **knock spots off** ▷ SPOTS; **put someone in the shade** ▷ SHADE

'shame on you!
You say **shame on you!** as a way of not too seriously telling someone that you think they have done something bad or shameful: *'Shame on you,' came the bantering reply, 'not to know one of your own local poets.'*

shape

in any shape or 'form
In any shape or form means 'of any kind', or 'in any way', or 'at all': *I would emphasize that we do not support in any shape or form the selling of tobacco goods to children under the age of 16.* □ *The company's lawyer said: 'You won't get a real opal in any shape or form for £3.50.'*

knock into 'shape or **lick into 'shape**
You **knock**, or **lick**, someone or something **into shape**, when you improve them, make them more organized, or more efficient: *'Don't worry, ma'am,' he laughed. 'We'll soon lick him into shape.'*

in 'shape
If you are **in shape**, you are physically fit and healthy.

in the shape of
You use **in the shape of** to give an example of a more general term, which you mentioned before: *The space-age has arrived here too, in the shape of ultra-modern satellite TV coverage.*

out of 'shape
You are **out of shape** when you are not as fit and healthy as you can be.
◇ SEE ALSO **out of condition** ▷ CONDITION

take 'shape

Something **takes shape** when it takes on a definite or recognizable form: *Now a new line of research is taking shape in the US to combat these and other toxic chemicals.*

shapes

all shapes and 'sizes

If you say that people, or certain things, come in **all shapes and sizes**, you mean that they exist in many different types and forms: *They tend to think they'll be cutting trendy hairstyles all day. But real people come in all shapes and sizes.* □ *Pasta comes in all shapes and sizes, some for specific recipes, such as the large sheets of lasagne.*

share

more than your fair share of 'such-and-such

Someone or something has had **more than their fair share** of a particular thing if they have had more of it than most, and perhaps too much of it: *It's an area with more than its fair share of disadvantages.*

your fair share of 'such-and-such

Someone or something has had **their fair share of** a particular thing if they have had a lot of it: *It's the titles that matter, and Martina, with 156, has her fair share of them.*

share and share a'like

Share and share alike is a saying which means 'share things equally': *In her will she thanked the thirteen people she considered important in her life and asked that they should simply 'share and share alike'.*

shave

a close 'shave

You have **a close shave** when you just manage to avoid having an accident: *Good gracious, that was a close shave, I'll have to sit down for a minute, I think I'll have a cup of coffee or something.*
◇ SEE ALSO **close call** ▷ CALL; **narrow escape** ▷ ESCAPE; **narrow squeak** ▷ SQUEAK; **close** or **near thing** ▷ THING

shebang

the whole she'bang (*informal*)

The whole shebang means 'the whole lot' or 'everything relating to the situation being described': *He was willing at first to take her to the latest 'in' restaurants and nightspots, charity balls, Henley, Ascot, the whole shebang.*

sheep

the 'black sheep

The black sheep of a particular group of people, such as a family, is someone who does not follow the rules of that group, often causing shame to the other members: *I wanted to be the black sheep. That was my role in life.*

This phrase is often found in the expression 'the black sheep of the family'.

count 'sheep

You **count sheep** when, unable to sleep, you imagine an endless number of sheep, jumping over a fence; counting them is supposed to help you fall asleep: *Dougal closed his eyes and tried counting sheep.*

may as well be hung for a sheep as a 'lamb

If someone says that they **may as well be hung for a sheep as a lamb**, they mean that if you are going to do something wrong, you might as well do something really bad which will benefit you even more.

Stealing a lamb used to be punishable by death, so it was worth stealing something bigger, because the punishment could not be any worse.

separate the sheep from the 'goats or sort out the sheep from the 'goats

Something such as a task, that will **separate**, or **sort out, the sheep from the goats** will show which people in a group are good, useful and efficient, and which ones are not: *Rationalizing a business, while keeping the enthusiasm and loyalty of one's staff can certainly separate the sheep from the goats in the management sense.*
◇ SEE ALSO **separate** or **sort out the men from the boys** ▷ MEN; **separate** or **sort out the wheat from the chaff** ▷ WHEAT

sheet

a clean 'sheet

You start with **a clean sheet** when you disregard any faults or mistakes you have made in the past, which may be to your disadvantage, and begin again: *It is rarely, if ever, possible to start with a clean sheet.*
◇ SEE ALSO **a clean slate** ▷ SLATE

shelf

on the 'shelf

1 Something that is put **on the shelf** is postponed, or put aside for a time. 2 If you say that someone, especially a woman, has been left **on the shelf**, you mean that they no longer have the opportunity to marry because they are now too old: *In those days, spinsterhood was seen as a mark of personal inadequacy, and I, as they probably all realized, was being left on the shelf.*

The idea of a woman being **left on the shelf** is rather an old-fashioned one now, but single women sometimes use the idiom jokingly to speak about themselves.

shell

come out of your 'shell

You **come out of your shell** when you become more confident and less shy; you **bring someone out of their shell** if you help them to be able to do this: *At university I came out of my shell. I actually talked to my fellow students and built up some relations with people.*

shine

take a 'shine to someone

Someone **takes a shine to you** when they decide very quickly that they like you: *I think he took quite a shine to you.*

ship

abandon 'ship

You **abandon ship** when you stop doing something before you have finished, because continuing with it would lead to disaster: *Do you think I'm trying to back out? Of course I don't want to abandon ship.*

run a tight 'ship

Someone who **runs a tight ship** is in control of an efficient, well-run organization: *We've run a very tight ship and we feel now is the time to increase the manager's budget.*

when your 'ship comes in

If you say that you will be able to do something **when your ship comes in**, you mean that you will be able to do it when you are rich: *The house needs a lot of work, I'm afraid, but perhaps we'll be able to do something to it one day, when our ship comes in.*

ships

like ships that pass in the 'night

You describe people as being **like ships that pass in the night** if they meet each other by chance, once, or several times, but never really get a chance to talk or get to know each other.

shirt

bet your 'shirt on or put your 'shirt on

If you **bet**, or **put**, **your shirt on** something, you depend completely on its happening: *The 1990s could be the decade of the European. But don't bet your shirt on it.*

have the shirt off someone's 'back

Someone who **would have the shirt off your**

back, is prepared to cheat you financially, without any feelings of guilt: *I'd watch out for those loan companies – they'll have the shirt off your back if you're not careful.*

keep your 'shirt on

If you say '**keep your shirt on**' to someone, you are telling them rather rudely, to calm down, and not to become so angry or excited: *All right, all right, keep your shirt on!*

shit

get your 'shit together (*informal*)

You **get your shit together** when you organize yourself, your life, or your possessions, for example: *Ryder returned home alone to get his shit together.* □ *What do they know about these mad drug stories and us not getting our shit together?*

hot 'shit (*very informal, slang*)

Something that is described as **hot shit** is very impressive or enjoyable: *Have you heard the new 'Elastica' album? Pretty hot shit.*

in the 'shit (*very informal*)

You are **in the shit** if you are in trouble: *'We're in the shit,' he said. 'The engine's overheating. The oil gauge is in the red. Christ, I can smell it!'*

◇ SEE ALSO **up the creek without a paddle** or **up the creek** ▷ CREEK; **out of your depth** ▷ DEPTH; **up shit creek** ▷ SHIT; **in the soup** ▷ SOUP; **in a tight spot** ▷ SPOT; **in trouble** ▷ TROUBLE; **in deep water** ▷ WATER; **in hot water** ▷ WATER

not give a 'shit (*informal*)

Someone who **doesn't give a shit** doesn't care at all: *Nobody seems to give a shit about my research.*

◇ SEE ALSO **not give a damn** ▷ DAMN; **not care a fig** or **two figs** ▷ FIG, FIGS; **not care or give a hoot** or **two hoots** ▷ HOOT, HOOTS; **not give a monkey's** ▷ MONKEY'S; **not care a sod** ▷ SOD; **not give a tinker's cuss** ▷ TINKER; **not give** or **care a toss** ▷ TOSS; **not care or give tuppence** ▷ TUPPENCE

'shit-for-brains (*informal, slang*)

If you call someone **shit-for-brains**, you are saying, very rudely, that they are stupid: *Guess who told them; shit-for brains over there.*

the shit hits the 'fan or the 'shit flies (*informal*)

If you say that **the shit hits the fan**, or **the shit flies**, you mean that the situation suddenly causes trouble for someone: *Everyone knew that Aristos was a frustrated dead loss, so if the shit did hit the fan it would be simple for Ocker to disclaim all knowledge of Aristos' actions.*

tough 'shit (*informal*)

If you say '**tough shit**' to someone, you mean, very rudely, that you have no sympathy for them, or that you do not care about what they think: *They told me to take my earring out when I go to have an interview. If they don't love me for what I am that's just tough shit!*

up shit 'creek (*informal*)

You are **up shit creek** if you are in serious difficulties: *She was in a mess, not only emotionally, but financially too. 'Up shit creek,' as Corky would have said.*

◊ SEE ALSO **up the creek without a paddle** or **up the creek** ▷ CREEK; **out of your depth** ▷ DEPTH; **in the shit** ▷ SHIT; **in the soup** ▷ SOUP; **in a tight spot** ▷ SPOT; **in trouble** ▷ TROUBLE; **in deep water** ▷ WATER; **in hot water** ▷ WATER

> This idiom is a more vulgar variation of the expression 'up the creek without a paddle' or 'up the creek'.

shits

give someone the 'shits (*informal*)

Someone or something that **gives you the shits** makes you feel frightened, worried or anxious: *That used to give me the shits. Every time I heard those shots I thought 'My turn tomorrow'.*

shiver

a shiver runs down your 'spine

If you say that **a shiver ran down your spine**, you mean that you had a sudden feeling of horror or fear: *It was like taking a step back into the past, and for a moment a little shiver ran down her spine.*

shivers

give someone the 'shivers

Someone or something that **gives you the shivers** gives you a feeling of horror or fear: *Miss Jarman looked at her – a long calculating look that gave Jess the shivers.*

shock

come as a 'shock

Something **comes as a shock** when it deeply upsets you, particularly because you were not expecting it: *Her death came as a terrible shock to us all.*

◊ SEE ALSO **a bolt from the blue** ▷ BOLT

'shock tactics

You use **shock tactics** when you do something unexpected in order to surprise someone and so gain an advantage over them, or try to teach them a lesson: *Shock tactics are being used to make young drivers more aware of danger on the roads.*

a shock to the 'system

You describe the effect of something good or bad as **a shock to the system** if it causes you to feel suddenly disturbed or disorientated because you are not used to it: *Dashes of brilliant colour can still be a shock to the system after the rather quiet, dignified grooming of recent seasons.*

short sharp 'shock

Someone is given a **short sharp shock** as a punishment when they are disciplined very severely over a short period of time, the idea being that this will 'shock' them into behaving lawfully: *The 'short sharp shock' detention centre regime for young offenders was introduced by Mrs Thatcher's Conservative government in the early 1990s.*

shoes

fill someone's 'shoes

You **fill someone's shoes** when you successfully replace them in their function: *And if you're to try and fill your mother's shoes, you'll need all the reminding I can give you.*

in 'so-and-so's shoes

If you say that you would behave in a particular way if you were **in** a certain person's **shoes**, you mean that you would act in that way if you were in their situation: *She really was making his life a misery. If I'd been in his shoes, I'd probably have lost my patience weeks ago.*

put yourself in 'such-and-such's shoes

You **put yourself in** a certain person's **shoes** when you imagine how they must feel under the circumstances: *She felt sorry for him. 'Please,' she said coaxingly. 'Put yourself in his shoes.'*

◊ SEE ALSO **put yourself in such-and-such's place** ▷ PLACE

step into someone's 'shoes

You **step into someone's shoes** when you take over their duties or responsibilities: *Who will step into the shoes of Lord Elton at the head of Britain's most important investor protection body?*

shoestring

on a 'shoestring

You do something **on a shoestring** if you do it using very little money: *We were living on a shoestring all the time he was enjoying himself down there.* □ *Fighting bankruptcy, living from day to day on a shoestring budget.*

shop

all 'over the shop (*informal*)

If things are **all over the shop**, they are scattered everywhere or in many places;

if you, or your behaviour is **all over the shop**, you are behaving in a disorganized, inconsistent way: *In between, Ballesteros was, for much of the time, all over the shop.*

shut up 'shop
If a business **shuts up shop**, it stops trading, either at the end of a working day, or permanently: *But as shopping habits changed many traders shut up shop and moved out blaming recession, traffic restrictions and fewer bus routes.*

talk 'shop
People **talk shop** when they discuss their professional concerns when they are away from the workplace: *'Don't tell me that you two are talking shop,' Andrew said. 'Don't you ever stop?'*

short

be caught 'short or **be taken 'short**
You **are caugh**t, or **taken**, **short** when you need to go to the toilet and find that there are no toilets nearby: *And you'd best go to the toilet before you leave. You don't want to get caught short.*

be short of
You **are short** of something if you do not have enough of it: *We're a bit short of 'milk. Could you get some?*

have someone by the short and 'curlies
You **have someone by the short and curlies** if you have them in a position where you can get whatever you want from them: *You'd believe anything. I can see they had you by your short and curlies the minute they got you into that uniform.*

short and 'sweet
Something that is described as **short and sweet** is shorter than expected, often pleasantly so: *His comments were short and sweet. 'Sam McKnight, I admire him because he is just so creative in his work.'* □ *I think I've got five minutes, which is probably more than some of you delegates have got, so I'll keep it fairly short and sweet.*

shot

be shot of
You **are shot of** someone or something if you have got rid of them, or if they are not there any more to bother you: *I bet you're glad to be shot of those ex'ams now.*

'big shot
A **big shot** is an important or influential person: *He is in London now, working in the theatre. He will be a big shot one day, she thinks.*

call the 'shots
If a particular person **calls the shots**, they are the person who gives the orders or is in charge: *Mother is in charge: she is the boss and she calls the shots.*
◇ SEE ALSO **call the tune** ▷ TUNE

like a 'shot
If you do something **like a shot**, you do it extremely quickly without hesitating: *As soon as she heard about the accident she was down the hospital like a shot.*
◇ SEE ALSO **like a dose of salts** ▷ DOSE

a shot in the 'arm
If something that is failing or faltering is given **a shot in the arm**, it is given something which has the effect of reviving its performance: *The 25 billion will be used to create jobs and generally give the economy a shot in the arm. But it still may not be enough.*

a shot in the 'dark
A **shot in the dark** is a wild guess which may or may not prove to be right: *Every appointment seems to be an outrageous shot in the dark.*

shotgun

shotgun 'marriage or **shotgun 'wedding**
1 A **shotgun marriage**, or **wedding**, is a marriage which takes place because the woman concerned is pregnant. 2 A **shotgun marriage**, or **wedding**, is also any kind of enforced joining together of two groups: *Others wanted Lloyd George to take over the leadership and unite the parties in a shotgun wedding.*

shoulder

give someone the cold 'shoulder
Someone **gives you the cold shoulder** when they act in an unfriendly way towards you, perhaps by refusing to speak to you: *Will they remember me? What will they say to me when I come back home? Will they give me the cold shoulder?*
◇ SEE ALSO **give someone the brush-off** ▷ BRUSH

put your shoulder to the 'wheel
You **put your shoulder to the wheel** when you begin to make a great effort or to work very hard: *I want you to put your shoulder to the wheel if necessary. You ready for it?*
◇ SEE ALSO **get cracking** ▷ CRACKING

a shoulder to 'cry on
You give someone who is upset **a shoulder to cry on** when you give them sympathy, and encourage them to feel better: *I felt very inadequate but at least I was able to provide a shoulder to cry on.*

shoulder to 'shoulder
If people do something **shoulder to shoulder**, they do it side by side, or in friendship and agreement: *The women went with their men in to the fields and byres and worked shoulder to shoulder.*

show

straight from the 'shoulder

You speak **straight from the shoulder** when you speak frankly and forcefully: *Sometimes he spoke straight from the shoulder and sometimes in puzzles and parables.*

show

get the show on the 'road

You **get the show on the road** when you begin doing what you have planned: *Thanks, Jim. Now let's get this show on the road.*

jolly good 'show (*old*)

'**Jolly good show**' is a rather outdated and upper class way of expressing satisfaction or pleasure.

> **Jolly good show** is now only used by most people in a humorous or mocking way.

just goes to 'show

If you say '**just goes to show**', you mean that things are not always as we expect them to be: *'And they seemed like such a happy couple.' 'Well, just goes to show.'*

a show of 'hands

If someone asks for **a show of hands**, they mean that they would like the people who relate to, or agree with, the case mentioned, to put their hand in the air so that they may be counted: *Let's have a show of hands. How many people think this project ought to be stopped right now before it goes any further?*

shreds

tear to 'shreds or rip to 'shreds

You **tear**, or **rip**, someone or something **to shreds** when you criticize them severely: *In a 'serious' election dealing with economic issues their manifestos would be quickly torn to shreds.*

◇ SEE ALSO **pull to bits** ▷ BITS; **pick holes in** ▷ HOLES; **pull** or **tear to pieces** ▷ SHREDS

shrift

give someone short 'shrift

You **give someone short shrift** when you are unsympathetic to their request or suggestion, for example: *He accosted me in the bar, asking for a glass of brandy, but I gave him short shrift.*

shudder

I shudder to 'think

You say '**I shudder to think**' a certain thing when it makes you alarmed, embarrassed or disgusted to think of it: *He pretended to my face that he admired and loved me dearly. I shudder to think what kind of life I should have had with him.*

shut

'shut it or shut 'up (*informal, offensive*)

'**Shut it**' or '**shut up**' is a very rude way of telling someone to be quiet.

◇ SEE ALSO **shut your face** ▷ FACE; **shut your gob** ▷ GOB; **shut your mouth** ▷ MOUTH

side (*see also* **sides**)

err on the side of 'such-and-such

You **err on the side of** something, such as caution, safety or prudence, when you take too much care to exercise that quality: *As a soldier he had been taught to err on the side of caution. It was always wise to work out a line of retreat as well as a line of approach.*

get on the wrong 'side of someone

You **get on the wrong side of someone** when you do something that makes them displeased with you: *You'll be okay if you don't get on the wrong side of Mr Forbes – he can be pretty ruthless if he doesn't like you.*

get up on the wrong 'side of the 'bed

You say that you **got up on the wrong side of the bed** when nothing seems to be going right for you on a particular day.

◇ SEE ALSO **get out of bed on the wrong side** ▷ BED; **not be someone's day** ▷ DAY; **one of those days** ▷ DAYS

give someone the rough side of your 'tongue

You **give someone the rough side of your tongue** when you criticize them severely and angrily: *She's likely to receive a piece of my mind, the rough side of my tongue and my boot up her backside.*

◇ SEE ALSO **send someone away with a flea in their ear** ▷ FLEA; **give someone hell** ▷ HELL; **give someone a piece of your mind** ▷ PIECE; **read the riot act** ▷ RIOT; **tear someone off a strip** ▷ STRIP

keep on the right 'side of someone

You try to **keep on the right side of someone** by doing whatever pleases them, and avoiding annoying them: *If you manage to keep on the right side of old MacGregor, you'll do well.*

know which side your 'bread is buttered

Someone who **knows which side their bread is buttered** knows exactly how to behave in order to get the greatest financial benefit: *The employees know which side their bread is buttered. They look around this area, they see the factories that have opened in the past few years.*

laugh on the other side of your 'face

You say that someone **will be laughing on the other side of their face** if you think that they will not be so pleased with themselves when they discover the unpleasant consequences of a certain thing they have done: *You wait, I'll get you and then you'll be laughing on the other side of your face!*

let the 'side down

You **let the side down** when you fall below the standard set by the other members of the group to which you belong, and so endanger its chances of success, or its reputation: *We don't want anyone to let the side down, so I'd like you all to be on your best behaviour tomorrow, all right?*

look on the 'bright side

You **look on the bright side** when you concentrate on the positive aspects of a situation, rather than the unpleasant ones: *Come on, look on the bright side – at least you won't have to move away from home now.*

◇ SEE ALSO **count your blessings** ▷ BLESSINGS; **half a loaf is better than no bread** ▷ LOAF; **thankful for small mercies** ▷ MERCIES

on the 'such-and-such side

Something that is **on the large**, or **small**, or **narrow**, etc, **side**, is a bit too large, small, or narrow: *Have you got the next size up? These are a bit on the small side.*

on the right side of the 'law

You are **on the right side of the law** if you are acting legally: *I would like my children to stay healthy, on the right side of the law, and lead fulfilling lives.*

on the wrong side of the 'law

You are **on the wrong side of the law** if you are acting illegally: *Producers believe the video may persuade some young people to think twice before they find themselves on the wrong side of the law.*

on the 'safe side

You do something in order to be **on the safe side** if you do it as a precaution: *'There's a train that goes at about half-nine, I think.' 'OK, we'll meet at half-eight just to be on the safe side.'*

on someone's 'side

Someone who is **on your side** supports you against your opponents: *Look, don't you understand? We're on your side! We want to help you!*

the other side of the 'coin

The **other side of the coin** is the opposite argument or view: *One must look at the other side of the coin. There has been a good reduction in the number of strikes; we must give the Government credit where it is due.*

see the 'funny side of something

You **see the funny side of something** if you are able to laugh about it: *It's all rather embarrassing for us, but I think we'll see the funny side in the morning.*

◇ SEE ALSO **see the joke** ▷ JOKE

side by 'side

1 Things or people are **side by side** if they are next to each other: *Stand side by side so we can see who's the tallest.* 2 Two people, groups, or ideas that are found **side by side**, are found together, when you would normally expect them to be separate or in different places: *In some situations this type of abrupt and complete switch-over is necessary since it is not possible to have both old and new methods running side by side.* □ *Dealers crowded out exclusive wine bars as well as the pubs. They would drink side by side with City workers, but would never quite bridge the communication gap.*

side of the 'fence

You **are on** a particular **side of the fence** if you hold a particular view or position in an argument: *Whatever side of the fence you are on, the debate is not going to disappear; the issue is here to stay.*

take 'sides or take someone's 'side

You **take sides**, or **take someone's side**, when you support one person or group against another in a conflict or argument: *The counsellor cannot afford to take sides, but should instead aim to help the whole family face up to the problems they are experiencing.*

This idiom is most frequently used with a negative form, or with a verb suggesting reluctance. Typical verbs and expressions found preceding it are 'refuse to', 'rather not', 'don't want to', 'would have to', and 'would be forced to'.

this side of the 'grave

Something that happens **this side of the grave** happens during someone's lifetime: *They parted as extravagantly as if they never expected to meet again this side of the grave.*

sidelines

stay on the 'sidelines

You **stay on the sidelines** when you do not get involved with something: *The officials tended to sit on the sidelines criticizing and always coming up with a reason why you couldn't do anything.*

sides

split your 'sides

You **split your sides** when you laugh very long and loudly: *And whatever were you up to? It looked like some amazing mime game. I nearly split my sides.*

side-splitting: *Twenty side-splitting comedy videos to be won!*

siege

'siege mentality
A **siege mentality** is a defensive and fearful attitude to life: *They have all played their part in creating a near siege mentality in the media.*

sight

at first 'sight
If something appears in a particular way at **first sight**, it appears that way to begin with, before it has been studied or considered more closely: *At first sight, you might think this machine is a new and sophisticated way of finding the meanings of words, but in fact it's just another cheap gimmick.*

catch 'sight of
You **catch sight of** someone or something when you begin to see them, or you get a brief view of them: *I thought I caught sight of someone in the back garden.*

get out of my 'sight
If you say '**get out of my sight!**' to someone, you are telling them, very angrily, to go away, probably because you are disgusted with their behaviour.

know by 'sight
You **know someone by sight** if you recognize them, but have never met them personally: *She knew him well by sight but she had never spoken with him before.*

lose 'sight of
You **lose sight of** someone or something when you can no longer see them; you lose sight of an aim or target when you are diverted from it: *Why are we doing all this? What do we want to achieve? If you lose sight of that, all the attention to detail in the world is not a great deal of use.*

not a pretty 'sight
Someone or something that is described as **not a pretty sight** is not pleasant to look at: *Derek had a big pasty face covered in spots and was not a pretty sight.*

out of sight out of 'mind
If you say that something is **out of sight out of mind**, you mean that because you do not see it, you do not think about it: *I don't worry about them when I'm away from home – I suppose it's a case of 'out of sight out of mind'.*

second 'sight
Someone who has **second sight** is believed to be able to know about the future, or what is happening in another place, or other people's minds, without being told: *It was like having second sight, the sense that*

something terrible was going to happen and there was nothing you could do to stop it.

a sight for 'sore eyes
A **sight for sore eyes** is a very welcome sight: *The mighty Cairngorm Mountains are a sight for sore eyes in any rambler's book.*

sights

lower your 'sights
You **lower your sights** when you make your aims less ambitious than before: *I once had ideas of sailing around the world, but work got in the way, and I had to lower my sights.*

set your 'sights on
You **set your sights on** someone or something when you decide that you will try to achieve it: *Few jobs are easy to get these days and, if you have set your sights on advertising, it must be worth extra effort.*
◇ SEE ALSO **set your heart on** ▷ HEART

sign

a sign of the 'times
If you say that something is **a sign of the times**, you mean that it shows how the world is changing: *What worries women most in the '90s is their husband or partner losing his job. This is a real sign of the times.*

signs

show signs of
Someone or something that **shows signs of** doing something seems to be changing in that direction: *The economy shows signs of im'proving.*

silence

silence is 'golden
1 '**Silence is golden**' is a saying which means that it is often better not to speak at all in a difficult situation. **2** People sometimes say '**silence is golden**' when they can suddenly enjoy a period of quiet after a lot of noise.

sin (*see also* **sins**)

live in 'sin (*old*)
Two people who **are living in sin** are living together in a sexual relationship, and are not married to each other: *'Well yes, she did happen to wonder about that.' Lucy giggled as she added, 'She feared you might be living in sin.'*

This expression, as well as the concept, is now considered old-fashioned, since it regards 'living together' as a shameful activity. People still use it jokingly, though, especially to talk about the opinions of people with very traditional ideas (as in the example above).

sincerely

Yours sin'cerely

You write 'Yours sincerely' at the end of a formal letter, especially one which you began with 'Dear Mrs, or Mr, or Ms, so-and-so': *I look forward to meeting you. Yours sincerely, Jack Marshall.*

◇ SEE ALSO **yours ever** ▷ EVER; **faithfully** ▷ FAITHFULLY; **yours truly** ▷ TRULY

Note that if you begin a letter with 'Dear Sir' or 'Dear Madam', you should write 'Yours faithfully' before signing your name.

sink

sink or 'swim

You describe something as a case of **sink or swim** if the people involved have been left to try to succeed by their own efforts at the risk of suffering complete failure: *That first week was an ordeal. She had been thrown in at the deep end and it was a question of sink or swim.*

◇ SEE ALSO **in at the deep end** ▷ END

sins

for your 'sins

If you say that something is the case **for your sins**, you mean, humorously, that you regard it as a punishment to you: *I happen, for my sins, to have been shadow Chancellor since the last election in 1987.*

sitting

be sitting 'pretty

You **are sitting pretty** if you are rich, successful, or in a pleasant situation: *I'm sitting pretty in a nice house with a success-ful businessman and you're left teaching a lot of nasty little children the ABC.*

situation

no-'win situation

A **no-win situation** is one in which whatever you do, the result will be unpleasant: *'I was effectively put in a no-win situation – there was nothing else I could do,' he said.*

◇ SEE ALSO **vicious circle** ▷ CIRCLE; **Catch twenty-two** or **Catch twenty-two situation** ▷ CATCH

sticky situ'ation

A **sticky situation** is one which may cause you embarrassment or difficulties: *I am extremely grateful to them for getting me out of a sticky situation.*

sixes

at sixes and 'sevens

If someone is **at sixes and sevens**, they are in a state of total disorder or confusion: *I'm sorry. I'm all at sixes and sevens. I really don't know what I'm saying.*

size

cut someone down to 'size

You **cut someone down to size** when you do something that will make them realize that they are not as important as they think they are: *Some of the older boys will probably think you need cutting down to size; they might be quite right, of course.*

pick on someone your 'own size

If you tell someone to **pick on someone their own size**, you mean that they should not attack someone who is too young, weak or inexperienced to defend themselves: *He should pick on someone his own size, not two young kids who were near to tears.*

try something for 'size

You tell someone to **try** a particular thing **for size** when you want to see what they think of it: *You may think you're quite good at solving mental problems. If so, try this one for size.* □ *Leonora, will you come to Wales next weekend? See my house – try it for size?*

skates

get your 'skates on or **put your 'skates on**

If someone tells you to **get**, or **put**, **your skates on**, they are telling you to hurry up: *We'd better get our skates on if we're going to be there on time.*

skeletons

'skeletons in the cupboard or **'skeletons in the closet**

Skeletons in the cupboard, or **closet**, are shameful secrets relating to someone's past: *Nothing's going to be hidden, no skeletons in the cupboard, no dark secrets, everything out in the open.*

This idiom is variable. For example, you may find **his** or **her** in the place of **the**, or **skeleton** (singular), rather than **skeletons**.

skids

put the 'skids under

You **put the skids under** someone or something if you cause them to hurry: *That really put the skids under them when they found out about the new deadline.*

skies

praise to the 'skies

If you **praise** someone or something **to the skies**, you praise them very highly: *It should be good. The critics have been praising it to the skies.*

skin

by the skin of your 'teeth

You manage to do something **by the skin of your teeth** when you only just manage to do it: *Consolation came with the Indiana result. He won, but only by the skin of his teeth.*

drenched to the 'skin or soaked to the 'skin

You are **drenched**, or **soaked, to the skin** if you, and all the clothes you are wearing, are very wet: *The rain lashed down unremittingly. By the time he had reached the shelter of the station he was soaked to the skin.*

get under someone's 'skin

When someone or something **gets under your skin**, they **1** annoy and upset you very much: *It was the sheer effrontery, the excessive assurance of them which got under my skin.* **2** cause you to feel a strong passion or attraction for them: *I know we haven't known each other long, but you've got under my skin like no other woman I've ever met.*

jump out of your 'skin

If you say that someone or something made you **jump out of your skin**, you mean that they startled or surprised you very much: *Do you have to make me jump out of my skin like that every time you come in?*

no skin off 'your nose

If you say that something is **no skin off your nose**, you mean that it does not cause you the slightest concern or nuisance: *Why should you worry what my mother says about you? It's no skin off your nose, is it?*

save your 'own skin

Someone does something to **save their own skin** when they do it to protect themselves from harm or danger, especially when doing this causes them to neglect someone else's safety or feelings: *He is intent only on saving his own skin. Sarah's feelings and the consequences for her are not considered.*

skin and 'bone

Someone who is described as **skin and bone** is thin in an unhealthy and unattractive way: *'You'll have to eat more, Mum,' he said urgently. 'You're only skin and bone.'*
◇ SEE ALSO **bag of bones** ▷ BAG

sky

the sky's the 'limit

If you say **'the sky's the limit'**, you mean that there is no upper limit to the amount of money that may be spent, or the things that may be achieved: *There's so much potential in this business – the sky's the limit.*

slap

slap and 'tickle (*old*)

'Slap and tickle' is a rather old-fashioned term for playful sexual behaviour: *But all Walter thought about at that time was slap and tickle in the grass.*

a slap in the 'face

A **slap in the face** is a rude or insulting rejection or refusal: *A failure by government to recognize this situation will be a cruel slap in the face to an arts world that has done so much to adapt to the market economy of the 1980s.*

a slap on the 'back

If someone gives you **a slap on the back**, they give you their congratulations by hitting you with the flat of their hand in the middle of your back: *The BMC deserves a hearty slap on the back for the organization of this year's festival and the quality of the speakers.*
◇ SEE ALSO **a clap on the back** ▷ CLAP; **a pat on the back** ▷ PAT

a slap on the 'wrist

A **slap on the wrist** is a gentle punishment or mild warning: *They usually get little more than a slap on the wrist and most know they can get away with it unchallenged.*

slash

go for a 'slash (*vulgar*)

If someone says that they **are going for a slash**, they mean that they are going to urinate: *I'd just been for a slash, and when I came out again, there was a great space cleared in front of the bar, and it was very quiet.*
◇ SEE ALSO **take a leak** ▷ LEAK

slate

a clean 'slate

You start with **a clean slate** when you disregard any faults or mistakes you have made in the past, which may be to your disadvantage, and begin again: *You'll be starting with a completely clean slate; there are no existing possessions that might prove difficult to accommodate.*
◇ SEE ALSO **a clean sheet** ▷ SHEET

put something on the 'slate

You **put something on the slate** when you postpone paying for it, and the supplier records the amount that you owe: *Could you put that one on the slate for me? I haven't got any cash on me just now.*

> A **slate** is a thin layer of dark grey rock that was used in the past for writing on.

wipe the 'slate clean

You **wipe the slate clean** when you decide to forget past mistakes, or arguments that you have had with other people, and restart a relationship or activity as if it had just begun for the first time: *An agreement* had been reached with the ANC on the details of an amnesty for political offenders which would 'wipe the slate clean and bury the past'.

slave

a slave to 'such-and-such

Someone who is a **slave to** a certain thing has let their life become controlled by it: *Yet Sally's no slave to fashion: 'I think fashion should be fun and you should wear what you feel comfortable in, not what people say you should wear.'*

sleaze

'sleaze factor

The **sleaze factor** refers to the extent to which someone or something is immoral or sordid: *The sleaze factor has been highlighted by the revelation that large chunks of the money were laundered via Switzerland into luxury flats in Docklands.*

sledgehammer

a sledgehammer to crack a 'nut

If you say that someone is using **a sledgehammer to crack a nut**, you mean that they are putting too much effort into trying to solve a relatively minor problem: *These measures could quite justifiably be regarded as something of a sledgehammer to crack a very small nut, since they are intended to deal with a problem the existence of which is almost totally unproven.*

A **sledgehammer** is a large heavy hammer used for breaking rocks.

sleep

not lose 'sleep over

If you tell someone **not to lose any sleep over** something, you mean that it is not worth worrying about: *He described Joe Kinnear's attack on his side as 'rubbish' and says he won't lose any sleep over his comments.*

put to 'sleep

Vets **put** animals **to sleep** when they kill them painlessly by injecting them with a lethal dose of a drug.

'sleep on it

If you tell someone to **sleep on it**, you mean that they should delay making a particular decision until the following morning: *It was clear to those around Mrs Thatcher that, although she said she would sleep on it, she was virtually certain to resign.*

sleep 'tight

If you say '**sleep tight**' to someone, especially a child, you mean 'sleep well'.

sleeve

have something up your 'sleeve

If you **have something up your sleeve**, you have an idea or plan that you are keeping secret from other people, which you may use at some later time: *Mr Major does not look like a prime minister with a secret agenda up his sleeve.*

laugh up your 'sleeve

Someone **is laughing up their sleeve** when they are feeling secretly very pleased with themselves for having successfully deceived someone: *I trusted him, and all the time he was laughing up his sleeve.*

sleight

sleight of 'hand

If something is done by **sleight of hand** it is done using skilful deception: *We may never know if he means this sincerely, or merely as sleight of hand.*

slice

a slice of the 'action

You get **a slice of the action** when you have the opportunity to get involved in a particular activity: *If you want a slice of the action tickets may still be available.*
◊ SEE ALSO **a piece of the action** ▷ PIECE; **a slice of the cake** ▷ SLICE

a slice of the 'cake

Your **slice of the cake** is your share of something, such as money or profits: *If the BBC started to take advertising, the commercial TV companies would see their slice of the cake get smaller.* **a piece of the action** ▷ PIECE; **a slice of the action** ▷ SLICE

a slice of 'life

You describe a story, a play, or a film as **a slice of life** if it closely resembles or represents real life: *He claimed that contemporary drama had encouraged the young movie industry to take 'the slice of life' as its subject-matter.*

slings

slings and 'arrows

The **slings and arrows** of someone or something are the problems, difficulties and damage caused by them: *the process of combatting, enduring or avoiding the slings and arrows of day-to-day living.* □ *This particular model was built to demonstrate at shows and has suffered the slings and arrows of a curious public.*

slip

Freudian 'slip

A **Freudian slip** is a small mistake you make when speaking, which reveals how you

really feel about someone or something: *I'd like you to meet my wife, sorry, I mean my assistant! How's that for a Freudian slip?*
◇ SEE ALSO **slip of the tongue** ▷ SLIP

give someone the 'slip
You **give someone the slip** when you succeed in escaping from them: *I decided to give the authorities the slip and went through the bathroom window of the hotel.*
◇ SEE ALSO **break free** or **break loose** ▷ BREAK; **make a break** ▷ BREAK; **cut and run** ▷ CUT

slip of the 'tongue
A **slip of the tongue** is a small mistake you make when speaking: *'The most painful ...'* *He paused, corrected a slip of the tongue, and went on, 'The most painless way is for us to keep out of each other's way until you can leave.'*
◇ SEE ALSO **Freudian slip** ▷ SLIP

slippery

slippery as an 'eel
Someone who is as **slippery as an eel** is dishonest and manipulative: *I was concerned about astonishing fluctuations in my popularity: 'He is,' they said most woundingly about me, 'as slippery as an eel.'*

An **eel** is a fish with a long snake-like body.

slope

the slippery 'slope
You are on **the slippery slope** if you have started doing something which reputedly leads to failure, ruin or self-destruction: *'Having another drink is the worst thing for a hangover and could put you on the slippery slope to alcoholism,' warns the magazine.*

slouch

no 'slouch
Someone who is **no slouch** on, or at, something, or at doing something, or in a particular 'department' is good at that particular thing: *No slouch on the guitar himself, Matthew has recently expanded his working instrument collection.* ◻ *It is hard to understand how none of these people received a mention. Chomsky is no slouch either.* ◻ *I mean, Emma's no slouch in the looks department, as you know, but this Cindy is like, well, absolutely perfect.*

slowly

slowly but 'surely
Something that is happening **slowly but surely** is definitely developing, but it is taking time: *If you concentrate on things*

that are maybe a week away instead of a month away then you'll gradually, slowly but surely, improve.*
◇ SEE ALSO **by degrees** ▷ DEGREES

sly

on the 'sly
You do something **on the sly** when you do it secretly: *The more anyone told me not to do a thing, the more I tried to do it. So we continued to meet on the sly.*

smash

smash-and-'grab
A **smash-and-grab** is a burglary where the robbers break a window, take as much as they can, and escape immediately: *In a sense, jewellers who keep valuable items in their shop-windows could be said to cause smash-and-grab raids.*

smile

wipe the 'smile off someone's face
Someone or something that **wipes the smile off your face** makes you feel suddenly foolish or regretful, when you had just been feeling very pleased with yourself: *Robyn glared; how she longed to wipe that infuriating smile off his face!*

smoke

Big 'Smoke (*informal*)
The **Big Smoke** refers to a big city, especially London: *It was really good to see him in London last month; I think I've been up and down to the Big Smoke more times since Christmas than I have in the past two years.*

go up in 'smoke
A plan **goes up in smoke** when it is completely ruined or comes to nothing: *We haven't worked all these months to have it go up in smoke now.*

no smoke without a 'fire
If you say that there's **no smoke without a fire**, you mean that if a lot of people are saying that something has happened, there must be at least a little truth in it: *In general, people tended not to believe them. But the 'no smoke without fire' theory remained in people's minds.*

smooth

smooth as 'silk
Something that is as **smooth as silk** is very smooth: *In fact her skin was smooth as silk and almost unlined.*

Silk is a very smooth, fine cloth.

snail

at a 'snail's pace

Someone or something that progresses **at a snail's pace** progresses very slowly: *They worked at a snail's pace in that place – I don't know how they ever managed to compete with other firms.*

A **snail** is a small animal, with a soft body and a shell, which moves very slowly.

snake

a snake in the 'grass

If you describe someone as **a snake in the grass**, you mean that they cannot be trusted: *She knew what she was doing, that snake in the grass, that viper! And I daresay she thinks she's succeeded.*

◇ SEE ALSO **a wolf in sheep's clothing** ▷ WOLF

snap

snap 'out of it

If you tell someone to **snap out of it**, you mean that they should take control of themselves and stop feeling sorry for themselves, or stop behaving foolishly: *I was miserable for weeks – couldn't snap out of it. It was dreadful.*

◇ SEE ALSO **pull yourself together** ▷ PULL

snappy

make it 'snappy (*informal*)

If you tell someone to do something 'and **make it snappy**', you mean, impatiently, that they should do it very quickly: *He broke off as his phone rang. 'Hello. Is that you again? Make it snappy – I have important visitors.'*

sneeze

not to be 'sneezed at

Something that is **not to be sneezed at** should not be disregarded or dismissed as being of little value: *They'll take her on because of the money. And she'll get all I have, which isn't to be sneezed at.*

◇ SEE ALSO **not to be sniffed at** ▷ SNIFFED

sniffed

not to be 'sniffed at

Something that is **not to be sniffed at** should not be disregarded or dismissed as being of little value: *We worked very hard, and we're very pleased. £7 million is not to be sniffed at.*

◇ SEE ALSO **not to be sneezed at** ▷ SNEEZED

snook

cock a 'snook

You **cock a snook** at someone or something when you show them obvious disrespect, especially when you know you cannot be punished for it: *Tom Keating spent a lifetime cocking a snook at the art world. He painted in various styles and passed them off as originals making a lot of money in the process.*

◇ SEE ALSO **thumb your nose at someone** ▷ NOSE

'**Cock a snook**' in its first sense refers to a gesture of disrespect or scorn. It involves putting your thumb on the end of your nose and holding your fingers out in an upright position, while moving them around.

snowball

not a snowball's chance in 'hell

Someone who **hasn't got a snowball's chance in hell** is extremely unlikely to succeed: *If you do not get active and stay active, you've not got a snowball's chance in hell of maintaining any weight loss.*

◇ SEE ALSO **not have** or **stand a cat in hell's chance** ▷ CAT; **not have a hope in hell** ▷ HOPE

Hell is usually imagined to be very hot, so a snowball would not have any chance of surviving there.

'snowball effect

A, or the, **snowball effect** occurs when something develops or increases rapidly and uncontrollably: *Their demand gathered its own momentum and benefited from a snowball effect. At the same time, technological changes were encouraging increased scale, pressures and stakes.*

If you roll a snowball along in the snow, it gradually increases in size.

snuff

'snuff it (*informal*)

Someone **snuffs it** when they die: *If I'm going to snuff it, I'd rather snuff it with a pint in my hand than one of their mugs of Ovaltine.*

◇ SEE ALSO **breathe your last** ▷ LAST; **kick the bucket** ▷ BUCKET; **cash in your chips** ▷ CHIPS; **pop your clogs** ▷ CLOGS; **shuffle off this mortal coil** ▷ COIL; **bite the dust** ▷ DUST; **give up the ghost** ▷ GHOST; **depart this life** ▷ LIFE; **go the way of all flesh** ▷ WAY

so

and 'so on

And so on is used at the end of a list to indicate that there are more things of the same kind that could be mentioned: *You can do things for yourself in the way of diet, exercise, good lifestyle, not smoking and so on.*

◇ SEE ALSO **and everything** ▷ EVERYTHING

'so-and-so

You use **so-and-so** instead of a name when you want to speak generally, rather than be specific about a certain person: *The atmosphere was cordial, and the talk was of what grandchildren were up to or what Dr So-and-so said about this or that particular problem.*

soap

soft-'soap someone

You **soft-soap someone** when you try to persuade them to do something for you by saying flattering things to them: *We know you were soft-soaping us, Appleton. We could see right through your crafty but loose propaganda.*

soapbox

get on your 'soapbox

You **get on your soapbox** when you give your opinions loudly and forcefully: *Last week the Prime Minister, on his soapbox, was being heckled with considerable passion by a young man carrying a banner.*

A **soapbox** is a small platform that someone stands on when they are making a speech in public.

sob

'sob story

A **sob story** is a story that someone tells you about some misfortune they have suffered, often in order to gain something from you: *She believed every sob story she was told, often ending up giving the food away.*
◇ SEE ALSO **tale of woe** ▷ TALE

You **sob** when you try to speak while you are crying, making short bursts of sound as you gasp for breath.

sock

put a 'sock in it (*informal*)

If someone tells you to **put a sock in it**, they are saying, rudely, that they want you to be quiet: *Put a sock in it, will you? You've caused more than enough trouble today.*
◇ SEE ALSO **button it** ▷ BUTTON

socks

pull your 'socks up

If someone says you should **pull your socks up**, they mean that you should make an effort to do better than you have been doing recently: *If we don't pull our socks up and actually start working, then it could happen to us as well.*
◇ SEE ALSO **get your arse in gear** ▷ ARSE

sod

not care a 'sod or not give a 'sod (*vulgar*)

You say that you **don't care**, or **give**, **a sod** about something if you do not think it is important, or have no interest in it: *She didn't care a sod about the child – she said she had no feelings for her whatsoever.*
◇ SEE ALSO **not give a damn** ▷ DAMN; **not care a fig** or **two figs** ▷ FIG, FIGS; **not care** or **give a hoot** or **two hoots** ▷ HOOT, HOOTS; **not give a monkey's** ▷ MONKEY'S; **not give a shit** ▷ SHIT; **not give a tinker's cuss** ▷ TINKER; **not give** or **care a toss** ▷ TOSS; **not care** or **give tuppence** ▷ TUPPENCE

sod 'all (*vulgar*)

Sod all means 'nothing at all': *I don't know how he got to become the manager. He knows sod all about football.*
◇ SEE ALSO **bugger all** ▷ BUGGER

'sod it (*vulgar*)

People sometimes say '**Sod it!**' when they are angry, or when they decide that it is not worth worrying about something any more: *Everybody is enthusiastic about doing up a house for the first three years. After that they think, sod it, that will do.*

Sod's 'law (*informal*)

Sod's law is the tendency that things have to go wrong: *It had been a perfectly bloody conference. Sod's law. Everything that could go wrong had gone wrong.*

sod 'off (*offensive*)

'**Sod off**' is a very rude way of telling someone to go away: *There must be times when they want to tell people to sod off. Everyone is that way sometimes.*
◇ SEE ALSO **bugger off** ▷ BUGGER; **get lost** ▷ LOST

softly

softly-'softly

If you take a **softly-softly** approach, you try to solve a problem in a quiet and reasonable way, rather than being forceful: *We tried a very softly-softly approach originally because we didn't want to push them too hard.*

sold

'sold on something

If you are **sold on** a particular idea, you are extremely enthusiastic about it or convinced by it: *I get the impression they're not altogether sold on the idea.*

something

count for 'something

If you say that something **counts for something**, you mean that it has some value and importance: *You already have experience of* *working in a sales environment and that counts for something.*

give so-and-so something to 'talk about

If you say that something **will give** a certain person or people **something to talk about**, you mean that it will give them an excuse to gossip: *Have you shocked them in the village? I do all the time without meaning to. And then I think, well, it gives them something to talk about.*

have 'got something there

If you say to someone **'you've got something there'**, you mean that they have made an interesting observation.

have something 'going with someone

You **have something going with someone** if you are having a romantic affair with them: *'Perhaps it would divert their minds if they thought I had something going with her,' he thought.*

a little 'something

A little **something** is a gift: *We've bought you a little something to say thank you for everything you've done.*

something 'else (*informal*)

Something else means 'special' or 'incredible': *That car of his really is something else – have you had a ride in it yet?*

something for 'nothing

You get **something for nothing** if you obtain something without having to pay for it in money, time or energy: *You can't have something for nothing, not in a capitalist market economy.*

son

son of a 'bitch

'Son of a bitch' is a very rude and offensive insult.

song

for a 'song

Something that goes, or is sold, **for a song**, is sold at a price much lower than its real worth: *Contrary to all expectations, the painting went for a song at Sotheby's last week.*

make a song and 'dance

You **make a song and dance** about something when you make a lot of unnecessary fuss about it: *There's no need to make a song and dance of it. Just convey the basic facts. Simple approach is the best, that's my advice, Stevens.*

soon

just as 'soon

If you say that you would **just as soon** do something as another, you mean that the first thing is as acceptable as the second,

and that you would slightly prefer the first: *I'd just as soon stay in a small pub as a hotel.*

sooner

sooner or 'later

If you say that something will happen **sooner or later**, you mean that it may happen in the near future, or in the more distant future, but it will definitely happen eventually: *Sooner or later someone will find out anyway.*

the sooner the 'better

If you say in reference to something you want to happen **'the sooner the better'** you mean you want it to happen soon: *'We'll have to do something about this situation.' 'Yes, and the sooner the better, as far as I'm concerned.'*

sorrows

drown your 'sorrows

People **drown their sorrows** when they drink alcohol in order to forget their problems: *With the first results of the exams due on Thursday night, you may be in the mood to celebrate or drown your sorrows.*

◇ SEE ALSO **hit the bottle** ▷ BOTTLE

sort

a good 'sort

Someone who is described as **a good sort** is a good, trustworthy and pleasant person.

nothing of the 'sort

'Nothing of the sort' is an emphatic negative which means 'not at all the thing just mentioned': *I smiled in a way that was meant to signify interest in this excursion, but Carla could see that it showed nothing of the sort.*

◇ SEE ALSO **nothing of the kind** ▷ KIND

sort of

You use **sort of** when giving a rough description or idea of something: *I feel sort of 'funny when I look at those photos.*

◇ SEE ALSO **kind of** ▷ KIND

sorts

it takes 'all sorts

If you say **'it takes all sorts'**, you mean that you can't expect everyone to like the same things as you, even if you cannot understand why they do or like certain things: *They've gone on a fishing honeymoon. Not my idea of romance – takes all sorts.*

of 'sorts

Something you describe as a certain thing **of sorts** is not a very good or very typical one of its kind: *This chapter is therefore an invitation of sorts – an invitation to pause before plunging into the issues that follow.*

◇ SEE ALSO **of a kind** ▷ KIND

out of 'sorts

You are **out of sorts** if you are not feeling very well: *He's seemed a bit out of sorts these past few days. It's probably nothing.*
◇ SEE ALSO **below** or **not up to par** ▷ PAR; **under the weather** ▷ WEATHER

soul

bare your 'soul

You **bare your soul** when you tell someone your deepest feelings: *I don't know what it is about you, Miss Abbott, but you make me want to bare my soul to you.*

The **soul** is the part of a person that is believed to consist of personality, emotions and intellect.

bless my 'soul (*old*)

'Bless my soul!' is a rather old-fashioned expression of surprise: *'So that's what gave me away. My shoes. Well, bless my soul,' he said, with an air of exaggerated surprise.*
◇ SEE ALSO **fancy that** ▷ FANCY

sell your soul to the 'devil

You **sell your soul to the devil** when you do something immoral or illegal in order to get something you want: *We were wondering if her essays were all her own work. She's sent them up to a London publisher. Do you think she's sold her soul to the devil?*

'soul mate

A **soul mate** is someone who has a similar way of seeing the world as you, and for whom you feel a lot of affection or love: *The film is a romantic comedy about a woman's search for a soul mate.*

sound

sound as a 'bell

Something that is as **sound as a bell** is undamaged and in very good condition: *It's twenty five years old, but it's sound as a bell – take it for a drive.*
◇ SEE ALSO **in mint condition** ▷ CONDITION; **in good nick** ▷ NICK; **in good repair** ▷ REPAIR

soup

in the 'soup

You are **in the soup** if you are in trouble or difficulties: *Democracy must be seen to work, or else we're all in the soup.*
◇ SEE ALSO **up the creek without a paddle** or **up the creek** ▷ CREEK; **out of your depth** ▷ DEPTH; **in the shit** ▷ SHIT; **up shit creek** ▷ SHIT; **in a tight spot** ▷ SPOT; **in trouble** ▷ TROUBLE; **in deep water** ▷ WATER; **in hot water** ▷ WATER

sour

turn 'sour

If a situation **turns sour** it becomes less enjoyable: *But as time went by the marriage turned sour.*

Milk that has turned sour has an unpleasant taste because it is no longer fresh.

space

'breathing space

You get, or you are given, **breathing space** when you get some time between two tasks to have a rest, reflect on what you have just done, and prepare for the next task: *They asked me to go away and come back again in a week which gave me breathing space and time at least to learn it properly.*

watch this 'space

You say, or write, '**watch this space**' when you want people to keep alert so that they will be ready to receive the next piece of information on the subject at a later date: *Will it be a hit? Only time will tell, but it's looking good – watch this space for further details!*

spade

call a spade a 'spade

Someone who **calls a spade a spade** speaks plainly without trying to make things seem better than they really are: *Let's call a spade a spade. The answer is no.*
◇ SEE ALSO **not mince your words** ▷ WORDS

A **spade** is a long-handled digging tool with a broad metal blade that you push into the ground with your foot.

spanner

put a 'spanner in the works

You **put a spanner in the works** when you spoil a plan or activity by introducing an obstacle which prevents it from progressing: *No, something always comes along and puts a spanner in the works and that upsets everybody.*
◇ SEE ALSO **spike someone's guns** ▷ GUNS; **put a spoke in someone's wheel** ▷ SPOKE

A **spanner** is a tool with one or two specially shaped ends which fit around a nut or bolt which can then be turned with the handle.

spare

go 'spare

You **go spare** when you become very angry: *Both of us need protecting. Old Stevenson would go spare if he knew.*

spark

bright 'spark

If you refer to someone as a **bright spark**, you mean that they are lively, witty or intelligent; people sometimes use the term '**bright spark**' to show that the person's cleverness irritates them, or sarcastically, when they think the person is actually rather slow: *The growers appeared to be facing ruin until one bright spark hit on an idea.* □ *Which bright spark has gone and put salt in my tea?*

sparks

sparks 'fly

Sparks fly when people become very angry with each other: *I know he made the sparks fly sometimes in council committees but most of that was good humoured.*

speak

speak for it'self

Something **speaks for itself** if it has an obvious meaning or significance and does not need to be explained: *Her success speaks for itself.*

speak for your'self

You say '**speak for yourself**' to someone who has just included you in a statement, which does not actually apply to you, even if it applies to them: *Whenever I read such a remark, I always feel like writing 'Speak for yourself' in the margin.*

speak too 'soon

You **speak too soon** when you say something optimistic and then find out that it is not the case: *I don't want to speak too soon, but I think I've been fairly consistent this season.*

◇ SEE ALSO **tempt fate** ▷ FATE; **tempt the gods** ▷ GODS; **tempt providence** ▷ PROVIDENCE

speak when you're 'spoken to

'**Speak when you're spoken to**' means 'don't take the initiative to speak to someone, because it will be considered rude': *No make-up allowed, mind. And only speak when you're spoken to. He likes, you know, silent women.*

to 'speak of

Nothing, or no-one, **to speak of** means nothing, or no-one of any size or importance: *'Have you got a decent resource library?' 'Well, nothing to speak of really.'*

spec

do something on 'spec

You **do something on spec** when you do it without having received or seen an offer or invitation, in the hope that there will be a place for you anyway: *You will not need an*

application form if you are seeing a single applicant who has applied for the job on spec.

spectacle

make a 'spectacle of yourself

If someone **makes a spectacle of themselves** they do something foolish or ridiculous that makes them the focus of attention: *She couldn't get on the bicycle – she would fall off and make a spectacle of herself.*

◇ SEE ALSO **make an exhibition of yourself** ▷ EXHIBITION; **make a fool of yourself** ▷ FOOL

speed

at breakneck 'speed

You do something, such as drive, **at breakneck speed**, when you do it very fast: *There speaks the man who drove us here at such breakneck speed that I began to take pity on his poor Ferrari's engine.*

◇ SEE ALSO **at a rate of knots** ▷ RATE

spell

under someone's 'spell

You are **under someone's spell** if you are so attracted to them, or fascinated by them, that you are prepared to do anything for them: *She may be ruthless and dangerous to those who fall under her spell. She is capricious, elusive and quite irresistible.*

A **spell** is a set of words or actions that are supposed to have magic power.

spick

spick and 'span

Something, especially a room or house, that is **spick and span** is very clean, tidy and fresh: *Everything was spick and span, more like a hotel than a home.*

spirit

enter into the 'spirit of

You **enter into the spirit of** an occasion when you get involved in the general atmosphere or feeling created by the people present: *Mr and Mrs Lewis entered into the spirit of the occasion but I thought I could see some sadness in Mrs Lewis's eyes.*

◇ SEE ALSO **let your hair down** ▷ HAIR; **get into the swing of things** ▷ SWING

spirits

in high 'spirits

You are **in high spirits** if you are feeling cheerful: *Such garments, he insists, will recall this golden age of Chinese socialism when people 'worked hard and were always in high spirits'.*

in low 'spirits
You are **in low spirits** if you are feeling sad or depressed: *Tom Poole, who had nursed his father devotedly at the end, was in low spirits.*

spoke

put a spoke in someone's 'wheel
You **put a spoke in someone's wheel** when you make problems and difficulties for them: *'They'll put a spoke in our wheel,' Lionel said. 'If they know what we're planning, they can out-manoeuvre us.'*

◇ SEE ALSO **spike someone's guns** ▷ GUNS; **put a spanner in the works** ▷ SPANNER

sponge

throw in the 'sponge
You **throw in the sponge** when you stop trying to do something because you know that you cannot succeed: *So I cycled, just for a fortnight, but it was fourteen miles there in the morning, and fourteen back at night, and I'm afraid I threw in the sponge!*

In boxing, if you throw a sponge or towel into the ring, you are admitting defeat.

spoon

born with a silver 'spoon in your mouth
If you say that someone was **born with a silver spoon in their mouth**, you mean that they have had a privileged, comfortable and sheltered upbringing: *But Mario – as he often liked to point out – hadn't been born with a silver spoon in his mouth; he couldn't afford the fare to Europe.* □ *She thinks that we have absolutely no understanding of anybody because we were born with a silver spoon in our mouths.*

spit

spit it 'out
If you tell someone to **'spit it out'**, you mean that they should not waste any more time and tell you exactly what it is they want to say: *Stephen stopped. 'Spit it out, Gus. I don't care what it is, I want to hear it. Right?'*

spot (*see also* **spots**)

have a 'soft spot for someone
You **have a soft spot for someone** if you, maybe privately, feel affection for them: *Dad had a soft spot for Auntie Nellie and perhaps Mum had something to be jealous about.*

◇ SEE ALSO **hold a candle for someone** ▷ CANDLE; **have a crush on someone** ▷ CRUSH

in a tight 'spot
You are **in a tight spot** if you are in a difficult position: *You're in a tight spot. If you refuse to co-operate I can force you to pay me the money you owe me.*

◇ SEE ALSO **up the creek without a paddle** or **up the creek** ▷ CREEK; **out of your depth** ▷ DEPTH; **in the shit** ▷ SHIT; **up shit creek** ▷ SHIT; **in the soup** ▷ SOUP; **in trouble** ▷ TROUBLE; **in deep water** ▷ WATER; **in hot water** ▷ WATER

on the 'spot
1 If you do something **on the spot** you do it immediately: *She preferred to make corrections on the spot.* 2 If you are **on the spot** when something happens, you are at the scene: *Companies appear to rely on the perceptions of their own managers on the spot, with a loyalty to head office.* 3 If someone puts you **on the spot**, they put you in a difficult position, especially one that forces you to take action or make a response when you would rather not: *Such a development would certainly put the directors on the spot.*

rooted to the 'spot
You are **rooted to the spot** if you are so terrified or shocked that you cannot move your legs: *Her feet seemed to be rooted to the spot as she saw the pram with baby Donald in it disappear over the bank.*

spot 'on
'Spot on' means 1 absolutely accurate: *He was spot on when he described the car as 'quite simply a revelation.'* 2 excellent or exactly what was required: *You look marvellous. Spot on. Can I get you a drink?*

◇ SEE ALSO **bang on** ▷ BANG ON

spotlight

turn the 'spotlight on
You **turn the spotlight on** something when you focus people's attention on it: *It is only by turning the spotlight on the suffering that we can hope to end it.*

spots

knock 'spots off
If one person or thing **knocks spots off** another, they are very much better than that other person or thing: *The policy review certainly knocks spots off anything attempted by the Conservatives in the run-up to the 1979 election.*

◇ SEE ALSO **put someone in the shade** ▷ SHADE; **put to shame** ▷ SHAME

spout

up the 'spout (*informal*)
Something that is **up the spout** is useless, ruined or damaged: *I'm doing this on a PC,*

as opposed to my typewriter, and for some reason the function keys are all up the spout.

spread

middle-aged 'spread
Middle-aged spread is the extra weight some people gain, especially round their waist, when they reach middle age [= aged between about 40 and 60]: *At 40, you developed something flabby, disgusting and unavoidable called middle-aged spread, and your waist disappeared along with your energy.*

spring

no spring 'chicken
Someone is described as **no spring chicken** if they can no longer be considered as very young, and are therefore not able to do all the things that young people can do: *But getting fit takes time and commitment and if you're no spring chicken, you have to take it easy along the way.*

◇ SEE ALSO **over the hill** ▷ HILL; **past it** ▷ PAST; **long in the tooth** ▷ TOOTH; **not getting any younger** ▷ YOUNGER

a 'spring in your step
You have **a spring in your step** if you walk in a confident and relaxed way which shows that you are feeling well and happy about something: *A red wine to put a spring in your step is the romantically named Castello Vicchiomaggio Chianti Classico 1986.*

spur

on the spur of the 'moment
If you do something **on the spur of the moment**, you suddenly decide to do it on an impulse: *We all buy things on the spur of the moment – this is what the retail trade calls an 'impulse buy'. It means a purchase that hasn't been planned in advance.*

square

back to square 'one
If you have to go **back to square one**, you have to go back to the place or position that you started from originally, with no progress being made; you are **back at square one** if you are in this position: *One drink, and you find yourself back at square one.*

squeak

a narrow 'squeak
If you have **a narrow squeak** you just manage to avoid disaster or serious injury: *Hunt's championship was a narrow squeak, achieved in a car that was far from being all-triumphant.* □ *Jeremy? He's fine.*

Going home tomorrow. He had a narrow squeak, that one.

◇ SEE ALSO **close call** ▷ CALL; **narrow escape** ▷ ESCAPE; **close shave** ▷ SHAVE; **close** or **near thing** ▷ THING

squib

damp 'squib
You describe an occasion as a **damp squib** if it completely fails or does not have the effect that was intended: *A member of the audience sitting behind me commented that it seemed more of a damp squib than a big band.*

> A **squib** is a kind of firework. If it is damp, it will not go off.

squint

have a 'squint at or take a 'squint at (*informal*)
If you **have**, or **take, a squint at** something you have or take a quick look at it: *After a bacon sandwich and a squint at the newspaper we were rounding the corner to Eastwood House.*

stab

have a 'stab at or make a 'stab at
If you **have**, or **make, a stab at something**, you try to do it: *Why don't you have a stab at it? You've got nothing to lose.*

stable

shut the stable door after the horse has 'bolted
If someone **shuts the stable door after the horse has bolted**, they take measures to prevent something from happening when it has already happened, and it is too late: *To lock up young car thieves is another example of shutting the stable door after the horse has bolted.*

> This idiom has many variations, such as **close, slam,** or **bolt, the stable door after the horse has fled** (or **bolted**). Sometimes it is shortened to '**it's a case of shutting the stable door**', or even '**it's a stable-door situation**'.

stack

blow your 'stack
If you **blow your stack** you become very angry: *Can't you have a reasonable discussion without blowing your stack every five minutes?*

◇ SEE ALSO **go off at the deep end** ▷ END; **have a blue fit** ▷ FIT; **blow a fuse** ▷ FUSE; **blow a gasket** ▷ GASKET; **let fly** ▷ LET; **blow** or **flip your lid** ▷ LID; **do your nut** ▷ NUT; **lose your** rag ▷ RAG; **fly into a rage** ▷ RAGE; **hit the roof** ▷ ROOF; **lose your temper** ▷ TEMPER; **blow your top** ▷ TOP; **throw a wobbly** ▷ WOBBLY

stage

hold the 'stage

If someone **holds the stage**, they speak to a group of people for a long time, without letting anyone else interrupt.

the stage is 'set

If **the stage is set** for something to take place, the circumstances indicate that it will happen: *These imbalances threaten the welfare of younger generations and of society as a whole – the stage is set for a profound confrontation.*

stakes

raise the 'stakes

You **raise the stakes** when you increase the reward that you or others are competing for: *Mr Major raised the stakes in the final phase of the election campaign last night.*

> A **stake** here, refers to a sum of money risked in betting.

up 'stakes

You **up stakes** when you leave home and move on to another place: *You don't imagine we can simply walk out of here, do you – up stakes and toddle off back to the world of boiled cabbage and beds with sheets?*

> **'Stakes'** here refers to the pegs which support a tent. You take them up when you are ready to move your tent to another place.

stand

make a 'stand or take a 'stand

You **make a stand** against something or **take a stand** on something when you state your position on some issue and prepare to defend it.

stand cor'rected

You say '**I stand corrected**' when someone points out that you have made a mistake and you accept that they are right: *Sorry people, I stand corrected, the game is on Tuesday night. I'll still be there though.*

stand up and be 'counted

If people have to, or decide to, **stand up and be counted**, they feel it is necessary to make their opinions known, even if doing so is going to cause problems: *I'm a Socialist, but it's a swear word now, well I am proud to be a Socialist, so I will stand up and be counted.*

standstill

come to a 'standstill or be brought to a 'standstill

Traffic, or a city, **comes**, or **is brought, to a standstill** when cars, etc, can no longer move freely on the roads; business or finance **comes**, or **is brought, to a standstill** when transactions cannot take place due to some kind of exceptional circumstance, such as war: *It is nearly six years ago since our wedding, when the traffic in the City was brought to a standstill.* □ *The unrest, which stems from their demand for higher salaries, has brought the day-to-day operations at the ministry of finance to a virtual standstill.*

stars

reach for the 'stars

You **reach for the stars** when you are very ambitious: *This was her chance to be her own boss, to give free rein to her design flair, to stand up and reach out for the stars.*

see 'stars

You **see stars** when you see flashes of light in front of your eyes after you have knocked your head hard against something: *With the blow on his head, Anton saw stars: flashing, exploding in his eyes blue and red and colours he had not known existed.*

thank your lucky 'stars

You **thank your lucky stars** when you realize and appreciate how fortunate you are: *As I escorted him to the door, I thanked my lucky stars for the hours of self-defence training that I had undergone.*

starters

for 'starters

You say that something is the .case **for starters** when that point is the beginning of a list of complaints or arguments: *Here's a couple of his weak points, just for starters. He's unreliable and he's totally irresponsible.*
◇ SEE ALSO **for a kick-off** ▷ KICK

state

in a 'state

Someone who is **in a state** is nervous, anxious or upset: *She's in a terrible state and she won't let them give her sedatives because of the baby.*

state of af'fairs

A particular **state of affairs** is a situation or set of circumstances, especially one that is bad: *Several factors are involved in this unhappy state of affairs.*

state of 'mind

Your **state of mind** is the way you feel: *It is a state of mind, one of shock and withdrawal.*

state-of-the-'art

You describe something as **state-of-the-art** if it is very modern, using recent ideas and techniques: *The keyboard player may be using £5,000 worth of state-of-the-art technology.*

stead

stand in good 'stead

Something **stands you in good stead** for a future activity if it prepares you well for it: *Conran is convinced, too, that his experience of manufacturing in the early days has stood him in good stead as head of a retailing company.*

steady

steady as a 'rock

Someone or something that is as **steady as a rock** is very solid, reliable, or trustworthy, or physically unmoved by fear or nervousness: *Rain drops shimmered on his dark, oily skin; the Kalashnikov in his hands was steady as a rock.*

steam

full steam a'head

If you say that an activity is, or is going, **full steam ahead**, you mean that it is progressing well and fast: *The Oxford team, now full steam ahead, were not going to be caught, eventually crossing the line at 36 to Cambridge's 35.*

get up 'steam or pick up 'steam

Someone or something **gets up steam** or **picks up steam** when they gradually become bigger, more active or more successful: *His campaign steadily picked up steam.*

let off 'steam

People **let off steam** when they do something that has the effect of releasing the anger or energy that has built up inside them: *He doesn't mean to get at you personally. It's just that he wants to let off steam, and you're the only person he can lose his temper with.*

◇ SEE ALSO **get something out of your system** ▷ SYSTEM

run out of 'steam

If something **runs out of steam**, it loses its energy or momentum: *Yes, I would write those short stories when I felt I'd run out of steam on the novels.*

under your own 'steam

If you get somewhere **under your own steam**, you get there by your own efforts: *Ask them if they can make it under their own steam on Saturday or whether they'll need a lift.*

step

mind your 'step or watch your 'step

If you **mind**, or **watch**, **your step**, you proceed with caution, taking care not to anger or offend others: *Better watch your step next time you drink whisky.*

a step at a 'time or one step at a 'time

If something is done **a**, or **one**, **step at a time** it is done gradually: *Changes must be made one step at a time, each step being an improvement on the preceding one.*

a step 'backwards

You take **a step backwards** when a task you are working on, or a process, is delayed, or part of it has to be repeated: *Any sort of stress such as moving house, illness or upset in the family may cause the child to take a temporary step backwards in behaviour.*

a step 'forwards

A step forwards is an advance made in a task or process: *The success of his operating systems took Mr Gates another giant step forwards.*

one step 'forward, two steps 'back

A situation is a case of **one step forward, two steps back**, when, despite all attempts to progress, you still find yourself in a worse position than you were in when you started: *It is no good signing up a new member and then losing two others. That's one step forward, two steps back.*

out of 'step

If something is **out of step** with, for example, current developments, it is not in harmony with them: *To watch the ceaseless spinning for too long made you feel sick and dizzy and a bit out of step with everything else.*

step by 'step

If something is done **step by step**, it is done gradually: *She stressed that talk of a re-united Germany was 'going much too fast. You have to take these things step by step.'*

a step in the right di'rection

You take **a step in the right direction** when you do something that brings you nearer to your goal: *Mrs Thatcher called the move 'a major step in the right direction'.*

'step on it

If you tell someone to **step on it**, you mean that they should hurry up: *The Corporal and I shouted at the Sergeant to step on it, as the explosions were getting closer.*

In driving, you **'step on it'** when you press your foot down on the accelerator to make the car go faster.

steps

retrace your 'steps

You **retrace your steps** when you go back over the way you have come, or look back at past actions: *Cross the stream, and keep going until you reach the path you used at the start, and retrace your steps to the car park.* □ *Retrace your steps, and try to remember everything you did on that night.*

take 'steps

If you **take steps** to do something, you take the necessary action to ensure that something is done: *The Government considered the need to take steps to improve public order.*

stew

in a 'stew

If you are **in a stew**, you are in a very worried or anxious state about something: *I've been doing this job for years now, but I still get in a stew when I have to speak in public.*

A **stew** is a mixture of foods, especially meat and vegetables, cooked slowly in liquid.

stick

give someone 'stick

You **give someone stick** when you tease or criticize someone for not doing something properly: *I had to win, or the rest of the boys would have given me stick, particularly Linford.*

in a cleft 'stick

You are **in a cleft stick** when you have to choose between two very important and difficult matters: *So it's a cleft stick. And it's difficult, very difficult to strike the balance.*

◊ SEE ALSO **in two minds** ▷ MINDS; **in a quandary** ▷ QUANDARY

more than you can shake a 'stick at

More of a certain thing **than you can shake a stick at** means 'a lot of that thing': *Truly a top class outfit with more experience than you can shake a stick at.*

sticks

out in the 'sticks

A place that is **out in the sticks** is a long way from any big towns or public facilities: *Living out in the sticks, I can't afford to lose my driving licence.*

◊ SEE ALSO **the back of beyond** ▷ BACK; **in the middle of nowhere** ▷ MIDDLE; **off the beaten track** ▷ TRACK; **out of the way** ▷ WAY

sting

a 'sting in the tail

If something such as a set of circumstances has **a sting in the**, or **in its, tail**, it has a part or consequence that is unexpectedly unpleasant or harmful: *The budget certainly had a sting in its tail, and the increase on fuel charges is a terrible shock for the elderly.*

An insect's or other creature's **sting** is a sharp part that can pierce skin and inject poison.

take the 'sting out of

If something **takes the sting out of** an unpleasant event or situation, it makes it slightly less painful or easier to accept: *The company took the sting out of a halved dividend by saying it thought the figures were the low point in its fortunes and the only way to go was up.*

stink

cause a 'stink or kick up a 'stink

If someone **causes**, or **kicks up**, **a stink**, they make a fuss by complaining loudly: *The decision was finally changed, but only after he had kicked up a stink.*

◊ SEE ALSO **raise hell** or **kick up hell** ▷ HELL; **raise Cain** ▷ CAIN

stir

cause a 'stir or create a 'stir

If something **causes**, or **creates, a stir**, it causes or creates an excited reaction: *The Dents owned the very first car in Baldersdale and that created quite a stir.* □ *Microsoft recently caused quite a stir in computer circles by announcing that it is using real people to test its products.*

stitch

not have a stitch 'on

When you **do not have a stitch on**, you are completely naked: *One hot day I remember leaving our clothes along the river bank and swimming without a stitch on.*

stitches

in 'stitches

You are **in stitches** if you are helpless with laughter; someone has you **in stitches** if they cause you to be helpless with laughter: *I thought the film was excellent. It had me in stitches a lot of the time and definitely wasn't just for the kids.*

stock

'laughing stock

You are a **laughing stock** if a lot of people are laughing at you because of something ridiculous or foolish that you have done: *Yellow! Mummy, you must be mad if you think I would be seen in a yellow frock! I'd be a laughing stock!*

take 'stock of

You **take stock**, or **take stock of** a situation, when you think carefully about every aspect of that situation, usually in order to make a decision about what to do next: *He needs to be completely alone. To take stock, to recharge his batteries.*

stomach

not have the 'stomach for

If you say that you **do not have the stomach for** something, you mean you do not have enough courage or determination to do it or face it: *He had begun so promisingly, so full of the future and then, had found he no longer had the energy, the stomach for getting on.*

sick to the 'stomach

Something that makes you **sick to the stomach** disgusts you: *Cara stared at it, unbelieving. She felt sick to the stomach.*

stone

carved in 'stone

Something such as a rule or regulation that is **carved in stone** is strict, and cannot be altered: *The rules aren't carved in stone – they're just there to guide you.*

◇ SEE ALSO **set in** or **written on tablets of stone** ▷ TABLETS

> This idiom is commonly used in the negative, as in the above example.

leave no stone un'turned

If you **leave no stone unturned**, you search for something in every possible place: *We shall leave no stone unturned in our search for the culprit.*

a 'stone's throw

Something that is **a stone's throw** away is very near: *It's got a great view and the station's just a stone's throw away.*

◇ SEE ALSO **in** or **within spitting distance** ▷ DISTANCE; **on your doorstep** ▷ DOORSTEP

sink like a 'stone

Something **sinks like a stone** when it drops very quickly below the surface of a liquid; your feelings **sink like a stone** when you suddenly feel depressed: *Experts said that the raft would become waterlogged and sink like a stone.* □ *My heart and spirits sank like a stone in a lake. I was filled with dread, and with paralysing fear.*

stone 'me (old)

Stone me! is a rather old-fashioned expression of surprise: *'Stone me Aunt Fanny,'*

said Archie, 'I've got nothing to talk to Sergeant Joe about.'

◇ SEE ALSO **stone the crows** ▷ CROWS

stools

fall between two 'stools

Something you do **falls between two stools** when it fails because you have tried to fulfil two aims, and have been unsuccessful with both, perhaps because you could not decide which one to focus on: *The film's attempt to combine serious social comment with an escapist action movie format cause it to fall heavily between two stools.*

stop

come to a full 'stop

Something that **has come to a full stop** has come to an end: *Will the company come to a full stop? Probably not, even though the next couple of years will be tough.*

> A **full stop** is the punctuation mark (.) which indicates the end of a sentence.

put a 'stop to

You **put a stop to** something when you ensure that it will not happen any more: *The law should once and for all put a stop to these problems.*

stop at 'nothing

Someone who will **stop at nothing** is willing to do anything, however immoral, to get what they want: *He was a coolly calculating, ruthless man who would stop at nothing to get where or what he wanted.*

◇ SEE ALSO **by fair means or foul** ▷ MEANS; **at any price** ▷ PRICE

stops

pull out all the 'stops

You **pull out all the stops** when you act with as much energy, determination or emotion as possible: *The staff pulled out all the stops to ensure patients had a magical day.*

◇ SEE ALSO **take the bull by the horns** ▷ HORNS; **rise to the challenge** ▷ CHALLENGE; **grasp the nettle** ▷ NETTLE; **rise to the occasion** ▷ OCCASION

> The **stops** here, refer to the devices on an organ, which, when pulled out, enable you to play the instrument as loudly as possible.

store

in 'store

Something that is **in store** is coming in the future: *We have some great music in store for you on tonight's show.*

storm

lay great 'store by
If you **lay great store by** something, you value that thing highly: *The market economy must lay great store by individual responsibility.*

storm

a storm in a 'teacup
If you describe a situation as **a storm in a teacup**, you mean that a great deal of fuss is being made over an unimportant matter: *This disagreement between the different schools of thought is more than just a storm in an academic teacup.*

◊ SEE ALSO **make a mountain out of a molehill** ▷ MOUNTAIN

take by 'storm
A performer or performance **takes** a place **by storm** when they gain rapid and widespread popularity or approval: *As a teenager, Carol took the local Theatre Royal by storm.*

weather the 'storm
You **weather the storm** when you survive in a difficult time: *Their vigorous reshaping programme last year helped the company weather the storm slightly better than some of its rivals.*

story

a 'likely story
If someone says '**a likely story**', they mean that they do not believe what someone has just told them: *They told her that Serge had been feeling ill. A likely story, she thought – probably a hangover.*

◊ SEE ALSO **a tall story** ▷ STORY

another 'story
1 Something that is **another story** is very different from the thing just mentioned: *He plays the piano quite well, but the trumpet's another story.* **2** You say '**that's another story**' to indicate that you are not going to start describing the event that has just been mentioned: *Cases have been reported recently in which animals do seem to be able to recognize their relatives, but that is another story.*

end of 'story
If someone says '**end of story**', they mean that they refuse to discuss the subject any more: *I'm not going and that's that. End of story.*

it's the story of my 'life
People say '**it's the story of my life**' when they are feeling depressed because something unpleasant has happened to them, and the same thing has happened to them several times before: *'More likely he's run off with another woman,' Laura said bitterly. 'It's the story of my life.'*

not the whole 'story
If you say that available information or facts are **not the whole story**, you mean that there are further facts or additional information that must also be considered: *The Chancellor has made it clear his present priority is to get inflation down. But that is not the whole story.*

the same old 'story
You use **the same old story** to refer to an unpleasant or undesirable situation that happens again and again: *And when the winter came, it was the same old story, everyone was short of work again.*

the story 'goes
You use the phrase '**the story goes**' when you are about to tell someone something that is said or believed by many people: *He was also a vegetarian, although the story goes that Chapman persuaded him to eat steaks after hearing that he sometimes felt faint when heading a ball.*

a tall 'story
A tall story is a story or excuse that you do not believe: *The judge obviously thought that he had told a tall story.*

◊ SEE ALSO **a likely story** ▷ STORY

that's my story and I'm 'sticking to it
If you say '**that's my story and I'm sticking to it**' you mean that although your excuse is not actually true, that is the excuse you are giving: *I'm afraid I couldn't come because I was ill. Well, that's my story and I'm sticking to it.*

to cut a long story 'short
You use '**to cut a long story short**' when you are about to summarize the end of a story in order to make the point clear sooner: *So to cut a long story short, in the end I managed to get a taxi home, at about four in the morning.*

straight

on the straight and 'narrow
Someone who is **on the straight and narrow** is living their life in a moral and principled way, especially after a period of criminal, immoral or unacceptable behaviour: *Many returned to the straight and narrow as the result of his firm but compassionate influence.*

straight as an 'arrow or straight as a 'die
Something that is as **straight as an arrow**, or **straight as a die**, is very straight; someone who is as **straight as an arrow**, or **die**, is very honest: *A wall goes down from the road straight as a die to East Gill.* □ *The other friend, who also decided to become a lawyer, was as straight as an arrow.*

straight as a 'ramrod

Someone who is as **straight as a ramrod** is holding their body in a rigid and upright position: *Her back was as straight as a ramrod, which made her feel a little more dignified while engaging in what she considered the unladylike art of cycling.*

A **ramrod** is a long thin rod that can be used for pushing things into narrow spaces.

'straight up (*informal, slang*)

'**Straight up**' is used to emphasize that what you have just said is true: *'They gave us all this free.' 'No.' 'Yeah, straight up – they were closing down – throwing loads of stuff away.'*

straw

draw the short 'straw or get the short 'straw

You **draw**, or **get**, **the short straw** when you are given the least pleasant task to do, or when you are chosen to do something that no-one wants to do: *I drew the short straw and could not drink as I had the job of doing the first two hours' driving.*

the last 'straw or the final 'straw

You say that something is **the last**, or **final**, **straw** when it is the last in a whole series of disagreeable events and is the one that makes you feel that you cannot tolerate any more: *The final straw was when the government put up the price of rice yet again.*
◇ SEE ALSO **the straw that broke the camel's back** ▷ STRAW

straw in the 'wind

A **straw in the wind** is a small incident that does not have great importance now, but which shows how things may be in the future: *The military revolt may have been premature and unsuccessful, but it was a significant straw in the wind.*

the straw that broke the camel's 'back

You describe something as **the straw that broke the camel's back** if it is the last in a series of disagreeable events, and is the one that makes the person or thing involved finally break down: *In fact, the proposed mass redundancy in and around the mining industry was probably the straw that broke the camel's back for the British people.*
◇ SEE ALSO **the last** or **final straw** ▷ STRAW

Straw is the dried cut stalks of corn and other crops, used as food and bedding for cattle.

straws

clutch at 'straws or grasp at 'straws

You **clutch**, or **grasp**, **at straws** when you try, in desperation, to get out of a difficult situation by means that are unlikely to succeed: *She was in love with him, a sort of frantic grasping at straws, in love with the idea of love, romance.*

Someone who is drowning or falling is likely to try to hold on to anything, however useless, to try and save themselves.

streak

on a winning 'streak

You are **on a winning streak** if you are enjoying a series of successes: *Michael picked up his cards and studied them carefully. He was on a winning streak tonight.*

talk a blue 'streak

Someone who **talks a blue streak** talks very fast without stopping: *He could talk a blue streak. It was said that they had locked him up for a bit of peace and quiet!*
◇ SEE ALSO **talk the hind leg off a donkey** ▷ LEG

stream

go against the 'stream

When you **go against the stream** you refuse to accept the situation as it is, and act differently from the others.
◇ SEE ALSO **go** or **drift** or **swim against the current** ▷ CURRENT; **go against the flow** ▷ FLOW; **go** or **swim against the tide** ▷ TIDE

go with the 'stream

You **go with the stream** when you do the same as everyone else, or accept the opinions held by most people, because it would be more difficult to do something different or to disagree.
◇ SEE ALSO **go** or **drift** or **swim with the current** ▷ CURRENT; **go with the crowd** ▷ CROWD; **go with the flow** ▷ FLOW; **go**, or **drift**, or **swim, with the tide** ▷ TIDE

street

'easy street

You are **on easy street**, or your life can be described as **easy street** if you are rich enough to live comfortably: *She couldn't believe her luck, it was easy street. Ahead of her lay years of photo calls in women's magazines.*
◇ SEE ALSO **in clover** ▷ CLOVER; **in the money** ▷ MONEY; **quids in** ▷ QUIDS

'street cred

Someone who has **street cred** is familiar with the most up-to-date fashions and liberal ideas of the place in which they live: *Wanted: Drummer for rock band hoping to increase street cred.*

'**Cred**' here, is short for 'credibility'. Someone who has credibility commands recognition or respect.

up someone's 'street
Something that is **up your street** is just the sort of thing that you like: *You like travelling. The assignment should be right up your street.*

This idiom is very often preceded by 'right', which gives it emphasis.

streets

on the 'streets
Someone who is **on the streets** is homeless: *Tenants who refuse to accept leases are given notice to quit and find themselves on the streets after years of loyal service.*

'streets ahead
You say that something is **streets ahead** of others when it is much more advanced or much better than they are: *The Scandinavian countries are already streets ahead in the area of alternative energy production.*

strength

give me 'strength
People say '**give me strength**' when they feel that they cannot tolerate a situation any more: *He moaned aloud and rolled his eyes to the ceiling. 'Give me strength,' he yelled.*

go from strength to 'strength
People or things **go from strength to strength** when they keep improving or becoming more successful: *For several years the business went from strength to strength.*

on the strength of
You do something **on the strength of** some circumstance or experience when the circumstance or experience persuades you to do it: *McNeill signed Jack for 650,000, largely on the strength of personal recommendation and 'video evidence.*

stretch

at a 'stretch
You do something for a certain length of time **at a stretch** when you do it continuously throughout that period: *They can't expect you to work for more than five hours at a stretch.*

by no stretch of the imagi'nation
Something that can **by no stretch of the imagination** be described in some way cannot possibly be described in that way: *Carl, by no stretch of the imagination, could ever be called good-looking.*

stride

get into your 'stride
You **get into your stride** when you begin to work or do something well or effectively: *I've had to cut back a little just recently, but I'm hoping to get back into my stride really soon.*

put someone off their 'stride
You **put someone off their stride** when you interrupt them and break their concentration: *Will you be ready to give a 30 second summary of what you are doing, or will that completely put you off your stride?*

strike

on 'strike
Workers go **on strike** when they officially refuse to work because of a disagreement with their employer.

strike it 'lucky
You **strike it lucky** when you have good luck in some respect: *Retired factory worker Tom Hayes has struck it lucky – with a £10,000 Mirror Bingo jackpot.*

string

another string to your 'bow or a second string to your 'bow
You have **another**, or **a second, string to your bow** if you have another ability or skill apart from your main occupation, which will give you a second chance if you lose your job, for example: *He decided to take the degree so he would have another string to his bow.*

strings

hold the 'purse strings
The person who **holds the purse strings** in an organization or group is the one who is in charge of looking after the money, and deciding how it will be spent: *Colleges will now be responsible for managing their own budgets but the Government will hold the purse strings.*

pull 'strings
If you **pull strings** you use your influence or your friendly relationships with influential people in order to get something done: *He's a manager. He can pull strings.*

no strings at'tached
If a situation or proposal comes with **no strings attached**, it has no undesirable conditions or limitations: *And there's no strings attached to the sponsorship that I received. I didn't have to stay with the company after I finished studying.*

strip

tear someone 'off a strip
You **tear someone off a strip** when you tell them off angrily: *Don't just tear them off a strip. Explain why what they are doing is wrong.*
◇ SEE ALSO **send someone away with a flea in their ear** ▷ FLEA; **give someone hell** ▷ HELL; **give someone a piece of your mind** ▷ PIECE; **read the riot act** ▷ RIOT; **give someone the rough side of your tongue** ▷ SIDE

stroke

not do a stroke of 'work

Someone who **has not done a stroke of work** has not done any work at all: *Her beautiful hands had visibly never done a stroke of work in their owner's life.*

on the stroke of 'such-and-such

Something happens **on the stroke of** a particular time when it happens at that time exactly: *She's bound to arrive on the stroke of seven. She's obsessed with punctuality.*

put someone off their 'stroke

You **put someone off their stroke** when you interrupt them and break their concentration: *It put him off his stroke and the chopper slipped, cutting his finger.*

stroke of 'genius

A **stroke of genius** is a very clever or imaginative idea: *It was a stroke of genius by the Prime Minister to make him Minister of the Arts, where he could shout his head off and do little real harm.*

stroke of 'luck

A **stroke of luck** is a sudden piece of good luck: *The final stroke of luck was a strong north-easterly wind which washed them ashore on Great Barrier Island.*

stroll

take a stroll down memory 'lane

If you **take a stroll down memory lane** you take some time to think about the past: *Enjoy a stroll down memory lane to relive some of the golden moments you've shared with the ones you love.*

> A common variation of this idiom is **'take a trip down memory lane'**.

stuff

hot 'stuff (*informal*)

Someone or something that is described as **hot stuff** is very exciting or interesting, often sexually so: *He had succeeded in persuading a girl called Jill into going out with him. Jill was reputed to be hot stuff.*

> Women are likely to find this term offensive if it is applied to them.

know your 'stuff

Someone who **knows their stuff** has a thorough knowledge of their subject: *We've used him in the past on a few projects. He's a good man and knows his stuff.*

◇ SEE ALSO **know your onions** ▷ ONIONS

stuff and 'nonsense

Something that is described as **stuff and nonsense** is untrue, ridiculous or foolish: *'Stuff and nonsense,' Mary Ann said. 'Diet*

indeed! With a little figure like yours? You're too thin to cast a shadow.'

stuffed

get 'stuffed (*informal, offensive*)

People say **'get stuffed!'** as a very rude and contemptuous way of dismissing another person or what they have said: *Then he shrugged and turned away. 'Get stuffed,' he muttered.* □ *If I found I didn't like it when it came, I'd tell them to get stuffed. It's simple really, isn't it?*

◇ SEE ALSO **get knotted** ▷ KNOTTED

> If someone advises you to tell someone to **get stuffed**, they probably mean that you should show them that you do not accept what they have said, but not necessarily that you should use those exact words.

stuffing

knock the 'stuffing out of

If someone or something **knocks the stuffing out of** a person or thing, it takes away their strength or power and makes them weak and feeble: *Mike Spence's death at Indy in 1968 knocked the stuffing out of me.*

style

cramp someone's 'style

Someone or something that **cramps your style** stops you behaving as freely as you would like: *He looked over at the crutches with an expression of deep distaste. 'I try not to let them cramp my style'*

do something in 'style

You **do something in style** when you do it the most expensive or elegant way: *Buy this new garden furniture and relax in the sun in style.*

sublime

from the sublime to the ri'diculous

You say that something goes **from the sublime to the ridiculous** if it starts off well, but quickly becomes laughable or very bad: *Constructed layer by layer, Ostrowski's paintings range from the sublime to the ridiculous, presenting many paradoxes in the process.*

success

suc'cess story

A **success story** is the story of a great achievement, particularly if the person involved has made a lot of money: *In France, his fans prefer to dwell on Mr Depardieu's street-to-screen success story.*

such

'such-and-such
You use **such-and-such** to refer to an unidentified or unspecified person or thing: *It is sure to have its critics exclaiming: 'She never mentioned so-and-so or said such-and-such.'*

sudden

all of a 'sudden
Something that happens **all of a sudden** happens suddenly, or unexpectedly: *And then all of a sudden the lights went out.*

sufferance

on 'sufferance
If something is done **on sufferance**, it is tolerated, but not welcomed or encouraged: *She had been there on sufferance for so long and yet she had never been quite brave enough to break free.*

suit

follow 'suit
If someone does something and you **follow suit**, you do the same thing as they have done: *When West Germany raised its interest rate last week, Britain was forced immediately to follow suit.*

◊ SEE ALSO **take a leaf out of someone's book** ▷ LEAF; **take your cue from someone** ▷ CUE

In a card game, you **follow suit** when you play a card of the same suit (diamonds, hearts, clubs or spades) as the player before you.

sun

every such-and-such under the 'sun
You use **every** one of a certain thing **under the sun** in order to emphasize number and variety: *I dyed my hair every colour under the sun.*

sure

sure as eggs is 'eggs
You say that something is the case **sure as eggs is eggs** if you want to emphasize that you know for certain that it is the case: *She'll wait up for us. Sure as eggs is eggs. You know what she's like.*

◊ SEE ALSO **for certain** ▷ CERTAIN; **beyond all doubt** ▷ DOUBT; **without a doubt** ▷ DOUBT; **without question** ▷ QUESTION; **beyond any shadow of doubt** or **without any shadow of doubt** ▷ SHADOW

sure 'thing (*informal*)
Sure thing means 'yes, of course': *'Can you find the phone number?' 'Sure thing. I'll check the Yellow Pages.'*

surface

scratch beneath the 'surface
You **scratch beneath the surface** when you deal with more than just the superficial elements of something: *Scratch beneath the surface and you'll find a gentle, sensitive, even fragile man.*

scratch the 'surface
You **scratch the surface** when you only deal with the superficial elements of something: *So far, research has done no more than scratch the surface of this potentially important topic.*

surprise

come as a sur'prise
Something that **comes as a surprise** is not expected: *It didn't come as a surprise to me that he'd been fired.*

surprise sur'prise
'**Surprise surprise**' is an ironic way of saying that you are not at all surprised by something: *Right, if there are no further questions about step one, we're now going to move on to, surprise surprise, step two.*

swear

swear 'blind
You **swear blind** that something is the case when you say firmly and for certain that it is true, even though other people have their doubts: *He used to swear blind he saw his mother standing at the end of the bed.*

sweat

'no sweat (*informal*)
'**No sweat**' is a very informal way of saying that something is not a problem for you: *I just returned from an exhibition and wrote a 6,000 word report in one burst in my hotel room. No sweat.*

sweep

make a clean 'sweep
You **make a clean sweep** in a series of contests when you win them all: *But he failed to achieve a clean sweep of the end-of-season awards.*

sweet

'sweet on someone (*old*)
Someone is **sweet on** another person when they like that other person very much, or they are in love with, or sexually attracted to them: *You should have heard the crowd. Some of the girls were sweet on him.*

sweetness

all sweetness and 'light
If you say that someone is **all sweetness and light**, you mean that they are behaving in

an insincerely friendly and pleasant manner: *We've talked several times. He's been all sweetness and light, promised nothing and done nothing.*

swing

get into the 'swing of things

If you **get into the swing of things** you become very involved in a particular activity, or sufficiently involved in it that you begin to enjoy it: *I have now been here for over a week, and am beginning to get into the swing of things. It is very hard work, but very enjoyable.*

◇ SEE ALSO **let your hair down** ▷ HAIR; **enter into the spirit of** ▷ SPIRIT

go with a 'swing

An event that **goes with a swing** is very successful and enjoyed by the people present.

in full 'swing

If something such as a party is **in full swing**, it is at its liveliest stage: *The holiday season begins to get into full swing as our schools close.*

swings

swings and 'roundabouts

You describe a situation as **swings and roundabouts** if it involves gaining one thing by losing another: *The advantages of a small company over a large one is a matter of swings and roundabouts.*

> This idiom is the shortened form, of 'what you lose on the swings you gain on the roundabouts'. In a fairground, if customers favour the roundabouts, the managers will lose money on the swings, and vice-versa.

swoop

in one fell 'swoop

A number of things are dealt with or done **in one fell swoop** when they are all dealt with or done at one time rather than gradually or in stages: *You are likely to suffer from headaches, lethargy and so on, if you try and cut the stimulants out in one fell swoop.*

sword

a double-edged 'sword

You describe something as **a double-edged sword** if it has its advantages, but also its bad points: *Being well-known is a double-edged sword. Sometimes it's nice to be recognized, but there are just as many times when it would be nice to be anonymous.*

put to the 'sword

Someone or something that **is put to the sword** is killed or disposed of: *Other public institutions were put to the sword elsewhere. □ He put the monk to the sword, killing him instantly; then he tipped the cart, complete with contents, into the stream below.*

sword of 'Damocles

You feel you have a, or the, **sword of Damocles** hanging over you, if you feel or know that something terrible is going to happen: *Oh well, I suppose it was inevitable. I'm relieved in a way. It's been hanging over my head like the sword of Damocles.*

> From the story of Damocles, who was forced to sit through a banquet with a sword suspended over him, held up by only a single hair.

swords

beat swords into 'ploughshares or turn swords into 'ploughshares

People **beat**, or **turn**, **swords into ploughshares** when they change to a more peaceful way of life, disposing of their weapons: *We shall develop a planned programme for the conversion of the means of war manufacture to peaceful production. It will mean changing swords into ploughshares.*

cross 'swords or have crossed 'swords with someone

When two people with different or opposite opinions argue, you can say that they **have crossed swords**, or that they **have crossed swords with** each other: *Nonetheless it is perhaps surprising that the librarian has not crossed swords with the law over obscene and indecent literature before now.*

◇ SEE ALSO **at daggers drawn** ▷ DAGGERS

sympathy

come out in 'sympathy with

You **come out in sympathy with** another person or group of people when you do the same thing as them in order to demonstrate your support for them: *To almost everybody's surprise, dockers began everywhere to come out in sympathy. Strikes were announced throughout the country.*

system

all systems 'go

'**All systems go!**' means 'let's go!'; if a project is **all systems go**, it is just starting, on a large and ambitious scale:

Blue skies and sunshine reigned supreme and it was all systems go for a great airshow.

get something out of your 'system

When you have been feeling anger, sorrow, or frustration, and you manage to **get it out of your system**, you succeed in getting rid of that feeling by expressing it openly: *Don't be afraid to cry; it's the best way to get it out of your system.*

t

T

to a 'T
To a T means 'perfectly': *Mmm-mmm. This beef is done to a T.*
◊ SEE ALSO **done to a turn** ▷ TURN

ta

ta-'ta *(informal)*
People say '**ta-ta**' as an informal way of saying goodbye: *'You off then, love?' shouted Mrs. Hennessy. 'Ta-ta. Have a lovely time.'*

tab *(see also* **tabs***)*

pick up the 'tab
You **pick up the tab** when you pay the bill: *We will pick up the tab for your hotel. Okay? And we will pay all your travel costs there and back.*

table

drink someone under the 'table
You say you can **drink someone under the table** if you can drink a lot more alcohol than they can before getting completely drunk: *He was 24, highly intelligent, could drink Malc under the table and had a dry, lightning wit.*

set a good 'table
Someone who **sets a good table** provides good, healthy and delicious food: *Anna prided herself on setting a good table; great lasagne pies, Virginia ham, as well as all the best fish, game and vegetables her friends in the country sent her.*

under the 'table
Something that is done **under the table** is done secretly, rather than publicly or officially: *Do you think he is playing under the same conditions as everybody else? Everybody keeps quiet but under the table he's making money.*

tables

turn the 'tables
You **turn the tables**, or **turn the tables on someone**, in a competitive situation, when you remove the advantage from one person or people, and take the advantage yourself: *'You're just mad now because I turned the tables on you.' 'I'm mad because you told me all those lies!'*
◊ SEE ALSO **the boot is on the other foot** ▷ BOOT

tablets

set in tablets of 'stone or written on tablets of 'stone
A belief or principle is **set in**, or **written on, tablets of stone** if it is fixed and cannot be changed: *The existing programmes will not stand still, set in tablets of stone, but will need to improve continuously and evolve to meet business needs.* □ *The Treaty is not written on tablets of stone, it allows for changes and improvements as early as 1996.*
◊ SEE ALSO **carved in stone** ▷ STONE

> This idiom commonly occurs in the negative form, as in the above examples. Other variants include '**cast** in tablets of stone', and '**engraved** on tablets of stone'.

tabs

keep 'tabs on
You **keep tabs on** someone or something when you watch them closely so that you know exactly what they are doing and where they are: *Make sure you keep tabs on the books you lend to people, otherwise you may never get them back.* □ *They keep tabs on the injured who they rescue until they leave hospital.*

tack

a different 'tack
1 If someone goes off on **a different tack**, they start talking about something which is not directly connected with the subject of your discussion: *'You're different. You're not at all ordinary. In fact,' said Owen, his mind beginning to go off on a different tack, 'you're altogether extraordinary.'* **2** If someone tries **a different tack**, they try a different way of dealing with a situation or problem, because their previous method was unsuccessful: *If he doesn't respond to criticism, try a different tack. Encouragement works better in some cases.*

◇ SEE ALSO **fly off at a tangent** or **go off at a tangent** ▷ TANGENT

tacks

get down to brass 'tacks
Two or more people **get down to brass tacks** when they start discussing the exact details of something: *Then they got down to brass tacks: how old was he? Was he married? How did he make his money?*

> '**Brass tacks**' comes from the Cockney rhyming slang for 'facts'.

tail

have your 'tail between your legs
Someone **has got their tail between their legs** when they feel or look ashamed and embarrassed; if they **go off with their tail between their legs**, they go away feeling or looking like this: *This fresh humiliation and the subsequent return with tail between my legs would be the final nail in my professional coffin.* □ *We took her in when she came back from London with her tail between her legs, and we fed her and gave her a roof over her head.*

on someone's 'tail
You are **on someone's tail** if you are following close behind them: *I only realized that I had been breaking the speed limit when I saw the police car on my tail.*

the tail 'end of something
The tail end of something is the end or the last part of it: *I just caught the tail end of the film.*

the tail is wagging the 'dog
You say that **the tail is wagging the dog** if a small and unimportant part of the situation that someone is in has started controlling their actions and decisions, when it should in fact be that person's actions and decisions that control the situation: *It sounds like a recipe for feeble government, with the tail wagging the dog.*

take (*see also* **taken** *and* **takes**)

you can't take so-and-so 'anywhere (*often humorous*)
1 You say that **you can't take** a certain person **anywhere** if they always behave badly or embarrass you in public: *Please help as we can't take her anywhere, she just goes mad!* **2** '**I can't take you**, or **him**, or **her**, **anywhere**' is also a humorous comment made about the unsocial behaviour of the person you are with: *You must excuse John's terrible jokes. I can't take him anywhere.*

taken

be 'taken with
You **are taken with** someone or something when you find that you like them: *I'm quite taken with your cousin. What did you say her name was?*

◇ SEE ALSO **be bowled over** ▷ BOWLED; **have a thing about** ▷ THING

takes

takes one to 'know one (*informal, disrespectful*)
If someone says '**takes one to know one**' as a response to an insult or criticism, they are returning the insult or criticism by suggesting that you can only recognize faults in them if you are guilty of those faults yourself: *'I'm working with bloody amateurs here!' 'Takes one to know one.'*

tale

live to tell the 'tale
Someone who **lives to tell the tale** manages to escape alive from a dangerous situation and is therefore able to describe what happened: *In order to survive the jungle and live to tell the tale it is important not only to have good companions, but also to have the best available equipment.*

tale of 'woe (*often humorous*)
If someone tells you a **tale of woe**, they tell you a sad story about the bad things which have happened to them: *She disliked the casual way in which he made decisions profoundly affecting other people's lives – choosing whose tale of woe should be front page news.*

◇ SEE ALSO **sob story** ▷ SOB

talk (*see also* **talking**)

all 'talk
You say that someone is **all talk** if you do not believe that they will really do what they say: *Politicians were the least respected group: 'They're all talk. They always break their promises.'*

'small talk
Small talk is the kind of pleasant, light conversation on unimportant subjects which you have in a formal situation with someone you do not know well: *He is massively informed, and completely charmless. It is a shock when he smiles. He has no small talk, except about politics and, possibly, cricket.*

the talk of the 'town
You say that a person or thing is **the talk of the town** if everyone is talking about them: *She used to have hair all the way down to her waist. Then one time she came back from a*

*job and had a trendy, short haircut. It was
the talk of the town.*

'you're a fine one to talk or **'you can talk** or
'you can't talk

If you say **'you're a fine one to talk'**, or **'you
can talk'**, or **'you can't talk'** to someone
who has been criticizing someone else for
some fault, you mean that they have the
same fault themselves: *'Your trouble is
you've been watching too much crime on
telly.' Nev was a fine one to talk. He
watched so much TV he'd get square eyes.*
◊ SEE ALSO **hark at so-and-so** ▷ HARK; **look
who's talking** ▷ LOOK

talking

now you're 'talking (*informal*)

You say **'now you're talking'** to someone
who is at last making a suggestion or an
offer that interests you: *'If you don't want to
be my employee, how about becoming a
partner in the business?' 'Now you're talking.'*

talking of 'such-and-such or **talking of 'so-
and-so**

You say **'talking of'** a certain thing or
person when you want to mention another
thing connected with that subject: *Talking
of funny things, have you seen that new
comedy on Friday nights?* □ *'I had a drink
with Julie last week.' 'Oh, talking of Julie,
can you give her a message next time you see
her?'*

tandem

in 'tandem with

Two people or things work **in tandem with**
each other when they combine to form a
system that works in a useful way: *But it
seems unlikely that many customers will rely
solely on the private network, instead using it
in tandem with British Telecom's lines.*

A **tandem** is a long bicycle for two
people.

tangent

fly off at a 'tangent or **go off at a 'tangent**

You **fly**, or **go**, **off at a tangent** when you
begin to think, talk about, or do something
unrelated to the original subject: *So I leave
what I was going to do, go off at a tangent
and do something totally different. So, you
know, it never gets dull, which is good.*
◊ SEE ALSO **a different tack** ▷ TACK

If you are swinging an object in a circle
around a central point, and then you let
go of it, it will **fly**, or **go**, **off at a tangent**,
moving in a straight line away from the
circle.

tantrum

throw a 'tantrum

Someone, especially a child, **throws a tantrum** when they become violently angry
about something relatively unimportant:
*Thomas kicked his legs. He went red in
the face. He yelled. 'He doesn't usually
throw tantrums,' Ashley said ruefully.*

tap

on 'tap

Something which is **on tap** is ready to be
used as soon as it is needed: *How useful it
must be, she thought, to have all this information on tap.*

Beer is **on tap** if it is served straight from
the barrel into the glass through a tap,
rather than being kept in bottles.

tape

red 'tape

If people talk about **red tape**, they mean the
official processes which must be completed
before a certain activity can start: *There's
an awful lot of red tape to get through, just to
make sure that it's safe and complies with
health and safety standards.*

In law and politics, official documents
are tied together with a bright pink
ribbon [= the 'red' tape]. This ribbon
has to be cut or untied before the documents can be read.

target

on 'target

You are **on target** when you are working at
the correct rate and will finish or achieve
something on time: *Employees and share-
holders will be pleased to hear that mid-year
sales figures were on target.*

a sitting 'target

You describe a person or thing as **a sitting
target** if they are a likely victim for some
attack because they obviously have no way
of defending themselves: *Anyone who is
driving a hire-car in Los Angeles will be
seen as a sitting target by muggers.*
◊ SEE ALSO **sitting duck** ▷ DUCK

In hunting, an animal which is sitting
still can be shot more easily than if it is
running.

task

take someone to 'task

The people in authority **take someone to
task** when they criticize that person
strongly for what they have done and
demand to hear an explanation: *I refuse*

to be taken to task over a decision which was made without my knowledge.

taste

give someone a taste of their own 'medicine

You give someone **a taste of their own medicine** when you punish them by giving them the same bad treatment that they have given you, or someone else: *Tired of the humiliation my husband's affairs imposed on me, I decided to give him a taste of his own medicine.*

◊ SEE ALSO **pay someone back in their own coin** ▷ COIN; **pay someone back with interest** ▷ INTEREST

in bad 'taste or in poor 'taste

Something that someone says or does is **in bad taste**, or **in poor taste**, if it is offensive and is likely to upset people: *It is curious that he should select such a subject for his essay, drawn from a newspaper announcement of a man's death. This verges on being in poor taste.*

leave a bad 'taste in your mouth or leave a bitter 'taste in your mouth

Something **leaves a bad taste in your mouth** when you feel uncomfortable or unpleasant after it has happened: *She had known the fear of being rejected, and it left a bitter taste in her mouth. Why couldn't he love her?*

no accounting for 'taste

You say that there is **no accounting for taste** when you are surprised that someone likes a certain person or thing, because you find that person or thing worthless: *I just don't know what she sees in that dreadful guy. Still, I suppose there's no accounting for taste.*

to your 'taste

Something that is **to your taste** is something you like or enjoy: *We have some beautiful ruby rings. Or maybe a small diamond would be more to your taste?*

tatters

in 'tatters

1 Clothes that are **in tatters** are badly torn: *His hair was matted and his clothes were in tatters.* **2** Something that is **in tatters** has been destroyed: *A year at teacher training college had left my confidence in tatters.*

tea

not for all the tea in 'China

You say that you would not, or could not, do something **for all the tea in China** if you are determined never to do it, or if you would never be able to do it: *Berenson had left the business for school-teaching and* *wasn't about to give it up, thank you, for all the tea in China.* □ *Albert had only to ring up. Which he couldn't do now for all the tea in China. He went to the call-box night after night, but there was no way of finding the nerve to dial.*

◊ SEE ALSO **not for love or money** ▷ LOVE

tea and 'sympathy

If you give someone who is upset **tea and sympathy**, you make them a cup of tea and try to comfort them: *The mothers can sit alone with their preoccupations, or share tea and sympathy and cigarettes with other women.*

teach

teach someone a 'thing or two

You **teach someone a thing or two** when you **1** are able to give them advice, perhaps unexpectedly: *The amateur can so often teach the professionals a thing or two.* **2** punish them because you think they need to be less proud or selfish: *I've overheard the Headmaster saying he would like to teach me a thing or two.*

tears

bored to 'tears

You are **bored to tears** when you are very bored: *I stuck it for about a year and then moved on to another. The move was really just a change for change's sake – I was simply bored to tears by it all.*

teeth

armed to the 'teeth

People are **armed to the teeth** if they are carrying a lot of weapons or other equipment which will be useful in a particular situation: *The army camped in the hills, armed to the teeth with machine guns.* □ *We were already armed to the teeth with mountaineering equipment.*

fed up to the back 'teeth with

You are **fed up to the back teeth with** someone or something if you have been patient with them for long enough and you feel unwilling to give them any more of your time or energy: *Smaller practitioners are fed up to the back teeth with all forms of regulation, and audit regulation in particular.*

get your 'teeth into

You **get your teeth into** an activity when you get involved and start working hard and enthusiastically on it: *He was a bit slow at first, but he's working much better now he's got his teeth into the project.* □ *It was the first role I'd had that I really felt I could get my teeth into.*

gnash your 'teeth

You say that someone **is gnashing their teeth** when they are expressing a strong feeling such as extreme anger, pain, or sadness: *She had come to the Centre in the depths of despair, weeping, gnashing her teeth and venting her hatred upon the doctors.*

An animal or person **gnashes their teeth** when they open and shut their mouth and show their teeth because they are angry or in pain.

grit your 'teeth

1 You **grit your teeth** if you press them together tightly so that you can, for example, bear pain more easily: *I watched him grit his teeth and try not to scream as I removed the shrapnel from his shoulder.* **2** You **grit your teeth** when you prepare yourself mentally for some unpleasant experience: *It wasn't going to be fun, but I decided to grit my teeth and get on with it.*

lie through your 'teeth

Someone who **is lying through their teeth** is telling you something which is completely untrue: *'Don't worry, Lavender, you'll soon catch up,' Miss Honey said, lying through her teeth.*

◇ SEE ALSO **pull a fast one** ▷ PULL; **sell someone a pup** ▷ PUP; **put one over on someone** ▷ PUT; **take someone for a ride** ▷ RIDE

set someone's 'teeth on edge

1 Something such as a noise **sets your teeth on edge** if it is so unpleasant that you find it difficult to bear: *The chalk scraped across the blackboard, setting my teeth on edge.* **2** Someone's behaviour **sets your teeth on edge** if it causes you to feel, but not show, anger: *'You're late,' he said tersely, and the abruptness of his tone set her teeth on edge.*

teething

'teething troubles

If people talk about **teething troubles**, they mean the problems which a project or activity often have when they are just starting and are not yet firmly established or working perfectly: *There were an awful lot of teething troubles in the first year or so, but it is working very well.*

When babies are teething [= getting their first teeth], they are often in a bad mood and cry a lot.

tell

I 'tell you (*rather old*)

You say **'I tell you'** when you are insisting on something and trying to persuade an-

other person to believe you: *'Don't be silly. You're worrying for nothing.' 'I'm not being silly. There's something wrong, I tell you.'*

tell a'part

You are able to **tell** two or more similar things or people **apart** if you know how they differ from one another, and are therefore able to say which one is which: *The twins are so alike. How do you tell them apart?*

'tell me about it (*informal*)

You say **'tell me about it'** when you want to indicate that you also have the problem that has just been mentioned: *'I always end up spending more than I expect.' 'Tell me about it.'*

tell me a'nother (*informal*)

You say **'tell me another'** to someone to show them that you do not believe what they have just said: *'She's French,' said Joe, 'with a job in some academy, teaching deportment. She gave me a cup of French coffee and we had a chat.' 'Tell me another,' said Dolly.*

◇ SEE ALSO **pull the other one** ▷ PULL

tell you 'what (*informal*)

You say **'tell you what'** as a way of introducing a suggestion or offer: *Tell you what. Why don't I get us both a nice cake to cheer us up?*

you never can 'tell

If someone says **'you never can tell'**, they mean that, even if something is unlikely, it may still surprise you by happening: *It is difficult to foresee any end to this task in the immediate future, but then you never can tell.*

telling

you're telling 'me (*informal*)

You say **'you're telling me'** to express emphatic agreement: *'Phew, that was a lucky escape.' 'You're telling me.'*

Sometimes this idiom is shortened to 'telling me'.

temper

in a 'temper

You are **in a temper** when you are angry: *Don't go near him today. He's in such a temper.*

◇ SEE ALSO **hopping mad** ▷ MAD

keep your 'temper

You **are keeping your temper** if you are managing to control yourself and avoid getting angry: *They were doing their best to annoy him, but somehow he managed to keep his temper.*

lose your 'temper

You **lose your temper** when you suddenly get angry and start shouting or behaving violently: *I didn't mean to lose my temper. I'm sorry.* □ *I'm about to lose my temper with this stupid puzzle.*

◇ SEE ALSO **go off at the deep end** ▷ END; **have a blue fit** ▷ FIT; **blow a fuse** ▷ FUSE; **blow a gasket** ▷ GASKET; **let fly** ▷ LET; **blow or flip your lid** ▷ LID; **do your nut** ▷ NUT; **lose your rag** ▷ RAG; **fly into a rage** ▷ RAGE; **hit the roof** ▷ ROOF; **blow your stack** ▷ STACK; **blow your top** ▷ TOP; **throw a wobbly** ▷ WOBBLY

temperature

raise the 'temperature

An event **raises the temperature** when it has the effect of increasing the pressure in an already delicate or difficult situation: *EC trade analysts said last night that the minister's words were likely to raise the temperature of the dispute to an even higher level.*

ten

ten to 'one

You say that it is **ten to one** that something will happen if you think that thing is almost certain to happen: *Find out what other parents really think. Ten to one you'll find that they hate the idea too.*

tend

I tend to 'think *(formal)*

You use '**I tend to think**' as a polite way of introducing your opinion: *I tend to think we should try a different approach in dealing with young offenders.*

tenterhooks

on 'tenterhooks *(rather old)*

You are **on tenterhooks** if you are nervous and excited because you are waiting for something to happen: *Loretta, who was ignorant of the etiquette attached to these affairs, had been on tenterhooks throughout tea in case anyone should ask her to dance.*

term

in the 'long term

You talk about a situation **in the long term** when you are considering how that situation will develop in the future: *It's easy to see what the immediate effects will be, but what about the consequences in the long term?*

in the 'short term

You talk about a situation **in the short term** when you are considering how that situation will develop in the immediate future: *In the short term at least, we will see some improvement in the economic situation.*

a term of en'dearment

A **term of endearment** is a name you give someone to show them affection: *Many women resent being addressed as 'my dear'. Well-meaning older men may not be aware that this term of endearment causes such a reaction.*

terms

come to 'terms with something

You **come to terms with something** such as a personal problem or difficulty when you learn to live with it and accept it: *It's a terrible illness, but she seems to have come to terms with it.*

in no uncertain 'terms

You give your opinion, usually a disapproving one, **in no uncertain terms** when you express it strongly: *I told him in no uncertain terms what I thought of his behaviour.*

on bad 'terms

Two people are **on bad terms** when they are angry with each other, and are maybe avoiding speaking to each other: *You can't work well if you're on bad terms with your colleagues.*

on 'first-name terms

You are **on first-name terms** with someone if you know them well enough to speak to them using their first name, rather than using the more formal Mr, or Mrs, or Ms, So-and-so: *The hostel was all very friendly and cosy; the hostel staff were on first-name terms with everyone in the group within half an hour.*

on 'nodding terms

You are **on nodding terms** with someone if you know them well enough to recognize them and smile at them if you meet them: *I was on nodding terms with her for years before we had our first proper conversation.*

on 'speaking terms

1 Two people who are **on speaking terms** know each other well enough to speak to each other when they meet in the street, for example: *I feel very isolated from everything around me, and I don't know the neighbours, and I'm only barely on speaking terms with the shopkeeper.* **2** You also say that two people who have had an argument are **on speaking terms** if they are no longer angry with each other, although they are still not behaving in a very friendly manner towards each other: *Daisy nearly made a rude remark, but stopped herself because it was so good to be on speaking terms again.* **3** Two people who are not, or who are barely, **on speaking terms** are so angry with each other that they do not even want to speak to each other any more: *The problem is there's no*

*point my going over there. Suzie hates me –
we were barely on speaking terms the week
before she left.*

test

put to the 'test
You **put** something **to the test** when you use
it in order to find out whether it works in
the way it is supposed to: *I'm looking
forward to starting this job and putting all
my new skills to the test.*

stand the test of 'time
Something which **stands the test of time**
shows its strength by lasting for a long
period of time: *Their relationship has stood
the test of time.* □ *The wit and wisdom of
Oscar Wilde has stood the test of time. His
perception of romance and politics at the
turn of the century was amazingly accurate.*

thank

have 'so-and-so to thank for
You **have got** a certain person or thing **to
thank for** something if they are responsible
for its existence: *If women in Britain are able
to vote nowadays, they've got the Suffra-
gettes to thank for it.* □ *We've got the Government's tax policy to thank for the state of
this country's economy.* □ *You have only
yourself to thank for the trouble you're in!*

I'll 'thank you to
You say **'I'll thank you to** do a certain thing'
if you are asking someone in a cold, unfriendly way to do that thing: *'Who was
that you were speaking to?' 'I'll thank you to
mind your own 'business.'*

so-and-so will not 'thank someone for
You say that a certain person **will not thank
someone for** doing something if the action
mentioned is likely to upset or annoy that
person: *He certainly won't thank you for
disturbing him while he's sleeping.*

thanks

thanks to 'so-and-so
Something happens **thanks to** a certain
person or thing if they are responsible for
it happening: *Such diseases could soon be
easy to cure, thanks to new medical techniques.* □ *'I lost the firm five thousand pounds
this morning, thanks to you.' 'Oh, it's my
fault, is it?'*

that

just like 'that
If you do something **just like that**, you do it
immediately and without any more thought
or discussion: *That boy learns amazingly
quickly. I only had to show him once and he
did it himself, just like that.*

that's more 'like it
You say **'that's more like it'** when you are
satisfied with a change that has just been
made: *I'll turn down the music and light
some candles. Ah, that's more like it.* □
*She sat back and said, 'There! That's more
like it,' with a rich air of satisfaction, as if I
were her masterwork.*

that's 'that
You use **'that's that'** to say there is no more
to be said or done about a certain thing:
*You are not going to the party and that's
that.*
◊ SEE ALSO **end of story** ▷ END; **that's flat**
▷ FLAT; **no two ways about it** ▷ WAYS

them

them and 'us
You use the expression **'them and us'** to
describe a relationship in which two groups
feel that they are in opposition to each
other, rather than working together: *Try
not to see the relationship with your employees in terms of 'them and us'.*

there

not all 'there (*informal, disrespectful*)
If you describe someone as **not all there**,
you mean that they think slowly, probably
because they are not very intelligent: *She's
very sweet, but she's not quite all there, is
she?*

so 'there (*informal*)
'So there' is used to emphasize a defiant or
obstinate statement: *I'm going and you can't
stop me, so there.* □ *'She's not shut away,
she's just ill,' Nick shouted. 'And Carrie has
seen her, so there!'*

there and 'then
Someone does something **there and then** if
they do it as an immediate and decisive
reaction to something: *I went to see the flat
and told the landlord there and then that I'd
take it.*

there you 'are or there you 'go (*informal*)
You say **'there you are'** or, informally,
'there you go' 1 when you are giving something to someone: *'Could I have that dictionary, please?' 'There you are.'* **2** to close
your remarks about a situation you have
described, that is unsatisfactory but has to
be accepted: *I was made redundant after
only six months in the job. But there you
go, that's just how things are.* **3** You use
'there you are' to point out that you were
right about something: *'I should never have
trusted that woman with my money.' 'There
you are, what did I tell you?'*

thick

in the 'thick of something

1 You are **in the thick of something** if you are very busy with it: *She didn't have time to talk because she was in the thick of her wedding preparations.* 2 You are also **in the thick of something** if you are at the point where the greatest amount of activity is taking place: *in the thick of the fight.*

thick as 'thieves

Two or more people who are as **thick as thieves** are very close friends.

thick as two short 'planks

Someone who is described as being as **thick as two short planks** is not at all intelligent.

thick and 'fast

Things happen, or come, **thick and fast** if they happen or come quickly and in great numbers: *Radio listeners' letters have been coming in thick and fast on this topic.* □ *But protests have come thick and fast from those who say it will bring even more traffic.*

through thick and 'thin

You do something **through thick and thin** if you continue to do it no matter what happens and despite any difficulties: *We've been friends since we were kids, and have always stuck together through thick and thin.*

thin

as thin as a 'rake

Someone who is **as thin as a rake** is very thin.

thing (*see also* **things**)

another 'thing or another thing alto'gether

You say that something is **another thing**, or **another thing altogether**, if your opinion about that thing is very different from your opinion of the situation referred to before: *Time off work for illness is one thing. It's another thing altogether to take time off for a hangover.* □ *I know I advised you not to leave your husband, but it's quite another thing if he's been beating you.*

the best thing since sliced 'bread

You say that someone or something is **the best thing since sliced bread** if you have a very high opinion of them, and you wonder how you managed without them before they appeared: *The Maastricht Treaty is not necessarily the best thing since sliced bread, there are problems with it.* □ *They don't exactly consider you to be the greatest thing since sliced bread, now do they?* □ *Honorable Members seem to think that the council tax is the best thing since sliced bread.*

a close 'thing or a near 'thing

1 The result of a competition is **a close thing** or **a near thing** if the winner only won by a small amount: *The judges all agree that it was a close thing, but we have finally agreed on a winner.* 2 **A close thing** or **a near thing** is also a situation in which you only just manage to avoid an accident or some other unpleasant event: *Near thing: It missed me by about six inches. It was terrifying. I'm just glad it landed on the stage and not on the audience. It could have been a disaster.* □ *We were all roped together, so we got him out, but it was a close thing. He could easily have drowned.*

◇ SEE ALSO **close call** ▷ CALL; **narrow escape** ▷ ESCAPE; **close shave** ▷ SHAVE; **narrow squeak** ▷ SQUEAK

do the right 'thing

You **do the right thing** when you act wisely or honourably: *I think you should do the right thing and hand the money in to the police.*

do your own 'thing

You **do your own thing** when you do what you want to do, rather than what someone else tells you or advises you to do: *I've never been on a package tour. I prefer to do my own thing when I'm on holiday.*

the easiest thing in the 'world

You describe something as **the easiest thing in the world** if you consider it to be very easy: *It's the easiest thing in the world to make a promise. It's keeping it that's the problem.*

first 'thing or first thing in the 'morning

You do something **first thing**, or **first thing in the morning** if you do it early in the morning just after you have got up: *Will you be up at eight tomorrow morning? I was thinking of calling by your house first thing.*

for 'one thing

You use '**for one thing**' to give one particular reason for something and to suggest that there are several others: *This was not at all like school. For one thing nobody seemed to think that a reading room was a place where you were meant to read.*

a good 'thing

If you say that it's **a good thing** something happened, you mean that you are pleased or feel lucky that it happened, because you have been able to benefit from it: *It's a good thing you checked those timetables.*

◇ SEE ALSO **a good job** ▷ JOB; **just as well** ▷ WELL

have a 'thing about

You **have a thing about** someone or something 1 if they make you nervous: *She's had a thing about rats ever since she had them in* *her house one winter.* **2** if you like or dislike them to an unusual degree: *I think she's got a bit of a thing about that guy Oliver.*

◇ SEE ALSO **be bowled over** ▷ BOWLED; **be taken with** ▷ TAKEN

it all comes to the same 'thing or **it all amounts to the same 'thing** or **it all boils down to the same 'thing**

You say 'it **all comes**, or it **all amounts**, or it **all boils down**, to the same thing' if you consider that there is no real difference between the things which have been mentioned: *Whether you're given the sack or made redundant, it all amounts to the same thing – you're jobless.*

When you heat a liquid for a period of time, it boils down to a smaller quantity of stronger liquid, containing all the essential flavours.

just the 'thing or **the very 'thing**

You describe something as **just the thing**, or **the very thing** if it is exactly what you need: *A pair of sheepskin slippers. They'll be just the thing for the cold winter evenings.*

last 'thing or **last thing at 'night**

You do something **last thing**, or **last thing at night**, if you do it at night, just before you finish work or go to bed: *Don't forget to go round last thing and turn off all the lights.*

make a big 'thing of something (*informal*)

People **make a big thing of something** if they treat it as important: *My family has never made a big thing of Christmas.*

the nearest 'thing

You describe something as **the nearest thing** if, although it is not exactly what has been referred to, it is the most similar thing available: *'Do you have these sandals in brown?' 'I'm afraid not. These ones here would be the nearest thing.'* □ *Dry sherry is probably the nearest thing to rice wine that you'll get in a supermarket.*

neither one thing nor the 'other

Something is **neither one thing nor the other** if it fits no exact description because it is a mixture of two different things: *The ceasefire hasn't brought peace, just a tense situation which is neither one thing nor the other.*

no bad 'thing

If you say that something is **no bad thing**, you mean it is beneficial, despite what people may think: *What it lacks is sophistication and complexity, which is no bad thing, in my view. It sets out to do one job, and it does it well.*

no such 'thing

1 No such thing means 'something completely different from what has just been mentioned': *He told me he was a doctor,*

but he's no such thing. **2 No such thing** also means 'no' or 'not at all': *We thought there would be a car waiting for us, but no such thing. They expected us to walk.* **3** You say that there is **no such thing**, or **no such thing as something** if the thing you are talking about does not exist: *How can you talk about a humane method of killing animals? There's no such thing.* □ *There's no such thing as the Loch Ness Monster, is there?*

not know the first 'thing about

You say that you **do not know the first thing about** a certain subject if you have no knowledge at all about it: *I don't know the first thing about molecular biology.*

not the done 'thing

If something is **not the done thing**, it is not socially acceptable: *You mustn't ask people how much they earn. It's just not the done thing here.*

on to a good 'thing (*informal*)

You are **on to a good thing** when you have discovered a way of benefiting yourself, especially financially: *She only married him for his money. She knew she was on to a good thing.*

one thing after an'other

You say it has been **one thing after another** if a lot of unexpected things have been happening which have all needed your attention: *I haven't had five minutes to relax all day. It's just been one thing after another.*

one thing leads to an'other

If you say **one thing leads**, or **led, to another** you mean that there was a series of events in which one small event caused the next, and so on, finally leading to a big, or important event: *John came around to my flat after work one day, one thing led to another and we went to bed together.* □ *At first he stole small amounts, but one thing led to another and he started taking more and more.*

People often use this expression to avoid giving details of a series of events which might shock or offend people, especially when the incident involves matters related to sex. They may say 'One thing led to another...' leaving you to use your imagination about what happened next.

the real 'thing

The real thing is a real example of something, as opposed to something which is similar: *Frozen pizzas are all right, but they are nowhere near as delicious as the real thing.* □ *I've had other boyfriends, but I've never been in love before. This time it's the real thing.*

sure 'thing (*informal*)

If someone says '**sure thing**' when they are asked to do something, they are agreeing to do that thing: *'Can we finish up here?' she asked. Candy nodded slowly. 'Sure thing. Go and take some time off.'*

> This phrase is more often used in American English than in British English.

the thing 'is

You use '**the thing is**' **1** to introduce an explanation: *I'm sorry I didn't get the work done on time. The thing is, my mother's been ill.* **2** before describing a difficult problem which is stopping you from being able to do something: *He wants me to marry him. The thing is, I'm not sure I love him enough.*

a thing of the 'past

You say that something, especially something bad, is **a thing of the past** if, as a result of new techniques or solutions, it no longer exists or happens: *Voice-sensitive credit cards could soon make card fraud a thing of the past.*

too much of a good 'thing

If someone says that you can have **too much of a good thing**, they mean that, even if you usually enjoy something, you will not continue to enjoy it if you have or do it too much: *I'll go off pasta if we have it every night. You can have too much of a good thing, you know.*

> This expression is often used in a humorous way when someone is talking about something which they didn't even like to begin with, for example: *Watching you play football once a week is enough. A woman can have too much of a good thing.*

what with one thing and a'nother

You use '**what with one thing and another**' to show that there are several reasons for something, without saying what they are: *I meant to get that work done, but what with one thing and another I never got round to it.*

things

all good things come to an 'end

People say '**all good things come to an end**' when they are sad, but accepting of the fact that something they have enjoyed doing is now finished.

all things being 'equal or all other things being 'equal (*formal*)

All things, or **all other things, being equal** means 'unless anything unexpected happens', or 'if other facts, after having been considered, make no difference': *Research has shown that, all other things being equal, the person who exercises regularly performs better in tests requiring mental agility.*

all things to all 'men or all things to all 'people (*slightly disrespectful*)

You say that someone or something is trying to be **all things to all men**, or **all things to all people** if they try to please whoever they are with, especially by regularly changing their opinions to agree with different people: *At its worst this results in a sort of tasteless Euro-soup, which by trying to be all things to all men, ends up being nothing to anybody.* □ *The firm abandoned the idea that it could be all things to all people and decided to focus on identified areas of expertise.*

> The expression 'all things to all men' comes from the Bible (1 Corinthians 9:22).

first things 'first

You say '**first things first**' when you are advising someone to be sensible and get certain important things done before starting the other things they are planning: *'I'll need new clothes for teaching.' 'First things first. They haven't even offered you the job yet.'*

'hearing things

You **are hearing things** when you imagine you are hearing noises that are not really there: *I didn't sleep at all last night. It was awful. I kept hearing things and imagining.* **2** If someone says that you **have been hearing things**, they mean that you must have imagined a piece of information you thought you had heard: *I think you've been hearing things. Nobody would say that about Katy.* **3** You wonder if you **are hearing things** when you cannot believe what you have just heard: *'Feel free to spend your weekends at Seaview, even when I'm not here, any time you like.' Was he joking? Was she hearing things?*

how are 'things? (*informal*)

You say '**how are things?**' when you are asking someone to tell you whether they are happy or not: *'So, how are things at work?' 'Fine.'*

i'magine things

You **are imagining things** when you believe that certain things are happening when in fact they are not: *Of course nobody's been following you. You're imagining things again.*

just one of those 'things

If you say a certain event or situation is **just one of those things** you mean **1** that it could not have been prevented: *'You must have been so disappointed to lose your job.' 'Well, I suppose it's just one of those things.'* **2** that it is difficult to explain: *I don't know why I love him. I guess it's just one of those things.*

◇ SEE ALSO chalk it up to experience
▷ EXPERIENCE

of all 'things
You use '**of all things**' to express your surprise at the fact that a particular thing is the case: *He's lost interest in sailing and has taken up stamp-collecting of all things.*

'see things
You **are seeing things** when you imagine you see something which is not really there: *Is that a boat on the horizon, or am I seeing things?*

stranger things have 'happened
You say '**stranger things have happened**' to show that, although you think a certain event is unlikely, you realize that it is still possible: *I don't expect I'll get the pay rise I want, but then again, stranger things have happened.*

these things are sent to 'try us
You say '**these things are sent to try us**' to remark, often in a humorous way, on a certain thing which is unpleasant, but which must be accepted: *They sent me this picture. I miss him, sure do miss him. Still, these things are sent to try us.*

> The verb 'to try' is used in this expression with the old meaning 'to test'. Some people think that God sends difficulties and problems to test our patience and courage.

things that go bump in the 'night
If people talk about **things that go bump in the night**, they mean imaginary things, such as ghosts, which make all the unexplained noises which frighten you when you are alone: *Here is a chilling collection of stories, packed with ghosts, ghouls and things that go bump in the night.* □ *The noise was similar to an axe being dragged across the floor. The researchers are hoping that whatever did go bump in the night will make a return appearance tonight.*

think (*see also* **thought**)

anybody would 'think
You introduce a statement with '**anybody would think**' when you want to indicate that their behaviour or what they say gives a particular impression which is not actually the case: *Inviting him for a meal, for goodness' sake! Anybody would think she was pleased to see him!*

as you think 'best
You deal with something **as you think best** when you deal with it in the way that you think is most sensible: *'I fear that your father would not agree to my methods.' Louise hesitated. 'Treat him as you think best, Doctor, but please hurry.'*

have another think 'coming (*informal*)
If you say that someone **has got another think coming**, you are saying with annoyance that they are wrong to expect a certain thing, because it is not going to happen: *His arms clasped her against him. If he thinks he's going to kiss me he's got another think coming, she decided firmly.*

that's what 'so-and-so thinks (*informal*)
You say '**that's what** a certain person **thinks**' when you know that that person is wrong in their judgement of a situation: *'He said if I met you again I'd be sacked.' 'But he can't do that!' 'That's what you think.'*

think a'gain
Someone advises you to **think again** about doing something if they think you would be wrong to do it: *If you were hoping for a swift end to the depression in the housing market, think again.*

think 'better of
You **think better of** doing something which you had intended to do when you change your mind and decide not to do it: *I opened my mouth to protest, but thought better of it.*

think 'nothing of
1 You **think nothing of** something, or of doing something, if you consider it quite normal or usual: *In my youth, I used to think nothing of cycling 100 miles in a day.* **2** If you have noticed something strange or different about a situation, but fail to recognize its importance, you say that you **thought nothing of it**: *I had been feeling a little sick, but had thought nothing 'of it.*

think nothing 'of it
You answer '**think nothing of it**' **1** when someone thanks you: *'Thanks for all your help.' 'Oh, think nothing of it.'* **2** when someone apologizes to you, so that they know that you are not angry with them.

'think straight
You say that you **are not thinking straight** when you are unable to organize your thoughts as well as you usually do: *Look, I'm sorry about some of the things I said. I wasn't thinking straight.*

think 'twice
You **think twice** about doing something when you take time to consider whether or not it is right or sensible before doing it: *I didn't think twice about giving him my address.* □ *Think twice before you exchange your company pension for a private one.*

to 'think
You use '**to think**' to refer to the surprise you feel when you consider how much a certain situation, or people's reactions to that situation, have changed: *I can't stand*

that woman now. And to think we used to be best friends.

who does so-and-so think they're 'kidding?
(*informal*)

You say '**who does** a certain person **think they're kidding?**' to express surprise at the fact that they expect you to believe them: *You can't tell me that the big national companies who pour money into the Tory fund don't have a say in their policy. Who do they think they're kidding?*

Thomas

a doubting 'Thomas

A **doubting Thomas** is a person who does not believe that something is possible until they have seen the proof: *I can disprove all those doubting Thomases who said that five small boys on skis was a recipe for disaster, not a holiday.*

Thomas was the name of the apostle in the Bible who demanded to touch Christ's wounds before he would believe that he had really come back from the dead (St John 20:24-29).

thorn

a 'thorn in your side or a 'thorn in your flesh

You describe someone or something as a **thorn in your side**, or a **thorn in your flesh**, if they continually annoy or bother you: *Despite attempts to reduce the spending power of various councils, local authority finances remained a thorn in the flesh of the Government.*

The expression **a thorn in the flesh** comes from the Bible (2 Corinthians 12:7).

thought

I 'thought as much

You say '**I thought as much**' when a piece of news confirms suspicions that you already had: *Outside the room, standing at the top of the stairs, he was told exactly what the doctor had said. He nodded grimly. 'I thought as much.'*

it's the 'thought that counts

If you say '**it's the thought that counts**', when referring to an unwanted gift, you mean that you are happy to have received the gift anyway, because the person's generosity is more important to you than the nature of the gift itself: *When people do things for you and give you things that you don't actually want, you must always remember that it's the thought that counts. Anything else would be sheer ingratitude.*

perish the 'thought

You say '**perish the thought**' to express **1** your hope that the thing which has just been mentioned never happens: *What was she doing staying home nights? Not that she wanted him to contact her – perish the thought!* **2** your disapproval of the thing that has just been mentioned.

'**Perish the thought**' is often used ironically. Consider for example: *The essential purpose was to disguise the fact that Dennis was an alcoholic. He wasn't out to get drunk – perish the thought! – but to savour the unique individuality of each wine to the full.*

the thought had crossed my 'mind

You say '**the thought had crossed my mind**' to show that you had considered the possibility of the thing just mentioned: *'Demand a refund if you're dissatisfied with the service.' 'Well, the thought had crossed my mind.'*

thoughts

collect your 'thoughts or gather your 'thoughts

You are **collecting**, or **gathering**, your **thoughts** when you become calmer and consider things more carefully: *I needed a bit of time alone to gather my thoughts.*

on 'second thoughts

You use '**on second thoughts**' to show that you have changed your mind about the thing you have just said: *Could you make sure this goes off in the last post, please? No, on second thoughts, could you get a courier? It's quite urgent.*

thousand

a thousand and 'one

You can use '**a thousand and one**' to mean 'a large number of': *I'm afraid I can't help you out. I've got a thousand and one things to do today.*

thread

hang by a 'thread

If you say something is **hanging by a thread**, you mean there is uncertainty about whether it will succeed, or continue to exist: *Peace is hanging by a thread this week as negotiations run into serious difficulties.* □ *She was devastated by the news of Liz and Owen's terrible accident – and the knowledge that their lives were hanging by a thread.*

In Greek legend, the sword above Damocles' head was hanging by a single hair, and was therefore likely to fall and kill Damocles at any moment. This story may be the origin of the expression '**hang by a thread**'.

lose the 'thread

You **lose the thread** of something such as a story, or of what you are saying, if you find that you are no longer able to follow the logic of the ideas within it: *If you do not make notes you will quickly lose the thread of the ideas with which you are trying to come to terms.* □ *'Next week – 'He seemed to lose the thread, then visibly pulled himself together. 'You won't get away for another day or two.'*

thrills

thrills and 'spills

If people talk about **thrills and spills**, they mean excitement and danger: *This provides a safe and sheltered location in which groups of all ages can experience the thrills and spills of watersports.*

throat

jump down someone's 'throat

A person **jumps down your throat** when they answer you in an angry and unreasonable way without giving you a chance to finish what you are saying: *'I was about to say, before you jumped down my throat, if your plans need altering in any way...' 'I won't allow them to be altered!'*

ram something down someone's 'throat

Someone **is ramming something down your throat** when they express strong opinions and try to force you to agree with them: *I'm quite capable of making up my own mind on subjects like vegetarianism. I don't want it rammed down my throat.*

> To **ram** something into a place means 'to push it there with great force'.

stick in your 'throat

1 Something **sticks in your throat** if you find it difficult to accept: *Imagine promising to love, honour and obey some man! That's what'd stick in my throat.* **2** If words **stick in your throat**, you try to say something without success, usually because of the strong emotions which you are feeling: *I longed to call out to him to help me, but his name stuck in my throat.*

throats

at each other's 'throats

Two or more people or groups are **at each other's throats** if they are fighting or arguing violently: *How can we hope to reach an agreement with the two main parties constantly at each other's throats?*

◊ SEE ALSO **fight like cat and dog** ▷ CAT

> When two dogs are fighting fiercely, they often bite at each other's throats in an attempt to kill or harm each other.

throes

in the 'throes of something

A person or thing is **in the throes of something**, usually something unpleasant, when the power of that thing is so strong that it is destroying them or taking away all their strength: *a nation in the throes of a bloody civil war.* □ *The early '90s saw Europe in the throes of economic recession.* □ *She was at that time in the throes of unpleasant divorce proceedings.* □ *He seemed to be in the throes of despair.*

> In its original sense, the word **throes** described the pain felt by a mother giving birth to her child, and the expression **in the throes of something** was used to refer to a painful, but productive, process. Now, however, it is more often used to refer to a negative situation.

through

through and 'through

Through and through means 'completely'; if someone or something is described as a certain thing **through and through**, they are a typical example of that thing: *He said you never could tell what anyone was really like until you knew them through and through.* □ *He's a Scotsman through and through.*

thumb

stick out like a sore 'thumb

Someone or something **sticks out like a sore thumb** if they are noticeable because they are so obviously different from the things or people around them: *But I don't speak French or Arabic so I'm going to stick out like a sore thumb.* □ *'Was the factory camouflaged in any way?' 'No it wasn't. It stuck out like a sore thumb.'*

thumbs

the thumbs-'down (*informal*)

1 You give someone **the thumbs-down** when you clench your fist and point one or both of your thumbs towards the ground in order to show that you are unhappy about something: *'How did your exam go?' I asked. She pouted and gave me the thumbs-down.* **2** Someone gives something such as a plan or idea **the thumbs-down** when they decide not to give their approval to it: *American and British reviewers* *gave the film a thumbs-down when it was released at the end of 1972.*

In Roman times, when one of two gladiators in a fight had won, the spectators had to vote on whether or not he should kill his opponent. They made a **thumbs-up** sign if they wanted his opponent to live, and a **thumbs-down** sign if they wanted him to die.

the thumbs-'up (*informal*)

1 You give someone **the thumbs-up**, or a **thumbs-up sign**, when you clench your fists and point one or both of your thumbs up as a sign of encouragement, or to show that everything is fine: *Give me the thumbs-up when you're ready.* □ *Sporting matted hair, an unkempt beard and purple sneakers, he even gave Charles and Diana a thumbs-up sign at the end of his performance.* **2** You give something such as a plan or idea **the thumbs-up** when you approve of it: *We're waiting for the official thumbs-up before we start work.*

See note at **the thumbs-down**.

twiddle your 'thumbs

You say you **are twiddling your thumbs** if you are waiting for something, with nothing else to do to keep you busy: *The last few months had been very quiet. 'We've been sitting around twiddling our thumbs for some of the time and people have been going home early,' he said.*

◊ SEE ALSO **at a loose end** ▷ END

Although it is traditionally a sign of inactivity or boredom, it is rare to see a person actually **twiddling their thumbs** [= holding their hands with the fingers locked together, and moving the thumbs in circles round each other].

thunder

look like 'thunder

Someone who **is looking like thunder** is looking very angry: *He looked like thunder, and when he finally spoke his voice trembled with rage.*

◊ SEE ALSO **a black look** ▷ LOOK

When there is going to be a thunder storm, the sky becomes very dark.

steal someone's 'thunder

Someone **steals your thunder** if they take people's attention away from something that you are about to do or say, usually by doing or saying it first: *The Minister had planned a speech of thanks himself during a visit to Stoke Mandeville Hospital, but five-year-old Adis Avdic stole his thunder.*

In the 17th century, the playwright John Dennis invented a machine to create the effect of thunder for one of his plays, but the idea was copied by his rivals and used in another play.

tick

in a 'tick (*informal*)

In a tick means 'in a moment': *Could you just wait here? I'll be back in a tick.*

It takes a very short time for a clock to **tick** once.

what makes so-and-so 'tick

If people talk about **what makes** a certain person **tick**, they mean that person's reasons for behaving, speaking and thinking in the way that they do: *Nicholson insists that everything he does on screen is in some way autobiographical, helping us to understand what makes him tick.*

ticket

just the 'ticket (*old, informal*)

If a person says that something is **just the ticket**, they mean that it is exactly the thing they need for a particular purpose: *We've been looking for a short, funny play to perform. I reckon this one might be just the ticket.*

ticks

in two 'ticks (*informal*)

In two ticks means 'in a moment': *Hang on. I'll be with you in two ticks.*

See note at **in a tick**.

tide

go against the 'tide or swim against the 'tide

You **go**, or **swim**, **against the tide** when you ignore what everyone else thinks or is doing, and continue with your own activities: *Despite international condemnation, the country continues to swim against the tide of public opinion.*

◊ SEE ALSO **go against the current** ▷ CURRENT; **go against the flow** ▷ FLOW; **go against the stream** ▷ STREAM

See note at **go with the tide**.

go with the 'tide or drift with the 'tide or swim with the 'tide

You **are drifting**, or **going**, or **swimming**, **with the tide** when you fit in with the people around you and accept their opinions, because you do not want to upset them by doing something different or disagreeing: *I was counting on him to make an* *objection, but he seems content to drift with the tide.*

◇ SEE ALSO **go with the crowd** ▷ CROWD; **go or drift or swim with the current** ▷ CURRENT; **go with the flow** ▷ FLOW; **go with the stream** ▷ STREAM

> If an object is floating in the sea, it will be pulled in the same direction the tide is flowing.

tightrope

walk a 'tightrope

You **are walking a tightrope**, or **walking a tightrope between** two things, if you are trying to maintain a balance between those things, but there is a high risk that you will fail: *Such companies must walk a tightrope between keeping investors happy and providing a good service.* □ *Parents of allergic children have to walk a tightrope – on the one hand they need to warn their child about things to avoid, but on the other hand they must not make the child over-anxious.*

> In a circus, the **tightrope** is a thin rope which is stretched tightly between two points, high above the ground, which acrobats walk across. Another name for the tightrope is the 'high wire'.

tilt

full 'tilt

Someone or something is going **full tilt**, or at **full tilt**, if they are running, travelling, or doing something as fast as they can, or with all their energy: *Martin moved faster and faster until he was running full tilt after the intruder.* □ *Production, amidst all the changes, continues at full tilt.*

> In the medieval sport of **tilting**, or jousting, two riders would gallop their horses towards each other as fast as they could, and each would try to knock the other off his horse with a lance [= a long weapon for this purpose].

time (*see also* **times**)

about 'time

If you say it is **about time** something was done, you mean that it should be done: *'The car's being serviced.' 'Good. It's about time someone had a look at it.'*

about time 'too

People say '**about time too**' when something that should have happened earlier has at last happened: *'Here I am.' 'And about time, too.'* □ *There'll be new shops, a new roof and better access. Local residents say about time too.*

◇ SEE ALSO **not before time** ▷ TIME

all in good 'time

If you say that something will be dealt with **all in good time**, you mean that it will certainly be dealt with, but since there is no need to rush, not immediately: *'I appreciate the importance of your discovery, but why don't you go to the police?' 'All in good time.'*

all the 'time

1 (*informal*) Something that happens **all the time** happens frequently: *I might like him if he didn't complain all the time.* **2** Something that was the case **all the time** was always the case even though you did not realize it: *I treated him as a close friend, and all the time he was spreading those terrible stories about me.*

all the time in the 'world

You say that you have got **all the time in the world** if there is no need for you to hurry because you have plenty of time: *And don't run: there's no need in this heat and we have all the time in the world.*

any time 'now

You say that something which you have been waiting for is going to happen **any time now** if you think it is just about to happen: *The referee should be blowing his whistle any time now for the end of the game.*

at a 'time

Something that involves one person or thing, or a certain number of people or things, **at a time** involves them singly, or in groups of that number, one after the other: *Don't rush, children. One at a time, please.* □ *He leapt down the stairs three at a time.* □ *Her illness meant that I often heard nothing from her for months at a time.*

at any one 'time

If you talk about the state of a particular situation **at any one time**, you are talking about that situation at a single point in time, or during a single period: *There should never be more than two students doing a particular experiment at any one time.*

be ahead of your 'time

Someone such as an artist or thinker who is **ahead of their time** has ideas that other people do not understand the importance of until much later: *Coleridge was in many ways far ahead of his time in his understanding of the unconscious mind, pre-dating Freud.*

before so-and-so's time

Someone or something that was **before your time** existed or happened before you were born: *Connie Shackelock – you've probably not heard of her, she's a bit before your time, but she used to sing on the last night of the Proms.*

bide your 'time

Someone who **is biding their time** is waiting patiently, but with the intention of doing something: *For three years I've been biding my time, doing small things, waiting for the big job.*

the 'big time

If people talk about **the big time**, they mean the top level in any kind of activity: *So many bands enjoy modest success without ever hitting the big time.*

'big-time: *We want to put the big-time suppliers behind bars, not someone who smokes a few joints.*

buy 'time

Someone who **is buying time** is making excuses or finding ways to delay a certain event: *Such unreasonable demands are the company's attempt to buy time before coming to a decision.*

do 'time or serve 'time

Someone who **is doing time**, or **serving time**, is in prison: *He admits his crimes openly, and is not afraid to do time for them.*

feeding time at the 'zoo

If people talk about **feeding time at the zoo**, they mean a meal which is noisy and disorganized: *I don't know how she copes with six kids. Meals at their house must be like feeding time at the zoo.*

for the time 'being

For the time being refers to the present situation, with the suggestion that a change will soon come or be needed: *The ceasefire seems to be holding for the time being.* □ *This'll do for the time being, but I'll need a proper machine when I start on the project properly.*

from time imme'morial or since time imme'morial (*formal*)

Something that has been the case **from**, or **since**, **time immemorial** has always been the case: *The sea has been a source of fascination, and of dread, since time immemorial.*

from time to 'time

Something that happens **from time to time** happens probably with some regularity, but not often: *He would phone me from time to time, just to check that I was okay.*

give me such-and-such every 'time or I'd rather have such-and-such any 'time

If someone finishes their comparison of two or more different things by saying '**give me**, or **I'd rather have**, a certain thing **any time**', they mean that they would always take the thing they have just mentioned if they had the choice: *I've never been keen on that nouvelle cuisine. Give me a plate of stew and dumplings every time.*

give someone a hard 'time (*informal*)

If someone **is giving you a hard time**, they are speaking to you in a critical and unkind way: *'You never do a single bit of housework.' 'Come on, honey. Don't give me a hard time.'*

give someone a rough 'time

If someone **is giving you a rough time**, they are being strongly critical of you and your behaviour: *The media have been giving you a rough time over your decision not to resign.*
◇ SEE ALSO **haul someone over the coals** ▷ COALS; **give someone a rap over the knuckles** ▷ RAP

have no 'time for

You **have no time for** someone or something if you dislike them or disapprove of them: *A lot of people seem to admire the Prime Minister, although I personally have very little time for him.* □ *I avoid getting involved in their arguments. I've no time for that kind of nonsense.*

have the time of your 'life

A person who **is having the time of their life** is enjoying themselves a lot: *From what I hear they're both having the time of their lives! My father has been buying Margaret a designer wardrobe and escorting her to all the best restaurants and clubs.*
◇ SEE ALSO **have a ball** ▷ BALL; **live it up** ▷ LIVE; **rave it up** ▷ RAVE

have 'time on your hands

You **have time on your hands** if you are bored because you have a lot of time and no special plans for how to use it: *I can't see the sense in leaving all the work to you, when I have so much time on my hands.*

have time on your 'side or time is on your 'side

You say you **have time on your side** if you have enough time to do something, even though that thing might take a long time: *It's going to be a massive job, but the good thing is we've got time on our side.* □ *Time is on our side in that it doesn't start until the end of the month. But we must be well prepared.*

in good 'time

You arrive **in good time** for an event if you arrive well before it is supposed to start: *We arrived in good time, and went for a coffee.* □ *Hurry up, will you. I want to be in good time for my meeting.*

in no time at 'all

Something that is done **in no time at all** is done very quickly: *The make-up artist worked quickly, and in no time at all I found myself transformed.*

in your own 'time

1 You do something **in your own time** if you choose to use your free time to do it: *I* studied French and German at school, and Italian in my own time. **2** You do something **in your own time** if you do it at the speed which is natural to you: *Don't be tempted to rush. Just answer the questions calmly in your own time.*

keep good 'time

1 A clock or watch that **keeps good time** is always accurate: *I can't understand why my watch has started going fast. It has always kept excellent time in the past.* **2** A person who **keeps good time** is never late for appointments: *It doesn't matter how good his work is. We can't employ him unless he learns to keep better time.*
'time-keeper: *I have always been a meticulous time-keeper.*

kill 'time

You **are killing time** when you find something to do to use up the time and stop you getting bored, for example during a period of waiting: *He had to meet Martin at four o'clock and he had to kill time till then. He did so by wandering the streets.*

live on borrowed 'time

1 A person **is living on borrowed time** when they live longer than is expected or is thought likely: *They've told her she's had three years more than she should've had, she's living on borrowed time.* **2** You also say that someone **is living on borrowed time**, or **is on borrowed time**, if they are still accepted as a member of a group, but are likely to be rejected very soon: *The Government is living on borrowed time. Party leaders have lost the confidence of markets, their Euro-partners and their own people.*

long time no 'see (*informal*)

If someone greets you with the words '**long time no see**', they are remarking that they have not seen you for a long time: *Hello, Barry. Long time no see.*

make up for lost 'time

A person who **is making up for lost time** is trying to gain as much experience of a particular activity as possible, or working particularly hard at something, because in the past they have not managed to do it: *He may not have travelled much as a young man, but he has now made up for lost time. 'Whenever I have a week off, I try and visit a new city in Europe.'* □ *Certainly, it will need to work hard to make up for lost time; the party has neglected the cause of democratic socialism in the North for far too long.*

mark 'time

1 Soldiers **mark time** when they move their feet up and down as if they were marching, but without going forwards, in

order to keep the marching rhythm: *The procession came to a halt, but the majorettes continued to mark time, still twirling their batons.* **2** You **are marking time** when you allow time to pass without making any advance in your activities: *Since this is a non-exam course there is opportunity for pupils to mark time without any serious results but to achieve personal development gradually.*

next to 'no time

It takes **next to no time** to do something if that thing can be done very quickly: *'Thanks for mending my bike.' 'That's okay. I did it in next to no time.'*

no time like the 'present

You say that there is **no time like the present** if you have decided, or are trying to encourage someone else, to do something immediately rather than waiting till later: *'Shall I phone her now, do you think?' 'Why not? There's no time like the present.'* □ *'When do you suggest we start?' she whispered. 'I always say there's no time like the present.'*

no time to 'lose

You say that there is **no time to lose** when the situation is so urgent that you will have to act immediately and as fast as possible: *Come on, there's no time to lose. We've got about quarter of an hour before the bomb goes off.*

not before 'time

You say that something is happening **not before time** if you think that it should have happened sooner or earlier: *I received my copy today. Not before time, I may add, since I needed it for a meeting tomorrow.*
◇ SEE ALSO **about time too** ▷ TIME

not give someone the time of 'day

You say that you would **not give someone the time of day** if you think they are so worthless that you refuse to take any interest in them: *I'm helping her really. He thinks I'm helping him but I'm not. I wouldn't give him the time of day.*

on 'time

Something happens **on time** if it happens at the time it is supposed to: *It seems that the only trains that leave on time are the ones I am a couple of minutes late for.*

once upon a 'time

Once upon a time means 'at a time in the past', and is the traditional way of beginning a children's story: *Once upon a time there were three bears...*

pass the 'time

You do something to **pass the time** if you do it while you are waiting for something else to happen, or when you are bored and have nothing else to do: *I just knit to pass the time.*

pass the time of 'day
You **are passing the time of day**, or **passing the time of day** with someone when you stop to have a friendly conversation with them: *Perhaps they might become friends, she thought doubtfully, or at least neighbours, passing the time of day if they met in the road.*

play for 'time
You **are playing for time** when you delay something such as an action or a decision, while trying not to show that you are unsure of yourself: *He had feared being confronted with an unexpected decision like this. He needed to play for time. 'I scarcely know what to say. You've obviously been very... busy.'*

small-time
A **small-time** activity is one that is carried out, but is not done well or in an organized, professional way; a **small-time** person or organization takes part in such an activity: *These people are just small-time criminals. You know, pickpockets and shoplifters.*

take 'time
Something that **takes time** happens slowly or gradually: *It takes time to build up a trusting relationship.*

take time 'out
You **take time out** to do something when you stop a certain activity, such as your work, for a short time so that you can do that thing: *I've decided to take some time out from studying so that I can see the world.*

time after 'time or time and a'gain or time and time a'gain
Something that happens **time after time**, or **time and again**, or **time and time again** happens often or repeatedly: *I have asked you to tidy up after yourself time after time.*
◇ SEE ALSO **again and again** ▷ AGAIN; **over and over** or **over and over again** ▷ OVER

time and tide wait for no 'man
If someone says '**time and tide wait for no man**', they mean that life moves on without waiting for people to make decisions or plans, and that you must therefore take opportunities when you can: *The drinking session that followed stretched until 4am; the players disproving the theory that time and tide wait for no man.*

time 'flies
If someone says '**time flies**', they mean that time passes quickly: *Good God is that the time? Doesn't time fly when you're having fun?*

People often say '**time flies**' to express their surprise at the amount of time that has passed without their noticing it.

time is getting 'on
You say '**time is getting on**' to remark on the fact that it is getting late: *Time was getting on, and I was anxious to start work.*

such-and-such time 'lucky
You say 'second, or third, or fourth, etc, **time lucky**' if you hope that your second, or third, or fourth, etc, attempt at the thing you are trying to do will be successful: *He blew on the dice and murmured, 'Third time lucky' before throwing them down with a dramatic air.*

time's 'up
If someone says to you '**time's up**', they mean that the time allowed for something, for example answering the questions in an exam, is finished: *Okay time's up. You can stop now please.*

time will 'tell
If you say '**time will tell**', you mean that it will not be known for some time whether things are working out as you hope: *There's no reason why, with a bit of luck, they shouldn't make a full recovery. Time will tell.*

timer

old-'timer
You call someone an **old-timer** if they are old, and especially if their main skills and interests are not modern, but were formed a long time ago when they were young: *The only old-timer to be pensioned-off appears to be Mick Skinner.* □ *New drivers have twice as many accidents as old-timers in the first two years after passing the test.*

times

at the 'best of times
Something that is not good **at the best of times** is normally bad: *I've left the flat because my flatmate was driving me mad. I never got on with her at the best of times.*

behind the 'times
Someone who is **behind the times** is old-fashioned in the way they think: *I learnt to keep house in Jamaica at my grandmother's side, watching everything she did. All this may seem a little behind the times to the modern generation and to feminists.*

fall on hard 'times
You say that a person who previously had no financial problems **has fallen on hard times** if their luck has changed and they have become poor: *He was a man of noble birth, whose family had fallen on hard times.*

for old 'times' sake
You do something **for old times' sake** when you do an action which you used to do regularly in the past, as a little ceremony to

show that your memories of that time are still important to you: *We met for a drink together, more for old times' sake than for any other reason.*

move with the 'times
A person or organization is **moving with the times** when they change and develop in order to fit in with social changes, for example in fashions or people's opinions: *The Church faces certain decline unless it can begin to move with the times.*

tinker

not give a tinker's 'cuss (*informal*)
If you **do not give a tinker's cuss** about something, you do not care at all about it: *She doesn't give a tinker's cuss what anyone thinks of her.*

◇ SEE ALSO **not give a damn** ▷ DAMN; **not care a fig** or **two figs** ▷ FIG, FIGS; **not care or give a hoot** or **two hoots** ▷ HOOT, HOOTS; **not give a monkey's** ▷ MONKEY'S; **not give a shit** ▷ SHIT; **not care** or **give a sod** ▷ SOD; **not give** or **care a toss** ▷ TOSS; **not care** or **give tuppence** ▷ TUPPENCE

tinkle

give someone a 'tinkle (*informal*)
If you say that you will **give someone a tinkle**, you mean that you will contact them by telephone: *Give me a tinkle when you get back from your holidays.*

tip

on the tip of someone's 'tongue
1 Something such as a name is **on the tip of your tongue** when, although you know it, you cannot quite remember it: *'I don't mean Carole Lombard, do I?' said Jannie. 'No, no. The name's on the tip of my tongue.'* **2** Something is **on the tip of your tongue** when you are about to say it but decide not to: *It was on the tip of my tongue to tell her what I thought of her, but I managed to control myself.*

'tip it down (*informal*)
It **tips it down** when it rains very hard: *The match'll have to be cancelled. It's tipping it down out there.*

◇ SEE ALSO **rain buckets** ▷ BUCKETS; **rain cats and dogs** ▷ CATS; **chuck it down** ▷ CHUCK; **bucket with rain** ▷ RAIN

the tip of the 'iceberg
If you say that something, such as a problem you are dealing with, is just **the tip of the iceberg**, you mean that it is just a small part of something much bigger, most of which is still waiting to be discovered or dealt with: *The 50 ecstasy-related deaths which have been documented are probably only the tip of the iceberg.* □ *Police have uncovered a hoard of stolen property which*

may be the tip of the iceberg in a million-pound series of burglaries.

Only about one ninth of the total mass of an iceberg shows above sea level. The rest of it is hidden under the water.

tips

be such-and-such to the tips of your 'fingers
You say that someone is a certain thing or has a certain quality **to the tips of their fingers** if they are full of the quality you are referring to: *He's an aristocrat to the tips of his fingers.*

tissue

a tissue of 'lies
A story that someone tells, especially a complicated one, is **a tissue of lies** if it is completely false: *I would rather not hear what she has to say since I imagine it is a tissue of lies, of excuses and complaints.* □ *He said the allegations made by 13 sacked staff were 'a tissue of lies'.*

tit

tit for 'tat
If you give another person or organization **tit for tat**, you harm them in order to pay them back for an injury which you have received from them: *I could give him tit for tat, but I don't see the point.* □ *The death toll will continue to rise if these tit-for-tat killings cannot be stopped.*

tits

get on someone's 'tits (*vulgar*)
If someone says that a person or thing **gets on their tits**, they mean that they find that person or thing annoying: *Her nagging has started getting on my tits.*

tizz, tizzy

in a 'tizz or **in a 'tizzy**
When someone gets, or is, **in a tizz**, or a **tizzy**, they get so anxious and upset that they find it impossible to behave in a normal, relaxed way: *Her mother took the phone – she was in quite a tizz – and said they'd get the next plane home.*

to

to and 'fro
To move **to and fro** is to move forwards and backwards or from side to side, or in all directions: *The long seaweed was waving to and fro in the gently moving water.*

◇ SEE ALSO **back and forth** ▷ BACK; **backwards and forwards** ▷ BACKWARDS

toast

propose a 'toast

At a ceremony, someone **proposes a toast** when they ask everyone present to raise their glass and drink in honour of the person or thing which they have mentioned: *Let me propose a toast ... To the bride and groom!*

tod

be on your 'tod (*informal*)

You say that someone **is on their tod** if they are alone: *Don't tell me you're spending Christmas day all on your tod? That's terrible.*

The word 'tod' is the short form of the Cockney rhyming slang 'Tod Sloan', meaning 'alone'. Tod Sloan was an American jockey.

toes

be on your 'toes

You say that someone **is on their toes** if they are ready and prepared for action: *The boss is coming round today, so you'd better be on your toes.*

keep someone on their 'toes

Something such as a possible event **keeps someone on their toes** if it prevents them from getting lazy and makes them perform as well as they can: *Leisure studies, interests and hobbies will keep you on your toes so if you're a couch potato or telly addict you'd better change your ways.*

make someone's 'toes curl

You say that something **makes your toes curl 1** if it makes you feel awkward and embarrassed for someone else: *His behaviour at dinner made her toes curl.* **2** if it causes you to experience an intense moment of pleasure: *'Very chic,' he said in a deep, cultured voice with a deceptively lazy lilt to it. It made her toes curl just listening to him.*

tread on someone's 'toes or step on someone's 'toes

You **tread**, or **step, on someone's toes** if you do something to offend them, especially by trying to do something that they themselves are responsible for: *She will have to discover where she can be most useful at the hospital, without treading on anyone else's toes.*

toffee

for 'toffee (*informal*)

You say that you cannot do something **for toffee** if you cannot do it at all: *I can't dance for toffee.*

◊ SEE ALSO **for peanuts** ▷ PEANUTS

toilet

down the 'toilet

Something, usually a plan or an organization, which goes **down the toilet** fails completely and may even cease to exist: *This government is letting the country go down the toilet.*

◊ SEE ALSO **down the drain** ▷ DRAIN; **down the pan** ▷ PAN; **down the plughole** ▷ PLUGHOLE; **down the tubes** ▷ TUBES

token

by the same 'token (*rather formal*)

By the same token means 'also' or 'in addition': *If a school trusts its pupils, then they, by the same token, must show themselves worthy of this trust.*

toll

take its 'toll

Something **takes its toll** when it begins to have an effect and to cause problems or suffering: *Forty months of non-stop work on one project were beginning to take their toll.*

Tom

every Tom, Dick and 'Harry or any Tom, Dick or 'Harry

If you talk about **every Tom, Dick and Harry**, you mean everyone, including people you do not know; if you talk about **any Tom, Dick or Harry**, you mean anybody at all: *He wanted to confide in her, but he didn't want every Tom, Dick and Harry knowing their business.* □ *He had been extremely negligent in allowing any Tom, Dick and Harry access to Wyvis Hall.*

You may hear the humorous non-sexist variant of this expression, 'Tom, Dick and Harriet'.

tomorrow

like there's no to'morrow or as if there's no 'tomorrow

Someone who is doing something **like**, or **as if, there's no tomorrow** is doing it in a wild and irresponsible way, without thinking about the future results of their actions: *They were knocking back drinks as if there was no tomorrow.*

ton

like a ton of 'bricks

You come down on someone **like a ton of bricks** if you speak to them angrily or punish them severely: *She thinks a lot of you, you know. I made the mistake of criticizing you and she came down on me like a ton of bricks.*

tongue (see also **tongues**)

bite your 'tongue

You **bite your tongue** when you want to say something but you stop yourself, because you feel that it would not be wise: *I wanted to tell her that I despised her, but I bit my tongue.*

◊ SEE ALSO **bite your lip** ▷ LIP

find your 'tongue

You **find your tongue** when you finally manage to speak after a short time during which the strength of your feelings has made you unable to say anything: *Somehow she found her tongue and shakily voiced her only fear.*

get your 'tongue round something

If you say that it is difficult to **get your tongue round** a word, you mean that it is difficult to pronounce: *She found it very difficult to get her tongue round the unfamiliar words. 'What does that mean? Ceol tradistiunta?'*

have your tongue in your 'cheek

You do or say something with your **tongue in your cheek** if the way in which you do it shows that you mean something different from, or even the opposite of, what your actions or words suggest: *Benet, who wrote 'Bury my heart at Wounded Knee' may have had his tongue firmly planted in his cheek, but there is something rather wonderful about American place names.*
tongue-in-'cheek: *her perceptive view of life and delightful tongue-in-cheek humour.*

hold your 'tongue (old)

You **hold your tongue** when you say nothing or keep quiet: *'Mother, you've no right to -' 'You hold your tongue, Sarah!'*

◊ SEE ALSO **hold your peace** ▷ PEACE

lose your 'tongue

If you ask someone, especially a child, if they **have lost their tongue**, you are asking why they are not answering your question, or why they are so quiet: *Tell me who is responsible for this. What's the matter, lad? Have you lost your tongue?*

speak with forked 'tongue

You say that someone **is speaking with forked tongue** if they are being dishonest by saying one thing and meaning another: *Even though the Honourable Gentleman occasionally speaks with forked tongue, I welcome the fact that he proclaims his support for the training scheme.*

trip off the 'tongue

A name or word that **trips off the tongue** is one that is easy to pronounce and remember: *The team has realized that it has to come up with a leaner, meaner, faster name. A name which trips off the tongue.*

tongues

start 'tongues wagging or set 'tongues wagging

A piece of news **starts**, or sets, **tongues wagging** when people start gossiping about it: *Having a boyfriend or husband who is young enough to be your son can still raise a few eyebrows and set tongues wagging.*

too

only too 'such-and-such or all too 'such-and-such

Only too and **all too** emphasize that something is the case to a particularly great, and often an undesirable, extent: *Your little darlings will grow up into rebellious teenagers all too soon.* □ *'Do you remember how happy we were when we were young?' 'Only too well.'*

tools

down 'tools

To **down tools** is to stop working: *We decided to down tools and have some lunch.*

tooth (see also **teeth**)

fight tooth and 'nail

You **fight tooth and nail** if you do everything you can to make something happen, or to prevent something from happening: *I'll fight tooth and nail to keep the school open.* □ *He had fought tooth and nail to be allowed to see the men in custody since the time of the arrests.*

long in the 'tooth

If you say that a person or animal is **long in the tooth**, you mean that they are old: *If I may say so, he's a bit long in the tooth to be starting a new career now.*

◊ SEE ALSO **over the hill** ▷ HILL; **past it** ▷ PAST; **no spring chicken** ▷ CHICKEN; **not getting any younger** ▷ YOUNGER

> It is possible to tell the age of a horse by looking at its teeth. In general, the older the horse is, the longer its teeth will be.

top

at the top of your 'voice

You say something **at the top of your voice** when you say it as loudly as you can: *He was shouting at the top of his voice into the microphone but nobody could hear a word because someone had cut the amplifier cable.*

blow your 'top

Someone **blows their top** when they get very angry and lose their temper or start shouting: *Graeme is more volatile and likely to blow his top if his demands aren't met.*

◊ SEE ALSO **go off at the deep end** ▷ END; **have**

a **blue fit** ▷ FIT; **blow a fuse** ▷ FUSE; **blow a gasket** ▷ GASKET; **let fly** ▷ LET; **blow** or **flip your lid** ▷ LID; **do your nut** ▷ NUT; **lose your rag** ▷ RAG; **fly into a rage** ▷ RAGE; **hit the roof** ▷ ROOF; **blow your stack** ▷ STACK; **lose your temper** ▷ TEMPER; **throw a wobbly** ▷ WOBBLY

come out on 'top

You **come out on top** when **1** you succeed after a period of difficulty: *It was the best match I have ever played in and proof that the underdog can sometimes come out on top.* **2** results show that you have performed best in a competition, election, match, etc: *League tables of exam results published today are being roundly condemned – even by some of those schools which came out on top.*

from top to 'bottom

From top to bottom means from the highest to the lowest point, or completely: *The building was shaken from top to bottom by the blast.* □ *We searched the apartment from top to bottom.*

from top to 'toe

'**From top to toe**' means 'all over the body', or 'completely' in reference to someone's appearance: *I was washed from top to toe in Mrs Joe's usual violent manner, and handed over, in my tightest Sunday clothes, to Mr Pumblechook.* □ *Beautifully co-ordinated from top to toe, he wore a soft wool coat that matched his eyes.*

let something get on 'top of you

You **let something**, usually a problem, **get on top of you** when you allow yourself to get so upset about it that you lose the ability to deal with it effectively: *I know you're going through a lot of stress at work, but you mustn't let it get on top of you.*

off the top of your 'head

1 If someone makes a statement **off the top of their head**, they are relying on their own spontaneity, knowledge or experience, rather than referring to notes or reference books: *I gave a short talk off the top of my head.* **2** If you tell someone that you cannot give them a particular piece of information **off the top of your head**, you mean that you do not know it, and will need to find it for them, in a book, for example: *We'll come back to you with the precise details. I just can't say off the top of my head.*

on 'top of something

Someone who is, keeps, or gets, **on top of something** such as their work has it well organized and under control: *It's a relief to feel I'm on top of all my paperwork at last.*

on top of the 'world

You are **on top of the world** when you are feeling happy, especially as the result of

something good that has just happened to you: *I don't know why, but I was on top of the world that morning.*

◇ SEE ALSO **walk on air** ▷ AIR; **thrilled to bits** ▷ BITS; **on cloud nine** ▷ CLOUD; **in seventh heaven** ▷ HEAVEN; **over the moon** ▷ MOON

over the 'top

You describe something as **over the top** if it is so extreme that it is unacceptable; you **go over the top** if you act in an unacceptably extreme way: *Her behaviour last night was over the top.* □ *It's nice to have some Christmas decorations, but they've just gone over the top.*

◇ SEE ALSO **go to extremes** ▷ EXTREMES

> The abbreviation **OTT** ('oh-tee-'tee') is often used in place of this expression.

sleep like a 'top

You say that you **slept like a top** if you had a good, peaceful sleep with no interruptions: *The bed was comfortable and I slept like a top.*

◇ SEE ALSO **sleep like a baby** ▷ BABY; **sleep like a log** ▷ LOG

to top it 'all

When you mention one last misfortune in a list of unfortunate events, you can introduce it with the expression '**to top it all**': *On hearing the news, her boyfriend promptly leaves her and her father has a fatal heart attack. To top it all her mother rejects her.*

◇ SEE ALSO **to cap it all** ▷ CAP; **to crown it all** ▷ CROWN; **to make matters worse** ▷ MATTERS; **what is more** ▷ WHAT

up 'top (*informal*)

When you talk about what someone has **up top**, you are referring to how intelligent they are: *'I'll never make a secretary, I've got nothing up top.' 'Don't be silly.' 'I'm not. I just can't grasp these things. Have you ever tried to do shorthand?'*

torn

'torn between

You say you are **torn between** one thing and another when you have a difficult choice to make between those two things: *I was pretty torn between my feelings of loyalty and my duty to tell the truth.*

toss

argue the 'toss

A person **argues the toss** when they openly disagree with what has been said or decided: *He grunted, 'Please yourself.' He had better things to do than argue the toss.*

◇ SEE ALSO **take issue with** ▷ ISSUE

not give a 'toss or **not care a 'toss** (*informal*)

If someone does **not give**, or does **not care**, a **toss** about something, they do not care at all about it: *Out on the motorway he let rip. He either wasn't a local or he didn't give a toss about the video cameras mounted every couple of miles along the motorway to catch the speeders.* □ *'Do you expect me to believe that?' 'I don't give a toss what you believe. What concern is it of yours?'*

◇ SEE ALSO **not give a damn** ▷ DAMN; **not care a fig** or **two figs** ▷ FIG, FIGS; **not care or give a hoot** or **two hoots** ▷ HOOT, HOOTS; **not give a monkey's** ▷ MONKEY'S; **not give a shit** ▷ SHIT; **not care** or **give a sod** ▷ SOD; **not give a tinker's cuss** ▷ TINKER; **not care** or **give tuppence** ▷ TUPPENCE

touch

the common 'touch

You say someone has **the common touch** if they have the ability to get on well with, or appeal to, a wide range of ordinary people: *De Gaulle's animated presentation and common touch in these interviews were disarming.*

the human 'touch

You say that someone has **the human touch** if they have the useful ability to be warm and friendly with other people: *He has an excellent record as a politician, but many claim he lacks the human touch.*

in 'touch

1 You get **in touch** with someone when you contact them by writing or telephoning; you are, keep, or stay, **in touch** with them if you meet, telephone, or write to each other regularly: *Get in touch and tell me your new address when you know it.* □ *I was hoping you could put me in touch with a good music teacher.* 2 You are **in touch** with a subject or situation if you have all the most up-to-date information about it, or if you are paying careful attention to it: *I try to keep in touch with the latest medical developments.*

lose 'touch

1 You **lose touch** with someone when you meet and contact each other less and less often: *We used to write to each other, but over the past few years we've lost touch.* 2 You **lose touch** with a subject or situation when you fail to keep your knowledge of it up to date: *It's easy to lose touch with what's going on in the fast-moving world of computers.*

out of 'touch

You are **out of touch** with a subject or situation if you do not have up-to-date information about it, or are not paying

careful enough attention to it: *'I'm a bit out of touch with this modern medicine,' Kate Maybury admitted. 'Does that mean she's cured?'* □ *Are you feeling out of touch with your own body* [= not paying attention to the way your body feels]?

touch and 'go

Something is **touch and go** when it is just as likely to turn out badly as it is to turn out well: *It was touch and go for a while after the operation, but her condition is now much more stable.*

touches

put the finishing 'touches on something or put the finishing 'touches to something

You **put the finishing touches on**, or **put the finishing touches to**, something when you do a final few things to make the thing you have been working on perfect: *The organisers are currently putting the finishing touches to this autumn's events.* □ *When they had finished landscaping their garden, they decided to put the finishing touches on it by designing and making their own garden furniture.*

tough

get 'tough

1 You **get tough**, or **get tough with someone**, or **get tough on something**, if you begin to deal more forcefully or severely with them: *If they still refuse to give us a refund, I think it's time to start getting tough with them.* □ *There is mounting public pressure on the Government to get tough on crime.* 2 You say that things **are getting tough** when a situation starts to develop severe problems or difficulties: *It's only when the going gets tough that you find out who your real friends are.*

tough (*informal*)

If someone says '**tough**' they mean, rudely, that the person or people in question will just have to accept the situation as it is: *I've got them a book each, and if they don't like it, tough.*

◇ SEE ALSO **hard cheese** ▷ CHEESE; **tough**, or **hard**, or **bad**, **luck** ▷ LUCK

tough as old 'boots

1 Something that is as **tough as old boots** is very tough: *Do you remember that steak I had there? It was tough as old boots.* 2 Someone who is as **tough as old boots** has a lot of determination and is not sensitive or easy to hurt emotionally: *Beneath her frail exterior, Kylie is as tough as old boots.*

tour

whistle-stop 'tour

A **whistle-stop tour** is a quick series of short visits to several places, which may be made, for example, by a politician: *Although brief, his whistle-stop tour of the South-East seems to have boosted his popularity.*

A **whistle-stop** was originally a small station which trains did not usually stop at unless they got a signal to do so. The meaning of the word developed to mean any small, unimportant town.

towel

throw in the 'towel

When a person **throws in the towel**, they are giving up and admitting defeat: *Especially important, we agree, is the likelihood that governments pursuing these policies will be forced by recession and rising unemployment to throw in the towel.*

In boxing, **throwing in the towel** is a sign that the boxer accepts defeat.

tower

ivory 'tower

You say that someone in authority is in an **ivory tower** if they are unable to have a real understanding of ordinary people's problems because they are protected from having any direct contact with them: *Groups of adults have sat around in various political and educational ivory towers, deciding what they think a 14-year-old should be able to achieve. □ There is a widespread feeling in the country that universities are 'ivory tower' institutions, whose staff are ignorant of the realities of the modern commercial world.*

a tower of 'strength

Someone is **a tower of strength** if they give you a lot of help, support or encouragement: *My wife has been a tower of strength to me throughout this difficult period.*

In Shakespeare's *King Richard III*, V iii, Richard reassures members of his own army by reminding them that 'the king's name is **a tower of strength**', which is sure to give them an advantage against the opposing army.

town

go to 'town on something (*informal*)

You **go to town on something** if you spend a lot of money on it or make a great effort in preparing it: *There wasn't much to drink at the party, but she had certainly gone to town on the buffet.*

◇ SEE ALSO **push the boat out** ▷ BOAT; **go to great lengths** ▷ LENGTHS; **go to a lot of trouble** ▷ TROUBLE; **go out of your way** ▷ WAY

paint the 'town red

When people **paint the town red**, they go out for a wild evening of pleasure and excitement which probably involves a lot of drinking and dancing: *The Noufara is an ideal meeting place to have cocktails before painting the town red.*

◇ SEE ALSO **a night on the town** or **on the tiles** ▷ NIGHT

trace

sink without 'trace or vanish without 'trace

Someone or something that **sinks**, or **vanishes, without trace** disappears completely: *Any rumours that he may be planning to return to boxing seem to have sunk without trace. □ I can't think where my passport has gone. It seems to have vanished without trace.*

traces

kick over the 'traces

You say that someone **is kicking over the traces** if they are refusing to respect authority in the way that they used to: *You start the weekend wanting to kick over the traces of convention and conformity. In fact, you're out to shock.*

The **traces** are the long strips of leather which join a cart or other horse-drawn vehicle to the harness of the horse which is pulling it. If a horse kicks over the traces, its leg passes over these strips, and the horse becomes out of control.

track

keep 'track of

You **keep track of** someone or something if you make sure you know where they are, what they are doing, or what is happening to them: *While the organisers did their best to keep track of all those who attended the conference, the list below is not complete.*

lose 'track of

You **lose track of** someone or something if you do not know where they are, what they are doing, or what is happening to them any more; you **lose track of** time when you do not know what time it is any more: *We wanted to invite the Collins twins, but everyone who knew them seems to have lost track of them. □ He said he felt disorientated, the blinds were drawn, and he lost track of time.*

off the beaten 'track

A place is **off the beaten track** when it is far away from main roads, public services and

centres of population: *I'd like to try and arrive before it gets dark. It's a bit off the beaten track and I don't want to get lost.*
◇ SEE ALSO **the back of beyond** ▷ BACK; **in the middle of nowhere** ▷ MIDDLE; **out in the sticks** ▷ STICKS; **out of the way** ▷ WAY

on the right 'track

You are **on the right track** if you are thinking or acting in a way which means that you will be successful or will find the correct answer: *If he wants to make me angry, he's on the right track.* □ *'You're not getting married, are you?' 'No, but you're on the right track.'*

put someone off the 'track or throw someone off the 'track

Someone **puts**, or **throws, you off the track** when they succeed in making you turn your attention temporarily away from something which they do not want you to discover: *I hoped to throw them off the track by suggesting alternative explanations for the recent events.*

tracks

make 'tracks (*informal*)

You **make tracks** when you leave a place: *Come on, Jen. Shall we make tracks?*

stop dead in your 'tracks

Someone who is walking or moving forwards **stops dead in their tracks** when they stop suddenly and remain standing in the same position: *There was a feeling of high spirits in the air. And then she saw them. She stopped dead in her tracks. Her mouth fell open.*

trail

blaze a 'trail

If a person or organization **blazes a trail**, they lead or show the way towards something new: *After years of quiet research, the company is blazing a trail in the development of an AIDS cure.*

hot on the 'trail

You are **hot on the trail**, or **hot on the trail of** someone or something, when you have almost succeeded in catching them: *Police are hot on the trail of the burglar who stole a CD player and sentimental items from a local couple's house last night.*

train

train of 'thought

Your **train of thought** is a connected series of thoughts: *I didn't want to interrupt your train of thought.*

transport

in a transport of de'light

A person who is **in a transport of delight** is experiencing a strong, temporary feeling of perfect happiness, maybe as a reaction to some surprise: *She was in a transport of delight, overwhelmed by the loveliness of his present.*

trap

shut your 'trap! (*offensive*)

If you say **'shut your trap!'** to someone, you are telling them rudely to be quiet: *'I told you this would happen.' 'Oh, shut your trap!'*
◇ SEE ALSO **shut your face!** ▷ FACE; **shut your mouth!** ▷ MOUTH

A **trap** is a small door.

travel

have such-and-such, will 'travel

In job advertisements, employers sometimes use the expression '**have** a certain thing, **will travel**', to show that the person they intend to choose for the job must have the skill which they have mentioned and be willing to go somewhere new to use it, probably to a foreign country: *Have language skills, will travel.*

The word 'will' in this phrase is used in its old-fashioned sense of 'be willing to'. A few people still claim that, when correctly used with the first-person subjects 'I' and 'we', 'will' expresses determination or desire, and is therefore not identical in meaning to 'shall' (used with 'I' and 'we' simply to signal the future tense). It is more common, however, to ignore this and to use 'will' in preference to 'shall' with all subjects.

treat

go down a 'treat

You say that a person or thing **goes down a treat** if they are greatly appreciated by everyone: *Her lively and helpful attitude went down a treat with the tourists.*

tree (*see also* **trees**)

bark up the wrong 'tree (*informal*)

You say that someone **is barking up the wrong tree** if they have the wrong idea about something: *We've been barking up the wrong tree all along. How could we have been so stupid?*

be out of your 'tree (*informal*)

If you say that someone **is out of their tree** you mean they are mad or crazy, or that they are drunk or acting strangely because they have taken a lot of drugs: *You've* decided to join the Foreign Legion? You must be out of your tree. □ 'Where's Mike?' 'In the corner over there, but I wouldn't bother speaking to him. He's out of his tree.'

trees

not grow on 'trees
You say that something, especially money, **does not grow on trees** as a way of reminding someone that that thing is precious and difficult to obtain: *I wonder where he got it all from? Large amounts of money like that don't grow on trees, you know.*

trend

set the 'trend
You **set the trend** if you start a new fashion: *Oh, I remember the Beastie Boys. Didn't they set a trend in vandalizing cars or something?*
'**trend-setter**: *She has a reputation as a trend-setter.*

trial (*see also* **trials**)

on 'trial
1 A person who has been accused of committing a crime is **on trial** when their case is being heard in a court of law: *She is on trial accused of murder.* **2** A piece of machinery, drug, or person is **on trial** when they are being tested to check that they work and have no serious faults before being permanently accepted or approved: *If you order it through a catalogue, you'll get it on trial for a couple of weeks before you decide to buy.*

trial and 'error
You do something by **trial and error** when you keep trying different ways or different things until you find the correct or the best one: *She taught herself to cook by trial and error.*

trials

trials and tribu'lations
If people talk about the **trials and tribulations** of a certain situation, they mean the many annoying problems which that situation involves: *He still brings dirty washing home at weekends. Oh, the trials and tribulations of being a mother!*

triangle

eternal 'triangle or 'love triangle
An **eternal triangle** or a **love triangle** is an emotional situation involving two women and a man or two men and a woman: *What had started as a casual affair with his best friend's wife had become an eternal triangle.* □ *And tomorrow in The Daily Star... read*

about Hollywood's most scandalous love triangle.

trick (*see also* **tricks**)

do the 'trick
Something **does the trick** when it does what you want or need it to do: *Don't call the plumber, I'll fix it with a piece of old cloth. There, that should do the trick.*
◇ SEE ALSO **do the job** ▷ JOB

every trick in the 'book
You say that someone is using **every trick in the book** if they are using a wide range of methods to try and achieve the result they want: *That child will try every trick in the book to avoid going to school.*

a trick of the 'trade
If people talk about **a trick of the trade**, they mean one of the ways of being successful in the particular activity they are referring to: *Monthly meetings will provide a forum for teachers to meet and swap tricks of the trade.*

trick or 'treat
Trick or treat is the children's activity, especially in the USA and Canada, of dressing up on Hallowe'en and visiting houses to ask the people who live there for sweets or money. It is traditional for the children to play a trick on people who do not give them anything: *I always kind of liked the idea of trick or treat when I was a kid, but my mom never let me go.*

tricks

how's 'tricks? (*informal*)
If someone asks you '**how's tricks?**', they are asking how you are: *'So, how's tricks?' 'Not bad. How's yourself?'*

The reply to this question is the same as if the person had asked 'how are you?', for example 'fine, thanks'.

up to your old 'tricks
You say that someone is **up to their old tricks** when you notice them behaving in the slightly unacceptable way which you have learnt to expect from them: *I see you're up to your old tricks again, flirting with women half your age.*

trifle

a trifle 'such-and-such
You use **a trifle** to describe something that exists or is true to a small degree: *I must say, I was a trifle surprised when I heard he was getting married.*

trigger

'trigger-happy

Someone who is **trigger-happy** is too willing or likely to use guns or general violence: *How can we be expected to negotiate with a bunch of trigger-happy terrorists?*

trimmings

all the 'trimmings

You say that a particular dish comes with **all the trimmings** if it is served with all the vegetables and sauces which people traditionally eat with it: *I used to look forward to Sundays. We always had a roast dinner with all the trimmings.*

trooper

smoke like a 'trooper

Someone who **smokes like a trooper** smokes a lot.

swear like a 'trooper

Someone who **swears like a trooper** uses a lot of shocking swear-words: *She looks so sweet and innocent, but she swears like a trooper.*

trolley

be off your 'trolley (*informal*)

If you say that someone **is off their trolley**, you mean that they are mad or crazy: *'I'll gather some seaweed and make soup with it.' 'Do you know something? You're off your trolley.'*

◇ SEE ALSO **be bananas** ▷ BANANAS; **off your chump** ▷ CHUMP; **off your rocker** ▷ ROCKER

trot

on the 'trot

You do a series of things **on the trot** when you do them one after the other: *I'm quite looking forward to staying in tonight. Three nights out on the trot has just about finished me off.*

trouble

'asking for trouble

You say that someone **is asking for trouble** if they are acting in a way that is likely to give them problems later on: *If you go on holiday without any insurance, you are just asking for trouble.* ☐ *He was of the opinion that a single woman wearing a short skirt was asking for trouble.*

go to a lot of 'trouble

You **go to a lot of trouble** to do something when you make a big effort or do a lot of work to get it done: *'I've made your bed for you, and your dinner's in the oven.' 'You shouldn't have gone to so much trouble.'* ☐ *They went to a lot of trouble to help us*

when Dad was ill – the least we can do is get them a Christmas present.

◇ SEE ALSO **push the boat out** ▷ BOAT; **go to great lengths** ▷ LENGTHS; **go to town on something** ▷ TOWN; **go out of your way** ▷ WAY

in 'trouble

1 A person or organization is **in trouble** if they have serious problems: *The company is in trouble, and is expected to announce more redundancies today.* ☐ *If you ever do that again, you'll be in big trouble.* 2 A child is **in trouble** when he or she has done something wrong and will be punished for it: *'If they catch you up here,' said Philip, 'you'll get into trouble.'*

◇ SEE ALSO **up the creek without a paddle** or **up the creek** ▷ CREEK; **out of your depth** ▷ DEPTH; **in the shit** ▷ SHIT; **up shit creek** ▷ SHIT; **in the soup** ▷ SOUP; **in a tight spot** ▷ SPOT; **in deep water** ▷ WATER; **in hot water** ▷ WATER

something is more trouble than it's 'worth

You say that **something is more trouble than it's worth** if you do not get enough benefit from that thing to justify the effort that you have to put into it: *I used to grow carrots, but they're more trouble than they're worth.*

'look for trouble

You say that someone **is looking for trouble** if they go out with the intention of finding and getting involved in a dangerous, illegal, or violent situation: *A jury heard yesterday that the young man, 20, went 'looking for trouble' after going out drinking with his flatmate.*

'no trouble

Something that is **no trouble** does not take much effort to do or deal with: *'Thanks for looking after the cat.' 'That's okay. It was no trouble.'*

take the 'trouble to or go to the 'trouble of

You **take the trouble to** do something, or **go to the trouble of** doing it, when you make the effort to do it: *You'd have seen there was no stamp on the letter if you'd taken the trouble to check before you posted it.*

take 'trouble

You **take trouble**, or **take trouble with** or **over something**, if you spend a lot of time doing it carefully or correctly: *It was obvious that he had taken a great deal of trouble over cooking the dinner.*

a trouble shared is a trouble 'halved

If someone says '**a trouble shared is a trouble halved**', they mean that it often helps people to feel better if they talk about their problems with a friend: *Many people will have experienced the relief of being able to talk to another person about* *their feelings and difficulties. It is at the heart of the old saying 'A trouble shared is a trouble halved'.* □ *'I'm not sure I want to talk about it.' 'Come on, a trouble shared is a trouble halved, remember?'*

trousers

catch someone with their 'trousers down

When you **catch someone with their trousers down**, you put them in an embarrassing situation by doing something which they do not expect, or discovering something which they would have preferred to keep a secret: *By combining different topics in his questions, the examiner caught a few students with their trousers down.*

◇ SEE ALSO **catch someone red-handed** ▷ CATCH; **catch someone with their pants down** ▷ PANTS; **catch someone at it** ▷ CATCH

wear the 'trousers *(disrespectful)*

The person who **wears the trousers** in a male-female relationship is the one who makes the decisions for both of them: *I'd like to take a bet on it that she wears the trousers in that marriage.*

truant

play 'truant

Children **play truant** if they are absent from school without permission: *More than seventy per cent of children at one school have played truant in the past year, according to the Government's figures published today.*

true

so such-and-such it's not 'true *(informal)*

If you describe a person or thing as being **so** something **it's not true**, you are making a comment on how well the description fits them: *We were both dabbling in drink, drugs, and all that. But now Don and I are so straight it's not true.*

'true to

1 You are **true to** your word or promise if you do what you have promised to do: *She said she would come, and when I arrived there she was, true to her word.* **2** You are **true to** your principles when you do what you believe is right: *I regard being true to my own principles as my number one priority.* **3** You are **true to** yourself if you behave in a natural and honest way, without any pretence: *How can you expect other people to trust you if you can't even be true to yourself?* **4** You are **true to** a particular person if you respect your relationship with them and accept all the duties and responsibilities which are part of that relationship: *And thus I found myself betraying my wife, even though I had promised always to be true to her.*

truly

yours 'truly

1 *(formal)* At the end of a formal business letter people sometimes write '**Yours truly**' before signing their name. **2** *(informal)* People sometimes talk about **yours truly** when they are referring to themselves: *She said she couldn't clean up the dog's mess, so guess who ended up doing it? Yours truly* [= myself].

◇ SEE ALSO **yours ever** ▷ EVER; **yours faithfully** ▷ FAITHFULLY; **yours sincerely** ▷ SINCERELY

> The two most important endings to remember when you are writing business letters are **1** '**Yours faithfully**', if you do not know the name of the person you are writing to, and started your letter by writing 'Dear Sir/Madam', and **2** '**Yours sincerely**', if you know the person's name and started your letter by writing 'Dear Mr/Mrs/Ms X'.

trump *(see also* **trumps***)*

'trump card

Your **trump card** is an advantage you have, which other people do not know about, and that you use to your benefit in a certain situation: *The unions have all the trump cards and they are in a good position to negotiate.* □ *The final item could include all the performers if there is time and opportunity to organize it – failing that play your trump card with a really stunning item to finish.*

> In card games, a **trump card** is a card which scores more points than a higher card of another suit, because it belongs to a particular suit which was chosen as 'trumps' before the game started.

trumpet

blow your own 'trumpet

You **blow your own trumpet** when you talk in a proud way about yourself and your achievements: *Unashamedly blowing his own trumpet, he considers that many of the people he selected for management roles are doing a better job than the people before them.*

trumps

come up 'trumps or turn up 'trumps

You **come**, or **turn**, **up trumps** when you behave or do your work successfully under difficult circumstances, especially when people do not expect you to do so: *And to think I doubted your commitment! You've come up trumps, Derek. I'm proud of you.*

In a card game, you 'turn up trumps' when you win a game unexpectedly by showing the other players that you were holding a trump card [see note at **trump card**].

trust

not trust someone as far as you could 'throw them (*informal*)
If you say that you would **not trust someone as far as you could throw them**, you mean that you do not trust them at all: *You can believe him if you like. But personally, I wouldn't trust him as far as I could throw him.*

trust 'so-and-so (*informal*)
If you say, in reference to something foolish that someone has done, '**trust them**', or '**trust them to do that**', you mean it is typical of them to do such a thing: *'Did you hear that Billy's been arrested for nude sunbathing in Hyde Park?' 'Oh, trust him.'*

truth

economical with the 'truth
You say that a person or a statement is **economical with the truth** if, without going as far as telling lies, they manage to give a false impression of something by not giving all the details they know: *I didn't say his statement was false. It was just, how shall I put it, economical with the truth.*

in 'truth or **in all 'truth** (*formal*)
You use '**in truth**' or '**in all truth**' when you want to emphasize the truth or reality of a certain situation: *We tried to behave as if nothing was wrong, although in truth we were very concerned.* □ *'I want you to marry me.' 'In all truth, I don't know what to say.'*
◇ SEE ALSO **in all truthfulness** ▷ TRUTHFULNESS

to tell you the 'truth
You say '**to tell you the truth**' to correct somebody when you think they have over-estimated your experience: *'What do you think of Martin Amis?' 'To tell you the truth, I haven't read anything of his.'*

truth will 'out
If someone says '**truth will out**', they mean that it is impossible to hide the truth about something for ever: *It may take time, but we will find out who was responsible for this. Truth will out, as they say.*

truthfulness

in all 'truthfulness
You use **in all truthfulness** to indicate that you are being completely truthful: *I can say in all truthfulness that I was unaware of her resentment towards me.*
◇ SEE ALSO **in truth** or **in all truth** ▷ TRUTH

tubes

down the 'tubes
Something, usually a plan or an organization, which goes **down the tubes** fails completely and may even cease to exist: *Britain's steelworking industry has gone down the tubes in recent years.*
◇ SEE ALSO **down the drain** ▷ DRAIN; **down the pan** ▷ PAN; **down the plughole** ▷ PLUGHOLE; **down the toilet** ▷ TOILET

tug

tug of 'love
A **tug of love** is an emotional situation in which two people are fighting with each other for the love of a third person: *But it is important that the baby doesn't become involved in a tug of love in between two warring parents.*

tug of 'war
A **tug of war** is a situation where two people or groups of people are trying to gain power or influence: *Both sides want to control the presidency, so there's a kind of congressional tug of war going on here.*

tune

call the 'tune
If a certain person **is calling the tune**, they have control over a situation: *Six countries will be represented, but the US envoy will be calling the tune in next month's peace talks.*
◇ SEE ALSO **call the shots** ▷ SHOTS

change your 'tune
Someone **changes their tune** if they express a completely different opinion from the opinion they held before: *'You've certainly changed your tune, anyway', Peter went on, 'I thought you were intent on warning me against her. Now it seems you rather approve of my choice.'*

You often use this idiom to show that you are suspicious of someone's reasons for changing they opinion so radically.

in 'tune with
You are **in tune with** other people or things if you are able to understand and fit in with them rather than opposing them: *Is your mind in tune with your body?* □ *Primitive human beings were much more in tune with nature than we are now.*

to the tune of 'such-and-such (*informal*)
To the tune of a particular large amount means having that amount as a total: *He demanded fees to the tune of ten million dollars.*

tuppence

not give 'tuppence or **not care 'tuppence**
(*informal, rather old*)

If someone does **not give tuppence** about
something, or does **not care tuppence** about
it, they do not care at all about it: *How
could he treat her like this? Clearly he didn't
love her, he didn't care tuppence for her!
Damn the man.*

◇ SEE ALSO **not give a damn** ▷ DAMN; **not care
a fig** or **two figs** ▷ FIG, FIGS; **not care** or **give
a hoot** or **two hoots** ▷ HOOT, HOOTS; **not give
a monkey's** ▷ MONKEY'S; **not give a shit**
▷ SHIT; **not care** or **give a sod** ▷ SOD; **not
give a tinker's cuss** ▷ TINKER; **not give** or
care a toss ▷ TOSS

turkey

cold 'turkey (*informal*)

When people talk about **cold turkey**, they
mean the unpleasant physical effects which
a person suffers if they suddenly stop
taking a strong drug on which their body
has become dependent: *Doctors don't inform their patients about what to expect. I
went cold turkey, and I had the worst three
days of my whole life.*

> The skin of a cold and shivering person is
> said to resemble the skin of an uncooked
> turkey.

talk 'turkey (*informal*)

When people **talk turkey**, they have a
serious discussion about things such as
work or business arrangements: *I'm ready
to talk turkey.*

turn

before you can turn 'round

If something happens **before you can turn
round**, it happens so quickly that you have
no time to do anything about it: *When he
met this one he fell for her. Before you could
turn round they'd got married, and soon
after that she was pregnant.*

◇ SEE ALSO **before you know where you are**
▷ KNOW

done to a 'turn

You say that food is **done to a turn** if it is
cooked to exactly the right degree: *This is
delicious. The beef is done to a turn.*

◇ SEE ALSO **to a T** ▷ T

a good 'turn

You do someone **a good turn** when you
make a special effort to do something that
benefits them: *One good turn deserves another* [= it is natural for a person to want
to repay someone who has shown them
kindness]. □ *I feel very grateful to old
Tom. He's done me many a good turn since
I moved here.*

have a 'funny turn (*informal*)

If a person or animal **has a funny turn**, their
behaviour suddenly changes and they act
strangely for a short period of time: *'Tell
me how you feel when you have these funny
turns,' he said. 'I get very dizzy.'*

speak out of 'turn or **talk out of 'turn**

You **speak**, or **talk**, **out of turn** when you
say something which is considered to be
unsuitable for the situation you are in: *I'd
better be careful not to speak out of turn if
he's going to be there, I suppose.*

take a turn for the 'better

If the state of a person or thing **takes a turn
for the better**, it suddenly improves: *At last,
I had a job interview. Things seemed to be
taking a turn for the better.*

take a turn for the 'worse

If the state of a person or thing **takes a turn
for the worse**, it becomes suddenly worse:
*The vet said that Caspar had taken a turn for
the worse overnight, and had died early in the
morning.*

a 'turn-up for the books or **a 'turn-up for the
book**

An event can be described as **a turn-up for
the books**, or **a turn-up for the book**, if it is a
surprise: *Fancy you being in New York too.
What a turn-up for the books!*

turns

take 'turns or **take it in 'turns**

People **take turns**, or **take it in turns** to do
something when they do it one after the
other: *We took turns holding the baby.* □ *I
knew a family of five devoted daughters who
took it in turns, when their father died, to
stay with their mother night and day.*

whatever turns you 'on (*informal*)

If you say **'whatever turns you on'**, you are
remarking in a humorous way that the
activity which has just been mentioned
may be enjoyed by certain people, but that
you yourself would not like it: *'He collects
railway time-tables.' 'Whatever turns you
on, I suppose.'*

twinkle

a twinkle in so-and-so's 'eye

You speak humorously about when someone was just **a twinkle in** one of their
parents' **eye** to refer to a time before they
were born, or even conceived: *Even those
who were just a twinkle in their father's eye
in the '60s joined in with the fun.*

twinkling

in the twinkling of an 'eye

In the twinkling of an eye means 'in a
moment' or 'immediately': *She'd come to*

perform a routine task, and suddenly, virtually in the twinkling of an eye, her entire life had been turned upside-down, and all its certainties challenged.

◇ SEE ALSO **in the blink of an eye** ▷ BLINK; **in the wink of an eye** ▷ WINK

twist

drive someone round the 'twist (*informal*)
You say that someone or something **is driving you round the twist** if they are annoying you very much: *He'll drive us round the twist with those drums of his.*

round the 'twist (*informal*)
If you say that someone is **round the twist**, you mean you think they are mad: *There was talk that Albert was round the twist. Especially since his old mother died.*

◇ SEE ALSO **round the bend** ▷ BEND

two

a 'such-and-such or two
If you talk about a certain thing **or two**, you mean one or two of those things, or a few of those things: *I suppose we'd had a beer or two, but we weren't drunk.*

put two and two to'gether
You **put two and two together** if you judge correctly what is happening in a certain situation from the obvious signs which you have noticed: *After a while, I started putting two and two together and wondering if perhaps Richard's disappearance might have had something to do with them.*

If you say that someone **has put two and two together and got five**, you mean that that person has made an incorrect judgement of a certain situation, by taking certain facts as proof of something which is not really the case.

that makes 'two of us (*informal*)
If you say '**that makes two of us**', you mean that you are in the same situation as the person who is speaking to you: *'I cannot stand that man.' 'Yeah, well that makes two of us.'*

type

not so-and-so's 'type
Someone that you say is **not your type** is not the kind of person you find attractive or interesting: *Christina pulled a face. 'Not my type. Too full of himself.' 'Good-looking though don't you think?'*

tyre

spare 'tyre
If people talk about someone's **spare tyre**, they are referring to the roll of fat which that person has round their belly: *This exercise is especially good for eliminating a spare tyre around the middle and also helps to straighten out a double chin!*

A **tyre** is the rubber covering which is filled with air, attached to a wheel. A **spare tyre** is an extra one that you keep in the car in case you get a puncture [= a hole in one of your tyres].

u

U

do a 'U-turn

1 *A vehicle or its driver* **does a U-turn** when
the driver makes the vehicle turn round to
face in the other direction. **2** *A person or
group such as a government* **does a U-turn** if
they change their minds completely about
something: *He needs to rebuild his reputation and authority, after a humiliating series
of U-turns and political defeats.*

◇ SEE ALSO **have a change of heart** ▷ CHANGE

non-'U (*rather old*)

Someone or something that is described as
non-U is not typical of, or used by, the
upper classes: *her (very slight) Cockney
accent, her generally 'non-U' turns of
phrase, and her inability to deal with the
simpler points of etiquette.*

'U' here, stands for 'upper', as in 'upper
class'.

ugly

as ugly as 'sin

Someone or something that is **as ugly as sin**
is very ugly: *Whereas James had been
referred to by more than one gossip colum-
nist as a sex symbol, Leo, bless him, was as
ugly as sin.*

◇ SEE ALSO **a face like the back of a bus** ▷
FACE

um

um and 'aah

You **um and aah** about something when you
take a long time to make a decision about
it: *Mr Eliot was most feeble and hesitant,
umming and aahing and throwing back the
questions with 'Is that not what I said?' or
'Does it not prove my point?'*

'Um' and 'aah' are supposedly the
sounds people make when they are trying to decide on something,

umbrage

take 'umbrage

If someone **takes umbrage**, they feel, and
show, that they are affected and upset by
what someone else has said or done: *Point-
ing out difficulties is riskier because it is far
from certain how people will take it. People
often take umbrage and start disagreeing.*

unstuck

come un'stuck

You **come unstuck** when you fail to achieve
the result you are aiming for: *These companies have moved into an area which they
are ill-equipped to deal with, and have come
unstuck.*

up

not up to 'such-and-such

You say you are **not up to** a certain activity
when you feel too tired to do it, or think
you cannot do it for some reason: *I don't
feel up to going out tonight. I think I'll have
to cancel it.*

on the up and 'up

Something that is **on the up and up** is improving all the time or becoming increasingly
successful: *Production is on the up and up.*

up a'gainst it

You are **up against it** when you have a
difficulty or challenge to face: *But when
you are really up against it there are times
when the only way to win is by a little crafty
reinterpretation of the rules.*

◇ SEE ALSO **the cards are stacked against
someone** ▷ CARDS

up and a'bout

Someone who is **up and about** is out of bed,
and can get on with their tasks: *Because
there was no pressing urgency to be up and
about he lay for a little, considering the day
ahead.*

up-and-'coming

Someone who is described as an **up-and-
coming** star, artist, designer, manager, etc is
one who is becoming successful or well-
known: *Up-and-coming executives use a
period of employment with a multinational
as a form of training in the methods and
values of big business.*

up and 'down

A situation that is **up and down** is not very
stable or predictable: *Things have been a bit*

up and down since Christmas, but we're confident of a better summer this year.

up and 'go

You **up and go** when you decide to leave a place: *He just upped and went off with that posh woman.*

up to 'here

You say that you are, or have had it, **up to here** with a particular thing, sometimes indicating the top of your head with the flat of your hand at the same time, when you are tired of, and have had enough of something: *Look, I've had it up to here with your excuses; just get on and do the work.*
◇ SEE ALSO **have had enough** ▷ ENOUGH

up-to-the-'minute

Something that is **up-to-the-minute** is the most recent of its kind; someone who is **up-to-the-minute** has all the most recent knowledge about something: *They took her to Vidal Sassoon's salon so that her hair could be cut in an up-to-the-minute style.* □ *He lacked up-to-the-minute information at the crucial moment; he didn't know what the others were doing.*

'up to something *or* up to no 'good

You say someone is **up to something**, or **up to no good**, if you think they are doing something secret or dishonest: *I'm sure he's up to something; every time I go into his office he hurriedly puts the phone down.*

up to 'you

If you say '**it's up to you**' to someone, you mean that they must, or may, make a particular decision: *You know what I think, but it's up to you now.*

well 'up on something

You are **well up on** a particular subject if you have a lot of knowledge about it: *Is that a pterodactyl? I'm not very well up on dinosaurs.*

upright

bolt 'upright

You are **bolt upright** if you are sitting or standing in a very straight, rigid way, possibly because you are afraid, anxious or shocked: *They all sat bolt upright in their seats, in business suits and ties, and remained silent.*

> '**He or she sat bolt upright**' can mean that the person moved into that position, or that they were already in that position.

ups

ups and 'downs

Something goes through a series of **ups and downs** when it goes through alternating periods of success and failure: *I have to*

try and accept it. Life is full of ups and downs and I know that there are going to be bad times to go with the good ones.
◇ SEE ALSO **ebb and flow** ▷ EBB

uptake

quick on the 'uptake

Someone who is **quick on the uptake** is quick to understand or realize something: *I thought it would be evident; you are generally very quick on the uptake.*

slow on the 'uptake

Someone who is **slow on the uptake** is slow to understand or realize something: *In fact I've had to conclude that I am generally rather slow on the uptake. Possibly even subnormal.*

use

a 'fat lot of use

Something that is angrily described as **a fat lot of use** is of no help at all to a situation: *Well that's a fat lot of use. I thought she was supposed to be available at all times.*

it's no use doing 'such-and-such

You say that **it's no use doing** a particular thing if doing it would not help the situation: *We don't think the product is right yet, so there is no use marketing it just now.*

no use to man nor 'beast

Something that is **no use to man nor beast** is useless: *I advise you to take some such steps yourself. Otherwise, my dear fellow, you will soon be of no use to man nor beast.*
◇ SEE ALSO **no good to man nor beast** ▷ GOOD

out of 'use

Something goes **out of use** when people stop using it: *They quickly went out of use when the new, cheaper model came on the market.*

put to good 'use

You **put** something **to good use** when you use it profitably: *They have been able to put the money to good use.*

what's the use of

You ask '**what's the use of**' doing a certain thing when you cannot see why it is necessary to do it: *What's the use of having a car if you never 'drive it?*

useful

make yourself 'useful

You **make yourself useful** when you help other people rather than, for example, watching them working: *Why don't you make yourself useful, get Jenny a drink or something?*

usefulness

outlive your 'usefulness

Someone **has outlived their usefulness** when they are still present in a place where they no longer have any function: *In order to enhance his credibility Fedora was allowed to expose John Vassall who by then had outlived his usefulness.*

user

user-'friendly

A product or machine that is **user-friendly** is designed to be easy or pleasant to use, or easy to follow or understand: *Technological progress has given us much more user-friendly software.*

usual

as per 'usual

You say that something has happened **as per usual**, if it happens more regularly or more often than you would like: *When he came back he was drunk as per usual. So my mother calmly said, 'I'm not opening the door to you now or ever.'*

utmost

do your 'utmost

You **do your utmost** to achieve something when you try as hard as you can to achieve it: *He promised them that he would do his utmost to find their son and deliver him safe from harm.*

v

vacuum

in a 'vacuum

You are **in a vacuum** if you are experiencing a feeling of emptiness or loss: *You will feel that you are in a vacuum for some time yet. Surround yourself with as many friends as possible.*

> A **vacuum** is a space that contains no air, gas or matter.

vale

vale of 'tears

People sometimes refer to life as a, or this, **vale of tears**, when they want to emphasize its sad and difficult side: *It's a vale of tears, girl. And it's better if you cry on your own, because no man's shoulder is strong enough to bear the tears of a woman.*

value

place a high 'value on something

You **place a high value on something** if you think it is important or useful: *Brian repeatedly emphasized that he placed a high value on incidental conversations with his staff.*

value 'judgement

A **value judgement** is a judgement of how important, useful or valuable something is, based on your own personal opinions and not on facts: *Her perception was not clearly defined by sensations and she made a value judgement not based on a logical process.*

variety

variety is the spice of 'life

If someone says '**variety is the spice of life**', they mean that we need change sometimes, even if it causes problems, because it makes life more interesting: *For him, variety is indeed the spice of life and he revels in his constant changes of pace, environment and attitude. □ Oh, yes, I'm fine. It all adds variety. You know what they say – the spice of life, and all that.*

> Note how the idiom is shortened in the second example. People often do this with proverbs, sometimes adding an expression like 'and all that', or 'as they say'.

veg

veg 'out *(informal, slang)*

You **veg out** when you spend time relaxing and doing nothing, or watching TV, for example: *All we did, was sit there all day Saturday and just veg out in front of the telly.*

> **Veg**, here, comes from 'vegetate', which means 'to live a dull and boring life with no activity or excitement'.

veil

draw a 'veil over something

You **draw a veil over** a particular action or state when you ignore it, decide to forget it, or pretend that it did not happen: *'Let's draw a veil over yesterday,' he suggested. 'It won't happen again.'*

vengeance

with a 'vengeance

You do something **with a vengeance** when you do it in a determined, intensive way: *Mark was now speaking out with a vengeance. For the first time in his life he was free from corporate restraints, to say what he really thought.*

vent

give full 'vent to

You **give full vent to** your feelings when you express them freely: *He moved away from the house before stopping and giving full vent to his fury.*

ventured

nothing ventured nothing 'gained

If someone says '**nothing ventured nothing gained**', they mean that if you never try anything, you will never achieve anything in life: *However, 'nothing ventured nothing gained', and you only improve at something by doing it.*

verge

on the verge of 'such-and-such

Someone or something is **on the verge of** doing a particular thing when they are likely to be doing it very soon: *Britain was on the verge of joining the Common Market, a move Conran, a staunch European at the time, embraced with great enthusiasm.* □ *At that time, the company was on the verge of bankruptcy.*

vessels

empty vessels make most 'noise

If someone says '**empty vessels make most noise**', they mean that the people who are talking or shouting most are likely to be those who know the least about the subject in question.

A vessel is a container.

victory

Pyrrhic 'victory

A **Pyrrhic victory** is a situation where someone is successful, but where the cost of winning is so great that it was not worth it: *Most political commentators believed that it was a Pyrrhic victory which had left him considerably weakened and vulnerable to a future challenge.*

Pyrrhus was a king who lost a lot of soldiers in a victory over the Romans in 280 BC.

view

colour someone's 'view of

Someone or something **colours your view of** someone or something when they cause you to see it in a less attractive way: *His overwrought state of mind colours his view of the world around him, and he is no longer able to distinguish between imagination and reality.*

in 'my view

You use **in my view** when giving your own opinion about something.
◇ SEE ALSO **in my book** ▷ BOOK

in view of 'such-and-such

You make a decision **in view of** certain circumstances when those circumstances influence your decision: *In view of the current situation, I think we should postpone our trip until a later date.*

on 'view

Something is **on view** when it is in a place where the public can see it: *An exhibition of recent paintings by Timothy Easton is on view throughout March at The Chris Beetles Gallery, London.*

take a dim view of 'such-and-such

You **take a dim view of** someone else's actions if you do not approve of them: *As a keen amateur astronomer I take a*

dim view of being mistaken for a fortune teller.

take the view that

You say that you **take the view that** something is the case when that is your opinion: *I think he'd take the view that the government needs to be 'educated.*

with a view to

You do something **with a view to** a certain purpose when you do it for that purpose: *They're taking me on for a trial period with a view to possibly employing me long term at a later 'date.*

with something in 'view

You do something **with** a certain purpose **in view** when you do it for that purpose: *He wrote on various subjects, all of them with one aim in view, namely to keep his name before the public.*

village

the global 'village

People sometimes refer to the world as **the global village** when they want to emphasize how much smaller it seems as a result of sophisticated modern-day communication systems: *Despite the view that television has created a 'global village', the presentation of sport on British television differs sharply from that of the United States or of France.*

villain

the villain of the 'piece

Someone or something that is described as **the villain of the piece** is the person or thing that is seen as being the cause of trouble on a particular occasion: *In mitigation Charles Foster said his client was not the villain of the piece and had lost £9,000 through his involvement.*

'The villain of the piece' originally referred to the evil character in a play.

vine

wither on the 'vine

Something **withers on the vine** when it disappears gradually: *Those New Year's resolutions rather withered on the vine, I'm afraid.*

Grapes wither on the vine when they slowly die while still attached to the plant.

violet

no shrinking 'violet

Someone who is described as **no shrinking violet** is an exhibitionist: *Julie T Wallace has never been a shrinking violet – which is probably just as well, as it would be almost* *impossible for her to fade quietly into the background.*

viper

a viper in your 'bosom

You have, or are nursing, **a viper in your bosom** if you are helping or protecting someone who is likely to betray you or cause you some harm: *He visualized the surprise and confusion of the household, their rude awakening to the viper in their bosom.*

If you hold a viper [= a kind of poisonous snake] close to your chest, it is likely to attack you.

virtue

by virtue of *(formal)*

You can use **by virtue of** to explain why something is true or is the case: *Once permitted and enabled (chiefly by virtue of legal aid) to petition for divorce, women have done so in ever-increasing numbers.*
◊ SEE ALSO **by dint of** ▷ DINT

make a virtue of 'necessity

You **make a virtue of necessity** when you make the best of a task or situation that you cannot avoid: *In these circumstances parents made a virtue of necessity; they believed that the experience of death could strengthen family ties, rather than act as a dissolvent.*

virtue is its own re'ward

If someone says '**virtue is its own reward**', they mean that the reward for acting on good moral principles is the knowledge that you have done so, and so you should not expect other people to praise you for it: *He has earned one peerage and an OBE or two, but otherwise virtue is its own reward.*

visit

a flying 'visit

You pay someone **a flying visit** when you call in to see them for a short time: *Lynch may make a flying visit to the French festival but he's a busy man, preparing three new films.*

voice

give voice to

You **give voice to** your feelings or opinions when you express them openly: *He paused as if to collect himself, allowing the crowd to give voice to their frustrations and 'feelings.*

in good 'voice

You are **in good voice** if your voice is in good condition: *The girl singer was in good voice by the pool, singing some sentimental Spanish favourites.*

keep your 'voice down

You **keep your voice down** when you speak quietly, so that people cannot hear what you are saying, for example: *He wondered why the old man kept his voice down. Who could possibly overhear them in a garden?*

make your 'voice heard

You **make your voice heard** when you make sure that people know about your opinions: *If you oppose this development then make your voice heard.*

raise your 'voice

You **raise your voice** if you begin to speak more loudly: *She raised her voice over the noise of the children playing around her.*

sink your voice to a 'whisper

You **sink your voice to a whisper** when you suddenly start speaking very quietly, or whispering, because you are saying something that you do not want other people to hear: *He sank his voice to a whisper: 'I could tell you a few things,' he said.*

with one 'voice

People speak **with one voice** when they are united in expressing the same opinion: *The important thing is that we present our proposals with one voice.*

volumes

speak 'volumes

An action that **speaks volumes** is very easy to interpret, even though the person in question has not expressed their feelings explicitly in words: *She remained silent, but the look on her face spoke volumes.*

vote

put to the 'vote

A matter that **is put to the vote** is decided on by voting: *When the issue was put to the vote in the House of Commons we had a majority of 127 and the campaign against us was left in ruins.*

vote of 'confidence

A **vote of confidence** is a vote taken to establish whether a government or person in authority still has the majority's support for their policies; it is also an official show of approval for something: *The Government, in its anxiety to win a parliamentary vote of confidence, has left itself little room for flexibility. □ The sport of mountain-bike racing received its biggest vote of confidence so far yesterday.*

vote of 'thanks

A **vote of thanks** is an invitation to an audience, usually in the form of a short speech, to thank someone for something: *We owe a particular vote of thanks to our loyal and hard working employees for all their efforts during the year.*

wagon

on the 'wagon

Someone who is **on the wagon** has decided not to drink any alcohol for a period of time, often because they have been an alcoholic, or because they have been drinking too much: *I offered him a drink out of courtesy. He said 'No thanks, I'm on the wagon now.'*

waifs

waifs and 'strays

Waifs and strays are people who do not have anywhere to live or stay: *He also made a special study of the outcasts, the waifs and strays of industrial society, the vagrants.*

wait

just you 'wait

You say to someone '**just you wait**' when you are giving them a warning or threatening them: *'Just you wait,' he said, 'I'll get you.'*

wait and 'see

You say '**wait and see**' to people to tell them to be patient about something, and not get anxious unnecessarily: *'What have you got in that box?' 'Wait and see.'*

wake

in the wake of 'such-and-such

One thing follows **in the wake of** another if it is caused by the other: *In the wake of the killings the Government was overthrown.*

The **wake** of a ship or aircraft is the line of disturbed water or air left by it.

wakey

wakey 'wakey (*informal*)

'**Wakey wakey**' is a friendly way of waking someone up; '**wakey wakey**' is also used sarcastically to someone who is not behaving very intelligently, or not acting very quickly: *Wakey wakey! Time for breakfast!* □ *Wakey-wakey! Come on, you're holding up production!*

walk

from every walk of 'life or from all walks of 'life

If you talk about people **from every walk**, or **all walks, of life**, you mean 'all kinds of people' or 'people from many different professions and backgrounds': *She was interested in men from every walk of life and divided her lovers into those from the streets, sailors, professors and factory workers.*

walk all 'over someone

If someone **walks all over you** they treat you without respect, especially when you have already helped them or trusted them in some way: *Don't let him get away with it! It's your house after all! Don't let him walk all over you!*

'walk it (*informal*)

If someone says, referring to a test or competition, for example, that you **will walk it**, they mean that you will easily pass or win it: *Come on, don't worry. After all the work you've done, you'll walk it.*

wall

drive someone up the 'wall

Someone or something **drives you up the wall** when they annoy you intensely, and make you feel very angry and frustrated: *For the rest of the day all the teenagers would drive their parents up the wall.*

go to the 'wall

An organization, such as a company, that **goes to the wall** is ruined financially: *It would be a tragic loss to theatre if such an important organization were to go to the wall. It's been the help of many actors, directors and playwrights.*

off-the-'wall

Something that is **off-the-wall** is strange and unusual: *No idea was too off-the-wall, no scheme too madcap. He was going to have fun.*

walls

climb the 'walls

You say that you **are climbing the walls** if you are intensely angry, frustrated or in pain: *A nightmare of pain. A period of almost literally climbing the walls.*

walls have 'ears

You say '**walls have ears**' as a way of reminding someone that even though no-one appears to be listening, they should be careful, as people may be listening outside: *She had heard often enough how careless talk cost lives, how even walls had ears. Somebody was bound to be listening.*

wand

wave a magic 'wand

You say that you can't **wave a magic wand**, or that so-and-so thinks you can **wave a magic wand**, if you are unable to immediately produce something that someone wants: *I cannot wave a magic wand and change everything around. But I will plan ahead.*

A **magic wand** is a thin rod that magicians or fairies are said to wave in order to perform magic.

wanderer

the wanderer re'turns

People humorously say '**the wanderer returns**' when someone who has been away for a while comes home: *Look who's here! The wanderer returns!*

wane

on the 'wane

Something that is **on the wane** is getting smaller or weaker: *Even in East Hampshire the party's popularity is on the wane.*

want

have someone right where you 'want them

You say that you **have someone right where you want them** if you have so much influence over them that you can persuade them to do what you want: *I can't believe we were so stupid. They've got us right where they want us now.*

◇ SEE ALSO **have someone wrapped round your little finger** ▷ FINGER; **have someone eating out of your hand** ▷ HAND; **have someone eating out of the palm of your hand** ▷ PALM; **have someone in your pocket** ▷ POCKET

warpath

on the 'warpath

Someone who is **on the warpath** is in an angry mood, and is looking for the person who caused them to feel that way: *The last thing he needed at the moment was an outraged husband on the warpath.*

wars

in the 'wars

You say that someone has been, or is, **in the wars** if they have been injured: *Another international player in the wars was Worcestershire's Graham Dilley, who underwent an operation on his left ankle at the end of April.*

warts

warts and 'all

Something that is presented to you **warts and all** has not been edited, censored or cleaned up in an attempt to make it more superficially attractive: *Our philosophy is an absolute open door policy where people can look at everything, warts and all.*

Warts are little hard lumps that grow on your skin, especially on your face or the backs of your hands.

wash

come out in the 'wash

If you say that a particular problem will **come out in the wash**, you mean that it will work out satisfactorily in the end: *He promised that the story of his stormy relationship with Flashman would 'all come out in the wash'.*

not 'wash

If you say that a particular explanation or excuse **doesn't**, or **won't**, **wash** with someone, you mean that they will not be convinced by it: *It does no good to say there is not as much crime there as in Chicago or Sydney. That does not wash. Crime has doubled since 1979.*

waste

go to 'waste

Something **goes to waste** when it is not used and has to be thrown away: *'Eat up,' Isabel said, 'we cannot afford to let things go to waste.'*

waste not 'want not

If someone says **waste not want not**, they mean that if you do not waste things, you will be less likely to find yourself in need of anything later: *'Eat up now,' Dad said. 'Waste not, want not.'*

waste of 'space

If you describe someone as a **waste of space**, you mean, very disrespectfully, that they are worthless: *So basically if you're going to tell somebody they're a waste of space, you should at least tell them why.*

watch

'watch it

You say '**watch it!**' to someone to warn them to be careful, or as a threat.

watch 'out

You say '**watch out!**' to someone to warn them that they are likely to be hit by a moving object if they do not move very quickly.

water

a lot of water has passed under the 'bridge since then or a lot of water has flowed under the 'bridge since then

If someone says '**a lot of water has passed,** or **flowed, under the bridge since then**', they mean that a lot of things have happened since the time mentioned, and that the situation is different now: *A lot of water has flowed under the bridge since we lifted the trophy. It is interesting to reflect on the members of the team and their fortunes since that afternoon.*

hold 'water

An argument that **holds water** is one that you can find no mistakes in, or that you can prove: *This argument just does not hold water. The whole system was ill-conceived from the outset.*

in deep 'water

You are **in deep water** when you are in trouble, danger, or difficulty: *Suddenly Sophie found she was in deep water. It would be foolish to appear evasive.*

◇ SEE ALSO **up the creek without a paddle** or **up the creek** ▷ CREEK; **out of your depth** ▷ DEPTH; **in the shit** ▷ SHIT; **up shit creek** ▷ SHIT; **in the soup** ▷ SOUP; **in a tight spot** ▷ SPOT; **in trouble** ▷ TROUBLE; **in hot water** ▷ WATER

in hot 'water

You are **in hot water** if you are in trouble.

◇ SEE ALSO **up the creek without a paddle** or **up the creek** ▷ CREEK; **out of your depth** ▷ DEPTH; **in the shit** ▷ SHIT; **up shit creek** ▷ SHIT; **in the soup** ▷ SOUP; **in a tight spot** ▷ SPOT; **in trouble** ▷ TROUBLE; **in deep water** ▷ WATER

like water off a duck's 'back

You say that someone's reaction to something is **like water off a duck's back**, if that person is not at all surprised or bothered by it: *It was like water off a duck's back to Nick, but I'm sure it upset Paul.*

pour cold 'water on or throw cold 'water on

Someone **pours**, or **throws**, **cold water** on your plans, for example, when they try to discourage you or make you less enthusiastic about them: *I don't want to pour cold water on things, but what if they didn't*

believe you? And think how embarrassing it would be.

◇ SEE ALSO **put a damper** or **the dampers on something** ▷ DAMPER, DAMPERS

test the 'water or test the 'waters

You **test the water** when you try something out tentatively before committing yourself to it: *Why do so many of us feel the need to test the water first? Is a period of living together any indication of how the marriage will fare?*

water under the 'bridge

If you say about something unpleasant '**it's water under the bridge**' or '**that's all water under the bridge now**', you mean that you want to forget about the things mentioned because they happened in the past and the situation is different now: *'Look,' he went on hurriedly, 'It's over. It's all water under the bridge; you don't want to hear it.'*

waters

muddy the 'waters

Someone **muddies the waters** when they cause confusion in a situation which had been clear up until that point: *Those who can pay but refuse to do so muddy the waters and make it more difficult for local councils to adopt collection policies.*

still waters run 'deep

If someone says '**still waters run deep**' they mean that reserved, quiet people often have deep feelings or a lot of knowledge about a subject: *It is said that 'still waters run deep'. I for one could never penetrate his thoughts, could never really feel comfortable with him.*

Compare this idiom with: '**empty vessels make most noise**' (at **vessels**).

Watson

ele'mentary my dear Watson

If someone says '**elementary my dear Watson**', they mean, humorously, that something is easy: *'But how are we going to get across the river?' 'Elementary, my dear Watson; we build a raft.'*

This idiom is supposed to be a quotation from the stories of Sherlock Holmes, by Sir Arthur Conan Doyle. In fact, Sherlock Holmes never said these words as a complete phrase.

wavelength

on the same 'wavelength

Two people who are **on the same wavelength** understand each other well and tend to have similar opinions about things: *I must confess I don't think I was on the same wavelength as the Prime Minister almost from the start.*

waves

make 'waves

Someone who **makes waves** causes trouble, or spoils a comfortable situation: *Outspoken people tread on toes, but they are often the ones who make waves and achieve something.*

◇ SEE ALSO **rock the boat** ▷ BOAT

way

by the 'way

You use **by the way** to introduce a point that you want to mention while you remember it, though it may not be relevant to the present subject: *Yes, I saw him yesterday. By the way, are you going to be at home tonight?*

downhill all the 'way

1 You say that it's **downhill all the way** with reference to a job or task when all the hard work has been done and the difficulties have been dealt with: *Two-nil up at home against moderate opposition – it would have been downhill all the way for most teams.* **2** You also say that it's **downhill all the way** when a situation gets worse from a certain point in time onwards: *I launched into a career as a journalist and for my health it became downhill all the way. I drank a bottle of scotch a day.*

◇ SEE ALSO **plain sailing** ▷ SAILING

go the way of all 'flesh

Someone or something that **goes the way of all flesh** dies or disappears finally: *Mother has to die some day, as do all of us. It's the way of all flesh. Who would want immortality?* □ *Another Main Street has gone the way of all flesh – shopping centres everywhere.*

◇ SEE ALSO **breathe your last** ▷ LAST; **kick the bucket** ▷ BUCKET; **cash in your chips** ▷ CHIPS; **pop your clogs** ▷ CLOGS; **shuffle off this mortal coil** ▷ COIL; **bite the dust** ▷ DUST; **give up the ghost** ▷ GHOST; **depart this life** ▷ LIFE; **snuff it** ▷ SNUFF

fight your way out of a paper 'bag or punch your way out of a paper 'bag

If you say that someone couldn't **fight**, or **punch, their way out of a paper bag**, you mean that they are weak, either physically or morally: *I've reached that point now. I couldn't fight my way out of a paper bag now.* □ *'The Tunnel Mob,' Danny explained, 'They're a bunch of nothings. Not one of 'em could punch their way out of a paper bag.'*

This idiom can be adapted to describe any kind of incompetence or inability. You might use expressions like 'could not find his way out of a paper bag' for someone who has a bad sense of direction, or 'could not act her way out of a paper bag' for someone who is not good at acting. You can add to the list to suit your own needs.

get out of my 'way or get out of the 'way

You say '**get out of my way**' or '**get out of the way**' when you are rudely telling someone to move because in their present position they are blocking your way or preventing you from doing something: *If you don't get out of my way, I shall have to use force. Now move!*

◇ SEE ALSO **get out of my,** or **the, road** ▷ ROAD

go all the 'way

1 To '**go all the way**' is to have sex, as opposed to just kissing and touching, etc: *You mean, you want to make love to her? Go all the way? Some of the girls allow petting on a date, but I don't know anyone who's actually done it.* **2** To '**go all the way**' is also to complete something that you have started: *I haven't toured for a few years now, apart from the World Cup and I made that an exception because I felt we could go all the way and win it.*

go back a long 'way

Two people **go back a long way** if they have known each other for a long time: *Oh yes, we go back a long way. I could tell you a few things about old Charlie here.*

go down the wrong 'way

Food **goes down the wrong way** when it gets stuck in your throat and makes you choke.

go out of your 'way

You **go out of your way** to do something when you make a particular effort, or disrupt your plans, in order to be able to do it: *They really went out of their way to give us a good time.*

◇ SEE ALSO **push the boat out** ▷ BOAT; **go to great lengths** ▷ LENGTHS; **go to town on something** ▷ TOWN; **go to a lot of trouble** ▷ TROUBLE

go your own 'way

Someone who **goes their own way** does what they want without considering others: *She is simply a normal balanced youngster who knows her own mind and goes her own way.*

have a long way to 'go

Someone or something that **has a long way to go** is not at all at the required standard yet: *Mason still has a long way to go before he can think of himself as a genuine contender for the world championship.*

have a 'way with such-and-such

Someone who **has a way with** a certain kind of thing or person is good at dealing with them: *He's always had a way with children – he'll be a great primary school teacher.*

have a 'way with you

Someone who **has a way with them** has an attractive manner and is good at impressing people: *He's a handsome man, oh yes, brown and glossy, with a light in his eye, and a smile on his lips and a way with him.*

have come a long 'way

Someone or something that **has come a long way** has developed or improved a lot: *Technology has come a long way since the days of the typewriter.*

in a bad 'way

Someone or something that is **in a bad way** is in a poor condition: *Poor girl, she was in a bad way. The doctor gave her some pills, and she's finally gone to sleep now.*

in a big 'way

You do something **in a big way** when you do it on a large scale: *Looks like they're going in to electronic publishing in a big way.*

lead the 'way

You **lead the way** somewhere when you guide someone there: *She led the way through the undergrowth to the spot where the body was lying.*

learn the 'hard way

You **learn the hard way** when you realize your mistake through experience, after having ignored someone's advice which would have enabled you to avoid making it: *There is a trick in making privatizations a success, something that the UK Government has had to learn the hard way.*

◊ SEE ALSO **to your cost** ▷ COST

learn your way a'round

You **learn your way around** when you accustom yourself to your new surroundings or duties: *When you've learnt your way around you'll be able to start enjoying yourself a bit more.*

look the other 'way

You **look the other way** when you pretend not to notice something: *Next time you see that kind of thing going on, don't just look the other way, do something about it.*

make way for

You **make way for** someone or something when you move aside to give them space: *Make way for the people getting off the 'bus before you try to get on.*

no 'way (informal)

You answer **'no way'** to a suggestion or proposal when you consider it unacceptable or impossible: *'Are you going to the concert?' 'No way. It's not worth £20.'*

'one way or another

One way or another means 'in some way': *Don't worry, we'll get there one way or another.*

out of someone's 'way

You keep **out of someone's way** when you try to avoid meeting them: *I try to keep out of his way when he's in one of those moods.*

out of the 'way

1 A job that is **out of the way** is finished: *When I've got this paper out of the way I'll be able to enjoy myself a bit more.* **2** A place that is **out of the way** is a long distance from any main roads or public facilities: *It's a bit out of the way – I suppose we'll have to take the car.*

◊ SEE ALSO **the back of beyond** ▷ BACK; **in the middle of nowhere** ▷ MIDDLE; **out in the sticks** ▷ STICKS; **off the beaten track** ▷ TRACK

pave the way for

Someone or something **paves the way for** something to happen if it makes it easy or possible for that thing to happen: *In a case which could pave the way for other people living near Sellafield to bring 'similar claims, the couple are suing British Nuclear Fuels.*

pay your 'way

You **pay your way** when you pay your own debts and living expenses as distinct from being dependent on someone else: *And incidentally, I always pay my way, whoever I'm with. Tonight will obviously be no exception.*

rub someone up the wrong 'way

You **rub someone up the wrong way** when you do or say something that annoys them: *Here she was, creeping around her own house like a burglar, trying to avoid a man who rubbed her up the wrong way.*

◊ SEE ALSO **drive someone round the bend** ▷ BEND; **get someone's goat** ▷ GOAT; **make someone's hackles rise** or **raise someone's hackles** ▷ HACKLES; **get on someone's nerves** ▷ NERVES; **get up someone's nose** ▷ NOSE; **get on someone's wick** ▷ WICK

see which way the 'wind is blowing

You **see which way the wind is blowing** when you try to discern how a person or group of people is thinking, so that you can act accordingly: *In this business you have to see the way the wind is blowing. What's in, what's out.*

take the 'easy way out

A person who has to decide between a number of possible actions **takes the easy way out** when they choose the one which is easiest or involves the least effort: *Because of her pain and the stiffness, the easy way out is to stay in her chair, but May is determined not to let pain master her.*

◊ SEE ALSO **cop-out** ▷ COP; **anything for a quiet life** ▷ LIFE; **the soft option** ▷ OPTION

that's the way the cookie 'crumbles

If someone says **'that's the way the cookie**

crumbles', they mean that unpleasant things happen sometimes in life, and that we must accept them: *Hey, that's the way the cookie crumbles; you can't always win you know.*

◊ SEE ALSO **life goes on** ▷ LIFE; **such is life** ▷ LIFE; **that's life** ▷ LIFE

there's more than one way to skin a 'cat

If someone says that **there's more than one way to skin a cat**, they mean that there are several ways of achieving the thing mentioned.

to 'my way of thinking

To my way of thinking means 'in my opinion': *To my way of thinking, there's no point in investing all your money in one product.*

◊ SEE ALSO **to my mind** ▷ MIND

under 'way

A project is **under way** when it has begun: *Plans are under way for a new bridge across to the mainland.*

a way of 'life

1 Your **way of life** is your lifestyle: *Here Leonard discovered the Greek way of life – its alternating rhythms of work and leisure, both on the seasonal and the daily basis.* **2** Something that has become **a way of life** has become ordinary to the person mentioned, even though it might appear difficult or unpleasant to others: *For Thompson, living with the knee injury became a way of life.*

wend your 'way

You **wend your way** towards a certain place when you go in that direction in a leisurely manner: *We wended our way home, glowing with triumph, each of us the proud possessor of a silver trophy.*

ways

can't have it 'both ways

If someone says **'you can't have it both ways'**, they mean that you should not expect to benefit from two situations, since each excludes the possibility of the other: *Listen, John, you can't have it both ways. There's no point in us meeting again until you've reached a decision.*

change your 'ways or mend your 'ways

You **change**, or **mend**, **your ways** when you start taking your responsibilities seriously after a period of unacceptable or irresponsible behaviour: *But really, Steve, I really do think you're going to have to mend your ways very considerably indeed if you're to succeed in this job.*

◊ SEE ALSO **turn over a new leaf** ▷ LEAF

in more ways than 'one

You say **'in more ways than one'** when you use an expression which is appropriate in both its literal, and its figurative, or idiomatic sense: *He celebrated his home debut with his first goal – he used his head in more ways than one.* [= he scored the goal with his head, and he used his intelligence].

no two ways a'bout it

If you say that there are **no two ways about it**, you mean that you refuse to discuss something any further because you have made your final decision: *I'm afraid there are no two ways about it; you're not going.*

◊ SEE ALSO **end of story** ▷ END; **that's flat** ▷ FLAT; **that's that** ▷ THAT

set in your 'ways

Someone who is **set in their ways** has been doing things in the same way for a long time and is reluctant to change: *A period of sharing your home is sometimes healthy, because it teaches you to be more adaptable and stops you from becoming too set in your ways.*

◊ SEE ALSO **creature of habit** ▷ CREATURE

ways and 'means

If you say that there are **ways and means**, you mean that there is a possible way, or ways, of solving a particular problem: *There are ways and means to deal with such a matter. The child could be adopted.*

wayside

fall by the 'wayside

Someone or something **falls by the wayside** when they fail in what they are trying to do, or get neglected and forgotten about: *One source of solace to the New Zealand team must be the rate at which Great Britain's best players are falling by the wayside.*

wear

wear and 'tear

Wear and tear is damage caused in the course of normal use: *The equipment needs to be checked for any signs of wear and tear well in advance.*

the worse for 'wear

Someone or something that is **the worse for wear** is in a poor state through too much activity, too much alcohol or too much use: *A few minutes later, feeling decidedly the worse for wear after the last Armagnac had been downed, Mark moved unsteadily into the lift.*

◊ SEE ALSO **have seen better days** ▷ DAYS; **in bad repair** ▷ REPAIR

weather

keep a 'weather eye on

You **keep a weather eye on** someone or something if you remain alert and watchful: *Every three months we will send you a statement. This lets you keep a weather eye on your finances.*

make heavy 'weather of

You say that someone **is making heavy weather of** something if you think they are making unnecessarily slow and difficult progress with it: *They made heavy weather of the opening sections, completely robbing the music of any momentum or atmosphere.*

under the 'weather

You are **under the weather** when you are not as healthy or well as you usually are: *Your own ability will vary. You will have off days when you are tired or a bit under the weather.*

◇ SEE ALSO **below** or **not up to par** ▷ PAR; **out of sorts** ▷ SORTS

wedding

hear 'wedding bells

You say that you **can hear wedding bells** if you think that two particular people are likely to announce their marriage soon: *The two were seen going everywhere together, and all her friends could hear wedding bells.*

> **'Wedding bells'** is also used to talk about marriage in general. People say they are 'waiting for wedding bells' [= waiting for a couple to announce their marriage], or that 'it's wedding bells' [= a couple has announced their marriage].

week

week in week 'out

Something that happens **week in week out** happens repeatedly over a fairly long period of time: *the businessman who goes off at eight in the morning and comes back at six, week in week out, year in year out, with perhaps four weeks' holiday.*

weekend

dirty week'end (*informal, humorous*)

If people talk about a **dirty weekend**, they mean a weekend away from home devoted to having sex with their lover: *Have I stumbled on some dark and desperate secret? Are you heading off for a dirty weekend together?*

a wet week'end (*informal*)

If you compare someone or something to **a wet weekend**, you mean that they are no fun: *You're about as exciting as a wet weekend under Southend Pier.*

weight

carry 'weight

Someone or something that **carries weight** has an important influence on others: *You do not just want someone whose opinion is going to carry weight but someone who is also going to provide persuasive evidence.*

a 'weight off your mind

If you say that something is **a weight off your mind**, you mean that you are relieved: *There is nothing wrong with you, nothing that a rest cannot cure. There, is that not good news? A weight off your mind?*

◇ SEE ALSO **a load off your mind** ▷ LOAD

pull your 'weight

You **pull your weight** when you do your full share of work, for example, in a team or group: *I can't tolerate incompetent, unreliable labour. If you're going to stay out your time here, you'll have to pull your weight. You understand?*

take the 'weight off your feet

You **take the weight off your feet** when you sit down for a rest: *Come in and take the weight off your feet. You look tired out.*

throw your 'weight about

Someone **throws their weight about** when they give orders to other people in an unnecessarily rude way: *Do not use the opportunity of promotion to throw your weight about.*

worth your weight in 'gold

Someone or something that is **worth their weight in gold** is very useful or helpful: *This is where experienced help is worth its weight in gold, since the correct set-up can only be established by an expert.*

welcome

outstay your 'welcome

You **outstay your welcome** when you stay at someone's house longer than they would like: *He is one of those people who gives you the impression that you have outstayed your welcome before you have even sat down.*

well

all well and 'good or all very 'well

Something that is **all well and good**, or **all very well**, is apparently satisfactory: *Exercises in a room were all very well, but they were no substitute for running every day.*

> **All well and good** and **all very well** are usually followed by 'but . . .'.

just as 'well

If you say that it is **just as well** that something has happened, you mean that you are pleased or feel lucky that it has happened, because you have been able to benefit from it: *It's just as well I didn't go in to work today, or I wouldn't have been in when you called.*

◊ SEE ALSO **a good job** ▷ JOB; **a good thing** ▷ THING

well 'off

1 You are **well off for** something when you have plenty of it. **2** Someone who is **well off** has plenty of money: *He would be well off now. As an ex-minister there was no doubt he would be able to pick up numerous lucrative directorships.* **3** You are **well off** when you are in a situation that you ought to be contented with: *Some people don't know when they're well off.*

whale

a 'whale of a time

You have **a whale of a time** when you enjoy yourself thoroughly: *She'd been on the floor for nearly every dance, and was having a whale of a time.*

what

what is 'more

You say **'what is more'**, when you are about to mention a final argument which supports a particular point you have made: *I have been fortunate to find a career that I love and, what is more, get paid reasonably for it.*

◊ SEE ALSO **to cap it all** ▷ CAP; **to crown it all** ▷ CROWN; **to make matters worse** ▷ MATTERS; **to top it all** ▷ TOP

wheat

separate the wheat from the 'chaff or sort out the wheat from the 'chaff

You **separate**, or **sort out, the wheat from the chaff** when you decide what is valuable and what is worthless: *In theory this filtering system should sort out the wheat from the chaff but the volume of material is so great that it is beyond any useful human assessment.*

◊ SEE ALSO **separate** or **sort out the men from the boys** ▷ MEN; **separate** or **sort out the sheep from the goats** ▷ SHEEP

wheel

behind the 'wheel

The person who is **behind the wheel** in a car is the driver: *With a sigh of relief, she got behind the wheel. She turned the ignition key. Nothing happened.*

big 'wheel

A **big wheel** is a person who holds an important or influential position in an organization: *He progressed up the ladder, bought the business, and became a big wheel in the East India Company, a founder of Williams & Glyn Bank and the local MP.*

wheel and 'deal

Someone who **wheels and deals** makes

business deals that are clever, but not very honest or moral: *He says that money will be made available for Glenn Hoddle to buy players and he will wheel and deal as he usually does to get the men he wants.*

wheeler-'dealer: *He suggested that many Western partners in joint ventures were blatant speculators, wheeler-dealers and the 'rejects of entrepreneurship'.*

wheeling and 'dealing: *Solutions turn not on principle and reasoned argument, but on compromises, accommodation and, on occasion, rather sordid wheeling and dealing.*

the wheel has come full 'circle

If someone says **'the wheel has come full circle'**, they mean that after a period of change, the situation has returned to its original state: *Strangely, the wheel had come full circle: I was back working for Alan Lewis, the man who'd given me my first music press job.*

wheels

oil the 'wheels

Something that **oils the wheels** of a particular activity makes it work more easily, especially when it involves use of influence or money: *Compliments oil the wheels of life. Even a bit of flattery doesn't go amiss.*

set the 'wheels in motion

Someone or something **sets the wheels in motion** when they cause an activity to begin: *With the sale of the manor off her mind, Jane set the wheels in motion to find somewhere small to live.*

while

worth someone's 'while

If you tell someone whom you have asked to do something that you will make it **worth their while**, you mean that you will pay them to do it, or give them something in return: *'That depends,' he said softly, 'On whether you make it worth my while.' Peter smiled a predatory smile.*

◊ SEE ALSO **for someone's pains** ▷ PAINS

whip

crack the 'whip

Someone who **cracks the whip** uses their power and influence over others in a severe manner: *He has been urging them to crack the whip a bit, arguing that the whole establishment needs reorganization before reforms can be introduced effectively.*

A **whip** is a long narrow strip of leather, or a narrow rope, attached to a handle, for striking people or animals with.

whirl

give it a 'whirl

If you say that you will **give it a whirl**, you mean that you will try something to see if it works or to see if you can do it: *On balance I decided that the only way to find out if I could do it was to give it a whirl!*

whisker

within a 'whisker

You are, or you come, **within a whisker** of something when you are very close to it: *He came within a whisker of losing his job.*
◇ SEE ALSO **a hair's breadth** ▷ BREADTH

An animal's **whiskers** are the long coarse hairs growing around its mouth.

whistle

blow the 'whistle

Someone **blows the whistle** on someone else if they make that person's illegal or deceitful schemes known to the public: *Mitchell, an oil rig welder, blew the whistle on safety violations by his drilling company, two months after the Piper Alpha disaster.*

wet your 'whistle

You **wet your whistle** when you have a drink to stop yourself feeling thirsty: *Get the kettle on and your whistle wetted!*

Here, **whistle** is a slang term for the mouth or throat.

white

white as a 'sheet or white as 'death or white as 'snow or white as 'paper or white as a 'ghost

Someone who is as **white as a sheet, as death, as snow, as paper**, or **as a ghost**, is very pale due to shock or illness: *Ethel turned white as a sheet. 'I don't know what you're talking about,' she said.* □ *He saw Oliver lying on the pavement, shaking, his face as white as death.* □ *Isabel, are you all right? You're as white as snow.* □ *He went as white as paper, and jerked upright in his chair. 'Drugs? What are you talking about?'*
◇ SEE ALSO **pale as death** ▷ PALE

whom

to whom it may con'cern (*formal*)

You address a formal letter '**to whom it may concern**', when you do not know who will be reading it.

whys

whys and 'wherefores

The **whys and wherefores** of a particular situation are the reasons and explanations behind it: *I want to find the answers to certain whys and wherefores which have puzzled me all my life.*

wick

get on someone's 'wick

Someone who **gets on your wick** annoys or irritates you: *Of course I care about you – you're my husband, aren't you? You just get on my wick at times, that's all.*
◇ SEE ALSO **drive someone round the bend** ▷ BEND; **get someone's goat** ▷ GOAT; **make someone's hackles rise** or **raise someone's hackles** ▷ HACKLES; **get on someone's nerves** ▷ NERVES; **get up someone's nose** ▷ NOSE; **rub someone up the wrong way** ▷ WAY

wild

wild-'goose chase

A **wild-goose chase** is a search that cannot succeed, usually for reasons unknown to the searcher: *He drove off into the night. He was aware that they could be setting out on a wild-goose chase, but he had to believe that they weren't.*

wildfire

spread like 'wildfire

Something, such as a piece of news, a rumour, or disease **spreads like wildfire** when it spreads very fast: *The news of his marriage had spread like wildfire through Florence.*

will

against your 'will

If you do something **against your will**, you do it because you are forced to, although you do not want to do it: *I'm not going to force you to do anything against your will – if you really have decided to quit the music business, then so be it.*

at 'will

You can do something **at will** if you can do it whenever, and however, you want to: *I'd love to be able to spend vast amounts of money at will.*

of your own free 'will

You do something **of your own free will** when you do it because you want to, and not because someone has asked you or told you to do it: *That he did not depart of his own free will is evidenced by the fact that he left behind all his belongings.*

where there's a will there's a 'way

If someone says '**where there's a will there's a way**', they mean that if you want something strongly enough, you will find a way of getting or achieving it.

with the best will in the 'world

If you say that **with the best will in the world** you cannot manage something, you mean that however much you would like to be able to do it, it is impossible: *With the best will in the world the police officer was unlikely to catch him.*

willies

give someone the 'willies or **get the 'willies** (*informal*)

Someone or something that **gives you the willies** frightens you; you **get the willies** when you are frightened: *I couldn't go to see that kind of film 'cos I get the willies, but some people enjoy being frightened don't they?*

wind (*see also* **winds**)

break 'wind

You **break wind** when you let gas out of your bowels through the anus: *He staggered into the seat and broke wind loudly, causing Sarah to purse her lips.*

get 'wind of

You **get wind of** something when you hear about it: *By February the local press had got wind of the affair.*

get the 'wind up (*informal*)

You **get the wind up** when you get anxious or alarmed; you **put the wind up** someone when you make them anxious or alarmed: *It was his mental state which put the wind up the hospital staff. The constant talking to himself.*

in the 'wind

Something that is **in the wind** is being planned or considered: *There were changes in the wind which may prove to be a sterner test of the depth of the market.*

it's an ill 'wind or **it's an ill wind that blows nobody any 'good**

If someone says 'it's an ill wind', or 'it's an ill wind that blows nobody any good', they mean that some good has come of an apparent misfortune: *However, it was an ill wind and some did profit by it, namely the undertakers.*

piss into the 'wind (*informal*)

Someone who is **pissing into the wind** is unlikely to be successful because what they are trying to do is going against the general tendency: *In a moment of weary despair, he turns to a colleague and says, 'It's like pissing into the wind!'*

run like the 'wind

You **run like the wind** when you run very fast.

◊ SEE ALSO **as fast as your legs can carry you**
▷ LEGS

sail close to the 'wind

Someone who is **sailing close to the wind** is taking a big risk, by being close to breaking a law or social rule: *He left a terrible mess behind him when he disappeared. He'd been sailing close to the wind for years and everything was just about to blow up in his face*

> If a boat sails too closely towards the direction from which the wind is blowing, it is likely to turn over.

take the wind out of someone's 'sails

You **take the wind out of someone's sails** when you make them suddenly lose belief in what they are doing or saying, especially when they felt very strongly about it before: *Wouldn't it take the wind out of his sails more thoroughly if she seemed indifferent rather than angry?*

a wind of 'change

If you say that **a wind of change** is blowing in a place or organization, you mean that there are signs of change, especially in political or social conditions: *There is a wind of change blowing through the corporate environment these days. That change is one of attitude.*

window

go out of the 'window

Something **goes out of the window** when it is lost, forgotten about, or disregarded: *It's always the same. He's working well, then as soon as love comes along, everything goes out of the window.*

winds

to the four 'winds

Someone or something that is scattered **to the four winds** is sent, or spread, over a wide area: *They fought a massive sea battle against the Empire fleet, sending half the Imperial ships to the bottom of the sea and scattering the rest to the four winds.*

wine

wine and 'dine

You **wine and dine** when you have, or go out for, a lot of expensive meals; you **wine and dine** someone when you take them out for expensive meals: *In the house he now wined and dined in a style that not even his grandfather had done.* □ *Tony bursts into a plush restaurant where Sharon is being wined and dined by a romantic Italian rival for her affections.*

wing

under someone's 'wing

You are **under someone's wing** if you are under their protection or guidance; someone **takes you under their wing** if they decide to protect or guide you: *Hattie had the wonderful ability of taking people under her wing. She was mum, sister – everything to all of us.*

ings

clip someone's 'wings

You **clip someone's wings** when you take away from them the power to do something: *Her nose wrinkled with distaste. 'Actually I've decided against having children – they clip your wings.'*

People sometimes clip birds' wings to stop them from flying away.

spread your 'wings

You **spread your wings** when you try to carry out your plans for yourself, rather than under someone else's guidance: *If you're interested in doing business with people who encourage you to spread your wings, why not make a date to come and see us?*

wait in the 'wings

You **are waiting in the wings** if you are waiting in readiness, for example, to take over someone's job: *Waiting in the wings, there was a young colleague of his. Charles wanted his protégé in and I happened to be in the way.*

The wings here, are the areas at each side of a stage in a theatre, where performers wait to enter, hidden from the audience.

wink

in the wink of an 'eye

Something that happens **in the wink of an eye** happens suddenly, or immediately: *You could look at someone and like them, be excited, hopeful, and then, in the wink of an eye, it could all turn sour.*

◇ SEE ALSO **in the blink of an eye** ▷ BLINK; **in the twinkling of an eye** ▷ TWINKLING

not get a wink of 'sleep or not sleep a 'wink

You **don't get a wink of sleep**, or you **don't sleep a wink**, when you do not go to sleep at all: *'Holiday!' he stormed. 'That was no holiday. I didn't get a wink of sleep.'*

winks

forty 'winks

You have **forty winks** when you go to sleep for a short time, especially during the day: *After I'd had forty winks, I felt a lot better.*

winner

on to a 'winner

You are **on to a winner** if you have found a person or situation that is likely to ensure you success: *He's not going to give up that easily. He knows when he's on to a winner.*

winner-takes-'all

A **winner-takes-all** prize, or competition, is one in which there is only a prize for the person who comes first, and not for those who come second, third, etc: *He collected his winner-takes-all prize of £27,000 after a dramatic finish.*

wires

get your 'wires crossed

People **get their wires crossed** when they misunderstand each other: *We have to talk. Somewhere along the way we seem to have got our wires crossed.*

wisdom

with the wisdom of 'hindsight

You understand a situation **with the wisdom of hindsight** when you understand it more clearly after it has occurred, since you are able to look at it more objectively: *With the wisdom of hindsight and the benefit of several years' experience, I now see that my decision was premature.*

wiser

none the 'wiser or no 'wiser

You are **none the wiser**, or **no wiser**, about something that has been explained, or that has happened, if you do not understand the explanation, or do not realize what has happened: *Thus, in 1973, we are no wiser than we were in 1948: the experience of twenty-five years has shed no more light upon the question.*

wish

make a 'wish

People **make a wish**, for example in fairy tales, or as a custom on special occasions, when they express a desire, often silently, which they are supposed to believe will be magically fulfilled: *I closed my eyes and made a wish – that everything would work out all right for her.*

wouldn't wish such-and-such on 'anyone

If you say that you **would not wish** some bad experience **on anyone**, you mean that it is so unpleasant that no-one should have to suffer it.

your wish is my com'mand *(humorous)*

People say to someone '**your wish is my command**' as a humorous way of suggesting that they will do anything that the person asks them to do: *And what about you, young lady? What do you fancy, then? Your wish is my command.*

with

'with it

1 You are **with it** when you are concentrating on, or paying attention to, what is happening around you: *Sorry, I'm not really with it today. What did you say?* **2** (*rather old*) Someone who is **with it** is fashionable: *I always used to wish my parents were a bit more with it.*

wits

at your wits' 'end

You are **at your wits' end** when you cannot think how to deal with a problem and are in despair about it: *What are you doing for those people who are at their wits' end? They can't afford it.*

◇ SEE ALSO **worried to death** ▷ DEATH; **at the end of your tether** ▷ END

> Your **wits** are your ability to think fast in a difficult situation.

collect your 'wits or gather your 'wits

You **collect**, or **gather, your wits** when you try to think calmly: *Eva gathered her wits together. She must concentrate hard so she could report in full detail when she got back.*

have your 'wits about you or keep your 'wits about you

You **have**, or **are keeping, your wits about you** when you are constantly prepared to deal with dangers and difficulties: *For this kind of interview you need all your wits about you, which means being well prepared and getting a good night's sleep beforehand.*

pit your 'wits

You **pit your wits** against someone when you compete with them in a trial of intelligence: *Here's your chance to pit your wits against the world champions.*

scared out of your 'wits

You are **scared out of your wits** when you are terrified: *Frightened? Sonny, I was scared out of my wits, and that's the truth.*

wives

old 'wives' tale

An **old wives' tale** is a piece of advice, often related to curing health problems, which was believed to work in the past, but which we now know to be ineffective: *'Oh come on, that's just an old wives' tale.' 'No it's not, it works.'*

wobbly

throw a 'wobbly (*informal*)

Someone **throws a wobbly** when they suddenly become very angry about something: *It's no good trying to work with someone who throws a wobbly every time something goes wrong.*

◇ SEE ALSO **go off at the deep end** ▷ END; **ha** a blue fit ▷ FIT; **blow a fuse** ▷ FUSE; **blow** **gasket** ▷ GASKET; **let fly** ▷ LET; **blow or fl** **your lid** ▷ LID; **do your nut** ▷ NUT; **lose you** **rag** ▷ RAG; **fly into a rage** ▷ RAGE; **hit th** **roof** ▷ ROOF; **blow your stack** ▷ STACK; **lo** **your temper** ▷ TEMPER; **blow your top** ▷ TO

woe

woe be'tide so-and-so

You say **'woe betide'** anyone who disobey a certain rule as a warning that they will b punished, or that you will be very angr *We were allowed to get two out of ten wron Woe betide you if you got three or mor wrong.* □ *She seldom smiled and woe betic anyone not paying attention.*

> In old English, **woe betide** literally meant 'misery happen'.

wolf

the big bad 'wolf

Someone or something that is referred to a **the big bad wolf** causes people to fee threatened or afraid: *I do get a bit tire of being the permanent big bad wolf. I hav occasionally been known to be kind to pec ple, you know.*

cry 'wolf

You **cry wolf** when you regularly ask fo help or give people warning of an imagir ary fear, so that when you really do nee help, or when there is a real danger, peopl no longer believe you: *He nearly said, 'M wife is ill,' but he had cried wolf too ofter*

keep the 'wolf from the door

If you do something to **keep the wolf fror the door**, you do it in order to keep awa poverty or hunger: *I work part-time in library, just to pay the mortgage and kee the wolf from the door. Really, I'm a writer*

a lone 'wolf

A **lone wolf** is someone who is very inde pendent, and who enjoys living and work ing alone: *You know how he is – a lone wol That's what made him a successful foreig correspondent.*

a wolf in sheep's 'clothing

Someone who is described as **a wolf i** **sheep's clothing** is a dangerous or cruel person who appears to be gentle and harm less: *The murderer was a really first-grad monster. A beast. A raving wolf in sheep' clothing.*

◇ SEE ALSO **a snake in the grass** ▷ SNAKE

wonder

chinless 'wonder

A **chinless wonder** is a weak or foolish, usually upper class, man: *a chinless wonder in a baggy suit and powder blue trainers, saying 'And where have you been all my life?'*

little 'wonder or no 'wonder or small 'wonder

If you say that it is **little**, or **no**, or **small**, **wonder** that something is the case, you mean that it is not surprising that it is: *The number of cases of skin cancer has more than doubled to at least 3,000. Small wonder that doctors are calling for the return of the parasol.*

wonders

do 'wonders or work 'wonders

Someone or something **does**, or **works**, **wonders** if they achieve marvellous results: *Have some of this, it works wonders for indigestion.*

wonders will never 'cease

If someone says **'wonders will never cease'** they mean, humorously, or sarcastically, that they are pleasantly surprised because they didn't expect the person in question to do or achieve something in particular, or the thing in question to happen: *I can't believe it! Wonders will never cease. How did you manage it?*

wood

can't see the wood for the 'trees

If·you say that someone **can't see the wood for the trees**, you mean that they are so concerned with detail that they cannot see the obvious or general point: *One of the main features of people under stress is that very often they can't see the wood for the trees.*

touch 'wood

You superstitiously say **'touch wood!'**, sometimes touching something wooden at the same time, when you have just said that things are all right, and you do not want them to go wrong: *I look on life with a great deal of optimism, and touch wood, I've been fairly lucky in my life.*

woodwork

come out of the 'woodwork or crawl out of the 'woodwork

People and things that **come**, or **crawl**, **out of the woodwork** make themselves known after having been hidden for a long time: *All sorts of secrets started crawling out of the woodwork after a few drinks.*

wool

pull the 'wool over someone's eyes

You **pull the wool over someone's eyes** when you deliberately deceive or trick them: *I'm not stupid. You can't pull the wool over my eyes like that. I'm not so easily fooled, oh no.*

word

as good as your 'word

Someone who is **as good as their word** keeps a promise: *She had always promised her schoolfriend a room when she got her own apartment. She was as good as her word.*
◇ SEE ALSO **true to your word** ▷ WORD

by word of 'mouth

You receive information **by word of mouth** when you hear it from people, rather than read it or hear it on radio or television: *Such events succeeded in attracting large audiences via word of mouth invitations.*

a dirty 'word

If you say that such-and-such is **a dirty word** for a particular person or group of people, you mean that they do not like the particular person or thing mentioned, and that they may react badly if you mention them: *In most 'serious' artists' studios, from Paris to New York, prettiness was indeed a dirty word.*

from the word 'go

Something that has been the case **from the word go**, has been so since the beginning: *The marriage was a disaster from the word go, although I didn't realize this until it was all over.*

the 'F word

People sometimes say **'the F word'** to talk about the word 'fuck': *Every other word they use is an F word!*
◇ SEE ALSO **four-letter word** ▷ LETTER

get a word in 'edgeways

You **can't get a word in edgeways** when someone else is talking so much that you cannot get a chance to speak: *Whenever Barker was allowed to get a word in edgeways, it was obvious that he would be fascinating if only Hamilton would remain silent long enough for him to speak.*

give your 'word

You **give your word** when you make a promise: *Francis, you promised! That was part of the deal! You gave your word, and now you're telling me it's not on.*

go back on your 'word

You **go back on your word** when you do not do something that you said, or promised you would do: *All sorts of doubts clouded my mind. What if the dealer had a cash-in-hand offer from someone else and went back on his word?*

have the last 'word

You **have the last word** in an argument when you make the final remark: *You always have to have the last word, don't you? Can't you just let it rest?*

the last word in 'such-and-such

Someone or something that is described as **the last word in** a particular thing is the best, most recent, or most fashionable of their kind: *The driver, anxious to be the last word in customer care, drove at a snail's pace so that passengers could walk beside the train and pick flowers.*

not breathe a 'word

If you say that you will **not breathe a word**, you mean that you will not tell a particular secret to anyone: *Do you promise not to breathe a word to anyone?*

not have a good word to 'say about

Someone who **does not have a good word to say about** a certain person or thing does not like them, and considers that they have a lot of faults: *His wife definitely was aware of the relationship and never had a good word to say about Mary.* □ *They don't have a good word to say for marriage.*
◇ SEE ALSO **have something against** ▷ AGAINST

put in a good 'word

You **put in a good word** for someone when you speak about them to someone influential in a way that gives a good impression of them: *Because he put in a good word for her, Ruth was given the job without references.*

say the 'word

If you tell someone to '**say the word**', or '**just say the word**', you mean that they should tell you as soon as they need your help, advice, etc: *What would you like now? Cereal? Toast? Fruit? Just say the word.*

spread the 'word

You **spread the word** when you make sure that as many people as possible know about a particular thing: *I'd like you to spread the word around and tell people what my business is, and that if they need me I'll be able to help and charge only a little interest.*

take someone at their 'word

You **take someone at their word** when you accept what they say as being true without checking that it is so: *The problem is whether to take a politician at his word when he is publicly declaring a desire for greater friendship and understanding with these people.*

take my 'word for it

You say to someone '**take my word for it**' when you want them to know that what you are saying is true, and that they should

trust you: *There are things I can't tell you guys, you'll just have to take my word for it*

there's many a true word spoken in 'jest

If someone says '**there's many a true word spoken in jest**', they mean that a lot of jokes people make actually have a basis in truth

true to your 'word

You are **true to your word** when you do what you say you will do, or keep a promise: *'Now Felix, if you stand there I shall lash out at the next off ball and knock you down.' Felix did not move and true to his word the batsman knocked him down.*
◇ SEE ALSO **as good as your word** ▷ WORD

word for 'word

1 You repeat something **word for word** when you say the exact words that you heard: *When she recounted word for word the interview she had had with Moran they exploded into wild laughter.* **2** You translate **word for word** when you translate into words that correspond exactly with those in the original language: *They recognize that it is inadequate and sometimes completely misleading to translate the text word for word.*

word gets 'round

You say '**word gets round**' to talk about the large number of people who have already heard about something: *It's very hard to get work, it's a very small community and if you're bad word gets around.*

a word in someone's 'ear

You have **a word in someone's ear** when you tell them something secretly, or when you tell them something that you think they ought to know: *I wonder if I could just have a word in your ear before we continue with the next point on the agenda?*

a word of 'caution

You say '**a word of caution**' to introduce a warning or piece of advice: *A word of caution: if you don't start working early on in the term, you'll never be able to complete all the assignments.*

words

eat your 'words or swallow your 'words

You have to **eat**, or **swallow**, **your words** when you are forced to admit that something you said before was wrong: *As soon as I've proved I'm not what he thinks, he'll have to eat his words.*

famous last 'words

You say '**famous last words**' when you think that someone has been too confidently optimistic about something: *Before going to prison he was allowed to go and see her, and she told him, 'I won't divorce you while you're in prison.' Famous last words.*

have 'words with someone
You **have words**, or **have words with someone**, when you have an angry argument with them: *You know. I was in a bad mood, and he kept pestering me, so we had words.*

in words of one 'syllable
You explain something **in words of one syllable** when you explain it very clearly and simply: *Everything has to be explained to them in words of one syllable. They're driving me mad.*

mark my 'words (*rather old*)
'**Mark my words**' is a rather old-fashioned way of saying 'take notice of what I'm saying': *I'm against it myself. It will lead to nothing but trouble, you mark my words.*

not mince your 'words
Someone who **does not mince their words** does not try to avoid offending people when telling them something unpleasant: *She told me that our separation was all my fault because I was too proud to admit I was in the wrong. She doesn't mince her words.*
◊ SEE ALSO **call a spade a spade** ▷ SPADE

put words into someone's 'mouth
Someone who **puts words into your mouth** states that you have said something that you have not said, or suggests that you are about to say something that you have no intention of saying: *I did not say that about you! Don't you dare put words into my mouth!*

take the words out of someone's 'mouth
Someone who **takes the words out of your mouth** says exactly what you were intending to say.

words 'fail me
You say '**words fail me**' when you are so surprised, overwhelmed or annoyed that you cannot express yourself: *Words fail me in praise of your company and its workforce.* □ *I cannot and will not tolerate incompetence. And as for you, Fiona, words fail me.*

work

all work and no 'play
When people talk about '**all work and no play**', or say '**all work and no play makes Jack a dull boy**' they mean that too much working and not enough enjoyment leads to inefficiency, and may make you bored, or boring: *Well, don't work too late. You know the old saying about all work and no play?* □ *It seems that all work and no play, even in the workplace, makes not only for a dull boy, but also one that is not as efficient.*

do someone's 'dirty work
You **do someone's dirty work** when you do the unpleasant jobs that they do not want to do, especially when it involves explaining or apologizing for mistakes, or telling people things that they will not like hearing: *They asked me to protest to get them off the hook. I told them to do their own dirty work.*

have your 'work cut out
You **have your work cut out** when you face a challenging task: *The leaders had their work cut out keeping the group together, and one or both had to remain at the back to motivate the slower ones.*

make light 'work of something
You **make light work of** a task when you do it very quickly and efficiently: *Make light work of cooking with the help of this electronic food processor.*

nice work if you can 'get it
People say '**nice work if you can get it**' when they approve of a particular arrangement or job that someone has: *She was lying on the bed as she studied Kim Basinger and Mickey Rourke indulging in the ultimate nice work if you can get it.*

workman

a bad workman always blames his 'tools
If someone says '**a bad workman always blames his tools**' they mean that it is typical of an incompetent person to criticize their equipment, or other external factors, rather than recognize their own failings.

world

all the world and his 'wife
If someone says that **all the world and his wife** were present at an occasion, they mean that large numbers, or crowds of people, were there: *It seemed that all the world and his wife were in Madrid for the Olympics.*

dead to the 'world
You are **dead to the world** if you are very deeply asleep: *I hadn't realized how tired I was till I saw that bed. Fifteen minutes later I was dead to the world.*

do you a 'world of good
Something that **does you a world of good** makes you feel much better: *Everyone should spend a week somewhere like this once a year. It does you a world of good.*
◊ SEE ALSO **bring some colour to your cheeks** ▷ COLOUR

give the 'world
You say that you would **give the world for** something, or to do something, if you would like to do, or have, it very much: *I'd give the world to have long legs like those.*
◊ SEE ALSO **give your right arm** ▷ ARM; **give your ears** ▷ EARS; **give your eyeteeth** ▷ EYETEETH; **give your right hand** ▷ HAND

worlde

go 'up in the world

You **go up in the world** if you are successful: *John's gone up in the world since he left school. I hear he's a merchant banker in the City now.*

have the 'world at your feet

Someone who **has the world at their feet** is very successful and admired by many people: *You've got the world at your feet, everything you've ever wanted, and look at you. You're still unhappy.*

in another 'world

1 Someone who is **in another world** is detached from everyday life, or very absent minded: *'He lives in another world half the time.'* **2** If you say that you feel like you are **in another world**, you mean that you feel good or strange, in a situation that is completely different from your normal life: *When the music starts I walk out on stage and the spotlight hits me. It's magic. Suddenly I'm in another world.*

◊ SEE ALSO **in a world of your own** ▷ WORLD

in a world of your 'own

Someone who is **in a world of their own** is detached from everyday life, and preoccupied with their own thoughts: *Never mind. The old man evidently lived in a world of his own; it's pointless blaming him.*

◊ SEE ALSO **in another world** ▷ WORLD

mean the 'world to someone

Someone **means the world to you** if you are very fond of them, or if you love them very much; something **means the world to you** if it is very important to you: *She means the world to me. That's why I've got to try, even though it looks hopeless.*

not long for this 'world

Someone who is **not long for this world** will probably die soon: *Even at a glance he was clearly not long for this world, yet between bouts of coughing he was giving instructions and advice to the surgeon.*

◊ SEE ALSO **at death's door** ▷ DEATH

out of this 'world

Something that is **out of this world** is marvellous, or excellent: *The food and the service there is out of this world.*

set the 'world on fire

Someone who **sets the world on fire** is very successful and makes a good reputation for themselves: *He hasn't exactly set the world on fire with his performance this year, has he?*

> This idiom commonly appears in the negative.

tell the 'world

You **tell the world** something, or about something, when you let as many people

as possible know about something, often something private: *Their honeymoon had been 'fabulous', said Diana, with enthusiasm and dying to tell the world.*

think the 'world of

You **think the world of** someone if you love or admire them greatly: *Lee thinks the world of that dog.*

watch the 'world go by

You **watch the world go by** when you sit in a public place and look at people as they go past: *The café terrace is an ideal place to relax and watch the world go by, and its à la carte restaurant has excellent food and is well known amongst the local residents.*

what is the world 'coming to?

People, especially older people, say **'what is the world coming to?'** when they are shocked at the things people do these days, compared to how they remember the world in their youth: *Honestly, 95p for a tin of grapefruit. What's the world coming to?*

the world at 'large *(formal)*

The world at large means 'people in general': *The question is, whether this policy will be accepted by the world at large.*

the world is your 'oyster

If someone says **'the world is your oyster'**, they mean that all opportunities in life are open to you: *These may be tough methods, but if you survive them, the world will be your oyster.*

> Some oysters have pearls inside them, and are therefore seen as a symbol of wealth and opportunity.

a 'world of difference

There is **a world of difference** between things if they are entirely different: *There is a world of difference between ham that has been sliced from the bone and the prepackaged wet and tasteless substance that so many people believe to be ham.*

wouldn't do something for the 'world

You say that you **wouldn't do something for the world** if you want never to do it: *All the effort is worth it. I wouldn't give him up for the world.*

worlde

olde 'worlde or oldy-'worldy

Something such as a building or town that is described as **olde worlde**, or **oldy-worldy**, is very old and traditional in an attractive, or possibly artificial, way: *Unspoilt Cornish and Devon countryside, old market towns, picturesque villages, olde worlde inns, ancient churches, charming little coves and a choice of lovely beaches.*

worlds

the best of 'both worlds

You get **the best of both worlds** when you can enjoy two things that cannot usually be enjoyed together: *Working and looking after children part-time gives me the best of both worlds.*
◊ SEE ALSO **the grass is always greener on the other side of the fence** ▷ GRASS; **have your cake and eat it** ▷ CAKE

'worlds apart

Things that are **worlds apart** are entirely different: *The Chinese food you get here and the food you get in China are worlds apart.*
◊ SEE ALSO **poles apart** ▷ POLES

worm

a worm's eye 'view

A **worm's eye view** is the way someone who is closely involved in something sees it: *Those accepted for training at Sotheby's will get a one year worm's-eye view of the company in three or more departments and they will be paid £9,500.*

This idiom is derived from the more common 'bird's eye view', meaning a good view, especially from above. Worms live in the earth, and so 'view' things from the inside.

the worm has 'turned

If you say that **the worm has turned**, you mean that someone who has suffered over a long period of time has decided not to tolerate an unpleasant situation any longer: *Ever since I came here, you have treated me like dirt! Well, the worm has turned, madam!*

worst

if the worst comes to the 'worst

You say that something may happen **if the worst comes to the worst** if you think it may happen if things develop in the most unfavourable way: *Look, if the worst comes to the worst and you really can't contact us, we'll just have to come looking for you.*
◊ SEE ALSO **worst case scenario** ▷ CASE

wounds

lick your 'wounds

You say that someone **is licking their wounds** when they are comforting themselves after something painful or disappointing has happened to them, especially if you do not feel a great amount of sympathy for them: *They had met at Ascot in June 1977 when Sarah was licking her wounds after her romance with the Duke of Westminster had ended.*

When an animal has been injured, it licks its wounds in order to help them heal.

wraps

keep under 'wraps

You **keep something under wraps** when you keep it hidden or secret: *All this has to be kept under wraps, Newman. You've signed the Official Secrets Act.*

take the 'wraps off

You take **the wraps off** something when you finally reveal it or expose it to public view: *IBM is finally ready to take the wraps off the parallel processing system it is developing.*

wreck

nervous 'wreck

Someone who is described as a **nervous wreck** is in a bad or exhausted state of physical and mental health: *By the end of that relationship she was a nervous wreck, and had to spend some time in hospital.*

wringer

put someone through the 'wringer

You **put someone through the wringer** when you ask them difficult questions in order to find out if they are doing their job properly: *Barry Fry wants to put Stan Flashman through the wringer by forcing him to account for yesterday's decision to sack him as manager.*

A **wringer** is a device that squeezes water out of wet cloth.

wrongs

two wrongs don't make a 'right

If someone says '**two wrongs don't make a right**', they mean that it is foolish to think that just because someone has hurt or angered you, that you should do the same to them in return: *I do not think there is any punishment in this world that would fit what they have done. My instinct would be to do the same to them, but two wrongs don't make a right.*

y

yard

not in 'my back yard

The 'not in my back yard' attitude is a reaction of people who ignore unpleasant things while others are suffering, and only protest when they themselves are directly affected: *People concerned about proposals that would spoil green fields with development, are often branded as 'NIMBYs' (Not In My Back Yard-ers), but there is nothing wrong with seeking to safeguard the beauty of the place you live in.*

> A back yard is a paved area behind a house.

yarn

spin a 'yarn

Someone **spins a yarn** when they tell you a story, usually with a great degree of exaggeration: *He spun me some yarn about coming face to face with a shark.*

> In this idiom, telling a long exaggerated story is likened to drawing out and twisting fibres.

yea

yea or 'nay

You tell someone **yea or nay** when you accept or refuse an offer, or agree to or refuse a request: *We accept its rules because we wish to do so. This right to say yea or nay clearly indicates the continuing supremacy of the Parliament.*

> Yea and nay are old-fashioned words for 'yes' and 'no'.

year

New Year's reso'lution

A **New Year's resolution** is a decision you take at the beginning of the New Year to stop doing something you consider bad, or to start doing something you consider good: *Mum's made her usual New Year's resolution – to lose weight.*

see in the New 'Year

You **see in the New Year** when you celebrate the arrival of the New Year at mid-night on the 31st of December. *The home video shows him enjoying a family Christmas but detectives believe he didn't live long enough to see in the New Year.*

since the year 'dot

Something that has been happening **since the year dot** has been happening since the beginning, or ever since you can remember: *Traditionally, scientists have been involved in war since the year dot.*

year in year 'out

Something that happens **year in year out** happens regularly and unchangingly over a very long period of time: *He had kept the same job, they had lived in the same house, they had rented the same seaside bungalow for a summer holiday, year in year out.*

years

put 'years on someone

Someone or something that **puts years on you** makes you look or feel much older: *I'm not keen on that beard – puts years on him.*

roll back the 'years

You **roll back the years** when you think about, or make people think about, the past: *Old Jimbo can still roll back the years and reach into his glorious past, and how he loved it as the crowd roared for him.*

you

how was it for 'you?

'**How was it for you?**' is a question that people supposedly ask their partner after having sex, in order to find out how much they had enjoyed it.

◇ SEE ALSO **the earth moved** ▷ EARTH

> This idiom is only used mockingly or in jokes now.

young

you're only young 'once

If someone says '**you're only young once**', they mean that you have to take advantage of being young, because there are some things you won't be able to do any more when you are older: *'Oh, I don't know.' Vi pursed her lips. 'You're only young once.*

May as well enjoy yourself. □ *'You're right, Pat,' she agreed. 'Life is short and they're only young once.'*

◇ SEE ALSO **live for the day** ▷ DAY; **seize the day** ▷ DAY

younger

not getting any 'younger

If you say that someone **is not getting any younger**, you mean that they are getting old, or that there are some things they cannot do as well as they could when they were younger: *A smiled curved her lips. 'Actually I think I'd rather like to have a child. Besides, we can't leave it too late, we're not getting any younger, you know.'*

◇ SEE ALSO **over the hill** ▷ HILL; **past it** ▷ PAST; **no spring chicken** ▷ CHICKEN

yours

up 'yours (*offensive*)

Up yours! is a very rude expression of contempt: *You think I look funny? Up yours.*

Z

zip

zip 'up (*informal, offensive*)

If you tell someone to **'zip up!'** you are telling them, rudely, to be quiet: *Can you please zip up, just for five minutes?*

A **zip** is a device for fastening clothes and bags, consisting of two rows of metal or nylon teeth with a sliding tab which you pull to make the two rows of teeth fit into each other. This idiom humorously suggests that you can close your mouth with a zip.

SUBJECT INDEX

You can use this index to find idioms related to a subject you want to talk or write about. You will find the idioms, with their definitions, in the main text of the dictionary at the page indicated.

A

affection
all over someone 7
the apple of someone's eye 8
bill and coo 26
blue-eyed boy 35
hold a candle for someone 46
have a crush on someone 76
cupboard love 77
ewe lamb 108
the light of someone's life 185
pride and joy 266
get under someone's skin 311
soul mate 317
have a soft spot for someone 319
a term of endearment 337

age
young at heart 149
over the hill 152
old as the hills 234
past it 245
Peter Pan 250
pushing such-and-such an age 272
no spring chicken 320
old timer 349
long in the tooth 352
olde worlde 384
not getting any younger 387

agreeing
agree to differ 5
be agreed 5
in agreement 5
in bed with 21
gentlemen's agreement 131
just so 164
that's just it 164
at one 235

quite so 275
too right 285
you're telling me 336

anger
go up in the air 5
throw up your arms 9
up in arms 9
like a bear with a sore head 19
beside yourself with something 24
bad blood 29
make someone's blood boil 30
raise Cain 45
cut up rough 78
curse the day 81
the devil to pay 86
go to the devil 86
drive someone mad 94
go off the deep end 104
have a blue fit 123
send someone away with a flea in their ear 123
blow a fuse 129
blow a gasket 131
in God's name 134
fly off the handle 144
lose your head 148
give someone hell 151
hornet's nest 154
hue and cry 155
have, or get, the hump 155
stew in your own juice 164
let fly 180
blow, or flip, your lid 182
a black look 191
if looks could kill 192
hopping mad 196
foam at the mouth 219
so-and-so's name is mud 222
do your nut 230
take it out on someone 238
give someone a piece of your mind 251
like a red rag to a bull 276

lose your rag 276
fly into a rage 276
rant and rave 278
read the riot act 286
get a rise out of someone 286
see red 300
give someone the rough side of your tongue 307
go spare 317
sparks fly 318
blow your stack 320
let off steam 322
cause a stink 323
tear someone off a strip 327
get something out of your system 331
throw a tantrum 334
gnash your teeth 336
set someone's teeth on edge 336
in a temper 336
lose your temper 337
on bad terms 337
jump down someone's throat 344
look like thunder 345
like a ton of bricks 351
blow your top 352
climb the walls 369
on the warpath 370
throw a wobbly 380
have words with someone 383

annoyance
drive someone round the bend 23
be in someone's bad books 33
browned off 39
rattle someone's cage 45
hot under the collar 63
drive someone mad 94
not hear the end of something 104
ruffle someone's feathers 118

(annoyance continued)
get someone's goat 133
make someone's hackles rise 141
beyond a joke 162
kick yourself 167
the limit 186
get on someone's nerves 225
get up someone's nose 227
a pain in the neck 241
try the patience of a saint 246
rub it in 291
get under someone's skin 311
so-and-so will not thank someone for 338
have another think coming 342
a thorn in your side 343
get on someone's tits 350
tread on, or step on, someone's toes 351
drive someone round the twist 362
up to here 364
drive someone up the wall 369
rub up the wrong way 373
get on someone's wick 377

things people say when they are annoyed or angry
give me a break 37
for Christ's sake 57
for crying out loud! 76
I'm damned if such-and-such 79
that does it 89
down with so-and-so! 92
drop dead 94
enough is enough 106
get out of my face 113
for God's sake 133
for goodness sake 135
for heaven's sake 150
what's the big idea? 156
knock it off 170
I don't know 171
look here 191
For the love of God 193
do you mind? 210
for Pete's sake 250
what's your problem? 268

appearance
bag of bones 14
bald as a coot 15

beauty is in the eye of the beholder 20
beauty is only skin deep 20
go beetroot 22
the belle of the ball 23
in your birthday suit 27
a bit of all right 27
black and blue 28
a blot on the landscape 30
like something the cat brought in 50
grin like a Cheshire cat 54
cut a dash 80
done up like a dog's dinner 90
look like a million dollars 91
an ugly duckling 95
grin from ear to ear 97
like nothing on earth 99
a face like the back of a bus 113
knee-high to a grasshopper 137
not a hair out of place 141
head and shoulders above 147
plain Jane 160
look your best 191
not much to look at 191
good looks 192
mutton dressed as lamb 221
dressed up to the nines 226
nose-job 228
no oil painting 234
pale as death 241
look the part 243
pigeon-toed 253
poker face 261
pretty as a picture 265
a drowned rat 278
put the roses back in someone's cheeks 290
not a pretty sight 309
a sight for sore eyes 309
skin and bone 311
spick and span 318
from top to toe 353
spare tyre 362
as ugly as sin 363
warts and all 370
white as a sheet 377
put years on someone 386

arguing
battle of wills 18
battle of wits 18
come to blows 30
have a bone to pick with someone 33

fight your corner 70
at daggers drawn 79
play the devil's advocate 87
ding-dong 88
fan the flames 123
have it out with someone 146
make an issue of something 159
a sore point 260
the rights and wrongs of 285
have a run-in with someone 292
have crossed swords 330
at each other's throats 344
have the last word 382

avoiding people and things
at arm's length 9
give a wide berth 24
stay clear of 59
keep your distance 89
a near miss 213
play hard to get 257
out of someone's way 373

B

birth
give birth 27
the happy event 107
the patter of tiny feet 246
breed like rabbits 276

boredom
bored stiff 34
browned off 39
dry as dust 94
at a loose end 103
have had enough 106
in a rut 293
twiddle your thumbs 345

C

taking care
make a fuss of someone 129
at someone with kid gloves 133
split hairs 142
in safe hands 145
nit-picking 227
please yourself 258

not caring
not give a damn 79
not care a fig 120

heart of stone 149
not give a hoot or *not care a*
  hoot or *not give two hoots*
  153
not give a monkey's 216
not give a shit 304
tough shit 305
no skin off your nose 311
not care a sod 315
not give a tinker's cuss 350
not give, or *care, a toss* 354
not give, or *care, tuppence*
  361
like water off a duck's back
  371

cause and effect

at the bottom of 35
get to the bottom of 35
the chicken and the egg 55
in consequence 68
by dint of such-and-such 88
down to so-and-so 92
get to the root of something
  289
the root cause of something
  289
one thing leads to another
  340
the thing is 341
by virtue of 368
in the wake of something
  369
pave the way for 373
whys and wherefores 377

certainty

feel it in your bones 33
for certain 51
make certain 52
bet your bottom dollar 91
beyond all doubt 92
without a doubt 92
beyond question 273
it's only a question of time
  274
without question 274
beyond any shadow of doubt
  302
bet your shirt on 304
sure as eggs is eggs 329

change

the boot is on the other foot
  34
for a change 53
have a change of heart 53
make a change 53
ring the changes 53
chop and change 56

put a different complexion on
  something 66
culture shock 76
the damage is done 79
from one day to the next 81
by degrees 85
go to the dogs 90
go downhill 92
down the drain 93
ebb and flow 100
turn of events 107
turn over a new leaf 177
in the making 197
break the mould 218
change out of all
  recognition 280
never the same again 295
a sign of the times 309
show signs of 309
slowly but surely 313
turn the tables 332
a different tack 332
fly off at a tangent 334
change your tune 360
take a turn for the better
  361
take a turn for the worse
  361
a turn-up for the book or
  books 361
U-turn 363
ups and downs 364
change your ways 374
a wind of change 378
variety is the spice of life
  366
a world of difference 384

not changing

die hard 87
you can't teach an old dog
  new tricks 90
fait accompli 115
a leopard never changes its
  spots 179
much the same 295
same as ever 295
set in tablets of stone 332

comparing people and
things

as against 4
a whole new ball game 16
for the better 25
it's as broad as it's long 39
tarred with the same brush
  40
not fit to hold a candle to
  46
carbon copy 70

like chalk and cheese 52
a chip off the old block 55
in a class of your own 58
have something in common
  65
beyond compare 66
by comparison 66
a far cry from 76
a cut above 78
same difference 88
six of one and half a dozen of
  the other 93
have the edge on someone
  100
head and shoulders above
  147
the spitting image of
  someone 157
a pale imitation 157
pale into insignificance 158
in keeping with something
  166
out of keeping with
  something 166
kettle of fish 167
the lesser of the two evils
  179
compare like with like 186
like as two peas in a pod
  186
meet your match 203
no match for 203
like-minded 212
cast in the same mould as
  someone 218
compare notes 229
on a par with something
  243
poles apart 261
in relation to such-and-such
  282
it remains to be seen 282
put someone in the shade
  302
put to shame 302
knock spots off 319
streets ahead 327
a world of difference 384

condition

in mint condition 67
have seen better days 83
in good nick 226
in bad repair 282
in good repair 282
sound as a bell 317
the worse for wear 374

criticism

pull to bits 28
put the boot in 34

(**criticsm** continued)
haul someone over the coals 62
ear-bashing 97
go easy on someone 100
in the extreme 109
pick holes in 153
face the music 221
pull to pieces 252
the pot calling the kettle black 262
bad press 265
a put-down 272
give someone a rap over the knuckles 278
pour scorn on 298
tear to shreds 307
give someone the rough side of your tongue 307
give someone stick 323
take someone to task 334
give someone a rough time 347

D

death
blow your brains out 36
breathe your last 38
kick the bucket 40
cash in your chips 56
shuffle off this mortal coil 62
pop your clogs 60
curtains for 77
pushing up the daisies 79
Davy Jones's locker 80
someone's days are numbered 82
dead as a doornail 83
at death's door 83
bite the dust 95
end it all 104
six feet under 119
the pearly gates 131
give up the ghost 132
beyond the grave 137
to an early grave 137
your hour has come 154
depart this life 183
give your life for 183
lose your life 184
meet your maker 197
in mourning 218
your number is up 230
last resting-place 256
the grim reaper 280
pay your last respects 283

lay someone to rest 283
put to sleep 312
snuff it 314
put to the sword 330
go the way of all flesh 372
not long for this world 384

making decisions
nail your colours to the mast 64
have the courage of your convictions 72
at a crossroads 75
come to the crunch 75
change your mind 210
make up your mind 211
in two minds 212
when push comes to shove 271
in a quandary 273
sleep on it 312
in a cleft stick 323
um and aah 363
New Year's resolution 386

getting what you deserve
get your come-uppance 64
have it coming to you 65
take the consequences 68
deserve whatever you get 86
get your just deserts 85
serve someone right 302

determination
over my dead body 32
take the bull by the horns 41
mean business 43
at all costs 71
at any cost 71
stay the course 72
hang on like grim death 84
have designs on 86
to the bitter end 105
put up a good fight 120
put your foot down 126
hold your ground 138
stick to your guns 139
with guns blazing 139
move heaven and earth 150
dig your heels in 150
come hell or high water 150
hell bent on 151
see someone in hell 151
keep at it 166
go to great lengths 179
for dear life 183

not for love nor money 193
you can't keep a good man down 200
by fair means or foul 205
grasp the nettle 225
rise to the occasion 232
stay the pace 240
at any price 266
never say die 296
stop at nothing 324
pull out all the stops 324
for all the tea in China 335
with a vengeance 366
where there's a will there's a way 377

difficulties
asking for it 10
have your back to the wall 13
the bane of your life 17
get out of bed on the wrong side 21
bite off more than you can chew 27
bogged down 32
cross that bridge when you come to it 38
can of worms 46
to cap it all 47
the cards are stacked against someone 47
set the cat among the pigeons 50
Catch twenty-two 51
poisoned chalice 52
when the chips are down 56
vicious circle 57
too many cooks spoil the broth 69
box someone into a corner 70
cost someone dear 71
up the creek without a paddle 74
have a cross to bear 75
to crown it all 75
lame duck 95
in at the deep end 104
keep your end up 105
one of those days 83
out of your depth 85
lead someone a dance 80
not be someone's day 82
the death of someone 84
fall about so-and-so's ears 98
set someone by the ears 98
the end of someone 104
to the bitter end 105
your own worst enemy 105

put a brave face on it 114
a fate worse than death 117
no mean feat 118
out of the frying pan into the fire 128
fun and games 129
up a gum tree 139
tear your hair out over something 141
play merry hell with 151
for the life of me 183
have a job 161
kettle of fish 167
tie yourself in knots 171
to make matters worse 204
make a meal of something 204
a hard nut to crack 230
against all the odds 232
a tall order 237
no picnic 251
queer the pitch 255
hard pressed 265
make a rod for your own back 288
there lies the rub 291
easier said than done 294
in the hot seat 300
in the shit 304
the shit hits the fan or *the shit flies* 304
up shit creek 305
no-win situation 310
sticky situation 310
slings and arrows 312
in the soup 317
in a tight spot 319
on the spot 319
teething troubles 336
in trouble 358
up against it 363
in deep water 371
in hot water 371
make waves 372

disagreeing
beg to differ 22
a bone of contention 33
on the contrary 68
not see eye to eye 110
you could have fooled me 125
the hell you are or *the hell you do* or *like hell* 151
take issue with 159
that's just it 164
at loggerheads 190
at odds with 233
with respect 282
argue the toss 353

disbelief
(not) believe your ears 98
(not) believe your eyes 111
believe something when you see it 23
if you believe that, you'll believe anything 23
not born yesterday 34
come off it! 64
do me a favour 117
don't give me that 132
too good to be true 135
the hell you are or *the hell you do* or *like hell* 151
hocus pocus 152
you're joking 163
you're kidding 167
don't make me laugh 175
a load of rubbish 190
tell that to the marines 201
never, or *not, for one minute* 212
never, or *not, for one moment* 215
pigs might fly 253
pull the other one 270
a likely story 325
a tall story 325
all talk 333
tell me another 336
hearing things 341
not wash 370
words fail me 383

dishonesty
cook the books 33
in breach of such-and-such 37
funny business 42
cock-and-bull 62
a guilty conscience 67
under the counter 71
sink to such depths 85
in bad faith 115
on the fiddle 120
have light fingers 122
have your fingers in the till 122
flatter to deceive 123
up to no good 135
a put-up job 162
a white lie 182
feed someone a line 187
shoot someone a line 187
funny money 215
monkey business 216
a pack of lies 240
foul play 257
tell porkies 261
sharp practice 264

under false pretences 265
pull a fast one 270
sell someone a pup 270
put one over on someone 272
take someone for a ride 284
have the shirt off someone's back 304
laugh up your sleeve 312
sleight of hand 312
slippery as an eel 313
on the sly 313
a snake in the grass 314
under the table 332
lie through your teeth 336
a tissue of lies 350
speak with forked tongue 352
economical with the truth 360
wheel and deal 376
a wolf in sheep's clothing 380
pull the wool over someone's eyes 381
spin a yarn 388

distance
as the crow flies 75
short cut 78
in spitting distance 89
on your doorstep 91
door to door 91
a hair's breadth 141
near, or *close, at hand* 144
a stone's throw 324

drink
hit the bottle 35
bottoms up! 35
Dutch courage 72
half cut 78
cannot hold your drink 94
the demon drink 94
drink to 94
drive someone to drink 94
the worse for drink 94
drunk as a lord 94
pink elephants 102
have had a few or *a few too many* 119
drink like a fish 122
the hair of the dog 141
out of your head 148
under the influence 158
here's mud in your eye! 220
a quick one 274
one for the road 287
one over the eight 236
well-oiled 234

(drink continued)
piss artist 254
piss-up 254
pissed as a fart 255
what's your poison? 261
rat-arsed 278
drown your sorrows 316
drink someone under the table 332
on the wagon 369

E

ease
and Bob's your uncle 32
chickenfeed 55
child's play 55
cop-out 69
crystal clear 76
take to something like a duck to water 95
easy as ABC 100
no hassle 146
kids' stuff 168
anything for a quiet life 182
second nature 223
nothing to it 229
the soft option 236
a pushover 271
plain sailing 295
the easiest thing in the world 339
walk it 369
elementary my dear Watson 371
downhill all the way 372
take the easy way out 373

effort
all out 7
get your arse in gear 10
break the back of something 12
break your back 12
beaver away 20
do your bit 27
take a bit of doing 27
blood, sweat and tears 29
sweat blood 30
can't be bothered 34
stay the course 72
in earnest 98
elbow grease 102
a fool's errand 125
bust a gut 139
work your guts out 139
huff and puff 155
go to great lengths 179
labour of love 173

be at pains 241
make a point of 259
put your shoulder to the wheel 306
a sledgehammer to crack a nut 312
pull your socks up 315
pull out all the stops 324
fight tooth and nail 352
go to town on something 355
go to a lot of trouble 358
take the trouble to or *go to the trouble of* 358
do your utmost 365
go out of your way 372
pull your weight 375

embarrassment
drop a brick 38
look a Charley 54
drop a clanger 58
curl up and die 77
I'd rather die 87
make an exhibition of yourself 109
faux pas 117
make a fool of yourself 125
put your foot in your mouth 126
I shudder to think 307
sticky situation 310
make a spectacle of yourself 318
you can't take so-and-so anywhere 333

encouragement
right behind someone 22
fingers crossed 121
go for it 133
knock 'em dead 170
break a leg! 178
better luck next time 194
good luck 194

enjoying yourself
have a ball 16
have a field day 81
live for the day 81
seize the day 82
halcyon days 83
let your hair down 141
lap it up 175
live it up 189
the life of Riley 183
make merry 207
a night on the town 226
make a night of it 226
sow your wild oats 232

take pleasure in 258
in raptures about something 278
rave it up 279
enter into the spirit of 318
get into the swing of things 330
have the time of your life 347
paint the town red 355
a whale of a time 376
you're only young once 386

enthusiasm
all for 6
eager beaver 20
champ at the bit 27
get the bug 40
bursting to do something 42
get carried away 48
jump at the chance 53
keen as mustard 166
a new lease of life 177
like mad 196
go overboard for 239
on a roll 288
sold on something 315

escaping
break free 37
make a break 37
do a bunk 42
cut and run 78
get the hell out of 151
leg it 178
on the loose 192
run a mile 209
do a moonlight flit 217
show a clean pair of heels 241
beat a retreat 283
on the run 292
run for it 292
scot-free 298
give someone the slip 313

exclamation
Christ Almighty 57
for Christ's sake 57
stone the crows 75
for crying out loud 76
damn it 79
oh dear 83
fuck it 129
bloody hell 150
hell's bells 151
Lord 192
in the name of God 222
for Pete's sake 250
that's rich 398
stone me 324

F

failure

go down like a lead balloon 16

bang goes such-and-such 17

fight a losing battle 19

beginning of the end 22

draw a blank 28

go a complete blank 28

blow it 30

burn your boats 32

miss the boat 31

not have a cat in hell's chance 50

a lost cause 51

blow your chance 52

have had your chips 56

run, or go round in circles 57

go off at half-cock 62

come a cropper 75

someone's or something's days are numbered 82

sound the death knell 84

sign your own death warrant 84

done for 91

bite the dust 95

if all else fails 115

fall flat 116

slip through your fingers 122

fluff it 125

dig your own grave 137

come to grief 137

not have a hope in hell 154

bring someone to their knees 170

miss the mark 202

make a muck of something 220

a nail in the coffin of 222

go phut 251

make a pig's ear of something 252

couldn't organize a piss-up in a brewery 254

on the rocks 287

Sod's law 315

go up in smoke 313

damp squib 320

fall between two stools 324

down the tubes 360

come unstuck 363

go to the wall 369

wild-goose chase 377

piss into the wind 378

fear

make someone's blood run cold 30

bottle out 35

brave it out 37

shit bricks 38

bundle of nerves 41

have butterflies 43

a chill runs down your spine 55

pluck up your courage 72

scare the living daylights out of someone 82

in fear of your life 117

put the fear of God into someone 117

get cold feet 119

the fright of your life 128

make someone's hair stand on end 141

heart in your mouth 149

heebie-jeebies 150

shake like a jelly 161

turn to jelly 161

shake like a leaf 177

lose your nerve 225

scare someone shitless 297

give someone the shits 305

a shiver runs down your spine 305

give someone the shivers 305

rooted to the spot 319

sword of Damocles 330

give someone the willies 378

get the wind up 378

scared out of your wits 380

flirting

roving eye 110

flutter your eyelashes at someone 111

make eyes at someone 112

a ladies' man 173

lady-killer 173

chat-up line 187

Latin lover 193

on the make 197

food

have a bite to eat 27

fit to burst 42

dig in 88

doggy bag 90

get such-and-such down you 92

your eyes are bigger than your belly 112

eat your fill 120

I'm so hungry I could eat a horse 154

eat someone out of house and home 155

a square meal 204

meat and two veg 205

a burnt offering 234

make a pig of yourself 252

set a good table 332

feeding time at the zoo 347

done to a turn 361

go down the wrong way 372

wine and dine 378

foolishness

look a Charley 54

have egg on your face 101

make an exhibition of yourself 109

get your fingers burnt 121

act, or play, the fool 125

a fool and his money are soon parted 125

a fool's paradise 125

make a fool of yourself 125

more fool you 125

fools rush in 126

act the goat 133

head case 147

lose your head 148

take leave of your senses 178

a mug's game 220

nut-case 230

laughing stock 323

stuff and nonsense 328

forgiving

let bygones be bygones 44

no hard feelings 118

make your peace 246

wipe the slate clean 311

draw a veil over something 366

water under the bridge 371

G

telling people to go away

beat it 19

on yer bike 26

go to the devil 86

never darken someone's door again 91

show someone the door 91

get out of my face 113

go to hell 151

(telling people to go away continued)
sling your hook 153
hop it 153
take a running jump 164
get knotted 171
go jump in the lake 174
get lost 192
get out of my sight 309
sod off 315
get stuffed 328

H

health
alive and kicking 6
bring some colour to someones's cheeks 63
off-colour 63
out of condition 67
have the constitution of an ox 68
catch your death 84
look like death warmed up 84
like nothing on earth 99
at a low ebb 100
not feel yourself 118
fit as a fiddle 123
on top form 127
pale about the gills 132
hale and hearty 142
out of joint 162
not look yourself 191
on the mend 207
back to nature 223
overdo it 239
below par 242
right as rain 285
in shape 302
out of shape 302
out of sorts 317
up and about 363
in a bad way 373
under the weather 375
do you a world of good 383
nervous wreck 385

help
aid and abet 5
to the aid of someone or to someone's aid 5
with the aid of 5
in bed with 21
for the benefit of so-and-so 24
the blind leading the blind 29
bottle-feed 35

charity begins at home 54
too many cooks spoil the broth 69
for the common good 134
give, or lend, a hand 143
lean over backwards 177
give someone a leg-up 178
a life-saver 184
lighten someone's load 190
through the offices of 233
a tower of strength 355

I

idealism
build castles in the air 49
cloud cuckoo land 61
head in the clouds 147
flight of fancy 124
never-never land 174
pie in the sky 251
a pipe dream 254
chase rainbows 277

getting information
pick someone's brains 36
have your ear to the ground 97
put out feelers 118
keep abreast of something 166
find out how the land lies 174
spy out the land 174
the lie of the land 182

insults
cry-baby 12
old bag 15
bird brain 26
bossy boots 34
cock-teaser 62
cradle-snatcher 73
give someone two fingers 121
lady muck 173
dirty old man 198
shit-for-brains 304
son of a bitch 316
takes one to know one 333

J

joy
walk on air 6
thrilled to bits 28
on cloud nine 61

warm the cockles of someone's heart 62
happy as a sandboy 145
in seventh heaven 150
joie de vivre 162
over the moon 217
at one 235
pleased as Punch 258
in high spirits 318
on top of the world 353

K

not knowing
not know someone from Adam 3
Christ knows 57
not have a clue 61
in the dark 80
not have an earthly 99
don't know one end of a such-and-such from the other 104
staring you in the face 114
not have the faintest 115
not have the foggiest 125
God knows 134
goodness knows 135
anybody's guess 138
heaven knows or heaven alone knows 150
have no idea 156
not have the remotest idea 156
ignorance is bliss 157
I wouldn't know 171
Lord knows 192
search me 299
not know the first thing about 340
none the wiser 379

L

talking about language
effing and blinding 101
English as she is spoke 106
excuse my French 128
bad language 174
strong language 175
four-letter word 181
mixed metaphor 208
to coin a phrase 250
a play on words 257
Freudian slip 312
slip of the tongue 312
get your tongue round something 352

trip off the tongue 352
in more ways than one 374
the F word 381
word for word 382

talking about life

accidents will happen 2
take the bad with the good 14
if you can't beat 'em, join 'em 20
no bed of roses 21
you've made your bed, now you'll have to lie in it 21
beggars can't be choosers 22
make the best of something 24
count your blessings 29
bite the bullet 41
turn the other cheek 54
from the cradle to the grave 73
all in a day's work 80
a necessary evil 108
chalk it up to experience 109
let's face it 113
a fact of life 114
the grass is always greener on the other side of the fence 136
you've got to laugh 176
life begins at forty 183
life goes on 183
life is a bowl of cherries 183
life is for living 183
life's rich tapestry 184
such is life 184
that's life 184
like it or lump it 186
live and learn 189
live and let live 189
you only live once 189
half a loaf is better than no bread 190
a man's gotta do what a man's gotta do 199
thankful for small mercies 207
needs must when the devil drives 224
you can't make an omelette without breaking eggs 234
take the rough with the smooth 290
sadder but wiser 294
the school of hard knocks 298

the school of life 298
just goes to show 307
look on the bright side 308
just one of those things 341
vale of tears 366
learn the hard way 373
that's the way the cookie crumbles 373
can't have it both ways 374
two wrongs don't make a right 385

liking people and things

be bowled over 35
take someone's breath away 38
get the bug 40
give me such-and-such any day 81
go into ecstasies 100
a flash in the pan 123
flavour of the month 123
suit down to the ground 138
after your own heart 148
to so-and-so's liking 186
sing the praises of 264
take a shine to someone 304
hot shit 304
up someone's street 327
hot stuff 328
be taken with 333
the best thing since sliced bread 339
have a thing about 339

love

sweep someone off their feet 119
plenty more fish in the sea 122
old flame 123
head over heels in love 147
heart skips, or misses, a beat 149
lose your heart 149
lonely hearts 149
the light of someone's life 185
love is blind 193
love nest 193
sweet nothings 229
nuts about 231
one in a million 235
on the rebound 280
soul mate 317

sweet on someone 329
mean the world to someone 384
think the world of 384

not liking people and things

have something against 4
into the bargain 17
bête noire 25
strangled at birth 27
not go a bundle on something 42
hold in contempt 68
not much cop 69
not what it's cracked up to be 73
not someone's cup of tea 77
leave a lot to be desired 86
take exception to something 108
pull, or make, a face 113
make someone's flesh crawl or creep 124
not take kindly to something 168
a dead loss 192
no love lost between 193
a black mark against someone 201
not much of a such-and-such 220
turn your nose up at something 228
no great shakes 302
no accounting for taste 335
have a thing about 339
have no time for 347
a dirty word 381
not have a good word to say about 384

luck

more by accident than design 1
fortune smiles on so-and-so 127
in the lap of the gods 175
a leap in the dark 177
a charmed life 183
bad luck 194
for luck 194
in luck 194
the luck of the draw 194
more by luck than judgement 194
not believe your luck 194
take pot luck 263
flying by the seat of your pants 300
thank your lucky stars 321

M

madness
be bananas 16
basket case 18
have bats in the belfry 18
round the bend 24
have a brainstorm 36
off your chump 57
go gaga 130
not right in the head 148
take leave of your senses 178
out to lunch 195
barking mad 196
mad as a hatter 196
midsummer madness 196
lose your marbles 201
go out of your mind 210
nutty as a fruit cake 231
up the pole 261
off your rocker 287
have a screw loose 299
be off your trolley 358
round the twist 362

manipulation and control
wrap someone round your little finger 121
have someone in the palm of your hand 241
have someone in your pocket 259
have someone by the short and curlies 306
under someone's spell 318
have someone right where you want them 370

marriage
the happy day 81
tie the knot 171
pop the question 274
shotgun marriage 306
hear wedding bells 375

money
an arm and a leg 9
bring home the bacon 14
not cost a bean 19
better off 25
in the black 28
bleed someone dry 29
keep body and soul together 32
cost a bomb 32
make a bomb 32
your bread and butter 37
break even 37

go broke 39
make a fast buck 40
make a bundle 41
go bust 43
cash in hand 49
hard cash 49
go cheap 54
on the cheap 54
take someone to the cleaners 59
in the clear 59
in clover 61
coin it 63
see the colour of someone's money 64
what's the damage? 79
dirt cheap 88
dollar signs in your eyes 91
go Dutch 96
cost the earth 99
false economy 100
at the expense of 109
fair and square 115
the fat of the land 117
a fool and his money are soon parted 125
make a fortune 127
a small fortune 127
go halves 142
hand over fist 143
put your hand in your pocket 144
golden handcuffs 144
pass the hat round 146
burn a hole in your pocket 153
vested interest 158
hit the jackpot 160
make a killing 168
king's ransom 169
beyond your means 205
within your means 205
have money to burn 215
hush money 215
in the money 215
make money 215
money does not grow on trees 215
money for jam 215
money is no object 215
money is the root of all evil 216
money talks 216
not made of money 216
put your money where your mouth is 216
spend money like water 216
throw good money after bad 216
throw money around 216

throw money at something 216
where there's muck there's brass 220
on the nail 222
feather your own nest 225
a nest-egg 225
on the never-never 225
pay through the nose for something 228
such-and-such is no object 232
over the odds 233
or nearest offer 233
cost a packet 240
cross someone's palm with silver 241
grease someone's palm 241
in the pay of 246
for peanuts 246
penny-pinching 248
penny wise, pound foolish 248
a pretty penny 248
not cost a penny 248
peppercorn rent 249
rob Peter to pay Paul 250
make your pile 253
he who pays the piper calls the tune 254
in pocket 259
line your pockets 259
out of pocket 259
the asking price 265
at a price 266
cheap at the price 266
put a price on something 266
quids in 274
be quits with someone 275
hold someone to ransom 278
get-rich-quick 284
daylight robbery 287
rolling in it 288
when your ship comes in 304
on a shoestring 305
know which side your bread is buttered 307
put something on the slate 311
for a song 316
born with a silver spoon in your mouth 319
easy street 326
hold the purse strings 327
pick up the tab 332
pay your way 373
well off 376
oil the wheels 376

N

names for different kinds of people

copy cat 50
tough cookie 69
culture vulture 76
cool customer 77
slippery customer 78
cheeky devil 86
legal eagle 97
earth mother 99
enfant terrible 106
square-eyes 112
fag hag 115
four-eyes 127
a big girl's blouse 132
goody-goody 135
greedy-guts 137
lager lout 173
cheeky monkey 216

O

giving an opinion

if you ask me 10
in my book 33
as far as I am concerned 66
all things considered 68
to judge from something 163
pass judgement 163
change your mind 210
speak your mind 211
to my mind 211
for my money 215
compare notes 229
for one 235
for my part 243
make your point 260
point of view 260
give your seal of approval 299
as far as I can see 300
get on your soapbox 315
stand up and be counted 321
I tend to think 337
in no uncertain terms 337
change your tune 360
value judgement 366
in my view 367
take a dim view of such-and-such 367
take the view that 367
make your voice heard 368
to my way of thinking 374

P

the past

in my day 81
halcyon days 83
the best days of your life 82
the good old days 83
those were the days 83
déjà vu 85

pessimism

I wouldn't bank on it 17
don't bet on it 24
don't hold your breath 37
fat chance 52
chance would be a fine thing! 52
count your chickens before they are hatched 55
don't count on it 71
that'll be the day 82
dream on 93
too good to last 175
a prophet of doom 269

poverty

badly off 14
bag lady 14
on the breadline 37
stone broke 39
tighten your belt 23
not have a red cent 51
make ends meet 105
not have a penny to your name 248
poor as a church mouse 261
on a shoestring 305
fall on hard times 349
waifs and strays 369

precision

bang on 17
hit the bull's-eye 41
right on the button 44
clear-cut 59
dot your i's and cross your t's 92
on the dot 92

pregnancy

bun in the oven 41
with child 55
in the club 61
up the duff 95
in the family way 116
in the pudding club 269
shotgun marriage 306

saying that something is not a problem

no bother 34
no sweat 329
think nothing of it 342
no trouble 358
no problem 268
no probs 268

punishing and being punished

bring someone to account 2
bring someone to book 33
throw the book at someone 33
cop it 69
make an example of someone 108
get it 132
for the high jump 164
bring someone to justice 164
take the law into your own hands 176
teach someone a lesson 180
get it in the neck 224
take the rap 278
a slap on the wrist 311
do, or *serve, time* 347
short sharp shock 305
woe betide so-and-so 380

Q

telling people to be quiet

button it! 44
cut the cackle 45
drop dead 94
shut your face 114
shut your gob 133
get knotted 171
shut your mouth 219
pack it in 240
hold your peace 246
give it a rest 283
shut or *shut up* 307
put a sock in it 315
zip up 387

R

rejection

give someone the boot 34
for the chop 56
get the chop 56
give someone the elbow 102

(rejection continued)
give someone the heave-ho
   149
*give someone their marching
   orders* 237
throw something overboard
   239
give someone the push 271
get the sack 294
on the scrap heap 298
a slap in the face ·311

repetition
again and again 4
once again 235
once too often 235
all over again 239
over and over 239
same again 295
as per usual 365
week in week out 375
year in year out 386

responsibility
someone's baby 12
*the ball is in so-and-so's
   court* 15
take something on board 31
pass the buck 40
carry the can 46
in charge 53
be lumbered with 195
*a millstone round someone's
   neck* 209

rest
recharge your batteries 18
have a breather 38
take it easy 100
put your feet up 119
breathing space 317
take the weight off your feet
   375

revenge
settle an account 2
*pay someone back in their
   own coin* 63
get even 107
*an eye for an eye and a tooth
   for a tooth* 109
*pay something back with
   interest* 158
get your own back 239
*give someone a taste of their
   own medicine* 335
tit for tat 350

taking risks
chance your arm 9
go for broke 39

throw caution to the wind
   51
cut it fine 78
dice with death 84
be a devil 86
court disaster 88
tempt fate 117
skate on thin ice 156
take your life in your hands
   184
risk your neck 224
stick your neck out 224
take the plunge 258

not taking risks
better safe than sorry 25
better the devil you know
   86

S

sadness
got the blues 31
weep buckets 40
cut up 78
in the depths of 85
in the doldrums 90
down in the dumps 95
cry your eyes out 112
long face 113
cry, or sob, your heart out
   148
have a heavy heart 148
heart in your boots 149
down in the mouth 219
hit rock bottom 287
in low spirits 319
tale of woe 333

**having, keeping, and
telling secrets**
spill the beans 19
let the cat out of the bag 50
in confidence 67
*take someone into your
   confidence* 67
keep your counsel 71
blow someone's cover 72
behind closed doors 91
blow the gaff 130
give the game away 130
*between you, me, and the
   gatepost* 131
*keep something under your
   hat* 146
in on something 157
keep something to yourself
   168

land someone in it 174
in league with someone 177
let something slip 181
my lips are sealed 189
hush money 215
mum's the word 221
on the quiet 275
skeletons in the cupboard or
   closet 310
*have something up your
   sleeve* 312
laugh up your sleeve 312
on the sly 313
under the table 332
walls have ears 370
not breathe a word 382
keep under wraps 385

self-importance
put on an act 3
put on airs and graces 6
smart aleck 6
know all the answers 7
think you are the bee's knees
   21
a bit of a lad 27
bold as brass 36
*like the cat that got the
   cream* 50
*think you are the cat's
   whiskers* 50
city slicker 58
too clever by half 59
clever clogs 60
delusions of grandeur 85
clever dick 87
beneath someone's dignity
   88
ego trip 102
go to someone's head 147
high and mighty 152
*be full of your own
   importance* 157
jumped-up 164
lord it over someone 192
queen it over someone 273
blow your own trumpet 359

sex
*as the actress said to the
   bishop* 3
go to bed with someone 21
the birds and the bees 26
bit on the side 27
the earth moved 99
get your end away 104
the facts of life 115
play footsie 126
hanky-panky 145
blow job 161
dirty joke 162

kiss and tell 169
have carnal knowledge of
   someone 172
get laid 173
an easy lay 176
get your leg over 178
red-light district 185
make love 193
man-eater 198
a dirty mind 210
the missionary position 213
one-night stand 226
spend the night with
   someone 226
get your oats 232
sow your wild oats 232
have it off with someone
   233
fancy the pants off someone
   242
make a pass at someone
   244
the oldest profession in the
   world 268
breed like rabbits 276
in the biblical sense 301
slap and tickle 311
go all the way 372
dirty weekend 375
how was it for you? 386

speed

like a bat out of hell 18
beetle off 22
like blazes 28
in the blink of an eye 29
go like a bomb 32
like nobody's business 43
go like the clappers 58
like crazy 73
like a dose of salts 91
on, or at, the double 92
not see someone for dust 95
fast and furious 117
as fast as your legs can carry
   you 179
like greased lightning 186
in the nick of time 226
at full pelt 247
quick as a flash 274
a race against time 276
at a rate of knots 278
no sooner said than done
   295
in two shakes 302
like a shot 306
at a snail's pace 314
make it snappy 314
at breakneck speed 318
just like that 338

full tilt 346
in no time at all 347
before you can turn round
   361
in the twinkling of an eye
   361
quick on the uptake 364
slow on the uptake 364
run like the wind 378
in the wink of an eye 379

spoiling things

upset the applecart 8
prick the bubble 40
put a damper on something
   79
do to death 84
flog to death 84
fly in the ointment 125
take the gilt off the
   gingerbread 132
cook someone's goose 135
spike someone's guns 139
put the kibosh on something
   167
make a mess of something
   207
foul the nest 225
party-pooper 244
put a spanner in the works
   317
put a spoke in someone's
   wheel 319
muddy the waters 371
pour cold water on 371
make waves 372

high status

anyone who's anyone 8
fat cat 50
big cheese 54
upper crust 76
top dog 90
big fish 122
have friends in high places
   128
the king of the castle 169
big noise 227
of note 228
the powers that be 263
the top rung of the ladder
   293
big shot 306
big wheel 376

low status

common as dirt 65
the rank and file 277
poor relation 282
riff-raff 284

the lowest rung of the ladder
   292

physical strength

have the constitution of an
   ox 68
firing on all cylinders 78
do something with all your
   might 208
with might and main 208
a tower of strength 355

success

have an ace up your sleeve
   2
bring home the bacon 14
pull something out of the bag
   15
go with a bang 17
make first base 18
half the battle 19
beat someone hollow 19
take a lot of beating 20
beginner's luck 22
under your belt 23
get the better of someone
   25
make it big 25
early bird 26
sweep the board 31
in the can 46
have, or keep, a card up your
   sleeve 47
carry it off 48
rise to the challenge 52
a fighting chance 52
in with a chance 53
not stand a chance 53
a sporting chance 53
fancy your chances 53
with flying colours 64
carry the day 81
live to fight another day
   82
save the day 82
go the distance 88
like a dream 93
an ugly duckling 95
with an eye to the main
   chance 111
so far so good 116
feather in your cap 118
fall on your feet 118
wipe the floor with 124
bear fruit 128
glory days 133
strike gold 134
make the grade 136
go great guns 139
give someone a hammering
   143

(success continued)
beat someone hands down 145
win hands down 145
hat trick 146
landslide victory 174
have the last laugh 176
in leaps and bounds 177
on the right lines 188
never look back 191
make it 197
the making of someone 197
the grand old man of such-and-such 198
the man of the match 199
hit the mark 201
make your mark 202
make mincemeat of someone 209
mission accomplished 213
cut the mustard 221
make a name for yourself or *make your name* 222
rise to the occasion 232
strike oil 234
come into your own 239
a purple patch 245
go places 256
pip someone at the post 262
rags to riches 277
riding high 284
get something right 285
run rings round 286
coming up roses 290
sink or swim 310
be sitting pretty 310
on a winning streak 326
success story 328
make a clean sweep 329
come out on top 353
come up, or *turn up, trumps* 359
on the up and up 363
Pyrrhic victory 367
on to a winner 379
winner-takes-all 379
go up in the world 384
have the world at your feet 384
set the world on fire 384

surprise
beyond belief 22
believe it or not 23
would you believe 23
be blowed 30
out of the blue 30
a bolt from the blue 32

I'll be damned! 79
in all my born days 83
not believe your ears 98
not bat an eyelid 111
not believe your eyes 111
your eyes nearly popped out of your head 112
eyes out on stalks 112
fancy that 116
funnily enough 129
can't get over 132
God Almighty 133
My God 134
too good to be true 135
in heaven's name 150
so-and-so's jaw dropped 160
you're joking 163
you're kidding 167
knock someone for six 170
not believe your luck 194
fancy meeting you here! 206
blow someone's mind 210
in the name of God 222
a new one on you 226
that's news to me 226
none other than so-and-so 227
the last person 249
you could hear a pin drop 253
you don't say! 297
have to be seen to be believed 301
come as a shock 305
shock tactics 305
a shock to the system 305
jump out of your skin 311
bless my soul 317
stone me 324
come as a surprise 329
of all things 342
to think 342
who does so-and-so think they're kidding? 343
wonders will never cease 381
words fail me 383
what is the world coming to? 384

sympathy and indifference
hard cheese 54
hard lines 188
bad luck 194
tough shit 305
tough 354

T

talking
shoot the breeze 38
a running commentary 65
bend someone's ear 97
so-and-so's ears are burning 98
chew the fat 117
the gift of the gab 132
talk the hind legs off a donkey 179
all mouth and trousers 218
big mouth 218
hush my mouth 219
motor-mouth 219
talk a blue streak 326
small talk 333
pass the time of day 349
find your tongue 352
at the top of your voice 352
a trouble shared is a trouble halved 358
talk turkey 361
speak, or *talk, out of turn* 361
get a word in edgeways 381

thinking
rack your brains 36
knit your brows 39
put on your thinking cap 47
someone's mental cogs 62
take something into consideration 68
under consideration 68
chew the cud 76

tiredness and sleeping
all in 6
sleep like a baby 12
dead on your feet 118
look like death warmed up 84
dog-tired 90
done in 91
fit to drop 94
at a low ebb 100
fading fast 115
drop like flies 124
hardly put one foot in front of the other 126
the land of nod 174
be on your last legs 179
go out like a light 185
sleep like a log 190
hit the sack 294
run out of steam 322

sleep like a top 353
not up to such-and-such
 363
forty winks 379
dead to the world 383

going to the toilet
go to the bathroom 18
the call of nature 45
the ladies' room 173
take a leak 177
powder your nose 228
spend a penny 248
be caught, or *taken, short*
 306
go for a slash 311

truth
above board 31
make a clean breast of it 37
lay your cards on the table
 48
come clean 59
come out of the closet 60
someone's true colours 64
look someone in the eye
 110
*written all over someone's
 face* 114
face the facts 115
God's truth 134
with your hand on your heart
 144
in your heart of hearts 149
I kid you not 167
no kidding? 167
lay it on the line 187
nothing in it 229
on oath 232
in the open 236
put someone right 272
set the record straight 281
straight from the shoulder
 307
bare your soul 317
straight up 326
swear blind 329
in truth or *in all truth* 360
to tell you the truth 360
truth will out 360
in all truthfulness 360
take my word for it 382

trying
have a bash 18
as best you can 24
do your level best 24
make it your business 43
have a crack 73
last-ditch attempt 89

give something a go 133
go for it 133
try your hand at something
 144
try your luck 194
as a last resort 282
have a stab at 320
put to the test 338
*nothing ventured nothing
 gained* 366
test the water 371
give it a whirl 377

U

not understanding and
misunderstanding
beyond you 25
clear as mud 59
at cross-purposes 75
double Dutch 96
*get hold of the wrong end of
 the stick* 104
it's all Greek to me 137
can't make head or tail of
 147
over your head 148
get your lines crossed 188

being unfriendly
give someone the brush-off
 40
cold as charity 63
cold as ice 63
cool customer 77
cut someone dead 78
look daggers 79
cold fish 122
treat like dirt 88
with your nose in the air
 228
a nasty piece of work 252
*give someone the cold
 shoulder* 306

W

wanting
give your right arm 9
could do with such-and-such
 89
your wildest dreams 93
be dying for something 96
give your ears for something
 98
have your eye on 110
feast your eyes 112

*give your eyeteeth for
 something* 112
please God 134
give your right hand 143
set your heart on something
 149
want jam on it 160
on your knees 170
wouldn't mind 211
cry for the moon 217
*I could murder a such-and-
 such* 221
out for something 238
set your sights on 309
make a wish 379
give the world 383

weather
rain buckets 40
rain cats and dogs 51
chuck it down 57
the heavens open 150
tip it down 350

work
busy bee 21
back in business 42
business as usual 42
get down to business 42
out of business 43
busy as a bee 43
busman's holiday 43
*burn the candle at both
 ends* 46
paddle your own canoe 47
watch the clock 60
get cracking 73
a dog's life 89
work like a dog 90
the donkey work 91
duty calls 96
elbow-grease 102
run errands 106
up to your eyeballs 111
up to your eyes 112
*work your fingers to the
 bone* 122
work your guts out 139
have your hands full 145
back in harness 146
hive of activity or *hive of
 industry* 152
jobs for the boys 162
up to your neck 224
*keep your nose to the
 grindstone* 227
the Peter principle 250
*put your shoulder to the
 wheel* 306
all work and no play 383

worrying

*beside yourself with
something* 24
a bundle of nerves 41
like a cat on hot bricks 50
worried to death 84
dread to think 93
drive someone to drink 94
on edge 101
at the end of your tether
103
*tear your hair out over
something* 141

have kittens 169
get your knickers in a twist
170
go out of your mind 210
on someone's mind 211
prey on someone's mind
211
out of sight out of mind
309
not lose sleep over 312
in a stew 323
*let something get on top
of you* 353

worthlessness

not worth a bean 19
full of crap 73
beyond help 151
count for nothing 229
*not worth the paper it is
written on* 242
scum of the earth 299
a fat lot of use 364
no use to man or beast
364
a waste of space 370

CHAMBERS
English

Other titles in the Chambers English series:

Chambers Essential English Dictionary
0 550 10680 4 *(paperback)*

Chambers Students' Dictionary
0 550 10732 0

Chambers Dictionary of Phrasal Verbs
0 550 10731 2